D1394002

A NEW HISTORY OF ENGLAND

410–1975

A NEW HISTORY
OF ENGLAND
410–1975

L. C. B. SEAMAN

THE HARVESTER PRESS

First Published in Great Britain in 1981 by
THE HARVESTER PRESS LIMITED
Publisher: John Spiers
16 Ship Street, Brighton, Sussex

British Library Cataloguing in Publication Data
Seaman, Lewis Charles Bernard
  A new history of England, 410–1975.
  1. England—History
  I. Title
  942   DA30
  ISBN 0-85527-697-5

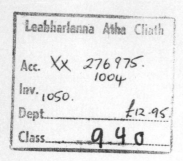
Photoset in Great Britain by
Rowland Phototypesetting Limited
Bury St Edmunds, Suffolk
and printed by
St Edmundsbury Press
Bury St Edmunds, Suffolk

To
F. C. S.

'It is the end that crowns us . . .'

Historians can use history to fulfil many of the social purposes which the old mythical pasts did so well. It can no longer provide sanctions for authority, nor for aristocratic or oligarchical élites, nor for inherent destinies clothed in national guise; but it can still teach wisdom, and it can teach it in a far deeper sense than was possible when wisdom had to be taught through the example of heroes.

J. H. PLUMB

The longer one studies history, the harder it gets to arrive at results which even the author, let alone the reader, can decently consider to be the truth.

V. H. GALBRAITH

CONTENTS

ix

Contents

PART FIVE

FREEDOM AND SUBORDINATION
Approximate Dates: 1653 until after 1780

PART SIX

CHALLENGE AND RESPONSE
Approximate Dates: from before 1760 until after 1860

Contents

PART SEVEN

FROM PAST TO PRESENT
Approximate Dates: 1860–1975

PREFACE

THERE are many reasons why we need a new history of England. As we change our vantage point in time, the whole historical landscape changes, and we need new guides. As the study of history itself becomes more specialised, we need new syntheses. There have been as many changes in the study of history over the last thirty years as there have been in England's place in the world.

Mr Seaman is concerned with England, not with Britain, although he cannot leave out English relationships with our fellow islanders in Wales, Scotland and Ireland. English society itself is rich and complex, so that England itself cannot be taken for granted by the historian. He has to explain how it came to be unified and integrated.

It used to be the continuities in the English story which attracted historians, and many of them believed that the continuities were a matter of pride. Now most historians start with the problems. There is less desire to escape into the past, though Englishmen find it difficult to avoid nostalgia, and there is more anxiety to explain. It is not only England itself which cannot be taken for granted, but most of the explanations of past success.

Mr Seaman does not lead us through to the preoccupied present. There is a gap between the end of his story and the story as it is now unfolding. What he does is to prepare us for a change of mood. Historians are influenced not only by their vantage points but by the social weather. This does not mean to say that they agree. They argue, and it is one of the merits of this ambitious study that it finds a place throughout for the arguments as well as for the agreed facts.

Some countries have very short histories, and there are some countries, too, which are more interested in the future than in the past. Moreover, national history no longer occupies the central place in historiography that it did thirty years ago. Such variations in perspective ensure that a new history of England becomes more, rather than less, interesting. So, too, do those variations in English perspectives which now prompt historians to find a place in the story for people whose names have been forgotten, some of them the failures of history, not its successes.

Mr Seaman's history speaks for itself, and his chapter headings by themselves reveal his plan. He identifies not one theme, but many. He seeks at every stage to draw the reader in, warning him in the words of the medieval historian Galbraith, quoted at the very beginning, that 'the longer one studies history, the harder it gets to arrive at results which even the author, let alone the reader, can decently consider to be the truth'.

Asa Briggs

ACKNOWLEDGEMENTS

SOME of these pages have been helpfully scrutinised by Angela Kent of Trinity and All Saints' College, Leeds, by Fred Dwyer of the University of Southampton and by Jack Watson of the Preston Polytechnic. On certain specific points within their particular specialities, I took advice from Dr Peter Brooks of Downing College and Dr Derek Fraser of the University of Bradford. Help with typing at various stages was provided by my daughter-in-law, Christine; and my daughter Mary helped with the proof correction. My former colleague, Gilbert Talbot also read the proofs with his customary thoroughness. To all these I am duly grateful. Most of all, however, I am grateful to my wife, who for so long endured without complaint the inconveniences of life with a husband apparently endlessly writing a history book. This work is rightly dedicated to her because, whatever its deficiencies, it is the biggest offering of the kind that I can make to her.

L.C.B.S.

INTRODUCTION

To attempt to write a one-volume history of England is to make an assault on the impossible. What Professor Lawrence Stone writes about the seventeenth century may be applied to all English history: it is 'a battle-ground which has been heavily fought over, and is beset with mines, booby traps and ambushes manned by ferocious scholars prepared to fight every inch of the way'. Academic historians, conscious of their limited knowledge even of the particular field to which they have committed their reputations, are too professional to venture into areas where their rivals have a monopoly of the maps and mine-detectors.

This commendable caution nevertheless creates a gulf between academic historians and the public as a whole. Hence, though interest in the past increases, knowledge of English history declines. Because it is so highly specialised, much of the new historical knowledge deposited within authoritative volumes and learned journals remains buried within their covers. For most of society, academic historians are unknown warriors whose labours earn them unknown graves. Even those dedicated tomb robbers, the school textbook writers, disinter only broken bones.

The professionalism of academic specialists, by fragmenting English history into 'periods', tends also to obscure its broader perspectives and continuities: the specialist bridles at any suggestion that what happened in 'his' period has resemblance or relevance to other periods, or could have its origins in earlier, or major consequences in later, periods. The proper conviction that every historical event is unique is emphasised to the point of overlooking the fact that human beings in one century are like, as well as unlike, those living in other centuries; especially when, as in England, they are members of the same continuing society.

Fragmentation, and a consequent inaccessibility of knowledge, also result from the proliferation of disciplines within history. Economic historians pay scant attention to other kinds of history, even social history. Social historians dissociate themselves from whoever in their own domain deals with what is austerely dismissed as 'old fashioned social history'. Demographic historians, like historians of 'families', express scarcely less dubiety than economic historians about any history that cannot be quantified. Practitioners of regional, urban and local history seek to bar all general statements about 'English history' by demonstrating that, despite what the big books have always said, they managed things in ways wholly their own in seventeenth-century Barsetshire or nineteenth-century Casterbridge.

Introduction

So, as all busily engage in updating or outdating one another's conclusions, history is in danger of becoming something communicable only from one academic historian to other academic historians. Yet history does have a social function. It ought to be able to provide at least an introductory or approximate answer to the question, 'What has been the history of England so far?' Of late years, the question has been largely unanswered.

This book is therefore a rash attempt to provide what few are prepared to take the risk of offering, a survey of England's history over the past fifteen centuries. I have not set out to produce a potted textbook or to be comprehensive. I have tried to trace some of the main trends in political, economic and social history as they have affected people as a whole. The subject matter ranges from wage rates to public concerts; from revolts, riots and strikes to births, deaths and marriages; from the making of laws to the creation of great gardens; from technology to mysticism; from cathedral schools to comprehensives; from manuring the fields to clothing the body; from the invention of factories to the evolution of the home; from taxes to sex; from theology to football. I have also concluded the book by examining, more closely than might be expected in such a work, the developments of the later as well as of the earlier decades of the twentieth century. To be able to see the past in its historical context is a private virtue; to try to do the same for the present is, though more difficult, something which perhaps all historians ought to try to do, since it is a task for which their discipline might be expected to equip them.

To keep the book within a reasonable length I have made it predominantly a history of the English in England. Not only does it contain little about Ireland, Scotland or Wales; it says relatively little about Englishmen overseas and omits much military and naval detail. It also says less than it might have done about the extraordinary achievements of their empire builders. It is thus a history book that could not have been written even thirty years ago. Yet, in a book surveying fifteen hundred years of English history, even the empire has to be seen as one theme among many.

I have tried, no doubt with imperfect success, to avoid discredited interpretations and not to present as historical facts what the best authorities consider exploded myths. While I apologise in advance for the errors, if not howlers, that only an unattainable infallibility could exclude from so presumptuous a book, I shall not be dismayed if from time to time I have made assertions that 'the latest research' is thought to have disproved. That is the necessary fate of whoever writes anything but the most eruditely original kind of history. Every year brings news that what was once 'the latest view' is now old hat, and that what was only recently a discredited theory is due for favourable reappraisal.

I would finally emphasise for the benefit of the unwary that this has no pretence to be in any way a 'definitive' or 'authoritative' English history. The most august of historical works is usually no more than an interim report on the subject matter with which it deals. If this book informs more often than it misinforms, it will be useful. If it provokes thought, that will be better. If it persuades its readers to turn to the work of other and more distinguished historians, it will have justified itself.

L.C.B.S.

A NOTE ON STRUCTURE

I have tried in this book to avoid parcelling English history into a number of neat packages called 'periods'. Although divided into seven parts, the book is intended to be read as a continuous whole. The dates assigned to each Part are in almost all cases approximate, and have been selected deliberately, but not perversely, to break down the artificial barriers that, for example, set the whole of 'the middle ages' apart as one 'period' or cut off the Tudor period from the Stuart period or just as misleadingly enclose them off together. I have, by making Parts V & VI overlap chronologically, tried to emphasise the continuity of political developments between 1760 and 1860 and to make it impossible to think of 'the Industrial Revolution' as something that was peculiar to, or the only historical occurrence of, the years from 1780 to 1830. By beginning the final part in the mid-Victorian years, I have tried to avoid presenting 'the Victorian Age' as if it possessed a unity; and to present the 1960s and early 1970s as consequential upon the changes of the past hundred years as well as of those of the previous twenty-five.

To maintain a readable narrative flow and an acceptable clarity of analysis, I have excluded from the text itself any reference to the many controversies that exist among historians about the interpretation of virtually every topic I have touched upon. This book will, however, be misunderstood unless it is realised to what an extent it is a synthesis created out of the writings of others and of their often contradictory interpretations. As far as possible I have tried to avoid too great a dependence on any particular interpretation, whatever topic or period I have been dealing with, since no interpretation is final. There is always something else to say, always a new point of view to consider, always a fresh piece of information to force one to keep an open mind.

PART ONE

FROM ROMANS TO NORMANS

Approximate Dates: 410 A.D.–1087

1

WARRIORS, SETTLERS, CONVERTS

The Problem of Sources

BETWEEN the withdrawal of the Romans from Britain early in the fifth century until the establishment of Norman mastery by the end of the eleventh, the basic ingredients of England and its history were put together. During those centuries England acquired a strong monarchy and entrenched local institutions, and became a member of the Christian community to which the rest of Europe belonged. The English became recognisable as a mixture of peoples who had struggled against one another for control of the land but had contrived, if with difficulty, to cultivate and administer it in cooperation. By 1100, the Romano-Celtic, Anglo-Saxon, Scandinavian and Norman elements, which contributed in varying degrees to the making of 'the English', had all been assembled and were not thereafter modified by further hostile invasion.

The major contribution to the settlement and cultivation of the land during this period was made by the Anglo-Saxons and Scandinavians. But the early stages of the process are impossible to describe either with accuracy or in detail. With the collapse of Roman power came political breakdown and the decay of trade, towns and literacy. As a result, the fifth and sixth centuries in particular have left few memorials for the historian to decipher. Few among the population could write; most of what was written was long ago destroyed. Wooden buildings quickly perished. Buildings of more lasting substance from the Roman past fell into disuse or served as quarries from which later generations pillaged their own building materials. Artefacts of beauty continued to be fashioned in precious metal since these offered the most reliable means to proclaim and preserve the wealth of those who could afford them, but they too could become objects to loot and dismantle, or to bury for safety and then to be forgotten when their owners were killed by enemies of their own race or by marauders from the sea. Though, in consequence, the archaeologist, the aerial photographer, the student of names and place-names, the occasional farmer turning up lost Saxon treasure in a twentieth-century field contribute much to modern knowledge of the Anglo-Saxon world, the interpretation of the evidence they provide is extremely difficult.

Thus, the uncovering of pagan burial places can tell us much, but also mislead. The failure to find them in any particular area will not necessarily indicate that no Saxons settled there in the period before the conversion from paganism to Christianity from 597 onwards. Their

3

burial places may well have been destroyed by later ploughing. Place-names, too, may reveal less than they seem to. The Scandinavian word *by*, meaning a farm or village, appears often as a suffix in such place names as Asgarby or Whitby; but though this will indicate that the place was settled by Scandinavian invaders in the eighth or ninth century, it does not necessarily imply that it had not previously been an Anglo-Saxon settlement. Suffixes in earlier use, such as *ham*, or names incorporating *ingas*, as in Hastings, appear to have had more than one meaning. *Ham* meant a town; but it could also refer to a region or to an estate. Though Hastings denotes an area settled by the *ingas*, kinsmen or followers of a leader called *Haest*, *ingas* could also mean a district or a large estate. It is not surprising that the more learned historians of Anglo-Saxon England tend to write with magisterial caution. They are dealing with historical material that makes confident assertion even more perilous than it is for those who write about the better-documented later periods. The few clues the Anglo-Saxon period has left behind have to be scrutinised with quite exceptional attentiveness.

The literary evidence, as it begins to appear from the mid-sixth century onwards, is no easier to assess because, being so scanty, it cannot be checked by reference to other literary sources. The only writer of the time known to have attempted to describe the Anglo-Saxon conquest in its earlier stages was a Celtic cleric, Gildas, whose *Ruin of Britain* was completed by about 550. A fervent call to the Romano-Celtic people to repent of the sins which had caused God to inflict pestilence and barbarian invasion upon them as a punishment, the *Ruin of Britain* itself contains an admission that much evidence about the immediate past had already been lost. Earlier writings and records, Gildas complains, 'have been burnt by the fires of enemies or carried far away in the ships which exiled my countrymen'. Even though he wrote during a pause in the Anglo-Saxon invasions, he refers to the 'cities of our country' as 'deserted and dismantled . . . because although wars with foreigners have ceased, domestic wars continue'. Though his tone is almost always hysterical and his reliability, for lack of supporting evidence, so difficult to check, Gildas has to serve as the basic source of what is known about the times in which he lived.

Bede's *Ecclesiastical History*, completed in 731, relies heavily, for information about the fifth and sixth centuries, on oral tradition. He apologised for the fact in his introduction: 'I have simply sought to commit to writing what I collected from common report, for the instruction of posterity'. Among his sources were lists of the kings of the various Anglo-Saxon kingdoms, learned by heart and passed on by word of mouth, sometimes as genealogies pure and simple or as part of stories or poems. Not only were these likely to be changed as they passed from one generation to another; a king's name might well be suppressed, and left out of a genealogy if at some later date he was thought for some reason to have set a bad example, perhaps by reverting to paganism from Christianity.. Bede was, however, careful to write 'It is said,' before noting facts of which he felt uncertain. He does so when recording the tale that the first leaders of the Anglo-Saxon invasion were two brothers, Hengest and Horsa, who were direct descendants of the great Anglo-Saxon god, Woden. Since, however, in Old English, 'Hengest' meant 'Gelding' and 'Horsa' meant 'Horse' the existence of these two brothers outside the realms of myth seems improbable. The original inclusion of two such impressive names, combined with their association with a major god like Woden, had obviously been intended to give an impressive look to the genealogy of the early kings of Kent, who claimed descent from Hengest.

Since these are no more than random examples of the difficulties with which historians must grapple when dealing with Anglo-Saxon England, it seems that certainty about the fifth and sixth centuries is unattainable; and though much written and other evidence survives from the remainder of the Anglo-Saxon period, it is incomplete enough to make the study of it a matter of the most painstaking scholarship. Over a thousand years after Bede, any account of the Anglo-Saxons ought still to imitate his careful use of the introductory phrase: 'It is said . . .'.

Conquest and Settlement

From the middle of the first century A.D. until the early fifth century, Britain was a remote province of the Roman empire. At the beginning of the fifth century, however, the need to defend the heartland of their empire against large-scale barbarian incursions across the Rhine and Danube caused the Romans to withdraw the garrisons that had protected Britain and maintained Roman power there. In the thirty years after about 410 A.D. the Romano-British population had to rely for its defence on a succession of 'tyrants'. Most of these were likely to be British, that is Celtic, chieftains who took over from the Romans the task of fighting off the Picts and the Scots who had been the chief threat to Roman Britain; the Romans had built Hadrian's Wall in order to keep watch on them.

Once the Romans had withdrawn, the principal danger was to come, not by land from the north, but from the east by sea. Since the middle of the third century A.D. the eastern and southern coasts of Britain had from time to time been attacked by marauding pirates known to the Celtic peoples as Saxons. These attacks were part of the same great migration of Germanic people and warriors which was now threatening the whole Roman empire. In Britain, both the Romans, and the 'tyrants' who took over from them, employed Saxon mercenaries in their battles against the Picts; and the downfall of post-Roman Britain was traditionally said to have been precipitated by the encouragement given to these Saxon mercenaries to establish permanent settlements.

By about 450, the Saxons began a large-scale migration into Britain and during the next fifty years firmly entrenched themselves on the eastern coast southwards from the Wash, and also in Sussex. Some time between 490 and 516, however, the Celtic British won an important victory in a battle at an unidentified place called Mount Badon, with the result that, for the next forty or fifty years, the Germanic peoples, though steadily consolidating their hold on the east and south, made little further advance. Only in the sixth century was that advance resumed, and on a scale large enough to establish, between 550 and 650, the several Germanic kingdoms that were to shape English history until the Viking attacks of the ninth century.

The Celtic peoples were all the while distracted by their own civil wars and by warfare against the Picts: the legendary British king, Arthur, to whom the triumph at Mount Badon is ascribed, may possibly have perished in a battle against the Picts on Hadrian's Wall. Their capacity to resist the Germanic advance was reduced by the inevitable tendency of the Celts to gravitate towards the western coasts giving access to the seas that linked them, commercially and culturally, with their fellow Celts in Ireland and Brittany. Those Celts who survived in the west eventually acquired from the newcomers the Germanic label, 'Welsh', meaning a foreigner. But although the invaders' word for a Celt was also that for a slave, it seems clear, particularly in the north-west, in what became the Anglo-Saxon kingdom of Northumbria, that a substantial Celtic population survived the English conquest. It may be that the quite rapid spread of the English language has disguised the extent to which many of those who learned to speak the invaders' language may in fact have been Britons, even as far to the south-east as Kent.

In general, however, the newcomers' language and customs were little affected by Roman or Celtic influences. Celtic upland farms and villages were deserted. The new arrivals preferred to plough in the valleys, so that though they acquired from their predecessors the names of rivers, forests and hills, and Roman towns, most of the place-names of the future would be of their own devising. They were very conscious of their German origin and, though in due time they looked with awe on the derelict Roman towns as 'the work of giants', most of the new settlers' towns were away from the urban centres built by the Romans. Among notable exceptions were London, Canterbury, York and Lincoln. Accustomed to timber or lath and plaster building, they had no desire to live in stone buildings they did not know how to maintain and for which their way of life had little practical use.

The newcomers were differentiated by Bede, the eighth-century monastic historian, as Angles, Saxons and Jutes. The Angles who settled in the north, and in East and Middle Anglia, came from the lands and islands between the Elbe estuary and Jutland. The Frisian islands are considered as the original home of some of these newcomers: the language used in the Frisian regions was closely related to English, and East Anglia retained into the Middle Ages a number of customs

paralleled in Frisia. The Saxons, Bede thought, came from the region of
the Lower Elbe, and settled in what became Essex, Wessex and Sussex.
The Jutes were from mid-Denmark and were held to have populated
Kent, the Isle of Wight and the mainland opposite it. The Jutes seem to
defy precise identification, though their name was often invoked by
later generations. The unusual systems of inheritance and land tenure
that long prevailed in Kent were alleged to be of Jutish origin, and the
legend long persisted that Kent was first settled under a Jutish leader
called Hengest. As late as the twelfth century the New Forest was
referred to as a 'Jutish' region.

The invaders had little if any sense of belonging to a particular nation
called Angles or Saxons. They came in the first instance in small groups
led by a warrior chieftain, in long, open boats, perhaps a dozen at a
time, slowly pushing up the river estuaries. Gradually, as settlements
were established, several groups would combine to form a large 'folk'
under a king, and in time populate a considerable geographical area;
and they would acquire their collective name from the area they
dominated.

The condition of Anglo-Saxon England during the centuries after 550
was so lacking in political unity, and marked by such frequent warfare
between kingdoms with indeterminate boundaries, that, compared with
conditions under the Romans or the Normans, it appears one of
confusion and anarchy. Yet the battles recorded by the bards and
chroniclers as full of fearful horrors and tremendous heroism were
usually small-scale encounters. The frequency with which the kings of
rival kingdoms were killed in such battles confirms this. The readiness
of lesser, or less bellicose, kings to acknowledge the overlordship of a
more powerful king suggests that the respect with which prowess in war
might endow a king could itself limit the scope of the fighting. Triumph
in battle was itself sufficient authentication of the victor's claim to
political paramountcy over areas beyond his own territory. The paramountcy would continue until he or a successor was in turn defeated by
another king. No king in the period before the Viking invasions had the
administrative or even military skills adequate to the task of effectively
controlling the Anglo-Saxon people as a whole. In a land only slowly
being won from forest and swamp, physical communications were bad
and lack of literacy made the creation of a bureaucracy or even the
transmission of orders extremely difficult.

Competing Kingdoms

By the middle of the sixth century it is however possible to distinguish
the principal kingdoms into which the Anglo-Saxons were divided.
Since he claimed, not very accurately, that there were seven such
kingdoms, it is to Bede's later *History* that this period owes its label, 'the
Heptarchy'. Bede's seven kingdoms included Middle Anglia and

7

Lindsey; but these were soon absorbed into the kingdom of Mercia. Northumbria and Mercia were the most important kingdoms before the coming of the Vikings; it was only at that point, when the existence of all English kingdoms was in doubt, that Wessex came into prominence. The other English kingdoms, of Essex, Sussex, Kent and East Anglia, were all in different ways rather apart from the others; but, facing the seas as they did, they were always liable to attack and domination from the landward side.

Of the lesser kingdoms, Kent was among the most stable. This may have been due to the survival of Roman or Romano-British influences. Among its first settlers were probably a number of Franks from northern Gaul, and there were close commercial and cultural links between Kent and the Franks, a circumstance which is reflected in the fact that the Roman church chose Kent as the region from which to begin the conversion of the English. For much of its history, however, the Kentish kingdom was to varying degrees subject either to Wessex or Mercia.

The kingdom of East Anglia depended upon its control of the Icknield Way, a main trackway from the north of Norfolk to the Berkshire Downs. Its trading links with Frankish Gaul and with Sweden made it a kingdom wealthy enough to attract Penda, king of Mercia (*c.*634–56). It was in the course of a battle fought by the East Anglians and Mercians in alliance, that both Penda and the East Anglian king, Ethelhere, were killed by the Northumbrians in 656. Little is known about East Anglian kings thereafter except that one of them was executed by the dominating king Offa of Mercia in 794; nevertheless, unrest in East Anglia was an important contribution to the ending of Mercian supremacy early in the ninth century. That East Anglia had a rich culture and a wide commerce was demonstrated by the celebrated ship burial excavated at Sutton Hoo in Suffolk in 1939. Loaded with treasure, but containing no body, the ship, 80 feet long and 14 feet wide, served as a cenotaph, possibly for the East Anglian king Raedwald.

The newcomers north of the Humber grouped themselves at first into two kingdoms: Deira, between Humber and Tees; and Bernica, north of Tees. Their amalgamation into a single Northumbrian kingdom under Bernician kings involved much warfare. Deira was first annexed by the Bernician king Aethelfrith (593–637) but it was not until 635 that Aethelfrith's son Oswald finally established the Bernician domination of Northumbria that lasted, though not without opposition, until 759.

Northumbrian kings waged continuous war with their neighbours. Wessex was attacked in 627. The Northumbrian conquest of Anglesey and the Isle of Man in 629 was but one incident in a succession of conflicts between the Northumbrians and the Welsh kingdom of Gwynedd. Oswald defeated and killed Cadwallon of Gwynedd, attacked Edinburgh and died in 643 while fighting the Mercians. Oswy of Northumbria (643–71) defeated and killed Penda of Mercia in a battle in which Penda's allies included the East Anglians, the king of Gwynedd and many disaffected Deirans.

The Northumbrians were unable to conquer Mercia because they became involved in an inconclusive struggle with their northern enemies, the Picts. For a time, the Celtic kings of Strathclyde recognised Northumbrian overlordship and in 756 a Northumbrian army, though destroyed immediately afterwards, captured Strathclyde's capital city Dumbarton. In the eighth century, Northumbria was usually at peace with its Pictish neighbours to the north and with the Mercians to the south mainly because it was riven by violent internal rivalries. These made it all the more difficult for the Northumbrians to resist the Vikings in the tenth century.

The Mercians, with a territorial base in Staffordshire and the Trent valley, were the most successful of the Anglo-Saxon kingdoms until the later emergence of Wessex. Little is known of them before the reign of Penda and information about him, as of his successors, derives from sources outside Mercia. Apart from his struggles with Gwynedd and Northumbria, he conquered the territory of the Middle Angles of what later became Leicestershire. This enabled his son Wulfhere (656–75) to subdue the East Saxons to the south east. Wulfhere made war as far south as the Isle of Wight, dominated the small kingdom of *Hwicca* in Worcestershire (bordering the kingdom of Wessex), controlled another buffer region in Herefordshire to hold off the Welsh, and annexed Cheshire. It was probably in Wulfhere's reign that the Mercians defeated Cynddylan, the Welsh prince of Powys, and destroyed his palace, thought to have been near Shrewsbury. Wulfhere's successors absorbed Lindsey, ravaged Kent and defeated king Ine of Wessex. Aethelbald, who became king of Mercia in 716, made himself overlord of all southern England, controlling the Middle Saxons of Middlesex and also London, previously part of the kingdom of the East Saxons.

Offa of Mercia (758–96) strengthened Mercian control of Essex and forced Kent, hitherto intermittently dominated by the West Saxons of Wessex, into dependence on him. From this subordination, Kent won a brief respite after what was apparently a victory over Offa at Otford in 776. Offa's successor Cenwulf (796–821), however, fiercely put down a Kentish rebellion in 796 and then made his brother king in Kent. Mercian control of Kent continued into the ninth century. Offa himself campaigned as far south as Hastings, so that Sussex, another former dependency of Wessex, also became dependent on Mercia. He defeated the West Saxons at Bensington in Oxfordshire in 779 and was certainly the most powerful Anglo-Saxon king in the centuries before the Danish invasion. He asserted as much by assuming, in 774, the title of *rex Anglorum*. He appointed and deposed kings in Essex, Kent and Sussex and married one of his daughters to a king of Northumbria and another to a king of Wessex. More impressively still, he sought to negotiate on terms of equality with Charles the Great, king of the Franks, celebrated from 800 onwards as Charlemagne the 'Emperor'. Offa refused to agree to a marriage between one of his daughters and Charles's son unless Charles agreed to give his daughter in marriage to Offa's eldest son Ecgfrith. Charles seems to have thought Offa's proposal presumptuous while Offa thought Charles's objections impertinent because Offa's family was far more ancient than Charles's. In consequence, the two kings embarked on a trade war.

Offa and his eventual successor Cenwulf (796–821) were also ambitious to control the church in England. They tried to undermine the prestige of Kentish Canterbury, first by persuading the pope to establish an archbishopric at Lichfield, in Mercian territory, and then by trying, without success, to transfer primacy over the church in southern England to London.

Offa also campaigned vigorously against the Welsh. He defeated them at Hereford and made war against them as far to the south-west as Dyfed. His determination to subdue or at least overawe the Welsh is commemorated by Offa's Dyke, the great earthwork called after him, running along most of the Welsh border from near Rhuddlan to near Chepstow. The construction of the dyke did not end the conflict. After Offa's death in 796, the Mercians killed Caradog, king of Gwynedd, in 798, ravaged Snowdonia in 816 and Dyfed two years later, and in the 820s annexed the Welsh kingdom of Powys.

The unification of the West Saxons into the kingdom of Wessex is dated from the late 680s, when their king, Caedwalla, established a supremacy over the Thames Valley Saxons, whom Mercian pressure had pushed into Hampshire and Wiltshire. Caedwalla's successor, Ine (688–726), kept control of Sussex, held off the Mercians, overawed Kent, completed the conquest of Devon, and defeated the Celtic people of Cornwall. Though Offa of Mercia was too strong in the late eighth century for Ine's successors to challenge him, the balance was now beginning to shift against Mercia. Whereas its geographical position gave it, at the outset, the benefit of inner lines of communication, by the beginning of the ninth century its power was overstretched. All its dependencies were restive; and although Wessex had the Cornish threat to its rear, the Welsh were a much more serious threat to Mercia.

The rise of Wessex was sudden. Egbert was its king from 802 until 839, but he did not challenge Mercia until the 820s. In 825 he defeated a Mercian attack at *Ellendun* (Wroughton, south-west of Swindon) and at once demanded, and got, the submission of Kent, Surrey, Sussex and Essex. This encouraged the East Anglians to assert themselves and inflict two heavy defeats on the Mercians in 825 and 827. The insubstantial structure of even an apparently powerful Anglo-Saxon kingdom was further shown by the fact that, when Egbert won an unhoped-for victory over the Mercians in 829, he was at once recognised as overlord of all the peoples south of the Humber and after marching as far as north Derbyshire was rewarded by the submission of Northumbria. Though

Egbert's supremacy was itself only a temporary tribute to his swift military triumphs, his immediate successors, though without much control in Mercia, Northumbria, London or East Anglia, were regarded as paramount from Devon to Kent as well as in Berkshire.

The existence by the first half of the ninth century of two fairly evenly matched kingdoms in Wessex and Mercia might have led to a protracted conflict between them. The Viking invasions brought this exclusively Anglo-Saxon phase of English history to an end. The emergence of one dominant kingdom in the south on the foundations laid in Wessex came only just in time to avert a wholesale Danish conquest.

Heathens, Celts, Romans

Roman Britain had been part of the 'universal' church catholic which had been coterminous with the empire of Rome since the early fourth century. As the Anglo-Saxons advanced, Christianity retreated westwards. It survived in Wales, part of Scotland, and above all in Ireland, but mainly in monastic form. When organised Roman society broke down, congregational worship was no longer possible. In the Celtic church the bishop was a monk, supervising monasteries rather than administering a diocese. The isolation of these Celtic communities meant that Celtic Christianity was more ascetic than the Roman, and placed great emphasis on meditation. But despite various other differences, mainly in externals, there were no great doctrinal divergences between Celtic and Roman Christians.

The religious practices of the invading Anglo-Saxons were those of a primitive people anxious to placate the adverse, and activate the beneficent, natural forces around them. Their major gods were Tiw, Woden and Thunor, whose names are enshrined in the calendar within every Tuesday, Wednesday and Thursday. Friday commemorates Frig, the bride of Woden. Woden was the god of death and battle, and his favourite bird was the raven, a legend surviving long enough to give added point to Lady Macbeth's words, used by Shakespeare a thousand years later, 'The raven himself is hoarse that croaks the fatal entrance of Duncan under my battlements'. Place-names such as Wansdyke and Wensley refer back to Woden; Thundersley in obstinately heathen Essex recalls Thunor; and Tisbury in Wiltshire enshrines the memory of Tiw.

To secure the cooperation of their gods, the Anglo-Saxons held feasts at which food was offered to them. When cattle were slaughtered in the 'sacrifice month' of September, and in the 'blood month' of November, there were also great religious feasts. The gods had their temples, sanctuaries and priests. Priests were not allowed to bear arms and could ride only on mares. Trees, stones and wells were venerated; elfish spirits haunted the misty marshes and sent forth poisonous darts; caverns and lakes were the homes of dragons and other monsters. There was a great reliance on incantations and charms. After a death, grain was burned to

11

protect the health of the survivors; children might be put in an oven to cure them of a fever.

Anglo-Saxon religion had little to do with ethics. Its primary concern was not men's relations with one another but with the mysterious forces of nature. Nor was it preoccupied with an after life. Man's highest reward was not, as with the Vikings, a hero's resting place in a post-mortem Valhalla but a surviving reputation for greatness and glory among one's posterity. Even so, the main preoccupation was not with right conduct by man towards man, but with ensuring the right conduct of gods towards man.

The official conversion of the Anglo-Saxon kings and aristocracy to Christianity took place over little more than half a century. Between 597 and 660, all the English, except those of the Isle of Wight and Sussex almost isolated by the great forest of Andredswald, had been converted, at least in the sense that their kings and large numbers of the population at large had been baptised.

The process began with the arrival in 597 of a mission from Rome. According to tradition, it was sent by Gregory I, the first of the great medieval popes, because he had been moved, by the sight of some Deiran slave boys in Rome, to a desire to save the souls of their kinsfolk. He did not, however, send St Augustine, his missionary, to Northumbria but to Kent, whose king, Ethelbert, had married a Frankish, and therefore Christian, princess. She had continued to practise her religion and had a Frankish bishop as her chaplain. Whether Augustine was sent to Kent merely because it was the part of England most accessible from Rome, or because Ethelbert was known to be sympathetic towards the faith is not clear. Kent was more politically stable than other Anglo-Saxon kingdoms at that particular time and more closely linked to Frankish Gaul. Ethelbert was thus more open to the consideration that, as a Christian, he would no longer be a 'barbarian' on the edge of what was still thought of as a 'Roman' world, but a monarch as sanctified as those whose kingdoms were nearer the centre of things.

Ethelbert was duly baptised soon after Augustine's arrival and this was followed, during the rest of 597, by the baptism of 'ten thousand' converts; the decline in the number of worshippers of Woden was said to have been dramatic. But Augustine had more ambitious aims on the pope's behalf. He was to consecrate twelve bishops and send a suitable man to York who in his turn would also consecrate twelve bishops, while Augustine was to transfer his see from Canterbury to London as soon as possible. This scheme, which was never fully completed, showed how the old organising temper of Rome had been absorbed by the papacy. The English were to be organised by the pope in much the same way as the British had been organised by the Roman empire. But it was not until after the industrial revolution that the province of York would match that of Canterbury in ecclesiastical strength and organisation. London, though the principal city of Roman Britain and an obvious choice for the site of the principal episcopal see in Christian England, was within the kingdom of the heathen East Saxons; and, despite the efforts of Cenwulf of Mercia on its behalf early in the ninth century, it had been fully christianised too late to challenge Canterbury. Canterbury's primacy of the south, and eventually of all England, became permanent, surviving the breach with Rome in the sixteenth century.

Though Augustine was able to establish bishoprics at Rochester and London before his death, and Ethelbert to command the East Saxons and East Angles to become Christian, there was a reaction under his son Eadbald. Eadbald refused to be a Christian and followed the not unusual custom of marrying his dead father's second wife. Augustine had been sufficiently alarmed by the tendency of the Anglo-Saxons to marry a stepmother or a sister-in-law to consult Pope Gregory about it. Gregory pronounced such unions as 'abominable', thus eventually bequeathing to the nineteenth-century parliament at Westminster the annually debated question of whether it should become legal for a man to marry his 'deceased wife's sister'. Laurentius, who had succeeded Augustine, frightened Eadbald out of his heathenism by telling him that St Peter had visited him by night and scourged him for thinking of giving up his mission to England altogether. He substantiated this tale by displaying, for Eadbald's benefit, the marks that the apostolic scourging had left upon his archiepiscopal person. Eadbald abandoned his idols, and his stepmother, and was duly baptised. This confirmed the conversion of Kent, even if it made little difference in Essex and East Anglia, and by 619 the monks of Canterbury turned their attention to Northumbria.

The Roman mission to Northumbria failed because the kingdom fell to Penda of Mercia, a determined heathen. Christianity was eventually brought to Northumbria by missionaries of the Celtic church. Though concentrating on preserving the faith of their own people in Ireland and the Celtic fringe of Britain, Celtic monks had always been at work in the remoter parts of Wessex and Northumbria, and Augustine had in fact been told to seek the cooperation of the Celtic bishops. Negotiations, probably in 602 or 603, seemed to have resulted in acrimony. The Celts would not give up their habit of celebrating Easter on a date different from that customary in the Roman world, and may have been upset by Augustine's own claim to be their superior. This is suggested by the story that the Celts arrived armed with the advice of a holy sage that they should accept Augustine if he were to rise to his feet to greet them; but, instead, he remained seated.

It was partly this failure of the two groups to act cooperatively that led to Northumbria's conversion by Celtic missionaries. Oswald, who won the kingdom of Northumbria in 634–5, had already become a Christian during a long exile among the Celtic monks of the island of Iona, off the west coast of Scotland, and may thus be considered the first Anglo-Saxon king to be Christian by conviction. At Oswald's request, the famous Ionan monk, Aidan, was consecrated bishop and began a mission in Northumbria. Aidan established his headquarters at Lindisfarne, off the Northumbrian coast. From this 'Holy Island', in typical Celtic fashion, he directed a mission which resulted in the conversion not only of Northumbria but also Mercia and the obstinate East Saxons.

Thus, by 660, the English were, though officially Christian, subject to the authority of Canterbury only within the kingdom of Kent, since its links with Wessex and East Anglia were extremely tenuous. Elsewhere, kings appointed bishops as they pleased, or accepted them from the community at Lindisfarne. If the English were not to form two distinct churches, a Celtic and a Roman, a decision would have to be made sooner or later to submit to Rome. There was little chance of the Celtic church assimilating all the English once Rome had made its presence felt. Even in Northumbria, the younger generation of Christians were becoming susceptible to the superior prestige and majesty of Rome, and beginning to find Celtic monasticism rude and barbarous by contrast.

The problem of the differing dates of Easter came to symbolise the conflict and, in 663 or 664, Oswy of Northumbria summoned what later came to be known as the Synod of Whitby to consider the matter. The Celtic claim to be right about Easter was based on a tradition sanctified by St John and the Irish monk, Colomba. The Romans took their stand on the principle of universality: the Celts, and the Celts alone, were out of step with the rest of Christendom. They reminded the Celts that Christ had given St Peter the keys of the kingdom and that he and St Paul were rather more important than an Irish saint called Colomba. Since the Celts were not really disposed to argue to the contrary, the issue was decided in favour of Rome.

The view that Whitby was the product of bitter controversy and that after it Celtic influence rapidly declined seems exaggerated. Nevertheless, the decision at Whitby appears in retrospect a decision in favour of Europe; or at least the establishment of ties with the Mediterranean world closer than those which had hitherto linked the Anglo-Saxons with Gaul and north-western Europe. England would remain in communion with Rome for 900 years. Nevertheless, the short-term results were undramatic. To the ordinary man, Christianity, whether Celtic or Roman, might seem a new sort of magic, to be used alongside the old, and treated, perhaps, as a new bottle for old heathen brews. To the more susceptible, the peregrinatory Celtic monk or bishop, who visited his flock on foot and not, like a haughty Roman bishop, on horseback in the manner of the world's great ones, may have seemed more effective as missionaries both before and after Whitby. Most Celtic monks seem to have accepted Whitby, pre-eminent among them being St Cuthbert, who flourished at Lindisfarne and allowed himself to be consecrated bishop of Hexham in 684 out of respect for the authority of Canterbury. Though his episcopate was short (he died in 687) he continued to travel widely, preaching to the people in their remote villages and administering confirmation. The Celtic tradition proved so strong that a council of the church thought it necessary to forbid Celtic priests to function within the province of Canterbury as late as 816.

The consolidation of the Roman organisation after Whitby was the work of Theodore of Tarsus, who became archbishop of Canterbury in 669 when already, by the standards of the time, an old man of 67. To assist him, the pope sent Hadrian, abbot of a monastery in southern Italy. Thus, the future of Christianity in England was shaped in the seventh century by Irish and Scots of the Celtic faith, by a Greek scholar from Asia only recently admitted to the Roman communion from the eastern Orthodox faith, and by a learned African fresh from a Neapolitan monastery. But if the Celtic influence was largely a spiritual one, Theodore and Hadrian would establish the organisation by which the faith could be systematically perpetuated.

Theodore established further dioceses with more bishops. Most existing bishoprics were either too large or lacked bishops altogether when he arrived. When he held his first church synod at Hertford in 672, there appear to have been only six bishops who could have attended, and only four turned up. Yet the council at Hertford was important not merely because of its regulations concerning the church: it was also the first national assembly in English history. Though there were still the separated, rival kingdoms, there was now only one church.

Theodore's dioceses were larger than elsewhere in the Roman church. When he established them he called them *parochiae*, i.e. parishes; the idea of a diocese as consisting of a large number of parishes did not yet exist. For a long time, much of the pastoral and evangelical work of the church was done from the monasteries. By the eighth century, district churches appeared, but often with small communities attached to them; they were more like regional monasteries than local churches, and were often called minsters, a word not greatly different from monastery. At these minsters, Christians would congregate on feast days; from them clergy would be sent out to remoter spots on Sundays, to celebrate mass in small wooden buildings or in the open air beneath tall stone or wooden crosses. Minsters were usually established in fertile valleys by the side of streams which could be used for baptisms, over which for some time minsters had a monopoly. Minsters were common in early Wessex, as is demonstrated by such place-names as Axminster, Beaminster and Warminster.

Monks, Teachers, Missionaries

For most of the period before 1066, the backbone of English Christianity was the monastery. The monasticism of the Benedictine rule was certain to find favour in a land already familiar with Celtic religion. In the reign of Oswy of Northumbria (643–71) the allied monasteries of Wearmouth

15

and Jarrow were founded; among the first novices at Jarrow was the future scholar and historian, Bede. The founder of Wearmouth was Benedict Biscop, a Northumbrian aristocrat who had acted as an English adviser to Theodore of Tarsus and had for two years been abbot of the monastery at Canterbury. By the beginning of the eighth century there were many other monasteries in Anglo-Saxon England, for example at Whitby, Chertsey, Malmesbury, Much Wenlock, Abingdon, Glastonbury and Evesham.

It was with the monks and the monastic schools that the history of formal education began in England. From the start, the Roman mission thought teaching as important as preaching. By the time of Theodore of Tarsus there were already schools in Kent and Essex, and Theodore and Hadrian themselves taught at Canterbury. Church music was taught to such effect that the Anglo-Saxons were the first non-Italians to use Gregorian chant. The teaching at Canterbury in the middle of the seventh century was considered superior even to that of the church in Ireland.

St Aldhelm (*c.*639–709) was one of the most famous Anglo-Saxon scholars of his times, though he was perhaps clever rather than profound. He had studied under an Irish man of learning in the neighbourhood of Malmesbury before going to Canterbury to study in 671. His various eccentricities, such as an obsession with word play and obscure riddles, and his habit of attracting audiences by singing religious songs near town gates or bridges have sometimes been ascribed to his Irish education, though the Anglo-Saxons themselves delighted in word play and riddles. Aldhelm founded monasteries at Frome and Bradford on Avon, visited Rome, was a strong supporter of the Roman against the Celtic cause and was for four years bishop of Sherborne. He studied Roman law, mathematics and astronomy. The first Englishman known to have composed Latin verse, he also had a considerable reputation as a poet in the vernacular, for which Alfred the Great later expressed considerable admiration. In one of his letters, he writes, while at Canterbury, that he is so busy with his studies that he cannot take time off for dancing at Christmas. In another he rebukes his fellow monks and priests for their indulgence in brightly coloured clothing. They ought, he thought, to give up their scarlet tunics and red fur shoes.

It was Northumbria, however, that became the chief seat of learning in England. Benedict Biscop enriched Wearmouth and Jarrow with numerous books brought from Rome, and it was this scholarly atmosphere, in a community which may have contained some 600 monks at the time, that produced Bede, by far the most famous of Anglo-Saxon scholars. He lived from about 672 until 735, and his enduring fame rests, not on his contemporary repute as a theologian, scholar and teacher, but on his *Ecclesiastical History of the English People*, a work written with some largeness of purpose. His aim was to demonstrate to the Anglo-Saxons that they were, through their membership of the Roman church, linked with their island's Romano-British past and with the wider Christian community across the Channel. It is perhaps not enough to call Bede the first English historian: in that he was the first man to try to give the Anglo-Saxons a sense of national identity within the whole religious and cultural structure of the western world, he may be said to have created English history.

It was partly due to Bede's inspiration that a school was founded at York which, from 778 onwards, was under the direction of Alcuin. Since he was in deacon's orders only and became a professed monk only at the end of his life, Alcuin can rank as the first eminent English school-master. He insisted that to provide men with spiritual learning was a major work of charity and that a large number of learned men was necessary for the world's welfare. His pupils were given specialist teaching in grammar, rhetoric, astronomy, arithmetic and biology, as well as church music and the scriptures. It is a tribute to Alcuin and to the quality of Northumbrian education that in 782 he became master of the palace school established by Charlemagne at Aix-la-Chapelle to provide an educated élite for his own still largely untamed dominions.

A notable characteristic of Anglo-Saxon men of learning was their zeal in conducting missions for the conversion of the heathen peoples of north-western Europe. The ideal of forsaking all in order to live apart to do God's work was strong at this time. Then, as later, spiritual merit was attached to the practice of making pilgrimages to far-off sacred shrines, above all to Rome itself. All such journeys were perilous at a time when any stranger was thought a potential thief and likely himself to be the victim of robbery. Regular hazards included shipwreck and capture by pirates or brigands, or destitution resulting from the ex-orbitant exactions of those from whom food and shelter were sought. Women pilgrims to Rome who did not freeze to death crossing the Alps might, so Bede averred, end up as adulteresses or harlots. Nevertheless the establishment in Rome of a special quarter in the Borgo San Spirito for the benefit of English pilgrims indicates that many of them did indeed reach their journey's end. But the most spectacular and enduring results of the religious wanderlust of the Anglo-Saxons of the seventh and eighth centuries were the conversion, by the Englishman, Willibrord, of the heathens of Frisia, and the mission of Winfrith, better known as St Boniface, to the Thuringians and the Bavarians. Willibrord died in 739 at Echternach, and Boniface, who has been called 'the greatest man of action in Anglo-Saxon history', was martyred at Dokkum, in Frisia, in 754. Even after this, Englishmen helped to convert the Saxons whom Charlemagne conquered.

This missionary enthusiasm to some extent limited the contribution of learned eighth-century churchmen to the political development of England itself. They did not regularly provide kings with a body of literate permanent officials, nor did they systematically seek to give kingship a broader basis than the primitive Germanic concept of a king as principally a conquering warrior and distributor of booty. The evangelistic spirituality inherited from the Celtic church led the clergy to see themselves as pastors, not rulers. The church exercised great cultural and educational influence, but played a relatively minor part in the evolution of a more ordered society. The consecration of Offa's short-lived son, Ecgfrith, by the church suggests that a closer collaboration between church and king might have developed but for the Danish onslaught that began shortly after this event. Before the ninth century, however, the aim of churchmen was to sanctify the person of the king, not to organise his government for him. Both Boniface and Alcuin had severely criticised kings; but they did so while devoting their real energies to converting heathens or educating Franks across the Channel.

Yet in one respect, the church enlarged kingship by its very existence. The clergy were sanctified persons whose protection became an additional function of kingship, since the king alone had the right and the power to defend them against attack or illegality. In consequence, churchmen considered the ordering of ecclesiastical affairs to be as much the king's concern as it was theirs. The long process by which the king's justice was gradually extended to all his subjects begins with the king's assumption of the right to protect his churchmen.

2
VIKINGS AND SAXONS

Danes and West Saxons

THE Danes, like the Norwegians who ravaged Ireland, Scotland and northern England, and the Swedes who moved eastwards into Russia, were major participants in the succession of migratory Viking invasions which, in the ninth and tenth centuries, left a mark on places as far apart as Greenland and Constantinople, Shetland and Sicily. Their initial reputation as fierce pagan warriors was the result of the great population pressures in their Scandinavian homelands which drove them across the seas in search of new territories in which to settle. Within a short space of time they assimilated the culture of the regions they conquered and allowed themselves to be baptised as Christians without much hesitation. Most of them were soon integrated as members of existing village communities in the areas they settled.

Resourceful seafarers and energetic traders who greatly widened Europe's horizons and infused it with new energy, the Vikings first appeared to the Anglo-Saxons as pirates and angels of death. Some, it was said, howled in battle like wolves, others fought frenziedly without armour and were known as *berserks*. But they were intelligent as well as ferocious. Their ships were better constructed, though not necessarily larger, than those built by their victims, and with their long, kite-shaped shields, their vicious long-handled battle axes, and their more general use of helmets and chain mail, they were better armed than Saxons. Their masterly use of forts and fortified bases also enabled them to establish themselves as more than mere raiders.

The Vikings attacked the British Isles by two main routes. The more northerly route was followed by the Norwegians and relatively few Danes. Permanent Norse settlements were made on the east coast of Ireland. From there, Norsemen raided and settled extensively in the north-west of England and also, by the tenth century, east of the Pennines, so that as late as 950 there was still the possibility of the establishment of a Norse kingdom stretching from Dublin to York. The sack of Lindisfarne and Jarrow as early as 793–4 probably took place during the first stages of this seaborne Norwegian advance.

The Danes took a southerly route, their main thrusts being upon the Rhine and northern Gaul and thence across the Channel to England, where sporadic raids on the Wessex coast, and a number of land and sea battles, by no means all Danish successes, took place between the 780s and the 870s. Well before 870, however, it had become apparent that there were easier targets than Wessex. As late as 860, though Danish raiders stormed Winchester, they were driven away again, and neither Wessex nor Mercia felt seriously threatened at that time. The Vikings' reputation for savagery was a reflection of the unpreparedness of the east coast: the Danes found Lindisfarne and Jarrow richly endowed with treasure but wholly without defences. Hence, between 865 and 874, a determined Danish assault on these eastern coasts overwhelmed the English. By 867 they had subdued East Anglia, overthrown Northumbria after a bloody struggle at York, and had set up a powerful base in Mercia at Nottingham. Their strongholds at York, Nottingham and at Thetford, in East Anglia, were a major contribution to the permanence of the Danish triumph.

By 870, the Danes had moved inland far enough to create another base at Reading. From there they threatened Alfred, king of Wessex (871–99), forcing him to make peace in 871. By 874 they had put down a rebellion in Northumbria, set up a new base at Repton in Mercia, and imposed a puppet king on that kingdom. In the first week of 878, in a surprise attack upon Chippenham, a Danish force under Guthrum secured control of much of Wessex, so that by that date all three major English kingdoms had lost their authority in little more than ten years. But for the diversion of a Danish force northwards in 874 to ravage Bernicia and attack Celtic Strathclyde, there might have been no English recovery.

Abandoned by many of his folk, some of whose leaders found it preferable to collaborate with the Danes rather than fight and be killed, Alfred took refuge in the Somerset marshes. He fortified the Isle of Athelney, from which he conducted guerrilla attacks on the Danes, still concentrated at Chippenham. The only adult ruler to have survived the overthrow of the early English kingdoms, Alfred managed to attract sufficient support from West Saxons in Hampshire, Wiltshire and Somerset to confront Guthrum's army at Edington on the Wiltshire Downs in the early summer of 878. He forced Guthrum back to Chippenham and besieged him there for a fortnight. There seems nothing 'berserk' in Guthrum's response to this development. He promised to remove his force from Wessex and agreed to become a Christian, staying with Alfred at Wedmore in Somerset for some days after being baptised. Withdrawing to Cirencester, Guthrum then returned to East Anglia in 879. Two years later, part of his army was detached to do battle in Gaul. From the Danish army that remained, Alfred wrested control of London in 886, and he and Guthrum agreed on a territorial demarcation between Dane and Saxon. The limit of the Danish con- trolled area, the Danelaw, was fixed on a line that ran along the rivers Thames and Lea, thence to Bedford, along the Ouse to Watling Street, and then north-west to Chester. Guthrum himself settled in Suffolk and died at Hadleigh in 890.

Guthrum's policy in the face of Alfred's resolution was realistic. The Danes' primary aim, the acquisition of booty, had already been realised.

Now, they wanted to ensure the survival of the Danish settlements formed in the wake of their victories. The new colonisers needed peace as badly as their Saxon neighbours. Newly arrived Danes were as vulnerable to disease among cattle and men as the indigenous Saxons. Danish sea-raiding parties, with their attendant women and children might, even at this stage, die of hunger if they failed to win sufficient good land to see them through their first winter. Guthrum's withdrawal from Wessex suggests that, for the time being, Danish power had been stretched as far as it could reasonably go, since Alfred's unexpected opposition was an obstacle with which the Danes had not been confronted elsewhere in England. Moreover, their victories farther north had not totally extinguished opposition, either in Northumbria or Mercia; indeed, the area of the Danelaw conceded by Alfred to Guthrum extended beyond the main areas of Danish settlement by including Suffolk and Essex, where few Danes were settled.

Alfred's resistance to Guthrum, and to a renewed Danish advance from Gaul by way of the Thames in 892, was founded on a considerable capacity for organisation. Though he was by no means 'the founder of the navy', he built new and better designed ships, and was thus the only king in Europe to attempt to match the Danes in their own element, the sea. He adapted existing methods of defence and made them more effective. He reorganised the Saxon militia, the *fyrd*, so that at all times some men were available to fight, some to man fortresses and some to till the soil. Hitherto summoned for the two former purposes only at moments of crisis, even men who did not prefer to stay in their fields were liable to arrive too late to fight. Landholders had always been expected to build and maintain fortresses, but Alfred and his son, Edward the Elder, constructed a coordinated network of fortifications which provided for defence in depth and were a refuge for men and cattle against Danish plunderers. The fact that they were constantly manned made these defensive *burhs* centres not merely of defence but of trade, commerce and local government. Few continental rulers showed as much competence in the face of Viking attacks, and Alfred's success meant that there was no repetition of the kind of calamity that had occurred at Chippenham in January 878.

From 880 until his death in 899, Alfred, previously the leader of a resistance movement among his own folk, became the organiser of something like a grand alliance against the Danes, a diplomat as well as an organiser of military victory. He secured the cooperation of the West Mercians by presenting not only London to the West Mercian leader (it had been Mercian before the Danes took it) but also his daughter, Aethelflaed, as a bride. The Danes were held off in 893 by a Wessex–West Mercian alliance; and Alfred also contrived to break up a dangerous conjunction between the Welsh of Gwynedd and the Danish kingdom of York in Northumbria.

The alliance with West Mercia survived into the reign of Alfred's son,

Edward the Elder (899–924). The Northumbrian Danes were routed, and English overlordship acknowledged by all the Danes of southern England. Thanks to Alfred's marriage treaty, his daughter, Aethelflaed, the 'Lady of the Mercians , controlled Mercia after her husband's death. She was a notable organiser of resistance to the Danes and built many burhs, among them Tamworth and Newcastle-under-Lyme. In 924, Athelstan, son of Edward the Elder, was accepted as king in both Mercia and Wessex. He was one of the most successful English kings, forcing the submission of Northumbria, securing recognition of his overlordship from Strathclyde and from the Scots and Welsh, and confining the Cornish to the western side of the Tamar. In a great battle at an unidentified place called *Brunanburh* he defeated a rebellious coalition of Scots, the Celts of Strathclyde and the Norsemen of Dublin. According to Irish chroniclers, five kings were slain at Brunanburh, and the fame of Athelstan's victory was such that it was recorded as far away as Iceland. It made good his claim to be 'most glorious king of the Anglo-Saxons and the Danes'. His prestige was international. One of his daughters married the Duke of the Franks and another the heir to Otto the Great of Saxony, the future Emperor of the Germans.

The monarchy established in England by Alfred and his successors between 878 and 975 was more durable than almost any other in the Europe of their time. Yet, neither triumph in battle, even over many foes at once, nor their concession of overlordship to him, guaranteed the survival of a king's power beyond the moment of his death. No English king could leave an assured heritage behind him. English kings could fight, proclaim laws, accept submissions, but they lacked a professionally trained army and a permanent bureaucracy. Without these there was little chance of establishing the idea of a government or of a continuing administration to some extent independent of the reigning king. In an age when personal loyalty to a warrior king was the principal basis of political stability, there was little certainty that that stability could continue for any length of time. This was all the more true given that England then had such indefinable frontiers to the north and west and was, after the Danish invasions, such a mixture of peoples. From 936 to 955, during the reigns of Athelstan's brothers, Edmund and Eadred, West Saxon control in Mercia and Northumbria was again almost non-existent. For most of the years from 940 to 954, hostile Scandinavian kings, one from Ireland and one from Norway, ruled in York. The Danelaw was beset by internal divisions between the Danes, particularly the Mercian Danes, and the Norwegians, and it was the Northumbrians themselves who overthrew the Norwegian king of York, Eric Bloodaxe, in 954. Mercian and Northumbrian acceptance of the overlordship of Wessex after that was not much more than a defensive alliance against further Norse attacks and proved the start of what was merely a longish pause before the Scandinavians overthrew the kingdom of Wessex some sixty years later.

The breathing space, during which the Scandinavian threat was in abeyance, enabled the chroniclers to say of Edgar of Wessex (959–75), 'God granted him to live his days in peace'. He had a sizeable fleet to guard the coasts and he made war in Glamorgan; but his principal contributions to kingship were ritualistic. He was crowned with elaborate ecclesiastical ceremonial in 973, and six or seven Scottish and Welsh kings rowed him, in similarly ceremonial fashion, along the River Dee at Chester. But whether this act was to acknowledge his overlordship or simply his leadership of an alliance of all the participants to defend the British Isles against raiding Danes and Norsemen is not clear.

Viking Conquest

In 978, Edgar's young son and successor, Edward, was assassinated at Corfe in Dorset. His place as king was taken by his brother Ethelred, then aged about eleven. Since Ethelred's mother and her Mercian associates were allegedly implicated in Edward's murder, Ethelred's reign had an inauspicious beginning. Whereas the murdered Edward was venerated as a saint, Ethelred seems to have been almost as disliked in his own day as he was despised afterwards. His name meant 'noble counsel' and his contemporary nickname was *unraed*, meaning 'evil counsel'. In later centuries he was given the even more derogatory label, Ethelred the Unready. The implication that he was merely vacillating and incompetent is perhaps misleading. He seems to have committed acts of treachery and injustice which made it harder to deal with his external foes because he intensified the hostility of powerful men in his own realm. The administrative limitations of English kingship, together with the respite of half a century's freedom from Danish attack, had encouraged a spirit of independence among the powerful notables of Northumbria and Mercia, leading to a number of complex quarrels between them. Over considerable parts of the north and north-east, Ethelred had no more authority than other Anglo-Saxon kings. In trying to assert such authority by involving himself in a succession of reckless interventions on one side or the other in these conflicts, Ethelred, so far from increasing his kingly power, diminished it by acquiring a reputation for arbitrariness and unpredictability. It was this rather than mere weakness that seems to have caused his 'unreadiness' when the Danes launched against him the most efficient attack they had ever mounted against England. The English collapse before the Danes on this occasion, as rapid as had been Alfred's earlier recovery against them, ensured for Ethelred as low a place in the records as Alfred's was high.

Ethelred's defects were not the sole cause of this collapse. The Danish attacks that began in 981 were, unlike earlier ones, wholly concentrated upon England and based on a strong, united kingdom of Denmark. Within England itself there were now well-established Danish communities disposed to welcome a Danish invasion if its outcome promised more settled conditions of life and a ruler from among their own people. Moreover, the new attackers were led by a highly trained professional force, aiming not at gradual settlement but, first, at despoiling, and then at controlling, a rich and ill-defended kingdom. From the early 990s until 1012 they consented to be bought off at intervals by large payments in cash. It was to obtain this Danegeld that Ethelred established in England the most effective and drastic system of taxation to be found anywhere in Europe.

The first great Viking leader of this period was Olaf Tryggvason, king of Norway. In 991 he defeated the men of Essex in a battle at Maldon; their heroism was commemorated in a moving Anglo-Saxon poem. Whether the absence during the succeeding twenty years of any large-scale pitched battles against the Danes by Ethelred was because of his incompetence or because the Danes preferred to wear the English down by hit and run tactics is uncertain. Ethelred's army was larger than the Danish and the Danes may therefore have relied on local battles of the kind they fought at Maldon, especially since they seem to have won most of them.

By 1013 the Viking enterprise was taken over by Swein Forkbeard, king of Denmark. His decisive intervention may have been due in part to a desire to revenge the killing of his sister, who had been one of the victims of the massacre of St Brice's Day (13/14 Nov) in 1002, when Ethelred had ordered the assassination of a number of his Danish subjects. It was an impolitic act since it lost Ethelred the support of many Norsemen who had previously been loyal to him. Swein's descent on the Humber in 1013 produced the submission of all the Danelaw and, after an undisciplined sacking of Canterbury by the Danes, such damage was inflicted in Wessex that Ethelred fled to Normandy. Even so, on Swein's sudden death in 1014, though the Danelaw submitted to his eighteen-year-old son, Cnut, the West Saxons took Ethelred back on the grounds that he was their 'natural lord'. All the same they begged him to rule more justly than in the past. Ethelred died in 1016, after doing nothing to consolidate his hold on the crown or on his people's affections, and was succeeded by his son, Edmund Ironside. Edmond, however, after being decisively defeated by Cnut at Ashingdon in Essex with many casualties, conceded control of all the Danelaw to Cnut and himself died shortly afterwards. The West Saxons, bereft of leadership, finally accepted Cnut as their king.

Ever since the advent of Swein, the issue had been not so much whether there should be an English or a Danish king as whether a land irreversibly Anglo-Danish could acquire a king capable of giving it good government. It is this which explains the various transfers of allegiance by powerful Danish personalities from Cnut to Ethelred or Edmund and back again. Many among the Anglo-Danish population wanted a return to the relatively stable kingship that had been enjoyed in the period between Athelstan and Edgar. The newly arrived Danes and Norsemen found it harder even than their predecessors to accept an English king.

Cnut offered stability to the former of these groups and his prestige to both of them. Ostentatious in his support of the church, a great Viking who was also king of Denmark and, for a time, of Norway, he symbolised his intention of being king of both Danes and Englishmen by marrying Edmund Ironside's young widow, Emma of Normandy. His reign revealed that the first real king of England would be a Dane.

Cnut was at pains to confirm his willingness to respect the traditional differences between English and Danish law, as Edgar of Wessex had done; and there was much kingly propaganda designed to make loyalty to 'the one Christian faith' synonymous with loyalty to king Cnut. He further advertised his royal and holy status by a visit to Rome in 1027, timed to coincide with the coronation of the Holy Roman Emperor so that he could appear not only as a devout pilgrim fulfilling a religious duty but as a great prince attending a solemn, sacred gathering in the company of the other great princes of Christendom.

His rule was nevertheless essentially that of a conqueror. He compelled payment of a huge further instalment of Danegeld to compensate those Danish forces that were returned to Denmark and then regularly imposed the onerous tax called the heregeld. This enabled him to maintain a fleet of warships and, using his personal bodyguard of 'housecarles' as its nucleus, to create a large and expensive standing army. The housecarles themselves collected the taxes from which they drew their pay. Cnut also habitually rewarded his military chiefs with great territorial earldoms. The word 'earl' derives from the Scandinavian 'jarl'; the greater nobles of the English kingdom had been called ealdormen. Of Cnut's sixteen earls, most were Danish, notably those of Northumbria and East Anglia, or half-Danish, and some English lords may have been dispossessed. But the loyalty of his powerful earls, the devotion of leading churchmen, and his command of an efficient army and a fleet, ensured Cnut a peaceful time in England.

Yet again, however, too much depended on the king's own person. Cnut died in 1035 when still a young man, leaving the succession to be disputed between his own two sons and the two sons of Ethelred the Unready. Weakened by these rivalries, exploited as they were by over-powerful earls, England seemed almost certain thereafter to submit either to the king of Norway or the Duke of Normandy.

Though the eventual triumph of the latter in 1066 was to mark the end of half a millennium of almost constant internal conflict and of vulnerability to seaborne invasion, England's social, legal and, to some extent political, geography long remained in basic respects as the Anglo-Saxon and Viking assaults and rivalries had left it. The unitary kingdom over which the Normans and Angevins would rule only slowly lost traces of the tripartite division into Wessex, English Mercia and the Danelaw that remained as a legacy of early Anglo-Saxon history and of Alfred's contest with the Danes. These divisions were still being acknowledged by the crown well after the Norman conquest. The most southerly counties, from Cornwall to Kent, together with Somerset, Wiltshire, Berkshire and Surrey, were markedly different in laws and customs from what had once been English Mercia: Oxfordshire, Warwickshire, Gloucestershire, Worcestershire, Herefordshire, Staffordshire, Salop and Cheshire. Both were different again from the Danelaw, throughout which the permanent Danish settlement established in the ninth century was sufficiently intense for the whole region to be considered Anglo-Danish, not Anglo-Saxon. Further north still, the combined effects of the two great Viking invasions was to create a considerable area whose ultimate political allegiance remained in dispute for much of the middle ages. Though Edgar of Wessex is thought to have recognised Kenneth of Scotland as king of all lands between Tweed and Forth, the Tweed could not yet be thought of as Scotland's southern boundary. Little of that part of Northumbria that lay between Tees and Tweed would be under the direct control of the English kings; for centuries to come it seemed more than likely that Northumberland, with its unruly, warlike earls, and Durham, after 1075 an almost independent ecclesiastical principality ruled by its bishop, would become part of Scotland rather than England. Even Lancashire, a region uneasily situated between English Mercia and Danish Northumbria, did not achieve the status of a distinct county under the English crown until after the Norman conquest.

Diocese and Parish

The ninth-century Danish invasions did great damage to the church. Its treasures were seized as booty, its manuscripts were dispersed if not destroyed, its diocesan organisation was so dislocated that some bishoprics disappeared for ever, and monks and bishops were forced into hiding. The library at York, considered one of the greatest in eighth-century Europe, was destroyed, and the Minster was so impoverished that for much of the two centuries before 1066 the see of York had to be held in plurality with the rich diocese of Winchester. The Lindisfarne community meditated flight to Ireland before eventually settling at Durham at the end of the tenth century. In addition, the Danelaw was everywhere settled by heathen Danes; and in English England there were many nominal Christians liable to revert to a similar heathenism because priests and monks could less often minister to them.

The Danes do not seem to have felt hostile towards Christianity and, like the Anglo-Saxons before them, may well have found little difficulty in assimilating what would appear to them as an additional corpus of useful magic into their already miscellaneous collection of charms and incantations. The church had adopted a pragmatic approach to heathen practices from the start; at this stage the church lacked the means and the intellectual resources that sustained the self-confident militancy of later Christianity. It is certain that heathen practices long survived in the Danelaw. As late as the eleventh century, over four hundred years after

Augustine's mission of 597, it was thought necessary to include in the laws of Cnut an 'earnest forbidding' of the worship of 'heathen gods, and the sun and moon, fire and flood, water-wells or stones, or trees of the wood of any sort'. Many Danes may have felt, on the other hand, that the gods of their former homelands might be unable to protect them in their new homes. Polytheistic, tribal religions do not seem to travel well or long survive in competition with 'universal' monotheistic religions. Christianity could offer a coherent interpretation of life, whereas the multiplicity of the older gods offered only a confused one. In baptism a man was initiated into membership, not of a tribe, but a whole 'world-wide' body of Christian people united together in one Christian society. Nor was this terrestrial community all: membership could last beyond the brief span between Christian baptism and Christian burial. Subject to good behaviour it was for eternity, and the church had the keys of that too.

Conversion or, in Anglo-Saxon England, revival, was accomplished by patient, pastoral endeavour as dioceses were re-established or reorganised under the rule of Alfred's successors. Bishops once more sent priests out into the villages from minster or monastery and in time, as more independent field churches were set up, the parochial system which was in operation throughout the land by the twelfth century began slowly to emerge. Saxon lords were encouraged by the kings of Wessex to settle among the heathen of the Danelaw and establish churches on their lands. Even modest landowners soon came to prefer more substantial memorials to their piety and their reputation than a mere open air cross or a rough-built chapel, and it became a customary act of piety for a lord to give land for the erection of a church and to endow it to provide it with a priest. Though the system of operating from minsters survived longer in the north, most English village churches were to stem from foundations begun before 1066. By that time the majority of Englishmen lived within reasonable distance of a church, and in the long run the work of these parish churches, though less spectacular than that of the monasteries, made the more permanent imprint.

Though most pre-Norman churches were small, fairly homely structures, many later Anglo-Saxon churches were skilfully constructed of stone, notably in Lincolnshire and Northamptonshire and within the Danelaw generally, and were finely ornamented, since English metalwork and church vestments were of high quality. In the towns, churches were built generously. By the eleventh century, Thetford, with a population of about 4,000, had twelve churches, York had fourteen churches for about 8,000 inhabitants and Norwich forty-three for rather fewer than 5,000.

The work of the spirit needed finance from the beginning; and as the church became endowed with wealth, some of its offices, originally established to serve God, came to be seen as offices of profit, leading to frequent confusion between the service of God and that of Mammon. On the one hand a church building belonged, spiritually, to the saint to whom it was dedicated, on the other it was a secular property. In Anglo-Saxon times a priest might pay a lump sum on taking over an incumbency and an annual rent thereafter. This could make the founding of a church by a landowner a form of property development as well as of piety. The landowner had the power to sell the church, divide its property, bequeath it to his heirs and to dismiss the incumbent at will. Yet, though the lay proprietorship of churches soon gave rise to scandal, its origins were not scandalous. Ninth and tenth century kings and bishops could not christianise the community without lay cooperation. In a time as unstable, and as heathen in its roots, as Anglo-Danish England, the protection of church and priest by landowners great and small was essential. Only in the thirteenth century, when society was more settled, was the church able to do away with lay investiture. The lord became a patron rather than a proprietor with the right to hire and fire. Though he continued to nominate the incumbent, the incumbent would in future be invested by a bishop. This new system of patronage survived beyond the Reformation, long preserving to the nobility and gentry the power to bestow upon persons of whom they approved one of the few occupations which carried security of tenure for life. In modified form it survived into the twentieth century.

Apart from donations and endowments of land, the church derived regular income from tithe (or tenth) and other dues. Tithes had a history going back before the days of Theodore of Tarsus and had originally been gifts to the church for many purposes, including alms for the poor or aid to holy pilgrims. The increase in parish churches caused tithe to be used chiefly for their maintenance. The laws of Edgar insisted on the appropriation of tithe to that purpose, and laid down that non-payment of tithe should be penalised by the seizure of most of the offender's tithable property. By Edgar's time, tithe consisted of the great tithe, representing ten per cent of the corn crop, due on All Saints' Day (1 November), and the lesser tithe, representing a tenth of the value of poultry, vegetables and young animals, payable at Whitsuntide. Originally paid in kind, tithe was increasingly paid in cash.

Another source of ecclesiastical income was church scot, referred to in the laws of Ine of Wessex (689–726). Originally a payment in kind, it could take the form of the first fruits of the grain crop, and was payable at Martinmas (10 November); the proceeds of church scot were the principal means of paying for the upkeep of the early minsters. By the eleventh century, other payments included plough-alms, a penny for every working plough team, payable within fifteen days after Easter, Peter's pence, a payment to the pope, which was due on St Peter's Day (1 August), and a thrice-yearly contribution of wax for church illumination. Soul scot was a burial fee, payable at the graveside. These dues were, in total, substantial enough to place a heavy burden on the peasant. The stiff laws of Edgar and Cnut against non-payment of tithe and church scot indicate that they were not always paid willingly.

Christian Kings, Monastic Ideals

The largely unchronicled missionary achievement of the growing number of parish churches was in part the outcome of Alfred's devotion, even while campaigning against the Danes, to reviving the learning of the church. Without learned churchmen there would have been no learning at all, and no literate men to assist the routine business of kingly rule. Alfred's concern for the church and its learning contributed as much as his successful resistance to the Danes to the creation of such unity as there was in England before the reign of Cnut.

The decline of learning when Northumbria crumbled provides the background for Alfred's allegation that by his time there were few men in England who could translate a letter written in Latin. By contrast, the learning which had been available in Northumbria before the Danish invasions had enabled Bede to become an admirable Latin scholar as well as a conscientious historian. He had been familiar with scores of Latin works by pagan and early Christian writers; his commentaries on the scriptures, like his *Ecclesiastical History*, had a European reputation. Northumbrian learning had qualified Alcuin to collaborate in the preparation of the Vulgate, remarkable, like Bede's *Ecclesiastical History*, for the near-classical quality of its Latin.

Since he was a king and a pious one, Alfred was more conscious even than Bede of the need to convince the leaders of the English people that they were heirs to a great historic religious tradition, and that access to this tradition depended upon familiarity with writings in the Latin language common to all western Christendom. Since Latin was now so little known, however, he set to work with a team of translators to render important Latin works into vernacular English. As well as Bede's *History* a whole library about the church was translated, in particular, Pope Gregory the Great's manual for bishops, *Pastoralis*, or Pastoral Care. Much of the clergy's success in the conversion of the Danelaw may have been due to the fact that they had the stuff of Christian teaching available to them in their own language.

Alfred's intention had been to create a laity educated in Anglo-Saxon and a clergy educated in Latin; but his patronage of the vernacular created a tradition which, by the end of the tenth century, resulted in English becoming one of the principal means by which basic Christian teaching was communicated. Aelfric, abbot of Eynsham (*c.*955–1020) wrote two sets of sermons in English for priests to deliver on great church festivals and Wulfstan, archbishop of York, composed a powerful address to the English, in their own language, to renew their faith during the crisis caused in 1014 by the flight of Ethelred the Unready to Normandy. The vernacular writings of Alfred and his collaborators, and of their tenth-century successors, made West Saxon the dominant form of English until the thirteenth century.

It was almost certainly at Alfred's instigation that his scribes initiated the Anglo-Saxon Chronicle in the English language. Beginning with an historical prelude based on oral tradition, on Bede and on fragmentary earlier records, it was continued as an account of the reigns of Alfred and his successors, and of their struggles against the Danes. It thus acquired the character of a national history rather than a mere dynastic chronicle. Copies of it were sent by the kings of Wessex to many English monasteries and various local versions of the Chronicle, containing varying degrees of detail, were continued for several centuries, one, at Peterborough, continuing until 1155. Its character as a sustainer of national morale is shown by the hostility of the chroniclers to Ethelred, so 'unready' against the Danes compared with his illustrious predecessor, Alfred. Yet it was sufficiently influential in maintaining the prestige of the dynasty of Wessex for that prestige to survive even Ethelred's catastrophes. On Swein's death, Ethelred was nevertheless accepted back again; and after the early deaths of Cnut and the two young sons who succeeded him, it was to Ethelred's son, Edward ('the Confessor'), that the English turned in 1042.

Monasticism was in decline after the Danish invasions, though perhaps it would be more correct to say that in addition to a reduction in the number of monastic houses there was, to a somewhat greater extent, a rise in the number of those who, though regarded as monkish, were only quasi-monks. There were many communities whose members were priests or, as they were usually called, canons or clerks, working outside the community. Members of these canonical communities served the minsters and the mission churches planted by them. Canons increasingly adopted such unmonkish practices as marriage and the ownership of property and were therefore much disliked by the ardent monastic reformers who became prominent in the tenth century. The reformers' zeal derived in part from a renewed insistence on an amplified form of the old monastic Rule of St Benedict, which was spread across western Europe by the pioneer reformed monastic house of Cluny, in Burgundy. Allied to an insistence on the basic Benedictine vows of poverty, chastity and obedience, was an emphasis on liturgical prayer at frequent, regular intervals throughout the day. The ideals of the movement were a powerful combination of an ascetic attitude towards the self with an elaborately aesthetic form of worship.

The monastic reform movement in England reached its culmination in the reign of Edgar and was presided over by Dunstan. A prominent member of the Wessex aristocracy, and a powerful and sometimes overbearing political force at court from the reign of Edmund (939–46) onwards, he was a renowned abbot of Glastonbury and held the sees of Winchester and London simultaneously; when Edgar became king in 959, the archbishop of Canterbury was demoted back to his former position as bishop of Wells so that Dunstan could become archbishop instead. It looks as if Edgar's reputation as an exceptionally Christian king might owe more to Dunstan than any particular saintliness on Edgar's part. The detailed administration of the monastic reforms of his reign was probably organised by Dunstan's hardworking contemporaries, Aethelwold, bishop of Worcester, and Oswald, archbishop of York.

Dunstan had earlier transformed the only partially monastic clerks of Glastonbury into a community following the Benedictine rule. Aethelwold and Oswald imposed monastic discipline on the chapters of Winchester and Worcester, even though it was far from certain that the life of a monk was compatible with the task of administering cathedral and diocese. The reduction in the number of secular cathedrals involved a reduction in the number of secular cathedral schools, institutions which, in France, were considerable centres of learning. Intellectual life in England was therefore somewhat backward until the foundation of the two English universities late in the twelfth century. This detachment from contemporary intellectual developments in Europe was also possibly accentuated by the interest of English churchmen in the vernacular.

Yet deficiency in intellectual training was accompanied by evidence of much monastic success in the encouragement of personal piety among the laity. The pre-Norman English were ahead of continentals in their devotion to the Virgin, and the English monasteries were probably the originators of the many legends about the Virgin, the so-called Mary Legends, that circulated widely throughout Europe in the twelfth century.

Dunstan and Aethelwold were mainly responsible for drawing up, in the 970s, an agreed rule for the conduct of the strict Benedictine monasteries of the time, the *Regularis Concordia*. From this it can be learned that, in winter, tenth-century monks would be roused for the first service of the day at 2.30 a.m. and would end the day at 6.30 p.m., the corresponding times in summer being 1.30 a.m. and 8.15 p.m. Work of all kinds was done in two hours during the morning, the rest of the day being devoted to an almost continuous round of liturgical duties. A total of five hours of psalm-singing, praying and scriptural reading was worked through even before daybreak. After masses and lesser offices every hour came vespers of the day, vespers of the dead and, finally, compline. As a result of this continuous liturgical activity few monks were scholars and much menial work had to be done by hired servants.

The reformed monasticism of the tenth century was dominated by the aristocracy and a strong sense of hierarchy. A distinctive feature of the *Regularis Concordia* is its emphasis on regular prayers for the king and the royal family; they were not, the rules insist, to be chanted too quickly. The elaborate coronation ceremonial organised by Dunstan for Edgar in 973 expressed in liturgical terms the resolve of a priestly aristocracy to exalt the king by affirming the priestly character of his office and also to exalt the priestly, aristocratic church which invested him with the symbols of his power. By the time of Cnut, secular and religious authority had produced an almost theocratic government. Cnut's charter of 1020 illustrates the lack of distinction between spiritual and temporal authority:

Now I beseech all my archbishops and all my suffragan bishops that they all be attentive to God's right, every one in his district which is committed to him; and also my ealdormen and command that they help the bishops in maintaining God's rights and my royal authority and the weal of all the people.

The monastic ideals of the age of Dunstan gave rise to a marked difference between the church in England and the church across the Channel. Cluniac monks tried to escape episcopal control, aiming to become autonomous save only for their allegiance to the pope. In England the great majority of the bishops themselves were monks. The longer term consequence of the Cluniac reform was a movement against lay patronage and against kingly and princely control over the church. By 1066 there were signs of this trend on the continent, but not in England. To English churchmen, the king was one of them; and to English kings the bishops were custodians, if not the guarantors, of what sense of national unity there was. Moreover, as Norman prelates found to their distaste when William of Normandy brought them with him, the English church was fairly casually organised in spite of the close association of king and church at the top. The real strength of the English church was less the alliance of aristocrat and king in a quasi-theocratic court than in its usually hardworking, austere and devotional bishops, its encouragement of simple piety, and the dedication of its craftsmen to the ornamentation of churches and the illumination of manuscripts. In religious art and painting, the English scarcely had equals in western Europe. The impression is of a religion of the spirit rather than of the letter, of a church not noted for its rigid enforcement of ecclesiastical discipline and, given its heritage from the Celtic church, and the size of its still not fully assimilated Scandinavian population, retaining much of the pastoral character of a missionary church whose first duty was that of patient conversion. It assisted, and gladly welcomed the aid of, secular great men, but did not, save in the case of exceptional characters like Dunstan and Wulfstan, offer them much more than moral guidance; as for the humble, it seems to have felt it imprudent to ask too much of them.

The monastic ideal had more general effects, many of which lasted beyond the pre-Norman centuries. Its emphasis on celibacy as the ideal state meant that to be married was perforce to be not quite fully Christian; the concept of 'holy matrimony' did not emerge until after the Reformation. The only hope, therefore, for the married, was that they could somehow make amends by the blamelessness of their lives in other respects. That the ideals of chastity and poverty were not put into practice by many Christians did not mean that they ceased to provide the criteria by which men's conduct was judged. People do not cease to respect established codes of behaviour merely by the circumstance of breaking them. The elaborate system of confession and penance, already established before the Normans came, was a recognition that the twin ideals of poverty and chastity provided the standards by which medieval men judged themselves and one another. Late twentieth-century man judged himself and others by the quite different ideals of affluence and sexual fulfilment. In medieval terms, this would be taken as a yielding to avarice and lust, two of the seven deadly sins.

Moreover, since medieval Europe was, in comparison both with the Roman Empire and Europe after 1800, relatively poor and 'backward', the propagation of the ideals of poverty and chastity to some extent conformed to reality. Chastity was not 'natural'; but to procreate was not only to breed sinners but to create mouths to feed where there was often not enough to eat, or bodies too weak to survive beyond infancy. In a society in which poverty was a fact of life for many and not just a rule for monks, it was gain rather than loss that riches should always be under judgment, even if the judgment were usually ignored. And the church reinforced these ideals by insisting that man's true life and meaning lay outside the visible world, for that was not his permanent habitation. Death was more important than life, both because it opened the way to eternity and because it came so much sooner to almost everyone than in the modern world; men had to prepare for it long before some of their remoter descendants would begin to give it a thought.

3
LAW, LIFE AND WORK

Kindred, Community, Law and King

UNLIKE the Romans, accustomed to look to a deified emperor as the ultimate source of all law and justice, the Anglo-Saxons, like the other Germanic peoples of their time, began with no idea of law as something imposed on them from above, and little or no idea of 'the state'. Their concern was almost entirely with loyalty to persons, whether the person of a king or a lord, or the group of persons who made up their kindred or their local community. 'Law' was not what they were told to do, but what custom required of them. A king could not 'make' law; law was not 'made' by any individual, however august, but was a large, rather untidy bundle of customs inherited from the past. It was proper for a king to remind people of customs that were falling into disuse and to propose punishments for those who ignored them. He could amplify, clarify and enforce custom, he could make the law known. But though Anglo-Saxon and later kings and governments certainly made new laws from time to time and had them enforced, this would be considered for centuries to be exceptional rather than normal.

The early laws of Anglo-Saxon kings were called, since the word 'law' was brought into the language by the Danes, 'dooms'. But a king would be at great pains to announce that his dooms were drawn up only after consultation with the best informed of his nobles and bishops, and in the presence, sometimes, of a positive host of witnesses; and the purpose of the dooms was nearly always the elaboration, enforcement or codification of already existing customs. The preamble to the laws of Ine of Wessex, in 690, insists almost obsequiously that they are set down only after the king had considered the views of his predecessor and taken counsel with two bishops, all his nobles (ealdormen), the most distinguished wise men (witan) of his people 'and a large assembly of God's servants'. In 920, Edward the Elder, seeking to make justice more certain in minor local disputes, begins by earnestly exhorting his wise men to help him in the matter. The king carefully avoids giving the impression that he is doing something new of his own accord. Instead, he declares what the law is, and lays down penalties for the breach of it, only after consulting those in a position to advise best on what custom requires.

Though kingship increased in prestige in the tenth century, it did not necessarily increase in effective power. The difficulty that early kings of Mercia or Wessex had in making their overlordship fully operative either in East Anglia or Kent, each with its own peculiarities of custom, was increased with the establishment of the Danelaw: the wholly imported character of the Danish population and of its social and legal customs always made unification under a Saxon king extremely difficult. When, in 962, Edgar wanted to put a stop to the universal crime of cattle stealing, his law on the subject, though reasonably firm in its admonition to the English, is repetitively deferential towards the people of the Danelaw: 'Moreover I will that such good laws prevail among the Danes as they may best choose, which I have always allowed, and will allow, to them in return for their fealty which they have always shown to me . . . let the Danes choose . . . what punishments they will exact'. Cnut's theocratically phrased charter of 1020 is hardly less exhortatory than the laws of his English predecessors, and still takes the form of an earnest request to his subjects to adhere more faithfully than before to the good customs bequeathed them by the past.

This seemingly deferential style of kingship arose out of the process by which the original raiders and migrants, arriving under the leadership of energetic fighting men, were grouped first into small and then into larger kingdoms and only thereafter subjected to the often fitful overlordship of a single king. The process was prolonged by the fact that the Danes of East Anglia, and of the whole region between the rivers Welland and Tees, were not fully assimilated until well after the Norman conquest. The strong element of personal freedom and economic independence that long survived in the Danelaw seems also to have existed among the Anglo-Saxons in the early stages of their own settlement. All later Anglo-Saxon customs and institutions were built upon the foundation of a warlike society composed of free peasants, or ceorls, who were also fighting men. But these legally free men were always aware of ties of loyalty binding them to their kindred, their lord (or thegn), who was usually in the first instance their military chief, and to their local community. For long, loyalty to the king consisted principally in paying him tribute in kind or cash; indeed, it was as a tax-gathering institution that the Anglo-Saxon monarchy was, by the eleventh century, at its most efficient.

Loyalty to the kindred was the most primitive form of mutual protection in Anglo-Saxon society. A man's kindred included his remoter cousins and, since marriage had to be with a partner outside the kindred, an injured wife would call on her own kindred to right her wrongs and to care for her children if she were widowed. It was the duty of the kin to avenge the killing of any of its members. This meant that the murder of one man by another could be the beginning of a blood feud or vendetta involving the kindred of both the slayer and his victim. Since this would be destructive of social order it quickly became customary to substitute, for the killing of the guilty party, the exaction of compensation (*wergeld*) in kind or money. Alfred and his successors sought to limit the blood feud. Alfred asked for recourse to the courts first. Edmund, in the tenth century, laid down that vengeance be wrought only on the guilty person himself. Nevertheless, though the church strongly supported its replacement by wergeld, the blood feud persisted throughout and beyond the Anglo-Saxon period.

In time, wergeld came to signify not so much what a man was worth if and when he were done to death, but his status while he was alive, as if a modern man were to be esteemed principally in accordance with the amount for which his life was insured. In practice, a thegn, even if he had less land than a prosperous ceorl, rated a wergeld from three to seven times that of a ceorl. One measure of the respect in which a king was held was the great size of his wergeld; though the fact that Viking kings in Northumbria had a higher wergeld than the king in Wessex doubtless reflected the greater risks attendant upon all attempts to wield power in the turbulent north.

The church was also fitted into the scheme. An archbishop had a prince's wergeld and a priest a thegn's. Difficulty arose if the slayer of an ecclesiastic refused, or was unable, to pay wergeld. The church constituted the priest's spiritual kindred, but ecclesiastics could not shed blood. This led the church to press the king to take over the responsibility, a foreshadowing of the still distant period when justice in general would become the king's justice.

Wergeld had its influence on the history of the law. Innocence or guilt was decided by a counting of oaths; the higher a man's wergeld, the larger the number of oaths his testimony counted for. A single ceorl's assertion of innocence would count for less than a single thegn's assertion to the contrary. The ceorl could perhaps make up the balance by getting other ceorls to swear to his innocence, but the thegn would need far fewer thegns on his side to secure a favourable verdict. Indeed, the kings of Wessex made it impossible for a ceorl to establish his innocence unless he could also find a thegn to swear for him. This process of oath-helping began as a means of demonstrating a man's respectability by the number or status of those who were prepared publicly to support him. But even before the Norman conquest, oath-helpers were coming to be treated as sworn witnesses as to fact rather than as simple guarantors of guilt or innocence.

The substitution of wergeld for the socially disruptive vendetta signified the establishment of a wider loyalty to the community than that to the kindred. Community, or folk, courts had, from the sixth century onwards, the right if not always the power to override loyalty to family or kin. By the eighth century, two separate kinds of folk court begin to appear: the small hundred court and the larger shire court. The hundred courts, which dealt with groups of villages within the shires, had obscure beginnings but were general by the end of the Anglo-Saxon period. They were open-air popular assemblies, meeting every four weeks to administer the customary laws, settle local disputes, punish thieves, and deal, in consultation with royal officials, with the matter of the king's taxes. In the Danelaw, the grouping of villages that corresponded to the English hundred was known as a wapentake. The development of hundred courts represented a gain for the idea of community over that of kin; but they also reflected a growth in the authority of the king, and were encouraged to that end. This applies even more to the shire courts. A shire was in origin the geographical description of a folk-group: Wiltshire had earlier been the shire of the men of Wilton, and earlier still merely the settlers on the river Wylye. The division of all England into shires with defined boundaries was a slow process, undertaken only with the growth of the influence of Wessex, and increasingly it took on the character of an administrative area created for the convenience of kingly government. Mercian shires such as Shropshire and Warwickshire bore little relation to folk-groupings and it is unlikely that those of the east Midlands did so either. What had begun as a natural association of the folk became an administrative grouping to create not only a sense of local community but of communal responsibility to the king.

A man's loyalty to his lord, however, was originally a matter of military discipline. Men hoping to win new land by fighting for it, or in later centuries trying to prevent Danes from seizing it from them, could succeed only by loyally fighting under their lord's command. Much Anglo-Saxon epic poetry is emotional propaganda designed to promote the idea that a man should fight to the death for his lord if need be. But, the original battle over, and regions and kingdoms won, king, lord and warrior inevitably found themselves translating their hierarchical military code into economic terms. The king took a lot of land, his lords took (or were given) large estates, his thegns smaller parcels and the ceorls enough for the maintenance of themselves and their families; while beneath them all were the many slaves, still, as late as 1066, constituting about ten per cent of the population. At first, there seems little evidence that the ceorl's social inferiority involved legal dependence on a lord other than that of serving on demand in his army. His basic obligations beyond those to his community were, like the lord's, to the king.

From the start, many villages were on a lord's estate and many more on the king's, and as time went on kings habitually gave lords more and more villages. Lordly power further increased as the shire courts developed, since the deliberations of great men carried most weight. Moreover, in times of pestilence or during the Danish invasions, peasant-ceorls, like many lesser thegns, sought protection by commending themselves to some powerful lord who would, in return, require from them a rent, in kind, in services or cash, or a combination of these. The growing demand for all three·by both king and church could also make it harder for the originally free peasant to preserve his economic, and therefore legal, independence.

By 1066, free ceorls were no longer numerous in the old kingdom of

Wessex. Even in the Danelaw, although there were many independent peasant proprietors, or sokemen, some of them substantial, some much poorer than an unfree ceorl in Wessex, such men were still required to acknowledge some great lord as their legal superior, even if the obligations this involved them in were few. Under Athelstan it was established that every man should have a lord. The literature of the time represents the lordless man as a sad, forlorn and defenceless person, a pathetic orphan; but from the point of view of public order he could also be considered a potentially dangerous character for whose acts nobody could be held responsible. Hence, a lord was answerable for his man's acts and required to produce him in court if charges were made against him. Though, in return, the man expected the lord to protect his interests, the emphasis of the time was very much the other way round. Alfred had insisted that a man should not pursue a blood feud if it involved him in fighting against his lord, and in the laws of Cnut, almost certainly under the influence of that great homilist, Wulstan, it is piously asserted, 'truly God will be gracious to him who is duly faithful to his lord'.

The growing power of the lord at the expense of the free peasant and, sometimes, of the hundred courts which mediated customary and kingly laws, is attested by the gradual establishment of a distinction between 'folkland' and 'bookland'. Folkland meant those areas in which there continued to be fairly direct relations between the community and the king. This relationship was concretely expressed in the duties and payments owed to the king. The heaviest burden was the tax known as the food-rent (the king's *feorm*). This originated from the early requirement that a group of villages should every year provide the king and his court with enough food to keep them going for twenty-four hours. When paid in kind, this could consist of varying quantities of ale, cheese, corn, butter, bread, honey and a number of beasts. The other ancient obligations were service in the king's militia (or *fyrd*) and the duty of maintaining bridges and fortresses for the king. Ensuring that these payments and duties were faithfully and equitably fulfilled by the peasants was one of the major functions of the hundred courts.

From the time of Alfred onwards, however, it became the custom, when land was bestowed upon a noble, for the fact to be recorded in a 'landbook' or royal charter; and this 'bookland' would be freed from all services to the king except fyrd-service and work on bridges and forts. Thereafter, the lord, in effect as a gift from the king, would himself receive the food-rent from the peasants on his lands, along with other services previously rendered to the king, such as the cartage of goods. More important for the landowner was that bookland could be sold to a third party or bequeathed in a will. Written documents of this sort had become essential once it became customary to give land to the church in perpetuity; and churchmen, like the laymen who acquired bookland, often paid money to the king for the sake of acquiring the revenue to which their charter entitled them.

Bookland also often formalised the lord's judicial powers over persons on his land. Lords had always had some judicial power over members of their household and their tenants, and these charters usually confirmed and widened the lord's right to a private court by conferring on him entitlement to 'sake and soke, toll and team and infangenetheof'. This routine legal formula gave the recipient three extremely lucrative judicial rights, namely, jurisdiction over misdemeanours and disputes among the peasants, the right to put a toll on the sale of cattle and other goods, and the power to decide cases of theft. The private courts of lords sometimes competed with hundred courts and sometimes took their place. Thus, English England could no longer be depicted as a society composed of communities of free peasant-warriors, even though the Danelaw shires of Lincoln, Leicester, Nottingham and East Anglia, with their many sokemen, retained, even beyond the eleventh century, some resemblance to such a society.

Shire courts developed later than hundred courts. Wessex was divided into shires in the eighth century, Mercia in the tenth. The bulk of the Danelaw shires were regions taken over by the various Danish armies of the first Danish onslaught. Men of these shires might still refer to themselves in their collective character as 'armies' in the eleventh century.

Whereas hundred courts were presided over by a local royal official known as a reeve, usually a man of thegnly status, the shire courts, which met twice a year, were headed by an ealdorman or a bishop, or sometimes a sheriff. The last-named was in origin a shire-reeve who acted as the ealdorman's deputy. Ealdormen were great nobles in their own right or members of the royal family and were the most exalted of those who combined landownership with service to the king, by whom they were appointed. By the time of Ethelred, ealdormen were usually responsible for several shires, with the result that, by 1066, the sheriff had become the king's principal official in the shires.

It was by way of the shire court and its sheriff that Anglo-Saxon kings eventually tried to establish regular administrative control over a realm generally governed locally, with kings merely issuing, from time to time, laws and exhortations demand that this local government be carried out more effectively. By the eleventh century the revival of learning had at last led to the emergence of a body of professional writing clerks in the king's chancery, where they developed a new and simple device for authorising grants of land and for conveying royal commands to the localities. This was a clear, succinct 'writ' in the English language. The old landbooks and charters had been in quasi-theological Latin and, since learning to write was a job for clerics and not for nobly born warriors, had been attested by 'signatures' that took the form of easily forgeable crosses. The writ, however, was not only short and to the point and instantly understandable to all who received it, it was also sealed with the king's own seal which was hard to forge or dispute. The use of the writ before the Norman conquest may have been neither general nor effective; on the eve of the Norman period the sheriffs to whom they were addressed were liable to be overruled by powerful ealdormen. As an innovation, however, the writ did more than testify to the seriousness with which the clerkly teachers of the time took the English language; it was without parallel elsewhere in Europe and a device which the Normans turned into a permanent feature of English law and government.

The issue of writs was also a consequence of the king's need to organise a national land tax to raise large sums of money with which to buy off the Danes. Normally, the king, as the greatest landowner in the realm, was expected, both before the Norman conquest and for five centuries after it, to 'live of his own', apart from the food rents or other services due to him. The levying of the Danegeld was so much of a novelty that it is described as the first regular land tax ever to be raised in Europe. That such considerable sums were obtained from it indicates the wealth of pre-Norman England and the surprising fact that Ethelred, reckoned so inglorious in military matters, should be so successful in getting his people to endure such exceptional taxation.

The geld was assessed in accordance with the most rough and ready calculations about the arable land each shire contained. The theory was that each shire contained an exact number of 'hides' on each of which was imposed a uniform tax. Originally a calculation of the size of a holding adequate to maintain a ceorl and his family, the area of a hide varied from shire to shire and by the eleventh century was not at all coincident with the real arable wealth of a shire. Even the comparable taxable unit in the Danelaw, the ploughland, though more recent in its origins, was notably more accurate. Nevertheless the geld was paid, first to appease the Danes and then, as heregeld, to support the fleets and armies of Swein, Cnut and their successors, and with what seems little protest. First levied in 991, the geld seems to have produced no physical demonstration against it until, in 1040, two collectors were killed in a tumult at Worcester. Perhaps the explanation of the general docility was that, as a punishment, the king's personal troops ravaged Worcester for five days. During Ethelred's reign, about £167,000 was raised. In 1018 Cnut squeezed a further £72,000 out of his kingdom, and £20,000 from London alone.

Though the geld was reduced under Edward the Confessor, with great damage to the national defences in consequence, the system was continued under William the Conqueror. Though its burdens were heavy, the system did possess a certain flexibility: it was possible, though doubtless difficult, to establish that the number of hides alleged to be taxable in a given area no longer reflected its real arable productivity.

The developments of the early eleventh century thus appear greatly to have strengthened the authority of the king, particularly if, added to his increased administrative competence, account is taken of the exaltation of the kingly office by the church. It is usual to assert that the Anglo-Saxon monarchy was the strongest in western Europe at that time. Yet, when Cnut provided England at last with a king whom both Danes and English could accept, he did what strong conquering kings were always liable to do: he enforced his authority by delegating much of it to his chief military followers. While Cnut lived, the powerful earls he thus created, many of them masters of several shires, showed due loyalty to their king. But during the thirty years after his death, with no king appearing who was capable of permanently commanding their respect or curbing their power, they obstructed kingly power as often as they supported it. In being better placed than earlier kings to impose his will, and therefore his fighting supporters, on the country, Cnut created dangers for kingship that the less militarily successful dynasty of Wessex seems to have avoided.

Other factors limited kingship's scope. One was the continuance of shire and hundred courts, and the seigneurial courts in the hands of individual lords. These ensured that for centuries to come most English government would be local government, since the Norman and Angevin kings after 1066 supplemented these courts and did not suppress them. Anxious, for propaganda purposes, to insist that he had conquered England only because he was lawfully entitled to rule it, even William the Conqueror announced his intention to maintain the laws of Edward the Confessor, the last king of the dynasty of Wessex. This implied that whatever a king might do in practice, in theory he still ought to respect ancient custom and rule, and proclaim the law, only after taking counsel with some group of nobles and churchmen who could be held to resemble the witan, a body of royal advisers common in pre-Conquest times. William's policy of affirming the continuing validity of old English custom despite having destroyed the old English monarchy and killed or dispossessed its nobility, had a long sequel. It preserved the conviction that, though kings could, and frequently did, keep themselves in power by force, that force was legitimate only if it preserved the known law. And when kings were too weak to impose their will or too feckless in imposing it, it was to ancient laws that, rightly or wrongly, and usually wrongly, men appealed to justify rebellion. Opposition to medieval kings was often accompanied by reference to laws which, so it was fervently claimed, derived fron Edward the Confessor and from his Anglo-Saxon predecessors. From the seventeenth century to the nineteenth, men would denounce kings and aristocrats alike by invoking the free institutions they believed to have been the mark of sturdy Saxons before the land had been subjected to 'the Norman yoke'. In the seventeenth century, the idea that law should maintain old custom and not introduce new was fiercely championed by the opponents of James I and Charles I by yet further appeals to scarcely understood pre-Norman traditions. They were even called in aid by some of the opponents of George III in the eighteenth century. Neither William the Conqueror nor later monarchs were able to impose the idea permanently on the English that the crown could make laws either of its own accord or arbitrarily. Historians long ago gave up looking on later ideas about 'English liberty' as an 'inheritance' from the Anglo-Saxons. This does not alter the fact that the combination of deep respect for monarchy with fairly dogged resistance to authoritarian control from the centre which marked later English history was also a feature of it before 1066.

The Land

The raw material of what was to become the English landscape was composed of moor, marsh and forest, if by forest is understood not merely the densely wooded forests of oak, but also extensive areas of scrub and undergrowth. The landscape that was slowly fashioned out of this difficult terrain was as much the work of man as the industrial conurbations that so many centuries later were said to be destroying it; the notion that God made the country and man made the town is a myth.

The transformation of the face of England into cultivable land capable of sustaining human existence had begun before the Romans, let alone the Saxons, but it is to the Saxons and their eventual Danish associates that must be ascribed the foundation of the villages in which most Englishmen were to live until the middle of the nineteenth century. The battles fought by Saxons against forest and marsh were more important than those between Saxons and Celts or Danes. Even so, their labours had still, by 1066, made little impression on the Weald, the Fens or the Chilterns, and sustained a population estimated at that date to be not much more than one and a half million.

The forests which originally covered so much of the land were seen as both malevolent and benign: malevolent because clearings had to be made in them before men could gain cultivable soil and because even after men had made their many small encroachments, they were still so extensive. The Andredswald in Sussex and Kent was thirty miles across and twenty miles long. The size of other great forests at that time may be assessed by the survival in place-names of references to forests which, if they survive at all, are now found only in attenuated form several miles away: the Cotswold village of Milton-under-Wychwood is considerably distant from the small area that survives as Wychwood Forest. In earlier Saxon times, forests were the natural home not only of bears and wolves but of robbers and outlaws.

Yet the forests were the major source of the raw materials of daily life. Whatever implements were not made of wood were smelted with the aid of charcoal. Almost all building was in wood and apart from peat it provided the only fuel. It was for economic reasons as well as a mere love of the chase that English kings and nobles, both before and after the Normans, were so anxious to preserve and extend their exclusive control over their forests. Encroachment upon them by villagers was continuous. The forest verges were regularly used by villagers to make up for the chronic shortage of grazing land, so that seedlings would be constantly nibbled and chewed by goats and pigs. Forests were also a regular source of firewood, itself a commodity hard to come by in the medieval period.

The number of place-names deriving from Saxon words referring to forests indicates how many villages began as forest clearings. Place-name endings such as 'den', 'dene' or 'dean' indicate what was originally a pasture cleared out of the woodland for swine or cattle. Endings in 'ley' and 'hurst' also indicate places first created out of the forest. But the major consequence of the contest between the English and their land was the foundation of the open field villages which predominated in that part of the country which extended from the river Tamar in the south-west to the Vale of York and the East Riding. Dedicated to arable farming, preferably on mixed soils of sand, gravel and clay, they were as dependent for their location on the waterways as the early cotton industry would be on fast-moving streams, and the iron industry of the mid-nineteenth century on coalfields.

Under the open-field system, villagers cultivated the arable land communally. Each villager's holding of land usually consisted of a number of long, narrow, scattered strips, and every year half to a third of the arable was left fallow. Though local conditions and traditions varied greatly, the open field village might be surrounded by two unfenced arable fields roughly totalling about 120 acres. In any one year, sixty acres would lie fallow. Of the other sixty acres, half might be devoted to one of the two autumn-sown crops, rye and wheat, and the other to a spring-sown crop of oats or barley. The use of a fallow year to enable the land to recover its fertility was dictated by the chronic scarcity of manure. Nor was the fallow merely left untended; it had to be ploughed and broken up as thoroughly as the cultivated arable acreage. Apart from this consideration, the fields were so large that there would have been neither time nor labour to keep more than half the land under full cultivation every year.

The scattering of individual holdings into strips, each amounting to an acre or half-acre, was also the outcome of practical considerations. Once ploughing with a team of oxen became possible, it was hardly likely that every cultivator would own sufficient oxen to make up a team of, as was occasionally the case, eight. The cultivators would in the beginning contribute an animal, or animals, or perhaps just the plough, to the local resources, and the ploughing would therefore naturally be done co-operatively. The strips ploughed in any one operation would be allotted

43

proportionately to the individuals who contributed to the team. In this way, too, newcomers could be the more easily incorporated.

Though certainty on the point is probably unattainable, the origins of the system may be ascribed to the fact that the first English settlers must have been concerned at first with producing enough from the soil to keep themselves alive. They needed to cultivate a large area, since yields were perhaps only a tenth of what would be considered normal in the twentieth century. Often the most they could have hoped for, initially was to be able to keep body and soul together; in a bad season, and during many winters, they might barely be able to manage even that. They had only the simplest of tools, their beasts were bred without benefit of the selective techniques of the stock breeder, while many beasts were killed off at the onset of winter because of an insufficiency of fodder and liable, since they grazed in common, to succumb to epidemics. The hardships of winter might, if the previous harvest had been poor, be followed by a hungry spring. A carefully regulated communal system of cultivation arose naturally during this pioneering period.

By the eleventh century, with the steady growth of lordship and kingship, few of the peasants who cultivated the arable were free peasants, at any rate within the area of the old kingdom of Wessex. Most of them paid rent in cash or in kind, or by labour services, to a lord. The distinguishing feature of the open field community by this time was that part of the land was appropriated to the lord, and known as his demesne. The peasants were expected to work on the demesne for part of the week and on additional days during the time of ploughing and harvest. Not only did lords have demesne land; the king had demesne lands and so, and on an increasing scale, did the church. Some royal and some monastic estates were, as it were, cultivated by direct labour rather than by the part-time efforts of men who had once perhaps been free peasants.

Though the peasant's life was hard, it was not one of unremitting toil. The calendar of the church was such that many of its holy days acquired the quasi-secular character of holidays. Sunday was a holiday from all but works of piety, essential service to the community and, of course, warfare; physical work for gain was banned on Sunday. Alfred the Great ordered that all but slaves and unfree labourers should have, as holidays, the twelve days from Christmas to Epiphany, work being resumed thereafter on what was long remembered by the church as Plough Monday. Other holidays were: the day on which Christ overcame the devil, the anniversary of St Gregory, as a reminder to the English of the pope who initiated their conversion, fourteen days at Easter, the feast of St Peter and St Paul, the whole week before the feast of the Assumption, and All Saints' Day. This led in time to some difficulty as the feast of the Assumption was on 15 August, an inconvenient date in the middle of the harvest season. There were disputes as to whether ploughing was or was not permissible on saints' days; and there was the perennial problem that, whereas men were liberated from work on holy days to 'hear God's service and the mass' and 'to spend the day in holiness' this was not what invariably happened.

That cattle were the most highly prized of Anglo-Saxon livestock is shown by the regularity with which kings, from Ine of Wessex onwards, tried to regulate the buying and selling of cattle, and to combat cattle-stealing. Oxen were used for ploughing for severely practical reasons. They were four times cheaper than horses, were less expensive to feed, and, when their working life was over, could be eaten. They were better able to cope with heavy land, and their slow pace was an advantage to the ploughman trying to control the Anglo-Saxon plough, which was a cumbersome implement. Indeed, though the horse collar made it possible from the ninth century onwards to use the horse as a draught animal on the farm, it was not used for this purpose in Anglo-Saxon England. It was bred for war and for sport. Its use for ploughing did not in fact become general until after the end of the eighteenth century.

At least before the eleventh century, the most characteristic beast was the pig. An indiscriminate forager, ready to eat anything, it was very much a poor man's animal, though usually a scraggy, razor-backed creature with little meat on it. Nevertheless, great herds of up to 2,000 or more swine were kept, and it was only in a few areas, such as Oxfordshire and Northamptonshire that more beef than pork was eaten. Peasants regularly made a cash payment known as pannage for the right to graze pigs in their lord's woods and it was a source of income the lords greatly valued.

By 1066, sheep may have been even more numerous than pigs, since they too could thrive in many different environments. Sheep provided milk, wool and meat, and their droppings increased the fertility of the land over which they grazed. Sheep provided most of the milk, butter and cheese of pre-Conquest England because the poor quality of pasture meant that yields of cows' milk were low and it was used mainly for the rearing of young stock. Sheep rearing was a subsidiary occupation among the majority of England's rural communities, but large-scale sheep farms had developed by Norman times in Essex, Norfolk, and in the west, where some flocks of over 2,000 were managed. One sheep farmer had grazing lands in the marshy lowlands of Essex for over 4,000 sheep. Sheep's wool and English woollen cloth were already being regularly exported across the Channel by the eighth century.

Goats helped, along with the sheep, to provide the milk, butter and cheese needed to compensate for the virtual absence of dairy cattle. Hens and geese were common, but no ducks appeared until the thirteenth century and few rabbits before the Normans. Bees were commonly kept since honey was the only available sweetening sub-stance. Honey was also the base of mead, the expensive beverage

45

favoured by the aristocracy. Though there were some vineyards in southern England, the Anglo-Saxons were fondest of their ale, made from barley. Beer made from hops was unknown until its importation from Holland at the end of the middle ages.

Ills of the Flesh

Few Anglo-Saxons could expect to enjoy either a very long life or a very healthy one. The majority of Anglo-Saxon skeletons which have been excavated provide evidence of rickets, tuberculosis and arthritis, often in an advanced state, partly because England was colder, damper and foggier in Anglo-Saxon times than in later centuries. Few surviving Saxon graveyards contain the remains of persons much over forty-five and most include a large number of children and infants. Old age was honoured as a testimony to exceptional health or good luck. Mortality would be high whenever storms destroyed the crops or murrain killed off the cattle. Even if famine did not result, ill-nourished physiques could not be expected long to endure backbreaking work in a land whose ample vegetation and many waterlogged stretches aggravated the effects of cold and damp. These conditions of life inevitably bound communities together and help to explain both the origin and persistence of social codes and economic practices whose emphasis was on the loyalty of a man to his lord, if he had one, and to his kith and kin whether he had a lord or not.

In Anglo-Saxon times war was not only a slayer in itself, but accessory to the spread of famine and epidemics. It is likely that the pestilence which accompanied the Viking invasions caused more fatalities than the fighting itself. Earlier, pestilence had once reduced the number of monks capable of singing the office at Jarrow to the abbot and one small boy called Bede. The collapse of Northumbrian power may well have been due to the continued pestilence there throughout the second half of the seventh century. The success of St Wilfred in converting the South Saxons to Christianity owed much, it was said, to his having taught them how to fish at a time when they were suffering a great famine. In the five years after the Synod of Whitby, the pestilence was so severe that, far from being the beginning of a new order in the church it was followed by a near-relapse into heathenism because of the death of most of the clergy. The link between war and famine and pestilence is suggested by the fact that Cnut's ordered reign contains no record of either. Most of Edward the Confessor's reign, however, seems to have been a time of pestilence, murrain among cattle and exceptionally severe weather.

The epidemics of the ninth to the eleventh centuries were probably the aftermath of famine caused by the devastations of war. Viking marauders would burn houses and corn, kill men, and kill or seize cattle. Without the systems of transport and communications developed in advanced countries only in the past two centuries, food supplies could not be moved from areas of plenty to one of shortage. Even in time of peace local famines occurred intermittently in England until the end of the middle ages. Famine was so common in the early Anglo-Saxon period that infanticide was countenanced at such times, and it is perhaps significant that the modern English verb 'to starve' derives from the Anglo-Saxon word 'to die'. Yet this state of affairs was compatible with the facts that, in relation to the small population, the Anglo-Saxons cultivated a large area of land and that, by the tenth century, the English were exporting corn, beer, wool, hides and cheese to Scandinavia.

The spread of pestilence was encouraged by lack of personal hygiene, and by the accumulation of filth in and around the ill-ventilated dwellings in which the population mostly lived. Diarrhoea, dysentery and scurvy were normal, the last being particularly common during the winter months owing to a lack of vegetables and fresh fruit; not much fruit was eaten before the end of the middle ages. Skin diseases were thus frequent, especially since cleanliness, far from being considered 'next to godliness', could be taken as a sign of excessive pride. The true ascetic would abstain as far as possible from so worldly an act as washing; St Wilfred's practice of washing his body every night of the year in holy water was regarded by the pope of his day as unwise. By contrast with modern men, however, the Anglo-Saxons seem to have suffered little from dental caries; their teeth were healthy but usually much worn down by having had to chew so hard on the coarse bread of the time. However, if teeth were once lost, nothing could be done about it; just as nothing was done about failing eyesight.

Medicine was primitive. Sickness was a 'bad' magic to be met with by the use of 'good' magic. The Christian gloss on this formula tended not to be an improvement: war, disease and pestilence were punishments for sin. The church would intervene with a call for repentance and prayers for forgiveness, and then apply the 'good' magic of blessing the victim, if possible with a holy relic. From classical times, prescriptions involving the use of herbs survived. Some of the prescribed herbs were unobtainable in England, while some prescriptions had been copied from ancient texts by scribes who, not understanding them, got them wrong. The words, 'With God's help no harm will come to him', appearing at the end of one Anglo-Saxon prescription perhaps reflected the fact that almost none of the herbs used in Anglo-Saxon medicine had the effects ascribed to it. However, fresh herbs might well have been a serviceable purgative and of use in combating winter scurvy. Nor would it be safe to assume that the use of herbs was confined to that indicated by the prescriptions of which we have knowledge; the evidence provided by the literate about the customs of villagers who are not literate is rarely conclusive. The majority of remedies can hardly have been effective. They might depend upon some magic number: 'three spoonsful a day or nine if the need is great'. Colours were significant: yellow-coloured remedies were necessary to cure jaundice. Since church bells were holy, rust from the church bell-clapper mixed in water was a cure for 'the flux'. Peony root would cure insanity. The eyes taken from a live crab (which had then to be put back into the sea) would cure 'swollen eyes' if then applied to a man's neck. Amber beads cured sore eyes and ensured safe pregnancy. Mugwort, the *artemisia vulgaris*, would, if carried on a journey, lessen fatigue and turn away the eye of evil men.

The perpetuation of these nostrums from generation to generation continued on through medieval times at least into the eighteenth century. Nor was this reliance on magical remedies compensated for by any understanding of the interior of the body or any great knowledge of anatomy. Although the monasteries, in quieter periods, did something to tend the sick, starting with sick brethren in the monastery itself, the church reinforced the heathen sense of helplessness in the face of unknown powers by regarding all physical ills as the work either of the devil or as a divinely ordained punishment for sin, and by teaching that the body and the material world were but the transient housing of souls whose larger destiny was in the world to come. Nor, at a mundane level, must it be overlooked that since war, pestilence and famine habitually killed off all but the toughest, suffering and sudden death were commonplace and not, as in the modern world, phenomena which, for all their persistence, appear as monstrous anomalies.

There were doctors of a sort. Since the church could not shed blood, laymen, called *medici* in Latin or in Anglo-Saxon *laece* (hence leeches) were needed for the primitive surgery of the time and for blood-letting. There is evidence that there was surgery of a sort; cutting off portions of the body was a normal form of punishment, and the surname 'wooden-leg' is frequent enough to suggest that some form of amputation was practised, as was trepanning. Minor surgery might consist of removing arrows from wounds with a pair of tongs. Stomach wounds would be stitched by needle and silk thread should the victim be royal or noble enough to warrant such attention. Blood-letting was the most popular of all remedies. It derived from a theory dating from classical Greece that excess of blood was the chief cause of disease: the disease or, in more sophisticated theory the 'evil humours', would be cured by drawing off blood from the appropriate part of the body. The notion gained credibility from the belief that blood was stationary in the body and did not circulate through it. Periodic blood letting was therefore part of preventive medicine until the nineteenth century, much as the taking of purgatives to ensure regular emptying of the bowel has remained part of folk medicine in the twentieth century. Some days were unpropitious for blood letting: one theory, ascribed to Theodore of Tarsus, was that it was dangerous to let blood on the fourth day of the moon because on that day the light of the moon and the tide of the ocean were both increasing. It was held by some that spring (Bede says from 25 March to

26 May) was a good time for blood letting; all dates in which the figure five occurred were considered bad by some, while others thought monthly bleeding on the fifth, fifteenth and twentieth nights of the moon the proper treatment for the palsy.

Trades, Crafts and Towns

Although the first concern of the early settlers was to produce enough to feed themselves and pay their dues to king or lord, there was almost always some production for a market. Particularly favoured areas would have a surplus to exchange for the products of others. Berkshire and Essex provided a surplus of cheese and the sheep farming regions produced wool for the market. From earliest times, the harvest of the seas and rivers was likely to exceed purely local needs and became a lively source of trade. The church forbade the eating of meat on Fridays and in Lent and this produced a great demand for fish in the inland areas. Herring, which could be salted, were widely fished, though large vessels for sea fishing were expensive. There were thriving fisheries on all major inland rivers and on the fens, and eels were fished in huge quantities.

The Anglo-Saxons could hardly have established their settlements without the work of such craftsmen as shipwrights and smiths, and most of the luxuries of the nobility and many of ordinary life's necessities called for specialised skills and the purchase of special commodities. The bronzesmiths and goldsmiths who made the elaborate brooches and jewels and the gilt and silver-gilt drinking horns used by kings and nobles were probably, in the first place, itinerant craftsmen; but goldsmiths in particular were so highly honoured that they were frequently rewarded with holdings of land. The various weaponsmiths and blacksmiths were ubiquitous, but regarded as of somewhat lowly status. Iron was used for many humdrum purposes as well as for weapons; it was needed for ploughshares, fish hooks, needles, locks and keys, cups, spoons, knives, rings, coins and nails. A number of place-names such as Smeaton and Smethwick suggest hamlets or even larger communities with a concentration of families specialising in iron. Iron was mined in various parts of the country, most notably in the Forest of Dean. Thence, puddled into bars, it would find its way to the blacksmiths. Some iron workers in the south-western shires paid part of their rents and dues in iron bars. The comparatively lowly status of the smith was due to the lack of demand for the specialised equipment of armour, harness and weapons to which the employment of armed horsemen in battle gave rise in continental Europe; there was almost no cavalry in the armies of pre-Norman England.

Since most building was in wood, society had great need of carpenters, some of whom would specialise as builders, shipwrights, wheelwrights and wainwrights. Other important craftsmen included weavers, cooks and bakers, sometimes from the slave class, together with the singers and musicians who entertained the nobility. The millwright played an increasingly important part in the development of Anglo-Saxon agriculture. There were few water mills in Roman Britain, but by the time of William I's reign there were over 5,000. The water mill marked a big step forwards in the harnessing of power compared with the previous laborious business of grinding corn by hand. By the time of the Normans, the mill was an important piece of capital equipment in the hands of the lords, who took care to compel all their tenants to make use of it in order to guarantee an adequate return on the costs of installation and maintenance. If the mill broke down, all the revenues would be lost until it could be repaired.

Native stonemasons were few in the early Saxon period, since they had no experience of stone-working in their Germanic homeland. Such stonework as there was before the eighth century was probably the work of masons brought over from Gaul. The stone crosses of that century were probably the work of native craftsmen, however, and there were many stone Saxon churches in the tenth and eleventh centuries. The Normans deliberately replaced most of them by their more elaborate churches. Work in stone seems to have been undertaken solely for the church. Most but not all of the stone would come from Roman ruins; there were also a number of local quarries.

The production of salt, which was a necessity for preserving meat, for the making of butter and cheese, and for the seasoning of vegetables, was widespread. It was carried on on the coast, or inland wherever there were brine springs from which the salt could be extracted by boiling the water. Names such as Budleigh Salterton and Sawtry are among the many which indicate places where salt was produced or traded. The greatest salt-producing town in pre-Norman England was Droitwich. Places without saltpans of their own relied on the salter's produce being transported to them by salt-pedlars.

Saltpans were made of lead, which was extensively mined, some of it being exported to the continent. Lead was even more important as an element in the minting of coins and for the roofing of churches. Derbyshire produced most lead, but there were also considerable lead mines in the Mendips.

There was also a considerable import and export trade, though many of the more splendid items of foreign manufacture, some from Byzantium and the Middle East, may well have reached kings and churchmen as gifts. Much glass and silverware was imported from the continent and the shores of the Mediterranean. Cheese, cloth and wool were exported and, throughout Saxon times, slaves. Bristol, which several centuries later prospered through the trade in African slaves, was a centre for the export of English slaves, for whom there was a considerable market in Muslim Spain and North Africa and also in Scandinavia.

English cloth was nevertheless the most notable of exports. Its high quality and bright colours were popular with both Christian and Muslim. Cloaks from England were exported from Mercia to the Franks. Charlemagne made strong complaints about some new cloaks he had received from Mercia which were of only knee length. They were, he said, too scanty to keep him warm in bed and, in view of the skimpiness of the material, poor value for money. The Frankish ruler's complaints arose during a quarrel with king Offa as a result of which both rulers closed their ports to the other's merchants. Evidently trade between Mercia and Frankia was substantial enough to make such sanctions embarrassing to both parties.

After the initial dislocation caused by the first Danish invasions, the growth of foreign trade was much stimulated by England's closer links with Scandinavia; the temporary severing of those links by the Norman conquest was something of a setback in this respect. Alarming though they were when they first appeared, the fact that the Danes came at all, that they stayed to settle and, in the eleventh century, established a temporary Danish rule over the whole land, indicates that pre-Norman England was a prize worth having, that its land had been made fertile and could be made more so, and its trade worth, if not capturing, at least sharing. The desire for part of other men's wealth, whether their land, their movable goods or their trade is common to raider, pirate and peaceful trader alike. The battlecry of the warrior will, once victory is gained, often transform itself into the less martial language of the market place. In the countryside, those who came wielding the battle axe would stay to speed the plough. Everywhere the Vikings went, though they set out to strike terror, they were soon to be found striking bargains instead.

In the earliest stages, much trade, both internal and external, had been based on barter. The splendid gifts from abroad that reached the king's treasury or the larger monasteries perhaps reflected the decline in the use of gold as currency from about 700 onwards. There was a change to silver currency in both Charlemagne's Frankish dominions and in Offa's Mercia; thereafter the economy of medieval Europe was based on silver, and not until the thirteenth century were gold coins again minted west of Byzantium.

The scarcity of gold in medieval Europe, combined with the rapacious search for it which was a principal motive for the great Discoveries of the fifteenth and sixteenth centuries, was not necessarily a sign of Christendom's poverty. Gold was too luxurious a currency for the kind of exchange which was normal within medieval Europe. The large number of silver coins in circulation in later Anglo-Saxon England reflects an expanding commerce in useful commodities as distinct from luxuries. For trade within Europe, gold was perhaps as inconvenient in the early Middle Ages as, inflation notwithstanding, ten pound notes would be for paying a local bus fare in the twentieth century. And if gold was really called for, good quality Byzantine and Muslim coins were available in the west. Nor were Anglo-Saxon pennies a form of small change. The approximate 'real' value of the silver penny might be that of a pre-1914 gold half-sovereign.

The adoption of this silver penny as the standard English coin was the work of Offa of Mercia in the last half of the eighth century. In the reign of Edgar, in the tenth century, there was a recoinage and the shilling came to be fixed as the equivalent of twelve pennies. The result was to give England an exceptionally stable and well-designed currency and to found the 'shillings and pence' tradition that lasted until 1971.

Most Anglo-Saxon towns grew up at the junction of ancient trackways or Roman roads with rivers, at points where the latter were bridgable or fordable. The insistence on the community's duty to keep bridges in repair shows their economic as well as their strategic importance. By the eleventh century the bridge at Oxford was more important than its ford; and the bridge over the Cam gave its name not only to the town but to the shire. Bristol's Anglo-Saxon name meant 'an assembly place by the bridge'.

Roman towns must, initially, have been targets of attack for the invading Saxons, but the development of Saxon towns out of Roman ones was usually dictated by the same factors that governed the location of their other towns. London, Canterbury, Colchester, Cambridge, Winchester and York continued as urban centres because all were at vital points where road or trackway met navigable rivers. It was because it lacked this advantage that Silchester was abandoned and that Wroxeter, Lichfield and St Alban's were Saxon substitutes for Roman towns somewhat further away from a suitable waterway.

The wars of Alfred and Edward the Elder stimulated the development of certain strategically placed centres which, owing to their use, or creation, as fortified bases against the Danes were called *burhs*. As a result, a word which had originally meant 'a defensive stockade' came to be used to indicate any place enjoying the particular privileges conferred by law on a town and passed from Anglo-Saxon into English as the word 'borough'. The alternative word for a town was 'port', originally meant any place where a market was held or coins were minted and only later was it confined to 'ports' on the coast. Many of the originally Roman towns preserved in their names some form (usually 'ceaster') of the Roman word 'castra', meaning a camp.

Towns thus developed at any place where geographical factors made it suitable for men to meet to exchange goods, to concentrate in readiness for war, or to establish an administrative or ecclesiastical headquarters. Many towns fulfilled all these functions simultaneously, as did York, Oxford and Winchester. But the establishing of towns also depended on reasonably good communications since without them merchants, armies, royal and ecclesiastical officials could none of them carry on their functions. At an early stage, kings took special steps to protect travelling merchants; the holding of periodic markets and fairs also made this necessary. From the seventh century, the main highways of Watling Street, Ermine Street, the Fosse Way and the Icknield Way were placed under the protection of the king. It was in any event dangerous to move about the country without blowing a horn or at least shouting; anyone who omitted to do so could legally be assumed to be a thief.

The characteristics of most boroughs, as they had developed by the eleventh century, were their fortifications, marking the origin of the medieval walled town; their right, by royal grant to hold a market and sometimes to mint coins; and an altogether special relationship with the king. Burgesses with property in the town held it directly from the king at a fixed rent. Even when boroughs were on lands granted by the king to ecclesiastical or secular lords, he retained overall control and, as well as being chief landowner in the borough, took part of the dues payable by the burgesses to their bishop, abbot or earl. There were distinctive laws for the boroughs and most but not all boroughs had courts of their own. Punishments for acts of violence within a borough were more severe than for similar acts elsewhere, the pursuit of a blood feud was forbidden inside a borough, and the crown tried to prevent all exchange of goods above a certain value taking place anywhere except inside a borough with a market.

The population of even the more important towns of the period was small by modern standards, though this did not prevent some of them becoming overcrowded, as is perhaps suggested by an early regulation in Canterbury that houses there should be built not less than two feet apart. All Anglo-Saxon towns had some arable and a large number of agricultural workers within their walls; and though, as a consequence of the Danish invasions, resident burgesses were reluctant to acquire land immediately outside the town's protective walls, most townsmen were likely to own rural property, combining their trade or craft with farming. As time went on, towns did not simply contain 'mere' merchants. Noblemen with estates at a distance from the borough would acquire town houses within the walls, and storeplaces for the surplus produce of their estates, the marketing of which would be supervised by the lord's reeve. Great lords would also want to own houses in towns of strategic importance and to plant in such houses loyal tenants who would pay them rent. The more important Anglo-Saxon towns were not simply market towns but centres which attracted a mixture of persons engaged in a variety of functions, military, social and administrative, both secular and lay, as well as purely economic. Small though they were by modern standards, by those of the times, London, York, Norwich, Lincoln and Winchester were large. By the middle of the eleventh century, about ten per cent of the population lived in towns, making England, before 1066, one of the most highly urbanised parts of Europe.

Royal control over towns went hand in hand with royal control over coinage. Edgar decreed that there should be only 'one coinage throughout the realm', Ethelred that no one could mint coins except by authority from the king, and that the punishment for doing so outside certain principal boroughs should be death. Moneyers who struck bad coins would have their hand cut off and displayed outside their workshops. This strict royal control gave tenth and eleventh century England coinage of the high quality it had earlier enjoyed only in the Mercian heyday of Offa. English coins were not only well designed and executed; their consistent silver quality made the currency unusually stable.

By 1066 there were between sixty and seventy mints in various boroughs and it has been suggested that the number of moneyers a town possessed gave a fair indication of its population. From this and other information it has been estimated that by 1066 the population of York was about, or perhaps in excess of, 8,000 and that of Winchester between 6,000 and 8,000. The estimated figure for Norwich is 5,000, for Oxford 4,000, for Canterbury 2,500 and for Southampton 1,200.

By contrast, London is thought to have had a population of about 25,000. Its pre-eminence dated from well before Norman times; Bede had written of its repute as an emporium for traders by land and sea. Londoners of the late Anglo-Saxon period enjoyed authority and legal rights far beyond the confines of the city itself, suggesting that it was a capital city whose powers covered a wide and indeterminate area of south and south-east England. It was this wide jurisdiction that gave strength to its usually independent posture towards the crown. By 1066 it was already one of the main terminal points of the great trade routes from Constantinople; and merchants from as far away as Novgorod, the Scandinavian trading centre in northern Russia, were to be found within its walls, as well as from German, Frankish, Flemish and Danish trading centres. By the Norman period, London provided the dies from which all English mints produced their coins, and no other town had a comparable volume of trade either then, or in the rest of the medieval period.

NORMAN CONQUEST

Downfall of the Old Monarchy

THE personal nature of kingship and the importance necessarily placed on a king's capacity as a warleader, meant that political developments almost throughout the first millennium of English history were liable to violent discontinuities. The accidents of mortality and of warfare, as well as the unpredictability of the behaviour of kings, though making little difference to ordinary daily life, were often decisive in the history of the nation as a whole. That its ultimate destiny depended on the accidents of death, battle and personal idiosyncrasy was never more obvious than during the thirty years that began in 1035.

The mischances of that time fully exposed the nature of England's perilous geographical position. Owing to the vulnerability of its eastern and southern coasts, English independence could be preserved only by a considerable fleet and a well-equipped, up to date professional army. At no time did it possess either in sufficient strength, if only because of the heavy cost; a major reason for the loss of English independence in 1066 was a tax-saving reduction of the navy and of the king's own fighting force in 1050. Security therefore turned in the end, as later generations came to understand, on the absence of strong, aggressive enemies on the opposite shores of the North Sea and the Channel. For three centuries, England's eastern shores had been subject to continuous, and in the main successful, attacks launched from Denmark and Norway. To this danger was added, in the eleventh century, that of an assault from across the Channel. These newer enemies were the Normans, who though by now largely French in culture derived their special characteristics from the conquest and settlement of Normandy by the Vikings of the tenth century. What is remarkable is not that by 1066 the old English monarchy had succumbed to a simultaneous conjunction of all these perils, but that it came so near to overcoming them.

The first in the catalogue of England's eleventh-century calamities was the unexpectedly early death of Cnut in 1035. This immediately produced rival factions among the Anglo-Danish earls. One was dominated by Cnut's widow, queen Emma, previously the wife of Ethelred the Unready. This group supported Cnut's only legitimate son, Harthacnut, king of Denmark. But Harthacnut could not leave Denmark in time to prevent a rival English faction led by Leofric, earl of Mercia, installing Cnut's illegitimate son, Harold, as king by the end of 1037.

But, when Harold died in 1040, Harthacnut quickly took his place. He reigned for two violent, oppressive years before he dropped dead in 1042.

Prompt demonstrations of popular support in London and elsewhere in the south then secured the coronation of Ethelred the Unready's surviving son, Edward, known to history as Edward the Confessor. The Anglo-Saxon dynasty of Wessex was thus restored, but in a not very favourable situation. King Magnus of Norway claimed the right to be regarded as Harthacnut's successor and until he died in 1047 continually threatened England with a Norwegian invasion. In England itself, Edward was surrounded by a formidable group of Anglo-Danish counsellors of whom the leader was earl Godwin, a man for whom the dynasty of Wessex meant nothing. Already forty years old, Edward had been an exile in Normandy for over twenty-five years. Not surprisingly, he made a number of Norman appointments, the most notable being Robert of Jumièges, who became bishop of London in 1044 and archbishop of Canterbury in 1051; but he did not import Normans in quantity and he neither challenged nor yet tamely submitted to Godwin. It was simply safer to work with him and his family for so long as Magnus of Norway was a threat. The Godwins themselves had to reckon with the hostility to them of the other great earls, Leofric of Mercia and Siward of Northumbria. In 1045, Edward married Godwin's daughter, Edith, and certainly by the late 1040s, the Godwin connection was formidably large. Godwin's own earldom included all the shires from Kent to Cornwall. His violent, disreputable elder son, Swein, was earl of Oxford, Gloucester, Hereford, Berkshire and Somerset, and his younger son, Harold, was earl of East Anglia, Cambridgeshire and Huntingdonshire.

Yet Edward was not the pious celibate he may have been in old age. Hot-tempered and vigorous, he took part personally in the successful repulse of three Norwegian coastal raids in 1044, 1045 and 1048. He disinherited his mother, queen Emma, for supporting the claim of Magnus to the English throne, and refused to lend his support to Godwin's family connections in Denmark and Flanders. Accordingly, the quarrel that began between Edward and Godwin in 1051 may have been due to ill-judged self-confidence on Edward's part. He may also have harboured a personal grudge against Godwin. In 1036, Godwin, then a supporter of the claim of the illegitimate Harold to the throne, had arrested Edward's brother, Alfred. Alfred had been blinded and had died from his injuries. Edward was said always to have held Godwin personally responsible for Alfred's death.

Once freed from the threat from Norway by the death of Magnus in 1047, Edward's behaviour was bad for himself and for England. He disbanded the fleet and stopped levying the danegeld, or, as it was now usually called, the heregeld. The large standing army which had sustained Cnut was much reduced. This weakened the king's power in the short run and also contributed to the inadequacy of England's military and naval defences in 1066. The immediate result of Edward's diminution of his armed strength was a threat of civil war. In 1051 he ordered Godwin to ravage Dover, a town in his own earldom, for allegedly maltreating the followers of Count Eustace of Boulogne, returning home from a visit to Edward. The punishment was not an unusual one for a breach of the king's peace within a town, and, as an earl was technically a royal official, Godwin was required to obey the king's instructions. Instead, he refused, and when summoned before the king in Gloucestershire prepared to resist by assembling a considerable army. Edward called in aid Leofric of Mercia and Siward of Northumbria. Godwin therefore thought it politic to agree to appear in due course before the witan. Determined to assert his authority, Edward called up the fyrd, or militia, all over England, demanding in effect that the thegns and ceorls of all the Godwins' extensive earldoms should rally to their king against their lord. When the witan met at Southwark in September 1051, Godwin and his men were outnumbered. Edward peremptorily ordered Godwin and all his family into exile and sent queen Edith to a nunnery.

Within a year the Godwins were back. Godwin and his son Harold mounted an attack by sea, secured the apparently willing support of the south coast ports, and sailed up the Thames to London. Edward's diminished fleet was unable to stop them. Outmanoeuvred, Edward gave way on all points, though he evidently took some persuading. Godwin's earldoms were restored, the queen fetched back from her nunnery and a Godwin nominee, Stigand, made archbishop of Canterbury. Robert of Jumièges fled the country.

It is perhaps in the brief period during which Edward had ruled personally that the issue of the succession of William of Normandy was first raised. Not only did Edward increase the number of his Norman advisers but also received a visit from William himself. The view that Edward then actually designated William as his successor may merely be Norman propaganda; but William was a blood relation of Edward's, and if it had not been for Norman protection in his years of exile, Edward might never have survived to become England's king.

The triumph of the Godwins in 1052 seems to have made it unlikely, however, that William could acquire the English throne peacefully. The Godwins' defeat of Edward was widely advertised and supported as a victory for patriotic Englishmen over a king with a deplorable predilection for Norman Frenchmen. Though Godwin died within months of his success, his son, Harold, appeared by far the most important man in England for the last thirteen years of Edward's reign. Aided by his brother, Tostig, who became earl of Northumberland in 1055, Harold had conducted several successful campaigns against the ambitious and formidable Gruffydd ap Llewellyn, prince of Gwynedd and Powis. Harold's prowess as a military leader may well be the reason why, in the end, it was Harold whom Edward after all nominated to succeed him. The only indication that favoured William was the story that, when visiting William in 1064, Harold had promised on oath to help William become king, an action Harold claimed to have been tricked or forced into. What may also have governed Edward's ultimate designation of Harold was the near certainty that William's claim would be opposed in England but that Harold's would not.

Edward died on 5 January 1066; on the day of the burial, Harold was consecrated king in the abbey church at Westminster which Edward had founded, and which had itself been consecrated only eight days before his death. In the nine months of his reign, Harold was to succeed in keeping his kingdom in being just long enough for it to fall wholly under the power of William of Normandy.

William was not Harold's only problem. Harold Hardrada, king of Norway, also wanted to be king of England. In addition, Harold faced a rebellion by his now disaffected brother, Tostig. With the help of Edwin, earl of Mercia, the Northumbrians had rebelled against Tostig in 1065 and compelled the king to make Edwin's brother, Morcar, their earl instead. As a result of these events it was Tostig who began the sequence of crises which culminated in the battle of Hastings.

In May 1066, Tostig attacked the Isle of Wight, and with sixty ships then attempted to get a bridgehead on England's eastern coast. By the summer he had been held off by Edwin and Morcar and with twelve remaining ships moved north to Scotland. Here he accumulated a considerable force which was to move against Northumbria in association with a seaborne invasion by Harold Hardrada. In the south, under the impression that Tostig's force was the vanguard of the expected Norman attack, the militia and the fleet were mobilised. But contrary winds delayed William's transports; wearied by the waiting, both the militia and the crews of the English ships grew so restive that the militiamen were despatched to their homes and the fleet withdrawn to London. At that point, news reached Harold that the combined attack by Tostig and the Norwegians had begun. Harold marched north, but arrived too late to take part in the grim battle at Fulford, near York, in which Edwin and Morcar were defeated. But while Tostig and the Norwegians were recovering from the effects of their costly victory and making plans to march south, Harold surprised and defeated them at Stamfordbridge. Both Tostig and Harold Hardrada were killed.

If the losses suffered by the Norwegians in their victory at Fulford contributed to their defeat at Stamfordbridge, the strain of both battles also told heavily upon the English. Three days later, the winds having changed, William of Normandy's army disembarked unchallenged at Pevensey Bay at a moment when the south was defenceless, when Harold was at York with not much more than his own personal army and when Mercian and Northumbrian forces were depleted by their struggle at Fulford. Yet within barely a fortnight, Harold, after first settling the north, had reached London, gathering such forces as he could on the way. It was physically impossible for men from shires at any great distance from his line of march to be summoned in time, let alone to join him. Nevertheless, when William attacked Harold on Senlac Hill, near Hastings he did so with a force that was smaller than Harold's. William's first advantage was surprise: he attacked before Harold's men were in battle order. His second was the superior training and discipline of his forces, though how far, on the day, the better Norman performance was due to their greater mobility as a cavalry force or to the exhaustion and disorganisation of the English forces remains matter for argument. The two-handled battle axe could be lethal against the relatively light armour of the Norman knights; and as for the celebrated feigned flights of the Normans which enabled them to wheel round and encircle their English pursuers, these were tactics that Harold himself is said to have used at Stamfordbridge. English resistance continued fiercely all day, inflicting much damage on the Normans; it broke only after Harold himself and his two brothers were killed, leaving the English forces leaderless.

'Norman Yoke'

That the Norman victory at Hastings proved decisive was due to William's fixity of purpose during the twenty years after the battle. His army was not large and he could nowhere expect the kind of support which Cnut, when he conquered England, had received from the people of the Danelaw. Despite the death of Harold, Edwin of Mercia and Morcar of Northumbria were undefeated, and in London it was hoped to make Edgar, a great-nephew of Edward the Confessor, king in Harold's place. William therefore made no swift, heroic march upon London after his initial success. Instead, carefully but ruthlessly, he set out to encircle it. He moved from Hastings to Romney, from Dover to Canterbury, building fortifications and ravaging the land on the way. One of the main reasons for William's success was this policy of building forts and subduing the neighbouring area with forces stationed on raised encampments. Neither the Anglo-Saxons nor the Vikings had attempted to overawe the native population by such a network of fortifications built for the express purpose of preventing local rebellions.

Deciding it was impossible to storm London Bridge, he burned Southwark and continued a purposeful, destructive march across Surrey, northern Hampshire and Berkshire and crossed the Thames at Wallingford. On the way he paused to exact or receive the surrender of important persons and places. He was giving the English time to grasp that the alternative to speedy submission would be the despoliation of every rich man's estate and the coercion of every obstinate town. By the time he reached Wallingford he had already been offered, by the

Confessor's widow, the submission of Winchester; and at Wallingford itself, Stigand, the archbishop who had improperly replaced Robert de Jumièges at Canterbury, waited upon William and swore fealty to him, perhaps hoping to keep his high position under the new order. When William then moved to Berkhamstead, he received the submission of Edgar, Edwin and Morcar, as well as of other London notables. Unmoved either by this, or by his own promise to them to be their good lord, William let his army despoil the whole twenty-five mile stretch of countryside that lay between Berkhamstead and London. This seems to have assured him what was probably an unopposed entry into London and his coronation at Westminster, on Christmas Day 1066, eleven months after that of Harold. A new element was thoughtfully inserted into the ritual. William could claim that he was related by blood to the Confessor, that he had, so he said, been named by Edward as his heir, that he came with blessing of the pope, and that leading Englishmen had submitted to him. But such legal frailties, however imposing they might appear, were not enough. Accordingly, all present were called upon, in English and in French, to acknowledge William as their king by acclamation. Thus the English were made to give public notice that they were a conquered people and the Normans made to acknowledge that the power they now had in England they held only as subjects of his kingly authority.

After six months during which the building of rudimentary castles at London and elsewhere was undertaken, the land heavily taxed and English estates confiscated or handed back only on payment of heavy fines, William spent much of 1067 in Normandy only to find on his return that everywhere there was disaffection. Only after a difficult siege of Exeter did William finally secure control of Wessex; and in the summer of 1068 he had to campaign energetically before he could secure the submission at York of a body of tough recalcitrants. The construction of Norman castles at Warwick, Lincoln, Huntingdon and Cambridge was a consequence of this campaign. But early in 1069 a Norman force in Durham was destroyed; and York being besieged by anti-Norman forces, William had to march north again to relieve it. English opposition in Northumbria revived yet again, with the landing of a Danish force sent by the king of Denmark. The Norman defenders of York came out from their castles to prevent their encirclement, only to be heavily defeated. But the Anglo-Danish force failed to exploit its victory or to prepare for the inevitable Norman reply, even though their victory had heartened potential rebels elsewhere. William's commanders had to combat risings in Devon, Cornwall, Somerset and Dorset and William himself had to fight a battle at Stafford to overcome a serious revolt in Mercia.

At that point, with the Danes controlling York, William once more turned to a systematic devastation of the countryside to the west and north of the city in order to isolate it, as he had earlier isolated London.

The Danes, always content with loot or cash whenever it seemed for the time being too hazardous to seek for more, decided to abandon York and allow themselves to be bought off. That done, William, after pausing to crush the Mercians for good in Cheshire, resumed his punitive campaign of deliberately devastating the rebellious region of Yorkshire, and then dealt scarcely less savagely with disaffected Cheshire, Shropshire, Staffordshire and Derbyshire. Twenty years later, great areas of the north, particularly the Vale of York, were still derelict.

In 1070, Swein, king of Denmark, himself appeared on the Humber. His forces, using the Isle of Ely as a base, attracted many Englishmen, including the legendary thegn, Hereward, who, with his Danish allies, made a successful raid on Peterborough. Though a treaty between William and Swein secured the latter's withdrawal, Hereward gained the support in 1071 of earl Morcar. But after William had retaken Ely, Hereward, with only a few followers, escaped to maintain a long remembered if minor guerrilla campaign. In the same year, William tried to finish off his operations in the north by invading Scotland, in an effort to persuade the Scots to stop supporting the still not finally abandoned hopes of Edgar. But, despite king Malcolm's submission, Scottish compliance was not to be permanent.

Thereafter William was much distracted by dynastic problems in France, involving his fractious eldest son, Robert, and the hostile king of France. During William's absence abroad, a rebellion, obscure in origin and purpose, was begun by two noblemen of the Confessor's day, Waltheof, earl of Northumbria and Ralf, earl of East Anglia, together with Roger, the Norman earl of Hereford. Both Waltheof and Ralf had been strong supporters of William; Waltheof's role in the rebellion was minimal and Ralf's actions may have had personal causes. The rebels posed a threat chiefly because Danish support was expected. They were, however, crushed without difficulty. Ralf fled to Brittany but Waltheof quickly repented of his role as rebel and tried to make his peace with William. William's own conduct afterwards was a grim warning to all the English. Roger was imprisoned and, though Ralf was unreachable in Brittany, Waltheof was beheaded, since in English law this was the usual fate of traitors. That Waltheof was the one highborn Englishman to be executed by William made him something of a martyr.

Northumbria and the far north proved a problem beyond even William's capacity to solve finally. Infuriated by the violence of the Norman knights who sustained the bishop of Durham, on whom William had conferred the earldom of Northumbria in 1075, a multitude assembled at Gateshead and murdered the bishop and his ecclesiastical and military supporters. Once again, punishment was dire. The areas from which the rebels had come were devastated, and to forestall any Scottish effort to acquire them, a farflung fortress was constructed at what later became Newcastle-on-Tyne. But Newcastle was fifty miles south of the Tweed and, from the west, Scotland's border was only two days' ride from York; yet the whole area of Northumbria, though now thoroughly cowed, was sullenly hostile.

Elsewhere, the king's Normans had firmly established an overpowering presence on the Welsh borders. From Hereford, Norman outposts were established at Monmouth and Chepstow. The earls of Chester dominated the Conway and beyond. The earldom of Shrewsbury was established to organise the defence of the eastern flanks of Plynlimmon. In 1081, William himself led a force as far as St David's.

In 1085, for the last time, a Scandinavian attack was threatened by an alliance of Cnut of Denmark and Olaf of Norway with Count Robert of Flanders. Great preparations were made on both sides of the Channel and though the assault never materialised it may have provided the reason for two of William's most significant acts: the extraordinarily detailed stocktaking of the taxable resources of the English kingdom known as Domesday Book, and the great council of Salisbury in 1086, when all the landholders of substance in the land (some hundreds of them) did personal homage to the king, promising to be faithful to him against all other men. In one sense neither of these actions was new. The pre-Norman geld had been levied on the basis of a careful assessment of the land's wealth, even though, by 1087, the assessment was quite out of date. Yet no investigation as thorough as Domesday was undertaken anywhere else in Europe. Similarly, the notion that loyalty to the king overrode all other loyalties would have seemed no novelty at least to the people of Wessex. But the conduct of the great earls after Cnut's death had scarcely conformed to it, and William's belligerent Normans were perhaps harder still to control. In proclaiming, through a great public act, that loyalty to the king came first, after twenty years of remorseless campaigning against his opponents and at a time when his hold on Normandy was being jeopardised by his uneasy relations with his eldest son, Robert, and by the ambitions of the king of France, William was asserting not so much a legal maxim that ought to be acknowledged as a fact that he intended to insist on.

The conquest of the old Anglo-Danish state and the establishment of Norman-French domination in its place was an awesome exercise of intelligent and disciplined violence. William seems to have been moved neither by caprice nor malice. In his different way, he was accounted as much a pious son of the church as Alfred the Great had been. If, from the Anglo-Danish state, the English inherited a respect for a continuing law, under William they were compelled into respect for strong monarchy well before other important European peoples. William I's twenty-year rule produced a strongly compacted compromise between the old English system and the new, a welding together of the Anglo-Saxon tradition of local government by royal behest with the hard new Norman fact of powerful kingship.

PART TWO

RATIONALITY AND LAW

Approximate Dates: 1066–1307

1
A EUROPEAN KINGDOM

Normans and Angevins

ENGLAND'S new position after the Norman conquest was paradoxical. On one hand, it became, like the contemporaneous Norman kingdom of Sicily, one of the most effectively organised states western Europe had known since the fall of Rome. The device of the writ, the intermittent levying of a highly productive national tax, and the quasi-theological rhetoric of charters and coronation rituals, show that much of the apparatus of strong government was in existence before 1066. Loyalty to kindred, community or lord had, however, been only partially or intermittently subordinated to loyalty to kings. In consequence, pre-Norman rulers and their advisers, lay and ecclesiastical, failed fully to unite the kingdom and in the end failed to defend it. Under the Normans, however, the old monarchy was made to work at full power. Royal authority became strong enough, as it had rarely proved before 1066, to survive even when, as did not occur often, the king himself proved weak. Henceforward, writs were far more likely to be obeyed, military duties more likely to be fulfilled, taxation to become more regular, and ecclesiastics be made to conform to new and more rigorous, if less amiable, ideas of efficiency.

On the other hand, though now indisputably a vigorously governed kingdom, and at last freed from the constant threat of foreign invasion, England had become part of a large territorial dominion and lost its pre-Norman character as an independent state ruled by men of its own race. Until 1154 it was part of a Norman, and after that date part of an Angevin, empire. Those empires, though they belonged to England's kings, did not belong to the English; and England's kings were not Englishmen. They did not use the English language. Their native tongue was Norman French, their official language Latin. In that these kings and the men on whom they relied had a culture and a homeland of their own, both were French. But in view of the widespread character of their well-calculated marriage alliances and their close association with the papacy, it is best to think of them as adventurous, capable and highly cosmopolitan Europeans. In the centuries immediately after 1066, almost every baron of political consequence was Norman French and all the more important posts in the church were held by men of continental birth and training. It is for reasons such as these that it is, for much of the middle ages, scarcely possible to distinguish between English and European history. It would be fair to say also that the only Englishman ever to rule over England after the death of Harold in 1066 was Oliver Cromwell.

The history of England was therefore now, as never before, continuously dependent upon events outside it. The starting point was William I's unwillingness to bequeath his entire heritage to his feckless eldest son, Robert. Unable to disinherit him in Normandy, William compromised by bequeathing England to his second son, William II (1087–1100), usually known as Rufus. Neither Robert nor all the Norman barons liked the arrangement, but a rebellion by Robert's adherents in England failed; and in 1095, inspired by the pope's call to Christians to save Jerusalem from the Islamic invaders of the Byzantine empire, Robert left Normandy to take part in the First Crusade. He raised the cash for his expedition by pawning the Norman duchy to William; but on returning from the Crusade in 1100, he found that Rufus had died in a mysterious hunting accident and that their younger brother, Henry, had been crowned king of England. Henry I (1100–35) bought Robert off by restoring Normandy to him; but Henry constantly intrigued against his brother, invaded his duchy in 1085 and defeated him at Tinchebrai in 1086. Henry thus once more reunited the Norman heritage.

In 1120, the accidental death of Henry I's only legitimate son in the wreck of the White Ship left the king's daughter, Matilda, as his sole heir. Married at eleven to the emperor Henry V and widowed in 1125 when she was twenty-three, she was duly acknowledged by the leading men in England as next in succession. But, conscious that controlling Norman lords was no job for a woman, Henry married Matilda, in 1128, to the powerful Count Geoffrey of Anjou. In addition to acquiring an ex-empress as a wife, Geoffrey was also to acquire both England and Normandy, an arrangement designed to end the longstanding hostility between Normandy and Anjou. Unfortunately, the Norman barons were even more unwilling to be ruled by Geoffrey than by Matilda. After Henry I's death, therefore, Henry's favourite and nephew, Stephen, became king with the support of many leading laymen and clerics.

Stephen's elevation represented something of a baronial reaction against the strong system of government which Henry had sustained; but Stephen, though reputed to be genial and chivalrous, lacked political or military skill and his reign was, in exaggerated fashion, looked back on as nineteen years of anarchy. Royal control over the barons lapsed. The empress Matilda and her husband, Geoffrey, and after them, their son Henry, all endeavoured to displace Stephen. Sporadic fighting took place between Stephen and Matilda from 1138 to 1145, each side being played off against the other by ambitious Normans. In 1138, a rebellion against Stephen by his half-brother, Robert, with Scottish assistance, led to the defeat of the Scots at the battle of the Standard; but at the same time, Geoffrey of Anjou conquered Normandy. In England, Stephen was captured in 1141 and Matilda entered London, only to be driven out within a week. After Stephen's release, the confusion continued until, in 1148, Matilda gave up the contest.

For the rest of his reign Stephen exercised less control over the powerful Norman earls than any king between 1066 and the early thirteenth century. The main issue was still the succession. Stephen wanted his son Eustace to be king, but a powerful party across the Channel now opted for Matilda's son, Henry. The Normans were as opposed to a divided heritage as ever, since most of them held lands in both Normandy and England. Henry was master over more than half of France, and his feats of arms made him an ideal candidate under whom the Norman and Angevin dominions could be united. War over the rival candidatures of Eustace and Henry was fortunately averted by the sudden death of Eustace. Stephen agreed that Henry should succeed, and he did so as Henry II in 1154.

Henry II (1154–1189) ruled England as the direct descendant, through his mother, Matilda, of Henry I; but his father's heritage and his own marriage to Eleanor of Aquitaine gave him dominion over Normandy, Brittany, Maine, Anjou, Touraine, Poitou, Aquitaine and Gascony. As a result, England was, for almost fifty years, part of an empire that stretched from the Tweed to the Pyrenees. It was a huge inheritance and, intelligent and energetic as he was, even Henry realised it was scarcely possible for one man permanently to control all of it with the efficiency with which, despite his many absences from it, he governed England. As time went on, he hoped, with the cooperation of his four sons, to run the empire through an Angevin family consortium. But all his sons plotted against their father and against one another and were encouraged to do so by the astute young French king, Philip II, steadily determined to remove Angevin power from his kingdom. Only the deaths of two of his sons, Henry in 1183 and Geoffrey in 1186, and of Henry II himself in 1189, averted total confusion and allowed Richard I to inherit from his father the whole Angevin empire.

More than any other English king, Richard I (1189–99) belongs to European rather than to English history. Virtually an absentee monarch, he spent scarcely ten months of his reign in England. He devoted his energies to countering the intrigues of Philip II and to reorganising the kingdom of Sicily. He was the effective leader of the Third Crusade, capturing Acre, defeating Saladin and negotiating a favourable peace with him. He was subsequently captured in Austria and held to ransom by the emperor Henry VI, an old enemy of his. All through his reign, England's wealth was systematically exploited to subsidise the crusading glories and dynastic imperatives of a spectacular international super-star.

Expensive though he was to maintain, Richard was a hero. His brother, John (1199–1216) was not a hero; but he was hardly less expensive, was wholly unpredictable and, forced by his failures to spend much of his time in England, rapidly acquired an evil reputation from which subsequent historical research has never wholly rescued him. Since his right to succeed Richard could be challenged on behalf of Arthur of Brittany, son of John's deceased elder brother, Geoffrey, it was only by faithfully accepting that Philip II of France was his overlord in respect of the Angevin dominion in France that John could hope to safeguard himself against Philip's hostility. Yet he foolishly laid himself open to attack from Philip by interfering with the utmost recklessness in a dispute over an inheritance in his Angevin dominion. He put away his own wife, married the female claimant in the case, and denied her male rival a fair hearing. Philip ruled that John had behaved illegally, declared his French lands forfeit, and invaded and conquered Anjou by 1203 and Normandy by 1204. In addition, though Arthur had certainly plotted with Philip against John, Arthur's mysterious death was universally believed to have been the result of a brutal murder planned by John.

Though John was determined to regain his possessions in France, the Norman lords in England refused to support him in a war against Philip, now rapidly acquiring the reputation that would earn him the appellation Philip Augustus. In addition, having foolishly challenged one of the greatest of medieval French kings, John had also quarrelled disastrously with Innocent III, the greatest of medieval popes. John's failures, his quarrelsomeness, his financial exactions, and his disregard for the normal rules of kingly and knightly behaviour lost him the personal respect that had attached to his predecessors, even including Rufus and Stephen. Not until 1214 did he manage to devise a plan to rehabilitate himself. He made his peace with the pope and formed an alliance against Philip with the emperor Otto IV of Germany, who was John's nephew. But an assault on the French which John hoped to launch from Poitou never got started and at the battle of Bouvines in 1214, Philip decisively defeated the emperor. John's plans had foundered.

In the long run England gained from the preoccupation of Richard and John with their continental and international ambitions. Since the country continued to be ruled efficiently throughout the long years of Richard's absence, it was already clear that such changes had been wrought by William I, Henry I and Henry II that it was possible to begin thinking in terms not merely of government by 'the king' but of government by 'the crown', an institution that could and should survive, whether the royal person were present or absent, capable or incapable. It was because John had alienated so much support by the arbitrary recklessness with which he had so spectacularly failed first to preserve and then to regain his French inheritance, that he found himself compelled to agree to Magna Carta in 1215; for that document was the ground on which would be erected the belief that neither a king nor his government could disregard law. Magna Carta was a baronial protest not so much against strong government as against bad government, and against the misuse of the crown as an institution.

John's son and successor, Henry III (1216–72) proved as airily ambitious in his own quite different fashion as his father and uncle. He too wasted his finances and damaged his personal repute in an endeavour to become a leading actor on the continental stage. A costly attempt to establish his younger son as king of what had once been Norman Sicily, and his brother as emperor of Germany, forced him to make what became a more substantial surrender of the purely personal powers of kingship. By the end of his reign Henry III had been forced to accept the demand of his leading subjects that their traditional role as councillors of the king should not only be respected but also enlarged to give them an authoritative voice in the business of government.

Henry III's continental failure was formally recorded in the treaty of Paris in 1259. Henry renounced his dynastic rights in Normandy, Anjou and Poitou; as Duke of Aquitaine he still held Gascony and other lands in south-west France, but as vassal to the French king. Hence, though the Angevin empire was gone, the French connection remained. His son, Edward I (1272–1307), made ambitious plans towards the end of his reign to reassert his independence from the French king, but failed to find the necessary continental allies and, more significantly, sufficient baronial or financial support from the English. Indeed, Edward was faced with a baronial attempt to curtail his freedom of action in England that only a monarch of his acknowledged ability could have survived. His efforts to coerce the French king were ended by an agreement in 1305. This still left Edward as the French king's vassal in respect of Gascony, and also provided for a marriage between Edward's son and the French king's daughter. Some thirty years later, in 1337, Edward III, born of that marriage, renewed the old rivalry by claiming the French throne. Thus began the first of the Anglo-French wars, known collectively as the Hundred Years War, which continued intermittently until 1453.

Treating with Rome

Pre-Norman England had always regarded the papacy with pious respect, but its remoteness from Rome meant that by the eleventh century the life and thought of its churchmen were somewhat behind the times. The Norman conquest brought England into an ecclesiastical association with Rome almost as close as its political connection with Normandy; and involved it as deeply in the disputes produced by the ambitions of popes as in those derived from the quarrels of Normans and Angevins.

Relations between the Normans and the popes were close. Popes relied heavily on Norman Sicily for support in their bitter conflicts with the German emperors for the right to be regarded as the supreme authority in western Christendom. William I arrived in England as one of the papacy's favourite sons. He was a loyal supporter of the papal programme of church reform and one of the various justifications of his invasion in 1066 was that he was to make effective the pope's decree that Stigand had become archbishop of Canterbury uncanonically. William not only removed Stigand in 1070, but replaced him with the Italian teacher and theologian, Lanfranc, who, while abbot of Bec, in Normandy, had founded one of the greatest centres of learning outside Italy. Essentially a tidy-minded, centralising administrator, he replaced the *Regularis Concordia* by a set of rules on French lines, remodelled the monastic cathedral chapters inherited from pre-Norman England, and saw to it that Normans were appointed to most of the abbeys, all the bishoprics and the most important positions in the cathedrals. He cooperated fully with the papal campaign against simony (the purchase of ecclesiastical offices for a cash payment) and against clerical marriage, and established the primacy of the see of Canterbury over that of York, going indeed further than his royal master by claiming for himself a primacy over 'all Britain'. Through a series of ecclesiastical councils he sought to frame a systematic code of church law in England and, with William's support, to set up separate law courts for the church, to deal with offences against ecclesiastical law and crimes committed by clerics.

This businesslike collaboration between king and archbishop in matters ecclesiastical was uncharacteristic of the Europe of the time. In the second half of the eleventh century a powerful intellectual movement, originating among the Cluniacs and vigorously propagated by Pope Leo IX and the even more ardent Gregory VII, worked to end that ecclesiastical dependence upon princely protection which had hitherto been normal in western Christendom. Without the protection of secular princes and their lords, the church could not have converted the Germanic invaders who broke up the old Roman Empire nor survived to convert the Scandinavian invaders of the ninth and tenth centuries. By 1050, however, the subordination of the spiritual to the temporal power seemed to have outlived its purpose. By that time, western Europe was no longer gravely threatened by either heathen or infidel. Even in Spain, Islam was already on the defensive; and the Byzantine empire was still an effective bulwark against it in the east. With the Viking threat also at an end, it seemed the time had come to assert in practice what almost everybody acknowledged in theory: that the pope, as Vicar of Christ on earth, was Christendom's supreme authority, that the princes were his inferiors, and that ecclesiastics should be appointed by and owe ultimate allegiance to the pope rather than to the kings who were the pope's spiritual vassals. Since princely and lay control of the church had corrupted it and made it worldly, papal attacks on simony and clerical marriage were among the first shots in the new campaign. But the great issue was the claim that the pope, and not kings and emperors, should appoint bishops and archbishops everywhere. During William I's reign, the refusal of the German emperor, Henry IV, to agree to abolish what was called the lay investiture of bishops led to his excommunication by the former Cluniac monk, Hildebrand, who had become Pope Gregory VII in 1073. The papal ban was lifted only after Henry had come to Gregory in 1076 at his castle in Canossa, to stand for three days in the snow as a barefoot penitent at its gates. Although, in the sequel, imperial forces drove Gregory from Rome to a death in exile in 1085, an agreement between the two rivals' successors in 1122 yielded much that Gregory had demanded.

Unlike the rulers with whom Gregory quarrelled, William I was zealous to remove abuses from the church and was unhampered by disaffected nobles who might espouse the papal cause in order to add respectability to their rebelliousness. Above all he was a Norman; and the Normans were Gregory's allies in Italy. William survived Gregory's pontificate unscathed. When Gregory asked William to do him homage for his English kingdom, claiming the long tradition of paying Peter's pence as a justification for the demand, William refused and Gregory climbed down.

The reign of William II, however, produced a protracted duel between a cheerful blaspheming rogue of a king and an ageing, monkish archbishop of Canterbury in St Anselm. This renowned philosopher was, in theological matters, wholly a product of the school of thought that exalted popes above princes. Though describing William as an untamed bull and himself as a weak old sheep, Anselm patiently upheld the principle that papal decrees were valid in England, and that papal legates could come to England, whether the king approved of them or not. He was even more successful against the more judicious and competent Henry I, and on no less an issue than the question of lay investiture that had divided Gregory VII and Henry IV of Germany. In 1107 Henry I agreed that in future the right to invest bishops with the symbols of their spiritual office on appointment to their sees belonged to the pope and not to the king. The agreement between Henry and Anselm served, in fact, as the precedent on which the issue was settled between pope and emperor in 1122.

In the centuries that followed, this symbolic change did not mean much in practice, if only because bishops continued to do homage to the king for the lands that pertained to their archbishoprics. But in theory (and in the medieval world theory often rated higher than practice) the crown had forfeited its supremacy over the English church.

Under Stephen, the crown lost actual control of the church. His ambitious brother, Henry of Blois, was made papal legate in England, a position which gave him virtual control of all ecclesiastical and monastic appointments. After 1143, Theobald, archbishop of Canterbury, was also papal legate; and just as the papal party had been influential in securing Stephen's recognition as king, so at the end of his reign it was an important factor in the negotiations leading to the accession of Henry II. But Henry II's determination to regain the royal control over the church that Stephen had lost led to the most celebrated personal conflict in the history of English high politics.

At first, ecclesiastical dominance seemed assured. Henry's chancellor, Thomas Becket, was an archdeacon high in the favour of the papalist archbishop, Theobald. But when, in the role of chancellor, Becket turned himself into a worldly despoiler of the church and became the king's closest companion, Henry chose him without hesitation to succeed Theobald at Canterbury. As Henry's man, Becket was clearly expected to cut the church and the pretensions of the papacy down to size. The power of the crown over the church, so diminished under Stephen, would, it was hoped, be fully restored.

Unfortunately, having earlier transformed himself from dutiful son of the church into a chancellor who robbed it, Becket now confounded the king by becoming, as archbishop, an intransigent defender of the freedom of the church from royal interference and of his own right to direct its affairs according to every interpretation of canon law that exalted papal authority at the expense of royal. Henry was exasperated by Becket's obstinacy into drawing up the Constitutions of Clarendon in 1164. They laid down that, without royal consent, no ecclesiastic could go to Rome, no appeals be made to the courts at Rome, and no magnate or royal official be excommunicated. The Constitutions were in fact little more than a precise definition of what had been accepted practice before Stephen's reign. As public definitions of royal authority, however, they were so contrary to contemporary ecclesiastical opinion that Becket's response was one of outrage. After first agreeing to them he recanted and fled abroad. He returned, briefly, to deny the king's right to put him on trial and to claim that as both cleric and bishop he was exempt from trial by a lay court. He then once more fled abroad and appealed to the pope.

For the issue on which Becket and Henry had quarrelled most violently had been yet another matter: Henry's insistence that churchmen who committed crimes ('criminous clerks') should be punished in the ordinary courts of law as if they had been laymen, and without regard to any penalties imposed on them by the church courts which had operated in England since the reforms made by Lanfranc. Becket insisted that to punish a cleric twice in this way was contrary to canon law. Not all canon lawyers agreed with him; but on this, as on all the other matters in dispute between Becket and the king, the pope had, in so public a controversy, no choice but to take Becket's side. Yet from the point of view of the king, and of many of his lay subjects, the leniency of the church courts, which tended to impose quite derisory penalties even for serious crimes such as murder, Becket's argument had little to commend it.

It was Henry's decision to have his eldest son crowned as king in his own lifetime that brought the dispute to its melodramatic climax. Since Becket had contumaciously fled the realm, Henry had the consecration of his son performed by the archbishop of York with the assistance of a number of the bishops. Becket's unappeasable anger at this flagrant invasion of his lawful primacy as archbishop of Canterbury culminated in his return to England after a six-year absence with the declared intention of excommunicating all who had crowned the king's son. It was Henry II's explosion of rage at this move that prompted four knights to murder Becket in his own cathedral at Canterbury in 1170.

In many ways, the conflict between Henry and Becket was more sensational than decisive. Henry had demanded a return to a past that no ecclesiastic of importance could accept. Even those bishops who had opposed Becket had done so out of fear of the king and dislike of Becket's intemperate attitude, not because they thought him wrong in principle. Becket, too, had tried to assert a degree of ecclesiastical independence and papal power that was beyond the limits of the practical. Henry did public penance in the streets of Canterbury and Becket was canonised. Beyond that, the Constitutions of Clarendon, though cancelled, continued to operate in practice. Otherwise, there happened what would have happened anyway. Appeals to Rome increased and canon law at last made the headway in England it had already made elsewhere, its application in detail, as in other parts of Europe, often being the outcome of a compromise, or of the occasional defeat now of the secular, now of the ecclesiastical cause.

The tide of papal power in England had yet to reach its highest point. John's reign, from 1199 to 1216, unfortunately coincided almost exactly with that of the formidable pope, Innocent III, whose pontificate lasted from 1198 to 1216. Innocent's aims were indicated by his choice of text for his first pontifical sermon. Taken from the prophet Jeremiah, it read 'See I have this day set thee over the nations, and over the kingdoms, to root out, and to pull down, and to destroy, and to throw down, to build and to plant'. Accordingly, at a time when John was losing Normandy and Anjou to Philip of France, Innocent enraged John by appointing the English cardinal, Stephen Langton, as archbishop of Canterbury, against the wishes of the king and the bishops, and of the monks of Canterbury itself.

John, with Angevin passion, countered this papal claim to determine who should hold the highest ecclesiastical post in England and the potential political power that went with it, by refusing to allow Langton into England. Innocent countered with an interdict: John was excommunicated. All the churches were closed and the only religious rites that could be performed were baptism and the hearing of the confessions of those about to die. The interdict lasted for seven years until, trapped by his desire to recover his empire from Philip and his fear that Innocent would authorise the French king to attack and depose him in England, John surrendered unconditionally. Langton came to England and absolved John. The interdict was lifted in 1214. John gave up all control of episcopal elections, declared himself the pope's vassal and thus acknowledged Innocent as England's feudal lord. Yet none of this prevented the collapse of John's simultaneous efforts to break the power of Philip Augustus. After his victory over the emperor Otto IV, at Bouvines, in 1214, Philip was impregnable. It was because he was now

73

in this humiliated, bankrupt position that John put his seal to Magna Carta in 1215.

Langton had all along avoided the bellicose heroics of a Becket, behaving with a politic moderation that caused Innocent to denounce the Great Charter and reprimand Langton for his statesmanlike part in helping to draw it up. Yet the first clause of the Great Charter registered, in words at least, a complete papal victory: *Anglicana ecclesia libera sit.* The church in England was to be free from royal interference and free, in consequence, to conduct itself in accordance with the decisions of the canon lawyers of Rome. Never before had papal authority been so great as it was in England for most of the thirteenth century. The resistance to it that developed later in the middle ages was never to be more than intermittent.

The conflict between popes and princes would not again simultaneously involve such outstanding figures as Rufus and Anselm, Henry II and Becket, or John, Philip Augustus and Innocent III. That the papacy had made good its larger claims was accepted as one fact; that it would pay neither popes to over-insist on those claims, nor princes to resist them head-on, was accepted as another. Relations between English kings and the popes were characterised by frequent recrimination and almost continuous friction. Not until the reign of Edward III (1327–77) did England give up promising to pay annual tribute to Rome as a sign of the feudal dependence upon the papacy created by John's submission. In important respects the clergy claimed, and preserved, great independence of lay authority. The pope's right to nominate incumbents to parishes and bishoprics, and canons to cathedral chapters, was legally unchallenged, and even then ineffectively, until parliament passed the statute of Provisors in 1351. Only in 1398, under Richard II, was there agreement that pope and crown should jointly appoint bishops; and only after that was it more or less automatic for the king's nominee to be appointed. Not until the fifteenth century did the frequency with which popes appointed foreigners to English appointments generally decline.

The papacy's right of taxation over the English clergy, a source of revenue the crown would dearly have liked to reserve to itself, was not resisted until after 1370. Only in the middle of the fifteenth century was it partly replaced by the payment to Rome, by newly-appointed prelates, of the first year's revenue of their benefices, the so-called 'first-fruits'. Appeals to Rome were not obstructed by statute until the statutes of Praemunire of 1353 and 1383 threatened with outlawry or expropriation all who had recourse to 'foreign' jurisdiction. The problem of criminous clerks that had so embroiled Henry II and Becket remained intractable. Clerics claimed immunity from crown courts while themselves claiming jurisdiction over matters of marriage and the ownership of benefices. The only major inroad here was Edward I's statute of Mortmain (1279), which limited the extent to which the church could acquire property; and a further royal edict which attempted to define, though scarcely to limit, the powers of the church courts. Not until the tempestuous Luther was papal authority fundamentally challenged in Europe and not until the days of Henry VIII would it be asserted that 'this realm of England is an empire', a sovereign state independent of all foreign authority. Only then could the words attributed to king John by Shakespeare be made good:

> . . . from the mouth of England
> Add this much more, that no Italian priest
> Shall tithe or toll in our dominions
> But as we, under heaven, are supreme head,
> So under Him that great supremacy,
> Where we do reign, we will alone uphold
> Without the assistance of a mortal hand.
> So tell the pope, all reverence set apart
> To him and his usurp'd authority.

There were gains for England from the closer involvement in the common European culture that necessarily resulted from the continuous presence in its midst of foreign clerics, not all of them venal, and many of them men of great learning. The two-way traffic with Rome in literate men of influence in great affairs, lay as well as ecclesiastical, is less easy to evaluate now, as then, than the yearly flow of cash into papal coffers. The Reformation, by detaching England from Rome, released new energies and made new opportunities. But it began the process by which England steadily distanced itself mentally from its European neighbours through the succeeding centuries. The grudging economic return to Europe in 1973 came only after England's independent role as pioneer industrialising and imperialist power had been played out to the full. By then it had been so long since any English matter had been submitted to the decision of an external authority that it is not surprising that this modern version of submission to Rome should have provoked many to wish for a new statute of Praemunire to forbid recourse to so 'foreign' a 'court' as that presided over by the European Commissioners in Brussels. But now, as had been so before the 1530s, 'this realm' was no longer an 'empire' either in the modern meaning of the word, or in the medieval sense of a state wholly free of external jurisdiction.

2
LAWS AND LIBERTIES

Lordship Enlarged

THE Norman irruption into England was not, like the Saxon and Danish incursions, a settlement of the land by a new race of pioneers. It was a take-over by a new monarchy and a new aristocracy. The English nobility being either dead or dispossessed, England came under a new management with little in common with the bulk of the population. The Danish invasions had, after the first onrush, added fresh men to the plough. The Normans did not come to plough, but to ensure that virtually every man in the land had a new, and Norman, master. They achieved their purpose in less than twenty years.

The transfer was soon arranged. Whenever William conferred land upon his followers, a writ to that effect was despatched to the shire court. Overawed by armed Normans, the court would have to give way. The absence of an English leadership capable of resisting this Norman pressure made it very effective. The new Norman masters began by building fairly crude castles on the edge of the main towns. From these they made raids into the shire to bully the inhabitants into rendering them all the dues they had paid to their previous lords, and perhaps more, for good measure.

In the general confusion, and given the rapacity of the Normans, some who perhaps found the lands they had acquired less productive or extensive than they had hoped, were not above seizing the lands of their fellow usurpers. One reason for ordering the Domesday survey of 1086 was the king's desire to discover just who had acquired the lordship of what, and whether he was entitled to it. The king's commissioners conducted at each shire court an inquisition not only into the value of each lordship but also into its ownership, or as the legal word of the time would have it, 'seisin'. The commissioners wished to know who had held the land in the time of Edward the Confessor, who was the present holder and on what date he had acquired seisin. Thus, the Domesday 'Book' deserved its nickname. It was the final day of judgment, not only as to the wealth of what the Normans had taken over; it was a final judgment as to which Normans held land by writ of their king and which had taken it without that authority.

Financial reasons, however, seem originally to have moved the king to order this extraordinarily detailed survey. Domesday was intended to record the potential yield of every lord's estate, on the basis of rents paid and services rendered, and of assets such as men, mills, plough teams and the amount of pasture and meadow it contained. Undertaken twenty years after the Conquest itself, it sought to establish, on the basis of the information it accumulated, what taxes and dues each lord's estate owed the king. It covered over 13,000 places south of the river Tees and provides a survey of economic and human resources for which no other European state of that time offers a parallel. Though it concentrated chiefly on places from which royal dues and taxes were collected, and omitted the names of other quite sizeable places as irrelevant to the compilers' purposes, it was an outstanding administrative achievement and an indication of the efficiency with which the Normans had infused the government they had taken over from the old English monarchy.

It is, however, misleading to regard the Norman Conquest as having subjected the English to a 'foreign' aristocracy which took perhaps three centuries to be assimilated as 'Englishmen'. To most people in the middle ages, 'foreigner' meant little more than 'stranger' or, more precisely, someone 'from outside'—and from outside *tun*, *vil* or *burh* rather than outside the country. That a new lord was Norman would matter less than that he was exceptionally ruthless in insisting on his rights.

The principle of loyalty to a lord and the legal necessity for every man to have a lord were established features of English life before the Normans. The Norman Conquest linked the system more precisely with land tenure. The Conquest also established firmly for the first time that ultimately all the land in England was held 'of the king'. This was because William, having conquered England, distributed it afresh among his principal followers. These became known as tenants-in-chief; they held their land directly 'of' the king.

The tenants-in-chief or 'magnates' at the time of Domesday numbered about 180 barons, together with a number of ecclesiastical landholders such as bishops, cathedrals, abbeys and minsters. The crown retained large areas for itself, since from one point of view the king can be thought of as a great lord who happened to wear a crown. Like his tenants-in-chief he needed land on which he and his household could feed and make a profit, from which he could draw a substantial personal armed following, and with portions of which he could endow his children and reward his supporters.

The tenants-in-chief in their turn divided their lands among their retainers, who would then sub-divide their tenancies among lesser sub-tenants. In theory, landholder A held of landholder B, who held of C, who held of D who, as a magnate, was a tenant-in-chief of the king. What prevented this from being much of a 'system' was that A could also hold a piece of land as an immediate tenant of C; and that C, who was a sub-tenant of D for one piece of land, might be D's overlord in respect of some other piece of land.

The theoretical purpose of the parcelling out of land to tenants was to

77

provide the Norman kings with a sufficient quantity of knights, that is to say armed cavalry. Each knight was to be able to report, fully armed, for forty days' service per year in the king's army in time of war. In theory, therefore, the tenant at the bottom of the chain of sub-tenancies which stretched upwards to the king was a fairly humble cavalry trooper. Land was assessed on the basis that every five 'hides' should support one knight. It was the function of the peasantry, who formed another network of tenantries further down the social scale, in effect to provide food for their military and ecclesiastical superiors. The close association of land tenure with the performance of military service in the king's army did not long survive. By the middle of the twelfth century the obligation was already being commuted for a money payment and what had once been primarily a unit providing the king with an armed man became a taxable unit known as a knight's fee. Most English land was held on this basis; but lands had by the thirteenth century been so divided and exchanged that whereas one holding might be rated at several knight's fees, others might be only a half, quarter or even tenth of a knight's fee. This tendency towards dividing knight's fees reflected among other things, the escalating cost of a knight's armament. By the fourteenth century, with the development of heavy plate armour, a knight had been transformed from a cavalry trooper into the operator of a rather cumbersome four-legged tank.

Increasingly, too, he was a mercenary. This was due to William's invention of the tax known as scutage, or shield money. He imposed this on his barons as an alternative to requiring them to supply him with a quota of knights from among their tenants. This gave Norman and Angevin kings a professional army, while allowing those who held land by knight's tenure to stay at home, manage their estates, involve themselves in the business of the shire courts and become the prototypes of the English country gentleman. The combatant knight was more likely to be a landless young man, victim perhaps of primogeniture seeking, by soldiering professionally under the command of king or baron, to win advancement and, in due course, land of his own. In the eleventh century, knights were still quite small fry; not until the twelfth century, as they became a more expensive form of weaponry did they begin to acquire the ceremonial trappings that passed into legend.

There developed an elaborate form of initiation for the young knight a night-long vigil in church, and a donning of expensive new robes after the rare luxury of a purifying bath. Whoever held land by knight' service continued to be compassed about with quasi-heroic formulas The tenant had to do homage. He was required to kneel, place his hand between the hands of his lord and declare 'I become your man from thi day forward of life and limb and of earthly worship, and unto you sha be true, and faithful . . . for the tenements that I hold of you'. Ther would then be a swearing on the gospels of the oath of fealty, at onc less personal but more specific: 'I shall be faithful and true unto you an faith to you shall bear for the lands that I hold of you, and I shall lawfully do to you the customs and services which I ought to do, so help me God and his saints'.

These solemn oaths were devices by which a belligerent society sought to overawe not only the humble but the mighty, since all who held land were required to swear homage and fealty to their liege lord. Norman kings regularly did so to the king of France in respect of their French possessions. William I was obviously impressed both by the sanctity of these oaths and by the frequency with which powerful men found reasons for breaking them. This is why, at Salisbury in 1086, William had demanded that landholding men, 'whosesoever men they be', should swear oaths of 'fealty to him that they would be faithful to him against all other men'. Hence, a man who swore homage to his lord thereafter did so 'saving the faith that I owe the king'. The Oath of Salisbury so powerfully reinforced the view that all men, however powerful, owed fealty to the king that it was now taken for granted.

The 'customs and services' promised by the oath of fealty demonstrate how firm the grip of lordship over vassal now was. Apart from his duty to do knight service to the king, or pay a tax instead, whoever held land by knight's service was required to pay his lord an 'aid' towards the costs the lord incurred when knighting his son or on the marriage of his daughter. When the tenant died, his successor had to pay the lord a tax known as a relief, like the Anglo-Saxon heriot or the later estate duty, before taking over. This was because, strictly speaking, land was not owned, but merely held, and not therefore a hereditary possession. Since it was convenient to the lord for a dead man's holding to be transferred undivided, with a minimum of delay or argument, to a new tenant capable of shouldering its responsibilities, this came to mean in practice that it passed in its entirety to the eldest son. Payment of the relief was a reminder to the new holder of the fief (as a landholding was called) that he was personally contracted to his lord. This system of primogeniture long survived, to fill the land with discontented younger sons. It was one of the several peculiarities of that county that in Kent the system known as 'gavelkind' prevailed, by which all a man's sons inherited a portion of his estate.

The eldest son was always held to have a moral duty, where primogeniture prevailed, to make some provision for his younger brothers. But the regularity with which an ill-used younger brother appears in tales and legends suggests that the Normans may have been more successful than most European rulers in preventing the excessive division of landholdings. On the other hand, the existence of land owing much less than a knight's fee indicates that they did not always succeed.

Two other rights over tenants were sources of dispute for centuries: the rights of wardship and marriage. Where an heir to a tenancy was under age, the lord had the right to full enjoyment of the land until the

79

heir, if male, was twenty-one or, if female, fourteen. The lord also had the right to marry his ward, male or female, to whomsoever he pleased. Both wardship and marriage were rights that could be sold: thus, the right to profit from the lands of a minor could be bought for cash, and the lord could also make money out of 'selling' a ward and his or her land by arranging a marriage with someone prepared to pay a good price. Originally, these rights were a form of social welfare, arising from a lord's duty to care for the children of prematurely deceased tenants; in a harsh world some such arrangement was sensible. But the only legal limitations upon how the lord carried out his responsibilities were that the land was not to be laid waste and that a ward should not be married to someone of inferior status. These safeguards proved inadequate.

Rights of lordship were also exercised by the king in his capacity as the greatest 'feudal' lord. The tensions between great landholders and the crown which make up so much of the high politics of English history on into the early seventeenth century were often concentrated on the king's tendency to demand excessive aids and reliefs, and on his, and his courtiers', often questionable habits over wardship and marriage.

Feudalism in Perspective

This arrangement of legal liabilities, by which land tenure was linked with the duty to perform, or pay others to perform, military service to the king, and by which vassals holding fiefs were bound to do 'customs and services' to their liege lords, constitutes the chief characteristic of what is usually called 'the feudal system' of 'the middle ages'. It is therefore relevant that the terms 'middle ages' and 'feudalism' were not invented until the sixteenth and seventeenth centuries respectively, by which time 'feudalism' in most of its aspects had disappeared. The men and women of the eleventh to the fifteenth centuries had no idea they were living either in a feudal society or in the middle ages. In much the same way, those who lived during the years of Angevin rule never knew that they were subject to 'Plantagenet' kings. The name was not applied to those kings until after they and their subjects were all dead. The use of the terms 'feudal' and 'middle ages' is at best a convenient form of historical shorthand. Their too frequent use suggests it is possible to say when the feudal system or the middle ages 'began' and when they 'ended'. It implies that they were wholly different from anything before or after them, that 'feudalism' was always 'feudal' in the same sort of way, and that the middle ages were all much of a muchness.

In England, feudalism was a phase or, more precisely, a succession of phases, in the continuous history of the tensions between men's loyalties to community, lordship and kingship that had begun with the Anglo-Saxons and were to continue at least until the beginning of the nineteenth century. In the first two centuries after 1066, loyalty to the local community was relatively weak; in the five centuries after that it was greatly strengthened. But all through the centuries labelled 'feudal' or 'medieval', lordship scarcely ever counted above kingship and whenever it did so, the most strenuous efforts were made by lordly barons to restore kingship at least to what seemed its legitimate strength. It may be true that, in continental Europe, feudalism was 'a compromise with anarchy'; in England it was always a compromise between lordship, or baronial power, and kingly power. The English were early to congratulate themselves, and to be congratulated by others, on their traditions of freedom. But their addiction to having, at the centre of things, a strong kingship which limited the ability of the powerful to dislocate the lives of the less powerful was a tradition at least as venerable, and feudalism represented no departure from it. The idea of freedom can itself be discerned in the fundamental feudal principle that no lord had 'right to do wrong', but it was a principle older than feudalism and one that outlived it. Moreover, while men expected kings to apply the principle to barons, all men, barons included, insisted that it also applied to their sovereign lord the king.

This continuing tension held all the elements, community, lordship and kingship, in permanent balance, so that when loyalty to the local community gained new strength from the developing institution of parliament, it failed, in the seventeenth century, to destroy loyalty to the idea of kingship and, in the eighteenth, to destroy the historic traditions of good lordship. 'Feudalism' was but one phase in the long history of the interplay between the ideas of freedom and community, kingship and lordship, liberty and law.

Kingly Justice and Power

Except during Stephen's reign, English feudalism during the Norman and Angevin period was in essence a form of aristocratic resistance to the growth of royal absolutism. The Norman and Angevin kings would all have ruled as absolutely as Roman emperors had they been able to. The power they left in the hands of the barons was a grudging royal concession to two practical limitations of their power: primitive communications, and a lack of educated, literate persons qualified to serve the king, not only in his court but also in the localities. Strenuously though they tried to undermine the powers of their barons, kings found it impossible to control the country without their assent, even if it was given unwillingly.

The king's earliest agents in the counties after 1066 were the sheriffs. They collected the income from the king's farms, presided over the shire courts, and were responsible for enforcing royal writs. Sheriffs were usually feudal lords of a middling sort; under William I, at least, they performed their duties well because both they and those with whom they had to deal were terrified of him. But, though to ignore a writ was a crime for which a man was required to answer personally to the king, it

could be months before a king found out that a sheriff had ignored his commands or neglected his duty; and more months still before the offending sheriff could be made to appear at the king's court to explain himself, particularly if he could plead sickness or urgent county business as valid reasons for not obeying the summons. Investigation of complaints about injustices committed by sheriffs could take years. The mere absence of means of communication that could operate at any speed much above a few miles an hour meant that the king could not govern at all without the cooperation of his feudal inferiors. Both Henry I and Henry II had to use drastic measures to remove unruly or oppressive sheriffs, and felt compelled to devise other means to limit their *de facto* independence.

Henry I is thought to have wanted to solve the problem by appointing resident royal justices in every shire, but before the new European universities of the thirteenth century had produced a large reservoir of highly trained graduates, the sheer lack of qualified men prevented him doing so. He compromised by setting up panels of royal 'judges in eyre', sent out at intervals from the king's own court to take over the shire court. When a shire court met on such occasions it became a branch of the king's court, the *curia regis*. The sheriff would have to do all the preparatory and coordinating work for the itinerant judges, and to this end was assisted by an official known as 'keeper of the pleas of the crown'. By the thirteenth century he was already being called a coroner.

It was through the persistent extension of the jurisdiction of the courts of the king, both at Westminster and in the shires, that large areas of law gradually ceased to be feudal, or private law, and became 'common law'. There had existed, long before the Conquest, the view that certain crimes were the king's special concern because they offended against 'his' peace. This was a sophisticated appropriation by the king to himself of the principle that a crime by one person against another, taking place on the premises of a third party, was an offence not only against the injured victim but against the 'peace' of the third party. The king therefore took the eight days of his coronation festivities and eight days at the time of each of the great Christian feasts of Christmas, Easter and Pentecost, under his special protection and turned crimes committed in these periods into crimes against the king's peace. Similarly, crimes committed on the four main highways of the land were treated as crimes against the king's peace because these highways were the king's, and regarded as legal extensions of his household.

By the time of Henry I, a whole miscellany of crimes had become justiciable in the royal court by being held damaging to the king's peace. They included housebreaking, ambushes, sheltering outlaws, flight in battle, and matters connected with shipwreck, treasure trove and the forest. The practice of extending the area of the royal forests, which often included large areas of farmland, was extremely unpopular in the middle ages and the consequent increase in the jurisdiction of the king's forest courts was much disliked. The severity of these courts was one of the complaints contained in Magna Carta. The extension of the crown's judicial authority was not therefore looked on as an unmixed blessing. The point was reached where an offended party had merely to assert in a private or shire court that the king's peace had been broken by the accused's actions for the case at once to be remitted to the king's judges.

By the end of the twelfth century crimes were coming to be described not only as against the king's peace but also as 'felonies'. 'Felony' took over into royal justice at large its original limited definition of the betrayal of one's lord, for which the punishment was death. Thus, capital punishment replaced the old traditional system of compensation. Violent acts which had once been followed by a blood feud and then by the payment of wergeld or compensation were now capital crimes against the king's peace. This would, it was hoped, be conducive to public order and to the augmentation of the crown's income.

By the time of Henry II, not only were virtually all criminal cases within the jurisdiction of the crown, but civil cases were being taken over also. Whoever had the money to pay for it and the patience to pursue an itinerant court could get a writ from Chancery ordering a debtor, for example, to hand over land or goods in payment of the debt. Failure to obey was contempt of a royal writ, punishable in the royal court. In Magna Carta, the barons tried to end the king's invasion of the private courts in this way, but without much success. The king liked taking over the profitable business of administering justice as much as the barons disliked losing it.

The royal courts of law evolved out of the *curia regis,* the court that the king held by virtue of his lordship over his tenants-in-chief. The *curia* was, indeed, the single cell out of which most institutions of English government were to emerge. By the end of the thirteenth century, its judicial functions had separated off from its varied administrative functions, and divided into three, of which the most important was the Court of King's Bench. Headed by the Lord Chief Justice, it consisted of judges who accompanied the king on his movements about the country. It was a royal court in a very special sense and, on occasions, the king still presided over it in person in the thirteenth century. Manifestly, its effectiveness was limited so long as it depended on the person of the king or on his court, for both were often away from Westminster when the king made progresses round the country and the king himself was, as often as not, absent from England altogether, carrying on the business of being ruler and warrior in Normandy or Anjou, or in Richard's case, being Christendom's chief defender against Saladin. The creation of the eyre courts in one sense made royal justice more accessible, but its object was primarily to make royal power more effective.

The development of the central courts, with visitatory courts going out into the counties, provided England with a common law in the sense that it was common to most parts of the kingdom and to almost everybody of standing, though as yet it hardly touched the villeins. It provided a sound basis on which a sense of national unity could develop. That they should be under the constraints and the protection of the same legal system as their fellows is one of the chief grounds on which men can nourish a sense of community. The legal systems of great nations and empires tend, for this reason, to outlive them; they offer a more durable bond than the political systems they underpin, and often last longer than their language. The English common law was often bad law. Almost from the start it was involved and archaic, and therefore expensive; but, ideally, it was a better commodity than private law because it was in theory easier to enforce and less capricious. In later centuries any claim that a king or mighty subject was trying to destroy it would provoke deep-throated warnings (the loudest coming from common lawyers themselves) that every Englishman's freedom was in peril. What had come into being to augment the income and exalt the authority of kings was used later on, and most of all in the seventeenth century, as a stick to beat them with. Moreover, the English common law eventually constituted one of the most notable of England's contribution to world history. Through the processes of colonisation, settlement and empire, it would become the basis of the legal systems of North America and the Indian sub-continent, as well as of parts of Africa, surviving in the late twentieth century wherever law was not derived from the Napoleonic code, or the Koran, or, though even there some acknowledgment of its ideas was made in the constitutional documents, from the ideology of Marx and Lenin.

Whatever exalted opinions later generations might have about the evolution of the common law, it looked to the powerful barons of the Angevin years like an attempt at royal despotism. To them it seemed that, while retaining his own particular justice over his tenants-in-chief, the king was also aiming at a monopoly of justice over all men, together with the power and profit that justice brought to whoever controlled it. In their increasing dislike of the way that royal power was diminishing their control over their knightly tenants, the lay barons of England were, though they lacked the religious sanction and the fanatical self-righteousness of the archbishop, in much the same position as Becket when he denied Henry the right to try criminous clerks. The barons had other causes for concern. To ensure their support, Norman and Angevin kings regularly summoned the great barons to meetings of the royal council. At such meetings, the barons, ordinarily immersed in their own affairs, were made increasingly aware that royal government was coming under the influence of a professional royal bureaucracy. This tendency dated from the latter part of Henry I's reign. The unsatisfactory outcome of his ecclesiastical conflict with Anselm caused him to give up that reliance on monastic officials which the Normans had inherited from the old monarchy, and to turn instead to the secular graduates of the great French cathedral schools, men who were clerics only in name. Henceforth busy-minded men with a tough intellectual training behind them maintained royal administration. Devoid of all trace of monastic unworldliness, they aimed at an efficiency which, while exalting the king's authority, would exalt their own powers too. Henry I's chief administrator, the first top civil servant in English history, was an obscure French cleric known, since Henry made him bishop of Salisbury, as Roger of Salisbury. Well rewarded by the crown and by the revenues of the wealthy bishopric the king had also bestowed on him, Roger founded a bureaucratic dynasty. His two bastard sons (as a bishop he could hardly have legitimate ones) were given the best education in the new French universities, and both were made bishops. One of them headed the royal Treasury in the 1130s, and his son, Richard, in his turn, became Treasurer to Henry II.

Others of Henry I's officials were set to work to purge the sheriffs, and one, Richard Basset, was in charge of the kingdom during Henry's absences in Normandy, a position to which the title of Chief Justiciar was given, and which acquired even more significance during the absentee reign of Richard I. The son of another of Henry I's officials, Aubrey De Vere, became the first earl of Oxford, and it is a comment on the common nineteenth-century notion, that 'De Vere' was the most aristocratic name imaginable, that the elevation of Vere, like that of Roger of Salisbury and Richard Basset, should have led to the contemporary charge that Henry promoted men 'from the dust'.

It is not surprising, therefore, that the barons were ready to support Stephen's claim to succeed Henry. Stephen, a genial, chivalrous warrior-baron with a soldier's outlook on life, had neither interest in, nor capacity for, the unmartial business of running a royal bureaucracy, least of all one that endangered the interests of the magnates he understood and admired as men like himself. The consequent revival of baronial power over the knightly class was in itself a reason for the general approval of the succession of so obviously throne-worthy a man as Henry II. The years of Stephen's reign had shown that, apart from a handful of powerful baronial families, everybody would gain from a restoration of the administrative and legal authority of the crown.

In the course of an energetic reform of the legal system, Henry II removed from the baronial courts all disputes about land tenure, insisting that no lawsuit involving any substantial piece of landed property could be begun except a writ first be obtained from the king's court of chancery. This still further tightened royal control over the knights and weakened baronial power over them. Henry also attacked the barons by demanding excessive reliefs and exercising his rights of wardship to the limit. More and more royal justices were despatched to the shires; more and more were the barons frustrated by the need to deal with unsympathetic royal clerks, liable to luxuriate in their power to delay, defer, postpone, or close their doors because it was either Easter or Michaelmas.

Richard I's reign demonstrated that even the absence of the king's person from the realm for years on end did not limit the royal greed for more justice and more money. Under Richard's Chief Justiciar, Hubert Walter, the great barons still faced the flow of writs from the efficient chancery of the time, writs which substituted royal justice for baronial, and ordered the payment of ever more exorbitant taxes. It is not surprising that when, in John's reign, the crown became associated with military and political humiliation, baronial patience was at last exhausted.

The Great Charter

John's double humiliation by Philip Augustus and Innocent III meant that he had sacrificed the one quality that had justified all his predecessors, success on the battlefield. The baronial rebellion which followed the disaster of Bouvines forced him to concede Magna Carta. But John repudiated it within months, and its survival as a document of historic importance owes most to his sudden death in 1216, when he was preparing to fight the barons who were in arms against him in the charter's defence. The charter was re-issued by the regents for the infant king, Henry III, in 1217, and duly accepted by them on his behalf. It was again re-issued in shortened form when Henry assumed power for himself in 1225. It was the 1225 version that became, and remains, part of English law.

Of the sixty-three clauses of the 1215 charter, at least twenty-four were about taxation, growing ever more burdensome under Henry II and Richard and, under John, ever more unpredictable. Richard's costly campaigns and the need to raise huge sums to ransom him from his captivity had already led to taxation on a scale without precedent. Carucage, a tax on ploughland, a virtual reimposition of the old Danegeld, was imposed, though on a much larger scale. In 1188, by the so-called Saladin tithe, a tax on personal and real property had been levied. John had imposed carucage as a matter of course and sharply raised the rate of scutage, levying it eleven times in sixteen years. In 1207 he demanded a tax amounting to a thirteenth of the value of all the chattels in the country. Though he consulted the barons on this occasion it was unusual for him to summon them to discuss or even to hear of his intention to impose taxes. In addition he exercised a gleeful ingenuity in finding ways and means to impose fines and extract exorbitant reliefs. He married off widows and heiresses in his wardship to the highest bidder no matter how unsuitable his person or his rank. He confiscated the estates of Norman nobles, and of bishops driven into exile by his feud with the pope. Those seventeenth-century opponents of the Stuarts who declared that Magna Carta gave legal sanction to their resistance to what they regarded as 'arbitrary' taxation have long been regarded as misguided by twentieth-century historians. Yet it certainly offered a precedent; and whereas in the seventeenth century Charles I chastised the gentry with the lightest of whips, John had chastised the taxpaying nobility of the thirteenth with scorpions. By its comprehensive assault on John's fiscal activities, Magna Carta was, among other things, a strong protest against arbitrary taxation. And since it led to a curtailment of the crown's feudal revenues it was followed, before a century was out, by a move towards introducing a national tax; and it was as a device for securing consent to such a tax that Parliament was to acquire its eventual importance.

In addition to the initial clause asserting the 'freedom' of the church, the privileges of the boroughs and of London were guaranteed; merchants and travellers were to be allowed freedom of movement; and areas designated as royal forest were to be curtailed. The most celebrated clause declared that no 'free man' would be arrested, imprisoned, deprived of his land, outlawed, or exiled or 'in any way brought to ruin' except 'by the judgment of his peers and the law of the land'. What exactly 'judgment of his peers', or 'law of the land' meant was for future generations to argue about; and though at the time the expression 'free man' certainly excluded the serfs, the potential significance of the clause, as the charter was successively renewed, was considerable. Like the establishment of a law common to the greater part of the community, the charter, and this clause in particular, helped to make the English ever ready to assert that their liberties were theirs by law and that no government had the right to take them away. The charter declared known grievances and appealed to known rights. It accepted that the crown existed as an institution, that it had feudal rights and had created a common law: Henry II's main legal reforms and his visitatory courts were specifically preserved in the charter. But it asserted other propositions that men had assumed to be facts until the behaviour of the Angevins, and of John in particular, showed increasing signs of ignoring them. One was that possession of the crown carried no entitlement to manipulate its institutions to the detriment of men's property and liberties. The other was that the law, whether feudal law legitimised by custom, or the common law that was being fashioned by the crown itself, were in some sense external to the king; they did not belong to him, nor were they instruments to be used to deprive his subjects of their rights. This view of the crown as an institution distinct from the king's person may well have been held most strongly by those among John's baronial opponents whose titles derived from the fact that their fathers and grandfathers had been officials ennobled by Henry I and Henry II: Count Robert De Vere was one of them. The charter was thus not the work merely of 'feudal' barons; it was also a protest against the king by the servants of the crown. It was the result of hard negotiation between the two groups, and was drafted in the king's own chancery. That both groups, as principal victims of John's rapacious taxation, were defending their own interests is true enough; but the rift between them and the crown inevitably gave them a certain corporate sense, a feeling that they were speaking for 'the community of the realm'. Though the makers of the charter were essentially practical politicians trying to get to grips with nothing but the problems of the moment, it is not altogether surprising that, when later opponents of the crown came to look at the charter, they saw more political theory in it than its compilers dreamed of.

The Charter's Legacy

A major problem remained: how to ensure the crown kept to the charter. Naturally enough, given their experience of John, the barons provided in the charter for a committee of twenty-five barons to act as watchdogs. If the king persisted in breaking the charter they would lead a rebellion against him. They were so engaged when John died; but the relevant article was left out of subsequent re-issues of the charter. Its original inclusion exposed too nakedly the fact that, when it came to it, the only effective sanction against any detested or oppressive medieval king was armed baronial rebellion. Much of the subsequent history of English government is a commentary on the fact that although the law had been declared supreme in 1215, the only sanction against a king who broke it was an appeal to force. The development of institutions which could keep royal government under surveillance and ensure its conformity to the law and the wishes of 'the community of the realm' was not achieved until the sovereignty of 'king-in-parliament' had become a reality in the early eighteenth century.

The events of the reigns of Henry III (1216–72) and Edward I (1272–1307) showed how hard it was to put the basic ideas of the charter into effect. Once in charge of his own court in 1225, Henry III revealed himself as pious enough to be rightly commemorated by the rebuilding of Westminster Abbey, but also as a man excessively committed to exalted views of his kingly office and a policy of somewhat effusive devotion to the papacy and its territorial ambitions. Not unexpectedly, he viewed his barons with suspicion and endeavoured to establish a purely personal government. Since his chancery, which was concerned with royal justice, and the exchequer, which dealt with finance, were liable to baronial interference, he tried to transfer as much business as he could to officials of his royal household, notably the wardrobe, and to claim that, as his personal servants, they were answerable to nobody but himself. His refusal to appoint royal servants in consultation with the barons of his council was a constant source of friction, particularly as Henry distributed official posts to a clique composed of his wife's French relatives.

The barons were finally provoked by the costly failure of his imperial and Sicilian ambitions, both undertaken at the instigation of the papacy and neither a really practical proposition. In 1258 the baronial party imposed on Henry the Provisions of Oxford, which in effect put the crown under the kind of supervision envisaged in the first version of the charter of 1215. A Council of Fifteen, consisting of various lay and ecclesiastical magnates, was henceforth to appoint and control all the great offices of state.

The leading personality on the Council was Simon de Montfort, a Frenchman whom Henry had made earl of Leicester. He had married the king's sister and had spent from 1248 to 1252 trying to end the near-anarchy into which Henry's possession of Gascony had degenerated. Not noted for tenderness towards troublemakers (he had driven the Jews out of Leicester and was the son of a renowned persecutor of heretics in southern France) Simon made enemies in the process, and Henry listened to them, publicly condemning Simon as a result. Even after an enquiry had exonerated Simon, Henry did not restore him to favour. Once again, as in the days of Henry's father, a king charged by his office to defend the law was being peevishly unjust. Simon had put forward the idea of the Council of Fifteen as the only way to ensure that justice should not be at the mercy of a single unjust man.

Yet the spectacle of an overmighty subject was no more acceptable to the barons, or to many of the knightly class beneath them, than that of an overmighty king. Simon may have been a born leader, but he had not been born an alternative monarch. Moreover, he quickly lost the support of those who had come to respect Henry's son, the future king Edward. Edward had three factors in his favour. Unlike his father, he was soldier-like and trustworthy and disapproved of his father's methods of personal government; and unlike Simon he had been born to be king. The Council of Fifteen accordingly soon collapsed. In 1262, Henry resumed power; but the discontent continued. Louis IX of France was asked to arbitrate between Henry and the barons; but as a noted exponent of chivalry and a king whose piety earned him canonisation as a saint, Louis was hardly likely to pronounce judgment against an anointed king. By ruling in 1263, by the so-called Mise of Amiens, that the Provisions of Oxford were an improper invasion of kingly rights, Louis left the barons with no alternative but rebellion. Despite the fact that Edward now supported his father's cause, Simon's forces compelled Henry's surrender after the battle of Lewes in 1264. But yet again, though Simon ruled sensibly enough by regular resort to the great council, the barons as a body wanted, not to be governed by a rebel, however farsighted, but by a king who ruled justly. The notion that rebellion was innately wrong was the most tenacious of men's ideas about kingship. The idea that the king should be above the nobility was a tradition more deeprooted than the belief that he ought to be subject to the law. The stigma of rebellion haunted the Lancastrian kings of the fifteenth century who acquired the throne by means of it; it would deny national assent to the government of the Puritan Commonwealth in the seventeenth century and cause those who replaced James II by William III in 1688 to take endless pains to insist they were not being in the least rebellious.

In 1265, Simon, his support dwindling, was defeated and killed at the battle of Evesham. The Dictum of Kenilworth, 1266, and the Statute of Marlborough, 1267, though reaffirming Magna Carta and the principle of government by consultation, restored the king's power to govern, and to choose and control his ministers.

Consultation and Consent

Although the thirteenth century was dominated by these clashes between king and barons, its most important long-term development was the increased association of the knightly class and, by Edward I's reign, the town burgesses, with the business not only of their localities but of central government.

The process began as a result of the increased taxation necessitated by the ambitions of Richard, the follies of John, the cost of Henry III's extravagant continental policies and the wars of Edward I. It became almost irreversible once Edward III was at war with the French from 1337 onwards. It was also a result of the diminished power of the magnates. With their powers over their knightly tenants so much reduced by the crown (and Edward I further reduced them) it could no longer be assumed, as in the past, that they could automatically answer for their knightly vassals. That the crown's demand for money should involve the towns was also to be expected since, in a period of economic expansion, merchants and traders had the ready cash that landowners often lacked. Moreover, the limit placed by the charter of 1215 on the crown's feudal impositions upon the barons is thought to have ensured them something of a tax holiday during the rest of the century. More money had therefore to be extracted from other groups. It was politic, therefore, to make some show of consulting them.

These reasons for the beginnings of the practice of summoning knights and burgesses to Westminster to meetings of what were coming to be called parliaments are perhaps somewhat too neat. Parliament's origins were far from deliberate, and the role of the knights and burgesses in its early history intermittent. In one sense, to summon two knights from every shire to Westminster from time to time was not much of a revolution. The crown's habit of ordering 'knights of the shire' to provide royal judges with local information as sworn members of 'juries' was well established. They might be appointed to keep custody of a suspect to make sure he appeared in the shire court when required, or deputed to report whether someone failing to attend the court on the grounds of ill health was malingering or not. Their instructions would reach them from the sheriff, acting in response to a writ from the crown. Men called to perform such services, though called 'knights of the shire' as a matter of courtesy, were often in practice esquires, gentlemen or even yeomen, who had never been ceremonially 'knighted'. It was no great step from issuing a royal writ requiring sheriffs to find 'knights' to perform the king's business in the shire to issuing one requiring their assistance at meetings of the king's great council at Westminster.

A 'parliament' did not at first depend upon the attendance of either knights or burgesses. Originally, it was an occasion when the crown met with the great council to confer on a matter of great importance; though it was relevant to the future of parliament as an institution that the matter to be discussed normally involved a demand for taxes. When, in 1207, John had persuaded the magnates to give their sanction to the special imposition of the 'thirteenth' of that year, the basic precedent for seeking the consent of those involved before taxes were levied on them was already in being. In the 1230s and 1240s, Henry III similarly imposed a tax (politely described as 'a gracious aid') with the consent of the magnates. But in 1258, 1264 and 1265, two knights from each shire were summoned to a parliament; and, on the third of these occasions, two burgesses from each of certain boroughs. Each time this occurred, however, the summons came, not from the king, but from Simon de Montfort; and the parliament of 1264 was concerned, not only to raise money, but to give its support to the Provisions of Oxford. It was thus, at the outset, associated with a revolutionary attempt to set up a limited monarchy. In 1264–5 it was hardly less revolutionary: Simon was trying to appeal to knights and burgesses over the heads of the great magnates who were by that time deserting him because they questioned the legitimacy of his rule.

Hence, though it is not altogether unreasonable to regard Simon de Montfort as 'the founder of parliament', its evolution into an institution thereafter depended on the fact that the crown needed money and could no longer get it by squeezing its barons. It was Edward I's urgent need for money to finance his simultaneous designs in Scotland and France that produced the 'Model' parliament of 1295. This included permanent councillors, magnates, bishops, representatives of the lesser clergy, and also knights and burgesses; and since this parliament was summoned by a king, even though a king under great pressure at the time from discontented magnates, it did much to establish that all these parties needed to be represented in any future parliament before the king could claim with justice to be acting (and taxing) with the assent of the whole community of the realm.

Even so, it was still very much *ad hoc*. The composition of a parliament, and the nature of its business, varied from occasion to occasion. If knights and burgesses were summoned, they often had to wait around until the king, his councillors and the magnates got to the point on their agenda when the presence of knights and burgesses was needed. As soon as the matter had been despatched, so were the knights and burgesses, and the parliament carried on without them. And there was only a parliament when the king felt he needed to explain his policies in public or when he could find no other way of raising money. Nor, since the summoning of parliament was usually followed by a demand for taxes, was it a highly popular institution. It was expensive and inconvenient for knights and burgesses to come to Westminster for an unspecified period of time and it was not unknown for the occasional knight to be so little aware he was assisting at the birth of a great institution for the defence of liberty that he would ignore the sheriff's writ that summoned him to it.

On the other hand, knights and burgesses found attendance upon parliament a convenient opportunity to present petitions, to ventilate grievances or to call the attention of the great men of the land to a variety of local and general legal or judicial problems. Some of this miscellany of petitions would be passed on to the king's courts. Some might lead to remedial executive action by the council. Occasionally, though rarely until late in the fourteenth century, they gave rise to an Act of parliament itself. For the most part, however, statutes were initiated by king and council, not by parliament.

By the 1330s, in Edward III's reign, parliament had nevertheless largely assumed the form it was to take until the seventeenth century. Knights and burgesses joined together to form the Commons, which beame a wholly lay assembly; the bishops and abbots came to parliament to sit side by side with secular lords; the lesser clergy met separately in the two convocations of York and Canterbury, often at the same time as parliament. By the middle of the fourteenth century the commons were able, by exploiting Edward III's wartime financial difficulties, to insist that customs be levied, not by royal pressure on the merchants, but only through 'a full parliament'.

The knightly class was also becoming more closely associated, not only with royal taxation, but with royal justice. The habit of sending out itinerant justices or, as they were called, 'judges in eyre', first introduced by Henry I, died out from Edward I's reign onwards, ceasing altogether after 1330. This was due in part to the increased efficiency of the judicial system during Edward's reign and partly because of the extreme unpopularity of the judges in eyre. They had been given such wide inquisitorial powers on the crown's behalf, covering political and administrative as well as judicial matters that, so far from being regarded as architects of a common law for the whole kingdom, they now seemed incompetent and interfering. They appeared in the shires perhaps at six or seven year intervals; in the ordinary way, what good order there was continued to stem from the traditional courts of the shire, the hundred and the manor rather than from either royal justice or the common law. The local courts dealt with commonplace offences a source; and since all concerned had to go on living together afterwards punishments were not usually excessive. Royal judges, indifferent to and ignorant of, local circumstances, might well be excessively eager to inflate their own power, and the king's, by exemplary punishment.

Accordingly, from the fourteenth century onwards, the administrative and judicial functions formerly exercised by judges in eyre were transferred to prominent local figures—members of the nobility, knights, lawyers and substantial yeomen perhaps—who were commissioned to act as justices of the peace. They had jurisdiction over various petty offences, but also became, in effect, the only official agents of royal government in the localities. By that time, too, it was becoming usual for local notables to be used as jurors for the purpose of determining guilt or innocence. In the past, juries had been witnesses as to fact or, as was the pre-Conquest fashion, a body of oath-helpers. The hundred courts had used juries of peasants to give evidence as to local customs, local property rights or the general repute of persons accused of crime. In the shire courts, juries of twelve knights had been required to denounce criminals to the sheriff or the royal justices: in effect to act as juries of indictment. Juries had been used, in short, to answer every sort of question except that of guilt. Guilt, it was felt, was for God to decide, since only God could know a man's heart. This theological principle provided the justification for trial by ordeal and the Norman importation of trial by battle. Since they were designed to invoke the judgment of the Almighty, both were religious ceremonies presided over by clerics. If, after a man had been subjected to scalding or a hot iron, the wound festered, this was one way in which God might establish a man's guilt. Worse still, God could prove a man guilty by making him choke to death upon taking sacramental bread into his mouth: before he actually did so, the priest would pray, 'O Christ grant that he who is guilty of this crime in thought or deed, when this creature of sanctified bread is presented to him for the proving of the truth let his throat be narrowed and in thy name let it be rejected rather than devoured'. The tale was that submission to this awful form of ordeal caused the death of earl Godwin.

The religious sanction of trial by ordeal ceased when, in 1215, Innocent III forbade the clergy to take part in such trials. By the middle of the thirteenth century judges decided to use, in addition to the often large jury of indictment which determined whether there was a case to answer, a small jury of twelve as a jury of verdict. That such a locally recruited 'petty jury' would be more than likely to arrive at exactly the same view as the larger (or grand) jury of indictment did not much worry the judges: they were busy men who preferred quick verdicts.

Jury trial was thus not instantly recognised as better than the ordeal. God's judgment was infallible; the verdict of twelve mortal men was another matter altogether. The ordeal did not instantly disappear after 1215, since royal justices were themselves doubtful about the value of a jury of verdict; and the accused could decline jury trial, thereby reserving judgment to God alone. Eventually, this inconvenient device was overcome by compelling a man to undergo *peine forte et dure* to force him to jury trial. This involved putting heavy weights on him until he either agreed or died. Even when the ordeal disappeared there were still valid reasons for endeavouring to avoid jury trial in this heroic manner. All the property of a man found guilty of felony was forfeit to the king for a year and thereafter reverted permanently to the felon's lord; often, the man's 'lord' was the king himself. But to die under *peine forte et dure* was to avoid a sentence of guilty; it thus enabled a man to die without leaving his wife and children destitute, quite apart from the evasion of the various penalties which attended felony: these ranged from the removal of various parts of the body to death by hanging.

Juries were not greatly welcomed in their infancy, either by judges or the accused, and were much subject to influence and intimidation whenever royal justice was weak and the power of lords overbearing. Nevertheless, the jury of verdict later proved a valuable means by which the community could resist repressive power. It was thanks to this royal invention of the middle ages that the government of the Commonwealth was prevented from condemning John Lilburne, that of James II from punishing the seven bishops who opposed him in 1688, and that of William Pitt the younger from punishing Thomas Hardy of the Corresponding Society in 1794. The continental method of employing torture to extract admissions of guilt, though used by the sixteenth-century prerogative courts of the crown, was opposed by England's common lawyers; but *peine forte et dure* did not become illegal until 1772.

Edward I: A Climax

In English history, Edward I's reign is much celebrated for the king's definitive establishment of royal justice and the common law. Yet, by the time of his death in 1307, the terms on which a king could or should govern the realm were still undefined and remained so for another three centuries or more.

During the first twenty years of his reign, Edward extended royal justice to the furthest limits it would reach at any time in the middle ages. In a series of statutes (so-called, though there is little evidence that the parliaments that approved them included knights and burgesses or were necessarily more than major sessions of the great council) he made a determined assault on surviving baronial rights of jurisdiction. If he did not greatly reduce them, he prevented their extension; and some of the legislation, by benefiting the king in his capacity as a great landlord, also benefited the baronial landlord.

By the statutes of Gloucester, 1278, and *Quo Warranto* of 1290, itinerant justices, armed with a royal writ, inquired by what right private baronial courts were held and asserted the right of the crown to abolish them unless it could be shown that they had been created by a specific royal grant.

The statute *Quia Emptores* of 1290 forbade the creation of new feudal tenures by the process of 'subinfeudation'. The subdivision of tenures, and the innumerable permanent or temporary grants of them to others, had created such a tangle of tenures that the principle that all land was ultimately held of the king, and therefore taxable by him, was becoming hard to enforce. In future, therefore, nobody who 'alienated his tenure' (sold it to somebody else) could become his new tenant's overlord. If B held of A and granted land to C, A would in future remain C's overlord. This prevented the loss by the overlord of the services and, more important, the taxes, due to him. In practice it greatly increased the number of tenants holding direct from the king and avoided the risk that royal rights might disappear in a jungle of sub-tenancies and sub-sub-tenancies. Further, by detaching the tenure of much land from feudal obligations to anybody save the king the transfer of land by grants or leases became easier. The system by which land was held by knight's tenure from the king survived until feudal tenures were abolished by the Puritan Commonwealth in the seventeenth century. By the clause of the second statute of Westminster of 1285 known as *De Donis Conditionalibus*, sub-tenants who were without lawful heirs were no longer allowed to dispose of their land. In future on their death it passed back to their overlord. This benefited the king greatly but was also lucrative for the great magnates.

Edward then took action against the church by the statute of Mortmain of 1279: no more land was to be given to the church unless a licence to do so was obtained from the crown. This was because the church, being an undying institution, could never be called on to pay reliefs; nor did church land, held as it was in perpetuity, provide the crown with the profits of wardship or the sale of marriageable widows and orphan heiresses. Nor was there any prospect that, through lack of an heir, church land would revert (or 'escheat') to the crown. The statute of Mortmain was a counter-attack on the church to which Edward was provoked by an attempt on the part of archbishop Pecham to extend the jurisdiction of the ecclesiastical courts. Edward asserted royal authority more pointedly by the issue in 1288 of the writ *Circumspecte Agatis* ('Mind what you are doing'). It sought to confine the jurisdiction of church courts over laymen to questions relating to marriage, wills and tithes and offences for which penances were prescribed.

Thanks to Edward's overdue reforms it was no longer necessary for litigants to sue personally at Westminster for judgment in civil actions. Writs arranging for a trial at Westminster now included an earlier alternative date on which the case would be tried by royal judges in the county assizes. Summonses to the hearing of such cases at Westminster would now contain the proviso *nisi prius*, meaning it would be heard there 'unless previously' heard in the assize courts. England was divided into circuits, and judges of the high court on assize henceforth dealt with *nisi prius* cases and also with 'gaol delivery', which meant trying all jailed prisoners. They would also hear and determine (or, as the bastard legal French rendered it 'oyer and terminer') all other cases involving the king's peace, such as murders, treasons and felonies. For the next six centuries the periodic arrival of the assize judges in the county towns of the land was a highly-charged demonstration of the majesty of royal justice.

Edward's reign also saw the high courts themselves assume the structure they would largely retain until the late nineteenth century. The court of the Exchequer dealt with fiscal matters. The court of Common Pleas dealt with cases between subject and subject. The court of King's Bench dealt with offences against the king's peace: either where the crown acted as plaintiff or where one subject claimed against another for breach of the king's peace on account of trespass, theft, poaching or rape. Together, the courts of Common Pleas and King's Bench became the main source of future developments in the common law, building up a great body of judge-made law founded on custom and precedent. In theory, because it was judge-made law and every new judgment created a new and binding precedent, the common law was regarded as more flexible than systems based on written codes of law, as was more usual elsewhere. In practice, this adherence to custom and precedent made litigation a hazardous and costly exploration of a jungle of law books and cases long ago. Nevertheless it helped perpetuate the idea of law as something other than the fixed decree of an all-powerful government or single legislator.

In the history of the rule of law, however, Edward I's reign was an end rather than a beginning. After his death, royal authority was never again as consistently effective until the 1530s. The abandonment of the habit of sending round the judges in eyre, and the transfer of their administrative duties to the often unsupervised, sometimes suborned and usually self-interested gentry who acted as justices of the peace was a reversion to earlier traditions of local government by local men of influence which would not be challenged until governments tried to bring JPs to heel at the end of the fifteenth century. Not until the establishment, in the sixteenth century, of the special royal Councils for the North and for Wales, did the crown again apply its inquisitorial powers systematically to areas where its justice was being neglected and its authority ignored.

Edward I's own reign ended by demonstrating how hard it was for the country to live with the institution of kingship. The reigns of Edward and his successors confirmed, as had the rule of his Angevin forbears, that the political nation would not stomach an unjust or incompetent king and least of all kings who either waged war unsuccessfully or preferred not to wage it at all. To one or other of these categories belonged John and Henry III and, among later medieval kings, Edward II, Richard II, Henry VI and Richard III. Yet the increasing cost of warfare, and the widening of the tax-consenting element in the nation to include knights and burgesses in parliament, was accompanied by increasing resistance on the part of those called on to foot the bill. Edward I, Edward III and Henry V were admired monarchs because they were splendid military leaders. A thousand years after the age of the fifth-century warrior-barbarians from whom they descended, Europeans still adhered to the tradition that a good king was above all a bringer of victory and a distributor of booty. Kings like John, who failed in this respect, or who eschewed it, as Henry VI did out of incapacity and James I, who did so out of distaste, were held in contempt. Nevertheless, those who best fulfilled the role of warrior king were often regarded as rather expensive luxuries; Henry V perhaps only escaped this dilemma by dying young. The two military Edwards faced opposition from subjects who, though ready to despise an un-warlike king as something less than a man, were obstinately unwilling to pay the inevitable cost of having a king who played the conqueror.

Fighting kings were also liable to an excess of ambition. Edward I was no exception. He began spectacularly with successful campaigns against the Welsh prince, Llewellyn ap Gryffudd, who had extended his power over the greater part of Wales and had refused to do homage to Edward. The Welsh acknowledged defeat in 1277, but rebelled in 1282. Llewellyn was then killed in battle and his brother, David, executed as a traitor; the statute of Rhuddlan of 1284 ended the existence of an independent Welsh principality. Though there were further rebellions in 1287 and 1295, Edward had achieved a sovereignty over Wales that had eluded all his predecessors. The memorials to his determination are the remarkable castles, such as those at Harlech, Conway and Caernarvon, which represent medieval military architecture at its highest peak of develop-ment.

Unfortunately, by 1296, Edward, having spent 1295 fighting the Welsh, was involved in a war with Scotland while simultaneously planning to fight the French. In that year there was what seemed the triumphant outcome of a complicated wrangle about Edward's rights of overlordship in Scotland when the Scots were defeated at Dunbar and Edward carried off to England the stone of Scone on which Scottish kings had tradition-ally been crowned. But, in 1297, a rising led by William Wallace with the support of Robert Bruce, compelled Edward to embark on a succession of campaigns against the Scots from 1298 to 1307 which, terminated briefly by the king's death, demonstrated what the defeat of his son, Edward II, at Bannockburn in 1314 would prove beyond argument: that to hold all Scotland by force of arms had been a vain hope from the start. Edward had, however, if only in 1296, become the first direct ruler of the whole of Britain and, when this is combined with his legislative achievement, certainly marks him as an outstanding king.

Yet he was trying, in the mid-1290s, to combine domination of all Britain with a reassertion of lost Angevin glories in France. But the Welsh, in 1294, and the Scots, in 1296, halted the departure of well-mounted expeditions to France; attempts to secure alliances with continental enemies of the French king proved abortive; and apart from the marriage

97

of his son to the French king's daughter, Edward gained nothing from his efforts.

The expense of all this military glory and hope created the kind of stiff royal demands for money that provoked, as it had in the past and would repeatedly provoke in the future, a resistance which easily swelled from being the normal resistance of normal men to parting with their money into active political opposition to the crown on the grounds that it was oppressively exceeding its lawful powers. Merchants endured a heavy duty on wool exports. Knights and burgesses granted parliamentary taxes in 1294, 1295 and 1296. The clergy were repeatedly mulcted. But in 1297, with the Welsh scarcely under control, Scotland in turmoil and plans afoot to fight the Fench, both the church and the magnates withdrew their support from Edward. With papal approval, the archbishop withheld ecclesiastical taxes and the nobles refused to permit a further tax on the laity without parliamentary approval. They even refused to go to Gascony to fight the king's war for him. Edward's departure for France left behind so unwilling a nation that the years from 1297 to 1300 saw the crown forced to make yet further concessions which added to the limitations on royal power which had been imposed since 1215. Most fundamental was that, by the Confirmation of the Charters in 1297, the king was not to levy taxes without the consent of the whole community of the realm. Edward was no more inclined than John to accept such limitations. By 1306 he had engineered both the overthrow of the archbishop who had led the opposition to him and his own release from his promises in the confirmation of the Charters.

And there, with Edward I's death in 1307, the issue was left unresolved. It remained in this uncertain state for over 350 years. During the whole of that time the English tried to run their country by a succession of *ad hoc* adjustments between kingly power and the will of the community without institutions through which the relations between the two could be conducted systematically. The institutions bequeathed by the thirteenth century provided the basis of English law and government for centuries.

3

THE GODLY ELITE

The Church Magnificent

As a result of the Norman conquest, the bishoprics and abbeys of England, in addition to passing from English into Norman hands, became feudal baronies. A few bishops and abbots held their lands by the tenure known as frankalmoign, which meant that the only service they rendered the crown was that of prayer. Most, however, became tenants-in-chief in respect of their often considerable lands, and then planted on them sub-tenants capable of providing the crown with knights. This assimilation of bishops and leading abbots into the baronage was to the advantage of the church as an institution. It never went unrepresented in the great council and might, through the archbishop or some other distinguished prelate, from time to time dominate it.

There was a larger significance in the presence in the council of ecclesiastical magnates whose allegiance was not solely to the king. It would be both flattering and erroneous to say of all these prelates that they regularly behaved as if their principal allegiance was to God; but it was true that, until the fourteenth century, they were conscious of speaking as servants of an international papacy which commanded, not only a universal spiritual authority superior to that of kings, but considerable wealth as well, and a political influence that affected every court in Europe. Whatever their personal failings, they were, by virtue of their ecclesiastical office, living witnesses to the principle that there were limits to what it was permissible for secular rulers to do; and from that principle all ideas about liberty in practice stem. By defending the liberties of the church, they contributed no less to the development of the idea of liberty than the barons, knights and burgesses did by the defence of their secular liberties. And whereas barons and knights could, in the last resort, appeal only to force, which by definition instantly became the crime of treason, resistance by a dissenting bishop carried the sanction of a spiritual power which was derived from God and, in the thirteenth century, backed by the richest and most highly organised institution in Christendom.

The collaboration between William I and Lanfranc proved the final manifestation of the old theocratic fusion of. the ecclesiastical and the secular which would survive only in the Byzantine, Orthodox east of Europe. Though the opposition of Anselm to Rufus and Henry I, like that of Becket to Henry II, was mostly an argument about what might be called applied theology, later prelates were often in the forefront of political resistance to royal power. Stephen Langton was the co-ordinating brain behind Magna Carta; archbishop John Pecham led the political opposition to Edward I in the 1290s; archbishop John Stratford led that to Edward III in 1341. On each occasion these men added to an opposition seeking to defend secular interests (which was what a 'liberty' was understood to mean in the middle ages) an opposition designed to protect the interests (or 'liberty') of an ecclesiastical system which, however excessive its privileges, was, at the time, the one legitimate source of the principle that secular government ought not to possess unlimited sovereignty.

It is therefore symbolic of, and appropriate to, the role of the church in England between 1087 and 1400 that its own freedom should have been the first of the freedoms which Magna Carta guaranteed. It could be suggested that one reason for the decline of men's respect for the church from the mid-fourteenth century onwards was that by then, the papacy had been robbed of its prestige by schism, and English bishops had become conformist appointees of the crown and no longer the leaders of national opinion they had been in times of crisis in the past. By the time of Wolsey's ascendancy in the 1520s, when it seemed the church was conspicuously concerned with no interests other than its own, men consented gladly to its despoliation by Henry VIII a few years later. When Thomas More and John Fisher accepted martyrdom in 1534 on the grounds that Henry VIII's laws were 'directly repugnant to the Law of God', they were performing the last act in the history of the medieval order in England. The absolute sovereignty that Tudor government sought to assert in sixteenth-century England was thoroughly un-medieval. It destroyed that medieval 'liberty of the church' which had once sustained secular liberties as well.

Nevertheless, great churchmen most often appeared to the laity all through the middle ages in their role as rich landholders and relentless tax-gatherers. Churchmen were thus likely to be far more easily identi-fiable with the king and his barons than with Christ and his saints. Many bishops were both saintly and learned; but such qualities were, by the nature of the episcopal office, exercised at a great remove from ordinary laymen. From the beginning, the Normans emphasised the new lordliness of the church by making it more visibly splendid. They pulled down Saxon churches and built larger ones to take their place. This may well have been because the discarded Saxon churches pro-vided unwelcome evidence to the Normans of the high standards of religious art and craftsmanship of a people they preferred to consider their inferiors. But the Normans were active most of all as the initiators of the great medieval tradition of cathedral building. Those at Durham, Norwich and Winchester are outstanding evidence of Norman willing-ness to undertake what were, for their time, huge construction works; but new cathedrals were begun, and old ones rebuilt or extended, throughout the middle ages and no less than the early medieval castles were designed to overawe. Castles and cathedrals were then the only large buildings, having to compete with no rival structures for men's attention. But while the medieval cathedrals added a splendid chapter to the history of architecture, what was perhaps more relevant to the age that created them was the enormous cost in relation to total resources both of the long process of building them, and the even longer one of maintaining their fabric and organising their complicated ceremonial and administration. Yet, in an age without printed books, when the knowledge even of the learned was greatly limited, when most men could neither read nor write, and the liturgy was conducted in a language laymen did not know, the existence of an all-powerful God could hardly have been proclaimed in a manner more emphatic or more immediately effective. And as well as glorifying God, the medieval cathedrals glorified their builders. In this they were so successful that, centuries after their own death and on into a time when the faith they proclaimed was itself fallen into decay, their work still survived, to elicit the admiration and often uncomprehending wonder of thousands of their remoter descendants.

Cistercian Revival

The Cluniac movement reinforced the tendency to build large cathedrals as fit settings for splendid processions and elaborate ritual. Most of the great medieval cathedrals were controlled by chapters of Cluniac canons, dedicated above all to liturgical worship. Indeed, so much of the time of regular Cluniacs was devoted to the liturgy that it was said they had little or no time left in which to commit the most venial of sins. In consequence, a monastic movement with a different emphasis developed. It began in a Benedictine abbey at Cîteaux (*Cistercium*) in northern Burgundy late in the eleventh century. From 1109 to 1134 its abbot was Stephen Harding, an Englishman, and in the first half of the twelfth century the Cistercian movement possessed, in St Bernard of Clairvaux, the outstanding religious figure of the age. In the thirty years or so after 1128, when the first small Cistercian house was founded at Farnham, in Surrey, seventy-six Cistercian monasteries were established in England, the most famous at Rievaulx, near York, and at Fountains, near Ripon.

The attraction of the Cistercians was their combination of the old with the new. Their newness was symbolised by their white monastic habits, contrasting with the traditional Benedictine black. Their conservatism lay in their effort to go back to the simplicity of the earliest Benedictine rule. More important was their effort to disentangle the monastic life from the secular world of feudal dues and rights. By the end of the eleventh century, the church throughout western Europe was becoming more efficient and bureaucratic, developing the formidable machinery of the canon law and working out an intricate system of theology. Religion was becoming formal, elaborate, aesthetic and intellectual.

The Cistercians restored old Benedictine asceticisms: such established innovations as the use of warm hoods, bedspreads, combs, and the extra foods which it had been decided were compatible with the rule, were forbidden. Excessive ornamentation was condemned: silver chalices were permitted but not ones of gold; crucifixes were to be of painted wood, not of gold or silver; vestments were to be of linen, not silk, and the more elaborate of them were forbidden. Enjoyment of such feudal additions to their income as revenue from mills, fairs, bakeries and courts was to cease. Cistercian houses were to have no villeins on their lands. Instead, they deliberately sited their houses in remoter places and cultivated the land for their own use by labour of their own. The almost total concentration of the Cluniacs on vocal prayer and liturgical ceremony was abandoned; the time thus saved was devoted partly to labour but also to private reading and private prayer. The pursuit of literary and scholastic fame was also condemned.

A Cistercian foundation was thus different from one housing the traditional black monks. By now, Benedictine houses were normally close to populous towns or to places of pilgrimage. Their cloisters and offices were surrounded by outbuildings for the accommodation of guests, pilgrims and the poor, and for the keeping of stores and provisions, all within an encircling wall. The lands of a black monastery consisted of scattered manors, each functioning economically and socially like manors held by the laity. This is why it must have been so hard for the men of the remoter English villages to see much difference between the men of God and the men of war and power. Both were distant 'lords'; both were made manifest by bailiff or steward devoted to the exaction of the rights of lordship, legalistically assiduous at getting the most they could in the way of rents and services.

Whereas, therefore, black monasteries tended to be centres of public devotion, and their abbey churches places of pilgrimage, Cistercian buildings were designed for monks who were to seek the life of perfection. Situated well away from the towns, the Cistercian abbey was a kind of religious castle or garrison dominating a large area of previously uncultivated or thinly cultivated land. Its monks divided their time between private prayer, manual labour and liturgical worship. At suitable points on the abbey's land were subsidiary farms or granges, normally no further than a day's journey from the abbey. Cistercian land was cared for, not by tenants owing rents and services, but by lay brothers. This was an attempt to bring ordinary people into the religious life. Lay brothers were assumed to be illiterate. They were to learn little more than the Lord's Prayer and the Creed by heart. They worked in silence save where their work made speech essential. They prayed together briefly at the beginning and end of the day, attended

Mass thirty or forty times a year as well as on Sundays, but received Holy Communion only seven times in the year. This may seem like substituting the rigours of a spiritual serfdom for those of the legal serfdom of the outside world. But it proved remarkably attractive to illiterate men in the early part of the twelfth century. Though monastic vows might, for a few humble men, be the prelude to advancement in the world, monasticism was still primarily what it had been in Bede's day, a vocation for members of the aristocracy. But the Cistercians, with evangelistic fervour, offered spiritual renewal and holiness to all. The eager response testified to the failure of their predecessors to spread their net wide enough. The anti-intellectualism of the Cistercians, and the little value they placed on learning, likewise attracted unlettered men.

Yet, by the end of the twelfth century, the Cistercians had acquired a reputation not unlike that of late twentieth-century property developers. Cistercian houses were almost all planted in the valleys of Lincolnshire and Yorkshire, districts hitherto thinly populated if not actually waste. The wool produced by Yorkshire and Lincolnshire sheep was of high quality; and though at first the Cistercians used the wool for making their own cowls and habits, they soon became major exporters of wool to the highly developed clothmaking cities of Flanders. Their enterprise as sheep farmers contributed much to restoring the prosperity of regions scarcely yet recovered from the devastation created by William I; and the northern barons, particularly active and ambitious in the unruly England of Stephen's reign, were as anxious to encourage the Cistercians to their lands as the Cistercians were to go to them. The landowners welcomed them because they created wealth and the Cistercians were glad of the welcome because the remoteness of the land offered remoteness also from the temptations of the world.

But it was as hard then as at any other time to go into the export trade and remain unworldly. Their rule did not forbid the Cistercians to possess, and profit from, animals; and as the numbers of monks and lay brothers increased, so did the gifts of land made to them. The temptation to enlarge Cistercian estates was the greater when it was resolved in 1153 that no new foundations be set up. Sometimes, since they could not accept villages and churches as gifts, Cistercian abbots would dismantle villages, hamlets and even churches on land they were given and substitute granges instead. In the end, they accepted both villages and feudal revenues like ordinary Benedictine houses. By Richard I's time, the Cistercian contribution of one year's wool output towards the ransom needed to release Richard from his imprisonment in Austria was so valuable that he tried to mulct them to the same extent a second time. John extracted large sums from them. Like other big businesses, they financed their operations by borrowing from Jewish moneylenders like the celebrated financier, Aaron of Lincoln. On a basis partly of fact and partly of envy of their commercial success, the Cistercians acquired, less than a century after their emergence, a reputation for sharp practice if not rapacity.

The Franciscans

The loss of its original simplicity by the Cistercian movement illustrated the recurrent difficulty facing the medieval church: each new attempt to revive its spiritual life was the victim of its success. Success brought in the crowds and attracted gifts. Increased numbers lowered personal, and increased wealth lowered corporate, standards. The result was widespread criticism, followed by a search for some purer way of satisfying men's aspirations. During the thirteenth century, popular religious movements abounded in Europe. This was due not only to the recurrent failures of monasticism but perhaps to its very insistence on withdrawal from the world. Consequently there developed a mania for miracles and marvels, and a superstitious devotion to dubious saints.

It was out of this turbulent climate of rigid legality on one side and often bizarre heresy on the other that there emerged one of the last major spiritual forces of the middle ages, St Francis of Assisi. A rich young man who sold all that he had in order to live a life of poverty he gathered around him in the early years of the thirteenth century a group of humble people, at first known as 'the penitents from Assisi', and then as the 'lesser brothers' (friars minor). It was not until 1220 that St Francis could be formally described as at the head of a new Religious Order.

The primary aim of St Francis was not to found an enclosed order, but to create a body of itinerant preachers, without possessions and without legal protection, living as beggars and manual workers. He never took priest's orders. His teaching was concerned above all with the humanity of Christ; he may be said to have been the first great teacher to have preached at all vividly the Christian doctrine of Incarnation: 'Behold your God, a poor and helpless child, the ox and the ass beside him . . . Your God is of your flesh, He lives in your nearest neighbourhood, in every man, for all men are your brothers'. Many centuries later, the Franciscan ideal was much sentimentalised. The Christmas crib, like the Victorian hymn, *Once in Royal David's City*, both descend from the incarnational theology of St Francis.

Innocent III saw the value of canalising this Franciscan piety; and the setting up of the Franciscan Order under his papal protection helped guard the friars against heresy. The final shape of the Rule imposed poverty on the individual friar, but not on the Order as a whole; and it made no mention of haphazard itinerant preaching. This was highly practical: the most itinerant of friars had to have headquarters somewhere, and these could not be maintained out of the proceeds of begging, quite apart from the abuses to which mendicancy could lead, given that the Order attracted all sorts and conditions of men. The limitation upon indiscriminate preaching was also realistic. Parish clergy might not have preached very much; but they did not want competitors who did.

To the accompaniment of much internal dissension as to the true nature of their calling, the Franciscans came to be organised as an international missionary force. Members were admitted to the Order as such, not to individual houses. These were no more than conventual headquarters, whose heads, in keeping with Franciscan ideals, were called 'ministers'. The aim was to preach and to serve the poor. At first the preaching was by the unlettered for the unlettered; but speedily, since in those days to be unlettered was no sign of low intelligence, it became necessary for friars to be given a considerable theological training. This was contrary to the intentions of St Francis. Franciscans continued, however, to live lives of considerable austerity, and the friaries which were their headquarters were never on the grand scale of monastic houses.

Between 1224 and 1240, thirty-four Franciscan houses were established in England and a century later the total had risen to fifty-three. The friars were as much men of the towns as the Cistercians had been men of the remote valleys; and, significantly, among the first towns in which they settled were the university towns of Oxford and Cambridge. Despite the differences between them and the original 'penitents of Assisi', the friars were received in England with the enthusiasm that had greeted the Cistercians. Some had an infectious gaiety; others impressed by their scholarship. The readiness of the majority of friars to move among the poor and sick distinguished them from the other religious and the seculars of their time. Their eloquence took religion out into the market place and the best of them spoke from both heart and head.

The most intellectual of Franciscans were always influenced by the movement's origins among the poor. The strong contingent of Franciscan teachers in the university of Oxford made it for a time the most intellectually exciting in Europe precisely because their views were radical and unorthodox. Two outstanding Franciscans, Duns Scotus and the Englishman, William of Ockham, who both taught at Oxford, were vigorous critics of officially accepted theology. Scotus criticised it with immense intellectual subtlety, but out of a profound conviction that it was rigid and arid and of little value to ordinary, fallen, suffering man. William of Ockham was more downright: he described the papacy as 'lusting after power', and thought it fraudulent of the theologians to suppose they could either explain or understand God. It was the fervent belief of another Oxford Franciscan, Roger Bacon, that the most truly spiritual man was an enquirer into nature, an experimental scientist.

Franciscan theology has been held by some to have been the first stirring of that revolt against the church magnificent that produced the later religious radicalism of the Lollards. Certainly, from the beginning, Franciscans could be as opposed to kings as to popes. Robert Grosseteste,

Oxford University's first chancellor and a saintly bishop of Lincoln, was at once a strong supporter both of the Franciscans and of Simon de Montfort; and a famous English Franciscan, Adam Marsh, was a close friend of both Grosseteste and de Montfort. A powerful poem about de Montfort's last battle, called The Song of Lewes, was the work of a Franciscan; and its main purport is to defend the view that the realm belongs to the community and not to the king and that where a king damages his realm, those who oppose him are being more truly loyal than the king. It was another Franciscan, a distinguished Oxford mathematician, John Pecham, who, when archbishop of Canterbury, led the political opposition to Edward I.

Dominicans and other Orders

Simultaneously with the Franciscans came the Dominicans. Founded by St Dominic, they were known as the Order of Preachers. The Order was quick to put its emphasis on learning, in the belief that piety of itself was not enough. Dominic believed it was the piety rather than the wickedness of simple people that led them into heresy, and the Dominicans became the 'domini canes', the hounds of the Lord, dedicated to the extirpation of heresy in all its forms. They were deeply involved in the work of the Inquisition, set up by papal authority to root out the heretical religious movements which had become widespread in all parts of thirteenth-century Europe. Strongest in southern France, the members of these often socially radical and bizarre movements were viciously put down. Yet though England was the first country in Europe in which the secular authorities enacted a law against heresy, there were few heretics in thirteenth century England and the Dominicans were less important in England than elsewhere. It was fortunate for the English that they were so orthodox at this particular time. Though the Dominicans had established houses in thirty-six towns in England by 1260 and had a total of forty-eight houses by the end of the thirteenth century, they did not bring the Inquisition with them. The result was that when, by 1400, the Lollard heresy began to spread, the authorities in England not only had no clear idea how to stamp it out, but, having seen its operations abroad, refused to allow the Inquisition to enter the country. Its harsh procedures included imprisonment on suspicion, the use of written evidence which the accused could not question, and the torturing both of witnesses and the accused. Had such methods been used in fourteenth century England the common law might not have survived to challenge their use in the sixteenth century.

The coming of the friars made preaching to the laity once more a regular and important function of the church. The friars also spread the practice of private confession, which was not greatly encouraged otherwise, owing to the somewhat miscellaneous character of the parish priests. The popularity of friars as preachers and confessors irritated the priests; it led to offerings and legacies going to the friars that the priests might otherwise have received themselves. Their superior intellectual training earned friars high positions in the more delicate operations of government. Dominicans were much used for difficult diplomatic missions, and many kings had Dominican confessors; their queens seemed to have preferred to confess themselves to Franciscans.

Other new religious orders appeared in the twelfth and thirteenth centuries. The Austin canons were small communities of priests; and it was from priories of such canons that St Bartholomew's and St Thomas's hospitals in London originated. The Austin priory of Our Lady of Walsingham was one of the few places of pilgrimage in England which attracted foreign pilgrims. Of the many English kings who went to Walsingham as pilgrims, the last was Henry VIII, in the hope, it is said, that this act of piety would lead to his Queen, Catherine of Aragon, becoming pregnant. The white canons, or Premonstratensians, were modelled on the Cistercians and built some twenty to thirty abbeys in remote areas. The Carthusians were an austere Benedictine order, living in private cells, coming together for liturgical purposes only and not, like other monks, sharing a communal refectory, dormitory and cloister. The only monastic order peculiar to the English were the Gilbertine nuns, whose devoutness was much respected.

Among the mendicant orders of the twelfth century were the Augustinian friars, with thirty-four houses, and the Carmelites who had thirty-seven by 1400. There were three houses for Franciscan women in England: they were known as 'the poor Clares' and practised the utmost poverty.

The Seculars

It is, however, the medieval parish that reveals how the church, like most large organisations in any age, was often inefficient at its point of contact with the ordinary individual. The great cathedrals and the recurrent revivals produced by monks and friars were related to day-to-day realities much as the alluring advertisements for international air travel are to the unreliability, the tediums and bizarre fare tariffs which afflict those who actually make use of it. Then, as ever, the gap between the episcopate and the parish clergy was wide, and the training of the latter inadequate.

Increasingly after the thirteenth century, bishops were men who had achieved high office either as servants of the crown or of the Papal court at Rome, or members of the aristocracy for whom a bishopric was a reward for political services to the crown. By the 1300s, monks, friars and men esteemed for their scholarship tended to be nominated only to the less important sees. Experience of diocesan administration, or of pastoral work, was rarely a prelude to episcopal status.

While the management grades in the complex business of the cure of souls consisted of men remote from ordinary life, the parish priests, the workers on the shop floors of Christendom, were a mixed lot indeed. Their one common factor was usually their lack of training for their task. Worse still, they were not necessarily required to carry out the duties of their office at all.

This arose largely out of the system of patronage, which had become more widespread since pre-Conquest times. The Crown, the chancellor, the lay magnates, the bishops and abbots, and in time the colleges of both universities, along with a whole miscellany of lay people of lesser estate, had all acquired the right to nominate parish priests. The appointment, like all other positions in the church, had two aspects. Under one aspect it was an office involving its holder in the performance of certain duties. Under the other, it was a benefice, namely, a form of property bringing in an income from emoluments, tithes, rents and fees. Accordingly, for kings, bishops and popes to grant a loyal servant a number of benefices became a normal method of bringing his pay up to a respectable level without the inconvenience of having to increase those emoluments directly out of the royal, episcopal or papal purse. The whole system of patronage, surviving as it did in one form or another in secular, as in ecclesiastical affairs, well into the nineteenth century arose for understandable and by no means discreditable reasons. For one thing, governments were always short of money because direct taxation was looked on with suspicion as 'extraordinary' and, even when collected, was usually inadequate. Graduated salary scales, regular increments, pensions, life insurance and the sophisticated machinery by which savings could be safely invested for a man's old age or for the provision of his children's education, did not exist. Consequently, men of ability were normally unable to live on the emoluments of office and lived instead off a plurality of ecclesiastical benefices. Secular government was in fact financially sustained all through the middle ages by the income and endowments of the church. It was as if, in modern times, there was so little money available to the government to pay the salary of the Chancellor of the Exchequer, that, to ensure him an adequate income, he would have also to be appointed Bishop of Chester, Master of one college at Oxford and another at Cambridge, Dean of Canterbury, Archdeacon of Liverpool, Principal of a large theological college, Vicar of Tewkesbury and headmaster of Lancing College. The only duties he would perform would be those of Chancellor of the Exchequer; the work of all the other posts would be performed by usually underpaid substitutes. In short, secular and ecclesiastical administration would have broken down without this system, for otherwise few officials in either sphere would have had enough to live on. Accordingly, virtually all public servants took religious orders so as to be entitled to benefices: 'clerk' and 'cleric' were synonymous.

The system was less the sign of an overweening church than of its invasion by laymen thinly disguised as clerics. Pragmatically defensible, it was patently open to abuse. The tendency to abuse was aggravated by the general lack, through so many centuries before the twentieth, of the idea of professional qualification. In practice, anybody could acquire a benefice provided he could find a sufficiently negligent or unscrupulous patron to present him to one. When one learns that, towards the end of his career, one English cleric was simultaneously Archdeacon of Shetland, Provost of Beverley, Rector of Wearmouth, a Prebendary of Lincoln Cathedral, Precentor of Lisbon Cathedral, and Prior of the Priory of St Agnes at Ferrara in Italy, not even the fact that he was a worthy and distinguished churchman appears particularly relevant.

Where the benefice was a parish, the practice was for the cleric upon whom it was bestowed to draw its emoluments and pay a substitute in priest's orders to do the work. The benefice might have an annual income of £50; a priest might be hired to perform the duties of the office for £5. The balance of £45 would either represent an addition to the annual income of the patron whose gift the benefice was, or be put to other (and not necessarily unworthy) uses if the patron were the king, a bishop or, as was increasingly true from the twelfth century onwards, one of the religious orders.

The system depended not only upon non-residence but also upon plurality, since only by holding more than one benefice could one normally derive an income worth having. Many pluralists were modest persons with only two benefices, and probably most held no more than three. The pope made rules to limit non-residence and plurality, but the exceptions were generous. There was no real limit to the number of benefices which could be enjoyed by important clerics in high secular or ecclesiastical office. One could be legally non-resident while studying at a university, so that the system was used by many bishops as a substitute for the modern university maintenance grant. Excessive plurality was the hallmark of a person of great estate; and, even so, the majority of the offices held by the great pluralists were cathedral rather than parochial appointments.

The system in no sense meant that all parish clergy were either unworthy or incompetent. Some beneficed clergy resided in their parishes, either from choice or necessity; and the unbeneficed clergy who acted as deputies for non-residents, and constituted the great majority of parish priests actually at work, were so poorly paid that it is probable that their most likely weakness would be ignorance. Some attended university; but those who did well there were probably drawn off into more lucrative administrative work. Even a highly educated secular priest was not supposed to know more of the Bible than was contained in the service books of the church, the breviary and the missal. Others acquired what learning they had from cathedral schools, from schools run by the friars, or from grammar schools. It was only as late as 1215 that the Papacy had made it mandatory upon Christians to make an annual confession to their parish priest and to make an annual communion at Easter; and it was perhaps as a result of this that, by the end of the thirteenth century, bishops were sending their parish clergy advice on how to carry out their pastoral duties. Various manuals of advice for parish priests also appeared.

Priests were told they must cross-examine people in the confessional about their religious knowledge as well as about their sins. They should advise pregnant women to suckle their young, as being in accordance with scripture and medical opinion. They should warn parishioners of the excommunications placed upon persons breaking various charters, including Magna Carta, a point which suggests one reason why the Charter found so unshakeable a place in the national folk memory. They were given advice on what to say about matrimony: it was on the whole a bad thing, and it was probably safer to marry an ugly wife than a pretty one. Care should be exercised in dealing with sailors, because their sins were greater than those of all other men, and wherever they went they contracted *de facto* matrimony with different women. Lords were to be told it was a sin to exact more from their tenants than was laid down by custom or contract; tenants withholding the services or rights due to their lords should know they were guilty of theft and perjury; prosperous villeins must be told not to conspire to cheat their poorer neighbours. Parishioners should be told that vain or profane conversation, fairs, markets, dissolute dances, games and stone-throwing were not to take place in churchyards.

Schools and Universities

Since a knowledge of Latin was essential to the conduct of any kind of business, illiteracy was far from universal, even in the early middle ages. Indeed, the illiteracy of men of importance derived partly from a lack of inclination, and partly from the availability of a considerable number of literate persons on whom they could rely for the conduct of correspondence, the engrossing of legal documents and the keeping of accounts. By the thirteenth century members of the nobility were almost without exception literate and by the fifteenth century most important towns had grammar schools, often endowed by the laity. Schools were also attached to cathedrals, to monasteries and some larger parish churches. Many unbeneficed clerics earned money as private tutors. Bishops exercised (to their profit) the right to license all schools and teachers in their dioceses. As a result, by the thirteenth century there would be at least one person in almost every village who could produce a document in a Latin which, if not classically elegant, was reasonably accurate. Bailiffs, too, would keep their accounts in Latin.

Universities in the sense of corporate or collegiate institutions devoted to the study of various academic disciplines through face-to-face contacts by teachers and students in a number of 'faculties', were a medieval European development. Before the twelfth century, higher learning had been largely a matter of 'wandering scholars' travelling from one revered or fashionable teacher to another all over Europe. Eventually, it was among a congregation of famous teachers at Paris that the concept of the university began to take shape. As a town where many important roads met, Oxford was also an obvious potential centre of learning, particularly as it was dominated by neither cathedral nor monastery. It had become a recognised centre for higher learning by 1170, possibly because in 1168 Henry II forbade English scholars and students to go to Paris. By 1200 the number of students was about 1500. It did not rise above 3000 in the medieval centuries. Cambridge became a university after a flight of students from Oxford when John had two scholars executed for the alleged murder of a woman. Its archives having been burnt during the Peasants Revolt of 1381, the early history of Cambridge is less well known than that of Oxford.

Oxford's reputation was high in the thirteenth and fourteenth centuries. Its scientific and mathematical tradition influenced continental universities; masters from Oxford were among the first teachers at the university in Vienna when it began in 1365. Firsthand observation and exact methods of calculation made Oxford celebrated for meteorological study. A first attempt was made to apply mathematical principles to physics. But this intellectual ferment did not survive into the fifteenth century. Roger Bacon's work was condemned by the church and William of Ockham was excommunicated in 1328. The most radical personality to emerge from medieval Oxford was perhaps the learned, disputatious heretic, John Wyclif, whose real or alleged responsibility for Lollardy led to Cambridge, rather than Oxford, receiving royal favours for the next two centuries.

The average medieval freshman was only fourteen or fifteen years old. It would be assumed that he knew some Latin, but neither his mental nor physical fitness was formally tested. He would already be a tonsured cleric; but the barber might well have been the sole officiant at his tonsuring. All beginners took the course for the Master of Arts degree, which was a general one including grammar, rhetoric, logic, arithmetic, geometry and astronomy, with an emphasis on natural, moral and metaphysical philosophy. Work was based on the detailed study of prescribed Latin texts, mostly translations from Aristotle, and as far as possible learned by heart. A distinguishing feature of the course was the disputation, in which a master or a senior pupil defended an argument against others in public. To achieve a Master's Degree, for which the examination was oral, took at least six years, with the intermediate status of Bachelor being attainable after three or four years. Thereafter, the good student proceeded to spend another eight years or so studying for a higher degree in theology, medicine or law. There was no compulsion to hurry. The time taken from entering the university to taking a higher degree could be anything up to twenty years. It is not surprising therefore that there was what would now be called a high wastage rate; only one in three became Bachelors and only one in six Masters. But those who lasted the course were a highly valued élite; they had learned to think and work with heroic industry and intense application, acquiring a sound memory and the ability to master a complicated argument and to speak readily in public. It produced sharply enquiring, if excessively niggling, minds. The occupational disease of medieval universities was less an acceptance of authority than a continuous hair-splitting criticism of it. Nor were universities primarily centres of religious education; this was the preserve mainly of those who took the higher degree in theology.

The life of most students in medieval Oxford resembled that advocated as desirable by some of their radical twentieth-century counterparts. At first, they attached themselves to any lecturer who attracted them (some touted for pupils) and who could hire a room to lecture in. The students lived in private houses or in halls of their own choice under a principal elected by themselves from among their own number. Not until the fifteenth century was it general for such principals to hold Masters' degrees. To these early freedoms was added a complete lack of inter-ference in personal behaviour until some time in the fifteenth century. In addition, there was a wide social range of students; few were financially supported by their parents. It was held to be a work of charity to support a poor student; many students, it has been said, who were ashamed to dig were not ashamed to beg; some were known to replenish their resources by highway robbery on the many roads that led to Oxford. Many students were non-resident holders of benefices, since it was possible for young boys to be canons of cathedrals and rectors of parish churches.

Not unexpectedly, university life was a matter of violence and drink as much as of study, particularly as undergraduates were mere boys and the academic life otherwise devoid of amusement. Nor was the violence confined to the young. One college warden was convicted of the offence of allowing his students forcibly to remove beer to the value of 12d (5p) from other students. One teacher was imprisoned for inciting his pupils to drag from the pulpit a priest who was announcing his excom-munication. Should a student kill someone, the offence was usually treated as manslaughter and punished by a short term of imprisonment. The most stupendous embroilment between students and the Oxford citizens occurred in 1355 after some students, disapproving of a taverner's wine, threw it over his head. The townsmen replied by attacking the students with bows and arrows, but were repulsed by a body of archers collected together by the Chancellor. The response was a general attack, in which halls were pillaged, books torn up, some students killed, and the rest forced to flee the town. The king severely punished the townspeople. Virtually all control of the town passed into the hands of the university, and it was not until 1825 that the university agreed to forgo the annual penance and fine which had been imposed on the town for an incident that by that date was 470 years in the past.

Although the colleges came into existence in the middle ages, they were then relatively minor institutions, originally intended as hostels to enable poor post-graduates to proceed to higher degrees. The first eight students of Merton, regarded as the earliest Oxford college, were all nephews of the founder and even when the number had risen to twenty, all were members of his family. There were six colleges by 1360, but their total membership is not thought to have been above seventy-five. The growth of the colleges did however result in discipline being tightened by the sixteenth century and the average student probably did more work by then. Corporal punishment became widespread and was administered to students under eighteen or, in some colleges, under twenty. Life continued spartan; it was considered self-indulgent to eat breakfast, and as late as 1580 football was permitted only within college precincts at Cambridge, offenders under adult age being flogged if they broke this rule.

4

TOWNSHIP AND BOROUGH

'Town and Field'

THE two or three centuries after 1066 were distinguished by what appeared a sharper legal division between a small ruling class and the great majority of the population than at any other time, before or since. It is sometimes suggested that medieval society was divided into those who fought, those who prayed, and those who worked. But both those who fought (barons and knights) and those who prayed (at any rate the important secular and religious clerics) were also in sole charge of central and local government and administration. They alone had a voice in public affairs or authority over others and they alone had, as yet, rights under the expanding common law. Aside from their fighting and their more frequent indulgence in hunting, the only ones among them who 'worked' were those monks for whom manual labour was part of of their spiritual vocation and the few who, by acquiring literacy at cathedral school or university, became so useful to the ruling class as bureaucrats that, like the De Veres and Bassets, they became members of the ruling classes themselves. 'Work' was otherwise the special mark of persons of servile status who laboured in the fields. Even those who traded in chartered towns were regarded by the crown as sufficiently servile to be liable, from Henry II's reign until parliamentary taxation became normal, to an arbitrary tax called tallage.

The peasants, farm labourers and artisans who made up the bulk of England's population, which stood at an estimated one and a half to three million during the two centuries after the Conquest, were regarded as a 'resource' from which the few thousand men who ruled the country drew their work force, their money and, when required, the rank and file of their armies. Few of this majority were slaves after 1066; but few of them counted as 'free men'. Most were legally bound to their lord and to the soil. The legally enforceable obligations which were the mark of their servile status, and ensured that dues and services could be extracted from them, made them part of what is often called 'the manorial system'.

As the Normans conceived it, the manor was the basic unit of feudal lordship, guaranteeing that knights were freed from the need to cultivate their land themselves so that they could fulfil their military and financial duties to their lord and the king. Theoretically, therefore, a manor ought to have been a village, with a manorial lord holding a manorial court in a manorial hall; and though much of the arable was

114

cultivated by the peasants for their own benefit, some of it was the lord's personal demesne land; as well as cultivating their own land, the peasants were legally compelled to cultivate the lord's demesne for him.

Fortunately for the men and women of the time, though less so for the historian, the realities of rural life, even in the areas where the manorial system existed (and it was chiefly confined to the open field areas pioneered before 1066), the 'manor' was always something of a legal abstraction, the result, perhaps, of a bureaucratic over-simplification contrived by the clerks and commissioners who produced the Domesday Book, in an effort to make their assessments look neater than the untidy realities of an already very complex society. Manor and village were only sometimes the same. Some manors consisted of several villages. Some manors were not villages at all, but a collection of isolated farms. There would sometimes be several manors within one village. Many villages had no manorial hall, and some, particularly those belonging to the crown, consisted entirely of demesne land leased out to tenants; and in yet others there was no demesne at all. Though large villages which were also manors were commonest in the Midlands, there, as in virtually every county, lords got more from their tenants in rents than in labour services; and by the thirteenth century money rents had in some manors replaced labour services altogether. This reflected the fact that from the start the manorial economy was not simply a form of subsistence farming; at least some of the produce of the lord's demesne had always been sold for cash in a market, and in the booming thirteenth century the peasants were doing the same for themselves.

From the strictly legal point of view a manor was an organisation whose affairs were managed by a manorial or 'customary' court to which all the tenants of the manor were answerable. Most tenants were villeins, owing the lord various services. Usually, in fact, the word 'manor' meant 'estate'. The estate might be one large village or several small ones or consist of parts of a number of villages. In the open-field areas of England it is better to think less in terms of the manor than of the village, though even this word (a Norman-French import) fixes attention too narrowly on the villagers' homes. Medieval Englishmen themselves spoke of 'town and field'. The town (from the Anglo-Saxon *tun*) was the village itself, clustered round the church; and town and fields together made up the 'township'.

The church was well established as the focal point of both town and field. It could be used when occasion arose as storehouse, courtroom, prison or fortress. Its churchyard was the only communal open space and might serve as local market place or pleasure garden. Not until after the Reformation were church and churchyard reserved for the exclusive use of the holy when busy with the business of being holy.

The villagers' houses, not greatly different from those of the Anglo-Saxons, were clustered together with a narrow space between them for a shed and a small patch of garden. Behind the houses were small closes or crofts which the villagers cultivated for themselves or on which they grew an additional crop for feeding their animals.

Beyond the 'town' the only likely change since Anglo-Saxon times was that there had developed either a three-crop rotation in two fields or in some larger villages a three-field system. The arable was still divided into strips and the cycle of the year's cooperative labour was to continue with little change for several centuries. In September, in a village with three fields, all three of the fields would be fallow, two showing the stubble of the recent harvest. The animals of the village would range over all the fields. During October the beasts were driven off the previous season's fallow, which would then be sown with wheat and rye and hedged to keep the animals out. Each villager had a precisely defined duty to assist with the erection and maintenance of this temporary hedging. In February the animals were driven off one of the other two fields. This was then ploughed and sown with spring corn, and hedged until the following autumn's harvest. The third field would remain fallow pasture, being ploughed twice in the summer before, when autumn came again, it was sown with the new season's winter corn.

'Customers'

The cooperative system by which villagers managed their own arable and pasture was extended to their labours on the lord's demesne. Relations between villagers and lord involved the normal feudal ceremonies of an oath of fealty, and the tenure of land on the theoretical basis that the lord gave protection and the man gave rents and services in exchange. In the relations between villein and lord of the manor, the jurisdiction of the lord was final. It was in the manorial court, from which there was no appeal to the courts of the crown, that a whole township might be fined for failing to 'wash the lord's sheep', or a woman be fined for dragging a man from his house by his hair, or a villein be compelled to pay his lord a substantial fine before obtaining permission to leave the village for good. In law, everything a villein had was his lord's; he could increase villeins' rents, and their services as he pleased and impose tallage on them at his will. He could even drive them off his land. Since the villein thus enjoyed no rights under the common law and was in fact little more than a chattel, the imputation of serfdom was a serious matter. In 1300 one manorial court fined a villager who publicly called his neighbours 'villeins'.

In spite of their servile status in law, many villeins were substantial peasant farmers with holdings which might amount to between ten and forty acres. Inferior to villeins were cottars, so-called because originally they had only their cottages; usually, the better sort among them would not hold more than five acres. Cottars gave fewer services than villeins, and because of their smaller holdings, different ones. A cottar who had no horse or ox of his own might have to serve as the lord's ploughman in return for the right to use the lord's plough team on his own land on Saturdays, a day when week-work was not normally done on the demesne. Lacking beasts to contribute to the plough team, a cottar's service might be limited to perhaps one day a week and consist chiefly of digging and threshing.

Legally superior to villeins, but not regarded as members of the ruling class were the freemen. Their fortunes varied greatly during the middle ages. Many free sokemen of the old Danelaw were pressed down to villein status after the Norman Conquest. Legal freedom bore no necessary relation to economic status; there was nothing to stop a villein hiring a free man to work for him. Indeed, by the end of the thirteenth century many freemen had turned to wage labour and become thatchers or carters, fullers or dyers. In the thirteenth century they discharged their duty to the lord by paying a rent. If they rendered services, they were of a managerial kind and they perhaps supervised villeins and cottars at harvest time. Those who prospered most came to be regarded as just below those who held by knight's service, rather than just above the villeins. In 1247 the crown ordered all freeholders of this sort who owned land worth 40s a year to be knighted in order to facilitate the work of the shire courts. By the end of the middle ages such men had acquired the usual designation of 'yeomen'. The traditional association of the term with the idea of 'sturdy independence' thus has at least some basis in history.

It was also possible for villein or cottar to acquire freedom, though usually only if he could afford to pay the lord a fairly stiff fine. A cottar might find it easier to buy release than a villein since his value, whether in rents or services, was less than a villein's. A runaway could obtain freedom if he could contrive to remove himself for a year and a day to the demesne lands of the crown or into the confines of a chartered town. A villein became free if he married a free woman and a villein's son became free if he took monk's vows, though here again the lord would demand a fine by way of compensation.

The real position of villeins nevertheless rarely corresponded with the law's contempt for them. Their relations with their lord were governed in practice not by the abstractions of Norman-French law but by village custom. This was why villeins were sometimes referred to as 'customers'. The lord's manorial court was a 'hallmoot' because in theory at any rate it was held in the lord's hall; but it was above all a customary court because its decisions were taken in accordance with the customs of the village, as avowed by juries of witnesses empanelled from among the villeins themselves. It would be wrong to imagine villeins as confronted in their daily labour by ruthless Norman lords bent on grinding the faces of a conquered peasantry. All but the poorest landowners employed at least one bailiff or steward, so that few lords had direct business dealings with the peasantry. The affairs of manor or village were conducted by people who knew that in an agricultural community where almost all work was done cooperatively, it would be dangerous to depart from custom. In an age when there was not much of a free labour market and little mobility of labour, and when the total working population was small, it would be counter-productive to overthrow custom and drive men too hard. For their part, the villeins knew that if they kicked too much they were unlikely to win. Whatever the law said to the contrary, they had security of tenure in practice; and even in times of social conflict they, like their betters, believed for centuries to come that the only thing to do in life was to adhere strictly to custom. So far from change being equated with something inherently good called 'progress', it was regarded with hostility. They were justified in thinking this, in the sense that any change proposed by the lords would probably be designed to squeeze more out of the villagers than was customary.

So committed to custom were village and manor at this time that the daily work of field and demesne was supervised by one of the villeins themselves, elected by them every autumn and known in most parts of the country as the reeve. To be, or have been, a reeve was one of the distinguishing marks of villein status. It reveals how thoroughly the cultivation of field and demesne was a cooperative activity based on custom that the man who had to see that it got done should himself be a 'worker' who knew, from being one of them, what the duties of his fellow-workers were. The reeve was usually a villein whom the others respected since they were held collectively responsible for his shortcomings. When chosen, he was freed of all services, was often also paid, and was entitled to such perquisites as perhaps being allowed to let his horse graze on the lord's pasture. In most manors he worked as the immediate subordinate of the lord's bailiff or steward: the two together had to maintain a balance between lord's rights and villeins' duties, and always within the framework of the traditions and customs of the manor. That it was an onerous task is proved by the fact that many villeins paid the lord a large sum to be excused service as reeve.

The reeve, chosen by the villeins, and the lord's ploughman, possibly chosen from among the cottars, were but two of the specialised servants of the lord and the village. The domestics employed about the lord's hall and demesne, such as dairymaids, house servants, carters and farm labourers, were frequently provided as part of the services due from particular holdings, especially the smaller ones. Of cardinal importance was the miller. The villagers were bound to have their corn ground at the lord's mill, but the lord usually farmed the mill out to a miller for a rent, the miller making his living by retaining for himself part of whatever was brought to be milled. It was normal to assert that the miller was a cheat. Lower in the social scale was the village blacksmith, usually one of the lesser villeins. As a return for the work he did for the lord during the year, the lord's plough teams might plough his land for him. The villein who guarded the lord's sheep would be relieved of week-work and had to see that the sheep were systematically hurdled in different parts of the land every day so that all the soil could benefit from their droppings. He was required to hurdle the sheep on his own land during the twelve holydays of Christmas; since they would then be doing his own land good, he would be more likely to keep an eye on them at this festive period. The hayward was almost as important as the reeve. He had to ensure that villagers' beasts did not stray from the common pasture into meadow or cornland. If necessary, he could impound such errant beasts. More important still was his duty to guard the crops at harvest time when there would be a number of 'foreigners' in the village acting as extra labourers.

Those villeins who rendered services as well as rents, worked on the lord's demesne for two or three days every week throughout the year and for more than that at ploughing times and at harvest. They were also to act as the lord's general carriers, and to use their own horses for the purpose. Villeins on certain manors of the church in Buckinghamshire, for example, not only carried goods to and from Oxford; they went as far as Gloucester in the west and Rochester in the south-east, to procure fish for their ecclesiastical masters. Thus, not every English villager was immured in his village for life. In particular villages, particular rents in kind were required. The lord might have to be given a hen at Christmas as a rent for the privilege of gathering wood from his woodland. Extra ploughing might be required in return for the privilege of making use of the lord's pasture.

The additional work done for the lord at ploughing time and harvest was referred to as boon work; unlike week-work, which went on all the year, it was specially rewarded. This preserved the socially soothing myth that this work, done for the lord at his time of greatest need, was performed by the villagers out of the goodness of their loyal hearts. At the same time it took some of the edge off the fact that the time of the lord's greatest need was also the time of the villagers' greatest need: they were called to the lord's ploughing and the lord's harvest just when they wanted most to be about their own. They might be given meat or fish to eat and ale to drink. All who contributed their oxen to the plough teams might be invited to supper at the lord's house. Similar meals were provided at harvest time, with the difference that the supply of ale might be more lavish at harvest. The fact that villein service and lordly largesse at these times were treated as a labour of love on one side and a free-will offering on the other did not prevent both service and reward being treated as customs and therefore as binding. Lords might fine villeins who absented themselves and villeins protest through their reeve if the quality of the bread or the ale was below standard.

Other recorded customs show that efforts were made to give a more personal touch to the relations between free lord and unfree tenant. Even where it was not a customary rent charged for the use of woodlands, it was also customary to give the lord a hen at Christmas as well as the almost universal egg at Easter. These acts were all at once valuable rents and ceremonial gifts. For his part, too, the lord usually gave a grand Christmas feast. This was not always as generous as it seemed. The villagers often sat down to eat food they had themselves contributed as a Christmas gift. They were sometimes told that it was because they had given most of the food that they were given the meal. On the other hand, even if all the lord did was to act as caterer for the occasion, this was something he alone had the facilities to provide. More obviously emollient devices for reducing social tension existed. After the mowers had mown one particular lord's pasture, it was his custom to put a sheep in the meadow. This, the mowers could keep; provided they could catch it. Elsewhere, at the end of mowing, every mower was allowed to take away for himself as much grass as he could lift with his scythe; but if he tried to lift so much that the scythe's haft broke under the strain, he could take nothing.

There were welfare benefits too. A villein could be released from week-work for up to thirty days if he was sick; and if he died, his wife was let off thirty days' service thereafter. In such cases, however, boon work was insisted on; and a substitute might have to be found and paid for by the villein or his widow.

Husbandry and Marriage

In most parts of the country, villein holdings, like the lands held by more exalted tenures, passed undivided to the eldest son, on the grounds that he was more likely to be old enough to assume full responsibility for the services due to the lord. Since this practice could leave young brothers unprovided for, there were areas where, on the grounds that his elder brothers were more able to fend for themselves, the holding passed to the youngest son. But whichever rule prevailed, it meant that villagers, like other social groups, added to social mobility by compelling landless sons to make their own way in the world. Not all of them necessarily left for the towns and even when they did they were, in theory at least, entitled, like the Prodigal Son, to take their 'portion'. Where the holding was large enough, it might be possible for the landless sons to find enough to do by staying. In return, they usually got their keep, but were not allowed to marry. A villein did not normally become a husband in the matrimonial sense of the word before he had also become, in the original sense of the word, a husbandman, that is to say, a peasant farmer with his own holding, and thus in a position to maintain a wife and family.

The consequence was that men married comparatively late in life, probably not until they were in their late twenties, in contrast to the nobility and gentry who married at a very early age. It was in one sense fortunate that expectation of life was low and that by the time a man was in sight of his thirtieth birthday his late-marrying father would already by that time have died, probably before he was fifty. The delayed marriages of the middle ages indicate the extent to which marriage was dictated by economic rather than personal or sexual considerations. There was no idea of romantic love; this, by the thirteenth century, had only just begun to make its appearance in the more sophisticated courtly circles of France. Outside what was then a limited and highly cultured minority even among the aristocracy, there was little in medieval society to encourage either the erotic or the idealistic in sexual relations. The almost universally low standards of personal hygiene, the prevalence of bad teeth, scurvy skin and body vermin can hardly have done much to stimulate either desire or imagination. The body was a shameful thing and women as such were most dangerous when least ugly. As far as the church was concerned, celibacy was the ideal and marriage a grudging concession to a fallen race living under the curse of Adam's first sin.

Moreover, excessive emotional commitment either to a spouse or to young children was scarcely appropriate given the high mortality rate of adults, the perils of childbirth and the even higher rate of infant mortality. Marriages were terminated by the early death of one of the partners at about the rate at which, in the late twentieth century, they were terminated by divorce; and around a quarter of all marriages were second marriages as a result.

It is perhaps not surprising, therefore, that medieval attitudes to the rituals of matrimony were for some time fairly casual. The effective ceremony was a secular one: the plighting of troths by the couple in the presence of witnesses, accompanied by the junketings now attendant upon the wedding ceremony. For the couple to proceed to a ceremony in church was considered less important and indeed as an unnecessary and expensive luxury involving the payment of fees. It was only in the thirteenth century that the church began to assert the idea of an indissoluble monogamous marriage, and to devise punishments for fornication and adultery, or try to deprive bastards of rights of inheritance. Even so, the marriage ceremony was not elevated to the status of a sacrament by the church until 1439; and both common law and manorial custom long regarded the secular plighting of troths in public as the key ceremony. This lay behind the long surviving custom of couples not proceeding to a church wedding until the bride was pregnant and the inextricable confusion of the marriage laws in England until the middle of the eighteenth century.

The position of women was reasonably protected by the law. At all levels, women could hold land; a lord of the manor could quite well be a lady, though such ladies, like heiresses, were much pursued. The records speak of a woman being required to shoe her lord's horses; but the duty was attached to her and rather than to her person. In the towns, women were often business partners with their husbands and when widowed they usually continued to manage their own affairs.

Fathers set aside a dower or marriage portion for their daughters much as they set aside a portion of their movables for their younger sons. At marriage, husbands endowed brides with land to be enjoyed during widowhood, and peasants' wills often indicated the expectation that a widow would live with her son and daughter-in-law.

A Developing Country

More and more during the two centuries after the Conquest, the manorial economy became concerned with production for the open market, regularly selling its surplus wool, corn, meat, hides and cheese for cash. Not only did the lord sell the produce of his estate; the villagers also took their surpluses to the markets. The poorer peasant, offering some of his produce for sale in the markets of the nearest small town or large village is a persistent figure who existed long before the coming of 'free enterprise capitalism', just as he obstinately survives where it has been officially abolished. The reliance of royal government on substantial money taxes since well before 1066 and the countless references, not only to money rents, but to money fines in the manorial courts, make it clear that lord, villein and cottar alike, from the earliest times, either sold their surplus produce for cash, or, if they were poor enough, sold their produce even when it was not a surplus, in order to pay their money debts. In thirteenth-century England as elsewhere, for instance, richer villeins acted both as employers of, and moneylenders to, the poorest villagers, especially the landless ones, whose numbers greatly increased in the century before 1300. Increasingly it is necessary to envisage the thirteenth-century village as a community in which an increasing number of cottars and other landless or almost landless men had to work for wages because they could not otherwise maintain themselves. Apart from harvesting, there must have been much occasional employment as carters, as assistants to carpenters and millers, and as weavers and spinsters. Village women frequently added to their income by selling ale.

Basic to the growth of a money economy was the doubling of the population between 1066 and 1300. There was a great expansion of the area under cultivation. Villages had brought more land under the plough and some larger villages had split into two or three. New villages had been created as fen and forest were cleared. Regions laid waste had been resettled. The pressure of population on the land was so great, however, that its exploitation for a cash return became an imperative; and fortunately there was an urgent demand in the developing cloth-making cities of Flanders for English wool. Accordingly, great lords and, combining piety with entrepreneurial zeal, the Cistercians and other great religious communities, took the lead in transforming England as a whole into Europe's most valuable primary producer. For a time it assumed towards the economically advanced Flemish cloth industry the relationship of the American South to the Lancashire cotton industry of the nineteenth century. The inflow of wealth, though channelled first of all towards the great nobles and the monasteries and mulcted by way of customs duties by the crown, was nevertheless a stimulus to economic development throughout the country. Sheep farming gave a new and highly profitable significance to thinly populated and less fertile areas outside the open-field heartland of England, particularly in Derbyshire, parts of Yorkshire and the Welsh Marches. But everywhere the demand for English wool encouraged not only landlords to develop great flocks, in almost every village the peasants, either singly or communally, had flocks which as well as serving their fertilising role in the cultivation of the arable, were a source of cash.

The quality of English wool was such that, as well as being in demand in Flanders, it attracted the attention of Europe's great international financiers, the Florentine bankers. They became the greatest buyers and exporters of English wool, partly because they were highly skilled practitioners in the business of organising international exchange, and partly because the great Florentine wool gild, which had a jealously maintained concern for the excellence of its cloth, insisted that its members should use only the finest English wool. The other reason for the interest of the Frescobaldi, the Bardi, the Acciaiciuoli and other Florentine financiers in English wool was that their initial appearance in England had been as papal tax collectors after the establishment of papal control following the surrender of John. Able, owing to their financial resources, to provide capital and credit to finance foreign trade not only in wool but in other exportable commodities, they lent money to kings and capitalistically minded barons, a function previously performed on a smaller scale by Flemings and, particularly in the twelfth century, by Jews. The latter, who had begun to enter the country in the wake of the Norman Conquest as 'Court Jews', had become increasingly unpopular after the onset of the Crusading movement; but one of the factors which led Edward I to expel them from the country in 1290 was the greater availability of Italian finance. The Jews were not allowed back until after the triumph of Oliver Cromwell.

There were growing numbers of English merchants in the thirteenth century. Many acted as middlemen for the great Italian buyers, since they were likely to be less unpopular than foreigners; and they also controlled the initial stages of England's own nascent cloth industry. They contributed also to the expansion of the older-established traffic in basic materials such as lead, tin, salt, iron and coal. The mining of iron in Gloucestershire, Yorkshire and Sussex was on the increase; the tin mines of Cornwall were profitable enough to be regarded by the Italian tycoons as a security against loans to the crown. Lead was now more extensively mined in Derbyshire, Somerset and the Yorkshire moors; and Newcastle thrived not only on trade with Norway but on the produce of England's largest medieval coalfield. The growing wealth of the barons led to a building boom that also absorbed much labour. The castles of the greater barons, often wooden structures in the eleventh century, were of stone by the twelfth, and by the thirteenth were both more elaborately fortified externally and more commodious within. Lesser barons and knights increasingly built themselves relatively substantial semi-fortified houses. The continuous building and extension of cathedrals and abbeys employed large numbers of men, both skilled and unskilled.

By increasing the demand for wage labourers of all sorts, these commercial and industrial developments helped to ease the problem caused by the fact that, although more land was being cultivated, it could not provide the whole of the increased population with a sufficient livelihood. Consequently, as more and more landlords either substituted rents for services on their demesne or leased their land out to farmers for a rent, wage labour became an increasing factor in village life and more and more was a purely agricultural wage supplemented by some form of rural industrial employment.

Economically, the England of the early middle ages was, in relation to Europe, a primary producer, outstandingly in wool, but also as a corn exporter; a medieval (but very aristocratically organised) version of nineteenth-century Australia, a country which a particularly tough and vigorous group from the European motherland had settled after 1066 and 'developed'. Accordingly, though its prosperity grew, its wealth was unequally distributed, and to a considerable extent, though decreasingly so, controlled by foreign finance. And, in keeping with its economically quasi-colonial position, its towns were mostly still no more than overgrown villages and their inhabitants still mostly at the very least part-time farmers.

Nor was the growth of trade synonymous with the growth of towns much before the nineteenth century. The ubiquity of such surnames as Skinner, Tanner, Sadler, Fuller, Weaver and Dyer are a reminder that up to half of the smallholders and landless men of the countryside worked part time in the cloth and leather industries neither of which, though leather work was certainly done in some towns such as Norwich and Stafford, was concentrated in urban areas. For the most part, merchants were a minority in the average town; it would derive much of its importance from its role as an administrative or ecclesiastical centre, or as the site of the shire court. Urban merchants were wholesalers. Most retailing took place at informal village markets; and wholesale exchange itself was long conducted at periodic fairs as at Boston in Lincolnshire, the St Bartholomew Fair in London and the later medieval cloth fairs at Northampton and York, as well as the fairs at Winchester, St Ives and Stourbridge, some of which were international in character.

A retarding factor in the development of towns was that the shackles of feudal obligation were scarcely compatible with the imperatives of trade. They prevented men moving about or disposing of their property to raise capital and made occupations more or less hereditary. There was no free bargaining, only conformity to custom. Hence, merchants congregated in towns in order to organise their liberation from feudal restraints on personal initiative. Merchants bought, from king or lord, charters of privilege and immunity. Townsmen would, as a result, hold their property by burgage tenure and collectively pay a fixed annual sum to their feudal superior. They levied and collected the cash themselves and in some cases chose a mayor, elected a municipal council and appointed a municipal treasurer. They became free of the tolls imposed by crown or baron on the movement of goods, acquired a monopoly over the town's trade and sought to exclude from it all 'foreigners', which meant either those living outside the town walls or burgesses of towns which did not have commercial agreements with them.

The economic instrument of urban monopoly was the gild. The habit of forming these originally social or sometimes religious fraternities among groups of neighbours or of members of the same trade or craft was widespread and in many towns the council responsible for urban administration consisted of gild members. Gilds regulated and controlled markets, protecting each individual's share of the trade. Where there were sufficient specialists, these would form craft gilds, such as those of the weavers of London and Oxford and the metal craftsmen of Coventry. The commerce of London was always on a sufficient scale for it to have craft and trade gilds at an early stage in its development. Of London's trade and craft gilds, the mercers, fishmongers, vintners and goldsmiths were the most important, constituting the important 'livery' companies.

Gilds had rules limiting hours of work, fixing prices, controlling quality and restricting recruitment and employment. They confined entry into their 'freedom' by heavy entry fees, limiting it to sons of gild members or, more generally, by imposing a seven-year apprenticeship culminating in a 'master test'. Even then it was hard to set up as a master on one's own account and many had to continue working as employees or journeymen.

'Flower of Cities All'

Town life was never as vigorous in England as on the continent. By the end of the middle ages, only about a quarter of all Englishmen lived in towns, mostly in some 250 places with about 900 inhabitants each. Bristol, Norwich and York each had between 25,000 and 30,000 inhabitants. By comparison with London, which was the largest city in Europe, all other English towns were local centres of minor importance, whereas Germany and Italy had cities powerful enough to be independent city-states and France had at least six cities larger than any English city except London. A much less literally 'civilised' people than their neighbours, the English would, as a result, later take their culture from the Italians, their manners from the French, their theology from the Germans, their commercial ideas and much of their technology from the Dutch.

Though the only place in his native land where the English could experience urban life as understood by their descendants or their European contemporaries, London was, as late as the seventeenth century, still largely confined within the area of the City of London itself. Congested and haphazard, its centre was barely a mile and a half away from green fields. Bounded on the east by the Tower, serving the crown as prison, mint and treasury, and still ranking as a royal palace, its westward limit was Temple Bar. Its northern limits were the gates called Aldersgate, Cripplegate, Moorgate, Bishopsgate and Aldgate, still closed at night with heavy doors or portcullises. Islington, like distant Hampstead and Highgate, was a country village where Londoners could go to shoot wild duck or to hear the cuckoo. Paddington was arable and meadow. Hackney's womenfolk came to London to sell turnips. It could be said, without causing laughter, that fairies danced at Bethnal Green. Charing Cross was an isolated village situated midway between London and the separate city of Westminster. There was hunting in Hyde Park and at Marylebone; and hawking where Liverpool Street station was eventually built. South of London Bridge lay St George's Fields and open country.

By the end of the middle ages, foreshadowing modern suburbia, wealthy Londoners were already building country houses in the surrounding fields, with their own orchards, gardens, walks, arbours and alleys. They built many such houses in Middlesex; but that county's chief distinction was its possession of some of the country's best farming land. Its wheat, particularly in the area between Heston and Pinner, was considered to be good enough to supply those who baked bread for the royal table. Cattle reared on its pastures were driven into Smithfield in the City and its village women took dairy produce and fruit to London twice or thrice a week. Essex sent London milk, butter and its largest cheeses; and there were red deer in its wide forests. The plentiful coppices of Surrey supplied much of London's fuel, and good corn was brought in from the fields between Farnham and Guildford. Croydon had an abundance of walnut trees and Dorking of boxwood. Kent sent fruit to the City from its profusion of apple and cherry orchards around Faversham and Sittingbourne.

Thus even London was as integrated economically with the countryside around it as were the smaller cities and market towns of the rest of England. Nor, for all its insanitary overcrowding, was it divorced from the rural even inside its close boundaries. The merchants' houses had attractive gardens, with pears, apples and gooseberries, along with daffodils, primroses, lilies and 'old' roses.

No other European city had a comparable river frontage or so great a quantity of shipping. The most characteristic sign of London's wealth and municipal magnificence were the buildings and furnishings of the medieval City Companies. By the end of the middle ages these were rich enough to be far grander charitable institutions than the monasteries. Not only were they a benefit society for their members; they founded schools and almshouses, maintained scholars at universities and left many endowments, surviving into the twentieth century, to be spent on the education of deserving young men. The Mercers, Skinners and, at the close of the middle ages, the Merchant Taylors, founded what were in due course to become public schools. The Merchant Taylors were also to be associated with the foundation of St John's College at Oxford. City companies did not hesitate to indulge in conspicuous expenditure to enhance their prestige. Splendid halls, rich with treasures presented to them by wealthy members, lavish feasts and well laid out gardens were all designed to impress, as was their habit of bestowing honorary 'freedoms' on leading public personages. Elizabeth I knighted Francis Drake; the City made him an Honorary Draper.

The City's principal thoroughfare was Cheapside. Broad and well-paved, its attractions consisted not only in the quality of the gold and silver vessels for sale in the shops but also in the excellent quality of the oysters to be bought there. Since, however, the Strand was a muddy lane running along the stables at the back of the noblemen's houses that fronted on to the river, it was the Thames that was the City's true main street. It was lined with bishops' palaces which, after the Reformation, would be replaced by the great houses of the new Tudor nobility. One such palace, at Lambeth, retained (and retains) its medieval status as the London residence of the Archbishop of Canterbury.

London Bridge, the only bridge across the Thames in what is now the whole London area until the 1730s, was considered a handsome structure; one patriotic Englishman rated it above the Rialto in Venice and the Ponte Vecchio in Florence. It had twenty arches, so that there was a fierce rush of water through them at high tide. The roadway was so narrow that it was hard for two carts to pass side by side; but it was completely roofed over, and flanked by shops and well built houses, inhabited by prosperous merchants.

The City of London's importance derived almost entirely from its trade and commerce. All through the middle ages it used its wealth to resist royal encroachment upon its privileges and to preserve the independent system of government which it retained in attenuated form in the twentieth century. Within the City walls its mayor occupied a place above all but the royal family and dukes of the blood royal; its MPs were paid about ten times as much in expenses as other members of the commons. Its privileges and immunities enabled it to grow rich without it ever becoming the intellectual, cultural or administrative centre of England. In ecclesiastical affairs, though the old cathedral of St Paul was, before the fire of 1666, the finest of the City's churches, it stood below Canterbury and York; and for both crown and nation, the religious heart of the land was the Abbey Church of St Peter at Westminster.

PART THREE

IRRATIONALITY AND DISORDER

Approximate Dates: 1300–1509

1
THE BATTLES OF FRANCE

Authority Diminished

THE years from 1066 to 1307 had seen the interaction of two coherent, rational principles. One was that of kingship, seeking to establish itself as sole guarantor of social order, justice and law. The other, of which the barons had been principal agents, was that the law and order provided by the crown should conform to the wishes and conduce to the welfare of the community of the whole realm. Though king and barons alike had resorted to force at times, they had usually done so in the service of coherent political motives. As a result institutions of law, government and consultation had been established of which many still survive in name, and a minority also in practical use, at the end of the twentieth century. The medieval rituals that survive in twentieth-century England are not simply a manifestation of 'quaintness' or an inability to acknowledge the realities of a changing world. They are justifiable tribute to the efficiency of the Norman and Angevin kings and barons who had devised, in crown, council, parliament and courts of justice, the institutions and precedents through which a not particularly manageable people could preserve their social and political cohesion for centuries to come.

But if rationality and order were, in the twelfth and thirteenth centuries, characteristic of the organisation of both secular and religious life, the fourteenth and fifteenth centuries were centuries of comparative confusion. The underlying causes, common to most of fourteenth-century Europe, were over-population followed by famine and plague accompanied by, and to some extent provoking, both damaging warfare and popular unrest. In the prospering twelfth and thirteenth centuries it was easier for rulers and subjects to conduct their relations fairly rationally; but the economically dislocated years of the fourteenth century posed problems which either explain, or were aggravated by, recurrent failures of leadership in all parts of Europe. The French monarchy, triumphant in the thirteenth century, slumped in the fourteenth into a weakness from which it did not fully recover until late in the fifteenth. Italy and Germany, neither at any time coherently organised, presented a picture of lawlessness in the former and virtual disintegration in the latter. In the east, Christian Byzantium shrank year by year under the advance of the Turk.

No less important was that the church lost much of its authority. The papacy appeared to have become the creature of the kings of France who, in effect, held successive popes captive in Avignon from 1305 to 1377; no worse than the general run of medieval popes and most of them rather better than many Renaissance popes, they were all Frenchmen, almost all extravagant and exceptionally insistent upon the collection of papal taxes. Worse still, by 1379 the 'Great Schism' had occurred. From then until 1417 there were two popes, one in Avignon and one in Rome, and, at the end of the period, three popes. Though unity was restored in 1417, the prestige of papacy and church did not recover until the emergence of Protestantism gave rise to the Catholic counter-reformation organised by the Council of Trent from 1547 to 1563. There was thus no possibility of the church maintaining its mediatory role in English high politics. Archbishops and bishops were now nominees of the crown, distinguishable from the rest of the aristocracy principally by the more permanent and indeed inalienable character of their great wealth.

Though England fared rather better than its continental neighbours, the crown too suffered something of a decline. This was partly the result of the biological hazards which might make an hereditary monarch, however able the sire who fathered him, wholly unfit to rule. But the abler kings of the period, by devoting themselves so conspicuously to warfare, inevitably exalted aristocratic pride and belligerence and put an undue strain on government finances. In an age dedicated rather to making war than to skilful government, crown, council, parliament and judiciary were liable to be less competent than previously, and more frequently manipulated by an aristocracy no longer held firmly in check by strong, efficient monarchs.

Thus, though in the fourteenth and fifteenth centuries parliament, and the commons in particular, seemed to become firmly entrenched, by the end of that time it showed signs of losing the key position it appeared at times to occupy in the reigns of Edward III (1327–77) and Henry IV (1399–1413). The commons acquired its own separate meeting place and its own Speaker, and the procedure for dealing with the introduction and discussion of bills was systematised. It became accepted practice that all major matters, particularly taxation, should be dealt with by parliamentary statute. Direct parliamentary taxes, known as subsidies, were important in the fourteenth century when the decline of the wool trade reduced the crown's income from the customs. But lay subsidies declined in importance in the fifteenth century. There arose repeated demands from the commons that the king should 'live of his own' and that he should cease the practice of giving away crown lands to recently ennobled favourites and take back lands he had alienated. The eventual fulfilment of this policy by Edward IV (1461–83) and Henry VII (1485–1509) by the end of the fifteenth century, together with the revived royal income from the customs, meant a decline in the financial importance of the commons. Its fiscal hold on the crown between 1307 and 1430 did not, therefore, outlast the wars with France; and by 1500 it had lost rather than gained as an institution. In the fourteenth century, the commons had usually been the independent voice of the gentry and burgesses. It was less consistently so in the fifteenth. Though only some MPs were aristocratic nominees and the divisions among the aristocracy were sufficiently confused to prevent any systematic management of the commons by the nobility, it was more than once packed by a momentarily triumphant king or overawed by armed men. Essentially an obstructive institution once it acquired the power to influence taxation, it was little used by the revived monarchy under Edward IV and Henry VII after 1471. They found other ways of raising money, called parliaments only occasionally and used them chiefly to add the assent of lords and commons to whatever the king happened to think it advisable, for propaganda purposes, to do with some public measure of formal consent.

The council underwent a process of regression by becoming increasingly secret. No longer a matter of royal consultation with the wise men of the realm, it became a small group of men privy to the king's secrets, operating, as Henry III had wished, through the household. No longer a kind of parliament-without-the-commons, it became answerable to nobody and no longer an independent institution apart from the persons who operated it. Despite intermittent complaints from the commons, the council became an aristocratic politburo whose members jostled for primacy in secret, seeking to use the king as a front man and parliament as a rubber stamp.

The steady growth of the formal powers of justices of the peace also represented something of a decline in royal power over the localities, since the justices were less able than judges in eyre to resist the power of the county sheriff. The transfer of the administrative and judicial functions of government to local nobles and gentry acting as JPs meant that from the fourteenth century until late in the nineteenth, the only official agents of central power regularly seen in the localities were the assize judges, once or twice a year trying complex cases or dealing with felonies by men of substance. The JPs tried all other cases, as well as conducting investigations into crown properties, and assessing and collecting local taxes. Their legal duties enabled them to pursue their feuds against rival landlords by trumping up accusations that acts they had committed were 'contrary to the king's peace'. Some of them, as knights of the shire, served as MPs and this gave them further scope for the protection of their rights as landlords. By 1390 they had secured the passage of the first game laws, forbidding anyone with an income from land of less than forty shillings a year to kill deer or rabbits, or keep hunting dogs. In 1432 they had voting rights restricted to persons owning freeholds worth forty shillings a year. In the past, local government had been undertaken not only by the king's command but also under the king's command. In the century after 1360 that control almost broke down. The recapture of the allegiance of the nobility and gentry who ruled the counties was one of the major tasks which the crown had to undertake in the last decades of the fifteenth century.

The decline in authority went beyond the decline of royal control of the JPs. The common law fell into disrepute. The need to obtain royal writs from the courts at Westminster was in itself productive of delay; but the weakness or corruption that prevailed in high places meant that a litigant who went to law without also enjoying the support of a royal councillor or courtier had little to hope for. This did not prevent litigation; it encouraged it. Any charge however dubious, any claim however illfounded, might stand a chance if some great man could use his influence in the right quarters. This quarrelsome age was intensely litigious.

One major development of the fourteenth and fifteenth centuries was the steady growth of the law of equity. The Lord Chancellor's court of Chancery came more and more into use to hand out decisions in response to petitions from victims of the defects and limitations, let alone the perversion, of the common law. This equitable or correctional jurisdiction was in any case necessary because of the need, which common law did not admit, to reconcile the law with common sense and with fairness. Equity led to common law being broken or overriden in particular cases, and often provided the speedy justice that common law had ceased to provide; for one thing any good lawyer could find perfectly good reasons for preventing a case coming to trial for some eighteen months. Unfortunately, the system of equity could become, and was often represented as, an arbitrary interference by the crown in the known law of the land. It would be centuries before remedial action by statute would become the rule, and though the Chancery court was a recognised and valuable part of the constitution by the end of the fifteenth century, it was fiercely attacked by the common lawyers and parliamentarians of the sixteenth.

Edward II: Violence at Home

The bloodthirsty strife of Edward II's reign from 1307 to 1327 was inflamed rather than caused by the humiliating postscript to his father's over-ambitious campaign against the Scots. This culminated in the Scottish victory at Bannockburn in 1314, which was followed by the expensive and damaging reluctance of the English to make peace and acknowledge Scottish independence until 1328. Association with military defeat was bad enough for any king's reputation, but Edward II also showed every sign of being homosexual. This led him to commit what in the view of virile fighting men was the objectionable offence of elevating ingratiating and unscrupulous personal favourites. In his early years, Edward was dominated by a Gascon knight, Piers Gaveston, whom he made earl of Cornwall. In his last years, a young courtier called Hugh Despenser appeared, by 1320, to be in complete control of government.

Both favourites, by ruthless rapacity, made enemies everywhere; both provoked armed rebellion; both were forced into exile by baronial pressure on the king; both were restored to favour, regardless of the king's undertakings to the contrary. But though the opposition to the king sometimes assumed constitutional forms, the struggle was essentially violent and personal and, indeed, vicious. The Ordinances of 1311, drawn up in an unsuccessful attempt to get rid of Gaveston, were a re-hash of the Provisions of Oxford of 1258, but were the work of barons simultaneously conducting private wars among themselves. Gaveston's execution in 1312 was not a vindication of constitutional legality but an act of personal revenge by the earl of Warwick. Edward's reign was less of a postscript to that of Henry III and Edward I than a foretaste, both in its military failure and in its violence, of the disturbed reign of Henry VI. It was, in fact, somewhat bloodier.

After Gaveston's fall, Edward was for some years overawed by Thomas of Lancaster, powerful lord over most of the midlands and much of the north. Lancaster was, however, primarily a territorial magnate too busy using his private army to wage war against other territorial magnates to have the time to establish systematic control of the king's government, and was rarely present at court. In consequence, Edward's last favourite, Despenser, was able, despite a sentence of banishment in 1321, to raise an army strong enough in 1322 to defeat Lancaster at Boroughbridge in Yorkshire, and then to execute not only Lancaster but many other lords as well.

What eventually brought down not only Despenser but Edward II himself, was a revolt led jointly by Edward's adulterous queen and her lover, Roger Mortimer, who had escaped from the Tower where he had been imprisoned for supporting Lancaster at Boroughbridge. Acting in the name of the king's son, the future Edward III, they had Despenser executed; then, with the authority of a full parliament, they organised Edward II's deposition.

The change made no appreciable difference. During the next three years, Mortimer acquired the title of Earl of March and a great deal of other people's lands and, as a Regent for the young Edward III, aroused the armed opposition of Lancaster's son as well as another conspiracy in which the Earl of Kent was alleged to be involved. The confusion was ended by a coup by the young king. Mortimer was seized and, again with parliament's assent, one more overmighty subject lost his head. Since Mortimer had been chief cause of his father's deposition and subsequent brutal murder at Berkeley castle, Edward could, in the context of this gory tale, be regarded as acting reasonably. More to the point, England now had a real king again.

Edward III: Violence Abroad

Edward II had damaged kingship by orchestrating aristocratic feuding at home. Edward III did it no less damage in the long run by organising aristocratic pillaging and plunder at the expense of the French. His more distinguished predecessors had combined military leadership of the nobility with the capacity to develop institutional means for keeping them subordinate to the political will of crown and government. But Edward III can hardly be said to have ruled the aristocracy; in effect, he became, to an extent that had been true of none of his Norman and Angevin forerunners with the significant exception of Stephen, a member of it. A great devotee of tournaments, he invented for his fighting companions the chivalric Order of the Garter. To show his genial concern for the nobility as a class, he restored the earldom of March to the grandson of his father's murderer and cuckold, Mortimer, and posthumously rehabilitated the Earl of Arundel, who had been executed for supporting Despenser. He also enrolled his sons as members of the aristocracy. All five of them, endowed lavishly out of royal or escheated estates, became dukes: of Cornwall, Clarence, Lancaster, York and Gloucester. The difference between the royal family and the barons was thus greatly blurred. Crown, councillors, judges, administrators had hitherto presented a fairly solid front against baronial ambition; baronial power, in alliance with knights and burgesses, had kept royal power within reasonable bounds. Now, the crown has become a property for control of which, before the fourteenth century is out, royal aristocrats, eagerly supported by non-royal aristocrats, will begin violently to quarrel. Government will cease to be the subject of rational debate; instead it will be the object for which men will contend in the course of a confused, family feud. In such circumstances kings can no longer protect lesser men from aristocratic domination and violence, for they are themselves the victims of it.

More than any other king, Edward III made violence the chief occupation of the aristocracy by actively encouraging the dubious values by which the successful organisation of war was presented as the fulfilment of the highest ideals of aristocratic chivalry.

It is no surprise that Edward's relations with his nobility were so cordial. He made them his brothers-in-arms in a high-hearted, profitable and, on occasion, enjoyable military escapade at the expense mainly of the nobility and people of France; though it bore heavily enough on the people of England too. A variety of rational causes may be alleged for Edward's inauguration of what is called the Hundred Years War; almost certainly the effective cause was the desire of a young, hearty, war-loving king to acquire glory.

He began in 1336 with a grandiose scheme: he would buy himself allies in the Rhineland, force the Flemings on to his side by rigging wool exports to create a shortage of their essential raw material and then invade France from the north. By 1340 his sole achievement was to have destroyed the French fleet at Sluys when it tried to stop him as he returned from Flanders to remonstrate with parliament for refusing to go on voting him subsidies. During the next five years he tried unavailingly to secure a permanent foothold on French soil in Brittany.

Not until 1346 did he at last find the glory he was looking for. In August, at Crécy, across the Somme, the English infantry overwhelmed the French cavalry. At Neville's Cross, in October, English forces defeated a diversionary exercise by the Scots designed to help their French allies. King David II of Scotland was taken prisoner. In 1347, the English made sure of Brittany and Calais. After an enforced pause due to the ravages of the Black Death, an army under Edward's son, the Black Prince, moved out from Bordeaux, in English territory in Gascony, to raid and pillage the French countryside as far south east as Narbonne on the Mediterranean and northwards towards Orleans. In 1356, at Poitiers in Poitou, the Black Prince was met by a much larger army led by the French king, John the Good. The English were again victorious and John became the second king to find himself taken captive.

The effects on France were dire. Political disunity followed the absence of the king. Pestilence and famine were compounded by a violent uprising of the French peasantry in 1358 and by the ravages of 'free companies' of Burgundian, French and English mercenaries, operating on their own account or on behalf of anyone who promised them booty regardless of whether or not an official truce had been declared. And though aristocratic foes might be treated courteously in these glamourised wars, civilians were another matter. The medieval equivalent of modern 'economic warfare' was to destroy the enemy's crops after first making sure that enough had been pillaged to keep the invader himself supplied. It was the continuance of raids of this sort which finally compelled the French to agree to the humiliating treaty of Brétigny of 1360. In return for a not very precise abandonment of his claim to the French throne, Edward became acknowledged master of almost the whole of south-western France, about a third of the whole kingdom, as well as of Calais. John's ransom was fixed at a sum equivalent to Edward's normal income for five years.

Edward's French ambitions were themselves excessive and his apparent success by 1360 was itself made possible to a great extent by the even greater follies of the French. Both Crécy and Poitiers were battles which the English had had small wish to fight, since on both occasions they were outnumbered and strategically at a disadvantage. A competently-led French army would have turned Crécy into a trap from which the English would have found it hard to escape. So little did the Black Prince, Edward's eldest son, look forward to fighting at Poitiers that he had tried to negotiate a seven-year truce in return for a safe conduct back to his base. Compelled to stand and fight at Crécy, Edward had won by adopting, in a position of local strength, defensive tactics which exposed a dashingly aristocratic cavalry charge by what has been described as 'the flower of the French nobility', to the devastating effect, on three sides, of the longbows of the English infantry, firing rapidly from behind fences and hedges. It was not that their reliance on infantry armed with longbows made the English less 'chivalrous' than the French nobles whom they impaled. Even though the French nobility regarded their own footslogging archers as an inferior rabble, the real difference was that the longbow could be fired three times as fast as the French crossbow, and that the English commanders combined pride in their aristocratic exclusiveness with a professionalism born of Edward I's difficult wars against the recalcitrant Welsh and Scots in terrain which gave little scope for heroic frontal assaults by panoplied horsemen.

Yet, for the English, the sequel to Crécy was no more than a long drawn out siege of Calais which a good French commander might have turned into a disaster for the invader. To the French, it taught no other lesson than that next time round they should resolve to win or die in the attempt. Hence, not only was Poitiers a battle joined deliberately by a French king besotted with chivalric fancies; it was fought by the French with the same tactics that had failed at Crécy, and with more disastrous results. It is a comment on the element of role-playing in the aristocratic behaviour of the time that, after his release from captivity in England, John, the French king who had lost at Poitiers, voluntarily returned to his imprisonment when one of the hostages he had left behind was dastardly enough to escape. The king continued to write sad letters to France telling his subjects how sorry he was for them.

The Forty Years' Failure

The arrangements made at Brétigny were thus likely to last only for so long as French leadership continued incompetent. In Charles V, France acquired in 1364 a monarch of ability. By 1369, the health of the Black Prince was giving way and Edward beginning a long semi-dotage. By 1375, the English had lost all their French possessions apart from Calais, the environs of Bordeaux, and a few precarious harbours in Brittany; and this despite another damaging march through France from Calais to Bordeaux, by an English army under Edward's second son, John of Gaunt, Duke of Lancaster, in 1373. Additional trouble had arisen from an expedition by the Black Prince, ultimately unsuccessful, to overthrow the French-sponsored usurper of the throne of Spanish Castile. This created a Franco-Castilian alliance and led to the destruction of a fleet of reinforcements being transported from England to Gascony in 1372, as well as to raids by French and Castilian ships on the English Channel coast. In 1377 the French burnt Gravesend and Rye. Punitive expeditions were mounted, one involving yet another spoiling English march from Brittany to beyond Paris and back in 1380. It was the cost of mounting this which induced the government to levy the poll tax that provoked the Peasants' Revolt of 1381. The existence of schism in the church next suggested to commercial and ecclesiastical interests the idea of a crusade under the bishop of Norwich (he was a Despenser) to defend Flanders against French influence, on the grounds that France was supporting a schismatic pope. The venture broke up in disorder in 1383 and for the next forty years the English hold on France was limited to Calais and Gascony. John of Gaunt consoled himself by attempting to make himself king of Castile; but though his invasion failed, he did enough to get himself bought off with a handsome sum in cash in 1389.

The English merchants who wanted to prevent France controlling Flanders and the magnates who wanted French booty were unreconciled to the failures of the English after 1360, least of all to the continuance of French seaborne attacks in the Channel. Conditions in England itself from 1370 to 1413 were much disturbed. Plague was both epidemic and endemic. The peasants in the east and south-east were seething with resentment after their revolt in 1381. There was much economic dislocation in part caused, and in part aggravated, by the warfare that profligated English financial resources, despoiled the French and damaged the trade with Flanders. Anti-clericalism and heresy embittered relations between secular and clerical magnates and for the first time added religious sanction to popular resentment against gentry and aristocracy. Both the commons and, in 1341, archbishop Stratford, had strongly opposed the financial burdens Edward III had sought to impose on knights, burgesses and churchmen in order to pay for his expensive plans for invading France. The commons had forced royal acceptance of the principle that lay taxation should be levied only with parliamentary consent. But, though parliamentary taxation was just bearable when war was prospering, it was altogether different after 1370. Parliament's recourse to the poll tax in 1381 was obviously an attempt to pass on the tax burden from gentry to peasantry; and the anti-clericalism of the same period was an attempt by government (then dominated by John of Gaunt) to avoid too frequent confrontations with parliament by mulcting the church instead. Wyclif, scourge of ecclesiastical wealth and pretension, owed his initial importance to his employment by John of Gaunt.

Worst of all was that Edward's capacity to rule did not last much longer than his brief period of glory as bringer of victories. By the 1370s he was an elderly widower dominated by his mistress, Alice Perrers, by his grasping former companion in arms, Latimer, who served as treasurer, and by the ambitious John of Gaunt. All were accused of graft by the so-called Good Parliament of 1376, but with little effect. Edward's death in 1377 increased the confusion. Owing to the youth of the new king, Richard II, power resided chiefly in Gaunt. It was his regime that produced the devil's brew of the poll tax, the Peasants' Revolt, Wyclif's anti-clerical turmoil, the crackbrained idea of the crusade to Flanders, and Gaunt's scheme to get himself the crown of Castile.

Richard II responded to the situation in a manner which if commendable in theory was in practice irresponsible and eventually self-destructive. He resented his formidable uncles, Gaunt, Gloucester and York, as well as the wealthy Earl of Arundel, not least because, in addition to their personal disapproval of him, they perpetually intrigued against one another. Perhaps the chief difficulty was that he seems to have dissented from the prevailing belief in the virtue of ravaging the French by land as, later on, James I was immune from the desire to ravage the Spanish by sea. Accordingly, Richard chose courtiers of less bellicosely virile temperament than the avuncular veterans set over him. The consequences were predictable. In 1386 parliament imposed upon him a council dominated by his uncle Gloucester (then still known as Thomas of Woodstock) and by Arundel; Richard nevertheless restored his own friends to favour, and the magnates took up arms against him and threatened to depose him. The 'Merciless' Parliament of 1388 subordinated the king to the leaders of the movement against him, the so-called Lords Appellant: Gloucester, Arundel, Henry Bolingbroke (John of Gaunt's son), Warwick, and Thomas Mowbray, the Earl of Nottingham. But though, by and large, Richard put up with them, he was unrepentantly convinced of the pre-eminence of his kingly office and deeply resentful of the curtailment of his personal authority.

In 1397 he made a dramatic bid for real power by organising a *coup*, perhaps deliberately styled as a mirror image of the Merciless Parliament of 1388. He was able to do so largely because the Appellants of 1388 were as hostile to one another as they were to the king. He arrested Gloucester, Arundel and Warwick. Gloucester died in prison at Calais, probably on Richard's orders, Arundel was executed and Warwick banished. Thomas Arundel, the archbishop of Canterbury, was also banished. To celebrate this uniquely successful royal assault on the most powerful men in the kingdom, Richard created five new dukes in one day: He made Bolingbroke Duke of Hereford and Mowbray Duke of Norfolk. A suitably overawed parliament granted him customs duties for life and empowered a committee to act in its name when it was not in session. With a concluding demonstration of royal majesty, Richard then banished both Bolingbroke and Mowbray, chiefly, it can be assumed, because though they had of late been his friends, they too had been among the detested Appellants of 1388.

Unfortunately, Richard's vengeance did not even stop there. When, in 1399, John of Gaunt died, Richard annexed to the crown the whole great Lancastrian inheritance to which, as Gaunt's heir, Bolingbroke was undoubtedly entitled. For the second time in his reign, Richard then went on expedition to Ireland. It is consistent with Richard's obstinate singularity that he should have flaunted his dislike of overbearing magnates who wanted him to fight across the Channel by choosing instead to fight, with the support of friends of his own, on the other side of the Irish Sea. He returned to find that Bolingbroke had secured the

The Battles of France

support of the northern Earls of Northumberland and Westmorland, and of the king's only surviving uncle, York. The outcome was a parliament which, with Bolingbroke's armed followers at the ready, deposed Richard on the grounds of his many misdeeds; he died in prison in 1400. There was no demur when, immediately upon Richard's deposition, Bolingbroke assumed the crown as Henry IV.

Richard was deposed in the end not because of his distaste for the martial arts but because he had behaved as badly towards the nobility as nobles tended to behave towards one another. The aristocracy required the king to be their good lord in the same way that lesser men expected good lordship from the great nobles. Richard had done nothing for the nobility but accumulate reasons why they should resent him. Hence there was no systematic appeal to community and law when he was deposed, only a list of aristocratic grudges. No undertakings such as had been demanded of John, Henry III, Edward I or Edward II by earlier aristocratic opposition, were demanded of Henry IV. Henry himself had no clear right through inheritance, by election or on principle, or even by successful rebellion, since he had returned from banishment claiming only his right to his personal inheritance as John of Gaunt's son. Though at pains, once he was king, to be respectful to both church and parliament, he allowed no suggestion that he owed his position to their support. The true situation was that in 1399 the crown had been seized by one of Richard's aggrieved aristocratic relations in temporary coalition with other aggrieved aristocrats, some of whom were also Richard's relations.

Henry IV's claim by inheritance depended on his descent from Edward III by way of Edward's second son, John of Gaunt. An arguably better claim resided in Edmund Mortimer, Earl of March. Mortimer was the grandson of Philippa, daughter of Edward III's eldest son, Duke of Clarence; and Richard II had named the Mortimers as his heirs. It is not surprising that Henry's authority as king was openly challenged as early as 1402 by Henry Percy (Hotspur), son of the Earl of Northumberland, the outcome being the battle of Shrewsbury in 1403, in which Hotspur was killed. This dangerous opposition to Henry IV, from the Percy family which had helped him to the throne, was continued by a rebellious outbreak by the Earl of Northumberland in alliance with the Mortimers and the Welshman, Owain Glyndwr, whose daughter had married a Mortimer. They proposed to overthrow Henry on the grounds that he was a usurper and then to give Wales to Glyndwr, the north of England to Northumberland and the southern counties to Mortimer. Not until 1409 was Henry able finally to destroy the conspiracy. Edward III's transformation of his sons into territorial aristocrats, and the deposition of Richard II, gave the aristocratic feuding that now prevailed the characteristics of a family quarrel made the more unmanageable by the fact that all the participants had so much to lose and so much to gain.

Equally disturbing at the time were the repeated efforts of parliament to restrict the crown's financial powers and its endeavours to stop the crown alienating crown lands, a device which by enriching the aristocracy reduced the crown's long term income and increased its demands for taxes. Under Henry IV, the Commons tried to nominate members of the royal council. The king, prematurely aged by constant military campaigning and constant friction with parliaments, contracted a nervous eczema which some took for leprosy and a sign of God's disapproval of a usurper.

His son, Henry V, who succeeded in 1413, had evidently been impatient to become king because, capable and energetic as he was, he was anxious to prove that the new dynasty of Lancaster was a glorious one. Already a veteran soldier at twenty-five, schooled in his teens by campaigning in his father's wars in Wales, he seems to have understood that he could secure the loyalty of the aristocracy only if he could assume the mantles of Edward III and the Black Prince and lead the nobles once again in battle against the French. How dependent royal prestige was on employing aristocratic energies in warfare outside the kingdom was revealed even as the new king's expedition was in preparation. Only a fortunate act of treachery averted a rebellion by Henry's royal relations, the Mortimers and the Yorkist family, both, like Henry V, descendants of Edward III and allied by marriage. But the prospects of glory and booty healed all divisions. Henry's own ducal brothers; his potential rivals, the Duke of York and the Earl of March (head of the Mortimers); and the head of the Percy clan, so recently in rebellion: all were ready to become a 'band of brothers' under a king who offered them the prospect, after the frustrating decades since 1370, of a return to the splendid days of Edward III.

War: Renewed and Lost

The situation in France in 1413 was worse than in Edward III's early days. Charles VI, a child king when he succeeded to the French throne in 1380, became a mad one in 1392 and remained so until his death in 1422, foreshadowing the similar life cycle of his grandson, Henry VI of England. To royal incompetence was added the rivalry between the dukes of Burgundy and a faction more or less associated with the French king's brother, and known as the Armagnacs. When, after managing, with some difficulty, to capture Harfleur as a base in 1415, Henry was confronted by the Armagnacs at Agincourt while en route for Calais, his depleted and tired army nevertheless won an overwhelming victory. Stationary archers yet again overcame chivalric horsemen, and about 7000 Frenchmen were killed. Agincourt was the last military victory of consequence to be won by the English on continental soil until Marlborough's battle of Blenheim in 1704, and the last memorable victory of this sort they were to win without the support of considerable allies.

The singularity of Agincourt soon became apparent, if only because of

Henry V's early death in 1422 and the protracted anti-climax of English military decline thereafter. But if early death saved Henry's reputation from the damage done to Edward III's by his survival into unsuccessful old age, Agincourt represented the peak of English martial achievement even more than Crécy and Poitiers. Edward III and the Black Prince had belonged to what was still a half-French dynasty; but whereas the Black Prince had been noted for his command of French, Henry V was probably the first English monarch habitually to use the English language. Agincourt was won by a ruler whose dynasty, for all its taint of usurpation, was almost wholly bred in England. Its aristocratic commanders also now seemed more thoroughly English, their territorial designations sounding like an heraldic roll call not only of noble persons but of noble cities and shires: Warwick and Salisbury, Bedford and Exeter, Gloucester, York and Northumberland. Agincourt, too, seemed one more demonstration of the superiority of the ordinary English bowman over the effete nobility of France, men who still regarded the idea that an army should rely on its archers with the aristocratic distaste early twentieth-century cavalrymen were alleged to evince at the mention of tanks.

Yet Henry's success in obtaining virtual control of all Normandy between 1417 and 1419 was less a consequence of Agincourt than of a simultaneous advance on Paris by the rebellious and powerful Duke of Burgundy. The murder of the duke by the Armagnac supporters of Charles VI's heir, the Dauphin, led to an alliance between Henry and the succeeding Duke of Burgundy which was the basis of English power in France for the next fifteen years. It was with Philip of Burgundy that Henry signed the treaty of Troyes in 1420 which, by giving him Charles VI's daughter, Catherine, in marriage, made Henry the mad old king's heir-apparent. In December 1420, Henry and Burgundy entered Paris; but in 1422, Henry died, aged thirty-five. Shortly afterwards, Charles VI also died; and the infant Henry VI became, in name at any rate, king of both England and France.

During the next six years, the English continued, chiefly under the leadership of Henry V's brother, John, Duke of Bedford, to extend their control over Normandy, Maine and Champagne. While the Duke of Burgundy held on to Artois, Flanders and Brabant, the English still also held Gascony, and had suzerainty over Brittany. Charles VI's heir, the Dauphin, controlled only the regions of France south and east of the Loire, his claim to be Charles VII being dismissed by his enemies on account of his alleged bastardy. But the English-Burgundian alliance, on which the position of the former depended, always worked badly. English leadership was harassed by faction at home and its commanders were less than scrupulous in their behaviour to the Burgundians.

Any positive move by the Dauphin was thus likely to make the Burgundians change sides, since they had no great desire to share control of France with the English; and in 1429 the reckless ambitions of armed aristocrats were suddenly transformed by the intervention of Joan of Arc. How far she led and how far she merely symbolised the successful liberation of Orleans from its English besiegers in that year is matter for dispute. What is clear is that thereafter the French cause at last began to prosper. Her most significant contributions were made after Orleans. Under her influence, Charles moved to Rheims, there to be crowned and anointed. Rationally, he should have aimed at Paris, the capital; but the ceremony at Rheims transformed him from an alleged bastard whom God had deserted into a rightful king whom rebels and foreigners had robbed of his inheritance. By the time Henry VI was crowned in Paris some months later, it was his coronation and not Charles's that looked the more of a charade. By that time, too, Joan had performed the greatest of her services to France. Captured by the Burgundians, she was handed over to the English, who had her burned as a heretic. Alive, she would have been a nuisance to everybody. There were already too many persons, male as well as female, in mid-fifteenth century Europe claiming to know more about things temporal and spiritual than their betters. But once dead, Joan could safely be used as a symbol of resistance to the English invaders.

By 1435 the Burgundian alliance had broken down. At a conference at Arras between England, France and the Burgundians, the uncompromising insistence of the English on their right to the French crown was rejected and soon afterwards Philip of Burgundy made his peace with Charles VII. In 1436, the English were driven from Paris. In 1444 a six-year truce was agreed, its guarantee being a marriage between Henry VI and Margaret of Anjou. It was imperfectly observed by the English forces still on French soil and in 1449 a well mounted French campaign culminated in the defeat of the English, with enormous losses, at the battle of Formigny. Unlike the more spectacular English victories earlier in the war, it was decisive. By 1453, of all their former possessions in France, the English retained only Calais. The French won not only the war but the undeclared peace that followed. During the next half century, France grew steadily in national self-consciousness and monarchical orderliness. The English endured thirty years of political confusion.

COLLAPSE AND RECOVERY

Things Fall Apart

FROM 1307 to 1422 crown and aristocracy had been chiefly concerned with the pursuit of glory and profit in a war they were unlikely to win. Their depredations in France were a medieval parallel to the barbarian invasions of Europe in the ninth and tenth centuries. In the end, the difference between the English invasion of France and the earlier Danish invasion of England was that the Danish attacks had been more successful. In the decades after Henry V's death, the glorious war turned into a steady drizzle of retreats. Worse still, not only had the aristocrats become defeated captains; they suddenly found themselves leaderless, in a situation in which the crown could not control them and they could not control one another.

Henry VI was nine months old in 1422. When his minority ended in 1437 it soon became apparent that, for him, childhood was prelude to a whole lifetime of second childhood. He proved intelligent enough not to be completely ignored, but incapable of framing and pursuing a policy of his own, except that of indiscriminately distributing pensions, pardons, wardships, offices of state (often, to avoid the pain of saying 'no', giving the same office to more than one person) to whoever could obtain access to his vaguely saintly presence. He would also readily release debtors from their obligations if they could get near enough to him to ask; and this at a time when the unsuccessful war had left the crown heavily in debt to creditors of all sorts, from great aristocrats to humble craftsmen.

The extreme reluctance of the nobility to get rid of Henry VI arose from the fact that to seize the king's power and use it in his name was less risky than to invite the hostility that rival aristocrats would instantly display to anyone who bore the stigma of usurpation. There was, too, a genuine difference of function between a king and a great aristocrat. The function of kingship was to dispense justice to all men and to govern and administer a whole realm. That of an aristocrat was to advance the interest and prestige of the family of which he was the head, to defend, exploit and expand the family territories, and promote the careers and influence of his family connections, dependants and clients. Any aristocrat who gained control of the council inevitably used the opportunities thereby opened to him to exalt his own family power at the expense of his aristocratic rivals. Even if he tried to govern well, an aristocrat occupying so high a place in the kingdom would be considered to be failing in his duty if he did not generously reward both himself and his followers, for it was by such means that he demonstrated that his authority was real. But this so enraged those who were excluded from power that nobody's tenure of it was more than temporary. What the aristocrats wanted was a king who would be a good lord to them all. The alternative, of replacing a king who failed in this role by an aristocrat primarily concerned with being a good lord to his own followers, and likely to be deserted by them if he were not, seemed no solution at all.

That Henry VI did not, like Richard II, have a policy prolonged the confusion. Henry VI survived because he meekly followed the dictates of whichever faction among the aristocracy had a temporary monopoly of access to him. Henry thus left the aristocrats with no alternative except to quarrel with one another. Yet for any one among them to take the crown seemed far more likely to increase confusion than end it.

As during Richard II's minority, affairs of state were in the hands of the king's aristocratic relations. Since John, Duke of Bedford, Henry V's most competent brother, busied himself with the war, the inevitable family quarrel was conducted between Henry V's other brother, Humphrey, Duke of Gloucester, and the king's great-uncle, Henry Beaufort, brother to Henry IV. As bishop of Winchester and manager of the wealth of the duchy of Lancaster, Beaufort financed the government and the war by lending the crown large sums of money at a considerable profit to himself. But while Beaufort systematically supported Bedford in his military cooperation with Burgundy against France, Humphrey did his best to end the Burgundian alliance by conducting his own private feuds with Burgundy. Twice he tried to oust Beaufort, in 1425 and 1432; on both occasions he was brought to heel by the intervention of Bedford, who, however, died in 1435.

When Henry came of age in 1437, power was gradually concentrating in the hands of the ageing Beaufort's chief supporter, William De La Pole, Duke of Suffolk. Suffolk's supremacy became complete when, shortly before the death of Beaufort in 1447, Gloucester also died: after Suffolk had had him arrested for treason. Henry not only gave Suffolk power; he showered money and all sorts of profitable economic concessions upon him; and Suffolk exploited his authority to its extremest limits, so that whoever could claim his protection could get away with anything. His most notorious protégé was William Tailboys who, with a retinue of strong-arm men, rampaged over Lincolnshire, subsequently being accused of four murders, eight assaults and sundry burglaries. He and his men forcibly prevented the assize court from functioning in Bedford in 1446; and in 1449 burst in on the council chamber itself with the intention of murdering the Treasurer, Ralf, lord Cromwell. But in 1448 Henry had granted Tailboys a royal pardon for all his offences; he was not punished for his attempt on Cromwell until after Suffolk's fall.

Among other local consequences of Suffolk's domination of the king was the impossibility of obtaining any sort of justice in Norfolk because he had its sheriff in his pocket. So impossible did it seem to bring any of Suffolk's clients to court that one county family took up arms against an Oxfordshire knight who enjoyed Suffolk's favour, since, though the knight had murdered one of their family, there appeared no other way of bringing him to book.

By 1450, all this, together with the imminent collapse of the war in France, led the commons to make an attack on Suffolk similar to, but even more comprehensive than, their descendants' later attacks on Buckingham in Charles I's reign: they tried to impeach him for treason. Since then, as in the seventeenth century, the abuse of power by a minister who enjoyed the confidence of a king could hardly be deemed treasonable, they had to invent various fictitious acts of treason to accuse him of. But Suffolk had been so grossly lawless that the Lords might not, had it come to it, have refused to find him guilty, as they were to refuse to condemn Strafford in 1641. Henry himself therefore vetoed the indictment and on his personal authority banished Suffolk for five years. But since Suffolk's offence was notorious, the matter did not end there. The ship carrying him to his exile was stopped in the Channel. He was taken aboard the intercepting vessel and murdered.

Suffolk's murder was only one evidence of growing popular revulsion against aristocratic lawlessness. Earlier in 1450, Adam Moleyns, bishop of Chichester, a leading member of Suffolk's ruling clique, had been seized and murdered by mariners at Portsmouth, alleging he was responsible for their arrears of pay. When Henry still made no move against the rest of Suffolk's friends in the council, the whole of northern Kent rose in revolt in June 1450 under the leadership of the evidently impressive, if mysterious, Jack Cade. Many thousands of yeomen, labourers, tradesmen and artisans, with the support of almost a hundred gentry from leading Kentish families, marched to Blackheath where they presented a 'Complaint' whose contents looked back to the Great Charter and forward to the Long Parliament's indictments of Strafford and Laud. They attacked evil counsellors who maintained that the king was above the law or pretended that men's goods and bodies were wholly at the king's disposal. They condemned the bribery of judges and juries and the notion that it was solely for the king to determine who was or was not a traitor.

Their remedies for these and other grievances, however, belonged precisely to their own time. The king was to resume control of the royal lands he had granted his courtiers, and choose different advisers; among them, they named the Duke of Norfolk, whose influence in East Anglia had been seriously prejudiced by Suffolk and, more significant for the future, Richard, Duke of York. Perhaps hopeful that a demonstration was enough, the rebels, when ordered to disperse, fell back on Sevenoaks, only to be spurred into further action by an attack from a royal force which they destroyed. In July, the king having removed himself from the capital, they were admitted to London, and insisted on the execution of two more of Suffolk's aristocratic henchmen. Encouraged by news of these occurrences, others gave way to their feelings. Riots and assaults against various of Suffolk's clients took place in Hampshire, Essex and Gloucester. In Wiltshire, the bishop of Salisbury, another of Suffolk's men, was lynched while saying mass. Even when Cade's men got so out of hand that they were expelled from London and dispersed and Cade himself died of wounds while resisting arrest, sporadic disorders took place in various southern counties.

Since, however, all that these outbursts amounted to was a demand that one set of aristocrats be replaced by another, they merely accelerated the substitution of one feud by another. The fall of Suffolk was followed almost at once by the revival of a longstanding quarrel between another Lancastrian aristocrat, Edmund Beaufort, Duke of Somerset, who succeeded Suffolk, and the disaffected Richard, Duke of York. A direct descendant of Edward III, Richard was one of the largest but least competent landowners in England and, since it then seemed likely that Henry would beget no children, the king's heir-presumptive. York had commanded the English in France but, after a quarrel, had been replaced by Beaufort and sent off to govern Ireland. That Beaufort, as Duke of Somerset, should now rise even higher as a result of the fall of Suffolk, provoked York to return to England. Fearful of their prospects under Beaufort's regime, many of Suffolk's clients turned to York, and for a time the commons also supported him. Unfortunately, between 1450 and 1453, York seemed to alternate between statesmanlike caution and demonstrations of armed force in a manner unlikely to assist him. Somerset ruled rather better than Suffolk, and the more it looked as if to substitute York for Somerset would require a civil war and set up yet another overmighty subject so soon after the uproar of 1450, the more York's chances declined.

There was sufficient aristocratic disorder as it was. In 1451, Thomas Courtenay, Earl of Devon, whose family would long support the house of York, led an armed force of about five thousand men against James Butler, Earl of Wiltshire, a Beaufort and therefore Lancastrian protégé; and in 1453 the great northern magnates, the Percies of Northumberland and the Neville family, whose head was the Earl of Warwick, engaged in armed attacks on each other in Yorkshire which the government was powerless to stop. Such attempts as were made to do so resulted in a face to face confrontation between Warwick and Somerset which was to turn Warwick into a supporter of York.

In August 1453, Henry suffered a mental breakdown which incapacitated him for sixteen months. Deprived of the king's support, Somerset found himself in the Tower and York became Protector. But in October 1453, Henry's determined wife, Margaret of Anjou, had, against expectation, given birth to a son; and, convinced that York meant to deny her child his crown, became York's enemy. So, when, in 1454, the king recovered sufficiently to take notice, Somerset recovered his power too. But this time, York and his clientele withdrew from London for the purpose of collecting an army. In 1455, in a pitched battle at St Alban's which is usually regarded as the first engagement in what Sir Walter Scott would eventually christen 'The Wars of the Roses,' Somerset was killed. The Yorkist victory resulted, naturally enough, in the implacable hostility of Margaret and the Beauforts; and since York had won it in alliance with Warwick, it also infuriated Warwick's sworn enemies, the Percies.

York found it possible neither to control the council nor pacify the kingdom. When, in 1455, the Earl of Devon and his two sons waged a campaign of murder and terror around Exeter, not only was York not powerful enough to enforce justice against them, but the king gave a pardon to both of the earl's two sons. By contrast, when one of York's clients took the law into his own hands in a dispute over the castles of Caermarthen and Aberystwyth, Margaret persuaded Henry to purge the council of all its Yorkists and replace them with Beaufort and the new dukes of Somerset and Northumberland. To complete the work, a packed parliament held at Coventry in 1459 while York was in Ireland and Warwick in Calais, attainted York and all his lordly confederates as traitors and declared their lands confiscate.

The answer to this came in 1460. Warwick, together with his father, the Earl of Salisbury, and York's eighteen year old son, Edward Earl of March, landed in England, occupied London and, after a battle at Northampton, captured the king and brought him back to the capital. York then sought to solve everything by announcing that he, and not Henry, was rightful king of England.

It did not seem much of a solution. In 1456, the Lancastrians had temporarily secured enough power to declare that all Yorkists were traitors. York was now using a probably no less temporary period of power not merely to label all the Lancastrian lords as traitors but to impugn the legality of every act of constituted authority since 1399. Since all the magnates, Yorkist as well as Lancastrians, had sworn allegiance to Henry, nobody could feel safe if York's claim were recognised. The only claim that could nullify that of Henry (let alone that of his infant son, Edward) was one based on conquest. But York had conquered nothing except temporary custodianship of the ineffective person of the king. Yet York was, all the same, the man on top at the moment. So the lords offered a compromise: York was to become Prince of Wales, protector of the realm and Henry's eventual successor.

The Lancastrian reply, organised by an indignant Margaret of Anjou, was immediate. Her forces trapped York's at Wakefield in 1460 and York himself was killed. A few weeks later, in January 1461, at another encounter at St Alban's, Warwick was also defeated and the king released from his Yorkist captors.

If the Yorkists were now to stand any chance of escaping the vengeance of a triumphant Margaret, they could hope to do so only by at last transforming a seemingly endless aristocratic feud into a genuine contest for the reality of power. They therefore declared their allegiance to the new Duke of York, Edward, Earl of March, as Edward IV. Not only Yorkist London but many previously hesitant magnates at last faced the fact they had been evading for almost thirty years, that only the re-establishment of an effective monarchy offered a solution to the problem of continuous political and social disorder. In March 1461, Edward and his supporters, aided by a small body of Burgundian troops, moved north against the queen and won the nearest approach to a major battle that the 'Wars of the Roses' produced, at Towton. Though Margaret, Henry and their son escaped to Northumberland, many leading Lancastrian lords were killed and others captured and beheaded.

Edward IV: A False Dawn

Though Edward did much to restore kingly authority, this was not, in view of the now ingrained habit of ignoring it, necessarily popular. Nor did it eliminate frequent outbreaks of feuding in the localities. Even worse, though rightly anxious not to become, like Henry VI, the tool of a faction, Edward was virile and genial and rather too self-confident in his treatment of the aristocratic elders who had elevated him. They wanted a king strong enough to subdue their enemies but not strong enough to subdue them. Accordingly when, by 1464, Lancastrian opposition seemed to have been overcome, he fell out with his chief aristocratic supporter, Richard Neville, Earl of Warwick, and his own jealous brother, George, Duke of Clarence. In part, the quarrel was a legacy of the Hundred Years War. Louis XI, the astute king of France seemed, on account of Edward's friendship with the Burgundians, to favour a Lancastrian comeback. Warwick therefore tried for a French alliance to scotch this idea, and hoped to cement the alliance by marrying Edward to a French bride. When Edward, who was not noted for sexual continence, instead married Elizabeth Woodville, whose mother had married her principal household official, all his lords were offended and Warwick most of all. As well as creating a family circle of his own, Edward was upsetting Warwick's diplomacy. Indeed, by marrying his own sister to the Duke of Burgundy in 1468, Edward annoyed Warwick still further. Accordingly, by 1469, Warwick was conspiring to make Edward's younger brother, Clarence, king, and succeeded in taking Edward captive. He had to be released soon afterwards, however, since nobody showed much interest in Clarence's allegation that Edward was illegitimate. But in 1470, Warwick, Louis XI, Margaret of Anjou and Clarence agreed together that Henry VI should be restored. Landing at Exeter with an Anglo-French force, Warwick caught Edward unawares; the king fled abroad to take refuge in the Burgundian Low Countries, and Henry VI, who had been held in the Tower since being captured in 1465, was duly released and once more solemnly recognised as king.

But it soon became clear that, though Edward's rights were not worth defending, neither were Henry's. He was now the creature of Louis XI and Margaret, both of them French. Warwick made this very obvious by trying to get parliament to honour the bill that Louis XI now sent in to his English friends, namely the cost of a war against Burgundy. Parliament refused, so that when Edward landed in the north in 1461 he not only had Burgundian support; he met with no organised opposition. His brother Clarence deserted the insubstantial Neville-Lancastrian-French coalition and at Barnet, in April 1471, an inadequate force under Warwick's command was destroyed, Warwick himself being killed. In May 1471, a belated Lancastrian resistance on Margaret's behalf was crushed at Tewkesbury: Margaret was taken prisoner and a further batch of Lancastrian peers were killed, as was her son, Edward. Before the month was out Henry VI died in the Tower, and in suspicious circumstances. Louis XI suspended his quarrel with the Burgundians and abandoned the Lancastrians. All that remained of the remnant was the Lancastrian Earl of Pembroke, Jasper Tudor, and his fifteen-year-old nephew, the obscure Henry Tudor, Earl of Richmond.

Since between 1471 and 1483 Edward IV did much to restore royal authority, he, rather than Henry VII, is considered the real founder of the revived royal supremacy once considered wholly the achievement of the Tudor dynasty. Yet, though neither Edward IV nor Henry VII was in any respect the creator of a 'new' monarchy, but a restorer of the medieval monarchy that aristocratic domination had destroyed, Edward IV achieved only a limited success in this respect. He was still sufficiently captivated by the traditions of the Hundred Years War to hope for territory or loot by exploiting the rivalry of Burgundy and France. In 1474 he was party to an improbable treaty by which Charles of Burgundy would partition France with him and allow him the title of king of France. By the time Edward reached France with a considerable force, in 1475, Burgundian power was so gravely weakened that he was glad enough to be bought off by Louis XI for a cash sum and a pension that was paid for about six years. This treaty of Picquigny in effect marked the end of the Hundred Years War; but it redounds rather more to the credit of Louis XI, who knew what he was doing, than to Edward. At the time of his death, Edward had gathered a large quantity of arms with the intention of invading France like his noble predecessors, particularly because by then Louis XI was dead and his successor was a minor.

End and Beginning, 1483–1509

At home, though he greatly reduced the hatred roused by old feuds, Edward's exaltation of his wife's family, the Woodvilles, by ennoblement and dynastic marriages, produced a disastrous feud between them and his Yorkist relations. Had this not occurred there would have been no doubt at all about Edward's right to be regarded as the real restorer of the crown's good lordship and government. But the Woodville-Yorkist rivalry which burst out as soon as he died in 1483 produced a political situation as alarmingly unstable as any that had existed earlier in the century. The new king, Edward V, was a boy of twelve. It was uncertain whether his father had wanted a regency controlled by the queen, Elizabeth Woodville, or a protectorate under his brother Richard, Duke of Gloucester. Gloucester had served his brother with great loyalty and had ruled firmly and competently in the north. But he was so sure that the Woodvilles were bent on destroying him that he arrested Earl Rivers, the head of the Woodvilles, personally took charge of the young king, and had himself proclaimed protector. Almost immediately, he accused Lord Hastings, formerly Edward IV's chamberlain and one of his own two chief supporters, of treason and had him summarily executed. He then declared Edward IV's marriage invalid and Edward V illegitimate, and was crowned in splendour as Richard III. Edward V and his younger brother were placed in the Tower and never again seen alive.

Such disregard for legality only a few months after Edward IV's death gravely imperilled Richard's reputation despite the fact that he gave every sign that in more favourable circumstances he would have been a firm and competent ruler. The judicial murder of Hastings, an act justified on no stronger grounds than that Richard held it treasonable in his friend to have corresponded with the Woodvilles, the baselessness of the claim that Edward IV's marriage was invalid and the never-rebutted charge that Richard had also killed Edward V and his brother are sufficient explanation of Richard's subsequent evil reputation. They can be explained only on the assumption that here was a man so passionately determined to defend his power against all comers that he could not see that by eliminating every possible rival he was depriving himself not merely of enemies but of friends. Presumably fearing that what happened to Hastings could happen to him, Richard's other principal supporter, Henry Stafford, Duke of Buckingham, deserted Richard before the end of 1483 and began overtures to the exiled Henry Tudor. But Buckingham's attempt at a rising on Henry's behalf proved a fiasco. Buckingham was captured and executed.

Nevertheless, such work of reconciliation as Edward IV had achieved was largely undone; certainly, the whole Woodville connection now turned towards the previously insignificant Henry. Though Richard showed every intention of governing well and undoubtedly had the capacity to do so, his violence and illegality had undermined confidence in him. It seemed, too, as if the wrath of the Almighty was pursuing him. His son died in 1484, and his wife a year later. Both events raised the hopes of the Lancastrians. Richard was haunted by the fear of a French invasion on Henry Tudor's behalf.

Expected in the spring of 1485, Henry did not arrive until August, fearing a repetition of the failure that had overtaken Buckingham. Landing at Milford Haven, he moved across Wales to Shrewsbury. The powerful Lord Stanley did nothing to halt the rebels; Richard's typical counter-measure against Stanley was to seize his son as a hostage for his father's good behaviour. Yet, when Henry faced Richard's army at Bosworth in Leicestershire, he had attracted little support. Henry's force of five thousand was outnumbered two to one; and though the unrepentantly Lancastrian Earl of Oxford, John De Vere (the thirteenth in the line to bear the title) was a competent soldier, Henry himself had little military experience. Richard, however, was undone by treachery; a treachery arising from the conviction that he was not the sort of king to risk death for. Stanley's forces were in attendance, but neutral. Richard detailed Henry Percy, Duke of Northumberland, to prevent Stanley intervening; but at the critical moment Stanley moved against the king and Percy did not stop him. The result was that when Richard, in a desperate display of chivalric recklessness, thrust himself forward in order to challenge Henry to personal combat, he was cut off and killed.

Though the overwhelming majority of the nobility and gentry had been 'but mutes or audience to this act', as they were to be at that other turning point when William of Orange landed in 1688, it marked the end of an old era and the start of a different one. They had no reason to think so at the time and rightly remained unconvinced for several decades that anything decisive had happened. Yet the monarchy that Henry now re-created was unlike any that England had known, except during the lucid intervals of Edward IV's reign, since the time of Henry I or Henry II. He avoided falling victim to the idea of war as glorious; he firmly kept the aristocracy in their place; and he was almost untroubled by parliaments.

Henry VII was so much more diligent, consistent and patiently calculating than the son and grandchildren who succeeded him that his reign bears little resemblance to theirs. After him, Tudor monarchy became so notable for both splendours and tantrums, for its vacillations and its alternations of expansive warmth with impolitic passion and prejudice, that the steady, calculated cold-bloodedness of the years from 1485 to 1509 seems a prelude to the 'Tudor Age' rather than a part of it. Few rulers could have accepted as completely as Henry did a situation in which what was possible was confined within such narrow limits, or have created so substantial a power on the basis of what had been, in 1485, no more than the unexpected good fortune of an almost penniless nobody.

The fact that he was a nobody meant that he could survive only by a most careful combination of severity with restraint. His hereditary claim was the weakest of any monarch since 1066, resting on his descent through two women. His grandparents were Henry V's French widow and her second husband, Owen Tudor. His mother was Margaret Beaufort, daughter of a younger grandson of Henry IV's younger

153

brother; and a statute existed that excluded the Beauforts from the succession. Since, therefore, nothing but Richard III's recklessness could have brought him to the throne, Henry moved with great wariness. He had already contracted to marry Edward IV's daughter, Elizabeth of York, in a bid to pacify the Yorkist faction and could not therefore impugn the legitimacy of the rule of either Edward IV or Edward V. Indeed, for the most part, he put a legal stop on punitive measures by an act preventing anyone being punished for supporting a *de facto* monarch; and though many of those attainted for treason by the Yorkists were rehabilitated, only some thirty of Richard's supporters were attainted. Henry appointed his principal royal servants from among those who had supported Edward IV, thus avoiding the strife that previous changes of regime had created. His policy of preserving continuity of administration both in the localities and at Westminster owed much, therefore, to Edward's statesmanlike choices and to the fact that Richard had himself destroyed, in Hastings and Buckingham, the magnates who would have most resented a change of dynasty.

The finality of Bosworth was soon put to the test, all the same. In 1487, a bizarre conspiracy to pass off Lambert Simnel, a ten-year-old Oxford boy, as the Yorkist claimant, the young Earl of Warwick, secured the support of the Marquis of Dorset, the Earl of Lincoln and not only Edward IV's widow but her sister, Margaret of Burgundy. Simnel was indeed crowned as Edward VI in Dublin, and Lincoln landed an army in Lancashire. It was almost Bosworth in reverse: a largely unopposed invasion faced by an unenthusiastically supported monarch. But there was no Stanley to betray Henry and he himself did not imitate Richard's heroics. Lincoln's defeat at Stoke in 1487 meant that never again did Henry have to face an army in the field.

The prolonged attempt of Yorkist interests at home and abroad during the 1490s to support the pretence that a French boatman, Perkin Warbeck, used as a sort of male model for a purveyor of fine clothes in Cork, was really Edward V's younger brother, revealed Henry at his most shrewdly competent. His agents (and in this at least he resembled his successors) systematically provided him with the names of the Warbeck plotters and when Henry suspected that his chamberlain, Sir William Stanley was implicated, he had him beheaded. There were other executions and hangings; and an itinerant commission investigated suspects in twenty-six counties. If Stanley's execution was a less spectacular exercise of royal power than Edward IV's similar process against his own brother, Clarence, in 1477, it was more forthright. Whereas Clarence was done away with in secret, to pass into immortality by way of the legend that he drowned in a butt of malmsey, Stanley was openly destroyed by an avowed and public act of royal power. That the Warbeck operation had failed by 1497 reveals the extent of the difference between Edward IV, falling captive to Warwick in 1469 and losing his kingdom altogether for a time in 1470, and Henry, unchivalrously destroying a great nobleman for a treason he had scarcely begun to commit.

The climax of Henry's careful war of attrition against even potential sources of disorder was the judicial murder of the imprisoned Earl of Warwick in 1499 for no better reason than that, while he lived, Yorkist conspirators would go on invoking his name. The king's diplomacy, too, was designed to distance him from his nobility. He was careful to enter the Tudors in the register of the dynasties of Europe: he married his son to Catherine of Aragon, daughter of the rising monarch of Spain, and his daughter, Margaret, to James IV of Scotland.

Throughout his reign, Henry worked systematically through a council of varying membership and a number of committees, continuing the process of making the operations of government as secret as possible. Unlike his Yorkist and Lancastrian predecessors, he did not allow power to be concentrated in too few hands. In relying more closely than had been usual during the two previous centuries on members of the knightly class to ensure better control of the localities he was in fact 'medievalising' rather than 'modernising' the monarchy. The myth that Henry VII employed 'new' men of low status meant little more than that, like Henry I, of whom the same complaint had been made, he made use of able though in the main still largely aristocratic servants whose loyalty was to himself rather than to some great territorial family.

He was of course making use of the prevailing winds. The old aristocracy had not disappeared; but the older generation of aristocrats who had not killed one another off had pretty well died out, and he himself made few new peerages, so that by 1509 the Duke of Norfolk was the only member of that rank in all England. In a century when to be forty was to be old, and to die much earlier than that in battle or on the block was the main occupational risk of aristocratic status, there was a sense in which most of Henry's subjects were 'new' men. By 1500, Agincourt was already two or three generations away for most people. The king himself was the step-grandson, and his wife, Elizabeth, the great-niece, of Henry V and by the end of the century both were nearing their forties. All but a handful of those who had been adult when the 'Wars of the Roses' had begun in 1455 were, by 1500, almost certainly dead. Men were growing less accustomed to a society whose principal occupation was foreign war combined with domestic violence.

Henry himself had no taste for foreign adventure, if only because its cost would put him at the mercy of both lords and commons. Like Edward IV, he put troops on to French soil and withdrew them on being offered, at the treaty of Etaples of 1492, an annual pension. But unlike Edward he had a more calculated aim, that of dissuading the French king from aiding the Warbeck conspirators, and in this he was successful. Apart from this windfall, he systematically acquired wealth in ways that earned him a reputation for miserly meanness and extortion and gave rise to the legend that he bequeathed his son untold riches. In 1486 he resumed possession of many crown lands previously alienated and gained a good deal from the confiscated estates of his enemies. He acquired the lands of the Yorkist earldoms of March and Warwick and annexed to the crown the duchies of Cornwall and Chester. He profited, too, from the fact that the Earl of Northumberland was a minor and therefore a royal ward, an event from which the Percies never recovered either in wealth or influence. He made a good income by demanding recognisances of good behaviour from the less reliable of the nobles and by imposing fines on magnates for breaches of the law. He ensured that he collected a satisfactory sum from them by first of all fixing a high figure and then graciously reducing it to the amount he had all along wanted. As well as increasing his income by such means he also increased royal authority.

He revived all the old medieval apparatus of feudal dues. Aids came back for special royal expenses, such as the marriage of his son, as did the profitable enjoyment of wardships, escheats, and payments to the crown whenever an heir entered upon his inheritance. It is a testimony to the efficacy of Norman and Angevin institutions that it was not by innovation but by a reversion to them that the Tudor monarchy took England from the fifteenth century into the sixteenth. Parliament was on the whole acquiescent; by avoiding war and exploiting the resources of a feudal sovereign he did not have to ask it for too much money and used it principally to add authority to his more significant acts of state.

Yet Henry could never be sure he had not laboured in vain. Like his successor, and his grand-daughter, Mary, he had little luck in the business of parenthood. In 1502 his elder son, Arthur, died at the age of sixteen and all now depended on the survival of the eleven-year-old prince Henry. The king was alarmed enough to make several attempts, when already in his elderly mid-forties, to represent himself as a highly eligible widower. But the young Henry grew up into exceptionally vigorous manhood; and his untroubled accession as Henry VIII in 1509 marked the conclusion of a period during which kings had seven times been driven from the throne by force and in which five sovereigns and two heirs to the throne had died by violence.

DEATH AND SURVIVAL

Famine, Pestilence, Revolt

THE social and political instability of the 150 years after 1307 reflected a widespread economic dislocation which gives to the whole period an appearance of unrelieved gloom. Yet, though there were undoubtedly (and occasionally literally) ill winds blowing across England during that time, as well as across most of Europe, they did not blow all the time and they were not such ill winds that they blew nobody any good. Indeed, it could well be argued that those who survived the worst of their effects did rather well out of them. England was a richer country by 1500 than in 1300; and if that wealth was concentrated in fewer hands, it was also probably better to be a villager in fifteenth-century England than it had been earlier, or was to be for several centuries to come. There was less surplus labour and therefore less poverty in rural England in 1500 than there was again until the end of the nineteenth century and the basic diet of the poor was to show little improvement on the standard attained in the fifteenth century until the beginning of the twentieth.

The heart of the matter was that, by 1300, the population was outgrowing the capacity of the soil to feed it. Yields began to fall. Intensive ploughing, coupled with a chronic lack of manure, had impoverished even the best soils; indeed, the fall in yield was most noticeable in the best ploughlands, which had been cultivated the longest. In areas of lower yield, brought under the plough since the Conquest, the effect was often that villages and hamlets began to be abandoned after 1300, particularly in the Yorkshire dales and the poorer chalklands of Hampshire and Wiltshire. Of other villages it seems that not until the beginning of the nineteenth century were some of them again as populous as they had been in 1300.

During the thirteenth century there had been a boom in land values. Competition had become so acute that the size of the average holding had diminished even though the total amount of land in cultivation had increased. Worse still, an increasing number of men were without land at all. But, by 1300, the boom was ending. As yields fell, so did land values, since by that time the profitability of land had come greatly to depend, both in the demesne and in villein holdings, on the sale of surplus product for the market. As the yields fell, more people, especially the poorest, began to suffer undernourishment, disease and perhaps even starvation. Famine prevailed in parts of the country in at least five years between 1271 and 1312; really critical were the bad harvests from 1315 to 1322. In 1315–17, England, like many continental countries, lost virtually the whole of two harvests, so that the price of cereals soared. Since the beginning of the thirteenth century too, the climate of north-western Europe had worsened, becoming colder and wetter; the sun shone so little that saltpans sometimes failed to dry and there was a shortage of salt for preserving meat for the winter.

It was among a population already thus affected by over-population and malnutrition that the Black Death made its first appearance, at Melcombe Regis, now part of Weymouth, in the late summer of 1348. The epidemic had spread slowly across the world's trading routes, by land and sea, from Central Asia, where it had struck first in 1338. Its ravages were not confined to the years 1348–9; less virulent outbreaks occured in the early 1360s and the mid 1370s. There were local outbreaks at various times in the fifteenth century and it did not finally disappear until after its last manifestation as the Great Plague of 1665. The bacillus of the disease was carried far and wide from Central Asia by infected black rats and by the black rats' fleas. The latter could find their way into cargoes of merchandise such as grain or cloth, in which they could survive for several weeks and thus spread the disease independently of the rats.

Plague manifested itself in three ways. The bubonic form began with boils or 'buboes', swellings of the lymphatic glands in groin, armpit or neck, and was quickly followed by vivid spots and rashes caused by the breaking of blood vessels beneath the skin. If the buboes burst within a week, the victim might survive, provided he could endure the agonising pain for so long. Normally, he was dead within five or six days. More lethal was the pneumonic variant of the disease. This produced violent fever, continuous coughing up of blood, and death within three days. This form, because of the coughing, was highly infectious. There was a third, septicaemic, form: transmitted from one victim to another by the human flea, it so infected the bloodstream that it could kill within a matter of hours.

How many were killed by the Black Death is impossible accurately to determine. One may suppose the population to have been between 3.5 and 4 million before the Black Death. If, to the deaths of the years 1348–9, are added those caused by later fourteenth-century outbreaks, the overall result could well have been to reduce the population by up to fifty per cent. It is a not unreasonable guess that, between 1348 and 1380, the Black Death and the later recurrences of plague killed between 1.5 and 2 million people.

The extent of the Black Death can be illustrated only by random samples from various parts of the country, bearing in mind that some areas were virtually untouched by it. In Shaftesbury in Dorset, four successive vicars died between November 1348 and May 1349. In one Bristol parish, the parson had to add an extra half-acre to his graveyard without proper authority, so great was the sudden increase in the number to be buried. When the miller in one Hertfordshire manor was struck down, his mill was declared valueless because no tenants remained alive to use it. In Farnham, Surrey, whose lord was the Bishop of Winchester, so many beasts were handed over to his reeve in consideration of heriots or reliefs due when tenants died that he had to pasture them on part of the demesne land; buyers were so few and prices so low that it was not possible to sell more than some of the twenty-six horses, fifty-seven oxen, fifty-four cows, twenty-six bullocks and twenty-six sheep which dead tenants' heirs handed over to him. At Westminster Abbey, they buried the Abbot and twenty-seven of the monks on one day. In one manor near Cambridge, twenty out of forty-two tenants died; in a second, thirty-three out of fifty-eight; in a third, thirty-five out of fifty; yet in two others hardly anyone died. In Lincoln, one hundred and five properties changed hands in twelve months owing to deaths from plague, the equivalent to the total for nine normal years. At the Cistercian abbey of Meaux in Yorkshire, the Abbot and five monks died on one day and shortly afterwards the prior, the cellarer, the bursar and seventeen other monks died too. At Cuxham, in Oxfordshire, when the reeve died in March 1349, one successor died in April, another in June and another in July.

Not all the deaths of 1348–9 were due to the plague, since the normal death rate was high; and the more cautious historian will nowadays say no more about the Black Death than that it accelerated economic trends which would have taken place without it. It is possible to suggest that it was a timely, or 'purgative' catastrophe, since the country was seriously over-populated. Though the extinction of some villages, notably in south Lincolnshire, was hastened, in others there was rapid recovery in the 1350s because the dead could so easily be replaced and because many of them had been under-employed. Although they were obviously a special case, new priests were notably easy to find even though the death rate among them had been high. To serve the 8,670 English parishes in 1348, there was an available total of at least 15,000 priests, so that at the height of the Black Death, every vacant benefice was filled within three weeks.

The calamities of the first half of the fourteenth century began a long period of low prices and rising wages. Prices which, before 1348, had steadily risen (subject to great seasonal fluctuations according to the yield of particular harvests) sank by ten to fifteen per cent by 1370 and only occasionally rose above this level for the next century. By contrast, there was a continuous rise in wages from 1325 until after the middle of the fifteenth century.

These trends brought drastic changes in the countryside. To protect themselves against the narrowing of their profit margins, many land-lords abandoned the cultivation of their demesne and farmed it out to individual 'farmers' for a term of years. This ensured the landlord a fixed income for the term of the contract, leaving the farmer to cope with seasonal fluctuations of price and the general upward movement of wages. Even so, by the fifteenth century, whenever contracts were renewed, the value of the farm had to be fixed at a lower figure than before. During the Wars of the Roses, political motives were added to economic. To secure themselves followers in the political, military and legal struggles of the time, many great landlords leased out part of their demesne lands for a whole life or a series of lives. In addition, less desirable parts of the demesne might be let out in small parcels to individual villagers. Demesne lands did not disappear altogether; but the farmer in the more modern sense of the word had arrived.

The practice of villeins commuting their work services by payment of rent was already common in the twelfth century. By the end of the thirteenth many villeins were allowed to render either rent or labour services and in such cases paid rent more often than they rendered services. In the fourteenth and fifteenth centuries commutation proceeded at such a pace that by the sixteenth century both labour services and most of the personal liabilities of villeins had disappeared. Attempts to stop the process were noticeable only in the years immediately after the Black Death. With population in decline, the only way to keep villeins was to lower rents and release them from services; otherwise, with the trends all in their favour, villeins could refuse to do work services or simply go elsewhere. In the thirteenth century men had been too plentiful; now they were scarce. When villeins fled, landlords might have to parcel the land among lesser men for lower rents, without demanding labour services. Otherwise, the land could go uncultivated. For the lower ranks of rural society, the Black Death and subsequent visitations of plague made the late fourteenth century a time of opportunity for all who were lucky enough to stay alive. With the fall in population, those smallholders and the cottagers who survived the pestilence were, if they were provident, at last able to acquire some land. And, for those who continued to work as labourers, wages on average more or less doubled. Thus it can be said that the fourteenth and fifteenth centuries were both a time of general agricultural decline and 'the golden age of the English peasantry'.

Naturally, landlords, particularly the middling sort, tried to stop these tendencies. Parliament passed a Satute of Labourers in 1351 in an effort to freeze prices and wages and to prevent labourers, bond or free, from changing their residences or breaking their contracts. It may or may not have worked for a while, but even in the short run it proved ineffective. Suggestive figures show a ploughman who earned 2s (10p) before 1348, was earning 7s (35p) in 1349–50 and 10s 6d (53p) the year after that. A year later he was still earning 6s 3d (31p); and in the seven following years he earned 7s 6d (38p) a year.

It has been argued therefore that those who took part in that other spectacular fourteenth-century event, the Peasants' Revolt of 1381, had little to revolt about. The rebels had not, however, read any economic history books, and thought they had much to complain of. There was undoubtedly resistance by landlords to the tide that was flowing against them and the poll taxes of 1377–81, imposed by the first parliament of Richard II's reign, can be regarded as a sign of this. A poll tax was a graduated direct tax upon every person in the land over sixteen years of age and thus an attempt, for the first time, to transfer part of the tax burden from the rich and propertied to the poor and unpropertied, who, it was perhaps felt, had 'never had it so good'. And it was the action of the people of Brentwood in Essex in driving from the town a commissioner come to enquire into evasions of the poll tax that set the Revolt in motion.

Within a week of the Brentwood incident, men all over Essex attacked manor houses and burnt the manorial rolls which recorded the dues owed by villeins to lords. Simultaneously, a rebel army in Kent seized Rochester, Maidstone and Canterbury and, under its leader, Wat Tyler, encamped on Blackheath on 12 June 1381 and listened to a famous sermon by the 'mad priest', John Ball. Declaring that nothing would go right in England until there was 'neither vassal nor lord' he asked the memorable question,

> When Adam delved and Eve span
> Who was then the gentleman?

He went on, 'For what reason do they thus hold us in bondage? . . . They are clothed in velvet and fine stuffs . . . while we are forced to wear poor cloth. They have handsome seats and manors when we must brave the wind and rain in our labours in the fields'.

A day later, they passed over London Bridge into the City of London. Here, they attacked Flemish traders on the grounds that they were draining the country's wealth; burnt down the Savoy Palace in the Strand because it was the residence of John of Gaunt, Duke of Lancaster, the acting head of government; and expressed their feelings about the laws of England by destroying the legal profession's headquarters in the Temple. At Tower Hill, they beheaded the Archbishop of Canterbury, who added to the offence of being the head of the ecclesiastical system the greater one of being Lord Chancellor. To complete their protest, they beheaded the Lord Treasurer as well.

On 15 June 1381, after first publicly confessing his sins in Westminster Abbey, the fourteen-year-old King Richard rode out to the rebels at Smithfield. Tyler made a long angry speech, there was an altercation with the king's guards, and Tyler was killed, chiefly through the action of Thomas Walworth, the Lord Mayor of London. That no further bloodshed occurred seems due to Richard's decision to ride forward to his rebellious subjects with a promise to give them all they desired if they would follow him. He then led them to Clerkenwell, issuing pardons and charters of freedom. The rebels, apparently believing they had won, then dispersed.

Revolt had also taken place in East Anglia. The prior of the monastery at Bury St Edmunds was beheaded and his monks compelled to grant charters of liberty to the rebels. The monks of St Albans were also forced to issue charters of freedom. The Lord Chief Justice was beheaded, partly for the offence of presiding over the Court of King's Bench, which administered the common law, and partly because he happened to be in East Anglia at the time. Led by a dyer called Geoffrey Lister and a knight called Sir Roger Bacon, rebels took control of Norwich, the second largest city in England, and were put down only because the city's bishop, a man of warlike character, led an array against them, defeated them, and had Lister hanged.

The rebels achieved nothing for their efforts. The king's promises were quickly broken. The new Chief Justice, with Richard accompanying him, went through the rebellious shires organising hangings. The manorial courts took the legal view that the rebellion and the burning of the rolls had caused all land to revert to the lords and that therefore villeins could receive them back only after payment of fines. The fact that the fines seem to have been paid is a further indication that these were not poor, half-starved rebels but robust men of some substance whose quality is misrepresented by the phrase 'Peasants' Revolt'.

The Peasants' Revolt, therefore, neither reversed old trends nor initiated new ones. One may suspect that in relation to economic factors it was a protest against the past as much as against the present, and a giving of notice that any attempt to re-impose that past would be resisted. Its connection with the burdens of villein tenure seems slight. The areas most affected, East Anglia, East Essex and Kent, contained only a minority of villeins and were traditionally freer than most parts of the country. It was an urban as much as a rural revolt. Many who took part in it were craftsmen, like the leader struck down by the Lord Mayor at Smithfield. He was, after all, Wat the Tyler, not Wat the Husbandman. Its real causes seem to have been wider. The attack on lawyers uncovered the kind of resentment that in the twentieth century would have been directed against politicians, since it was lawyers who then made 'laws' rather than politicians in parliament: Shakespere's Falstaff was to suggest two hundred years later that the first thing to do on taking over England would be to 'hang all the lawyers'. The presence of John Ball among the rebels suggested the hostility of many ordinary people towards the wealth and power of the church. There was more to the Peasants' Revolt than either objections to an inefficiently collected poll tax or to a villeinage that hardly existed in the places where the Revolt principally took place.

Its connection with the virtual disappearance of the old style villeinage in many parts of the country by the end of Henry V's reign is also unclear. Certainly, in the forty years after 1381, an increasing number of villeins simply moved away, to find work in a town or a freeholding in a distant village. Deprived not only of villeins, but of men willing to give labour services, and plagued by high wages and low prices, more and more lords leased their demesne to tenant farmers, resulting in a splitting up of demesne lands that made labour services impossible to organise. Thus villeinage declined, whether as a form of land tenure or as a form of personal status. Those who descended from former villeins came to be known as copyholders, tenants holding their land in accordance with the terms of a title deed which was a 'copy' of an agreement between tenant and lord, recorded in the manorial court. However, by the end of the fifteenth century, lawsuits involving copyhold were being dealt with in the ordinary courts: the villein had made good his escape from the justice of the lord to that of the king. The admission of copyholders into the ranks of the political nation was, however, long delayed. They did not get the right to vote for their county MPs until the Reform Act of 1832. Their economic status is nevertheless impossible to define from the fifteenth century onwards. These legally liberated peasant farmers might be, or become, men of substance by acquiring various pieces of land and take over the influence in the village once exercised by the lord of the manor. Others were much poorer men to whom the richer peasant seemed something of a grasping *kulak*.

Commercial Loss and Gain

Radical changes took place in the structure of English trade and commerce during the fourteenth and fifteenth centuries. They were accompanied by much uncertainty, caused by political interference and disorder at home, war abroad, and the intermittent dislocation and depression which affected the greater part of Europe for most of the time. There was, overall, a decline in the wool trade and an increased trade in cloth; but both the production of wool and the manufacture of cloth underwent important shifts of location. Though pestilence caused trade to contract by drastically reducing the population, the fact that many of the fewer who survived were the richer for it meant that it did not contract in every respect. Trade in luxury goods was increasing by 1500.

Exports of raw wool reached their peak around 1300 and then began to decline. Total production declined also, despite the sustained foreign demand and the additional market provided by the growing English cloth industry. The decline in population suggests one reason; but this was most relevantly reflected in the leasing out of the Cistercian and other sheep grazing estates in Yorkshire, Lincolnshire and the duchy of Lancaster. This meant that what had formerly been well-organised big business in a few concentrated areas became a matter of small peasant flocks widely dispersed throughout the country. Whereas Hull and

Boston had been the leading places of export for the wool of the large estates of Yorkshire and Lincolnshire, the best wool now went through Southampton and London, clipped from the backs of the sheep of the Cotswolds and Wiltshire. Both Flemings and Italians were to be found purchasing wool from the sheep farmers whose new prosperity is still commemorated by the churches and domestic architecture of such towns as Stow-in-the-Wold and Chipping Campden.

Wool exports to parts of Europe other than Italy were increasingly funnelled through English-owned Calais by a monopolistic organisation of English merchants known as the Company of the Staple, established there in 1363. There was a political reason for concentrating woollen exports at a 'staple', a word originally signifying a military supply depot. Edward III needed the Staplers to ensure him the solid financial backing of English merchants after he had bankrupted the Italian banking houses of Bardi and Peruzzi of Florence in the 1340s by defaulting on the loans he had contracted with them to pay for his war. The king gained handsome sums from the Staplers in return for their right to a monopoly of the wool export trade; and the Staplers farmed the customs for the crown, to its great convenience and their own profit.

Though it was important in the long run that the Staplers loaded their cargoes on to English ships, whereas, before 1300, most wool export had gone out in German, French or Flemish bottoms, wool was overall a declining export. The North virtually ceased to export its wool and the trade through Hull and Boston fell dramatically. Southampton's days as a great wool exporter were past by the end of the fifteenth century, its exports then having dropped by two-thirds. Even London, on which the Staplers chose to concentrate, exported less wool by a third than it had done in 1300. By contrast, by the middle of the fifteenth century at least as much wool was being exported in the form of woollen cloth as was being exported in the raw state. One encouraging factor for the native cloth industry was that exported cloth paid a much lower customs duty than wool exports, so that English cloth could undercut its continental competitors in their own markets.

Weaving may well have attracted many landless men to urban clothmaking in the late-thirteenth century, or escaping villeins in the early fourteenth. But it was only in its early stages, when its markets were probably more local than international, that the cloth industry was predominantly urban, at such towns as York, Lincoln, Coventry, Oxford, Stamford and Colchester. By the first half of the fourteenth century, its future lay in the country. The reason was the adoption by clothmakers of water power, hitherto confined to corn milling. The fulling mills used water-driven hammers to clean, thicken and felt the rough cloth, thus replacing the traditional method by which men stamped hard on it with their bare feet. The dependence of the fulling process on water took the industry out of the towns into country places where there were suitable running streams. In doing so, it also liberated the trade from the restrictive practices of the urban weavers' gilds. Places where waterpower was available were usually in good sheep country, too, and therefore conveniently close to the industry's basic raw material. Clothmaking flourished most in the fifteenth century in the West Riding, on the Mendips, on the downs above the Kennet and Thames, and in the Stour valley in Suffolk and Essex. From these areas came cheap serviceable cloth, exported all over Europe as far as Novgorod and Constantinople.

The trade with Europe was still much under foreign control during the fifteenth century. Trade with the Mediterranean was dominated by the galleys of the Venetians and Genoese from about 1430 onwards, and that with the Baltic firmly in the hands of the Germans of the Hanse towns. The Hansards had, since the thirteenth century, enjoyed privileges in England similar to those deriving from the so-called Capitulations imposed by nineteenth- and twentieth-century Europeans on imperial Turkey and China; they enjoyed virtual immunity from the law. By the fifteenth century, their walled headquarters, at the Steelyard by the Thames near Cannon Street, was virtually an inviolate foreign state, planted in the midst of England's mercantile capital. Hostility to foreigners was one further element in the unrest in London and elsewhere at the time of the Peasants' Revolt, and it was in the crisis year of 1450 that Hanse merchants drove English merchants out of the Baltic, and English fishermen from the waters of Iceland.

The Englishmen who 'adventured' abroad to sell their cloth to the Netherlands, therefore grouped together to form what became, after 1407, the chartered body called Merchant Adventurers, though for most of the fifteenth century they conducted their operations independently. Most London merchants dealt in cloth or wool, and Merchant Adventurers might also be members of the wool Staple. The dominant element included the London Mercers, importing an increasing quantity of silk and linen; members of other London Companies, such as Grocers, Drapers and Haberdashers were also prominent. They thus had enough capital and enterprise to compete with the Hansards on a scale beyond that of the less commercially powerful fourteenth-century exporters of Boston and Hull. London was soon exporting more broadcloth than all foreign merchants put together and almost as much as the total export of all other English ports. This meant that by 1500 two-thirds of all England's exports went through London. Its close association with Antwerp, where the Merchant Adventurers had their overseas headquarters, contributed to making that city the commercial metropolis of all Europe.

To venture overall generalisations about the economic fortunes of Englishmen in these two centuries is thus more than usually hazardous. Violence, rapine and piracy, added to pestilence, disorganised European trade in the mid-fourteenth century and drastically reduced the buying power of the rich export markets of northern France and parts of

Flanders. The decline of wool exports harmed some at home; the rise of cloth exports benefited first some areas and then others. Against the arrogance of the Hansards must be set the energy of London merchants in general. The worst time was probably the period when political disorder was also at its worst. In 1447, Sandwich, in Kent, exported 182 sacks of wool, but in 1449 only 25; and overall wool exports in the 1450s were only half the already lowered rate of 1400. Cloth exports fell in mid-century by nearly a third; imports and exports of other commodities all showed a decline. Nevertheless, a general recovery of trade began during the reign of Edward IV and continued unchecked for another hundred years.

The years of pestilence, by reducing the population, had brought better nutrition. The working people of the fifteenth century had a better intake of fish and meat protein than those of the nineteenth. Not only was more meat being eaten; higher wages meant a greater consumption of wool and leather goods. The England of the fifteenth century may have had a contracting economy, but it was not simply sagging. Even the overall decline in cloth exports was in proportion to the fall in population; they retained their monetary value and enjoyed a steady market at home. Between the 1330s and 1500 the assessed taxable wealth of the nation increased threefold. Though Lancashire and the north-western counties remained poor, there was a great increase of wealth south of the line from the Severn to the Wash, particularly in the south-east. London increased its proportion of the assessed wealth of the country from two per cent to nine. Though Oxford, Winchester and Lincoln declined, Coventry and East Anglia flourished and new prosperity came to the Cotswolds and to Wiltshire. Bristol, though less of an exporter than earlier, became an important shipbuilding city; there was a brisk increase of coastwise shipping on the east coast, from Berwick, Newcastle, Hull, Yarmouth and Lynn, almost all of it concerned, significantly enough, with internal trade. Coal and iron were mined in Durham, and one forge in Weardale was producing two tons of iron a week.

The Hundred Years War itself was a far from unprofitable enterprise. From the English point of view, it had the great advantage of being fought wholly on French soil. The rewards which Shakespeare caused Henry V to promise on the eve of Agincourt to whoever should 'outlive this day and come safe home' omitted the most probable one, which was financial. Pay was good and expenses small, since the English army lived off the French people, their lands and property. The astuter captains often did well on the side, either by defrauding their less quick-witted soldiery, or by indenting upon their superiors for pay for soldiers who had died in previous engagements. The great glory in defeating a noble opponent lay in the fact that, the more noble he was, the larger the ransom to be exacted for his release. Chivalric ideals required that no ransom be so great as to leave the captive's family destitute of their inheritance; but the captive's powers of negotiation on the subject were limited. Ransom money was divided between the captor and his military superiors, everybody, up to and including the king himself, taking a cut. Sometimes captives were sold direct to the crown for a lump sum payment. Though the French captured some Englishmen, all the battles in which men of high rank were made captive were won by the English. The French came nowhere near the English total of noble captives, which included three kings (one French and two Scottish) and a large number of royal princes. And although in the end the English lost, the French got rid of them partly by paying them handsomely to go away.

Booty, too, was a principal objective. Civilians were despoiled extensively and the English gained much from the French noblemen's habit of taking their jewels and plate with them on their campaigns. Nor must it be forgotten that, for a quarter of a century, almost all the officers who sailed with Henry V's armies held, and profited from possession of, a town, a castle or even whole provinces of France. Relatively short though it was, the English conquest of France had been, in its way, almost as profitable to the occupiers as the Norman Conquest had been to the first followers of William the Conqueror.

There may well have been a connection between manifestations of discontent among the lower orders and the fact that the profits of this lengthy undertaking were imperfectly distributed. The Crown paid for the army's equipment and for part of its wage bill; and this meant heavy taxation, direct and indirect. Worse still, when the king made a profit (and the crown made none after the death of Henry V) he kept it to himself; the notion of a separate budget for the expenses of state as distinct from the royal household was yet to evolve. The cost of the war bore heaviest on the French. It bore hard on the Flemings too, because a stiff duty was put on the export of wool, to the detriment of the Flemish cloth industry and the benefit of the English; and it bore heavily on the English villager throughout the period from 1336 to 1453. But while the Flemings and the French had nothing to show for their losses, it is fair to assume that some of the English people's taxes percolated back to them through the lavish spending of those who had done well out of the war. Like their marauding Saxon, Viking and Norman forbears, the English of the fourteenth and fifteenth centuries made substantial material gains as a people out of invading and capturing other people's lands and properties. And the great English landed aristocracy came out of it richer than ever.

4
THE LIGHT AND THE DARK

Nobles and Gentlemen

BY the later middle ages, the main social divisions that were to prevail almost unchanged into the twentieth century had already emerged out of the slow dissolution of Norman and Angevin 'feudalism'. The major cleavage was already that which divided the inferior majority who worked from the superior minority who did not. The conviction, inherited from the ancient world, that manual work, or any kind of 'practical' or 'useful' work, was the mark of persons so low in status that they were not considered fit for membership of the political nation proved almost indestructible; it could be said to have survived even after formal political rights had been conceded to such people in the nineteenth and twentieth centuries.

Throughout English history, all those who were above this dividing line were members of one ruling class. To divide them into aristocracy and middle class is in many respects artificial. The middle class mostly consisted of persons connected with, and dependent upon, the aristocracy. They imitated the aristocracy; and their desperate anxiety to join it is an important reason why an aristocracy continued to exist.

Nevertheless, the later middle ages saw a sophistication of the distinctions between the families above the dividing line. Originally, they were all thought of as noble (the *nobilitas*); but by the end of the fifteenth century it was evident that there was a small group of 'great' nobles, and a large group of 'lesser' nobles. At the end of the thirteenth century, the nobles consisted of about a dozen hereditary earls, together with another three thousand owners of land worth £20 a year or more. By the end of the fifteenth, there were about fifty or sixty lords whose rank and privileges marked them off distinctly from the rest. It was in this period that the hereditary ranks of duke, marquess and viscount were invented, and the old, vague title 'baron' now denoted only the lowest rank of the peerage. From about 1500 onwards, it was only by an excess alike of courtesy and inaccuracy that one would describe any one outside this narrow circle as 'noble'. Another manifestation of this new development was that only persons with these highest ranks were entitled to the king's personal summons to parliament which, during these centuries, was permanently separated into a House of personally summoned Lords, distinct from the elected House of Commons. This made the terms 'lord' and 'peer of parliament' synonymous.

The consequence of this more rigid hierarchy, associated as it was with the Crown's anxiety to reward the great nobles who commanded its armies against the French, was not so much that a middle class 'rose' but that in a sense it 'fell', because it lost its title to nobility. This was the more irritating in that, economically, members of the middling classes were often more influential than the lesser nobility. But they could always derive consolation from the fact that they were still officially designated 'armigerous' and, confirmed civilians though most of them were, entitled to a coat of arms. They were increasingly careful, too, to preserve the designation that proclaimed their armigerous status and their degree within it: a knight ranked above an esquire, and an esquire above a gentleman (or *generosus*). It is clearly because 'gentleman' was once the lowest armigerous rank that punctilious letter writers, observing that their correspondent was not 'Sir John Smith', long preferred to write 'John Smith, Esq.' on the envelope. Though not a knight, he was obviously a gentleman (one would not otherwise be writing to him); but it was safer and more courteous to treat him as someone rather more than a *mere* 'gentleman'. The fashion for coats of arms was considerable enough in Tudor times to lead to 'Visitations' by the heralds to suppress their unauthorised use; these continued at intervals until 1686.

The artificiality of these distinctions at the lower end of the table of degree might well reveal itself in the courts, where accuracy of description was mandatory. It was not unknown for a litigant to be described as 'James Brown, yeoman *alias* merchant *alias* gent'. A yeoman was not *generosus* for so long as he worked on his land himself; a merchant was not *generosus* for so long as he was only a merchant and had no land. But that one man, originally a yeoman, should at some stage of his life be something of a merchant also, and be on the verge of ceasing to work his land himself, because he had become rich enough to employ others to do it for him, is a reminder that ultimately the system was based on wealth. Gentility, it was said, was 'ancient riches'; but then as always, present wealth was often a sufficient entrance fee. Few families, whether of the major or the minor *nobilitas*, were as ancient as all that.

Thrusting ambition, however, was considered bad. Quite apart from the obvious fact that the ambitions of great men in the fifteenth (and sixteenth) centuries all too often led them to the executioner's block, it was felt that social disaster would result if men rejected the principle of 'degree'. This suggests how much men thought they had to fear from the ambitions of their equals and inferiors. The idea of degree protected status in other ways. A man should not be asked to demean himself by performing actions appropriate to someone of a lower degree. One cleric claimed that since by reason of his great learning he was *generosus*, and thus a gentleman, it was improper that he should be asked to engage in the menial task of preaching sermons in church.

The fluidity and uncertainty of the social scene required the utmost care in the matter of right designation. One sought the protection of a great lord by laying it on thick: 'Right high and mighty prince and my right good lord'. Even a mere gentleman was addressed by an inferior as 'Right Worshipful'. The king addressed his Lords as 'Right trusty and well beloved' and his Commons as 'faithful and loving hearts'. This did not merely indicate a hope that the Lords would be trusty, and feel beloved, and that the Commons would have such faith and love in their hearts that they would not grudge voting the king taxes. The first step to winning a man's support was to pay due deference to his rank.

The pretensions of the gentry and their anxiety to secure the patronage of a 'good lord' who would protect and advance their interests was a natural consequence of aristocratic dominance during a period of weak kingship. With the crown only occasionally capable of exerting its control, the nobility were in one sense free and in another almost compelled to pursue their interests with more than ordinary zeal. Local aristocratic feuding was endemic throughout the fifty years after 1422. The term 'Wars of the Roses' is no doubt misleading, since the time spent in actually fighting the battles that took place in the course of the contest between Lancaster and York amounted all told to about three weeks or so in the whole of the thirty years after 1461. But the pitched battles like Northampton and Tewkesbury, or even Towton and Bosworth, were only part of the story. It was a time of frequent trespasses, assaults, sieges of country houses and ugly brawlings. The local war waged round Bath and Taunton between the Courtenays and the Boleyns, the violent feuding in Yorkshire between the Percies and the Nevilles, and the freebooting activities of Suffolk's henchman Tailboys, were among the more striking examples of how the normal peace of at least some parts of the countryside might be shattered. That many areas escaped, and most were only intermittently disturbed, was less significant in determining what people thought about the age they lived in and what they wanted done about it. Disorder does not cease to be important merely by not being universal.

In pursuing their feuds, the aristocrats needed civilian as well as armed supporters; and the only defence the gentry had against the dangers of aristocratic injustice and depredation was aristocratic protection. The most famous manifestation of this was the practice of 'livery and maintenance'. This was largely a new version of the earlier notion, based on military service, private justice and land tenure, that every man had to have a lord; but since this was now a voluntary contract, based on the payment of fees, it has been christened 'bastard feudalism'. The term is perhaps unnecessarily opprobrious. It could equally be called 'pre-natal patronage' since patronage is what it mostly was. It derived from the wartime practice by which captains signed indentures with their men in order to 'retain' their services, often in theory for life. This practice spilled over into peacetime, with the difference that whereas in wartime the king paid the retainer's fees, in peace his 'lord' paid them. The practice once more took on a military character during the Wars of the Roses, though even then the retainer's duty was to serve his lord first and foremost in peace. The employment of men as temporary retainers was also common, though this had been illegal since the reign of Richard II. It was seen as particularly offensive that retainers wore their lord's livery, thus seeming to constitute a private army. Hence, it was against the law for liveries to be worn in peacetime or outside the lord's own household. When Edward IV and Henry VII made their own legal enactments against livery and maintenance they were reasserting old law, not proclaiming new.

To have a number of retainers on call was principally to assure the attendance of a sufficient following when the lord was in England. Retainers were part-time members of a noble household and often themselves of noble birth, a procedure parallel to noblemen's habit of sending their sons to be pages in other noble households. Retainers would ride with their lord when he toured his estate, went on a pilgrimage, or when he was summoned to court, council or parliament. Not to be attended by a large following would have been to admit not only to poverty but to an apparent lack of power over others.

The system was used to ensure that the great magnates had influence everywhere. They paid fees to the king's courtiers and to the principal officials in the great offices of state. Country gentry received annual fees or pensions from a nobleman to assure him of their loyalty in all matters. He was thus able to help his friends and thwart his enemies. To his clientèle he gave 'good lordship', advancing their fortunes along with his own. A fourteenth-century Earl of Devon had one hundred and thirty persons in livery; dependent upon him also were his five closest male relatives, seven highly esteemed knights, forty esquires, fifty-two yeomen, four minstrels, eight parsons, three unmarried women, six pages and fourteen lawyers. The consequence was that it was the beginning of worldly wisdom for any man who wished to advance his career and protect his interest to find a great noble to provide him with 'good lordship'. Some men were sufficiently concerned for their interests to accept retainer fees from two or three different lords without necessarily performing any particular service for any of them. In the relations between patron and client, as traditionally in those between master and servant, the 'exploitation' and advantage were not always as one-sided as they seem.

Good lordship often meant bad justice; or no justice at all. In the worst times, aristocratic feuding was a substitute for going to law. During less violent periods and in areas where violence was rare, both judges and juries could be overawed by armed retainers. This procedure would be resorted to by those who were too tempestuous, too short of ready cash, or whose cause was too dubious for them to rely on bribery. Outright bribery of juries was not always necessary. Since jurors were still expected to be witnesses as to fact, it was not unreasonable for my lord's man to inform the jury of 'the facts' beforehand. And where money did change hands, this at least meant that justice was being perverted (if it was) by something more civilised than the violence that went on at other times. Powerful men do not bribe men they can bully; nor are they content merely to bully men they can safely kill. To overawe the courts or to 'fix' their procedures was to recognise the court's intrinsic legality. Perverted royal courts were better than private courts of justice and better than the processes of armed vendetta. And if a strong king emerged again, royal justice might re-establish its independence. Even so, as late as the 1530s, enactments were still being passed to punish bribery of sheriffs and juries.

Custom and Usage of Noble Chivalry

It is difficult, when surveying the disruption of the two centuries after 1300 to accommodate such facts as that the reign of Richard II saw the re-emergence of English as a literary language for the first time since before the Norman Conquest, in Chaucer's Canterbury Tales; the building of Westminster Hall and of the naves of Winchester and Canterbury cathedrals; the painting of the Wilton Diptych; or that in Edward III's reign English perpendicular Gothic was established by the rebuilding of the choir at Gloucester, to reach its peak with the beginning of King's College Chapel in the reign of Henry VI. Yet there is a certain appropriateness in much of this aesthetic achievement. The Wilton Diptych and Westminster Hall celebrate the artistic and hieratic splendour within which Richard sought to embalm the idea of kingship. The rebuilding of the choir at Gloucester was Edward III's way of publicly hallowing the otherwise deeply sullied memory of his deplorable father, Edward II. The chapel at King's, like the foundation of Eton College, represents at once perpendicular Gothic at its best and, in its relative isolation, one of the few major architectural glories which fifteenth century England could set beside the achievements of the contemporary Florentine Renaissance.

It is perhaps Chaucer whose singular skill best illustrates the paradoxes of an age which all but the most elaborate studies are liable to represent as a time of gloom and uncertainty. The Canterbury Tales were the work of a sophisticated courtier and travelled diplomat. They depict a society secular, cheerful and boisterous. Almost the only emotions and values they sustain are the romantic and amorous ones derived from chivalry. It is clear enough that the church actually exists; but, save for the Poor Parson and the poor Oxford clerk, its representatives are a worldly Friar, a hunting Monk, an extremely ladylike Prioress, a lecherous official of the ecclesiastical courts, and a 'Pardoner' selling indulgences for cash, pretending that purchasers would, in consequence, not be punished for their sins. Chaucer's view of the church may be unfair; but it suggests what worldly men thought of it. His secular characters are as untouched by the religion of their day as the characters in a nineteenth-century French farce. The prosperous

Franklin, sometime knight of the shire, the much-husbanded Wife of Bath and the crafty Reeve, clearly belong to a society which it would be absurd to describe as deeply conscious either of sin or any other Christian mystery. Chaucer saw his fellows through the amused camera eye of a man chiefly at home at the elaborate court of Richard II; but it is significant that this period should have produced a cool portrayal of itself that is as bright and attractive, and as unemotional, as a coloured picture postcard.

The chivalric code which is glimpsed in Chaucer's poetry embodied various rules of behaviour which were in the first instance an attempt to civilise uncouth cavalry troopers. It broadened the basic imperative of the loyalty of a man to his leader to include loyalty to one's comrades-in-arms; and then further enlarged it to encompass the ideal of friendship. It sought to present the career of arms as a pursuit of justice rather than personal gain. The rebel Simon de Montfort was lamented after his death as the flower of knights because in his fight against Henry III he had loved right and hated wrong. The code nevertheless required a man to show audacity, and to have such skill with sword or lance as would enable him to perform the deeds of valour that would guarantee him a reputation for knightly prowess and honour. Knights were expected to adventure far and wide to establish such a reputation. The 'parfit gentil knight' of whom Chaucer wrote had displayed his knightly qualities in places as far away as Spain, Egypt, Russia and Asia Minor.

Chivalry was an attempt to limit the savagery of warfare. Noble opponents were to be fought by fair means and be treated honourably in defeat. The courtesies observed by Richard I and Saladin during the Third Crusade impressed men profoundly because they were thought to conform to such ideas. Richard was also an exemplar of the view that audacity, involving rashness, fearlessness and indomitability, was to be admired and that any attempt to avoid danger was shameful.

As a code for the guidance of a fighting aristocracy in their personal relations, particularly with their women, chivalry was on the whole a matter of one law for the rich and handsome in their dealings with one another, and with the occasionally-encountered helpless and harmless orphan, young girl or old woman, and another for their dealings with the majority of the human race. In practice, the sacking of cities, the destroying of crops, the violent affrays and the besieging of country houses were rather more typical than the rescue of the occasional distressed demoiselle. It was also a young man's creed and tended to implant youthful, immature ideas into the general European consciousness, since though they may claim to detest aristocrats, the lower ranks of society usually end up by imitating them. It was a code particularly appropriate to young men at a stage in life when they are particularly given to going about in close-knit gangs, to falling romantically in love with one kind of female in the intervals of seducing, or being seduced by, servant girls, and in indulging in self-display and bouts of aggressive violence. But chivalry flowered at a time when, since up to forty per cent of the population was usually under fifteen and men were old before they were forty-five, it was true to say that nearly all the world was young.

Almost all the decision-makers were certainly young. In not becoming kings of England until they had reached the advanced age of twenty-eight, both Henry V and Henry VII were unusual. Richard II began to be effective king of England at the age of fourteen. Edward III was eighteen when he secured personal control of government by his coup against Mortimer and brought confusion to affairs of state by surviving, sick and failing, into the senility of his sixty-fifth year. Just as Henry II had been an acknowledged commander of ability before he succeeded Stephen at the age of twenty-one, Edward IV was scarcely nineteen when he claimed the throne of Henry VI, but elderly and sick when he died at the age of forty-one. Henry VI was an old man when he died in 1471 at fifty. Henry VIII, coming to the throne as a golden boy of eighteen, almost paralysed the processes of government by living on into his dotage until he died at fifty-six.

Several of England's kings thus presided over government or commanded armies at an age when able twentieth-century young men would be thought fit only to captain a first eleven or to qualify for a trial as a university freshman. So, in the 1640s, Prince Rupert, Charles I's nephew, was a cavalry commander with a European reputation at an age when he might, in the twentieth century, have hoped for no higher glory than that of school prefect.

Rich young men, aware that time's chariot was bearing them rapidly towards an early death in any case, had therefore every incentive to express their personalities extravagantly and to defend their rights and make good their claims with vehement passion. In consequence, though chivalry gave Europe the youthful unrealities of romantic, idealised literature and art and of romantic, idealised love, it failed to equip its devotees with more than the irreducible minimum of compassion. Magnanimity was easy to display to a fallen knight on whose behalf a ransom might be expected. To kill such a defeated foe was not only a breach of the rules by which like protected like, but bad business. No such calculations demanded the display of courteous and piteous behaviour to a mere foot soldier. And by the middle of the fifteenth century, the men of chivalry, their military occupation gone, and their energies devoted to a jumble of angry quarrels about land and marriage and wardships, looked on the code chiefly as a source of nostalgia. It became a sentimental dwelling on battles long ago, most of which had probably never taken place. Sir Thomas Malory's great panegyric on chivalric ideals, *Le Morte D'Arthur*, was a late-fifteenth century funeral dirge for a past so unreal that it projected back into fanciful Arthurian times legends that had first been put together two hundred years earlier. Malory himself was not much of an advertisement for chivalric ideas in his own behaviour, one unkind version of his character being that he was 'a thug who died in prison'.

Nevertheless, chivalric ideas were not everywhere and always merely hypocritical or sentimental. Personal loyalty meant more to medieval men than to modern men, taught first and foremost to be loyal to the independent, omnipotent sovereign state of which they are passport holders. Fealty to a lord was the nearest most men of those centuries could get to a sense of public duty; and the parallel system, by which men would swear to be brothers-in-arms, might be their nearest approximation to a sense of obligation to their fellows. The swearing of such an oath might be solemnised by the two men concerned receiving communion together at mass. The obligations of a brotherhood-in-arms meant that each was bound to share all the spoils of war with the other, to assist the other in any civil or legal dispute, to defend the other's honour in all things and be a source from which his 'brother' might expect to receive honest counsel and intimate advice. These obligations were considered all but binding in law, and certainly in honour.

The various medieval orders or fraternities of chivalry were extensions of this concept of brotherhood-in-arms. It may, in origin at least, have played its part in the system by which men made themselves retainers of others, and have contributed to the special respect felt by normally unmanageable barons for any king who was a military leader of personality and prowess. The disrupted reigns of Henry III, Edward II and Richard II, none of them fighting men of quality, suggest that feudal loyalty held fast only when reinforced by the loyalty of brotherhood-in-arms. This would explain the esteem of fighting barons (and even of taxpaying commons) for Edward III. As well as waging successful war, he was magnanimous and courteous; and no English monarch secured in his lifetime the loyalty to himself and to one another of such able and martial sons. Edward's foundation of the Order of the Garter with its motto, *Honi soit qui mal y pense*, expressed a sense of chivalric brotherhood hard to appreciate by those who watch the procession of miscellaneous and usually unmartial persons who constitute the Order some five hundred years later.

Henry V has been called the ablest man ever to rule England. But what gave him his enduring prestige was that he seemed the last and culminating personification of medieval chivalry. Regarded as having been a better soldier than Edward III, Henry V obviously secured great loyalty. Malory wrote of 'that victorious and noble King Harry the Fifth and the captains under him', and Shakespeare, when providing Henry with his speech on the eve of Agincourt elaborates the theme:

> We few, we happy few, we band of brothers.
> For he today who sheds his blood with me
> Shall be my brother.

The words recalled a social institution still remembered in Tudor times, that of men joined in a brotherhood of arms that made the names of each indeed familiar in their mouths as household words, because such a brotherhood might involve familial closeness and bring them in fact into a common household.

Rich Men's Tables

The requirement that great men should, in conformity with the chivalric virtue of open-handed generosity, 'keep up a great state', helped to perpetuate the tradition that noblemen should not only wear splendid clothes but also give great feasts. 'Largesse' was inherent in the chivalric code and great lords were unwilling to appear to be counting the cost when giving a feast or making a public display of themselves. Though not many noblemen were such poor men of business as deliberately to ruin themselves, it was a chivalric precept that to die in debt proved that a great man had indeed been truly honourable. For centuries, it was a nobleman's duty as well as his pleasure to be gorgeous in his apparel, lavish in his entertainment, profligate in his spending.

This munificence was a device which assured to the great the deference of their inferiors and the esteem of their equals. It signified publicly that here was one with patronage at his disposal, the ability to dispense lands, benefices, sinecures, wardships, influence at kingly and episcopal courts and glittering prospects of advancement. The splendour of the great feast was exclusive to the powerful, and exclusive even to them in their public moments. The dwelling places of all classes were dark and ill-heated. Window glass was too costly for domestic use. Openings for light and air were small, and shuttered in bad weather, thus excluding light as well as the cold. Rags and straw would be stuffed round the edges to keep draughts out. Very small windows might be fitted with pieces of thin horn or mica. The clear flame of the wax candle was the best available form of interior illumination but too expensive save for the greatest of occasions and then only for the high table. Torches of rope steeped in pitch, tallow or oil or tallow dips fashioned out of kitchen fat, with rush wicks, were more usual. The effect was smelly and smoky; and one may suppose that only the most richly coloured and brightly ornamented of clothing could be effective in such ill-lit, shadowy surroundings. The problem of illumination helps to explain why at many feasts the business of eating was usually concluded by sunset, leaving the evening and night for dancing. Dinner in the houses of the gentry was usually eaten between ten a.m. and noon.

The great hall had changed little since Anglo-Saxon times. The more imposing resembled those still to be found in the colleges of Oxford and Cambridge. The company sat on benches, the exalted personages at a high table on a dais at one end. At the other end, a screen, sometimes carved and emblazoned with armorial bearings, hid the servants in the buttery and the passages to kitchen and cellars. Above the screen might be a minstrels' gallery. Not until the sixteenth century did the hall begin to acquire its later, less exalted status as the approach to a staircase leading to a large banqueting room on an upper floor. The walls were not likely to be much decorated with tapestry until the fourteenth century, but antlers and the heads of boars killed in the hunt might adorn the walls; and in the grander halls, heraldic banners might hang from the tie beams of the roof.

The hosts' favourite hawks might have a high perch somewhere in the hall and hounds moved around, hoping to be fed. The floors continued to be strewn with rushes; when they wore thin, fresh ones were laid on top, making a breeding ground for vermin of all sorts. This provided further evidence that the medieval nose was no sensitive organ. It adds point to a thirteenth-century reminder that as much light as possible be provided since to 'sup in darkness' was 'perilous on account of flies and other filth'.

With increasing prosperity, it was usual at great feasts presided over by the nobility or great ecclesiastics for the food to be brought in in silver vessels. Drink was in pots, goblets, jugs and bowls of silver; Venetian glass was in use also. If it were a royal feast, some vessels would be of gold. A favourite table adornment was a vessel shaped like a medieval ship, containing perhaps the salt cellar, small towels, or knives and spoons. The bringing in of successive, and above all special, dishes was done with inordinate ceremony, and perhaps to the sound of trumpets, so that the host might impress the guests by the solemnity, if not the number, of his household servants. The proceeedings were supervised by a marshal or a steward provided with a wand of office. Assisting him were a butler, a 'panter' (for the pantry), servers (head waiters), cooks and, a key figure on these occasions, the carver, whose task was onerous. Great quantities of meat would have to be transferred from the huge joints to individual guests, and carving required not only skill but strength. Whole roasted sheep and oxen had to be cut up before the guests and carved according to elaborate rules. Whoever was skilled at an art or craft in the middle ages was not just a master of it: he was skilled in its 'mysteries' and made sure they were as mysterious as possible. Hence, carving had a language as obscure as heraldry. Few creatures were actually 'carved'. A lobster was 'barbed', a hen was 'spoiled', small birds were 'thighed', a duck was 'unbraced' and a pike was 'splat'. The carver must put only two fingers and a thumb on his knife. This was no menial's work. It was to his credit that the young Squire in Chaucer's *Canterbury Tales* was fit to 'carve before his father at the table'. The carver presented pieces of meat to the guests on the point of his knife. Forks being unknown in England until the early seventeenth century, guests took the carver's offerings with their fingers. At large feasts there were several carvers, each armed with towels and napkins to cope with the splashes and for periodic wiping of the hands.

Guests needed towels and napkins during the meal because they were thus continuously handling their food. The only pieces of personal equipment were a knife, a spoon and a trencher. By the end of the fourteenth century most food was spooned on royal occasions, the provision of whole roasted animals being by then perhaps considered insufficiently courtly. The best cooks preferred to serve most dishes in semi-liquid form, chopped, mixed, squeezed, mashed and cunningly disguised with sauces and spices. If almost liquid, it could be spooned; if less slushy, it was scooped up with the fingers though, again, this seems not to have been the practice at court by 1400.

The trencher was either a flat, rimless piece of wood or a piece of coarse bread. If it were of bread, it would soak up all the sauces and juices of the meal and then be eaten by the guest himself or by the servants. Sometimes the food-permeated trenchers would be given to the poor. Sauce could be mopped up with a small 'sop' of bread but only exceptional ladies like Chaucer's Prioress were able to execute this manoeuvre without dropping food on to the person, the table, or down among the teeming life in the rushes on the floor. Not till the last decades of the fifteenth century were serviettes or small towels much used for washing before and after the meal. As late as the 1780s a French observer did not think the English used anything but the tablecloth for this purpose during the meal itself.

While manuals concerning 'etiquette' or social behaviour in any period are doubtful sources of information about real life, one dating from the first half of the fifteenth century, the *Boke of Curtasye*, suggests that table manners were far from elegant; later works of a similar nature suggest that they had changed little even by the days of Elizabeth I. It was apparently necessary to tell guests at the tables of the great to have clean finger nails, not to talk or laugh with their mouths full, not to leave greasy finger marks on the table, and not to spit on or over it. A guest should not blow on his food or use the tablecloth to wipe his eyes, nose or teeth; nor should he dip his meat or fish in the common salt cellar. If he must blow his nose, he should wipe his hand discreetly with the skirt of his apparel afterwards. If he had bad teeth, a guest should not bite on meat that was to be touched by others. He should remember neither to 'rend his meat asunder' nor to belch in anybody's face.

Much of the elaborate ceremony that surrounded the feast was designed to heighten the contrast between the large quantities of varied eatables made available by the largesse of a great nobleman and the monotony of the normally restricted diet even of the rich. The mother of Edward IV took boiled beef and mutton for supper on three days in the week; on days of strict fast she had salt fish and two dishes of fresh fish for dinner; and on less strict fasting days salt fish, one fresh fish and butter for dinner and salt fish and eggs for supper. Breakfast for the average member of a great household in the fifteenth century would consist of bread, beer and salt fish. The quantities appear at least adequate; the variety negligible.

The staple diet of villagers at least until the fifteenth century was black bread, 'white meat' and occasional bacon or fowl. White meat was dairy produce: milk, eggs and cheese. Most villages that grew wheat did so mostly as a cash crop; for their own bread they used oats, barley or rye. Few villagers ate meat unless they acquired it unofficially by poaching, or officially at a feast rewarding them for boon-work. On these occasions the meal was mainly of bread, fish and ale. Save at such feasts, most villagers drank milk, whey or water. There was evidently an increase in meat-eating among villagers in the fifteenth century, since there were complaints that the agricultural changes of the mid-sixteenth century were depriving them of meat.

Cooking was probably too expensive a luxury for many villagers. Heating arrangements were primitive, and in the arable lands there was as chronic a shortage of wood for fuel as there was of land for pasture; and most if not all of it belonged to the lord. There is evidence that a bundle of dry underwood could cost as much as a bushel of grain. Hence, porridge or gruel would often be eaten uncooked, and many households would occasionally pay others to bake their bread and cook their food as well as brew their ale. The lord might maintain a village oven; like the mill, it would be his monopoly and he would charge for its use.

Town craftsmen and workpeople ate more meat than villagers. Breakfast was solid: bread, pickled herring, cold meat, cheese and ale. By the sixteenth century, the midday meal might be eaten at a tavern or be bought at a cookshop, and consist of meat pies, stews or soups, with bread, cheese and beer. More meat, usually cold, with bread, cheese, ale or beer, made up the evening meal. The only vegetable much in use was the cabbage, which was shredded into soups. The general fear of fruit contributed to the prevalence of scurvy. Men consoled themselves that the blotches and sore places on their faces produced by their lack of vitamin C were a sign of the impurities being worked out of their systems.

To all this, the lordly feast was a telling contrast. Even so fruit and vegetables counted for very little. The bulk of the meal consisted of meat and fish, often served together. A typical 'meat' course might be of beef, but accompanied by eels and salt water fish. There might be several separate fish courses; sweets would appear at various stages in the meal. Where fruits appeared at all it was sometimes thought best to eat them first, on the ground that they were difficult to digest. The fish and the birds used for table in the middle ages included swan, peacock, cormorant, vulture, heron, whalemeat or whales' tongues and seal. The search for novelty and for dishes that could be consumed without the aid of forks gave rise to a preference for mixing everything up. A 'great pie' might be a mixture of beef, suet, capons, hens, ducks, rabbits, woodcocks, teals, yolks of hard boiled eggs, dates, currants, cloves, cinnamon and saffron, to name only the majority of the ingredients. Oysters were served in a sauce made by boiling together ale, strained bread, ginger, sugar, saffron, pepper and salt.

Virtually everything was spiced; the art of cooking consisted in disguising rather than preserving the distinctive taste of different foods. The most likely reason for the generous use of spices was that, since cattle were slaughtered at the beginning of winter, for most of the year meat was not fresh, but cured and salted. It was also thought that spices stimulated the stomach to digest the great quantities of meat, fish and fowl habitually eaten at great feasts. Perhaps what began as a necessity endured as a tradition. Certainly the cost of spices was the largest single item in the food budget of a great household. Meat, game, fish, poultry, and even fresh fruit such as strawberries and cherries, were spiced and so were wines. Sugar was classed with the spices on account of its enormous cost. It was used to flavour pork. Lean pork was often ground fine, boiled with ground almonds and rice flour and then strewn with sugar and powdered ginger mixed with almonds.

Most of the wines that were drunk would have come from Guyenne, Anjou, Poitu, Gascony and also the Rhineland. Nineteen different wines were imported in the fourteenth century, and five times that number by the sixteenth. The fact that many of them were highly acidic explains why they were often spiced with ginger, cinnamon, sugar or honey. One could pause in the proceedings to take a 'wine sop', a piece of bread which had been dipped in wine, as an aid to digestion and for the 'purging of the filthiness of the teeth' and because it also sharpened the eyesight; though, for best results with the last of these defects, it was thought preferable for the wine sop to be toasted.

Alternative Visions

The Peasants' Revolt and Cade's Rebellion were sharp reminders of the existence among the normally acquiescent majority of humbler people of a continuous feeling of resentment against those who ruled them. For most of the time the lower ranks of society endured whatever misfortunes befell them and nursed their grievances in secret. They would go on doing so for century after century; but intermittent popular outbursts like those of 1381 and 1450 occurred, in varying forms, on a smaller or greater scale, in every age. Mostly, they are punctuation marks in the prose narrative of English history: usually commas, sometimes semi-colons, but never full stops. Time and again, rebellions, riots, or big or little waves of strikes would occur, usually localised and quickly suppressed. They tended to be sudden, angry protests, without larger purpose or, as with the risings led by Wat Tyler and Jack Cade, constructive sequel.

Nevertheless, all had certain simple themes in common, which would recur in each new manifestation of unrest from the late-fourteenth century to the late-twentieth. Each was a cry of anger against the luxurious ways of the few, uttered on behalf of (though rarely by) the poor and the hungry. As soon as a society contained a sufficient number of men who could earn an independent living by their skills as craftsmen or artisans, and who could read or be read to, the history of popular social protest had begun; and by the late-fourteenth century England was already such a community. In the hundred years or so between the accession of Richard II in 1377 and the final deposition of Henry VI in 1471, there were more signs than usual of a growing disenchantment among the middling and inferior sort of men with the whole character of the society in which they lived.

Political disorder and graft, the intermittent breakdowns of the judicial process, the greater luxury enjoyed by the aristocracy, and the increasing comfort of the better-off gentry, went hand in hand with the spiritual and intellectual lassitude of the ecclesiastical system. The materialist, secular world was no longer under judgment. The church that should have judged it was itself dominated by secular minded men too often greedy for gain. Suddenly, fundamental assertions were being put, as they would be again and again in the future: that the great and glorious cathedrals and churches of the age had been built by the labour, and at the expense, of the poor and humble; that the wealth that had gone into the making of their stained glass, statues and rich ornament had been wealth thereby denied to those with empty bellies; and that, since those who ministered in such places were often so remote, so overweening and so lacking in concern, their exalted positions could not be justified. Men were calling attention to a disturbing fact: that the greater the splendour of a society's high culture, the greater is likely to be the relative poverty of its masses.

Hence, in this particular century, not only did men cry 'woe' to those who were rich; the claim was advanced that men mattered more than monuments or even than sacraments; and that God could be known, even by the most orthodox among the faithful, by a direct experience that needed no ecclesiastical mediation. Thus, apart from, but almost simultaneously with, popular social protest, there developed both intellectual and popular heresy and the growth of a world-renouncing mysticism.

The dissatisfaction behind the Peasants' Revolt found its most moving expression in William Langland's *Vision of Piers Plowman*, almost contemporaneous with Chaucer's *Canterbury Tales*. Langland's poem synthesises social with religious protest. Intended to be read mainly by urban craftsmen and traders, its demand is for justice to be grounded upon charity. Scholarly theologians, power-hungry popes, greedy friars, merry holiday-making pilgrimages, like those of Chaucer's characters to Canterbury, are all condemned. Piers the poor Plowman is in the end identified with St Peter, the founder of the Church, and the true recipient of the power of Christ. The writer's catalogue of the suffering humanity of his day is a strange comment on the jolly pageantry of the Prologue to the *Canterbury Tales*:

> Old men and hoar, that be helpless and needy
> And women with child that cannot work,
> Blind men and bedridden and broken in their members,
> And all poor sufferers, patient under God's sending,
> As lepers and mendicants, men fallen into mischief,
> Palmers and pilgrims, and men robbed perchance,
> Or brought low by liars, and their goods lost,
> Or through fire or through flood fallen to poverty,
> That take their mischiefs meekly and mildly at heart.

Though Langland's writing was of little consequence outside the limited circle for whom he wrote, Wyclif's career as an incorrigible heretic during the 1370s, when he enjoyed the patronage of the all-powerful John of Gaunt, left a permanent mark. Wyclif's background was remote from the world of humble persons with whom Langland was concerned. Yet there is a connection, suggesting that movements of protest in the fourteenth and fifteenth centuries were manifestations of a well-established but usually surreptitious current of opinion whose origin goes back to St Francis. Langland was a devout admirer of St Francis, just as that symbol of a different kind of popular protest, Joan of Arc, seems to have had several Franciscans in her entourage. Wyclif, in more sophisticated fashion, was also indebted to Franciscan insights. His opinions were those of a renowned doctor of divinity, a highly academic end-product of the intellectual radicalism of the Franciscans who had dominated thirteenth century Oxford, and produced in William of Ockham an advocate of what amounted to democratic liberties and human rights.

Wyclif was a formidable exponent of a basically anti-clerical tradition and lent his academic authority to the opinion that, since the wealth of the church derived from gifts and bequests from the laity, it ought not to resist royal demands for taxation, or indeed the state's expropriation of the endowments of the church in a national emergency. These opinions greatly suited John of Gaunt, desperate to extract money from the church in order to finance the continuance of the Hundred Years War with France. Subsequently, Wyclif aided the government by vehement attacks against the higher clergy. When the Bishop of London attempted to put Wyclif on trial for his offensive opinions, there were riots in the streets. Pope Gregory XI therefore condemned various of Wyclif's propositions, and the bishops and the Oxford authorities imposed silence on him.

That Wyclif was not excommunicated as a heretic was due partly to the inexperience of English bishops in dealing with so un-English a phenomenon, and partly to the disastrous collapse of papal prestige as a result of the 'Babylonish captivity' in Avignon, and the Schism that began in 1378. The disarray of the papacy saved Wyclif personally; and added force to the opinions he propagated.

Wyclif's experiences impelled him towards the furious and comprehensive heresy of a disillusioned, angry old man. Even before his intervention in politics he had failed to secure preferment consonant with his reputation; afterwards, he had been hounded for his opinions and little rewarded by a government anxious to get money from the church but not to stir up heresy. Accordingly, like Luther after him, having been resisted when challenging the church upon particulars, he proceeded to challenge it on the widest possible front. He had opposed various ecclesiastical practices on the grounds that they had no warrant in scripture. Thence, with impetuous intellectual passion, he proceeded to the opinion that virtually all ecclesiastical institutions were contrary to scripture, the literal truth of which he declared to be understandable by the simplest of laymen. This clearly involved the availability of the Bible in the vernacular. Also destructive of the ecclesiastical system was his emphasis on the doctrine of predestination: only the elect were saved. The rest were foredoomed to damnation, and Christ alone knew who belonged to which of these categories. The elect were saved by God's grace, not by the operation of the church; the Pope himself might turn out in the end to be on the list of the damned rather than of the elect. Wyclif also asserted the supremacy of the secular authorities over the church, and undermined the whole basis of the priestly idea by denying the doctrine of transubstantiation. Wyclif insisted that at mass the priest did not transform the bread and wine of the eucharist into the body and blood of Christ.

By 1382 this proved too much even for Oxford and a commission of twelve learned doctors decided (though only by a majority of two) that his doctrines were false. Wyclif thereupon withdrew to his neglected parish of Lutterworth, where he lived (writing heresies unceasingly) until his death in 1384.

Wyclif, though exceptional in English history for his pertinacious refusal to change his opinions under pressure, was perhaps not so much the founder of the Lollard movement for which he was at first blamed and then, after the Reformation, excessively honoured, as its intellectual counterpart. Even the Lollard vernacular Bible seems to have owed little to Wyclif, and the stock-in-trade of Lollard beliefs might well have been the same anti-clerical hotch-potch had he never existed. Some early Lollards were certainly younger Oxford disciples of Wyclif; but the condemnation of 1382 virtually ended intellectual Lollardy and it was thereafter essentially one manifestation, never nationally organised, of the widespread tendency among the fourteenth-century laity to express their religious feelings by a turning away from the corporate life of the church. It was a time of genuine moral fervour among the increasingly literate lay population. It was a period of private devotion, a time when persons of substance had private chapels and their own private confessors, who used portable altars and, since they had no parochial duties, were free from episcopal supervision. The new spirit was biblical, evangelical and anti-clerical, with a strong emphasis on immediate personal contact between the believer and his God.

If for the Lollard it was to Holy Writ rather than to Holy Church that he turned for the strengthening of faith, there were others whose religion was a direct, mystical communion with their God. The late fourteenth century, and the early fifteenth, were exceptional in English history for producing a number of such mystics. These included the anonymous author of the *Cloud of Unknowing*. This advocated a turning away both from good works and from intellectual enquiry into an absorbed and quite private love of God:

> . . . the higher part of contemplation . . . hangeth all wholly in the darkness, and in this cloud of unknowing; with a loving stirring and a blind beholding into the naked being of God Himself only.
>
> . . . love may reach God, but not knowing. All the whiles that the soul dwelleth in this deadly body, evermore is the sharpness of our understanding of all spiritual things, but most specially of God, mingled with some manner of fantasy; for the which our work should be unclean . . .

A no less vivid directness of religious feeling is found in *Revelations of Divine Love* by the anchoress, Mother Julian of Norwich:

> He showed me a little thing, the quality of a hazel nut, in the palm of his hand; and it was as round as a ball. I looked thereupon with my understanding and I thought, What may this be? And it was answered generally thus: It is all that is made. I marvelled how it might last, for methought it might suddenly have fallen to nought for littleness. And I was answered in my understanding: It lasteth and ever shall, for that God loveth it . . . In this Little Thing I saw three properties. The first is that God made it, the second that God loveth it, the third that God keepeth it.

Thomas à Kempis, whose *Imitation of Christ* was widely read, was equally aloof from heresy, and hostile to intellectual disputation. 'At the last judgment,' he wrote, 'we shall not be asked how many books we have read, but how we have lived.' He urged his readers to suppress their 'appetite to know' because 'great deception' lay in it. They should seek to know 'no other thing than Christ crucified'.

Orthodox faith may have been as much strengthened as weakened by the disasters of the Black Death. The figure of Death acquired awesome significance. Its scythe swept mercilessly and indifferently, and more and more saints were invoked for protection. The sufferings of Christ on Calvary acquired a new relevance to the plague-stricken. A new and deeper veneration for the Mother of God became widespread, as did the doctrine of her Immaculate Conception, not made official dogma until four hundred years later. In an age of pestilence, social conflict and shifting social divisions, the patronage of Christ, His Virgin Mother and the saints became the spiritual counterpart of the 'good lordship' that noblemen extended to their retainers in the troubled temporal world.

Lollardy was contemporaneous with these developments and an assortment of protests against them. Lollards condemned expensively caparisoned statues, and representatives of Christ in Majesty. Pilgrimages, prayers to the saints and the use of images should be replaced by regular preaching and by devotional reading. They agreed with Wyclif that man was a worthier representation of God than the eucharist. Lollards would stand and not kneel in the presence of the Host at mass and would keep their heads covered. Almsgiving was preferable to adoration of the Host, and Lollardy thus linked religious to social dissent. Devotion to the vernacular Bible extended to a refusal to have their wills written in Latin. Lollards were at pains to emphasise in dramatic English their spiritual unworthiness and their contempt for their bodies and to demand that this 'stinking carrion' be buried with minimum expense or ceremony.

Lollards were not all obscure hunted men. A number of men of knightly status are known to have maintained Lollard preachers on their lands and to have compelled their tenants to accept their ministry. Such men, powerful at court, protected Lollards and made no secret of the fact. The bishops were usually loth to persecute even humble Lollards, since there was no tradition of heresy hunting in the church in England and its leaders were tolerant, sceptical men. Lay patrons could not be interfered with; and worldly landed men who were bishops were in no hurry to quarrel with worldly landed men who happened to hold heretical beliefs known to command much public sympathy. Even after the passing of the statute for the Burning of Heretics in 1401 only two Lollards suffered the extreme penalty before 1413, and the searching out of heretics was often perfunctory.

Not until 1414 did lay Lollardy receive a mortal blow. This followed the escape from the Tower, where he had been placed for his Lollard views, of a former captain in Henry V's service, Sir John Oldcastle. Evidently an acknowledged leader in Lollard circles, he sent agents to various parts of the country to raise armies of supporters. News of the plot leaked to the authorities; when the ill-armed groups reached the neighbourhood of Westminster the king's forces suffered not a single casualty in defeating them. The rebels seem principally to have been weavers, shoemakers, glovers, tailors, carpenters and ploughmen, with the weavers the most numerous. The areas from which Lollardy drew its strength included Leicestershire, various places in Essex, such as Coggeshall, Kelvedon, Halstead and Colchester, and places in and near the Chilterns, such as Amersham, Missenden and Wycombe. Woodstock and the neighbouring Oxfordshire villages of Bladon, Handborough and Kidlington also produced a few rebels. There were thirty-one executions. The bodies of the seven of them adjudged guilty not

185

only of treason but also heresy were afterwards burnt. Oldcastle himself eluded this fate until captured in 1417.

From time to time thereafter there were spurts of activity. In 1428 Wyclif's body was dug up, his bones burnt and thrown in the river. An Abingdon weaver was executed for distributing handbills advocating taxing the church to pay for the war. In 1452, a Hertfordshire butcher was accused of opposing baptism and the veneration of images, and of asserting that there was no God but the sun and the moon. There was a brief revival in the villages between Henley and Wycombe in the 1460s, led by a blacksmith from Bristol. In 1481 a Derbyshire widow was put on trial for denying both the Virgin Birth and the sacrament of Baptism.

Lollardy had no academic theologians on its side after 1411, none of the landed gentry after 1414. So far from leading to reform of the Church it served to preserve it in all its late-medieval imperfection by provoking it to make a stand against heresy. Oldcastle's identification of Lollardy with treason further ensured that the lay leaders of society, at Westminster and in the localities, would continue to support a church that had the power to continue in existence but lacked the power to inspire. Loyalty to the faith was increasingly expressed in private devotion. The continued use of the Latin Vulgate meant that the mass itself became an occasion for spiritual meditation by the individual against a vaguely-heard background of liturgical muzak.

Yet the later middle ages were not much less generous in pious works than earlier centuries. It was a great age of church building rather than cathedral building. The ostentatiously splendid churches of the Cotswolds and East Anglia were endowed not only by men grown fat by trade but also by warriors enriched by the wars. Pious works of a tangible sort ceased to be the largely aristocratic actions they had earlier been. The new family pride also expressed itself in religious terms. The endowment of chantries, where services and masses for the dead were to be performed in perpetuity, was an almost universal habit in the upper reaches of the gentry, and a great source of employment to the over-populated clerical profession. Not to request in one's will, and if possible to provide the financial means for, intercessory prayers for one's soul was almost to be heretical. It was a great drain on family resources; and it depended upon the widespread acceptance of the view that, after death, man's soul spent a period in purgatory, either temporarily suffering for past sins before being made acceptable for heaven, or perhaps being trained to be ready for the beatific vision that heaven would reveal. This process could be actively assisted by the prayers of those left behind on earth. The endowment of the apparatus for offering such prayers was a personal, or at its widest a family, substitute for the older and more aristocratic practice of endowing monasteries; and as is usual when lesser men do on a lesser scale what their betters formerly did in a grander manner, they were sternly criticised. Chantries were condemned by Wyclif as nothing but a device for the vain perpetuation of family names. A perhaps similar un-conscious snobbery has led to too much being made of the absence of great saints and spiritual leaders in the late middle ages and too little of the fact that general standards of literacy, of behaviour and, in many instances, of devotion, were higher than they had been in the more splendid age of aristocratic Christianity.

PART FOUR

OBEDIENCE AND REBELLION

Approximate Dates: 1509–1653

1
NEW DIRECTIONS

Tudor Perspectives

IN their reassertion of royal power and justice, Henry VII and, in his best period, Henry VIII, were both, like Edward IV, in direct descent from Henry I, Henry II and Edward I. In their exaltation of their office, Henry VII, Henry VIII and Elizabeth I would have been recognised by both Henry III and Richard II as having succeeded where they had tried, but failed. This tradition, indeed, outlived the Tudors: the aloof dignity of Charles I was not unlike that to which Richard II had aspired.

The Tudors, at their best, therefore represented not a new monarchy but an improved version of the old. Yet theirs was no uninterrupted success story; neither was their success peculiarly personal. The alacrity with which, throughout the Tudor period, aggrieved or merely ambitious noblemen indulged in armed rebellion attests the fragility of the Tudor peace and the persistence into the sixteenth century of the traditions of the overmighty subject that had so dominated the fifteenth. Henry VII had always feared rebellion on behalf of pretenders to his throne, since neither he nor his subjects could know that his triumph at Bosworth would prove irreversible. In Henry VIII's reign, the Duke of Buckingham was executed for combining royal blood with putative royal ambitions; and the rebellion in the north in 1536 known as the Pilgrimage of Grace was an aristocratic as well as a religious protest against Henry's rule. The phenomenon of the overmighty subject reappeared in the reign of Edward VI, in the person of his uncle, John Dudley, Duke of Northumberland. To preserve, after the young king's early death in 1555, the power he had acquired during Edward's lifetime, he tried, though without success, to prevent the accession of Henry VIII's daughter, Mary, by making his own daughter-in-law, Lady Jane Grey, queen instead. Yet the rapidity with which his coup was defeated indicated how much times were changing. Nevertheless, Elizabeth I had to face two badly organised plots to unseat her on the part of the Duke of Norfolk; and a pointless rising by her disgruntled favourite, Robert Devereux, Earl of Essex bore, as late as 1601, a strong resemblance to the behaviour of overmighty subjects in the age of 'bastard feudalism' that Henry VII is held to have destroyed.

These incidents indicate, as does the preoccupation of Shakespeare's historical plays with the subject of armed rebellion, that political conflict might still have to be decided by real, if short-lived, battles. And if more men were executed for treason under the Tudors than were guilty of it, that too reveals how greatly treason was feared. Not until the end was the Tudor peace triumphant. The unexpectedly peaceful accession of the Scottish Stuart, James I, when the Tudor dynasty ended, is the only certain turning point. In consequence of it, by the time men found themselves on the brink of rebellion in 1642 they teetered long before going over it and, once in, fumbled with the indecisiveness of men to whom the habits of civil strife were long unfamiliar.

The Tudors were much prejudiced by their limited ability to beget healthy male heirs. Henry VII's first son, Arthur, had died young. Henry VIII's famous matrimonial endeavours endowed the kingdom with one short-lived consumptive son, Edward VI, king from 1547 to 1553, and two daughters: Mary who reigned from 1555 to 1558 and was barren, and Elizabeth I. Elizabeth, queen from 1558 until 1603, compelled to make political capital out of her virginity, was so acclaimed for doing so that it is clear how surprising an achievement it was. More than once in Henry VII's reign and again from 1529 until at least 1588, the dynasty's continuance, and with it not only the peace but also the independence of the kingdom, was in constant jeopardy, giving to the politics of those years a feverish intensity.

The achievements of the three enduring Tudors, the two Henries and Elizabeth I, by no means sprang wholly from their own political skills. All relied on intelligent, loyal servants. On balance, it was Henry VII, rather than his son or grand-daughter, who chose, and cooperated with, capable royal servants most consistently. From 1514 to 1529, Henry VIII served his crown, his finances and his country badly by giving power to the arrogant Wolsey, whose policies, both foreign and domestic, were mostly wasteful and misconceived. The king's last seven years were years of vacillation, marked, like his first, with foolish wars. Only during the 1530s, when Thomas Cromwell was secretary to the council, was England efficiently, if ruthlessly, governed. As for Elizabeth, she was by nature at once imperious and vacillating, a glorious queen and a great miser; and it is to William Cecil, Lord Burghley, the pilot who weathered the storms of royal temper or becalmed stretches when the royal mind refused to be made up, and who negotiated the rocks and shoals of religious and political controversy at home and dangers from abroad, that much of the credit for his queen's eventual triumph was due. He had worked for her during her sister's reign and served her as secretary from the beginning of her reign in 1558 until his death in 1598, only five years before the death of the queen herself.

Tudor sovereigns thus had devoted servants who worked to preserve royal power regardless of the fact that the wearer of the crown might be capricious, procrastinating, cruel or ungrateful. Yet, throughout the Tudor years, as in the past, the majority of councillors continued to be aristocrats since, though the crown might fear their hostility, it could not govern without their cooperation. It was not a matter, therefore, of the employment of 'new' men by the Tudors, but rather that, during the sixteenth century, new ideas about the responsibilities of government were becoming part of the intellectual stock in trade of many of the men who mattered.

Civic Virtue

The sixteenth century provided an intellectual climate which encouraged a positive and serious attitude to the conduct of public affairs. The predominant conventional view had hitherto been that life on earth was no more than a prelude to life after death. The world was a prison house where men endured punishment for Adam's sin, a place where every pleasure lured men's souls from the right path to salvation. In consequence, the solitary and the contemplative life was superior to one devoted to the affairs of the world. But the rediscovery of Aristotle by Italian scholars during the latter part of the thirteenth century had confronted them with the idea of man as a social being and of society as perfectible through the exercise of human reason. The humanist scholars of fifteenth-century Florence taught Europeans to regard learning as a preparation for public life. In the past, the ideal scholar had been intellectually apart from the world, as the ideal monk was ascetically remote from it. There also spread outwards from late-medieval Florence the view that commerce and the getting of wealth were virtuous if practised for the common good. In the earlier middle ages, the church had regarded profit-taking as wicked. It had condemned the charging of interest on loans, on the basis of Christ's 'Lend hoping for nothing again' and of an Aristotelian sentence implying that it was unnatural for a barren substance like gold to 'breed'. The ecclesiastical ban on 'usury' had been widely circumvented; but, just as commerce was uncomfortably exceptional in a world of feudal tenures, so was it unacceptable in one where all things material were sin and dross. Thanks to the Renaissance humanists, too, not only active public service, but also an active family life at last received philosophical justification. The ideals of renunciation, and of mortification of the flesh, gave way to those of worldly virtue, worldly wisdom and worldly success; and this implied a new attention to, and a new respect for, education. The aim of that education should be to prepare a man not for the profession of cleric or for a life of contemplative study, but for constructive social activity in commerce and affairs.

These Italian ideas had been percolating into England for some time. Englishmen had long visited Italy to study canon and civil law. Chaucer was familiar with the writings of Dante, Petrarch and Boccaccio. Officials of the papal court came to England not only to collect papal taxes but to spread new ideas and to advise English scholars and bibliophiles. The most celebrated of these was Humphrey, Duke of Gloucester, Henry V's turbulent brother. He built up a collection of books which an Italian prince would have envied and which laid the foundation of English humanism. He employed Italians as secretaries and commissioned translations of Italian humanist writings. Another aristocratic patron of humanism was John Tiptoft, Earl of Worcester, gathering a collection of texts, some translated by himself, which made possible the humanistic heyday of the first thirty years of the sixteenth century. The principal achievements of the humanists were to conceive of the educated man as one for whom the highest virtue lay in the fulfilment of his civic duties; and to see man, individually and socially, as possessing dignity, freedom of choice, and the power to change his own and society's destiny by the exercise of wisdom and virtue.

Although these ideas helped to foster among the more influential servants of the crown in Tudor times that sense of concern for the common weal for which the best of them were distinguished, it would not do to make too much of this humanist influence. Despite the reputation of Thomas More and Colet and their master, Erasmus, the atmosphere of Tudor England after Henry VIII's break with Rome in 1534 was far from conducive to the free play of the intellect, as the execution of More, and the careful evasiveness of Erasmus on the major religious issues of the time, would both suggest. Though tending to get lost sight of during the aristocratic turmoil of the fifteenth century, the thirteenth century's notion of the king as agent and interpreter of a law independent of, and superior to, the person of the king, long pre-dated sixteenth-century humanism. But humanist ideas gave new impetus to its re-emergence in Tudor times. It made the servants of the crown readier to respond to the idea that they, no less than monarchs, were custodians of the common weal. The fuller significance of this trend would not be clear until the first half of the seventeenth century; but it helps to explain the developed sense of public duty which characterises Tudor government, the caprices of Tudor monarchs notwithstanding.

Institutional Education

Enlightened humanist ideas influenced individuals rather than educational institutions, despite the impression created by the sojourn of Erasmus at Cambridge, by Colet's foundation of St Paul's School, and by the number of Edward VI and Queen Elizabeth grammar schools of the period. The new literacy and the higher ideals of public service and civic responsibility were encouraged by educational expansion; but that expansion was not initiated by humanism and the universities were little affected by it in the long run. More of the sons of the wealthy had been going to the Universities since the fifteenth century; but few of these young men stayed at university for more than two years, and the motives for their going there were primarily social. University reforms were adumbrated and Regius professorships were established; but the tradition that professors and lecturers did not lecture often, or at all, was soon established, to endure into the nineteenth century. The Inns of

Court had served as a secular university for the sons of nobles, knights and gentry since the fourteenth century, but the influx of students was so great by the sixteenth century that the lawyers who should have taught them could not find the time to spare from their commitments in the courts.

Just as the sons of the gentry and nobility were becoming so numerous at the universities as to crowd out the poor scholar, so, already by the fifteenth century, an increasing number of gentry and yeomen were sending their sons to schools hitherto reserved for clerics. Perhaps thirty per cent of the population could read by the fifteenth century and forty per cent by the mid-sixteenth, though rather fewer would have been able to write. Few of the schools were attached to, though some were separately endowed by, cathedrals or monasteries; these had ceased to be cultural centres. Many were endowed by the burgesses of towns such as Ipswich, by gilds, as at Stratford and Chipping Norton, or the City Companies, as at Walthamstow and Horsham. Many were chantry schools, set up when the endowment of the chantry was generous enough to enable the chantry priest not only to say masses for the dead but also to teach the young. When the chantries were dissolved in the 1540s the schools attached to them were often continued with a stipendiary lay teacher, or handed over to the local inhabitants. More than one King Edward VI grammar school founded at this time was a former chantry school under a new endowment and a new name; just as more than one Queen Elizabeth grammar school founded later in the century was so called as a compliment to the queen and in no way indicated a royal endowment.

The endowment and re-endowment of grammar schools in the fifteenth and sixteenth centuries testifies to a new enthusiasm for education and is the sign of an important shift in men's attitudes. Their forbears endowed, not schools, but monasteries, seeking honour in the eyes of God and man by the encouragement of those who would withdraw from the world. Now they acquired merit by devoting their charity to preparing the young to be active in the world's affairs. In that the religious element survived, it did so less with an eye to eternity than to the fashioning of loyal citizens. Here the 'modern' may be said to emerge from the 'medieval'; it marked the start of the process by which the clerisy of those in holy orders was to be replaced by the secular clerisy of those who teach. Yet, as with the proliferation of educational institutions in the second half of the twentieth century, the increased number of schools and the crowding of young men into the universities, did not necessarily produce results to correspond with the time's ideals. The study of Latin language and literature was still the principal function of the schools, with physical violence as the principal teaching aid. One improvement, however, was the greater attention to the writing of good English in Latin classes. This helped to compensate for the discouragement of spoken English in schools. Though the medium of argument in the courts was English by Edward III's reign, Henry V was the first English sovereign to use English in his correspondence and it was not until the eighteenth century that English finally became the official language of the law courts. Until 1650, pleadings were in Law French and statutes written in Law Latin. This system had degenerated into the kind of pidgin evidenced by the report of the Salisbury assizes in 1631; it was recorded of a man found guilty of a felony that 'puis son condemnation' he 'ject un brickbat a le justice que narowly mist'. As a result, a further indictment 'immediately fuit . . . drawn . . . et son dexter manus ampute et fix al Gibbet'.

It has also been claimed that the requirement that teachers be licensed by bishops ensured religious orthodoxy rather than sound teaching and resulted in a prescribed Grammar, a prescribed Catechism, a prescribed Primer and, ultimately, a prescribed Bible. Here and there the regimen of boredom and beatings was mollified by gifted teachers for whom humanist scholars had not, after all, written wholly in vain. Nor was religious orthodoxy universally instilled. The protection of powerful private patrons, or the quiet obstinacy of town burgesses, enabled many Puritans, despite royal disapproval, to teach in schools, or lecture in the universities, in Elizabeth's reign. Oliver Cromwell learned his Puritanism from his Huntingdon schoolmaster. In the late Elizabethan years, when Lord Burghley himself was vice-chancellor at Cambridge, and the Earl of Leicester vice-chancellor at Oxford, Puritanism was widely tolerated in the universities. Both men used the educational system to compensate for their inability to get their royal mistress to tolerate Puritanism officially. Indeed, it may have been chiefly through this unofficial Puritan element in formal education that the ideals of virtuous service to the common-wealth survived the Elizabethan period at all. The generality of those about the court became increasingly corrupt by the end of the reign; every kind of corruption flourished about the person of James I. What made early Stuart MPs more educated than their predecessors was, perhaps, not so much that more of them had received a formal higher education, but that so many of them had absorbed from Puritan teachers and dons (or lawyers at the Inns of Court) a robustly serious and practical concern for the commonwealth in contrast to the frivolous hangers-on of James I or the pedantic narrowness of the ministers of Charles I.

For the unregenerate majority, however, the tradition was already being established that formal places of education should provide a social rather than an intellectual preparation for life. The 'good' school and the university were places where those who were to govern the land, at Westminster or in the shires, learned to assess one another's characters and to note which among their fellows could most profitably be cultivated as patron or ally. Like Falstaff and Shallow at the Inns of Court (which performed a similar function) they heard the chimes at midnight, often enough with Jane Nightwork and her kind in attendance, forging those bonds of solidarity which derive from, and are deepened by, lifelong acquaintance. If they acquired intellectual maturity, they usually did so by other means and after their formal education was over. In these respects, the best schools and older universities changed little from the fourteenth century to the twentieth.

The expansion of the universities in the sixteenth century had important consequences for the seventeenth. Graduates were produced in excess of their opportunities for responsible employment. This frustration among the sons, and particularly the younger sons, of the gentry, added its quota to the accumulating grievances which were to issue in civil war. The over-production of graduate clergy by the early seventeenth century also had untoward effects. If they had Puritan leanings they were at odds with the bishops and might therefore spread Puritan ideas as lecturers in towns or chaplains in private households, attacking the existing order with all the fury of an intellectual scorned. If they were orthodox they tended to be at odds with their parishioners because their academic cast of mind, and their now higher social status, cut them off from their congregation; as did their tendency to preach intricately theological sermons on the theme of implicit obedience to the government. The fulfilment in the early seventeenth century of the historic medieval demand for an educated clergy worked, ironically enough, largely to the church's disadvantage.

Informal Education and the Printed Word

Perhaps even more important than institutional education in increasing literacy and enlarging men's minds about public affairs were developments in informal education in the fifteenth and sixteenth centuries. The education of the youngest children in the home by their parents came to be considered an essential element in family life. The employment of private tutors sometimes supplemented and sometimes replaced education at school and university, especially among wealthier families. It was also in the company of a tutor that young men of substance, whether they had been to university or not, undertook a course of foreign travel in late adolescence. By the eighteenth century the habit had produced the Grand Tour, whose purpose was often specifically cultural and artistic; but in the early modern period the object was to obtain first hand knowledge of the customs, languages and resources of foreign countries. This might well prove useful to a prospective courtier and lead to employment on a foreign embassy. Here, too, medieval habits give way to modern. The young man abroad was no longer a wandering scholar in search of learned masters or a pilgrim seeking merit in the eyes of God; with his tutor to guide and direct him he became (ideally at any rate) an earnest student of the ways in which they ordered things differently abroad, so that he could apply this knowledge to the conduct of his own, and society's, affairs on his return.

Tutors were naturally of all sorts; but where they were of the better sort, much was gained by the 1:1 teacher-pupil relationship. More important, all three types of formal education, by parents, the tutor at home and the tutor abroad, benefited greatly from, and were to some extent made possible by, the one genuinely revolutionary educational development of the time, the invention of the printed book. Once literacy was achieved, the printed book did more than strengthen the resources of schools. There were manuals in great number to assist parents to teach their children, and to give much needed advice to parish priests on the techniques of the sermon. Law books made up for the deficiency of the training in the Inns of Court, so that one could now actually 'read' for the Bar. There were manuals to teach merchants accounting, double-entry book-keeping and foreign languages (chiefly French, Spanish and Italian), subjects which were not available in the schools. The printed book could compensate the literate man, as it has done since, for the deficiencies, or even for the lack, of formal schooling, or liberate others from the narrowness of the universities. It could make a conscientious private tutor more valuable and an inadequate one less of a handicap. More important, church, monastery and university no longer enjoyed that monopolistic hold on knowledge which had unavoidably been theirs when books were copied by hand and upon which their pretensions about themselves had been based. Inevitably, since the printed book could lead to independence of mind and to the exercise of private judgment, the church, the universities and the secular authorities did all they could to restrict printing by licence and by censorship. But in the long run they failed to prevent the growth of a world in which the literate for the first time had reasonable access to knowledge thanks to the printer and bookseller and the private library. This was educational revolution in the broadest sense.

Its effect was to add a new dimension to the problem of public order. On the one hand, government became increasingly energetic, through a judicious combination of propaganda and espionage, to ensure the stability of the state; on the other, the religious cleavages of the time, themselves essentially a product of growing literacy, encouraged a dissent which resisted the state's more rigorous demand for obedience and for ideological conformity. The disputatious pamphleteer, the contentious preacher, the underground printer provided a new and, in the end, irrepressible source of anxiety to governments, at first supplementing and then, in the early seventeenth century, supplanting, the discontents of over-proud aristocrats as a major cause of political disaffection. That the consequent crisis was postponed until after the Tudor dynasty had ended testifies to the skill and toughness of the principal Tudor sovereigns and their often astonishingly faithful advisers; but it is a reminder that keeping the now dwindling minority of unruly nobles in check and securing the adherence of the more responsible among them was but the lesser part of the Tudor achievement. It meant that, in addition to their routine use of the more normal instruments of government, such as detailed surveillance, cruelty and more or less judicial murder, the Tudors succeeded, by the force of their personalities and by a highly intelligent use of visual and verbal propaganda, in building up among the greater part of the now much enlarged politically conscious nation a loyalty to the crown that was also a loyalty to the common weal. Even when their sense of what was due to the common weal led strong-willed men to be critical of the crown, they would be so in the conviction that, as Tudor propaganda was forever preaching, the nation's security depended on a continuing harmony between strong sovereigns and loyal subjects.

For the whole of the second half of the sixteenth century, the thinking and believing part of the nation would be divided into three ideological camps: the religious, and sometimes also radical, Protestants who acquired the nickname of 'Puritans'; the surviving Catholic adherents of the 'old religion' which until the 1530s had united all the English in at least a formal allegiance to Rome; and a 'middle' party denouncing Puritans as revolutionaries and Catholics as foreign agents, and standing squarely for a national church preaching obedience and ideological consensus. That it was this middle party that came through, and with such success that, by 1642, men were prepared to take up arms to defend so recent and so theologically mixed-up an institution as the Church of England, is the measure of how artfully the Tudor sovereigns and their councillors (Elizabeth I and hers in particular) had navigated their course through a time when Europe was everywhere rent by unbridled religious conflict or subject to the most deadly repression.

Nevertheless, the new directions which men's minds were taking impose limits on the extent to which the sixteenth and seventeenth centuries may be looked on as principally a time of religious conflict. Growing wealth and widening educational opportunities were making a society that was increasingly secular in its outlook. The religious ferment of the sixteenth century came at a time when the validity of religious institutions was a diminishing commodity. Luther's Ninety Five Theses against papal indulgences in 1517 was a triumphant piece of propaganda, not simply because it was so widely disseminated by the printers, but because it was a furious protest against the secular greed of a secular-minded papacy. But Luther's generation had produced two other revolutionaries. In 1513, Macchiavelli's *The Prince* was completed. In it, for the first time, statecraft was treated for what it usually was: an autonomous activity divorced from theological considerations. Whether they read him or not, most European rulers and statesmen of the next two centuries, and virtually all the successful ones, behaved in accordance with his a-religious ideas, whatever religious causes they espoused in public. In England, Thomas Cromwell, Elizabeth I, her secretary, Cecil, and in his own slippery fashion, Charles II, all succeeded because their minds were predominantly secular. Edward VI, Mary Tudor and Charles I, with religious minds, were political failures.

More revolutionary still, in the long run, was Copernicus who, in 1543, published what amounted to a declaration of independence on behalf of the entire solar system. By insisting that the earth revolved round the sun, he endowed the universe with its own pattern of behaviour independent of, and contrary to, that laid down for it by the church. Like Machiavelli's view of politics, the Copernican view of the solar system was condemned by all right-minded persons as well as by the rulers of church and state. But the religious zealotry of the sixteenth century, whether Catholic or Protestant, had much of the character of a desperate struggle by traditionally-minded men against the advancing tides of secularism. The difference between the Catholic and the Protestant response was largely that whereas the Catholics declined to compromise with the secular trends of the time, Protestants contrived to absorb some of them while stifling others. So, in late-seventeenth-century England, Isaac Newton, while labouring amid general esteem to construct, on sixteenth-century foundations, a universe obedient to immutable mechanical laws, continued to cultivate a private obsession with the interpretation of the Book of Revelation.

2
REALM AND EMPIRE

Overmighty Prelate

FOR much of the time and in most respects, the government of England in the twenty years following Henry VIII's accession in 1509 was conducted with an extravagant irresponsibility that nevertheless destroyed the prestige, not of the crown, but of the church. This was because affairs were, from 1514, run almost single-handed by Cardinal Wolsey, ruling as a virtual despot in the king's name. Henry's own personality was manifest in various acts of cruelty; in vigorous devotion, appropriate to a handsome, athletic grandson of the virile Edward IV, to the task of enjoying himself; and in a lively but far from coherent desire to cut a military dash on the fields of France.

To demonstrate that he was an altogether more open, warmhearted man than his stingy, extortionate father, he began his reign by having Henry VII's unpopular financial ministers, Empson and Dudley, attainted for treason. Innocent though they were, their judicial murder was useful propaganda. In 1521, when he was already perturbed by his lack of a male heir, Henry made a pre-emptive strike against Edward Stafford, Duke of Buckingham, a nobleman of great wealth and one of the king's own associates. Buckingham disliked Wolsey and failed to discourage suggestions that, as a descendant of Edward III's son Thomas, Duke of Gloucester, he himself might make quite a good king. Buckingham too, was therefore executed for treason. His elimination was a last footnote to the Wars of the Roses; but it was also a sign that, on the issue of providing for the succession, Henry would be resolute.

Henry's fancy for the traditional role of warrior king may well have had its usual effect of keeping the aristocracy sweet-tempered during the always dangerous first years of a young king's reign, particularly as his ventures had some success. He defeated the French in the so-called battle of the Spurs in 1513 and, a month later, an English army destroyed 10,000 Scotsmen, including their king, James V, at the battle of Flodden Edge. But from then until 1527, during Wolsey's supremacy, the English indulged in various theatrical military gestures in the course of the cardinal's busily unsuccessful attempt to establish England as a powerful intermediary in the struggle then going on between the Valois kings of France and the Habsburgs, who by then ruled the Empire in Germany as well as Burgundy and Spain. Italy was their favoured battleground and Wolsey hoped to appear as so loyal a supporter of the pope in Italy that he might eventually become pope himself. Wolsey therefore engineered a series of treaties, and set up leagues and alliances which fell apart as soon as they were made. Fortunately for Henry, and in many respects for England too, the failure of these schemes could all be laid at Wolsey's door and thus serve as prelude to a spectacular resumption of royal power by the king.

Wolsey also served the king well in the long run by his even more detested policy at home. His ambitions ruined the national finances. He imposed high taxes. He forced loans out of the propertied classes so onerous that Henry had to intervene to stop their collection and to pardon defaulters. Wolsey further upset the landed gentry by trying to stop them enclosing their lands, on the grounds that a vast pool of rural unemployment was allegedly being created by landowners turning peasant holdings into huge pleasure parks or sheep runs. His only valuable achievement was to strengthen the chancery court by greatly increasing its business and thus building up a large volume of equity case law. Having no legal training, Wolsey had little patience with the pedantries of the common law: since no new kind of writ could be developed, common lawyers took the unhelpful view that if there was no writ that could put right a particular injustice, the injustice was not an injustice. Chancery knew no such obstacles; and it was by prosecutions in chancery that enclosing landlords were attacked. More controversially, he extended the chancellor's jurisdiction in criminal cases. Chancery became the court in which the government enforced all its statutes and proclamations and punished contempt of court and bribery of juries. It also took over cases of forgery, libel and perjury, offences that Wolsey, as an all-powerful churchman, could remove from ecclesiastical jurisdiction into a court of the crown without raising a murmur. He also attempted to make justice available to poor men. He gave up when he discovered how much so many poor men had to complain about.

Nevertheless, the overall effect was to strengthen the judicial authority of the council and therefore of the crown. This was unlikely, as it had been under the Angevins and would be under the Stuarts, to find favour with the men of property or the common lawyers, particularly now that most substantial men of property had themselves had some legal training. But it was the more unpopular for being the work of an overweening prelate. Wolsey was too arrogant to see that he was strengthening the institutions of monarchy in a way that made it certain that he would reap the unpopularity, leaving the king in due course to gather this rich harvest of power to himself.

Wolsey also served another of the king's purposes: that of still further distancing royal power from its traditional political dependence on the aristocracy. In a sense, Wolsey was a great leveller, an important catalyst in the process by which all men, whatever their rank, were being made to feel themselves obedient servants of one sovereign authority. Aristocratic resentment at this painful process explains the contemporary allegation that he was the son of a common butcher in Ipswich. Hence, too, his vulnerability. He who was himself, after all, one of the king's subjects was behaving as if he were master of the whole realm. Confronted by this all-powerful—but unaristocratic—overmighty subject, men became unusually anxious for the king again to become their one, rightful good lord.

Matrimonial Cause

Wolsey fell from power because the failure of his foreign policy made it impossible for him to get papal approval of Henry's determination, from about 1527 onwards, to get rid of his wife, Catherine of Aragon, so that he could marry Anne Boleyn, a niece of Thomas Howard, Duke of Norfolk. To legitimise his desires, Henry took his stand on the legal technicality that Catherine had previously been married to Henry's deceased elder brother, Arthur. Though canon law forbade a man to marry his sister-in-law, it had been overridden in Henry's case by a papal dispensation. Henry, however, began to insist that the dispensation must have been invalid and his marriage sinful because God had clearly indicated His disapproval by allowing all Catherine's male children to die at birth or shortly afterwards. The pope was therefore duty bound, Henry thought, to announce that Henry and Catherine had never been man and wife. Henry could then proceed to a true marriage with Anne and thereby satisfy his conscience, his carnal appetite and his proper and politic anxiety to ensure an undisputed succession after his death.

Papal unwillingness to accommodate Henry was, to begin with, scarcely concerned even with technicalities. Catherine, unfortunately for Henry, was a Habsburg princess whose father was king of Spain and whose nephew was the Holy Roman Emperor, Charles V. Charles had just made himself the most formidable prince in Europe by defeating the French at Pavia in 1525. In particular he was now dominant in Italy, for control of which he and the French had been contesting; and this involved control over the pope in Rome. Wolsey at once made matters worse by cobbling together a league of various powers to resist Charles; with the result that Charles sent his troops towards Rome where, mutinous and ragged after long campaigning, they sacked the city for four days. In the outcome, the pope, Clement VII, became the emperor's prisoner. The likelihood that the pope would now feel free to announce that, owing to an error by his predecessor, the emperor's aunt had been living in sin for nearly twenty years was therefore remote. As for Wolsey, he had made himself an enemy of the emperor at exactly the wrong moment. The signal that he had come to the end of the road was the signature, by Charles and the king of France, of the treaty of Cambrai in August 1529. Though theoretically at that time an ally of the French, Wolsey was not consulted.

In the same month of August 1529, writs were issued for the summoning of a parliament. In October, Wolsey was dismissed and indicted, but survived, through an unusual display of mercy by Henry, until 1530, when he died on the way to trial. But the parliament that had its first meeting on 3 November 1529 would not be dissolved until 1536. Out of the ruins of Wolsey's career a revolution would be constructed.

'Down with the Church!'

To apply the word 'Reformation' to royal policy towards the church in the early 1530s is to ascribe to the king and his advisers intentions they did not possess. The only first cause was Henry VIII's anger at the failure of Wolsey and the pope to grant his divorce. Hence the king's dismissal of Wolsey, agent of cooperation with the papacy, and the summoning of a parliament for use as the instrument of an attack on the power and wealth of the church in an effort to frighten the pope into giving way. Only when this policy failed did Henry proceed to abolish papal power in England. But though this enhancement of the authority of government was of revolutionary importance, the intention was not, save in a minimally legal sense, to 'reform' the church, but merely to put it under state management.

Moreover, given that the king and the cardinal had by now exhausted the large fortune left by Henry VII, state control of the church, once envisaged, offered immediate and alluring financial advantages. The clergy did pay taxes to the king; but they paid them much more regularly to the pope. Through the device of bestowing high ecclesiastical offices and therefore their emoluments upon royal officials, the church had been subsidising the expenses of government for centuries; but it nevertheless possessed large quantities of land and capital. Conveniently, too, to threaten to cut off taxes to Rome, initially simply as a form of diplomatic pressure, would raise once again the old issue of whether such payments were justifiable as such. To threaten the wealth of the church within England itself would likewise provoke searching questions about the propriety of the possession of so much wealth by men who professed to serve God.

Hence, to summon parliament, to add pomp and circumstance to the crown's campaign to secure a royal divorce, would unleash for the first time for over a century the resentment against the church which had long been simmering among taxpaying property owners, a resentment made the more intense by the rapacity and arrogance of the unpopular cardinal. It was scarcely realised, when this process was begun, that these essentially secular acts, set in motion by a money-minded court in league with a money-minded parliament, would involve changes in religious belief pregnant with ideas potentially subversive of the social order. The implications were seen soon enough, however, with the result that 'reformation' of the church in England in the more radical sense of the word was continuously resisted and almost indefinitely postponed.

By the time the Long Parliament of the Reformation met, the years of Wolsey's domination had produced a wave of anti-clerical feeling that led at once to an angry concentration on the faults of a church which by and large was not notably worse than it had ever been, but whose deficiencies seemed the more apparent because of its failure to keep in step with the increased education of the majority of propertied laymen and the greater personal devoutness of the faithful minority. The Venetian ambassador reported, 'Now with the commons is nothing but down with the church'; an English chronicler noted that complaints men had hitherto feared to make lest they be accused of heresy could now be made openly because God had 'at last opened the king's eyes'.

The grievances of the laity demonstrated how greatly the church preyed on secular men for its own secular advantage. High fees were charged by church courts for proving wills, and by priests for burying people in consecrated ground. One MP claimed that a priest would let children starve rather than forgo the cow he demanded as a fee for burying their father. Church officials were accused of imprisoning for heresy men whose only fault was to criticise their parish priest. Bishops were accused of extorting excessive fees from clergy before allowing them to enter upon their benefices. It was claimed that bishops conferred livings on 'young folks, calling them their nephews', a charge not unconnected with the fact that Cardinal Wolsey's natural son had enjoyed the profits of twelve church benefices while away studying on the continent. Hints of the Puritan future showed up in complaints that there were too many holydays in the year, thus causing working men to fall into 'abominable and execrable vices'; and that pluralism and non-residence caused parishioners to lack 'preaching and true instruction of God's word, to the grave peril of their souls'.

Benefit of clergy was another scandal, and one with a long history. Over 350 years earlier his attempt to deal with it had involved Henry II in his quarrel with Becket. The sensation caused by the murder of Becket in his cathedral at Canterbury in 1170 had made sure that the complicated problem of how far the church rather than the crown had jurisdiction over 'criminous clerks' should remain unresolved throughout the middle ages. By the sixteenth century it was still possible for a first-time offender, charged with capital crime short of treason, to avoid prosecution in the king's courts by successfully claiming to be a clerk in orders. In theory he could be prosecuted in the church courts and, if found guilty, imprisoned until twelve or more other clerks swore to their belief in (not in the fact of) the prisoner's innocence. The abuses to which this led were obvious, if only because, episcopal prisons being small, convicted clerks would be let out merely to make room in the jail. Criminals could thus use the system to commit their first crime free of serious risk. Worse still, the system applied not only to those in holy orders (i.e. sub-deacons, deacons and priests) but also to those in the minor orders of ostiarius, lector and acolyte. These minor 'clerks' were laymen who, after a perfunctory test of their literacy, did part-time odd jobs about the church on Sundays and holydays. Since minor orders involved no commitment to celibacy, and literacy of a sort was not hard to come by, it was taken for granted that any potential criminal would take the precaution of getting himself admitted into minor orders.

Rights of sanctuary were equally offensive. Persons accused of felonies could escape justice by going to particular churches or areas. Again in theory, they were to confess within forty days and then abjure the realm. Whole towns and districts under the jurisdiction of the church, such as Beverley, Ripon and Durham, were sanctuaries, and therefore permanent refuges for criminals.

The contrast between such abuses and the service rendered to the community by the parish clergy was glaring. Absenteeism and pluralism were now general. Inflation made the income of less well-endowed livings inadequate for men of ability. The unbeneficed chaplains who did duty for absentee incumbents were poor, ignorant of the Bible and out of date in their ideas even when they were conscientious. The resistance of the bishops to vernacular translations of the Bible, for fear of Lollardism, prolonged clerical ignorance. The laity's low opinion of clerics inhibited bishops from punishing delinquent incumbents for fear of making scandal more scandalous. If an incumbent were deprived, he became a disgruntled chaplain elsewhere; and since the incumbent had a lay patron, the latter might cause trouble too.

Further difficulties arose from the fact that neither the changes in church government made by Henry VIII, nor those of his Tudor successors, systematically tackled these abuses. Efforts to exclude even minor orders from benefit of clergy failed until 1550. For those in holy orders it did not finally disappear until 1827. Sanctuary for crime was not everywhere abolished until 1623, while for civil cases it lasted until 1697, most notably in Whitefriars, in London, between Fleet Street and the Thames. The site of a former ecclesiastical sanctuary and nicknamed Alsatia in Charles II's reign, it was a notorious haunt of criminals who had evaded arrest. Pluralism and absenteeism survived into the nineteenth century.

Henry's dismissal of Wolsey, however, was seen as a major victory for the anti-clerical cause. As well as being Henry's chancellor and a papal cardinal, he had been archbishop of York, a permanent papal legate and, in his own mind, an eventual pope. As papal legate he exercised so crushing and arbitrary an authority over the English church that he made the papal power he represented unacceptable even to English bishops. His conspicuous rapacity shocked his contemporaries. He acquired, in addition to the see of York, England's wealthiest abbey, St Albans, and its wealthiest bishopric, Winchester. He began to build Hampton Court Palace; he made money by bribery and extortion. His hold over the church was so great that, when Henry dismissed him for failing to secure the divorce, the church was incapable of resisting the king's attack on it.

In 1530, after allowing the commons to express its general disapproval of the church, Henry declared the entire clergy guilty of praemunire; charged them a handsome sum for pardoning them for this offence; and got their unwilling acceptance of a formula declaring that the king was their 'singular protector, only and supreme lord, and, as far as the law of Christ allows, even Supreme Head'. Since canon law (the nearest anybody could get to 'the law of Christ') would allow no such proposition, this may be regarded as the first example of the Church of England's traditional resort to formulas that meant less than they said.

Forced by all this to examine first principles in his turn, the pope would still not give way. His papal authority had been challenged; and the matters of law raised by Henry's matrimonial situation became more complex the more they were looked at. The pope therefore made only one concession: he approved the consecration of Thomas Cranmer as the new Archbishop of Canterbury. Cranmer was Henry's choice because Cranmer believed in the royal sovereignty and because Cranmer was therefore ready to pronounce the marriage to Catherine void and to make Anne Boleyn Henry's one true wife. Since Anne was now pregnant it was imperative that her child be born in wedlock. With maximum irony, the child, when born, was not the much desired son but another daughter. She was christened Elizabeth.

Once Cranmer became archbishop, a Protestant reformation of religion became something of a long term probability, since Cranmer, though of infinitely cautious temperament, acted upon genuinely felt principles. With Thomas Cromwell also now acting as Henry's right hand man, the abolition of papal authority in England became a certainty. Cromwell was quick to see that the whole climate of opinion was working towards the exaltation of royal power at the expense of papal and towards a system of national churches in Europe that would mark the abandonment of the now unacceptable consequences of the medieval attempt to sustain a church that was international. It was due to Cromwell's energy that all the anti-papal proceedings after 1530 were given the force of law by statutes drafted by him and carried through parliament. By the Act of Appeals of 1533, all appeals to Rome on matters testamentary or matrimonial were prohibited. This, by allowing Catherine no right of appeal, led to Cranmer's excommunication; to insulting English references to the pope thereafter as 'bishop of Rome'; and to further statutes stopping all payments to Rome (including Peter's Pence). That these latter statutes had relatively little to do with 'reform' of the church but aimed, in modern terms, to 'nationalise' it and confiscate part of its wealth to the state was demonstrated by statutes of 1534 exacting annual payments from the church considerably in excess of the sums previously paid to the papacy.

To demonstrate beyond argument that an irrevocable constitutional revolution was nevertheless taking place, another statute made it high treason to deny by any public act the legal validity of Henry's marriage to Anne Boleyn. At the end of 1534, parliament summed up the new situation in a short Act of Supremacy. It proclaimed that the king 'justly and rightfully is and ought to be Supreme Head of the Church of England'. All this great flurry of statute-making, for which there was little precedent, was skilfully organised by Cromwell and rarely obstructed by a firmly anti-clerical parliament. Almost the only consistent protest the commons made was against the shabby treatment accorded to Queen Catherine, the first and the most demonstrably innocent victim of 'the English Reformation'.

Crown Imperial

The members of the Long Parliament of the Reformation scarcely realised (and would not have minded if they had) that, in allowing Henry VIII to make good, as William Rufus, Henry I and Henry II had failed to do, the claim that 'this realm of England is an empire governed by one Supreme Head and King', they had created a new Leviathan, the independent sovereign state. Between 1530 and 1536 the medieval theory of the two powers, the spiritual and the temporal, was, as far as England was concerned, demolished. From now on, no external authority could limit the competence of whoever at any time ruled over England; a state of affairs that would exist until the signature of the Treaty of Rome in 1973. Henceforth, too, no subject of a ruler of England could, on the grounds that it pertained to the realm of the spirit, claim that an action taken against him by that ruler was in excess of that ruler's powers. Theoretically, in fact, the power henceforth exercised by English monarchs was exceptionally all-embracing. There was scarcely a state in western Europe whose rulers possessed, as England's rulers now possessed, not only the traditional divinity of kingship, but also the complete subservience of a church hardly less hierarchical and authoritarian than when it had been in communion with Rome. In none was that comprehensive power buttressed by a representative body, of which the lower house was elective, and the whole of which, however factious it was later to prove, assented to the proposition that ultimate authority in all things resided in the crown. Even when civil war came in 1642, both sides professed to be fighting for king and parliament. None of the absolute monarchies abroad, whether Catholic or Protestant, had so obsequious a church. None could claim the added reinforcement of their authority referred to in Henry VIII's pronouncement of 1543: 'We are informed by our judges that we at no time stand so high in our estate royal as in time of parliament assembled, wherein we as head and you as members are conjoined in one body politic'.

Supremacy over church as well as state had been affirmed by means of statute partly because Henry and Cromwell knew that what they wanted, parliament wanted too; and because it was good public relations when throwing off a foreign, if internationally venerable, jurisdiction, to claim to be doing so with the assent of the whole political nation. But, having helped to endow the crown with power over the church, parliament would in time want to call it to account for the way it exercised that power. And monarchs would resist that interference. For, in 1535, as far as 'the Reformation' was concerned, the unsolved problem of what sort of church the English people were to submit themselves to now it was independent of the papacy had scarcely been considered. Conflict between crown and parliament on this issue seemed scarcely likely at the time; but in less than a century it would provide men with the slogans of civil war.

In the 1530s, however, there was no impediment to the energetic exercise of the crown's newfound supremacy. The monasteries were expeditiously dissolved and their wealth expropriated because this was instantly profitable to the crown and popular with the commons, to whom it was easy to represent monks and friars as agents of papal pretensions, improperly enjoying too much of the national wealth. It would be contrary to the evidence to assert that the monastic way of life had permanently outlived its usefulness; but in England, though perhaps rather less so than on the continent, it seemed to have done so by the 1530s. The laity felt that the approximately ten thousand monks and two thousand nuns did little to justify the wealth of the religious orders. Too many of them had taken their vows when they were too young to know what they were doing. This would seem to be confirmed by the fact that after the dissolution twenty-five per cent of the nuns married and rather more of the men. Except perhaps in the north and west, monks did relatively little for the poor; their hospitality was mostly reserved for the wealthy traveller. Official pronouncements that monasteries were dens of vice need not, however, be taken seriously.

The monastic lands were taken over by a Court of Augmentations, which Cromwell had set up by statute, and in effect nationalised. Movables were auctioned, lead stripped from roofs and sold, woodwork left to rot, pilgrimage shrines plundered. There was a holocaust of images, manuscripts and archives. This was symptomatic of the fact that increased literacy introduced into religious attitudes a topsy-turvily superstitious detestation of all visual aids to piety, particularly if they were of great beauty.

The authorities rather undermined their vilification of monks and nuns by showing a greater regard for their persons than their property. Heads of houses were usually well compensated; most monks and nuns, though described in advance as guilty of all kinds of vice, received a pension and a lump sum. Many of those in priest's orders got ecclesiastical posts, with the result that there were relatively few ordinations for another twenty years. This mild treatment was, however, reserved for the majority, who agreed to go quietly. Those who did not, felt the force of Tudor ruthlessness. The abbots of Colchester, Reading and Glastonbury were among those executed for declining to surrender their abbeys voluntarily.

The wealth of the religious orders has been estimated at 175% of the crown's annual average income. There was, however, a loss on the confiscation of some smaller houses owing to the liability for pensions for the dispossessed monks, and for the annuities which, in the absence of insurance companies, monasteries had sometimes sold to lay people in order to acquire ready cash. The crown sold most of the monastic lands to the landed classes, and it was soon evident that Catholic as well as Protestant families had become owners of monastic lands. Though parliament let Mary Tudor restore the authority of the pope in England in the 1550s, it would not hand back the monastic lands.

Though the dissolution of the monasteries was the most spectacular manifestation of the royal supremacy, more important in the long run were Cromwell's masterful efforts to strengthen and extend the power of the crown in matters secular. The administrative structure of government was much improved, and permanently so, by Cromwell's energies. The amorphous royal council, which might contain over a hundred members, was reduced to a more workmanlike privy council with roughly only a score of members. Though it was composed exclusively of nominees of the crown, its functions were those of a modern cabinet, which, in theory, is still an executive committee of the privy council. The council further tightened its grip on affairs by itself trying and punishing offenders, acquiring, when it functioned in this capacity, the eventually detested title of Star Chamber.

As important and as permanent was his transformation of the office of the king's principal secretary into that of the crown's chief executive and coordinating minister. In future the effective head of government would be not, as in the past, the chancellor, but the secretary of state, wholly concerned, as a primarily judicial functionary like the chancellor could not be, with administrative and political business. After Cromwell, the post was usually divided between two men, each of whom could act in the absence of the other. As late as 1782, English governments would still have these two secretaries of state more or less dividing home and foreign affairs between them. Only with the loss of the American colonies in 1783 did one of them become the secretary for foreign affairs and the other the secretary for home affairs. Technically, the later multiplication of secretaries of state in government administrations was still supposed to involve the ability of any one of them to act for any of the others. The downgrading of the office of secretary of state by the proliferation of departments headed by 'ministers' was a twentieth-century development. The title was not known before Lloyd George's appointment as minister for munitions in 1915 and his subsequent creation, when prime minister, of such ministries as those for Labour, Supply, and Health between 1916 and 1919.

Far more important for the crown than its acquisition of monastic lands was Cromwell's establishment for the first time of the supreme executive and judicial authority of the crown over the whole territory of the kingdom. By a succession of statutes, as thoughtfully drawn up by Cromwell as those which had drawn all ecclesiastical jurisdiction into the king's hands, all those feudal liberties were abolished which had previously excluded the crown from exercising sovereignty over particular parts of the country. According to the impressively worded preamble to an act of 1536 (of which both Henry II and Edward I would have unhesitatingly approved) 'Sundry gifts of the king's most noble progenitors' had removed from royal control 'divers of the most ancient prerogatives and authorities of justice appertaining to the imperial crown of this realm'. These lost rights were to be 'recovered'. They were in most need of such recovery in the north and on the Welsh Marches.

For the first time, in effect, the king's peace would be extended to the five most northerly counties. Northumberland, Cumberland, Westmorland and Durham had not been covered by Domesday, either because they were in the hands of the Scots or because they were thought too poor and turbulent for it to be safe or worth while to survey them. Durham and Chester sent no MPs to the Commons. Their inhabitants had the reputation of being notorious cattle stealers who, after raiding the neighbouring countryside, could retire within their palatine boundaries, safe in the knowledge that the king's writ did not run there. Northumberland and Cumberland were long an Anglo-Scottish no-man's-land administered by their feudal nobility in complete independence. General lawlessness was accentuated by the existence of the clan system on the English as on the Scottish side of the border.

By 1530, Chester and Lancaster had passed into the Tudor patrimony; Durham's palatine privileges were extinguished in 1536. After the revolt known as the Pilgrimage of Grace, Thomas Cromwell set up a permanent Council of the North, directly controlled by the crown. A last outburst in 1569, when the Revolt of the Northern Earls against Elizabeth took place on behalf of the Catholic Mary, Queen of Scots, was followed by widespread executions and confiscations which finally subordinated the north to the control of the crown. Final assimilation was achieved by the abolition of the separate Council of the North in 1641.

Similarly, a Council of Wales was established in 1536 to administer both the common law and act as a Star Chamber court in Wales, though in 1543 common law became the function of four Courts of Great Session in the Welsh counties. The act of 1536 extinguished the petty liberties and quasi-kingships surviving on the borders of England and Wales and incorporated them into the existing English or Welsh counties, or into the five new counties of Brecknock, Denbigh, Monmouth, Montgomery and Radnor. Henceforth, Wales was fully incorporated with England, thus compelling the historian, however anxious to respect the separate nationality of the Welsh, to write of their country as if it were part of England.

By 1536, therefore, the desire of a self-willed king to replace an elderly and now barren wife by a young and fertile one had set in motion a process which, once started, settled in a great rush issues which had been unresolved for the greater part of English history. The temporal power had won the victory over the spiritual that had eluded the tempestuous Henry II, and the king's peace was at last, as kings had wanted it to be since before the coming of the Normans, established throughout the kingdom. Of all the various dates which historians have suggested as marking 'the end of the middle ages' in England, the one about which there can surely be least argument is the year 1536 when, Henry VIII and Thomas Cromwell having completed their authoritarian revolution, their willing accomplice, the Long Parliament of the Reformation, was at last dissolved.

3
GROWTH, POVERTY AND AFFLUENCE

People and Prices

WHEN Henry VIII's reign began in 1509, the years of stable prices, stationary population and limited economic growth were ending. From 1510 to the mid-seventeenth century, food prices multiplied by seven and the prices of industrial products by three. It was the longest period of inflation in English history.

This long-term price rise was temporarily accelerated on its path by fortunately short-lived government policies and perhaps prolonged by events across the Atlantic. A relatively brief but damaging rise was caused by the debasement of the coinage in 1526–7 and from 1544 to 1551, on a scale large enough to produce, from then until 1560, the highest rate of inflation in the century. The earlier debasement of 1526–7 was provoked by the costs of Wolsey's diplomacy; the later by foolish wars projected by Henry VIII in his years of physical and mental decline. In the 1550s, the coinage, quite exceptionally in English history, was almost the worst in Europe. Initially, this tactic of reducing the amount of silver in the coinage increased the royal revenues; but, like modern increases in the money supply, it drove up prices so fast that the initial gain was soon lost. When Northumberland took over government in Edward VI's reign, he started, though his methods were clumsy, to rehabilitate the coinage so that, had debasement been the only cause, inflation would have slowed down after 1560. In fact it continued.

A more long term factor, which certainly much increased the money supply in Europe, was the inflow of American silver following the Spanish discovery of the silver mines of Peru and Mexico. But how much of this silver found its way into England and at what date, is uncertain. Inflation, already evident before the debasement of the coinage and continuing long after it, was well in evidence before the likely dates when Spanish silver reached England (some time after the 1560s) and must therefore be attributed to other causes.

That food prices rose so much more than other prices reflects what was probably the underlying cause. Between 1520 and the end of the seventeenth century the population of England and Wales seems to have risen from about 2.5 million to about 5.2 million. This contrasts with the fact that population had risen hardly at all since the Black Death and that from 1650 to 1750 it rose only by a further million. Interrupted by bad harvests, with or without outbreaks of plague, influenza, smallpox and dysentery in the 1550s, 1580s, 1590s and 1630s, the overall rate of growth in the hundred years after 1550 is comparable to that of the first decades of the industrial revolution.

The renewal after almost two centuries of a situation in which there were more mouths to feed greatly stimulated both agriculture and industry. It inflated prices and, by creating a surplus labour force, depressed wages and reduced their real value. But an increased number of mouths to feed meant a larger market not only for the products of the land but for the brewers, butchers, bakers and millers. With more bodies to clothe, the textile, clothing and leather trades expanded; so did crafts associated with transport, such as makers of carts, wheels, saddles and harnesses. New opportunities for profit encouraged new luxury products and an unprecedented boom for all the crafts involved in building.

The increase in the number of wage earners aggravated the problem caused by a population growth outrunning the capacity of the soil to feed it. The manufactures catering for other than more immediate neighbourhood needs were carried on principally outside the arable areas, in regions where the soil was relatively unproductive, notably woodland and forest areas. These were also subject to population increase, under-employment and high food prices. Towns also expanded, since they were the most obvious organisational and distribution centres for the surrounding countryside. Towns endured, as well as their own natural increase, that caused by the immigration of additional workers. London's population increased more than tenfold from 1550 to 1750; and though in the century after 1550 the populations of such towns as Birmingham, Worcester, Exeter and Plymouth doubled, London dominated English life more emphatically in Tudor and early Stuart times than it was to do again until the last half of the nineteenth century. Urban growth further inflated food prices by creating yet more wage earners dependent largely on the market for their food; and up to one-third of the rural population had become landless wage earners (or would-be wage earners) in agriculture and rural industries.

Like any other inflationary period, these years sharpened the division between winners and losers. Those who were likely to lose were the landless, or those with little land; the poor and unfortunate; and those whose economic life was tied to longstanding customs and regulations. The undoubted winners were enterprising men of all ranks, most particularly substantial yeomen, gentry, traders, merchants and lawyers. Though wages lagged well behind food prices, they did not lag far behind industrial prices, so that manufactured goods became relatively cheaper, thus stimulating demand and therefore employment. All these effects were unevenly distributed both in time and place and subject to the effects of bad harvests, outbreaks of plague or the dislocation of exports by international conflicts. It was, throughout, a period of disturbing change that nevertheless produced sufficient economic growth to outweigh, in the national balance sheet, the considerable social distress and the intermittent crises.

Ironically, though the fear that social distress might cause grave disorder led to legislation to protect the destitute from the worst of poverty's disasters, the most conspicuous victim of the long inflation would turn out, by the seventeenth century, to have been the crown. More powerful in the 1530s than it had ever been, inflationary pressure had, by the first decade of the seventeenth century, almost fatally weakened it. Moreover, the most difficult decades in the Tudor dynasty's history, the 1540s and 1550s, coincided with the worst period of inflation and of social disorder. This greatly aggravated the political and religious problems of those years and made the subsequent recovery under Elizabeth I seem all the more remarkable.

Agrarian Change

The stimulus of high prices and an expanding market led to great changes in agriculture. The need for more grazing land was urgent. More animals had to be grazed, if only to overcome the chronic shortage of manure so characteristic of medieval agriculture. Sheep and cattle rearing were encouraged by the growing demand for meat and for wool. The reviving cloth trade led to some change from arable farming to pasture, though there was not much enclosure for sheep farming alone, and little of it after the 1520s. More common was the trend towards mixed farming, since to increase the pasture was an essential contribution to improved arable husbandry. The need for better pasture to increase arable yields was also evident from the 1590s onwards in the growth of the techniques of convertible husbandry. This involved keeping the land under grass for between seven and twelve years, followed by a five to seven year period under the plough. Grazing over a long period fertilised the land, improved the quality of stock and, when the time came to put it under the plough, greatly increased yields. About three quarters of the land might be under grass at any one time, but the smaller area of arable could produce twice the yield of land permanently under the plough.

Conversion of open-field arable to permanent pasture, mixed farming or convertible husbandry was difficult to achieve without resort to the procedures known as enclosure and engrossing, both of which were subject to intense popular hostility. Enclosers and engrossers were, along with Catholics, the chief villains of Tudor and Stuart popular polemics. Engrossing meant amalgamating several small farms into one large one. Enclosure meant that the landlord extinguished common rights over arable and pasture and re-arranged strips into compact holdings marked off by hedges or fences. In this way the landlord acquired, more obviously even than before, the status of an entrepreneur capable of squeezing out smaller rivals. His share might include all or some of the common pasture and, where it was reasonably cultivable, parts of the waste and forest also. Smallholders or landless squatters

215

were liable to be evicted. Enclosing and engrossing landlords thus earned the ill-repute attracted by persons involved in take-overs and asset-stripping in the late twentieth century. Both pastoral farming and convertible husbandry were less labour-intensive than arable farming on the old style, and in those districts where the change took place there was a measure of rural depopulation which made the total situation, of too many landless men in a world of rising food prices, even worse.

Sixteenth-century enclosure and engrossing affected only about three to four per cent of the total arable acreage and they enabled agriculture to contribute significantly to the task of feeding, though at a lower standard than during the previous 150 years, a much increased population. Even so, though most of the open fields survived to be enclosed in the late eighteenth century, Tudor enclosures could affect up to thirty per cent of the arable in midland counties such as Northamptonshire and Leicestershire. Many smallholders were reduced to the status of casual wage earners or unauthorised squatters on forest or waste.

Even here they might still be at the landlord's mercy. Landlords would want to take in waste or forest either to cultivate it or to cash in on the timber shortage that was already compelling the use of coal as domestic fuel in towns. Enclosure and disafforestation, together with the parallel landlord activity of reclaiming the fens, were among the major agrarian grievances voiced by the more extreme radicals during the civil wars of the 1640s. Their champion, Winstanley, declared, 'True religion and undefiled is to let every one quietly have earth to manure'. The remark not only points up how precious a commodity manure was. It demonstrates how, before men had heard of an economic interpretation of history they had perforce to express economic concepts in the one intellectual vocabulary they had, that of religion. The contrary view to Winstanley's was framed in terms no less homely: 'A hedge in the field is as necessary in its kind as government in the church or commonwealth'. Yet both propositions were valid. The purpose of the hedge, as often as not, was to mark the boundary of a holding designed compactly to enclose enough pasture to guarantee sufficient manure for the effective use of the arable.

Not only was enclosure not universal throughout the open field areas; the outcry on the subject obscured the irrelevance of the issue to other rural communities. In the areas of woodland pasture, on the heavier soils of the Weald, north Essex and south Suffolk, and parts of Wiltshire, enclosure had long been usual. Open field arrangements were rarely applied to land which, in a rising market, was taken in from waste or forest. The higher moorland zones of the west, from Northumberland to Devon, had long been devoted to open pasture farming, mainly cattle and sheep rearing. In such areas there was a combination of enclosure with common rights which involved fewer of the traditional rules and customs of the kind whose disruption in the open field areas caused so much and, in the total agricultural context, disproportionate, controversy.

Industrial Expansion

The concurrent expansion of manufacture at this time was sufficient to cause some historians to speak of a sixteenth century 'industrial revolution'. There was, however, little or no technological innovation. Instead, there was chiefly a better organised use of the growing body of unemployed or under-employed rural labourers, in particular to meet the overseas demand for cloth, as well as the expanding home market. Woollen cloth exports in the 1550s were three times greater than in the depressed 1450s, and it has been tentatively estimated that in money terms textile exports increased fifteenfold between the 1480s and the early eighteenth century.

This increased production could be achieved with a minimum of capital investment and without the kind of technological innovation that launched the late-eighteenth century expansion of the cotton industry. The basic manufacturing processes were of a sort that could be carried out in (or 'put out' to) workers' own cottages and be undertaken by the various members of their families. Children could card the wool, the women spin it into yarn and the men do the weaving and finishing processes. Spinning wheels and looms were common articles of household equipment which villagers used to supplement an income from the land which rising prices made inadequate. Almost invariably, cloth manufacture developed where farms were too small to provide a sufficient income. It was by the end of the sixteenth century that the word 'spinster' began to be synonymous with 'unmarried woman', thus indicating that the state of virginity in rural England now automatically involved an economic function.

The system was so advantageously based on simple rural equipment that there was no need to resort to the capital expense involved in concentrating workers into a purpose-built factory. That John Winchcombe ('Jack of Newbury') set up a textile factory in the early sixteenth century with a number of looms in it is important only in the sense that he was almost alone in doing so. The putting-out system was admirably designed to function wherever there was a good deal of idle or semi-idle rural labour and this seems to explain its concentration during the sixteenth century in the West Country, Gloucestershire, Wiltshire, parts of Somerset, and Devonshire; in East Anglia, especially Suffolk and north Essex; and, to a lesser extent, in the West Riding. Significantly, these were all, for the most part, pastoral areas, often thought of as part of 'the forest'.

Other industries, though less significant in the development of English overseas trade, probably equalled clothmaking as a source of employment, most of it rural. Only three sixteenth-century towns,

217

Worcester, Coventry and Norwich carried on substantial textile manufacture. Workers who turned cloth into clothing—hatters, cappers and
tailors—were for the most part urban craftsmen; so were the leather-
workers, though the London shoemakers got their leather from Suffolk;
and Northamptonshire became a boot- and shoe-making area soon after
1650. Though half the leather was produced for footwear and much of
the rest for saddles and harnesses, it was also in demand for book-
binding and for buckets. The demand for leather was threatened for a
time by the success of clothmaking in capitalising on the rising
prosperity of yeomen and successful artisans. They now felt they could
afford to ascend from the ranks of those who wore leather to those who
could afford cloth. But the leather workers benefited from the fact that
boots and shoes were beginning for the first time to be worn by some of
the poorer classes.

Although metal workers were ubiquitous and most metal utensils
were made locally, already half the work force of Sheffield was producing cutlery and other metal goods by the sixteenth century. Coal
mining was, naturally, highly localised, principally in the Newcastle
area, the Forest of Dean, the west Midlands and west Cumberland.
England was already so short of timber as to be the biggest coal producer
in Europe. The Newcastle coal mines have been called 'the first really
large scale bulk-producing industry in the western world'. Nevertheless, although fires fuelled by coal brought by sea from Newcastle were
already sending their smoke into the skies of Tudor London, coal
mining employed only one tenth of the numbers engaged in the leather
crafts.

More widespread, given that fifty to eighty per cent of the rural
population was engaged more or less full time in agriculture and
therefore dependent on wooden implements and structures, was the
miscellaneous body of full or part-time woodworkers. The more
specialised of these operated in the forest areas, as much the workshops
of an agricultural society as coal and iron areas were to be of an industrial
one. Building expanded considerably; but since the cottages of the rural
poor were of the simplest construction, the highly skilled building
craftsmen were found more often in the towns. For unskilled work,
some wealthy landlords, when building their new country houses,
conscripted their tenants—and anybody else they could lay hands on—
into their labour force.

Conspicuous Consumption

The building of great houses was the largest capital undertaking of
Tudor and early Stuart times. In some counties, more such houses were
built in the fifty years before 1620 than in any other half-century. Nobles
and wealthier gentry often found ample supplies of building material to
hand when they acquired monastic sites. Many also built town houses,

particularly in London; in most prosperous towns there was much building of substantial warehouses, merchants' houses and, to a lesser extent, shops. Most country houses were large. Like the feudal castles they superseded, they were intended to dominate and impress, each one defying rival gentry and nobles to build larger. The challenge was usually accepted; and a great man's completion of a fine country house often signalled his impending financial ruin. The nobility also built large to provide suitably impressive hospitality for the queen. Though the court was less peripatetic than it had been, the close-fisted Elizabeth was always eager to feed at her wealthy subjects' expense. Thrifty men viewed these royal visitations with gloom; but the nobleman who shut his house and left it rather than entertain his sovereign found on his return that the queen's men had nevertheless got into the house, arranged for the queen's entertainment and were in process of sending him the bill.

The size, grand frontages and the splendour of the more remarkable larger Elizabethan houses, such as Burghley and Longleat, made them palaces rather than homes, and justifies Sir John Summerson's description of them as 'prodigy houses'. After the 1620s, a better understanding of Italian Renaissance ideas, as well as a realisation of the cost and inconvenience of sheer size, led to less ostentatious styles. Nevertheless, once built, the old large houses had to be kept up. This particular aristocratic dilemma was not peculiar to the twentieth century. Yet, as the surviving visual evidence confirms, the spectacular 'prodigy houses' were greatly outnumbered by the dozens of solid farmhouses built, or rebuilt, between about 1570 and 1640, right across the southern half of England.

The rebuilding of rural England in this way was the biggest, but not the only, stimulus to the economy that resulted from the luxurious habits of the better off. Butchers and brewers prospered greatly because the nobility and gentry of England were already notorious as enormous meat eaters and beer drinkers. In large households, five to eight pints of beer per head were consumed daily. It was also a fashion-conscious age. Both Elizabeth I and James I had an eye for a well dressed youth, and male gorgeousness was enhanced by costly materials such as crimson velvet, scarlet cloaks and ermine. Embroidery was so extravagantly indulged in that its cost could exceed that of the garment itself. Imports of silks and satin increased by leaps and bounds after 1560. James I and Charles I set their subjects an even more outrageous example than Elizabeth. During one seven-year period, James bought a new suit every day, a new waistcoat every three weeks, a new pair of gloves every day. In one year, Charles I bought 513 articles of footwear. Expenditure by courtiers could not fall too conspicuously short of these standards. Puritanism, with its emphasis on sobriety in dress and behaviour was something of a natural reaction against the conspicuous waste displayed by a very affluent society.

Commercial Adventure

The growth in the trade in cloth which began in the 1470s was sustained for the next eighty years, though accompanied by a downward trend in wool exports. By 1550, cloth accounted for three-quarters of all English exports. The proportion exported via London rose from fifty to ninety per cent, thus markedly adding to the prosperity of the south-east and making London more than ever the country's richest trading centre. The dominant position of the Merchant Adventurers was helped by successful commercial treaties negotiated by Henry VII; and the select body of merchants who belonged to the 'company' attracted hostility by their success in keeping so-called 'interlopers' from taking part in the trade. They were the better able to do this because Antwerp, the site of their continental headquarters, controlled virtually all movement of cloth to the rest of Europe.

The 1550s, however, in this as in other respects, was a time of some difficulty. The debasement of the coinage meant that, in terms of foreign currency, the cost of the English pound fell by nearly sixty per cent, so that the Merchant Adventurers were among the few who did not object to the debasement, since it created an export boom. But there was a corresponding slump when Northumberland once more restored the silver content of English coins. As well as the exporters, the farmers who had turned arable into pasture during the boom and the clothiers and the weavers who worked for them faced loss or unemployment because of over-production. Matters were made worse when France and Spain went to war and bankrupted each other in 1557; there were bad harvests, and political ill-feeling between England and the Habsburg rulers of the Netherlands. The Merchant Adventurers had to quit Antwerp in 1564 and find other continental headquarters. Even though they returned later, the bitter campaigns fought by the Spanish Habsburgs against their rebellious Protestant subjects in the Netherlands led to the ruin of Antwerp as a great commercial centre. By 1598, when the Merchant Adventurers settled in the northern, Protestant Netherlands, they had ceased to be adventurous except in name. Though they no longer had the German Hansards to compete with in London, their chief function had become that of making sure that an export trade that was twenty per cent lower than it had been in 1550 was firmly defended against 'interloping' English merchants who were not of their company.

The fact that the Merchant Adventurers had obtained, at a price, a legal monopoly from the crown was symptomatic of a problem both economic and political. In the war-ridden condition of sixteenth-century Europe, traders were in genuine need of government support and protection. At the same time, the crown needed both the cash they could pay in return for these monopolistic rights and the loans that could be raised from them. But though this guaranteed cash to the crown and profit to the monopolist, the resultant branding of all other potential rivals as interlopers stimulated criticism of the crown for selling commercial privileges to the favoured few. But by and large, the Tudor concept of civic virtue was little more favourable to freedom of economic enterprise than to freedom of religion. Elizabeth's Mr Secretary Cecil, though Protestant by persuasion and a quiet patron of the emphatically Protestant Puritans, was so far from equating the Protestant religion with the entrepreneurial spirit that he disapproved of the expansion of the cloth industry because he thought it encouraged those who worked in it to be 'unruly'.

Fortunately, the energies of other nations were offering the English quite different opportunities. By 1540, the Portuguese had found a direct route to south-east Asia and beyond; and after Columbus discovered the existence of America, Cortes and Pizarro had uncovered its wealth of precious metal. As a result of these events Europeans ceased to belong merely to a civilisation pitched hazardously between the Baltic and the Mediterranean and began to transmit their influence across all the oceans. The great age of the Hansards and the Italians was coming to an end; the successful traders of the future would be those who faced outwards from Europe towards the oceans. The oceanic pioneers could not, however, make good their bold original claims. The Spanish American empire was of unmanageable size (in theory it was held to include all the Americas except Brazil); and a small nation like the Portuguese, with a population of around a million, could hardly expect long to dominate, as it did to begin with, maritime trade routes that stretched from Lisbon by way of the Cape of Good Hope and Zanzibar as far as Goa and thence to beyond the Spice Islands. The Portuguese and Spanish achievement was thus a stimulus to other nations first to emulate and then, as far as possible, attack them. Significantly, the most persistent and eventually most successful rivals of the two pioneer Catholic states were the Dutch and English, able to claim that they were advancing legitimate trade and championing the Protestant faith all in the same operation.

The voyages by the Cabots on Henry VII's behalf to Newfoundland and, later, to Hudson's Bay, were of little immediate consequence, but the endeavour of Willoughby and Chancellor in 1553 to get to Far Cathay by way of Archangel led to the formation of the Muscovy Company which for a time dominated Russian trade with western Europe. Other such trading companies, most of them undertaking voyages on a joint stock basis, were formed in Elizabeth I's reign. Among them, the Levant Company temporarily enjoyed as fruitful a relationship with the Sultan's government as the Muscovy Company had done with that of the Czar. In 1600 came the formation of the most momentous of all English trading organisations, the East India Company. Other joint stock ventures included Drake's circumnavigation of the world, 1577–80, in which the queen had a share not only of

221

the risk but of the immense profits; and Hawkins's Africa Company which, in the 1560s, laid the foundation of England's deplorable but profitable participation in the trade in negro slaves. Early Stuart trading companies were the Plymouth Adventurers to New England (1620), and the Providence Island Company (1629) whose members included some of Charles I's most famous parliamentary opponents.

Attempts to found colonies in North America, though approved of as a possible answer to the population problem, were abortive, and neither the companies nor the colonies were systematically encouraged by the Tudor governments; the foundation of Empire was a Stuart achievement. What Elizabeth and her advisers were mainly concerned to do was to regulate and profit from such activities and, in the case of Drake and Hawkins, use their plundering ventures for as long as possible as a cheap and safer alternative to an official war with the Spanish. Moreover, all such companies were subject to political attack as soon as they were chartered, and, by their opposition to 'interlopers', they contributed to building up that resentment against 'privilege' which was so strong a feature of political strife in the early Stuart period.

Economically, such trading as was carried on by these companies and with such colonies as had been established by the 1640s—in New England, Virginia, Maryland and a few Caribbean islands—did not greatly increase England's overseas trade in the century after 1550. It did, however, produce that great increase in the merchant navy which would enable the English, in the second half of the seventeenth century, to compete with the Dutch for the domination of the greater part of Europe's maritime carrying trade.

Multiplying Gentry

A major cause of social change in Tudor and early Stuart England was the wider distribution of land ownership, producing a great increase in the numbers of the gentry. In the century after 1530, when the total population doubled, the number of esquires and gentlemen more than trebled; and their average wealth in the more prosperous counties may have risen fourfold.

This large scale transfer of land was probably stirred up initially by the sale by the crown, in the decade after 1536, of the expropriated lands of the monasteries; and the phenomenon of continuously rising food prices made land ownership a greater potential source of wealth than ever. The process was kept going by the frequent sales of its own extensive lands by the crown, which was desperate, in a time of intermittent wars and non-stop inflation, to lay hands on ready cash. Although most monastic and crown land went first to the nobility, the latter re-sold much of it to the gentry, probably because of the same inflationary pressures that had caused the crown to sell to them. The lavish expenditure expected of the peerage contributed to this tendency.

At the lower end of the scale, small copyholders and short-lease holders, victims of high rents and high prices, also often sold out to yeomen and gentlemen.

Considerable wealth was thus transferred from crown, church and larger landholders to the gentry. In the general scramble, though the poor got poorer, the aristocracy found it hard to preserve its old economic and political preponderance. Numbers of the peerage were also low. There were only 43 peers in 1509; though there were 62 in 1559, by the end of Elizabeth's reign there were only 36, since in old age the queen had a crabbed unwillingness to reward or ennoble anyone. That there were 126 peers by 1628 was due entirely to the sale of peerages and, worse still, the right to nominate to peerages, by James I. This down-graded the peerage without necessarily augmenting its wealth. One peer asserted in 1628 that the commons could buy the lords up three times over; statistically dubious though the plaint may be, it is still significant. Much of the prestige attached to a peer derived from his noble lineage; but in 1628, 44% of the peers were first-generation noblemen and manifestly not sprung from noble loins at all.

By contrast, the prestige of the gentry was increased rather than diminished by the expansion of the legal profession and bureaucracy and the increased wealth of the more important merchants; the most influential of these last were the hundred or so engaged in the export business, concentrated, apart from a minority in Bristol and Exeter, in London. Virtually all members of these groups would be sons of yeomen and younger sons of gentlemen. Those who prospered in these callings established, not dynasties of lawyers, public servants or merchants, but new families of gentry. Any man of good repute who could acquire freehold land worth £10 a year, or who had movable possessions worth £300, could buy himself a coat of arms from the College of Heralds. Such purchased ascent into the ranks of the armigerous could be given added propulsion by the fashionable and dubious antiquarianism of the time. This could endow a 'new' gentleman with ancestors as exalted as they were remote. Townsmen paid tribute to the rising prestige of the gentry by choosing armigerous country gentlemen rather than urban burgesses as their MPs.

The use made by the crown of the leading county gentry as justices of the peace also strengthened royal influence. Though the chairman of the county justices, the Lord Lieutenant, was a nobleman, executive tasks were in the hands of the gentlemen justices, and were so manifold as to provoke one critic to ask in 1601, 'Who almost are not grieved at the luxuriant authority of justices of the peace?' The trial of petty offenders, the maintaining of bridges, the enforcement of laws against Catholics, wage-fixing, the supervision of poor relief, were only some of the matters to which the council now required JPs to devote continuous, unpaid service. In a society so conscious of upward and downward mobility, the confirmation of a man's standing which derived from holding a justice's commission from the crown was reward enough in itself. To lose that commission could be so damaging a loss of status that, all through the Tudor period, the most that JPs would do to express disapproval of a policy they were required to implement would be to do so laxly. Even then, the council was likely to be vigilant in its demand for more punctilious service.

Inflation worked hand in hand with the centralising ambitions of the Tudors to take power out of the hands of noblemen with large numbers of armed dependents and clients, and place it instead in the hands of those who combined the benefits of substantial money rents with the enjoyment of direct or indirect, paid or unpaid, crown patronage. Peers were transformed from overmighty subjects, able to mobilise their loyal tenantry as an armed force, into landlords not conspicuously more wealthy than the gentry around them, relying, like them, on their rent rolls. What peers needed in an inflationary world was cash, so that what principally remained of their feudal rights were irritating privileges, such as entry fines and rights of wardship. If they cultivated the demesne at all now, it was as sheep farmers and cattle ranchers. Their relationship to the countryside was that of partly absentee landlords, detached from the manpower that worked their land and concerned more and more with optimum financial returns. Their differences from the wealthier gentry worked to their disadvantage. Some clung to the older tradition that a nobleman should not oppress his tenants, would hesitate to inflict the full penalties on offenders in manorial courts, and not take legal action against a tenant until he was at least eighteen months in arrears with his rents. If adhered to in the sixteenth and seventeenth centuries, these practices marked a nobleman as a beloved landlord likely to die heavily in debt.

Another sign of the times was the number of decayed castles in the sixteenth century. Those in remoter parts were abandoned for more congenial habitations nearer London and the court. Those in more desirable areas were modernised with large mullioned windows and thus rendered indefensible. In contrast to thick-walled fortresses, in which to concentrate ready for a fighting sortie against an outside world turbulent with enemies, the new country house had a fine facade open to a milder landscape; one which had been thoroughly valued and assessed by a competent surveyor, protected from hurt by clever lawyers and above all fertile with rack-rents. Nor were the sons of the gentry enrolled in noble households to learn, as in the past, how to be at once assiduous toadies and impetuous fighting men. The sons of the gentry, like the sons of the nobility, went to school instead. That youths of gentle birth should act as servants to noblemen was incompatible with the more independent spirit of a wealthy gentry which had learned to look down on servility.

Honourable Fashions

To fix attention wholly on processes which worked so slowly as not to be complete until after the middle of the seventeenth century is to ignore the tensions of the Tudor century. Old ways were changing, but there were many who pursued old habits all the more ardently now that they were ceasing to be socially and politically acceptable. Noblemen did not cease to have retainers merely because Henry VII passed statutes against the practice. As late as 1572 there was yet one more statute against the wearing of livery, and the decision that no retainer could be a JP caused much pain in aristocratic circles. Without the armies raised by the nobility, the crown would have been unable to fight any of the various wars of the sixteenth century, since neither the conscript militia nor 'trained bands' which the crown caused to be raised from the countryside were much better than the forcible Feebles and roaring Bullcalfs of Justice Shallow's country. Not until the 1630s did the nobility at last lose their fighting ardour, the final cause being the practical one that there had by then been so few big wars for them to fight for over half a century. That overblown favourite of James I and Charles I, George Villiers, Duke of Buckingham, was the last of the ennobled bullyboys to have hundreds of armed retainers. It was one of the reasons why he was so detested.

As opportunities for heroic warfare declined, the nobility strained hard to preserve the outward signs of their social superiority; and in doing so set fashions that would be aped by the aspiring gentry. Noblemen clung desperately to the old chivalric concepts of honour and generosity as being the special marks of their status. Impulsiveness was a virtue (though its more tetchy manifestations have been ascribed to the alleged prevalence of dyspepsia). In tribute to old ideas about brothers-in-arms, loyalty to a friend, in however pointless a quarrel, was an imperative. Swiftness to revenge an injury was the measure of the true man. The more pushing among the gentry could emulate their betters, since gentlemen, like nobles, carried their weapons at all times, in order to manifest to the world that their right to be deemed armigerous was no empty formality. When not employing their weapons, they poured out spleenful torrents of oral or epistolary abuse or indulged in offensive horseplay, galloping through puddles past an enemy to spatter him with muddy water, knocking his hat off, pulling out his hair, his beard or his teeth. The rivalry of court factions spilled into the London streets. Peers of the realm and their followers engaged in bloody affrays in the Strand, Fleet Street and the Inns of Court. In the counties, personal and family quarrels among the gentry were often intense and enduring. In remoter parts, the ancient institution of the blood feud still survived. A man involved in one of these might not go to church without first bolting and barring his house against his enemies and posting guards and a look out to summon help if an attack should come.

During Elizabeth's reign, the heavy broadsword gave place to the rapier. The former required so much muscular effort that the mere business of brandishing it might dissipate the tempestuous ardour of one infuriated by a slight upon his honour. The rapier, however, was swift to penetrate, and could kill for a trifle, or by mischance. Pistols were more perilous still, since they could be concealed about their persons by the lowest of men, though their possession was illegal for all below the rank of gentleman. Among the armigerous, the rapier at least had the effect of reducing the beatings up in the streets and of substituting the less brawling rituals of challenge and single combat. But this, too, got out of hand. The overblown concept of honour made the issue of a challenge mandatory for the smallest offence and the refusal to accept it the mark of the coward. Put on stage as they were in the midst of this profligate obsession with honour, Shakespeare's Lancastrians, his Hamlet, his Romans and even his Venetians were, for all the universality rightly attributed to them, as much figures of late-Elizabethan and early-Stuart times as Bottom, Dogberry, Pistol and Mistress Quickly. Many promising young men of those years, taught to think, like Hotspur, that 'it were an easy leap To pluck bright honour from the pale faced moon' ended quickly like him as 'food for worms'. Romeo feels 'unmanned' by his refusal to accept Tybalt's challenge to a duel. His love for Juliet has made him 'effeminate' and 'soften'd valour's steel'. He recovers his belief in his honour only when, after stoking up his virility with a strenuous invocation to 'fire-eyed fury', he kills Tybalt to revenge Tybalt's slaying of Mercutio, Romeo's friend and comrade. Hamlet's special tragedy is his inability to prevent 'conscience' from making a 'coward' of him, since 'honour' requires him to sweep 'instantly' to revenge his father's death. He vilifies himself repeatedly for his laggard-liness and states the code's case against himself in extremest form:

> Rightly to be great
> Is not to stir without great argument
> But greatly to find honour in a straw
> When honour's at the stake.

So, Coriolanus, for all his Roman attitudes, is a stiff-necked, over-mighty Tudor lord, with a self-destructive addiction to honour, a mouth ready with phrases of self-adulation, a vocabulary rich in invective, and a mind blinded by its contempt for his inferiors. In his own cloying fashion, Antonio, too, follows the Elizabethan pattern, persisting to the point of death in his lightly given undertaking to the spendthrift Bassanio. By contrast, the most vivid condemnation of the creed's absurdity (*'What's honour? A word . . . Who hath it? He that died o' Wednesday'*) comes from Falstaff, the buffoon whom Prince Hal must cast off as soon as it is time for him to become the soul of honour and the victor of Agincourt.

These follies were in part the product of the idleness of men without wars to fight and whose lands were leased to others to farm. They also followed from the increasing attraction now exercised by a more stationary court, from which all honours and rewards flowed, and from which no ambitious nobleman could afford to absent himself. Even if all he achieved was debt, this might bind him still more to the queen since, to increase her hold, she might lend him money. For all their touchiness about their honour they were also better educated than their predecessors and therefore drawn to court by the ideals, as well as by the pickings, of public service. Country life was boring, and London so much the only town of importance in Tudor England that it was the only place where one could do even private business of importance, buy fashionable clothes or exchange ideas. With her customary mixture of caution and cunning, Elizabeth, with Cecil to second her, avoided clamping down on the more violent elements, dealing with them chiefly by excluding them from her innermost circle. Nor did she take sides. She let the noble factions undermine their strength by incessantly quarrelling among themselves. She encouraged them to become mendicants and flatterers. By the end of her reign they were exalting her royal state in language that only sounded intolerable when, in the time of James I, it issued, not from the lips of subjects, but from those of the monarch's own person.

The Poor and the Law

Tudor governments, though prepared to accept that some indiscipline was only to be expected of the aristocracy, were as watchful over troublesome members of the unpropertied classes as over potential rebels among the nobility. They believed in order, not so much out of a conscious desire to be repressive or tyrannical, as on general philosophical grounds. Order, stability and hierarchy were good in themselves because they produced a society in which all men were harmoniously at peace with one another. Each man would receive the honour and accept the duties proper to his degree in society. Anything that encouraged restlessness and strife among the unpropertied, particularly a desire to change or greatly improve their status or occupation, was resisted. Government, itself nearly always putting pressure of some sort on the men of property, had no wish to have their tempers worsened by attacks on them from the lower orders.

It was therefore natural that, as the effects of steep inflation, bad harvests and high mortality rates due to plague became apparent by the end of the 1550s, there should have been an attempt at the statutory limitation not only of wages but of the freedom of movement of the labour force. These were the main objectives of the Statute of Artificers of 1563. That its terms were rarely enforced does not lessen its value as an exposition of what sort of society Tudor governments wished to preserve.

First, JPs were to fix maximum wages. If the maxima were exceeded, the labourer could be fined or imprisoned. His employer could also be fined, though less heavily, but not, of course, imprisoned. So much was this an attempt to legislate on behalf of a theory and in response to a temporary crisis that, by 1604, owing to the contraction of the cloth industry, JPs were being ordered to fix not maximum but minimum wages. In the eighty years after 1563, though money wages rose slightly, inflation kept them consistently below the rise in prices. Ironically, this rarely enforced Tudor act of 1563, originally passed to keep wages down and then used to stop them falling too low, was repeatedly invoked by distressed labourers and craftsmen in the bad years of the Industrial Revolution and the Napoleonic Wars. It established among the rural population a firm tradition that wages should not be left wholly to the operation of market forces; and the refusal of the authorities to implement the act in the years between 1790 and 1815 was considered a base betrayal.

The 1563 act also tried to keep semi-skilled men at their jobs in agriculture or in their craft, and to keep women at work as domestic servants. The social interests of the gentry were reflected in the rule that none should enter the skilled craft of weaving unless he had served a seven-year apprenticeship; and none was to enter such an apprenticeship unless he was the son of a gentleman or a freeholder with land worth above sixty shillings a year. This attempt to exclude most of the rural population from the cloth industry may be measured by the fact that the qualification for a parliamentary vote in the counties was land worth forty shillings. Although rarely enforced in any respect, the act clearly showed the desire of the gentry to keep those whose rank was not gentle strictly in their proper subordinate degree. Likewise, an act of 1555 had forbidden country weavers to own more than two looms, and another of 1576 was designed to stop clothiers setting themselves up as country gentlemen in the west country by forbidding them to buy more than twenty acres of land in those parts.

The issue of enclosures provoked action by both council and parliament that discloses how the Tudor concern for order involved a consciously benevolent paternalism. From the reign of Henry VII until that of Charles I, governments responded repeatedly by a succession of statutes to public outcries against enclosers and engrossers. They were almost all ineffective. But it is noteworthy that the last bill to limit enclosures was introduced into the commons in 1656 under the Puritan Commonwealth and rejected as an outmoded piece of quasi-royalist interference with the rights of landlords.

Tudor bills included one in 1515 which tried to have recently enclosed land reconverted from pasture to tillage, and one in 1533 enacting that no person should own more than 2400 sheep. In 1589 an act ordered that every cottage built should have four acres of land attached to it. These measures reflected conservative social views about the rural population

which were still current during the eighteenth century enclosure movement, the free trade controversies of the 1840s and the agricultural
depression of the 1880s. It was an article of faith that it was by men who
guided the plough that the country was enriched in peace and defended
in war. The fear that the country might come to depend for corn upon
foreigners was also invoked. No less important was the opinion that
arable farming had the advantage over pastoral, that it kept more men
busily at work, and gave them less time for idleness and drunkenness.

The high point of the enclosure controversy occurred, however, in
1548–9 when, with agrarian distress aggravated by bad harvests and the
effects of debasement, responsibility for the whole of the countryside's
misfortunes was blamed upon enclosing landlords, not only by those
who rose up against them but by men in the highest counsels of government. In the eyes of many, civic virtue required the gentry to act justly
towards their inferiors and to avoid 'that greedy and devouring spirit of
covetousness' which Nicholas Ridley, bishop of London declared, as is
the habit of moralists, to be peculiarly characteristic of the times he lived
in.

Edward Seymour, Duke of Somerset, then ruling on Edward VI's
behalf as Protector, was much impressed by these ideas. Considering it
his duty to stop the enclosures that were said to be depopulating the
countryside and filling the roads with hungry and resentful vagrants, he
appointed commissions to halt the enclosing process. Many enclosures
in the midlands were ordered to be destroyed. In 1549, to make it less
profitable to enclose land for pasture, he persuaded a reluctant commons to put a tax on every head of sheep.

Encouraged by these signs of goodwill from on high, and infuriated
by the reluctance of landlords to change their evil ways, a Norfolk
yeoman, John Ket, was able, in 1549, to transform a local anti-enclosure
riot into a demonstration by sixteen thousand men, who stationed
themselves outside Norwich. Somerset, torn between his concern for
social justice and his responsibility for maintaining social order, tried, by
the offer of a general pardon and the redress of some of their grievances,
to persuade Ket to disperse his followers. This having no effect, the
Marquess of Northampton was sent against them with an armed force;
but beat a hasty and inglorious retreat as soon as the rebels showed
signs of resistance.

This kid-gloved ineffectiveness was unacceptable to Somerset's
colleagues on the council, and particularly to John Dudley, Earl of
Warwick (who became Duke of Northumberland in 1551). Dudley's
strong feelings were heightened by his jealousy of Somerset's position
as Protector and perhaps by the fact that one of his own parks had been
done away by Somerset's anti-enclosure commission. With a substantial
force, Dudley arrived outside Norwich and at once hanged as many
rebels as he could lay hands on; and when Ket ordered resistance, three
thousand of his followers were killed in the battle. Ket, his brother and

229

about fifty others were executed for treason. Since there was also a still unsuppressed rising in Cornwall against the government's religious policy, the principal political consequence of Ket's rebellion was the discrediting of the aggrieved rural population's would-be champion, Somerset. In a matter of weeks, he was replaced by Dudley, and died, like Ket, by execution.

Like the Peasants' Revolt in Germany in the 1520s, Ket's rebellion ensured that when governments ceased to be Catholic they were still as determined as ever to keep the rural population firmly in its place. Ket's rebellion is nevertheless a reminder that, though enclosure may not have been the sole cause of the distress of the mid-century, and though its extent was small in relation to the total area under cultivation, it was exceptionally hard on those who suffered as a result of it. Villagers deprived by enclosure of their common land, which had been an element essential to their economic survival for hundreds of years, suffered a deprivation that is not to be minimised by the statistical circumstance that there were fewer of them than was believed at the time.

Tudor government never ceased to be disturbed by the social effects of a decline in the traditional open field economy. The traditional organisation of husbandry in the arable almost certainly produced a more disciplined population than forest, pasture land or the towns. The forest areas had long been notorious, first as the hiding place of outlaws and then as the home of unmanageable free craftsmen, and now because of the vagrants who squatted in them. Parishes in such areas were usually large and the population little troubled by lord of the manor, parson or justice of the peace. This perhaps encouraged the growth among them of those do-it-yourself systems of religion that verged on irreligion and of morality that verged on immorality, which burgeoned into the wilder Puritan sects of the 1640s. Similar social indiscipline was noted among itinerant rural craftsmen, building workers, pedlars, and workers in the rural cloth industry.

This association in the popular mind of the forest with freedom and with robbing the rich to help the poor had perhaps a closer connection with fact than one legendary Robin Hood. When Shakespeare's melancholy Jaques for the first time 'looks merrily', it is because he has met 'a fool i' the forest'; but his merriment derives from the forest fool's cynical detachment from conventional values. He

> . . . laid him down and bask'd him in the sun
> And rail'd on Lady Fortune in good terms,
> In good set terms, and yet a motley fool.
> 'Good morrow, fool,' quoth I. 'No, sir,' quoth he,
> 'Call me not fool till heaven hath sent me fortune.'

—and then, after deriding the slavery to the clock of those who engage in regular toil, he mocks all normal endeavour:

And so, from hour to hour, we ripe and ripe
And then, from hour to hour, we rot and rot;
And thereby hangs a tale.

The feckless indifference of 'fools' such as these to the rules of an ordered society committed to the idea of 'degree' made Shakespeare's Forest of Arden less merry than it seemed. Footloose people on the move from overcrowded villages or spilling into and out of the forests, were, to the government, vagrants and 'sturdy beggars' and a threat to law and order. At first, they were to be whipped and branded and sent back whence they came. In 1531, JPs were ordered to issue to those of the poor who were 'infirm' a licence to beg, thus rendering begging by the sturdy poor an offence. This measure showed an important ability to distinguish: those whose poverty was *prima facie* the result of the natural infirmities of the flesh were separately classified. In 1536, parishes were ordered to collect alms for the infirm poor, find them work and apprentice their children to a trade. In 1601, all earlier acts were codified into the 'Great' Poor Law. Two overseers of the poor in each parish were to collect a poor rate to be applied to the purposes laid down in 1536. The infirm were to be cared for in hospitals and almshouses; idle rogues and vagabonds were to be placed in houses of correction. An act of 1610 extended the definition of 'vagabond' to all able-bodied men or women who threatened to run away from their parish. Supervision of the overseers of the poor was in the hands of the JPs.

The Poor Law of 1601 remained the basis on which the poor were aided until 1834. It did nothing to solve the chronic under-employment of the intervening centuries and, although its administration was sometimes lax and sometimes heartless, it did at least admit that poverty was a problem requiring social action. This was as well. At any one time in the seventeenth and eighteenth centuries, a fifth of the population were likely to be paupers. The poor law was the sole means by which they kept alive. Up to half the population could look forward to the possibility of having to rely on it. And though the poor law was perhaps created chiefly to keep the able-bodied workless in order, its long continuance did establish the principle that the amelioration of poverty's worst effects should, through the poor rate, be a permanent charge upon the wealth of the propertied. The negligible role of the poor in the Civil war, which caused such a tumult of hopes and ideas among their betters, may perhaps be due in part to the fact that, by comparison with other European countries, seventeenth-century England was already something of a welfare state.

4

THE TRIUMPH OF MAJESTY

Religion by Crown Command

THE crown's destruction of papal supremacy over the church in England in the 1530s met with little opposition because there was no personality powerful enough to make his voice heard amid the general anti-clerical clamour, and little opportunity to organise resistance in the face of the efficient speed with which Henry and Cromwell operated. Anne Boleyn was unpopular and Catherine of Aragon much pitied. But the few pious people who did object were swiftly silenced. The so-called Nun of Kent, Elizabeth Barton, and five of her supporters, were hanged in 1534 because, under the influence of one of the monks of Canterbury, she had published an attack on the king's second marriage. The so-called Pilgrimage of Grace of 1536 was principally one more rebellion by the northern nobility, this one provoked by Cromwell's authoritarian secular policies. The religious rising that accompanied it was led by a devout Yorkshire lawyer and landowner, Robert Aske who, by October 1536, had gathered a force of thirty thousand men near Pontefract. They protested at the dissolution of the monasteries, called for 'the preservation of Christ's church' and the restoration of papal supremacy. By promising a general pardon and the redress of various of their grievances, the Duke of Norfolk, on Henry's behalf, secured a cessation of the pious Aske's activities; a trusting, godly man, he had no mind to resist a king or doubt his promises. When others, less willing to trust the word of a prince, then renewed rebellion, Norfolk acted violently against both the new and the earlier rebels all over the north. Aske and up to two hundred others were hanged, previous promises of pardon notwithstanding. The establishment of the Council of the North was the revolt's only permanent result. In the south, throughout the troubles, there had not been a flicker of sympathy for the northern rebels.

The one possible focus of effective opposition had already been removed before the Pilgrimage of Grace had begun. Sir Thomas More, who had succeeded Wolsey as Chancellor and resigned rather than condone the marriage to Anne, was of national and international repute for his learning and the probity of his character. Henry was determined to get either More's public approval or his head, and pursued that policy with single-minded harshness, finally getting More convicted of treason, to a large extent on rigged evidence, and executed. More had been at infinite pains to maintain his private opposition to the divorce without recourse to any overt deed or word that could be construed as treasonable; but Henry got him in the end. When it came to it, More died for the principle that no parliament could alter the word of God or lay down precisely what a man ought to believe. At the same time, John Fisher, bishop of Rochester, whose hostile views had been so far publicised as to persuade the pope tactlessly to make him a Cardinal, was also executed, as were half a dozen inoffensive but obdurate Carthusian monks. On the whole, the general view was that both More and Fisher had been unreasonable in opposing what all other responsible men had had the sense to accept; and that, as monks, the Carthusians had only themselves to blame.

The fate of More and Fisher, as of Elizabeth Barton, Robert Aske and the Carthusians nevertheless made it evident that the subjects of the crown were now in a quite novel situation. Hitherto there had been no necessary conjunction between heresy and treason. To hold ideas of one's own about the nature and destiny of man had not so far been liable to be considered a crime against the king's majesty. But, after 1536, the crown became the ultimate arbiter as to what constituted heresy, thus making it, potentially, a crime against the state; and, in a society whose basic principle was that a man's first duty was to obey his sovereign, this was to create a dilemma even more complex than a conflict between the demands of the state and the dictates of private conscience. In sincere men it could become an almost irreconcilable conflict between two contrary dictates of the same conscience: one, to hold certain principles as sacred, and the other to deny those principles because to hold them was to disobey the crown.

The dilemma was the greater from 1536 onwards because the state failed to establish any permanent, or permanently acceptable, 'party line' in religious belief and practice. Consequently, yesterday's spiritual conformist became today's dissident. Today's dissident would be tomorrow's religious commissar. In practice, this strengthened royal authority. To risk one's neck by dissidence today, when by falling back on the duty of obedience, one could survive eventually to enjoy finding oneself orthodox again, was behaviour confined, for the rest of the sixteenth century, to a handful prepared to accept the risk of martyrdom, or to simple men too lowly placed in society to understand what their betters understood perfectly. His Fool would in due time tell Lear that a man was indeed a fool to support a man or a cause condemned by those in authority: 'nay, as thou canst not smile as the wind sits, thou'lt shortly catch cold.' It was an age where the only sure survivors in public life were either cynical time-servers or, at the other extreme, sincere but above all patient men, prepared to double-cross their sovereign by combining with their outward conformity the covert encouragement of dissident beliefs and believers, against the time when the wind changed for the better. To survive the shifts and the vacillations of their sovereign rulers in matters religious, those in public office were required to be wiser than serpents, while taking infinite pains to appear more harmless than doves. For royal control veered hither and thither doctrinally during the last twelve years of Henry VIII's reign, moved towards one extreme during the six years of Edward VI's, to the opposite extreme for five years under Mary, and 'settled' under Elizabeth into a muzzy compromise that still left major questions of faith and observance obscure. Yet amidst all the changes, it is true to say of most people that, whenever they were ordered by the crown to change their religious beliefs forthwith, they did what they were told.

Henry's own preference was for an England Catholic in everything except obedience to the pope and toleration of monasticism. But until his execution in 1537 (for being too Protestant in both domestic and foreign policy, and for finding Henry a fourth wife who was insufficiently attractive) Cromwell, like Cranmer, operated in favour of genuine reform. Henry's own position depended on the ascendancy of particular factions at court, or on whether or not he happened temporarily to be seeking Catholic or Lutheran allies abroad. Thus, under the reforming influence, he ordered a copy of Coverdale's vernacular Bible to be put into every parish church, only to abandon the programme before it was completed. From his Catholic mood came the Statute of Six Articles of 1539, which affirmed the validity of the main doctrines of Catholicism; but it was for a short time only that it was used against 'heretics'. Nevertheless, royal supremacy in church and state was effective and confusing enough for three Lutherans to be burnt for heresy in 1540 and three Papists to be hanged for treason.

Edward VI, child of Henry and his third wife, Jane Seymour, was only nine when Henry died in 1547. The regency acting in Edward's name contained more reformers than conservative Catholics and was headed by Somerset, whom the council declared Protector. Under Somerset (though Edward himself was a precociously dedicated Protestant) chantries were abolished and their endowments confiscated on the grounds that, purgatory having been declared non-existent, prayers for the dead were superstitious. In 1549 came Cranmer's first Prayer Book. Its use was made compulsory by an Act of Uniformity. Though in many respects an English translation of the Latin formulas of the Catholic church, this in itself was revolutionary for a society hitherto accustomed to the use of Latin on almost every formal public occasion, religious or lay. Nor, at a time when spelling, vocabulary and pronunciation were still far from standardised, can it have been as 'easy and plain for the understanding' as was claimed. Yet only among some of the faraway parishes of Cornwall did feeling against the change spark off a rebellion. Its unluckier participants were hanged for so foolishly defending what they had been told all their lives to hold sacred. Had they waited four more years they could all have had their Latin back again in 1553.

Somerset's successor, Northumberland, sought power and profit, from 1551 to 1553, in the promotion of Protestantism and the despoliation of churches. His exercise of the crown's religious sovereignty included the destruction of altars as superstitious and their replacement by tables, the banning of vestments by clergy officiating at communion, and the issue of Cranmer's second Prayer Book in 1552. Altogether more Protestant in content than its predecessor, it was accompanied by a stiffer Act of Uniformity, making attendance at church compulsory and participation in any other kind of religious service punishable by imprisonment. Other activities included the confiscation of a great deal of church plate, a witch hunt for 'heretical' books in the university libraries and the virtual confiscation, chiefly for the benefit of Northumberland, of the whole wealth of the bishoprics of Winchester and Gloucester.

Between them, however, Northumberland and the precocious sixteen year old king did Protestantism grave damage in 1553, as it became clear that Edward's death from tuberculosis was imminent. Together they conspired, on the one hand to perpetuate Northumberland's domination of government, and, on the other to perpetuate the Protestant religion by a wholly illegal decision to disinherit the king's elder sister, Mary, Catherine of Aragon's Catholic daughter, whom Henry VIII's will had named as Edward's successor. On the sole authority of the dying boy-king's decision (though naturally and not undeservedly Northumberland shouldered all the blame) it was announced that the crown should pass to the Lady Jane Grey, recently become the bride of Northumberland's eldest son. The plan was objectionable because it disinherited not only Mary and Edward's other sister, Elizabeth, but because it also disinherited the Stuart family, descended from the elder of Henry VIII's two sisters. Jane Grey's descent was from Henry VIII's younger sister, Mary, Duchess of Suffolk. Consequently, as soon as Edward's sister, Mary, made clear that she would defend her right to the crown, support for Northumberland collapsed. Not even the Protestants supported him. He and his secular minded associates had discredited the faith by their rapacity and illegality and his doom seemed a just judgment from God. Within a month of Edward's death, Mary was welcomed into London with noisy enthusiasm and Northumberland went to the Tower and to execution.

Mary's triumph in 1553 demonstrated neither a general dislike of Protestantism nor a general desire for a return to 'the Old Religion'. It was a revulsion against Northumberland's breach of the one article of faith that would survive the disputes of all the divines, that of obedience to the rightful wearer of the crown. Mary's reign also proved that the royal supremacy over religion was both inescapable and, even in the extremest circumstances, effective; and even though its operations had, by 1558, become objectionable to many, it was by yet another exercise of royal sovereignty that the work of her five years of power was undone.

Obedient to their Sovereign Lady Mary, parliament now gave assent to the repeal of all anti-papal acts passed since the fall of Wolsey and all the 'reforms' of her brother's reign. They further consented to kneel *en masse* formally to ask for pardon and reconciliation, and for the restoration of England to the universal church Catholic. All they were prepared to insist on in return was that those of them who held monastic lands should keep them. The scrapping of Edward's reforms certainly did not please all of them; the repeal of Henry VIII's anti-clerical legislation can have pleased virtually none of them. Yet, when Sir Thomas Wyatt, the poet, led a rebellion by three thousand men of Kent (some perhaps descended from those who had followed Wat Tyler and John Ball) and all but entered the City of London, the rising failed. The claim that it was undertaken on behalf of Mary's Protestant sister, Elizabeth, put Elizabeth's own life at risk; but it attracted no additional support in consequence.

Mary's policy as a devout Catholic queen was a disaster for the future of her faith among Englishmen. By her insistence on marrying Philip of Spain she made it possible for Protestant reformers to represent Catholicism, for the first time, as an alien import, dependent for its existence on the domination of England, not by foreign priests, but by a foreign power. By imposing on them a titular king as dedicatedly Spanish as he was Catholic, Mary wounded Englishmen's pride (and her own) still further by involving the country in a war against France for purely Spanish purposes. The outcome was the loss of Calais, England's last possession on the continental mainland. Thereafter, the Channel Islands would be the sole surviving relic of vanished Norman and Angevin grandeurs.

Historians would treat the loss of Calais as a fortunate disaster, compelling England finally to look to the oceans as the true source of future greatness in the world. To the men of 1558 it was deeply shaming. To their successors it confirmed beyond argument their conviction that Catholicism meant foreign domination and national humiliation. When, almost a century later, Cromwell announced, 'Spain is Anti-Christ, Spain is our natural enemy, our Jesuits are Spanish-inspired', he was indeed speaking in the role of 'God's Englishman'. The effect of Mary's calamitous reign was to make anti-Catholic xenophobia so much a part of the stuff of English patriotism that it would manifest itself time and again in each succeeding century; even after it had died down in England itself, its voice would still be harshly audible in the streets of Ulster over four hundred years after Mary's death.

The burning of just under three hundred heretics, most of them ordinary working people, was without precedent in England; and care was taken to ensure that it would never be forgotten. Neither Mary's security as queen, nor the preservation of England's traditional faith, required these deaths; the victims were a danger to neither. Protestantism, on the other hand, did need them: in the centuries ahead, those who would most earnestly read their Bibles would be most likely also to read Foxe's *Book of Martyrs*, which recorded in gruesome detail the burning of men and women whose only offence had been to hold to their own religious faith with as much sincerity and with as little political realism as Mary herself held to hers. Though children might recall her unknowingly in the nursery rhyme, 'Mary, Mary, quite contrary,' their elders would remember her with fervour as 'Bloody Mary'.

The educated classes would no less persistently remember the burning of Hooper, Ridley and Latimer, bishops respectively of Gloucester, London and Worcester, because they had neither fled the country in 1553 nor been willing to renounce their beliefs at the queen's command. Cranmer, too, was burned. A liturgist of acknowledged genius, it was he, through his prayer books, who could claim to be the real founder of what was to become the Church of England. His Book of Common Prayer was to enrich the religious life of that church and the literature and common speech of most of those for whom English was their native tongue. Its final form, in 1662, was often an awkward compromise between its earlier and differing versions; but to worship according to the formularies of the Prayer Book would be the one characteristic peculiar to those who would eventually be labelled 'Anglicans', distinguishing them from the other non-Roman religious bodies that grew up over the centuries, even though all of them might borrow heavily from it. Though excessively praised by those who resisted its virtual abandonment by the Church of England in the decade from 1967 onwards, there was much to be said for the concomitant opinion that what took its place was conceived by men with a weaker liturgical sense and a feebler command of language.

The manner of Cranmer's death was as significant as More's. Cranmer's submission to Mary's Catholic commands would have sustained her system as More's submission to Henry's anti-papal legislation would have sustained his. Cranmer suffered the greater inward turmoil in that submission to royal authority was embedded more deeply in his religious beliefs than it had been in More's. Cranmer's view had already been anticipated by Wyclif: 'Since clerics are liege men to kings in whose lands they be in, kings have power of God to punish them in God's cause both in body and in chattels'. Cranmer's extreme reluctance, like that of so many others of character and attainment, to oppose the crown can be understood only as a manifestation of that fundamental notion to which all propertied and learned men subscribed, that the first duty of a subject was to obey his sovereign. For this reason, Cranmer recanted his Protestantism under royal pressure, but when he nevertheless came to be burnt he revoked that recantation. Only at the very last, when the fires were reaching up to him, and his Sovereign Lady, Mary, could have no further claim on him did he finally acknowledge, at the moment of death, that his Protestant faith meant more than his belief, while he lived, that he must obey his monarch.

Mary therefore achieved the opposite of her intentions. Protestantism was now no longer what it had too often been since 1530: a display of envious avarice by men greedy to rob the church of its wealth, or of oafish ignorance by others uncouthly proclaiming the superstition that God could tolerate only those who worshipped him with words, and that images, ornament and ceremony were always and everywhere 'idolatrous'. By 1558 it could be represented as a faith which sustained patriots and inspired martyrs. Moreover, by causing so many, at the start of her reign, to take refuge in Protestant cities abroad, such as Frankfurt, Zurich, Strasbourg and Geneva, Mary enabled them to add a new dimension to their dissidence. At her death, English Protestantism was strengthened by these returning exiles through being influenced, as it had not widely been before, by the disciplines of continental theology: Lutheran, Calvinist and Zwinglian. Protestantism ceased to be mainly a form of anti-clericalism. Thanks to Cranmer, it was able, at the first opportunity, to resume use of the Prayer Book upon whose essentially verbal modes his gift of tongues had bestowed an aesthetic quality that would slowly win men's hearts. But now, in addition, it was a faith sustained by its small army of martyrs and rendered self-confident by its capacity to exploit the passions of patriotism; and fortified by theological concepts which, though often repellent to Catholics and indeed to other Protestants, they would wish fiercely to impose on everyone.

Obedience and Recusancy

On hearing of Mary's death and realising that she had actually survived the hazards of being Anne Boleyn's daughter long enough to become queen herself, Elizabeth quoted the Latin verse of psalm 118, translated in the Authorized Version as 'This is the Lord's doing: it is marvellous in our eyes'. Yet her survival until 1603 proved a greater marvel than her accession in 1558. Throughout those years, Catholicism and the various Protestantisms of Europe were engaged in a struggle that ignored dynastic frontiers and faced most Christian rulers with the threat, or the fact, of rebellion, war or civil war.

Elizabeth knew that, as Anne Boleyn's daughter, and the saviour from Rome for whose coming Protestants had patiently waited throughout Mary's reign, she could not be Catholic. But neither would she be as extreme a Protestant (or 'Puritan') as the returning Marian exiles demanded. Her temperament inclined her to a policy calculated to cause the least offence to the unregenerate majority who, as ever, preferred their theology to be vague and their faith to be undemanding. Accordingly, the royal supremacy alienated by Mary to Rome was resumed. Elizabeth's Act of Supremacy made her 'Only Supreme Governor' of the church but this was little more than a linguistic concession to those who winced at the thought of a church having, as its 'Supreme Head', a member of the female sex. A new Act of Uniformity in 1559 imposed the use of Cranmer's Prayer Book; the 1552 version was to be used, modified at certain vital points to accord with the more Catholic forms of the 1549 version. Further to establish her determination not wholly to abandon Catholic ideas at the behest of the Puritans, clergy were to officiate in surplices and, at the communion service, wear vestments.

Elizabeth's system turned out to be almost as near as the post-Catholic English church would ever get to a genuine 'settlement'. Yet, when in 1563, her Archbishop, Matthew Parker, issued the Thirty-Nine Articles of Religion which purported, with some lack of precision, to state the official doctrine of the church, it was the fifth different set of such articles to which Englishmen had been required to subscribe in less than twenty-five years, not counting the circumstance that during the five years of Mary's reign they had been required to believe that all articles of religion devised by Protestants were damnable heresies. Not unnaturally, the majority accepted the Elizabethan order much as they had accepted the old. None could tell when they would next be told to believe something different. But, since the version of Cranmer's prayer book which was imposed in 1559 lasted until the 1640s and the Thirty-Nine Articles were important only to the clergy (and not always to them), men grew attached to the Elizabethan settlement merely because in a short time it acquired the basic virtue of any religious system, namely permanence.

The most numerous body won over by the passage of time were the Catholics. Theoretically, these constituted one hundred per cent of the population in 1558, at the end of Mary's reign, quite apart from the fact that everyone over thirty would have been brought up in the old religion. Yet within a decade the number of English Catholics had dropped to about 150,000. This great fall was due to the lack of help from a Catholic Europe caught up in its own divisions and to the deliberate leniency with which the new system was enforced. Legally, there was a fine of one shilling for each absence from church and a requirement upon all office holders to swear on oath that they accepted the queen's supremacy over the church. Neither provision was energetically carried out. The crypto-Catholic was not required to receive holy communion; this made it possible for him, by at least attending church, to keep within the law. The real problem was the absence of mass priests. All but one of Mary's Catholic bishops had refused to accept the Elizabethan Settlement and were deprived of their sees. Of about 80,000 beneficed clergy, up to 200 were deprived for the same reason, a calculation which implies that the other 79,800 were apparently content to switch from the mass to the prayer book communion service by royal command. This in itself would mean that most laymen would conform and become 'Anglicans' in imitation of those who until 1558 had been their mass priests.

Mass was still, nevertheless, said in remote places. In rural (as distinct from urban) Lancashire a predominance of Catholic JPs meant that recusancy fines for non-attendance at church were not much collected. Catholic nobles and gentry in various parts of the country supplied themselves and their tenantry with a mass priest, perhaps disguised as a secular household officer. Elizabeth resisted parliamentary pressure to enforce the laws against Catholics rigidly. A secular-minded woman with a highly developed gift for self-preservation, she took the view that 'church Catholics' who, despite their convictions, nevertheless attended their parish churches thereby adhered to the one faith of interest to her, that of obedience to her laws.

Between 1570 and 1588, Elizabethan Englishmen, over-simplifying but not fundamentally misreading a complicated situation, saw themselves faced with a threat to their independence from a revived Catholicism that was everywhere on the offensive against those who had abjured papal authority. From across the Channel they heard atrocity stories about Spain's treatment of the Protestants of the Netherlands, whose leader, William of Orange, was assassinated by a Catholic fanatic. From the Atlantic they heard stories of English seamen voyaging, though not peacefully, to the New World, being seized by the Spanish masters of the Americas and delivered to the torturers of the Inquisition. France was in the throes of a long civil war of Protestant against Catholic, in the course of which occurred the Massacre of St Bartholomew, when numbers of Protestants were murdered by Catholics without warning. And in 1570, in an access of zeal and in disregard of the proper procedures, Pope Pius V issued a bull of excommunication against Elizabeth, declaring her deposed and her subjects free to murder her. More frighteningly, in ways with which the twentieth century was to become familiar, enemies from without seemed to be encouraging enemies within the land. Foreigners engineered Catholic plots to replace Elizabeth by her Catholic cousin, Mary Stuart, Queen of Scots. Driven from her throne for her scandalous marital exploits, Mary took refuge in England in 1568 and, for almost twenty years, became the centre of these plots to Catholicise England. Though all failed, being mostly the work of scoundrels or fools, the queen's ministers managed to get Mary to incriminate herself sufficiently in 1586 for an order to be signed for her execution, a step which Elizabeth had avoided for years and tried to repudiate as soon as it was taken. With Mary gone, Philip of Spain took her place, little though he relished the role, as the destined agent of Catholic aggression. The Anglo-Spanish war, of which the fight with the Armada in 1588 was but the opening campaign, was not to end until after Elizabeth's death.

A 'spy scare' was provoked by the activities of young English Catholics in exile. Across the Channel, at Douai and Rheims, a Jesuit college, founded by an Englishman, William Allen, trained these young men to return as missionaries to the minority at home who held fast to the old religion but were unable to receive the Catholic sacraments. Forbidden to take part in politics or even, despite the Bull of 1570, to seduce Catholics from their allegiance to the queen, they were nevertheless inevitably regarded as agents of a hostile power. Elizabeth was therefore unable to resist the mounting patriotic zeal of the commons and her council, and approved a succession of penal statutes against the Jesuit 'invaders' and their protectors. In 1581 it became treason to convert any one to the faith of Rome or to be converted to it. In 1585 all priests ordained by Rome since 1558 were to leave the country. All Englishmen educated in Jesuit seminaries were to return home, or be adjudged guilty of treason. To harbour such priests became a capital offence; to fail to give information about them was punishable by fines or imprisonment. A fine of £100 for each offence was imposed for arranging for one's children to be educated in seminaries abroad.

Between 1585 and 1603, between 140 and 150 Catholics were executed, 98 of them missionary priests. All claimed to have been condemned for their religion; the government insisted that they had died for treason. There was not much to distinguish between the two, given the frenetic atmosphere of Catholic plots at home and Catholic threats from abroad. Nevertheless, the treatment of Catholic laymen had become less rigorous by the end of the reign because of the diminution of the danger of a Spanish invasion, and the loyalty of the English Catholics while it had existed. Catholic numbers increased a little. There was a greater output of Catholic books; being dedicated, by permission, to Catholic peers, they escaped censorship. Elizabeth and her council, unwilling to add to their disputes with the peerage, turned a blind eye.

The accession of James I raised hopes of increased toleration. He had hinted at this in advance, so as to enlist support from Catholic powers abroad for his claim to the English throne. Unfortunately, English Catholics were, by 1603, divided between a rational but leaderless majority and an irreconcilable minority led by Jesuits. A small group of hotheads sought to settle the issue with the Gunpowder Plot of 1605. Its discovery made it possible yet again to treat Catholicism as synonymous with treason and murder. For long, the Anglican prayer book contained special forms of service to commemorate, not only the accession day of Elizabeth I, which had delivered the land from Marian persecution, but also the nation's escape from the Gunpowder Plot.

True, the severer laws against Catholics that inevitably followed were only intermittently enforced; but henceforth English Catholics remained few in number until emancipated from their civil disabilities in 1829 and augmented by Irish immigration and by conversion during the nineteenth century. Until then, they were chiefly peers and well to do landed gentry, with children educated at home by Catholic private tutors, and with a social influence rarely extending much beyond the boundaries of their estates. In these, they lived lives as apart from the restored Catholicism that emerged on the continent after the reforms of the Council of Trent as from the main stream of the life of their own country. An estimate of 1780 was that only eight peers, nineteen baronets and 150 of the landed gentry were Catholics and that very few Catholics were engaged in trade.

Gloriana Enthroned

In the eyes of her subjects, Elizabeth I's chief glory was that she had brought England safely through a period when its national survival had seemed in deadly danger. War had ceased by now to be the mainly aristocratic pastime it had previously been (and would again become in the eighteenth century). It had become a clash of ideologies in which all men might feel themselves deeply involved. The persecution of Mary's reign, combined as it had been with a Spanish marriage culminating in the loss of Calais, had stimulated not only a fierce hatred of Catholicism and of foreigners but a conviction, much encouraged by the view of Foxe, in his *Book of Martyrs*, that the English were an Elect Nation. It was Elizabeth's good fortune that the circumstances of her early life as Anne Boleyn's daughter set her up at the moment of her sister Mary's death, as a unique, living symbol of a surge of patriotic feeling which may perhaps have made England for the first time an almost united political nation.

That this was Elizabeth's obvious status at the start of her reign made her as vulnerable as she was indispensable. The international situation took a turn for the worse soon after her reign began, when France plunged into a long religious civil war which made that country no longer an adequate counterbalance to the overpowering might of Catholic Spain. The aftermath of the Council of Trent proved to be a line of determined popes, grimly uncompromising towards heretics and fortified by the missionary zeal of the newly founded Society of Jesus. The basic situation in Scotland constituted a permanent hazard. Its allegedly beautiful, certainly impolitic, and emphatically Catholic queen, Mary Stuart, was, through her descent from Henry VIII's sister, the obvious heir to the English throne if Elizabeth died. Supported at times, though never wholeheartedly, by the French or the Spanish, both before and after her Scottish subjects' expulsion of her, she was hardly less of a symbol of the foreign Catholic threat than Elizabeth was of England's will to resist it.

Elizabeth's task therefore was both to represent English patriotism and keep it within prudent bounds. The expenditures and extravagances of the years since the 1530s had gravely damaged the crown's finances; there was no means of determining exactly how disaffected the English Catholics were; it was hard to prevent the commons from forcing her into a radically Puritan form of church settlement that would activate Catholic hostility at home as well as abroad; and, worst of all, she was a woman. When she became queen, the Venetian ambassador reckoned her reign would not last more than six months.

Fortunately, Elizabeth had political skills of a high order and of a kind possessed by few of her predecessors and few of her successors except perhaps Charles II. She adhered firmly to the idea that it was always best, in a position of weakness, to temporise, to eschew the heroic gesture (though not necessarily the heroic phrase) and to rely instead on the continuous exercise of guileful patience and politic vacillation. In an age when rulers and ruled all over Europe were filled with passionate conviction, she remained sceptically cool, impervious to religious extremism and determined never, if she possibly could, to put any grave matter to the test until she was sure there was no choice. She had her full share of imperious Tudor temper and all the Tudor pride in the high dignity of monarchy, but she had almost none of the cruel obstinacy that was the mark of the other Tudors.

To the exercise of these tactics she brought a witty, educated mind and a gift for pageantry and propaganda: 'We princes are,' she said, 'set as it were upon stages in the sight and view of all the world'. Above all she had a capacity for political speechmaking which makes the oratory of English politicians, Churchill included, seem laboured by comparison. She was adept at turning aside the grumblings of the commons with soft words and at conceding tactical victories to them in terms that seemed to add to her queenly dignity rather than subtract from it. And, if by the last years of her reign her evasions and postponements would bequeath to her successor a legacy of almost insoluble problems, her success in making procrastination into a high form of political art in the first thirty years of her reign not only ensured England's independence, but established a national unity that not even the civil war of the 1640s could succeed in destroying.

Among her political successes was the virtue she made of her unnatural position as an unmarried queen. Apart from the obvious difficulty that nobody believed that a woman should rule over men, her lack of a husband meant that the Catholic queen of Scots was her legal heir. The result was strong parliamentary pressure on Elizabeth to marry and bear children to eliminate the possibility that England should again have a Catholic queen. In the extreme Catholic view, both before and after Elizabeth's excommunication in 1570, Elizabeth was, as the Protestant daughter of Henry VIII's marriage to Anne Boleyn, not a true queen, but an illegitimate heretic. But Elizabeth seems to have had a strong disinclination to have her freedom of action circumscribed by a man. After all, it was only by the most elaborate avoidance of commitment to anybody that she had contrived to stay alive long enough to become queen at the age of twenty-five. Nor was her sister's experience as wife to a Spanish prince an encouraging precedent, and her cousin Mary Stuart's first marriage, to a French prince, had scarcely endeared her to her subjects. For Elizabeth, a foreign marriage would be a foreign alliance: but a Catholic marriage would upset the English, a Spanish marriage would annoy the French and a French marriage annoy the Spanish. A Protestant marriage would commit her to a confrontation with international Catholicism and lead to a spread of Puritan radicalism at home which she was bent on preventing. As for marriage to an English nobleman, whatever her supposed feelings for Robert Dudley,

Earl of Leicester, that would inevitably re-fuel all the ancient fires of aristocratic jealousy and rebellion whose suppression was the Tudor monarchy's originally proclaimed mission. So strong was Elizabeth's belief that she could rule safely only if she remained wholly unencumbered that she even baulked at the thought of giving birth to an heir; for he, as she had been in her youth, would be a potential pawn in the hands of a hostile faction. In this, as in most other matters, Elizabeth preferred, when it came to it, that her head should rule her heart; and though she would have favourites, she never let them stop her governing the realm with the aid of men of good sense.

In consequence, judiciously alternating anger with sweet words, she obstinately resisted all parliamentary attempts to discuss the question of her marriage. Since she all but died of smallpox in 1562, parliament was understandingly pressing in 1563; that their sovereign might die at any time, leaving a disputed succession, was after all a reasonable political calculation. It would have required an altogether irrational act of faith to take it for granted that Elizabeth would be so untypical as to live for another forty years and continue to play a valuable political game by pretending she might marry this, that or the other hopeful prince for nearly another twenty. Her angry mood was formidably expressed:

> I am your anointed queen. I will never be constrained to do anything. I thank God I am endued with such qualities that if I were turned out of the realm in my petticoat I were able to live in any place in Christendom.

Her placatory style was correspondingly disarming:

> Do not upbraid me with miserable lack of children, for every one of you, and as many as are Englishmen, are children and kinsmen to me.

In all other matters she pursued a similar policy. She refused Puritan demands for the persecution of Catholics until the crisis of the 1580s made it a political impossibility to do otherwise. She refused to act against Mary Stuart for twenty years. She resisted the Puritans' demand for the purging of the Catholic elements in her religious system long enough to give Anglicans like Hooker and Bancroft time to endow the English church with an intellectual and theological basis in many respects more defensible than that on which Puritanism was founded. Hating the waste and cost of foreign war, she gave but limited help to the beleaguered Protestants of the Netherlands against Catholic Spain, or to the French Huguenots against the Catholics of France. In her dealings with Spain, though not discountenancing unofficial acts of war at sea, she sought as patiently as Philip II himself to postpone official war for as long as possible. In all these policies of restraint she contrived, while seeming to be the crowned symbol of English Protestant patriotism, to act persistently counter to the desires of those passionate English patriots who wanted her to champion not only English Protestantism but European as well. She survived because her extreme political isolation as a virgin, Protestant queen made her indispensable. She alone stood between England and aristocratic and religious faction at home and the religious imperialism of the Spanish Habsburgs. As a result, the English faced the crisis of the Armada year of 1588 as an undivided people. By holding them back for thirty years both she and they were ready for it.

All the same, it was a close run thing. The Armada had been launched against a barely solvent monarchy which had at its disposal a far from adequate naval force. Neither was the Armada, though an ambitious project, an undertaking planned and executed by incompetent fanatics. Its achievement in reaching and sailing up the Channel intact was a considerable feat of seamanship which the English found almost impossible to impede. Not until it became vulnerable to English fire-ships off Calais, and was thereafter battered by the English off Gravelines and then shattered by foul weather, was its defeat possible. The English commanders were far from satisfied with their own performance and the commemorative medal which gave credit for the victory to the Almighty (God blew and they were scattered) suggests that their confidence in their special relationship with the Creator rather than an inflated notion of their own capabilities was the essential foundation of the Elizabethans' patriotism. Englishmen considered the world they lived in so dangerous that they thought their victory rather more miraculous than it really was; and they were too clearsighted to suppose that 1588 was the end of the matter. It was only the start. All the same, queen and people felt vindicated: God had given them a sign.

Queen and Commons

Whereas in previous centuries the drama of high politics had taken the form of aristocratic struggles within the council and on the field of battle, it was in the Tudor years that the commons became for the first time the principal stage on which political conflict was enacted. The change marked a civilianisation of politics, a step towards divorcing it from its more primitive character as a form of aristocratic warfare. It was because politics had for so long involved either armed rebellion, or the threat of it, that it was not until the beginning of the nineteenth century that the organisation of a coherent group of even wholly civilian politicians into a consistent political 'opposition' to government at last acquired respectability. The idea of 'opposition' still bore, even in the eighteenth century, the taint of its medieval origins as a potentially rebellious faction.

The Tudor house of commons, however, was in no sense an 'opposition'. It would have regarded the idea as treasonable and impious. It left opposition to the crown to manifest itself in the traditional way, in the various ill-conceived and thinly supported

245

aristocratic rebellions that took place. But armed rebellion was no longer the rule but the exception in the sixteenth century. The real political issues of the age were, from 1529 onwards, worked out by the council (after Thomas Cromwell's time more accurately described as the privy council) in association with the house of commons, just as the detailed administration of public affairs was conducted by the same privy council through the justices of the peace. By Elizabeth's time, though her councillors were aristocrats, it is fair to say that government conducted its business no longer solely nor even mainly through the aristocracy but through the gentry; if only because the boroughs as well as the counties were now represented by members of the landed gentry and because MPs and JPs were often the same people.

The Tudors, or perhaps to be more accurate, first Henry VIII and Thomas Cromwell, and then Elizabeth and William Cecil, made frequent use of the commons because the multiplying gentry were accumulating an increasing proportion of the country's wealth and had to be consulted if the crown was to finance itself and implement its legislation with any degree of public harmony. As Elizabeth's reign proceeded, inflation, the alienation of crown lands, and the cost of war with Spain, all made the goodwill of the commons increasingly necessary. But there were always elements other than the merely financial. Just as Henry VIII had needed the commons in order to represent the abolition of papal supremacy and the despoliation of the church as a manifestation of the national will and not the mere fiat of a presumptuous tyrant, so Elizabeth needed the commons to demonstrate to the world that her queenly status, though denied by foreign Catholics, was wholly legitimate in the eyes of her loving subjects.

But Tudor use of the commons was more than a matter of propaganda designed for foreign consumption. It was avowedly a sustained exercise in public relations at home. It would be wrong to say that in any formal sense the Tudors governed 'by consent'. Elizabeth herself said that, as head of the political system, she was not going to take orders from its 'foot'. But consultation with parliament, and the increased recourse of government to legislation by statute, gave to her system so striking an appearance of government by consent that, except for the queen and her council, who so assiduously stage-managed parliament's business, it convinced almost everybody. It certainly convinced a powerful Puritan minority among MPs; and though Elizabeth held her own against them, the political ineptness of her Stuart successors would result in making government by consent of the commons not merely an appearance but a reality.

The growing importance of the commons may be measured by its increased size and the wide range of its business. In 1509, the commons had 74 knights of the shire and 224 borough members. Since boroughs could now be relied on to elect landed gentlemen, Henry VIII created 14 new borough seats, Edward VI 34, Mary 25 and Elizabeth 62. In addition, Cromwell's reorganisation in Wales had added a further 25 MPs to the total. The commons thus almost doubled in size, while that of the lords decreased. The monastic spiritual lords disappeared; and Elizabeth's reluctance to grant peerages meant that membership of the lords fell from over sixty to less than forty.

The tasks that parliament, now numerically dominated by the gentry in the commons, was called on to perform testified to the energy of Tudor governments. Apart from the major statutes affecting the church, the ineffective ones against enclosure or for freezing wages, and the successive poor laws culminating in the act of 1601, statutes were passed providing for the 're-edifying' of Norwich, Nottingham, Shrewsbury, Gloucester and other towns, parts of which had become 'desolate and vacant'; others were passed imposing penalties on persons throwing dung or other filth into the Thames or stealing piles from the river for use as ballast. It was enacted that the unruly people of Wales should play no games at all except shooting with the longbow. There were statutes to limit the entrance fees of apprentices and to provide for a bounty of twopence a dozen for crows and rooks in order to reduce damage to crops. Parliament imposed penalties on sheriffs who 'packed' juries and on jurors who gave false verdicts. It ordered JPs to levy taxes for the maintenance of bridges and forbade tolls on the towpath of the river Severn, ordered towns to maintain their gaols, made rules for the dyeing of woollen cloth. It enacted that bakers, brewers and surgeons should no longer be legally classified as handicraftsmen; and ordered the paving of the Strand and the draining of Plumstead Marshes.

This bustling activity nevertheless derived its impetus almost entirely from the council, which also had the power to legislate on its own account by issuing proclamations which were no less legally valid than statutes. Many privy councillors were members of the commons, elected there by voters only too glad to have as their representatives exalted persons known to have regular access to the queen, fount of honour and justice as she was. Not only were various other MPs likely to be aristocratic or, more significantly, crown, nominees; the Speaker himself was a royal appointment, required to keep the house in order not for its own sake but for the queen's. Nor were the commons permitted to suppose that they could control either the queen or the council. She repeatedly averred that such matters as her marriage, the fate of Mary, Queen of Scots, and, more controversial still in the long run, her supreme governorship of the church, were concerns falling within her prerogative as queen and not therefore susceptible of parliamentary interference. She tried strenuously, though with less success than she would have liked, to maintain the principle that, though the commons had freedom of speech, it was only upon such matters as she chose to lay before them.

In consequence, there were frequent storms. The most notable of them were caused by the persistent campaign of the loquacious Puritan

MP, Peter Wentworth, to get it established that the commons could freely discuss any matter of public importance and propose legislation to deal with it. Fortunately for Elizabeth, the commons as a whole regarded Wentworth, despite his sincere protestations of loyalty to the queen, as a dangerous hothead. Only when the crown had passed to a monarch as unperceptive as Charles I would Peter Wentworth's bluntness of speech and largeness of view about the house's role be acceptable even to its other members. As it was, of the two occasions when Wentworth went briefly to the Tower for his impudence, the first was at the behest of the commons itself; and on the second, when he was confined on the orders of the queen, she was as careful not to make a martyr of him as he was not to concert any plots against her.

Until 1588 at least, the queen was even more politically necessary to the commons than the commons were to her. But her last decade was something of a trial. It was a time of bad harvests, soaring prices, declining trade and high taxes and of crisis for the royal finances. These were already so seriously prejudiced by inflation, high expenses and the repeated alienation of crown lands that the 'eating canker of want', of which James I was to complain, was already gnawing at the economic foundations of the crown's political independence. The cost of fighting Spain always exceeded the profits of the privateers and plunderers at work in the Atlantic and the Channel. The maintenance of a force to assist the Netherlanders against Spain cost two million pounds over a period of eighteen years, and the suppression of an Irish revolt cost twice that sum, to a government whose total supply of ready cash in the year of the Armada had been about £185,000. The queen's badly paid officials resorted to graft because she neither would, nor could, pay them adequately. The royal device of awarding monopolies to favoured persons was one result of the crown's shortage of money that aroused intense opposition from the commons. A courtier might be given a monopoly as a reward or obtain one for cash down. The monopoly would give him the sole right to make, or sell, or import commodities of various sorts, many of them in general demand. This inevitably put up prices. Worse still, monopolists had legal power to restrain and punish would-be competitors. Monopolies were thus seen as a particularly objectionable means by which the queen could, at her subjects' expense, do a good turn simultaneously to herself and a few favoured courtiers.

First raised by the commons in 1597, the matter was still unresolved by the evasive queen four years later. Her prevarications caused so much disgruntlement that in the end she had to produce one final demonstration of her lifelong policy of never bringing any matter to the test if it appeared politically profitless to do so. Out of the plenitude of her queenly prerogative she caused a proclamation to be issued announcing the imminent end to all harmful monopolies and a redress of all the commons' grievances about them. Surprise and anger, she said, were her feelings on discovering that monopolies had been oppressive to her people; and on being thanked by the commons for her gracious bounty, she turned defeat into victory in a reply that, with rare humility, not only put on record her view of her past achievement, but laid bare the foundation upon which she believed that achievement had rested:

Though God hath raised me high, yet this I count the glory of my reign that I have reigned with your loves . . . . I was never so much enticed with the glorious name of a king or royal authority of a queen, as delighted that God had made me his instrument to maintain his truth and glory and to defend his kingdom from peril, dishonour, tyranny and oppression . . . . Though you have had and may have many mightier and wiser princes sitting on this seat, yet you never had nor shall have any that will love you better.

5
STUART BREAKDOWN

Elizabethan Legacy

ELIZABETH I's special achievement had been to survive more of the nation's problems than she solved. Only with hindsight can it be seen as settled by 1603 that England would not be a client state of Spain and never again return to Catholicism. In 1603, war with Spain continued and, across the Channel, Catholics and Protestants were still at each other's throats. Elizabeth had grappled with inflation by obsessive meanness and by raising money in ways that upset powerful interests; but how, if at all, the nation was to be persuaded to contribute adequately to the costs of government was still undetermined. She had wooed, and usually won, the support of the commons; but such successes were personal triumphs conceded in a time of external danger. They merely disguised the fact that the country had a ramshackle constitution which, in a more divisive time, might prove unworkable.

Outside London, crown and council were without professional administrators. This left unanswered the question of how government could be effective if the gentry who controlled the counties as well as the house of commons were no longer disposed to cooperate. Sir Walter Raleigh described the gentry as 'the garrisons of good order throughout the realm'. This was true, but it meant that the crown could not afford to upset them: it had no real garrisons. The crown had weakened the aristocracy without enquiring how a monarch could survive if he could no longer summon great magnates to rally a subservient tenantry to the royal cause in a crisis. Despite Tudor legislation about trade and commerce, it was still wholly uncertain whether in such matters it was the business of government to encourage or merely to regulate and restrain. Finally, the great debate as to what kind of England should result from the second rejection of Catholicism in 1559 was still unresolved. This was not a 'religious' problem in the later, narrower sense of the word. It posed fundamental questions about the nature of society. Under the weight of so many ambiguities, the established institutions of the state were to collapse within forty years of Elizabeth's death, producing two decades in which military dictatorship seemed the only alternative to anarchy.

Poor Kings, Powerless Parliament

The point of stress from which the breakdown originated was the impoverishment of the crown and the inadequacy of its revenue.

Despite frequent resort to the unpopular use of traditional prerogative rights to raise money, the crown was coming to rely more and more on 'extraordinary' direct taxation, for the levying of which the consent of the commons was a legal requirement. But this consent was obtainable only if the crown's policies were those of which the commons approved; and one policy of which the commons most strongly disapproved was the raising of taxes by use of the prerogative. In reply, the king would insist that commons had neither the right nor the capacity to interfere with the prerogative and that parliaments were wholly subordinate to him.

These royal ripostes exacerbated the situation the more for being grounded in law and fact. Government was the responsibility of the crown, and a council permanently in being. Parliament did not select the council's members, could not control their actions, and had no power to dismiss them. Parliament was a rarely-meeting debating assembly. In the forty-four years of Elizabeth's reign there had been only thirteen parliamentary sessions, each averaging only ten weeks in length, and occurring, on average, only once every three years. In 1593, Elizabeth had accurately defined the position in terms neither James I nor Charles I improved on:

It is in me and in my power to call parliaments; and it is in my power to end and determine the same; it is in my power to assent or dissent to anything done in parliament.

The crown might find it increasingly difficult to govern without summoning parliaments; but parliament's legal power to influence government included neither a right to its own existence nor a say in the policy pursued by the government it subsidised.

Even parliament's power to withhold extraordinary direct taxes, technically referred to as 'subsidies', has looked greater to later observers than, even in the reigns of James I and Charles I, it really was at the time. The method of assessing the subsidies was much out of date. It took no account of inflation; and the amounts collected were so inadequate to the crown's needs that the commons understood that, beyond a certain point, subsidies were not often worth making an issue of. Before 1629, the Stuart kings usually got their subsidies; the commons knew that if they proved obdurate, the crown could send them all packing, and continue to manage on the proceeds of prerogative taxation; in particular by increasing customs duties. This did not require parliamentary assent and was a source of revenue which kept pace with inflation and was buoyed up by increasing trade. Hence, James I ruled from 1610 to 1621 with only one brief parliamentary interlude (the 'Addled' parliament of 1614, so-called because its refusal to vote subsidies helped to make it so distinctive); and Charles I ruled without any parliament at all from 1629 until 1640. As for controlling the king's ministers, no progress could be made. An unpopular minister could be removed only by impeachment, a process by which the commons accused the minister of treason and the lords acted as his judges. But, in the most explosive attack on a minister of the years before 1640, the attempt to impeach Charles I's favourite, Buckingham, in 1626, the jealousy of Buckingham felt by peers envious of his too rapid elevation to ducal status counted as much as did the commons' disapproval of his policies. And even if Charles had not squashed the attempt by dissolving parliament, there was no way by which a king's minister could be found guilty of treason against the crown for so long as the crown approved of his actions. The king's ministers were the king's servants, not parliament's.

'Great and Growing Mischiefs'

Crown and parliament therefore squabbled their way through the years of James I's reign, each trying to persuade or bully the other because both institutions were too weak to stand securely on their own feet, the crown through its lack of money, parliament through its lack of power. But though parliament had, in the last resort, little power over the king in peacetime (he could raise revenue by prerogative without them), a king was almost powerless without parliament in time of war. Not only did he then need the national support they could give to his cause; in wartime, he had to have their subsidies. It was therefore on the issue of peace and war more than anything else that a genuine conflict, involving fundamental principles, was most likely to emerge, and only in time of war that parliament might find itself acquiring effective power as an institution. Between 1529 and 1590, crown and parliament had been broadly agreed on the common aim of asserting and preserving national independence of both Rome and Spain. But the commons became convinced that, first James I, and then Charles I, were indifferent to, if not opposed to, this great national cause. Since wars, the most costly of government's activities, were so likely to increase his dependence upon the commons, James ended, in 1604, the war with Spain that had begun in 1588. Followed as it was by two decades of apparent subservience to Spain, this aroused in English hearts the frustrated hostility created among their descendants by the devotion of Baldwin and Neville Chamberlain to the policy of appeasing the European dictators. Still bloated with the patriotism of the Elizabethan years, gentry and merchants saw this as a betrayal of England's divinely ordained role as defender of commerce and the reformed religion. And, though it saved the government money, it was bad for those who had invested in privateering expeditions against the Spanish, on which, when successful, there was a high return of interest, and the plunder from which had constituted up to fifteen per cent of total imports for some twenty years.

Matters worsened with the outbreak of the Thirty Years War in 1618, when Catholic Spain and Austria threatened the survival of Europe's

Protestant states until they were rescued in the later stages of the war by the Catholic French. The defiant Protestants of Bohemia began the war. Rather than accept the Catholicising Austrian emperor as their ruler, they invited a Calvinist prince from Heidelberg, Frederick, the elector Palatine, to come to Prague as their king instead. The Bohemians were crushed; after one winter in Prague, Frederick became an exile, minus not only his Bohemian kingdom but his palatinate as well. Unfortunately for James I, his own daughter, Elizabeth, was Frederick's wife. Her emotive Christian name and her plight as a Protestant exile made her the heroine of the English parliamentarians. The commons at once demanded that James fight Spain, by land and by sea, to right the wrong done to a Protestant queen who was also an English princess. In a seventeenth-century Christendom about to commit itself to a generation-long war of dynastic rivalries dressed in the borrowed religious clothing of Catholicism on one side and Protestantism on the other, James was indeed its 'wisest fool' in trying to seek a policy of peace. Immune to the Armada tradition in which the parliament men had been bred, he took the view, more sensible in 1620 than in 1938, that Prague was in a faraway country about which England could do very little. With more folly than wisdom, however, he expressed his anger at the attempt of a bellicose commons to dictate his foreign policy by personally tearing the relevant page out of the commons' Journal.

All through the 1620s, the foreign policy of James and Charles, increasingly dominated by their swaggering favourite, Buckingham, did much to erode the commons' almost inexhaustible belief in the duty of a subject to be loyal to his king. There was a royal plan, sensible enough when first conceived, but now naive in its hopes and foolish in its execution, to restrain Spanish violence in Europe by means of a marriage alliance. When the plan collapsed, and Charles returned from Madrid without a Spanish Catholic bride, London cheered almost as if the Armada had been destroyed again. Convinced that this showed that an anti-Spanish policy would be the best means to win parliament's support, Buckingham at once formed an alliance with Spain's traditional enemy, France. As a pledge of this sudden, new Anglo-French accord, Charles was, before parliament could meet to forbid the banns, married to the French Catholic princess, Henrietta Maria. Faced with the *fait accompli* of a Catholic marriage after all, with all that it involved in the future increase of Catholic influence at court and over the education of the royal children, the commons were convinced that Buckingham was reckless, godless and unpatriotic.

His political errors multiplied. Ill-equipped conscripts were sent to help the Dutch against the Spanish, and returned a disconsolate rabble. An attempt to raid Spanish treasure ships led to a defeat off Cadiz as humiliating as an attempted landing against La Rochelle, the result of a pointless new quarrel which Buckingham now contrived with the French. The commons attempted in 1628 to impeach Buckingham, on grounds histrionically summarised by the intemperate MP, Sir John Eliot: 'Our honour is ruined, our ships are sunk, our men perished, not by the enemy but by those we trust'. Charles's reply was frigidly royal: 'I would not have the house to question my servants, much less one that is so near to me'. To have, at the king's command, too much power and to use it recklessly and dangerously, broke no law. It took the assassination of Buckingham by an army officer with a grievance to end the impasse.

To all this, the government added sins of omission. From 1629 to 1640 there was no parliament; and without parliamentary taxes, war was impossible. This seemed no blessing to Protestant patriots, remembering the brave days of Drake and Hawkins. Now, unpunished, pirates infested home waters, some of them Barbary corsairs snatching Devonians into oriental slavery. When, in 1623, East India Company traders were killed in Java by their Dutch rivals, James refused to move on the Company's behalf. When English merchants sought naval protection for their trade in the Mediterranean, Charles told them not to sail there.

Pockets and Consciences

The crown's financial devices caused deep rifts. Over each issue, what began as an argument about money ended as passionate debate about the fundamentals of government. For all its powerlessness in practice, the commons had warned that this might happen. In an Apology drawn up in 1604 to advise James about the rights of parliament (though it was never presented to him), the commons noted that everywhere in Europe despotic monarchy was becoming normal: 'The prerogatives of princes may easily and do daily grow: the privileges of the subject are for the most part at an everlasting stand'. Long before the slogan was invented, there were those in the Stuart house of commons who were already aware that the price of liberty was eternal vigilance. To the charge that they were not 'really' defending liberty, but only their pockets, the gentry and merchants opposing the Stuarts' prerogative taxation could have answered that, in the real world, every demand for liberty is a demand for the right to power and property; and that resistance to attacks on individual rights, power and property is a defence of liberty.

Of the specific issues, two illustrate all. Desperate to pay for the cost of Buckingham's wars, Charles appointed commissioners to force propertied persons to make him a patriotic 'loan' assessed in proportion to their income. On the grounds that this amounted to an unparliamentary tax, some gentry refused to pay, and were imprisoned. In 1627, five of them applied for a writ of habeas corpus. This, if granted, would secure their release unless it could be shown they had broken the law of the land. But the council informed the court that the offenders had been imprisoned 'by special command of the king'. The judges, though themselves victims of the king's forced loan, decided that the council's reply made the release of the prisoners impossible. This decision, correct in law, meant that the king could mulct his subjects as he pleased, send them to prison for objecting, and then keep them there. Not surprisingly, Charles got almost as much money from the Forced Loan as he would have done from the subsidies that parliament had refused to grant him.

The more celebrated matter of ship money arose in 1637. Previously payable only by coastal towns in lieu of a contribution of ships to the king's navy, it had been extended in 1635 to inland counties on the sensible ground that the navy protected the whole country. John Hampden refused to pay, declaring it was a direct tax levied without consent of parliament; and parliament had not met since 1629. The judges decided, though by a majority of only seven to five, for the crown. They had the difficult task of applying purely legal principles to a matter wholly political. In law, the king had a duty to recognise an emergency when he saw one and to take steps to meet it. Therefore he must have his money. There was no machinery within the law for asserting that there was no emergency and that no taxes were therefore required. But the dissenting judges saw the implications: no man was secure in life or property if the king could, at any time by prerogative, proclaim an emergency and then impose what taxes he pleased. John Hampden was a rich man; Charles honestly applied ship money to improving the navy, which badly needed it; but the issue was the larger one of liberty versus absolute authority.

The raising of money by straining the crown's fiscal prerogative to the limits of the law was the respectable part of Stuart policy. From James's accession until Buckingham's death in 1628, the court was a bazaar where everything a king or an all-powerful favourite had to bestow could be bought for cash. Knighthoods were sold almost to all and sundry. The new honour of the baronetcy, created in 1611 to fill the gap between the knights and the peerage, was obtainable for money from the beginning. Buckingham freely sold both peerages and the right to nominate to a peerage. The farming out of the right to collect customs duties was another means of saving and raising money. So was the right to collect the additional duties, known as impositions, placed upon luxury goods. The fortunate 'farmer' paid a lump sum to the crown and a fixed annual 'rent'. In a period of expanding trade he could safely rely on a profit. Buckingham was the top customs farmer. He got the right to the Irish customs for ten years, and made over £3,000 a year out of it. Other peers paid the crown for the right to an income from the collection of the impositions on currants, sugar and coal, and of the tax on aliens.

Other purchasable sources of income included the right to collect certain of the king's feudal revenues; to exercise a monopoly in new industrial processes; to collect fines payable for the breach of various economic regulations, or to sell exemptions from them. Under James, some individuals acquired for cash the right to collect recusancy fines from Catholics who failed to go to church on Sunday.

The commons complained vociferously about all these practices from the latter days of Elizabeth on into the 1620s. But with no nationally organised bureaucracy and a wholly inadequate revenue, the crown would have found it impossible to carry on the business of government had it not employed these miscellaneous and often dubious means of raising or saving money. Without them, few of the few public servants the crown employed would have been paid at all. Unfortunately, government was, under James, extravagant and wasteful. In less than two years, James made gifts to various peers of over £63,000. He distributed annuities and pensions so lavishly that a third of all peers were at one time pensioners of the crown. He allowed courtiers to borrow regularly from him, vaguely hoping to get the money back from their heirs. All this greatly embittered the normal hostility dividing those who enjoyed royal favours and those who did not. In time it would encourage a more significant division: between those who believed that monarchy had the right to be magnificent, and to be munificent to a favoured minority while demanding the obedience of all; and those to whom monarchy came to be seen, by its very nature, as spendthrift and corrupt.

The Puritan Contribution

When rebellion eventually came in the 1640s, it differed greatly from the aristocratic rebellions of the middle ages. At the outset, the king's leading opponents did think of themselves as engaged in a conflict on traditional lines, as upholders of the original Magna Carta, determined to reinforce its legal barriers against excessive royal power. They were, in many ways, a whole parliament of Henry Bolingbrokes descending upon Whitehall to claim back their lawful rights from a king whose aloof dignity, sensitive artistic taste, Byzantine cunning and Byzantine identification of himself with the true church made him in more ways than one a latter-day Richard II.

That the result was two decades of turmoil pregnant with ideas that were to reverberate through the centuries, to be echoed back from New England in 1776 and from Paris in 1789, was the particular contribution of Puritanism. It was because of Puritanism that the civil war produced victory neither for parliament nor king. It was Puritanism that threatened an apparently triumphant parliament with social revolution. It was Puritanism that sustained the Cromwellian dictatorship by which that social revolution was averted. England was not the only west European country to have rebellions against princely authority in the mid-seventeenth century. France, Spain and Holland faced rebellions too; but only the English rebels of that time were later to be hailed as progenitors of the revolutionaries of the modern world, honoured by Marxists as founding fathers of bourgeois revolution. This was because Puritanism added to the Great Rebellion a dimension that those who initiated the struggle in 1641, for all that most of them thought of themselves as Puritans, had not expected.

The most accurate definition of Puritanism, because it is the most imprecise, is the Elizabethan view that Puritans were 'the hotter sort' of Protestant. They considered the Elizabethan church too proximate to Catholicism in organisation and ritual and still too marred by the abuses of which parliament had complained in 1529, to be acceptable as a genuinely reformed church. What precise further reforms they wanted they rarely agreed upon. All wanted a 'preaching ministry'; but who should constitute the ministry and what exactly they should preach was uncertain. Most objected to pluralism and absenteeism; but few agreed on how else to select and finance the parish clergy, particularly as the more radical among them wanted to abolish tithes. Some wanted a Presbyterian system, governed by lay elders; but, despite much Puritan hostility to bishops ('swine, dumb-dogs and non-residents' as one polemicist called them), Presbyterianism took no deep roots in England. Other Puritans thought that a national church should be a purely cooperative organisation whose basic unit should be the completely independent Puritan congregation.

Though divided as to means, Puritans were reasonably agreed as to ends. They desired a more sincere and more seriously understood religion than the tepid conformism which was all that the Elizabethan church had sought, but fiercely opposed all attempts to achieve those ends when made by zealous bishops and divines who did not share Puritan ideas about the liturgy or about church organisation. They wished to impose on themselves, and on others, a more sober standard of conduct than that which prevailed in late Elizabethan and early Stuart England, while, again, resisting every effort by the established ecclesiastical authorities to do the same thing. But solemn, earnest, persons of this temperament, concerned principally with moral self-improvement, do not make revolutionaries unless greatly provoked. Moreover, obedience to the crown was more deeply embedded in Protestantism than in Catholicism. Without secular princes there would hardly have been Protestantism anywhere, let alone Puritanism.

What provoked Puritans into opposition was the steadily growing belief, between 1603 and 1640, that the Stuart kings were betraying the Protestant cause. James's friendship with Catholic Spain, Buckingham's with Catholic France, Charles's marriage to a Catholic queen, the increasing Catholic influence at court, the favour given to Catholic peers, hardened Puritan sentiment, particularly in the commons, where, since Puritans were men of drive and determination, it was strongly represented.

More alarming still, was the development by the Church of England of a theology of its own, divergent from that of other Protestants. Anglican divines began to insist that the church was itself a source of spiritual truth no less than the Bible. They restored old rituals. The communion table was again shifted to the east end of the church, was referred to as an altar, and sometimes railed off and honoured with frequent genuflections. This seemed thoroughly popish; though Cranmer's prayer book nowhere mentioned the word 'Protestant' neither did it use the word 'altar'. Puritans, illogical though it may seem, prided themselves on their freedom from superstition. To be asked to receive communion kneeling and not standing was offensive enough; to be asked to bob up and down before an altar was intolerable. They were also offended when the new young graduate clergy, so favoured by the bishops in the 1630s, began to preach the duty of non-resistance to the crown. This was unbearable at a time when the crown was failing to support Protestantism abroad; was refusing to summon parliament but still levying taxes with the full weight of the prerogative; and, when through Archbishop Laud, the most powerful prelate since the detested Wolsey, it was enforcing objectionable ceremonies in almost every parish church in the land.

Considered further evidence of a drift back to Rome was the abandonment under Laud's regime of the common Protestant doctrine of predestination. This claim that, since God knew everything and was all-powerful, he must have decided from the beginning which human beings were to be saved (the 'elect' few) and which were to be damned, suggests there would be no rejoicing in heaven if a sinner repented, but surprise; and the idea that man, who was, by Protestant definition, a worm, could surprise an omnipotent and omniscient God was held to be both blasphemous and illogical. The new doctrine of Arminianism taught, like old popery, that salvation could depend on whether a man responded to the divine grace or did not respond to it. It admitted the possibility that, having received grace, a man might fall from it. Arminianism thus destroyed the primacy that Puritanism placed on personal morality. It demolished all certainty about moral behaviour. The immoral might after all be saved by a change of heart at the end; and the moral might, through a late fall from grace, be damned. (Oliver Cromwell for one was deeply perturbed at the thought that this possibility existed.) That the Arminian doctrine of free will would seem to accord more closely to the teachings of the new testament would not necessarily commend itself to Puritans. To the Puritan, the whole Bible was a sacred text; he was therefore likely to be more influenced by the old testament than the new, since there was so much more of the old testament. The Romish practice, by which congregations sat during readings from the old testament but stood during readings from the gospel, was considered wrong by Puritans because all parts of the Bible required equal reverence. In contrast to the Lutheran insistence on the inherent worthlessness of the individual, and the theological determinism of Calvinism's theory that, save for the elect minority, all men were predestined to eternal damnation, Arminianism represented a major step forward in the liberation of the human spirit. But it was considered tainted by its origin in a court dominated by a detested archbishop and by its association with ceremonies reminiscent of the rituals of Rome.

These new ceremonies were rigidly enforced. Laud was a member of the royal council and also of the prerogative courts which enforced his religious jurisdiction. The outstanding outcome of this was the case of three university graduates, Prynne, Bastwick and Burton. For publishing pamphlets attacking bishops they were pilloried at Westminster, had their ears mutilated, and were sentenced to life imprisonment. That their attacks were scurrilous mattered less than that they were respectively, lawyer, doctor and parson. Gentlemen were unaccustomed to men of their rank being given punishments appropriate to the lowest ranks of society.

Laud's domination of the church and his emphasis on 'the beauty of holiness' enabled it to transmit to the future a better balanced theology and a more uniform and ordered ritual than it had had previously. But neither the worth of his reforms nor the sincerity of his motives could alter the fact that this fussy, irritable, well-meaning man made it impossible for the Church of England ever to be the church of all Englishmen. His efforts were too late. The inefficient censorship of the years from 1534 to 1630, and the political rivalries which had ensured that Puritans had once had powerful episcopal as well as aristocratic protectors, had enabled Puritanism to strike roots too deep for Laud to destroy. It was because of Laud's policies that, when the storm broke, the Puritans felt themselves conservatives, protecting the church from Laud's 'innovations'. It was because the Puritan side in the civil war contained so many whose minds had been shaped before the Laudian drive for uniformity and the introduction of new-fangled notions of non-resistance to the king, that the average parliamentarian was ten years older than the average Royalist. By 1640 it required an effort of memory to recall the time when there had been even one bishop on the episcopal bench whom a Puritan could confidently describe as a genuine Protestant. The Puritans who challenged Charles I in 1641 were not young men in a revolutionary hurry. They were mature conservatives who wanted to destroy neither state nor church, but to preserve both from 'dangerous innovations'.

6
UNWILLING WARRIORS

A Nation of Lawyers

WOUNDING though it may be to the national pride, the fact is that, in every major crisis of the seventeenth century, the preservation of English liberties was owed to the intervention of foreigners. The collapse of Charles I's non-parliamentary government in 1638 was initiated not by an English, but by a Scottish, rebellion. The division of the English, by 1642, into two distinct parties, one ready to fight for Charles and the other against him, was in large measure due to a rebellion by the Irish. The army that restored Charles II in 1660 was launched from Scotland. The Revolution of 1688–89 which ended the last Stuart attempt at authoritarian government was due wholly to the fact that at the critical moment Louis XIV of France decided not to help James II whereas William of Orange, a foreign sovereign prince, decided to support James's opponents with an army brought over from Holland.

The whole tortuous confusion of English history in the half century that ended in 1689 arises from the fact that the English were a nation, not of fighting men, but of lawyers. They were not even barrack room lawyers. To the English, armies were anathema, as engines of tyranny. The fact that from 1646 to 1658, their chief of men, Oliver Cromwell, was the one great English soldier of the age, was in itself sufficient to prevent him obtaining that consent to his rule for which he yearned. The civil war was begun by men who thought of it mainly in civilian terms, almost as a makeshift military equivalent to a general election to decide which group of men should form the king's government. Had this alternative civilian device been available they would unquestionably have adopted it. For almost the whole of the first two years of the civil war, the parliamentary side fought with the fumbling uncertainty of His Majesty's Loyal Opposition, forced by intractable circumstance to take up arms they wished to lay down at the first decent opportunity. The fighting spirit and the ideological ardour of the New Model Army, which defeated the king in the end, were repudiated by the bulk of the parliamentary leaders the moment victory was won. The English of those years give every impression of being passionate, rhetorical, fanatical and disorderly, but at the same time resolutely legalistic. The gentlemen of England strongly disliked the government of Charles I in the 1630s, the armed Puritan minority of the 1650s, and the armed pro-Catholic minority of the 1680s. But in each case, the initiative in the use of force was taken by men other than themselves.

260

Rebel Scots

In 1637, in order to achieve a greater religious uniformity between the two kingdoms, an attempt was made to impose upon the Scots a modified version of the English prayer book. The Scots resisted this Laudian attack on their quasi-presbyterian church. Charles resolved to behave 'as a brave prince should'. He tried to fight the Scots; failed; made a truce; and then summoned parliament in England, hoping to get money out of it by appeals to its patriotism. Instead, taking full advantage of the opportunity that Scottish resolution had given it, this Short Parliament attacked all the practices of the government since 1629. Charles dissolved it after only three weeks and renewed the war with the Scots, with even worse results. The Scots crossed the border, occupied Newcastle, Northumberland and Durham, and demanded to be paid the sum of £850 for every day they stayed there. Expecting a patriotic response, Charles summoned an assembly of lay and clerical notables to a Great Council at York. They did not rally to the head of the aristocratic order; they advised him to summon another parliament. The war having cost more than his total annual revenue, Charles took their advice. The Long Parliament assembled in November 1640. It did not technically disappear until 1660.

'I cannot tell you, sirs . . .'

Words later used by Cromwell reflected the thoughts of many in 1641: 'I can tell you, sirs, what I would not have; though I cannot tell you what I would have'. What the commons 'would not have' was the system of government by which the crown, by prerogative, could impose taxes and punishments on its wealthier subjects in disregard of parliament. The commons would not have it that the king should again exercise the untrammelled sovereignty that he had exercised since 1629. They were the more determined on this point since Charles's non-parliamentary government had been efficient. But on the issue of how much of the prerogative should be transferred to parliament for the future, they could not agree. The civil war emerged from the fact that some of the commons and most of the lords turned royalist when they became afraid that, if the king lost too much of his prerogative, the social order would break down.

The Long Parliament's first act was to encompass the execution of Strafford, the king's deputy in Ireland, where he had amassed an army which might be used to suppress the English instead of the Irish. It indicates the temper of the commons that, though Laud was also sent to the Tower, his trial and execution were delayed until 1645. Their first priority was to preserve legality from military usurpation; a point which gives weight to Cromwell's assertion that 'religion was not at first contended for'. During the rest of 1641, all taxation, direct and indirect was placed under parliamentary control and all the prerogative courts were abolished, thus bringing all England and all Englishmen (and Welshmen) for the first time under the common law. The king was not to dissolve the existing parliament without its consent; there were to be parliaments, of at least fifty days' duration, every three years. Little of the legislation passed in 1641 was modified by the Restoration of the monarch in 1660. Henceforth the crown would find it more difficult than ever to govern or finance itself without parliamentary consent.

On these points there was unanimity. But once the problem moved from what the commons would not have to what they would have, divisions appeared which were to produce civil war. In matters of religion all were agreed that the existing bishops were a bad lot, that bishops' powers should be limited and that the ceremonial interpretation of the prayer book imposed by Laud should be ended. But Puritan demands for the abolition of episcopacy 'root and branch' and for drastic Puritan changes in the prayer book of a kind which would have anticipated by three hundred years the amputations practised on it in the 1960s produced a division that was never healed. Those who saw an attack on episcopacy as an attack on social order and the rights of property were among the earliest royalists.

They were soon joined by those who resisted the Puritan demand for parliamentary control of the army. This arose because, with the removal of Strafford's strong hand, the Irish burst into rebellion. All thought the Irish were barbarous papists who ought to be put down. But an army raised to do the Lord's work in Ireland might then be used to do the devil's in England. Many saw the issue as a choice between an army serving the lawful sovereign, and an army serving the Puritan leader, John Pym, not only a superb contriver of majorities in the commons but also a sedulous organiser of riotous crowds outside it.

Heartened by signs that his enemies were falling out, Charles once more assumed the role of 'brave prince'. He went in person to the commons to arrest five leading MPs on a charge of treason. This action violated more than one sacred legal precedent and, like most of Charles's attempts to act decisively, was bungled. The plan was leaked in advance; the MPs were already in the safe keeping of the citizens of London when the king arrived. Charles abandoned his unfriendly capital, and after eight months of proposal, counter-proposal and propaganda on both sides, war began in August 1642.

Taking Sides

Most of those who took an active part in the civil war did so because they were forced to do so by their betters. Those (the majority) who were able to, stayed out of it. Those who chose freely did so chiefly according to their views on law and social order. Such views might, or might not, originate from or be reinforced by religious conviction. Many who found themselves on the parliamentary side between 1642 and 1646, particularly those who served in the New Model Army or who, as apprentices and small tradesmen in London, took part in the various affrays which at first helped to coerce the king and then to alarm parliament, might undergo a process of indoctrination, part-religious and part-political, which would lead them to oppose all the initial combatants and to demand the overthrow of all existing institutions. But, given the uncertainty as to the aims of both sides in the first civil war, men could choose between them only with much dubiety. The original parliamentarians lost active support rapidly when it became clear how little they knew what they wanted; and though royalism was too basic to be eliminated, the English royalists did little more, when the king was restored in 1660, than cheer the Restoration after it had happened. They did little to bring it about.

Attempts to establish the war as a conflict of economic 'interests' founder in a sea of human uncertainties. In some towns, merchants and traders who wished to participate in economic activities from which they were excluded by royal grants, charters and monopolies might be parliamentarians if, as in London, there were sufficient other parliamentarians to join. Catholics would be neutral if they could; if not, they would be royalist in the expectation, false as it turned out, that they had more to fear from Puritan rule. There were peers, gentry, merchants and lawyers on both sides. Parliament could hardly have got an army together without a measure of aristocratic support. For the view that this was a revolution by the bourgeoisie against the feudal aristocracy there are no supporting facts. The decline of the feudal aristocracy was not a result of the 'English Revolution' but one of its causes; and it was because it had already ceased to be feudal before 1640 that the aristocracy emerged from that 'Revolution' more powerful than when it had begun.

The Victory of the Independents

Since, apart from the king's nephew, Prince Rupert, younger son of the defeated Elector Palatine of 1620, there were few experienced commanders in England, the war was fought in diffident fashion on both sides. Neither side was sure what it could do with victory if it won it. If Charles won, this left unanswered the question of how he could hold the country down afterwards. If parliament defeated the king, there was no knowing how he could be made to keep any promises they might force from him. Both sides therefore fought in the hope that the other would give in.

This worked to the king's advantage. If parliament jogged along under the uninspiring command of the Earl of Essex, who went into battle accompanied by his coffin for fear of the worst, people would weary of prolonged rebellion and, as was said at the time, 'the king will come and say which of us is to be hanged first'. To extricate them from this dilemma, parliament secured an alliance with the Scots, a people more accustomed to war by now than the English were; and then, in 1645, organised the New Model Army, of regularly-paid professionals, recruited for service in all parts of the kingdom. These two developments assured the king's defeat; but they made impossible an agreed solution of the fundamental problem of how the country should be governed.

With the end of effective royalist resistance, Charles surrendered to the Scots at Newark in 1646. The first cause of the confusions that followed was Charles's readiness to negotiate interminably and with total lack of sincerity with whichever of his opponents cared to approach him. Second, the Scots, as the price of their help, had committed parliament to the establishment of a Presbyterian church. This aroused determined opposition from the Independent Puritans. Independents were as much opposed to a uniform system of church government by presbyters as to one imposed by bishops. They wanted a federation of more or less independent congregations, a demand which, in somewhat ambiguous fashion, made them pioneers of religious toleration. The final element was the emergence among the army rank and file and some of its officers, as well as among elements in the civilian population, of yet other Puritans whose blueprints for the future would eventually lead their opponents to bestow on them the label, 'Levellers'.

It was Cromwell who, slowly, unwillingly and always a little uncomprehendingly, found himself impelled (or, as he would have said, moved by the hand of the Lord) to become the man to bring these discordant elements into subjection. He had first made himself prominent as the stern advocate of fighting for outright victory. It was his success in achieving this aim which made him the man of the hour, even though all the ills with which he had to grapple derived from the victory he had insisted on. The key to his importance was that he was determined to preserve Independency from Scottish Presbyterianism in alliance with parliament. But he believed also in military discipline, in the authority of parliament, in the rights of property owners, and in a system of government which, in his usual vague fashion, he thought ought to have 'somewhat of the monarchical' in it. After great hesitation, which he called 'waiting upon the Lord wondrously to reveal Himself in events', he allowed the army to purge parliament of its more obnoxious Presbyterians and to snatch Charles into military instead of parliamentary custody. When, as a result, English and Scottish royalists and parliamentary Presbyterians provoked a second civil war in 1648, they were defeated. When powerful elements in the army at once pressed for the execution of Charles, not only for the now manifest reason that no one could trust him, but also as a prelude to the wholesale democratisation of society, he yielded to this pressure since, if he lost the support of the army, he could not preserve the Independency of which he and the army were sole defenders. Charles thought that he died to preserve the Church of England; it would be nearer the truth to say that he was executed to preserve religious toleration and non-conformity. For so long as Charles lived, Cromwell and his soldiers, who believed in both, could be certain of neither. In this particular aim they were successful. It was not only Charles I who died on 30 January 1649; as an effective force, so also did English Presbyterianism. The monarchy, the lords, the commons and the church would all survive the king's death. But so also did nonconformity.

'Fond Imaginary Hopes'

Cromwell had other work than this: to preserve the social order from the threat of what looked like, and sometimes avowedly was, anarchy. The summoning of parliament in a sudden crisis in 1640; the phenomenon of a war against the king which had the support of men of substance and which had ended first in victory and then in the treacherous fact of a second war; the execution of a king, not by unnamed assassins working in secret as agents of wicked men greedy for power, but in public, after a trial conducted, so it was declared, in 'the name of all the good people of England'—all this aroused the hopes of humble men whose welfare had been on nobody's mind when the struggle opened in 1640. Yet as early as 1642 it was being noted that 'the vulgar mind' was 'now fond with imaginary hopes'; and the fearful question was being asked, 'what will the issue be when hopes grow still on hopes?'

Encouragement of 'imaginary hopes' in 'vulgar minds' began as soon as the Long Parliament met. To whip up its own morale and that of whoever could read (particularly in London), Puritan preachers were invited to deliver sermons to the commons; they were afterward published. Many of them, long silenced by Laud, announced confidently that the Laudian system at home and the Thirty Years War abroad were signs of the reign of anti-Christ and were portents of a cataclysmic millennial event after which Christ would return to pronounce the Last Judgment and establish his eternal kingdom of justice upon the earth. The abolition by parliament in 1641 of the government's coercive powers over church and state had also swept away the machinery of censorship. This meant that everywhere, not only did unbeneficed Puritan preachers and lecturers, but ordinary laymen, each fortified by direct communication from God, deck out in religious language virtually every protest that could be made, not only by aggrieved persons who possessed property, but by aggrieved persons who had none. With the end of censorship, anyone who owned or had access to, a printing press, could produce a pamphlet venting his pent-up feelings about the wickedness of these present times and his demands for an immediate Utopia. Perhaps for the first time in English history (and, for almost three centuries, the last) ordinary men were free violently to proclaim their wrongs and demand their rights. They did so

265

when the English language was at a stage of its development peculiarly fitted for resounding denunciation, richly concentrated assertion, and phrases charged with virile emotion. Cranmer's prayer book and the King James Bible, both of them now deemed largely beyond the comprehension of the English people, constituted the basic vocabulary of the age, and gave to the utterance of the humblest of those who were literate a dignified cogency as great as that of their betters.

Characteristic of a mere artisan's readiness to appropriate to himself what had been intended to apply only to gentlemen at odds with their king, was the young man who declared, 'Afore, I looked upon the scripture as a history of things that passed in other countries, pertaining to other persons; but now I looked upon it as a mystery to be opened at this time, belonging also to us'. And a whole social revolution could germinate in the ground on which he based his claim to speak out: 'I am as the Paul of this time; he was a mechanic, a tent-maker . . . I am a tailor'. It was natural, therefore, that others should claim that lesser yeomen, craftsmen, small traders and mechanics (though probably not the really poor) were also a 'part of the nation' and entitled to equal rights with the gentry and the clergy; and that a Colonel Rainborough should claim that 'the poorest he in England' had a right to live 'as much as the greatest he', and the right, not 'of submission but of consultation, of debating, counselling, prophesying and voting'.

It was small wonder that a distressed parliamentarian should sadly write, 'When we mention the people, we do not mean the confused, promiscuous body of the people'. The fifty per cent of the population who lived by their labour alone were not, in the minds of those above them, entitled to be looked on as 'a part of the nation'. As Cromwell's principal adviser, his son-in-law, Ireton, put it, 'No person hath a right to an interest or share in the disposing of the affairs of the kingdom . . . that hath not a permanent fixed interest', by which he meant property. That it was not until the twentieth century that this principle, already challenged by the Levellers and other Puritan groups in the 1640s and 1650s, was finally abandoned, testifies to the radical lengths to which some Puritans found their doctrines leading them, and to the thoroughness with which they were defeated.

That the gentry who had heated their resolve to fight the crown by stoking Puritan fires should soon find the flames too warm for their comfort fulfilled prophecies made repeatedly by princes and prelates since the start of the Reformation. The Puritan attack on Catholic practices as superstitious might merely mean that, instead of kneeling before the sacrifice of the mass on a consecrated altar, a group of sober, respectable men and women should sit or stand to partake of the Lord's supper distributed from a simple communion table. But it could so blur the distinction between the sacred and the profane as to produce the spectacle of a determined person of Puritan convictions urinating on the altar in Canterbury cathedral, perhaps in the knowledge that such an action was one of the few methods by which an altar can be 'deconsecrated'. It was a simple progression from demanding the abolition of bishops to wanting the abolition of all clergy and, indeed, of 'ministers of any kind'. If told by their betters that purgatory and the worship of saints were superstitions, plain men could easily conclude that baptism, the miracles, the resurrection and heaven and hell were superstitions too. The Wiltshire rector who believed women were the only heaven and marriage the only hell, and behaved accordingly, had a counterpart in the lady who stripped naked during a service in the chapel at Whitehall with a cry of 'Welcome the Resurrection!' The group known as Ranters were not the only extreme group who pursued the Puritan attack on superstition to the point of regarding the Bible itself as a superstition. It was variously described by such men as the cause of all the blood that had been shed in the world; as so plainly contradictory to itself that it could not possibly be the word of God; as 'the plague of England'; and 'a pack of lies'.

Hardly any of those who propagated these ideas contributed to the history of the Commonwealth and Protectorate that followed Charles's death; they were, rather, its principal victims. This does not lessen their significance. Just as the Protestant Reformation and the Puritan development of it among the learned and the propertied produced no theological proposition that had not been put forward by Wyclif (to name no others), so the extreme social, political and religious heresies it precipitated among the unlearned and the unpropertied were at least as old as Lollardy and may be detected in the background of every revolt in which the common man had taken part since 1381, including the risings of the 1530s and of 1549. Of the Protestants who had perished in the fires of Smithfield during Mary Tudor's persecuting efforts to destroy Protestantism in the 1550s, almost all were artisans and craftsmen. Radical ideas appeared in spate in the late 1640s because the civil war temporarily destroyed the machinery for suppressing them. As soon as that power revived, they were roughly hustled off the stage. But just as Levellers, Diggers and Ranters and the rest were kindred spirits of the Lollards of two centuries earlier, so were they of the Luddites and Chartists of later centuries.

'To Prevent Our Ruin'

The problem at the end of the 1640s was that many of these ideas were propagated by an articulate minority in the New Model Army. While Cromwell and his senior officers, ironically labelled 'The Grandees', were religious Independents but social and political conservatives, some junior officers and cavalry troopers were Levellers, whose demands went beyond independency in religion to include something like universal suffrage. This was seen by the Grandees as the prelude to the replacement of the power of the gentry by a sovereignty of the propertyless people. Outside the army, these ideas were carried further. The Diggers, who also called themselves the True Levellers, wanted to end not only tithes but rents, enclosures, and all private property in land. To demonstrate their views, Digger communities in various parts began to dig village wastelands and plant vegetables on them. The land, they said, belonged to the people and should be held in common. Anticipating Marxist thunders, one Digger pamphlet proclaimed, 'None is our bread but what we work for . . . therefore those that do not work have no right to eat'. That these Diggers, or 'True' Levellers were anathema to the political Levellers in the army was disastrous to both. The Diggers had no defenders when attacked; and the political Levellers could be condemned by the Grandees because of the excesses to which their doctrines tended.

Cromwell and the army Levellers had much in common at the end of the first Civil War. It had been with a moral and intellectual earnestness as great as theirs that he and Ireton had debated with them for days in the parish church at Putney in 1647. But Cromwell acted without hesitation when Leveller agitation issued in an army mutiny. The Levellers of the New Model were, after all, soldiers. Their leaders were officers, and members of the gentry. The Levellers gained a hearing because their potential followers belonged to a close-knit body of men endued with a new-found dignity by their membership of a victorious fighting force. But, because these followers were soldiers in a highly-disciplined army led by a resolute commander, military discipline proved stronger than Leveller eloquence.

Since Leveller ideas were not confined to the army, they rumbled menacingly on when the execution of the king was followed by the establishment of a council of state appointed by what was left, after several purges of Presbyterians, of the original Long Parliament and known, unflatteringly as 'The Rump'. Since this did nothing to end commercial and industrial privilege, conscription, land speculation or the newly invented and detested excise, or to meet the demand for a reform of the law, there were renewed army mutinies in 1649, accompanied by furious denunciations of Cromwell. His suppression of the mutineers in the spring of that year marked the end of the army's Levellers. Civilian Levellers continued turbulent in London, led by the courageous John Lilburne and an energetic pamphleteer, William Walwyn. They staged various demonstrations in the streets in 1653. Lilburne was sent to the Tower, charged with treason. Significant of the capital's mood was his acquittal by a London jury. But though Lilburne soldiered on during the 1650s, this feverish battering against the brick walls of privilege with eloquent appeals for the cause of social justice can rarely be long sustained. Lilburne ended his days in that Puritan sect which was the first to seek solace from the failure of action by relapse into quietism: he became a Quaker.

Yet both Cromwell and the army remained more radical than the Rump. The latter regarded itself as the last remnant of legality and looked on the army as its mere servant. When it persisted in refusing to give place to some more representative body, as the army demanded, Cromwell dissolved it by force. An argument that had begun in 1641 as to whether crown or parliament should control the army had concluded with the destruction of both crown and parliament by a military coup d'état.

Cromwell's innate conservatism and legality of mind was deeply offended by the nakedness of the military power he now exercised. He sought to dispose of his authority to some civilian body that would somehow pacify the army without upsetting his susceptibilities as a gentleman deeply devoted to good order and the rights of property. The result was a council of state and a parliament whose members were nominated either by leading army officers or by selected congregations in England, Wales and Scotland.

The reputation of this, the first assembly to contain representatives of all three kingdoms, did not survive the jokey circumstance that one of its members was named Praise-God Barebone. The real cause of the ridicule was that it contained many very minor gentry, very few lawyers, and, among its 144 members, about forty radicals who thought the civil war ought not to have been fought in vain. This 'Barebones Parliament' thought the Chancery court so tardy and obstructive that it should be abolished; and that the legal system should be simplified and codified down to the proportions of a book. Union with Scotland, reform of the treasury, reorganisation of the national revenues, an enquiry into the workings of the poor law and into the appointment and duties of JPs, and a reduction in the number of public offices were all discussed. Though they refused to legalise divorce for adultery, they did establish civil marriage before a JP for the rest of the 1650s. They also wished to end tithe. This had become even more objectionable since the expropriation of the monasteries had made the tithes previously payable to monastic houses payable instead to the secular landlords who replaced them. They also wished to end lay patronage of church benefices. These were for the most part sensible reforms; so far from behing ahead of their time, they were mostly well behind them. But their attack on tithe, distressing in itself as an attack on property, was the more alarming because it provoked renewed Leveller stirrings in the London streets. The majority in the assembly therefore astutely put through a vote in favour of its dissolution at a time when the radicals were absent at a prayer meeting. Thus, the scabbard was once more removed from Cromwell's sword. Those radicals who tried to keep the assembly in being were, like the Rump two years before, dispersed by soldiers.

The collapse of the Levellers and the end of the Barebones Parliament, thereafter carefully derided as a gathering of 'daft', 'ridiculous' and 'little' saints, marked the end of all chance of a 'Puritan Revolution'. The whole course of events in England between 1641 and 1661 can, in most respects, be referred to as a 'revolution' only in the word's original meaning. It was a circular movement terminating in its point of departure.

PART FIVE

FREEDOM AND SUBORDINATION

Approximate Dates: 1653 until after 1780

1

THE MANIPULATORS

Back to Legality

THE Restoration may be said to have begun when Cromwell was installed as Lord Protector in Westminster Abbey in 1653 and entered into residence in the royal palace of Whitehall in 1654. From then until his death in 1658, he ruled either in a state of conflict with parliaments elected under newly-written constitutions or by means of major-generals who imposed military rule on the localities. By 1657 things had so far moved backwards (or forwards) that Cromwell was urged to become king. He refused; to do so would have made him look more than ever a traitor to what he and his soldiers had fought for.

The instant acceptance of his son Richard as Protector when Cromwell died in 1658 showed how near to monarchy the Protector had come. But Richard, though not the stupid Tumbledown Dick of royalist legend, soon resigned. Out of renewed quarrels between parliament and army emerged the inscrutable General Monk, commander of the English armies in Scotland. Moving slowly south in order, so he said, 'to protect parliament' he eventually caused all the excluded MPs to be summoned back to the Long Parliament, which thereupon dissolved itself and ordered the first free elections since 1640. The new convention parliament contained sixteen Rumpers, some presbyterians, and a substantial majority in favour of a restoration. Charles issued the Declaration of Breda, offering a general pardon and liberty (of religion) 'to tender consciences'. The new parliament resolved, on 1 May 1660, that the government of England 'was and ought to be by King, Lords and Commons'. A week later, Charles II was proclaimed king and before the month was out entered London in triumph.

The Restoration signified that the game of looking for the needle of consent in the haystack of rival ideals and interests let loose by the civil war was over. The Commonwealth's enduring achievement was to reinforce the belief that sovereignty belonged ultimately to the legitimate wearer of a heritable crown. Although Charles II's reign produced the two rival factions, Whig and Tory, from which political parties were later to develop, they were almost identical twins. Each believed as firmly as the other in the maintenance of monarchy; each at different times adopted policies previously pursued by the other; and it is not far wrong to say that, though not recognised at the time, the idea of 'a loyal opposition' was born in the late-seventeenth century.

The preoccupation of mid-twentieth century historians with the so-called 'Puritan Revolution' has tended to obscure the fundamental importance of the thirty years after 1660, which was perhaps better understood before it became fashionable to regard as major historical changes only those alleged to have resulted from armed revolutionary struggle. The Restoration of 1660, by restoring crown, church, lords, commons and squirearchy, put Englishmen back once more under a system of government which, proven unworkable by 1629, had been made more unworkable still by the legislation forced upon Charles I in 1641. Prerogative taxation, and the prerogative courts of Star Chamber, the Councils of Wales and of the North, and the Court of High Commission, by which the crown exerted day-to-day control over affairs secular and ecclesiastical, had been abolished; yet the crown's power to dissolve or prorogue parliament had not. And the blunt instrument of impeachment was still the only means by which the commons could call ministers of the crown to account on major issues. With a king on the throne who still wanted to govern, and a group of dissatisfied men in parliament who wanted his government to be controlled by them, conflict was hard to avoid. That even a civilian revolution did not happen until after Charles II's death in 1685, and at that date seemed more unlikely than ever, was due to Charles II's own character and the political nation's intense desire to avoid the risks of another civil war and another Cromwell.

Property and Popery

Genial, sceptical and witty, and inheriting, through his mother, Henrietta Maria, the approachability and adroitness of Henri IV, best-loved of the post-medieval kings of France, Charles II was the one Stuart prince whose political acts did not appear designed to ensure that his cause would speedily become a lost one. Though doomed to be remembered chiefly as the 'Merry Monarch' with more mistresses than Henry VIII had wives, Charles was distinguished even more by his political agility and coolness. He could display cheerful courage in a crisis and skill at deciding when to yield to his opponents and when to stand up to them. Wide open to the charge of unscrupulousness, he nevertheless used that lack of scruple to preserve the English from subjection to doctrinaire fanatics and to mob rule.

At heart, Charles wanted to be like his formidably rich and powerful cousin, Louis XIV of France, a monarch untroubled by parliaments and loyal to the Catholic faith. Louis XIV, bent on the destruction of the Dutch and the humiliation of his dynastic rivals, the Habsburg rulers of Austria and Spain, wanted England's support, if he could get it, and its neutrality if he could not. A powerful clique of noblemen emerged, led by the Earl of Shaftesbury, calling themselves the 'Country' party to indicate their hostility to the 'Court'. They put themselves at the head of all those elements, mercantile, patriotic and dissenting, who could be persuaded that Louis XIV and Charles II constituted a dangerous threat to parliamentary liberty in England and to Protestantism everywhere. This danger was not very real in Charles II's reign. Charles was at once too lazy and too astute to pursue policies, or to support ministers, likely to imperil his own position as king. In 1670, by the Secret Treaty of Dover, he promised Louis XIV, in return for an annual pension from the French king, to fight the Dutch and promote the Catholic cause in England. It was a package Charles could not deliver. Parliament forced him to cut short his Dutch war and abandon even the smallest attempt to relax the penal laws against Catholics. Charles at once confused his opponents by appointing as chief minister, Danby, well-known to be anti-French, devoted to the Church of England and skilled at managing the commons. There is no evidence that Charles was much mortified by what his father would have brooded on as a humiliating political retreat. Indeed, it was only after Charles allowed Danby to arrange a marriage between Mary, the Protestant daughter of the king's brother James, Duke of York, and the Dutch prince, William of Orange, that Louis XIV cut off Charles's pension.

There then followed the sardonic circumstances of Louis XIV paying the Country party cash, to encourage them to oppose Danby's anti-French policy, and, when the French and Dutch made peace in 1679, of Louis revealing to the Country party that it was Danby himself who had (unwillingly) negotiated the last of Charles's financial transactions with his French patron. All this could be used to prove beyond doubt that neither Charles, nor even the supposedly most patriotic minister he chose to employ, could be trusted. Only by dissolving a parliament hitherto obstinately loyal to him, for all its bouts of opposition, could Charles save Danby from impeachment. The one chance the Country party had had of whipping up widespread opposition to Charles was that of a dissolution, followed by a general election. They could not have brought this about by themselves; it was done for them by Louis XIV. The three-year crisis that then enabled them to get to the point of threatening renewed civil war could not have occurred without the financial and political support given them by the king of France.

The Country party worked on two fronts. They demanded an Exclusion Bill, to exclude James, Duke of York, from the succession, on the grounds that he was a professed Catholic who had recently acquired, as his second wife, a Catholic bride. To popularise their cause, they exploited the so-called Popish plot invented by the renegade Jesuit, Titus Oates. In the summer of 1678, Oates announced that, under orders from the Pope, the Jesuits were planning to murder Charles, put James on the throne with the aid of French troops, and organise the simultaneous murder of all London Protestants. Though he was exposed in the king's own presence as a liar, two circumstances gave Oates's tale the appearance of truth. One 'conspirator' named by him, the secretary to James's wife, was found to have asked Louis XIV for money to help in the 'utter subduing' of the 'pestilent heresy' of Protestantism in England. Worse still, the London magistrate, to whom Oates had confided his sworn statement about the plot, was shortly afterwards found dead on Primrose Hill, apparently murdered. Who killed Sir Edmund Berry Godfrey (assuming that he was in fact killed) remains a mystery; but it was not hard to spread it around that this good Protestant magistrate had been murdered by the papists because he knew too much.

That Charles, James and Louis XIV were indeed engaged, each in his different way, in what could, with some colour of truth, be called a 'Catholic plot', was true enough; sufficiently true to have rendered Oates's 'plot' superfluous as well as imaginary. But to the Country party, who knew it was an invention, it was a godsend. With their encouragement, Oates was allowed to organise an anti-Catholic witch hunt. Not until over twelve months later did the judicial murder of Jesuits and other Catholics on the false evidence of Oates and his accomplices come to an end. The trials of these victims took place in an atmosphere of panic kept at fever pitch by the Country party, so that whatever lies were told in the courts by Protestants were accepted as truths, and whatever truths were told by Catholics were held to be lies because, being Catholics, they were considered perjurers before they had even spoken. This was more than a reflection of the seventeenth century's primitive ideas about the laws of evidence. It was an aspect of the hysteria of the times. Most of the men of the 1670s had lived through civil war, the execution of a king—an unpardonable national crime— a military dictatorship, the unexpected miracle of Charles's Restoration in 1660, the horrors of the Great Plague of 1665, the unparalleled conflagration of the Great Fire of London in 1666, and the national disgrace of the descent of Dutch ships upon Chatham dockyard to burn British vessels there. Already unnerved by so much that was extra-ordinary, men could easily be convinced that the Great Fire had been started by the Catholics. In the absence of statistics of any kind, they could easily be made to believe the country was running alive with secret Catholics eager to come out of their hiding places to murder all good Protestants in their beds. Indeed, to express doubts on the matter was, at the height of the panic, deemed both irreligious and unpatriotic. Shaftesbury and the Country party, in the cause of civil liberty and true religion, did all in their power to keep the frenzy alive.

In parliament, they pressed on with efforts to get James excluded from the succession. Compelled by his political weakness to make no move as innocent subjects of his crown were hanged, drawn and quartered to appease an excited populace, Charles, with great coolness, played for time, countering venom with sweet reasonableness. He would accept every sort of limitation upon his successor; but he would not alienate his brother's lawful right to the succession. To the suggestion that he wriggle out of the difficulty by divorcing his barren wife and marrying a more fertile spouse, his answer was that the number of his illegitimate offspring indicated that he had already wronged his wife sufficiently as it was. And the Country party began to overreach itself. Shaftesbury and some of his adherents appeared to flirt with the notion that the succession should pass to Charles's handsome, worthless, bastard son, the Duke of Monmouth. The Whigs were merely exploiting Monmouth's popularity with the crowds, and not seriously advancing his candidature. But the suspicion that they were doing so implied a proposal to legitimise bastardy in a fashion that would imperil the expectations of the lawful sons of most great landowners. The Country party's line that, under James, landowners would lose their abbey lands to Catholics, would also look less valid if accompanied by a scheme to transfer the most important property in the realm from its rightful heir to a bastard. Charles further aided his cause by nearly dying in August 1679. It brought a whiff of reality into the situation. Hitherto frightened into silence by the anti-Catholic hysteria, the 'Tories', as opponents of the 'Whig' Country party were now being called, began to rally.

To hold off his opponents, Charles dissolved the 1679 parliament after three months; prorogued for a year a further parliament elected in the October of that year; and dissolved it in January 1681. The Whigs thought Charles could not play this game for long, through lack of money. But Charles was fortified, not only by a welcome rise in his income from the customs, but by a renewed flow of cash from Louis XIV. The French king, having cut off Charles's supply as a punishment for appointing Danby, opened his purse to him again in 1681 to avert the danger that the Country party might give England an anti-French king, whether it be the Protestant profligate, Monmouth, or James's Dutch son-in-law, William of Orange. Thus encouraged, Charles summoned the third parliament of the exclusion crisis to Oxford. There, since there was no London mob to be called up against him, the presence of his own Life Guards would provide an adequate show of force. After an initial confrontation with parliament, in which he again refused exclusion, declaring, 'I will not yield, neither will I be bullied', he next appeared before them crowned and robed in the manner appropriate to the one ceremony they had not expected; and one which, but for Louis XIV's money, he might have been powerless to perform: that of the parliament's dissolution. With characteristic sense of comedy, Charles had had the requisite ceremonial properties brought secretly to the meeting in a sedan chair.

The Whig opposition collapsed at once. Instead of resisting they fled, some of them abroad. Neither they, nor the bulk of the propertied classes, were again prepared to risk social chaos by armed resistance to a king. In 1681, caught wholly unawares, armed resistance seemed their only resource against him. Charles had called their bluff.

The rest of Charles's reign made it clear that the highest priority in English political life would henceforth be given to the protection of the rights of property. The card the Whigs had played had been that Catholicism was a threat to all Protestant property owners. The Tory reply now was that the Whigs had threatened every man's property by flirting with civil rebellion and by proposing to instal a puppet king (or a foreign Dutchman) through whom they would exalt dissenters and oppress the Anglican gentry. So, from 1681 to 1685, the political nation indulged in euphoric celebration of its deliverance from the threat of a second civil war. Charles was able to purge the judiciary and most borough corporations of Whigs, so that, in addition to compliant judges, he would have compliant MP's elected by compliant burgesses. And, to emphasise that the danger of another Cromwell had been finally averted, sermons were everywhere preached on the duty of non-resistance to a divinely appointed and anointed king. It was as if Laud had been privileged to anticipate Judgment Day, and to experience his resurrection in advance.

Towards Civilian Revolution

The conviction that to overthrow a king was to court disaster again dictated the conduct of the peerage and gentry when, so much against their will, they combined in 1688 to carry out, after all, the more respectable part of the Whigs' exclusion policy and to put William of Orange on the throne in James's place after James had reigned for only three years. James had failed to grasp that the royalist enthusiasm of the early 1680s had been a national thanksgiving for the turning aside of the threat of civil war and for the rescue of the Church of England from the dissenters. He took the talk of non-resistance and the obsequiousness of his first parliament at their face value. He imagined, too, that the revulsion against the Whigs had been a revulsion against anti-Catholic policies. He was wrong. James sought, if not to impose Catholicism on his subjects, at least to impose Catholic officials on them. To his astonishment, this instantly roused men's deepest fears for their property and their consciences. James put Catholics in high places by claiming the prerogative right to 'suspend', or 'dispense' with, the statutes that made such action illegal. Charles II had tried to do the same after his Secret Treaty of Dover with Louis XIV. In 1672, he had, by a Declaration of Indulgence, released both Catholic and Protestant dis-senters from the penalties and disabilities imposed on them by statute. In reply, Parliament had forced on Charles the Test Act of 1673, disbarring Catholics from public service. Henceforth public office could be held only by persons who were communicant members of the Church of England and who were prepared to declare their disbelief in transubstantiation. In 1687 and 1688, James II issued Declarations dispensing with this Test Act. Like Cromwell before him, he wanted, in the name of religious toleration, to impose a religious minority on the country with the backing of a strong army officered by members of that minority.

On the grounds that the Declaration was illegal, the Archbishop of Canterbury and six of his bishops petitioned the king against it. A version of their petition became a manifesto of national resistance; and, when James imprisoned them on the grounds that their petition was a seditious libel, the seven clerics were apotheosised as The Seven Lamps of Freedom. Their trial was a major spectacle; their judges were divided; and, amid general jubilation, the jury acquitted them.

At this point, James's Catholic wife gave birth to a son, thus creating the prospect of a dynasty of Catholic monarchs. Yet there was still no armed resistance. The king's opponents were as helpless as the men of 1640 would have been without the rebellion of the Scots. Everything therefore now turned on the fact that Danby had married James's elder daughter, Mary, to William of Orange. As its Stadtholder, William was effectively the ruler of the Dutch Republic and thus had an army, a fleet, and a European reputation as a defender of Protestantism. As ruler also of the minute independent state of Orange, near Avignon, in France, he was, like his father-in-law, a sovereign prince. Desperate to avoid starting another Great Rebellion, Whig and Tory leaders therefore combined to invite William of Orange to save them from such a catastrophe. A struggle between William of Orange and James II would be a contest between one sovereign prince and another, not a rebellion by subjects against their king. The aristocracy certainly wanted to preserve England from popery in 1688; but, unlike the aristocrats of earlier centuries, they were first and foremost civilians with a rooted objection to armed rebellion.

Fortunately for them, their own unwillingness to take up arms was matched by the unwillingness of James's supporters to fight for him. Deserted by his younger daughter, Anne, and his military commander, John Churchill, the future victor of Blenheim, James fled to France. He had patriotically refused French help earlier, so that at the moment of decision, Louis XIV had made no move to prevent William's departure from the Netherlands. Louis assumed William would be resisted and that the ensuing strife would effectively neutralise England for some time to come. The winds, too, blew in harmony with the King of France. Turning obligingly Protestant, they kept James's fleet in port, so that William moved unimpeded to his chosen landing point at Torbay. There was virtually no resistance. It was too much to expect men to fight for a monarch who, his nerve quite gone, had run away. The Grandees who had engineered William's arrival were thus left with the task of convincing themselves and their countrymen that to call on a foreign prince to dethrone their king and to deprive that king's son of the right to succeed his father was a wholly legal and conservative undertaking.

By what eventually became the Bill of Rights, it became illegal henceforth for the crown to override statute, as James had done, by the use of

279

the prerogative. There was to be no standing army such as James had had (though there was in fact one for ever afterwards). No Catholic could wear the crown of England. But there was no appeal to fundamental principles. For one thing, William had his own views. He had come to England, he told the Spanish ambassador, 'to restore the religion, laws and liberties of the English people, not to remove the rights of the Crown'. From the Tories, the Whigs got no more than a grudging admission that it was possible to regard the throne as having become 'vacant' even though its lawful occupant was still alive. This was the only 'revolutionary' principle to be established by what, on most inadequate grounds, the Whigs were later to christen 'The Glorious Revolution'.

And So To Hanover

Little was instantly settled by these events, beyond their confirmation of the resolute determination of the English not to fight a civil war. The Catholic Irish fought for James II in 1690 and were defeated, to their lasting harm. Catholic Highlanders fought for James's son, the Old Pretender, in 1715, and for his grandson, the Young Pretender, in 1745. Both these Jacobite rebellions alarmed the northern counties but both were disasters. This was not because the English were devoted to the sovereigns who succeeded James II. Mostly, they disliked them. But they disliked civil war (and Catholicism) even more. A more immediate anxiety was the shortage of suitable persons for the task of maintaining 'the Protestant Succession' after William's death. William and Mary were childless; and by 1700 it was certain that Mary's Protestant sister, Anne, would be survived by none of her eleven children. This led to the Act of Settlement of 1701, whose outcome was that, on Anne's death in 1714, George, Elector of Hanover, became George I. He was chosen because he was the grandson of James I's daughter, Elizabeth of Bohemia, parliament's Protestant heroine of the 1620s. This made him the one available prince who combined hereditary Protestantism with at least a proportion of blood in his veins inherited from the lawful Stuart dynasty.

The Bill of Rights, the Act of Settlement and various statutory and other changes of the years from 1689 to 1701 laid, at long last, the foundations of a new and eventually stable political system. But at no time before the 1720s did the political nation behave as if it thought anything had been 'settled' by the 'Revolution Settlement'. It was a time of ceaseless political faction-fights conducted by backstairs court intrigue, fierce pamphleteering, and unscrupulous appeals to crude prejudice that recalled the months of the Exclusion crisis. Thus, William had no intention of becoming the tool of the Whigs, for all that they could reasonably claim that his being king at all had been their idea in the first place. Anne, when she succeeded in 1702, had a strong personal devotion to Anglicanism, whereas the Whigs supported the toleration of Protestant dissenters. By launching England into the war against France from 1689 to 1698 known as the War of the League of Augsburg, William was at once attacked for subordinating English interests to those of the Dutch. The identification of the Whigs with England's participation in the long anti-French War of the Spanish Succession from 1702 to 1713 further assisted the Tory cause in that this war, like the previous one, was financed out of a land tax which bore heavily on the middling and lesser Tory landlords.

The 'Whig Revolution' of 1688–9 therefore failed to eradicate the Tory sentiments which had renewed their hold on the localities so firmly in the early 1680s; and the Tories thus found themselves participating in a system of government of which they fundamentally disapproved. The Act of Settlement of 1701, which provided for the eventual succession of George I, was passed by a Tory ministry. But, by passing it, they were committing themselves to the Revolution; so, at the same time, they included clauses all designed to put additional limits upon the powers of William's successors. But this was to behave almost as if they were converts to the principles of Shaftesbury's Country party. The Act stiffened the regulation that the monarch should not be Catholic by insisting he must be a practising Anglican. This was a true Tory thrust at William's Calvinism and at Whiggish toleration of Dissent; but it was a further assertion of the primacy of statute as against the crown. Further to circumscribe the powers of crown and government, the king was not to leave England, nor involve the country in the defence of his foreign possessions, without parliamentary consent. Ministerial decisions were to be taken formally at privy council meetings and not elsewhere. This would help the commons to know where to apportion responsibility. In an attempt to protect the commons from government influence, membership was to be denied to many office holders. The crown was also to be deprived of power over the judges. Henceforth they could be dismissed only by joint action by both houses of parliament. It was on the basis of the Act of Settlement that the famous doctrine of 'the separation of powers' was based: that executive, legislative and judicial functions should each operate 'independently' to prevent the executive (the government) controlling legislators and judges for its own purposes. In fact, this rigid separation has never existed in England; but since, in matters of government, men are more attracted by theories than facts, the ex-Englishmen who founded the United States endowed it with a constitution of which the separation of powers was the corner stone.

Niceties of constitutional theory were not the chief preoccupation of the decade that followed, however. As the 'Whig' War of the Spanish Succession dragged on, year after year, Tory anger continued to mount. To clinch their campaign against the Whigs they needed more than the relatively rational arguments that the war was offensively burdensome to taxpayers and conducted for the interest of England's Dutch and Habsburg allies rather than for England itself. Accordingly, they raised the old cry, 'The Church in Danger!' It had been used by the Whigs and Titus Oates in 1678 to set off the anti-Catholic terror against James II before he became king and by Whigs and Dissenters to unseat him in 1688. In 1710, the same cry was used by the Tories; and with such success that the Whigs were driven into a political wilderness from which they emerged in 1714 very largely through sheer luck.

What halted the Tories' effort to stay permanently in power was the flirtation of a few of them, notably the speciously clever Bolingbroke, with a plan for the accession of James II's son, James Edward (the Old Pretender), instead of Hanoverian George, despite the fact that it was by a Tory statute that George was to be made king. There was little chance that the plan would succeed, since James Edward refused to abandon his Catholicism. But the sudden death of Anne, at a moment when it was becoming known and feared, not least by the now imminent George I, that at least some Tories were prepared to contemplate a Jacobite plot to keep the Hanoverians out, led to their political eclipse for the next half century.

By their flirtation with James Edward, the Tories provided, in 1714, a mirror image of the Country party's seeming flirtation with the idea of crowning Monmouth in 1680; and Anne, by dying so suddenly, deprived the Tories of political power as effectively as Charles II had undone the Whigs by his dissolution of 1681. Thus, by 1714, both Whigs and Tories had given exhibitions of political extremism which, for the rest of the century, gave to any political group opposing government the discreditable label of 'a faction'. It was perhaps out of a rational disapproval of such unbridled factionalism, and not on the basis of political theories, that in the half-century after 1714 the English turned aside from religious and political activism and began to learn the more serviceable if often more deadening techniques of compromise. The political wisdom of the mid-eighteenth century was perhaps most aptly expressed by at least the first line of Alexander Pope's famous couplet:

> Let fools for forms of government contest:
> Whate'er is best administered is best.

The 'English Revolution' Perceived

Not until the accession of George I in 1714, the failure of the Jacobite rising of 1715 and the triumph of the Whigs in the general election of that year, does it become possible to say with assurance that there had been an 'English Revolution' since 1603. By 1715, it was finally established that, though Puritan values would continue to permeate English life, there had been no 'Puritan Revolution'. The proper title for the years from 1642 to 1660 would always be that of Clarendon's eye witness history of it, 'The Great Rebellion'. The only Puritans in the seventeenth century who could claim indisputably to have effected a 'revolution' were the Calvinist Dutch, by their successful rebellion against their Catholic Habsburg rulers; or the Scots, who, though in a less clear cut fashion, preserved their Presbyterianism well enough against both Charles I and Cromwell for it to survive even an Act of Union with England in 1707. The fact that, from 1714 onwards, the English could insist that they possessed 'a limited monarchy' constitutes the only safe definition of what they had achieved since 1603, or 1640. And it was enough of a revolution to distinguish England from virtually all other monarchical states in Europe, and to establish that the basic issue in seventeenth-century England had been about the monarchy rather than about parliament. By 1630, parliaments were everywhere coming to seem, on their record, medieval survivals, universally obstructive of ordered government. The tide was running against them all over Europe; and the view that, in seventeenth-century England, it was running steadily in parliament's favour can derive only from hindsight. When the Apology of 1604 averred that the power of princes was daily growing, its authors, whoever they were, showed a sharper understanding of their time than some later historians. James I and Charles I, of set purpose, systematically exalted the idea of monarchy, building on a tradition already flourishing in the reign of Elizabeth I. That James indulged in garrulous pedantry on the subject and was personally somewhat grotesque did not prevent his apotheosis on the Rubens ceiling of Inigo Jones's Banqueting House in Whitehall as the bringer of peace and uniter of kingdoms. In an age which used symbolism rather than ideology, James was the island's Prospero. Had it been thought worth depicting the house of commons, it would have been as Caliban. Charles I had most of the qualities required of an absolute monarch: an inborn or acquired capacity to radiate dignity and a passion for glamorising monarchy through a lavish patronage of the arts that was the more effective for being governed by sensitive discrimination. In the 1630s, he fortified the crown's majesty by a political and administrative independence of parliament that collapsed, despite his Stuart lack of drive, only because of one false move in Scotland. All through the years of the Great Rebellion, the prestige and mystique of monarchy survived the most furious assaults on it, so that, having executed Charles I in 1649, Cromwell had, to all intents and purposes, to restore him in his own rough-voiced person in 1653.

Under Charles II and James II, the establishment of a centralised monarchical despotism in which parliament played a minimal part was still the dominant political programme, as Shaftesbury's unscrupulous Country party had always insisted. Financed as it was in the 1680s by Louis XIV, architect of monarchical absolutism in the greatest and most populous civilised Christian state, this programme nearly came off. It is arguable that the decisive decades in seventeenth-century English history were the 1670s and 1680s, rather than the 1640s and 1650s. Shaken though it was—in 1638, 1640, 1642, 1649, 1679 and 1688— monarchy still managed to survive or revive. Each of these dates is a punctuation mark; only by 1715 is there a full stop. The events of 1653, of 1660, and of 1681, demonstrated the belief of the political nation that monarchy must be preserved: the Interregnum had convinced them that Charles I had been right to say that, if a republican-minded minority could take his crown away, there was safety for no man's property. The issue after 1660 was always how men of property could protect that property both from an absolutist king and from a levelling republicanism. That limited monarchy could provide a solution permanently acceptable both to the monarch and to the propertied parliamentarians who would devise the limitations, would be in doubt for as long as absolute monarchy had, in the Tories, a party in the state that adhered to a system of paternal centralism sustained by an exclusive and authoritarian church. It would be in doubt, too, for as long as there existed across the Channel, as Christendom's dominant ruling sovereign, an absolutist Catholic ruler prepared to patronise the Catholic absolutist cause in England. By 1713 the power of the French to interfere in England's domestic politics had been eliminated. The accession of George I in 1714 meant that by 1715 the Tory party had been rendered politically ineffective, and English Jacobitism reduced to the character of a skeleton for Whig ministers to rattle in public for the purposes of propaganda.

The extent to which there had been a revolution indeed since 1603 cannot be minimised. That it was a revolution that preserved the liberties of men of property implies the dismantling of the Tudor and early Stuart system of paternalism from the centre which, particularly in economic and social matters, sought to protect the poorest from the power of the wealthy. For the whole of the eighteenth century, and well on into the nineteenth, central government intervened as little as possible in local affairs, leaving local bodies of all sorts to manage their business as they pleased. The propertied classes were not, as they were elsewhere, troubled by paid or unpaid royal officials requiring them to conform to central government decree. The ability of the aristocracy and gentry freely to exploit the resources of their lands was a major cause of the entrepreneurial vigour of eighteenth-century England and one reason for the tremendous struggle that had to take place in the nineteenth century to re-establish the government's right to interfere in social and economic affairs. This degree of liberty was possible only because the Whigs, the party which had inherited so much of its thinking from the Commonwealth, had become dominant in the state by erecting a monarchy which, because of its limited nature, enabled them to govern without the risk of reawakening any of the revolutionary republicanism the 1650s had taught them to be so afraid of. That the liberty of the propertied was less oppressive than it might have been was due to the survival in the countryside of so many Tory gentry who continued to administer local affairs in the old, relatively paternalistic way.

There was also intellectual revolution. In Europe, the religious practice of the subject had to be acceptable to his sovereign. In England, the religious practice of the sovereign had to be acceptable to his subjects. There was thus no dictation of belief by authority from above. The years after 1640 enabled England to throw off the censorship of thought and expression which a dominant and exclusive Anglican church would have continued to exercise under absolutist rulers, and to escape the much fiercer censorship which prevailed in those important European states whose monarchical absolutisms were sustained by the authoritarian Catholicism that emerged from the Council of Trent. The contribution of this liberation to the development of a spirit of free enquiry, and of a free and often scurrilous press, was considerable.

What finally impresses the observer of the struggles of the years from 1603 to 1715 is not simply the bitterness, unscrupulousness and cruelties, and the exploitation of prejudice, of which both sides were guilty, but the sustained underlying significance of the issues which had divided them. That they should subsequently look on the system they had contrived to create out of it as the most perfect that could be devised may now seem absurd. This should not obscure the fact that their achievement excited not only their own admiration but that of intelligent foreigners for generations to come.

Taxpayers and Rentiers

Amid all the uncertainties of the half century after 1660, the foundations were being laid of a more efficient and stable system of government. In particular, taxation was never again quite the burning constitutional issue it had been under the early Stuarts. After 1660, not only did parliamentary taxation come under parliamentary control; it became more effective and less capricious.

Most pleasing to great landowners in particular was the abolition of feudal tenures in 1646. They were not revived in 1660. The effect was to release landowners from the infuriating depredations of wardships and reliefs and greatly to strengthen their ability freely to administer and develop their estates. They could now minimise the chances of estates being broken up on account of debts at the owner's death. Consolidation of their estates by great landlords, and the relative depression of the lesser gentry, greatly increased the influence of the peerage after 1660. Its skilful employment of its wealth during the eighteenth century maintained social stability by reducing the aspiring gentry to the status of clients, whose advancement once more depended, as in the fifteenth century, on the patronage of their betters.

Parliament's need to raise money to fight Charles I led to the introduction by John Pym of the excise, imitated from the Dutch. An inland duty payable on the sale of various commodities, it was easy to collect and very productive, since it affected food, clothes and drink. The Commonwealth's Dutch war produced the land tax. The only direct tax until Pitt introduced income tax in 1799, the machinery for assessing it was, ironically, derived in the first place from that used by Charles I to collect ship money. The land tax was always a potentially explosive political issue. It was as patrons of the expansion of England's commerce that the Whigs supported William's wars against Louis XIV; but the Tory landed gentry claimed it was they who had to pay for this Whig war, through the land tax. This, combined with Tory resentment of the Whigs as allies of Dissent and as therefore enemies of the church, does much to explain why every election from 1689 to 1714 produced a Tory majority.

The third main source of revenue continued to be customs which, at a time of expanding trade, provided a steadily increasing return. By 1688, both excise and customs were no longer farmed, but collected by officials appointed by the treasury itself. This made for more efficiency and less corruption. Perhaps more important was that, though unpopular, they were not, like early Stuart taxes, arbitrary, capricious or specifically directed against the wealthier and therefore most potentially troublesome ranks of society. Both indeed, affected some transfer of tax from the rich to the less rich.

After 1689, parliament was no longer an occasional affair. Henceforth, authorisation of taxation and of the pay and discipline of the army were dependent upon an annual vote by parliament. Moreover, the Triennial Act of 1694 and the Septennial Act of 1716 provided for regular elections. A permanent institution with power to approve excise, customs and the land tax, all efficiently collected, was in a stronger position to attract credit than the former monarchy, chronically unable to 'live of its own' and always failing to extract, from infrequent parliaments, subsidies big enough to pay its debts.

Just as the war had produced the excise and the land tax, so the long, costly struggle against the French after 1689 led to the creation of the National Debt and the Bank of England. In 1693, a £1 million loan was raised, to be guaranteed by parliament on the security of the excise; and in 1694 the Bank of England was created to lend, in the first instance, £1.2 million to the government. Henceforth, governments neither looked for credit to a narrow circle of City financiers nor relied on the always doubtful security of the word of a king. Instead, the security offered was parliament's sovereign powers over all taxation; and the investors who put money into government funds now came from all parts of the country and from abroad. As England's military successes mounted during the Spanish Succession war, the Dutch invested steadily in London's parliament-backed securities. Dutch banks, insurers and ship owners; widows and retired sea captains; French Huguenot pastors, American colonists and Prussian army officers, all supplemented widespread investment by individuals as well as schools, colleges, charities and local corporations at home. For the first time, too, women could, by acquiring government securities, compensate in some measure for the legal obstacles which prevented them from effectively owning land or raising capital on it.

For long it was thought neither prudent nor moral for the government to accumulate a national debt so vast that there seemed no hope of paying it off. In the 1750s the theory that the debt was incurred on particular taxes was dropped; and it was made to depend on a single consolidated fund, to which all duties were transferred, and from which all interest was paid. In effect the debt was made perpetual; and a new three per cent stock, known forever after as 'consols', was simply an income guaranteed by the British government. The stock could be transferred from investor to investor; but there was now no further pretence that the original loans would ever be repaid.

The national debt bound the propertied classes to the post-revolutionary regime much as the expropriation of the monasteries had bound their forbears to Henry VIII, since it associated them with a parliament which the propertied themselves elected. The confidence the government inspired may be judged by the low rate of interest of three per cent it could afford to offer by the 1750s, compared with the ten per cent rates normal in Elizabethan and early Stuart times. Not only did the system aid the accumulation and concentration of capital. It compelled all classes to contribute through taxation to the maintenance of government credit and to the incomes of investors in it. Early nineteenth-century radicals fiercely criticised the use of taxation to pay interest to rentiers. Its practical value was that it made the financing of government ordered instead of capricious, reduced the need for swingeing tax increases in wartime and offered material gains to precisely those social classes whose fury at government fiscal policies had produced the civil war.

Although this technique of transferring some of the costs of government from the pockets of the living to those of the unborn kept taxation within bounds, it was only by the most careful political management that opposition to the tax system was held in check. Some heat was taken out of the discontent by the widespread practice of smuggling. When in the 1730s, Sir Robert Walpole proposed to impose the more easily collected excise instead of customs duties on a number of commodities the outcry was so great that he abandoned the scheme. Excisemen were detested because they were pretty ruthless and reasonably efficient; revenue men were easier to evade. In consequence, all through the century there were few well kept tables in England that were not regularly furnished with smuggled commodities. It is possible that as much as three-quarters of all the tea imported into eighteenth-century England was smuggled, as well as much of the wine and brandy, since another estimate is that smuggled goods accounted for a third of all French imports into the country.

Age of Patronage

The collapse of the Tories at the death of Anne may be compared with the collapse of the Whigs after Charles II's coup at Oxford in 1681. But whereas that event inaugurated less than a decade of Tory domination, the death of Anne began almost half a century of what was virtually one-party government operated exclusively by the Whigs. When, in the 1715 election, the number of Tories was reduced to 217, this result can be ascribed to public doubts about Tory loyalty to the Protestant Succession rather than to crown patronage, since George was then but newly arrived in England. But the king's desire to perpetuate the Whigs' majority soon augmented their own determination to do so. George's conviction that the Tories were his enemies was confirmed when, later in the year, there occurred the rising on behalf of the Stuart Pretender, James Edward. This had the result that crown patronage was henceforth put at the disposal of the Whigs; and this, added to their own patronage, enabled them to manipulate both electors and elected MPs to ensure themselves a permanent if not always reliable parliamentary majority. At the time of Anne's death there had been 376 Tories in the commons and only 137 Whigs. The Tory slump to 217 proved only a beginning; by 1761, there were only 113, a minority inconsiderable enough to provoke Horace Walpole to the frivolous assertion that by that time the only Tories who had not become Whigs were either Jacobites or fools.

Since it is usual to regard the long duration of Whig rule as largely the product of a cynical exercise of the patronage system, it is worth suggesting that the odium which attaches to eighteenth-century patronage derives in part from its gradual replacement during the next two centuries by a social system committed to the ideas of universal suffrage and of qualification. By the late-twentieth century political power was thought to be legitimate only if based on the successful manipulation of an electorate comprising the whole population. Preferment and promotion in public life are regarded as due only to those possessing merit as defined either by a successful past record or by the acquisition of a qualification through a publicly administered examination. Politicians may not promise voters personal favours. Applicants for posts are expected not to be related to those who make the appointment. To assume that the reward of serving as a local councillor should be that one's firm receive the contract to build the town centre is to confess to a state of mind which, though normal two hundred and fifty years ago, is now considered quasi-criminal. The MP who assumed that a promise regularly to vote for the prime minister in the commons would result in his relations being given commissions in the army, livings in the church and clerkship in the customs and excise would be thought either naive or wicked. Public service is supposed to be divorced from personal advantage; and in that this ideal is thought not to have been fully achieved, the system is to that extent still held to be slightly iniquitous.

The eighteenth century, like most of the nineteenth, operated a system which combined the inheritance of a distant past with concepts of its own derived *post facto* from the Glorious Revolution. It continued the fifteenth-century concept of good lordship and the sixteenth-century idea that the best of good lords was the monarch. From its victory over the Stuarts the eighteenth century acquired its institutionalised devotion to the twin concepts of freedom and property. It was thus wholly in accordance with the spirit of the times that whoever wished to rise in the world sought out a lordly patron who could open the door to an office of profit in church or state.

The return to the patron was the sedulous nourishment of his social and political aims, whether by word or deed. Yet, since all men of gentle or learned degree were now held to be free, the patron had a duty to show favour to those who supported him. This was indeed a necessity, for it was then probably harder to put pressure, physical or legal, on men of property, however humble, than either before or since.

The post-feudal and pre-modern notion of an absolute title to property extended to the right to vote, the enjoyment by a parliamentary borough of its privilege of returning two members to parliament, and to the possession of offices of profit in government service, the army, a local corporation, a school, a college or university or, of course, the church. All these offices were manipulated as sources of income. A university chair, a church living, a government post, an appointment as a schoolmaster were only secondarily looked on as a means of doing work. What mattered was the income. The work itself could perhaps be done by an underpaid hack or, as often in the universities, not done at all. The obligation which an employee felt was not so much to his employer as to the patron through whom the employment was obtained.

The conduct of political and public life thus involved an elaborate operation by which the powerful disbursed jobs and sources of income to approved persons who were recommended to them by other approved persons. Hence, whatever one's talent, whether for writing or engineering, one sought a patron who would reward it. If one's talent was for oratory, a resounding speech at the Oxford Union might, if heard by a suitably powerful nobleman, secure one a seat in the commons. If one had no talent at all, there was always a chance of finding a patron with a sinecure to spare.

Patronage did not universally result in the employment and promotion of the incompetent. Alexander Cruden did not stay long in his post as reader to a noble lord when the latter. discovered that, when asked to read his lordship a book in the French language, his employee pronounced every French word as if it were an English one. There were qualified professionals even in the age of the patron. The navy, the customs service and to a less extent even the army, all insisted that patronage be supplemented by qualification. Thus, Samuel Johnson had a patron who offered to secure him a headmastership. Because he lacked the Oxford M.A. which the endowment's regulations required, and because his patron was unable to persuade Oxford to give him an honorary M.A., Johnson was not appointed. Nor ought it to be overlooked that a high proportion of the technological innovations which heralded the industrial revolution was due to the aristocracy's intelligent, businesslike eye to the profitability of new mechanical contrivances.

The charters enabling parliamentary boroughs to return two members each to the commons were also valuable properties because some of these boroughs had few electors and some had none. Only about twenty boroughs could count their electors in thousands. Of the two-thirds of all boroughs which had fewer than five hundred voters, half had fewer than a hundred. The smallest boroughs were particularly important politically: since their electors, if any, could be so easily controlled, they constituted safe seats for ministers of the crown. In those parliamentary boroughs which were corporate towns, the right to vote might be restricted to the self-nominating members of the corporation; or the handful of voters might all be employees of the treasury, the customs and excise or the admiralty and could therefore be relied on to vote for the candidate put forward by the government which provided their employment. In some boroughs, members were nominees of peers or clients of great enterprises like the East India Company. Boroughs of this sort were bought and sold by party managers. By the time this practice was ended in 1809 they could command over £5000.

Whereas there were 419 borough members for England and Wales, the 52 counties returned only just over ninety members. County constituencies were difficult to manage since there had been a uniform county franchise since the fifteenth century. All who owned freehold property worth at least forty shillings a year had the vote. It was in the counties, and in the boroughs with large electorates, that party managers found it difficult and sometimes impossible to achieve reliable results. County freeholders were assiduously courted. They were well aware of the value of their votes and sought the maximum benefit from the fact. Managers often had to resort to buying vote-carrying property both in counties and boroughs. The cost of managing the electorate was enormous, and this explains why the group in office at Westminster rarely lost an election. It had the resources of crown patronage, whereas its rivals had not.

The exercise of this expensive influence was possible because there was open voting at the hustings. This too was the mark of free men. When introduced in 1872, secret ballot was condemned as unmanly. It could take courage to declare one's vote in the face of a hostile, drink-primed mob; and in stormy times, those who had no votes could exercise direct physical influence over those who had. It is not to be overlooked that it was a general election held under this dubious system which, in 1831, returned a house of commons with a majority pledged to remove its worst anomalies. Normally, however, party managers preferred to fix things in advance. Where Whig and Tory, or one noble family and another, were at daggers drawn in a two-member constituency they tried to avoid a contest altogether by agreeing that each should nominate one candidate only. In many general elections there were fewer than sixty contests. In 1747, in only three counties was there a contest; in twenty-nine boroughs there were no contested elections for over forty years after the 1720s.

For rewarding voters, MPs and their clients, or peers and their clients, crown patronage was freely used. Apart from government service itself and the army and navy, the crown was the largest employer in the land. The court itself had a thousand employees and, as a major landowner, the crown was patron of hundreds of livings and most cathedral benefices. Walpole would use secret service funds to make payments in cash, particularly to Scottish MPs. The episcopal bench was more subservient than ever, and every church benefice in the patronage of crown, bishops or leading aristocrats was likely to be occupied by a political nominee. In the crown's gift, apart from the posts to which duties were attached, were sinecures which had none. Thus the faithful might be rewarded with the post of gentleman usher to a princess not yet weaned, or clerk of the cofferer of the household, or usher of the receipt. One can but speculate as to the duties and emoluments of the practising barrister who held the post of clerk of the king's silver in the court of common pleas.

All public office was treated as providing opportunity for the accumulation of private wealth. Since salaries were small, men looked on the pickings of office as a just return for their sacrifice of their time and money in the service of the state and as an insurance against the uncertainties of public life.

The ubiquity of patronage was a measure of the power and the prestige of the commons in the century after 1688. The church was subordinate to it, the crown financially dependent upon it. Outside parliament, the press, though vituperative and energetic, was not, before the 1760s, the power it would become later; it was looked on as a scarcely lawful, and certainly not politically respectable, nuisance. Though industry and commerce flourished, they still functioned in the shadow of their social inferiority to landowning; and whereas, in the nineteenth century, they would demand freedom from government regulation, they were still, in the eighteenth, insistent that government (which meant the commons) had a duty to aid and protect them. England's transformation after 1688 into a commercial and maritime great power enhanced the prestige of the commons not only at home but in Europe. French admiration of it contributed to the loss of confidence in the Bourbon monarchy which led to the French Revolution. The machinery of political patronage was defended at the time on the grounds that it preserved the stability of a glorious constitutional system which 1688 had made perfect, and which, in the eyes of the world, bore the hallmark of success. Yet, in practice, that stability was more vulnerable than it seemed. That an MP should be free to speak his own mind, express the opinions of the political nation outside Westminster and be ever vigilant against government encroachments upon liberty— this tradition was contained by the patronage system, sometimes dulled by it, but not suppressed.

'Bluff Bob alias Bob Booty'

The decades of Whig supremacy were presided over by Sir Robert Walpole and his collaborators and successors, the Pelhams, Henry and Thomas. Walpole was principal minister from 1721 to 1742. Henry Pelham held office from 1721 onwards and was chief minister after Walpole's fall until his own death in 1754. Thomas Pelham-Holles, Duke of Newcastle, was in high office from 1717 and nominally principal minister of the crown after Pelham's death until his own fall in 1762. Since Pelham had a quiet, unspectacular character and Newcastle was an eccentric,neurotic valetudinarian, it was Walpole who seemed most clearly to exhibit the characteristic features of this particular era. Yet, taking them overall, the years from 1714 to 1760 are the age of George I and George II and of Newcastle. For it was the first two Georges, convinced against the facts that all Tories were Jacobites, who put crown patronage at the Whigs' disposal, and Newcastle who coordinated the management not only of crown patronage but of his own, which, since he had land in thirteen counties, was considerable. Moreover, though Walpole made a fortune out of his political career, Newcastle's forty years of ducal dedication to politics and the task of keeping himself, Walpole and Pelham in power, were spent mostly on the verge of bankruptcy. His expenditure, most of it for direct or indirect political purposes, was so great that, in 1738, he had to sell so much land to pay his creditors that his income was halved as a result. When he died thirty years later he was heavily in debt.

It was Walpole, however, who saw to it that the resources of patronage were concentrated in the commons, where they were most continuously needed. He was the first great minister to stay for so long in the commons; he did not go to the upper house until his downfall in 1742. Not until Stanley Baldwin's more respectable heyday in the 1920s and 1930s was the leader of an administration so careful to study and assess the characters of his fellow members of the commons.

Walpole's survival was due to more than the mere manipulation of men through the disbursement of cash or the bestowal of jobs. He consistently alleged that he was the country's surest defence against a

Jacobite rebellion. He was adept at out-manoeuvring potential rivals for power within his own administration. His sound and effective economic policies had a calming, stabilising effect at a time when court, parliament and country were all still somewhat demoralised by the collapse of the manic burst of speculation created by the South Sea Company, whose 'Bubble' burst in 1720; though even here what mattered initially was not what Walpole did, but his refusal to panic and his cultivation of the myth that he had never been implicated in or a supporter of the South Sea Company. The years revealed, however, that he was a tireless worker, always attentive to detail, and mentally and physically tough. Above all, he was the average sensual man of his time, who understood and, in his own special way, represented, the average sensual men who constituted the bulk of the nation's political leadership outside London. Like them, he knew when he was on to a good thing, and saw to it that he amassed a fortune out of his long tenure of high office. While in power, he found lucrative jobs for his relations, built himself fine country houses, filled them with works of art, and entertained lavishly. He ate and drank hugely, was coarse in his language and East Anglian in his accent, and encouraged the legend that he gave the highest priority, when dealing with correspondence, to letters from his game-keeper. This undoubtedly Whiggish minister was, for all his anti-Jacobitism and his indifference to the church, very much of a Tory squire writ very large and rich. It was his special achievement to reconcile the Tories in the localities to Whig ascendancy in court and parliament, and to drag the ruling Whig party along with him on the path of peace that Tories preferred because it kept the land tax down. In return for what he got out of it, Walpole gave the state some twenty years of peace and stability; and after what English society had experienced of religious and political dissension in the previous two hundred years, it cannot be regarded as an altogether bad bargain.

Patronage Not Enough

The age of Whig supremacy was not one of political torpor. Without patronage, no government could have secured a majority; but even with it, a majority could not be guaranteed, nor opposition stifled. It is true that the number of placemen, i.e. MPs holding jobs or sinecures provided by government, rose from around 120 under Anne to nearly 190 under Walpole; and that, under Newcastle, as many as 260 MPs were thought to be linked by patronage to the government. But, with a maximum normal attendance of 450 out of a total membership of 558, governments had always to reckon with over 200 independent MPs, including most of the 92 knights of the shire. Some independents were Tories whom the king would not permit to hold office; but others were independent Whigs who, in contrast to the court Whigs, did not want office. Tending to pride themselves on their confident sway over their shires or their pliant boroughs, the 'country' Whigs and Tories continued to act out the traditional MPs' role of critic and watchdog. They were hostile to the administration but without the desire to take its place. Dangerous opposition to government was almost always the result of the ambitions of its own principal supporters and, since party organisation scarcely existed, could be led from within its own ministerial ranks. One reason governments survived was that such trouble makers within the ranks of the court Whigs could rarely look to country members for systematic support; while the country members themselves were always a miscellany of political irregulars, not a coherent force.

There were four issues on which opposition might focus. Country members forever charged the government with corruption. This on the whole had more effect outside political circles than within them, since it was all too easy to allege that independents who condemned corruption did so mainly because they did not themselves benefit from it. Excessive taxation was another issue. When Walpole tried to extend the excise the outcry was such that, fearing he might be dismissed, many placemen withheld their votes from him, either to make him give the scheme up (which he did) or to ensure themselves a good standing with whoever might replace him. Most effective were allegations that government was subordinating England's interests to those of the crown's possessions in Hanover and that it was deficient in patriotism. It was on the latter issue that Walpole fell. He had failed to respond to the reviving power of France and the growing demand for the protection of British trade in Spanish America; and, during the war that began in spite of him in 1739, proved a poor war minister. But although in 1742 the patronage system was still effective enough to keep the Whigs in power for almost another two decades, it was not strong enough to keep Walpole in office. He fell for the most constitutionally respectable of reasons, that of losing the confidence of the house of commons.

2
LATITUDINARIANS AND ENTHUSIASTS

Tolerant Saints

THE Interregnum's permanent achievement was to preserve religion and, therefore, in the long run, intellectual life, from the dead hand of uniformity. Thanks to Cromwell, Presbyterian uniformity did not replace Episcopalian; and though Puritan rule was intolerant, its intolerance was moral rather than theological.

In 1654 a commission of 'triers' was established to approve incumbents presented to them by lay patrons; and another, of 'ejectors', could expel ministers and schoolmasters who caused scandal through being swearers, perjurers, papists, adulterers, gamblers, drunkards, defenders of maypoles and stage plays, critics of the government, non-residents or users of the prayer book. Beyond these commissioners there was no ecclesiastical organisation, no precise code of discipline, no creed or confession requiring sworn assent. It is doubtful if England has ever had a better system of ensuring that parishes had incumbents likely to do their work sensibly. Despite the comprehensive definition of scandal, there was leniency in practice. Users of the prayer book were not greatly hounded. The figures suggest that a number of parishes were served by men who, though ordained in the Laudian high summer, were able to sit out the Puritan winter and still enjoy the returning springtime of the Anglican Restoration.

For two groups, the Protectorate was almost beneficent. The laws penalising Catholics for non-attendance at the parish church were repealed in 1650; and no action was taken against Catholics attending mass at foreign embassy chapels in London. In 1656, Cromwell admitted Jews to England for the first time since the reign of Edward I, ignoring a furious protest by that Prynne whose ears Laud had had lopped, to the effect that it was an affront to the Son of God. The wilder Puritan sects were intermittently persecuted, notably the Quakers, whose early history was the reverse of pacific, and whose insistence on not removing their hats, even in courts of law, aroused a fury like that of army officers convinced that if other ranks do not salute them, all discipline has utterly broken down.

The Church Untriumphant

Inevitably, the Restoration restored the bishops; but the years since 1630 had built up too much dislike for episcopalianism and the formularies of the prayer book for these ever again to be the basis of a truly national church. Comprehensiveness, even with Presbyterianism, proved un-attainable and the first instinct was to revive old habits of persecution. But the motives behind the so-called Clarendon Code (notably the Corporation Act) of 1661–5, and the Test Act of 1673, which excluded from the church, the universities, schools, the armed forces and municipal and public office all who were not communicant Anglicans, was primarily political. Puritanism had been revolutionary and might be so again; while Catholicism appeared in the 1670s once more as the spearhead of attacks on liberty and national independence. And since religious conformity was primarily a test of loyalty to the state, many who would have preferred not to conform were the more ready to do so to purge themselves of the suspicion that they wished a return to the chaos of the 1640s. Religious militancy was everywhere in retreat out of fear of social disorder. Persecution for religious diversity as such fell out of favour. It had both caused, and been a consequence of, the Great Rebellion. Thus the nonconformists' response to James II's Declaration of Indulgence was at once to take advantage of the freedom to worship it provided, but to protest that they wanted it based on the assured legality of statute, not the arbitrary exercise of a prerogative whose principal aim was papistical and thus destructive, like Laudian Anglicanism, of social unity. This nonconformist adherence to the supremacy of parliament cemented the alliance with the church which produced the invitation to William of Orange.

By the 1680s, the Independents, now mainly classifiable as Baptists and Congregationalists, were no longer social revolutionaries. Even the persecuted Quakers were moving towards the quietism which was soon to distinguish them; those few who supported Monmouth's rebellion against James II in 1685 were disowned by their brethren. From both ends of the spectrum, the papist and the Quaker, came new and mainly secular arguments in favour of toleration. Though unwilling to be bound by the oaths concerning faith and allegiance that others took so lightly, both insisted on their belief in non-resistance to authority. Toleration came to be considered good for trade, because it enabled men of all sorts peaceably to pursue their livelihood. Whatever men's particular religious beliefs, their natural instinct, it was now thought, was to be loyal to the society within which it had pleased divine providence to place them.

Such movements of opinion suggest that Charles II and James II, whatever their political aims, were truer to the spirit of the age than the Whig patrons of anti-Catholic hysteria in the 1670s. The Toleration Act of 1689 that resulted from the Glorious Revolution did not originate freedom of worship for Protestant dissenters; it confirmed by statute what James had granted by prerogative in 1687. Papists and Unitarians were not given this freedom, however, and neither the Test nor Corporation Act was repealed. Dissenters were acknowledged as citizens by the Toleration Act; but only as second class citizens.

By 1710, over 2500 places had been registered for dissenting worship, a fact which suggested that many who had once attended church had really wanted to go to chapel. Indifferentists also benefited. There now being no place of worship which all were bound to attend, they could fail to go to their parish church and forget to go to chapel. Perhaps it was a sign of these changes that in one Nottinghamshire village 200 out of 276 qualified parishioners attended Easter Communion in 1676, whereas the corresponding figures for an Oxfordshire village in 1730 was 20 out of a possible 220.

A Rational Church

Anglicans disliked the Toleration Act, since toleration, once legal, would tend to make Anglicanism, for all its official and social privileges, one 'denomination' among several. Hence, it tried to bolster its morale by a continuing insistence that, through the bishops who ordained them, the Anglican clergy, unlike dissenting ministers, were in direct apostolic succession from Christ's first disciples. The matter had greatly pre-occupied Clarendon during the Interregnum. He feared that if Charles II's Restoration were too long delayed, there would be no Anglican bishops left alive to lay hands upon the ordinands of a restored Anglican church and the apostolic succession would thus be irretrievably lost.

It was a claim which, though Rome derided it, was held to distinguish the Church of England from all other Protestant communions. It carried little weight outside ecclesiastical circles. To detect even vestigially apostolic qualities among some eighteenth-century bishops would have signified not faith but credulity. As the century proceeded, episcopal incomes grew larger and increasingly reserved for men of high birth. In mid-century, with all twenty-six bishops being Whigs, the Whig party had become allies, not so much of dissent, as of the church they had penetrated and emasculated.

The long Christian campaign against magic had by now given birth to the scientific spirit, which was first of all conceived of as an attempt to search out and understand the mysterious workings of God's ways. But this process of investigation led to the thought that if God could be explained by rational enquiry, there was less need to attach importance to the teachings of the ancient fathers or to the traditions of the church. It was thus not surprising that some of the clergy as well as the laity began to turn to Unitarianism and that the church failed to hold either London or the newer industrial towns. The bishop whose reply when asked his views on the deplorable conditions of life in the West Riding textile towns was, 'No gentleman ever goes into the West Riding' suggests why Anglicanism was becoming principally the religion of the small towns and the purely agricultural village. These, however, were still at any rate the birthplaces of most people; and in many of the 10,000 parish churches of the land a simple piety based on the ten commandments and the catechism, supplemented by a little schooling provided by underpaid curates to augment their exiguous emoluments, still maintained a permanent link between the common people and the educated political world. In that it existed at all, the stability of eighteenth-century society was perhaps based on this slender, if pious, foundation. The assertion that religious belief was unfashionable has to be balanced against the fact that the number of the fashionable was small.

Dissenters Deflated

In 1689, there were at least 75,000 Dissenters at a time when the total number of persons aged over fifteen in England and Wales is estimated at rather less than 3.5 million. Many were latitudinarian enough to communicate occasionally at their parish church (and communicating was a rare event even among Anglicans) in order to qualify for office under the terms of the Test and Corporation Acts. Tory attempts to proscribe this practice of 'occasional conformity' were shortlived. Eighteenth-century office-holders were later accommodated by an annual act of indemnity, which waived the penalties against them. The tactic of occasional conformity diluted both Anglicanism and nonconformity. It generalised among both a watered-down Puritanism, a respectable, orderly sobriety. It also began the process by which nonconformists who were socially successful might signalise the fact by becoming Anglicans. Dissenters themselves believed their numbers were declining after 1715; but this may have been a reflection of the apostasy of the few peers, and of some of the gentry, who had been Dissenters in Charles II's reign.

Dissenters were nevertheless the first modern pressure group. Their involvement in trade gave them a disproportionately large voting strength in urban constituencies of permanent value to the Whigs; and Dissenters also controlled some of the municipal corporations. During much of the century, the higher education provided by the dissenting academies was broader than that offered by the universities. With the blurring of denominational boundaries the universities later recovered their influence, though the Presbyterian academy established at Warrington in 1727 has been considered one of the most important centres of higher education founded in the century. Joseph Priestley, discoverer of oxygen, was on its teaching staff.

Significantly, Priestley was a Unitarian; and Unitarianism eroded traditional dissent as well as traditional Anglicanism. Unitarianism enabled men to come as near as possible to rationalism without altogether forfeiting the claim to be Christian. The Unitarians' denial of the Trinity and the particular divinity of Christ, together with their belief in human goodness and rationality, caused their exclusion from the terms of the Toleration Act until 1813. The first openly Unitarian congregation had however been established in 1774, in London.

Healing Streams Abound

A measure of the decline of enthusiasm among the heirs of the Puritan tradition is the fact that when large scale religious revivals came they originated within the established church: the Wesleyan revival which separated from it, and the later Evangelical and Tractarian revivals which remained within it.

Society's disapproval of Wesley's revivalism is perhaps best understood by reference to the contrasting popularity, when it began to appear in the 1770s, of Gibbon's *Decline and Fall of the Roman Empire*. Educated Englishmen took it to their hearts because they thought themselves the true heirs of Rome, separated from it only by intervening centuries of little worth marked, in Gibbon's illuminating phrase, by 'the triumph of barbarism and religion'. The House of Commons saw itself as a Roman Senate. Its members delighted to display their Latinity. The English, like the Romans, had magnanimously admitted other peoples, such as the Scots, into citizenship and imposed their rule on lesser tribes, like the unfortunate Irish. They had established colonies and trading stations across the seas and built a system of law and government which was the envy of the world. They had established a society based on civic virtue and settled order combined with a formal though solemn religion designed chiefly to teach the humble to defer to the great.

These Roman attitudes were reinforced by a classical education and the legacy of the Italian Renaissance. Both conditioned the instructed mind to think that only exalted beings could experience exalted feelings. If emotions were permitted at all, they were appropriate only to the noble, the beautiful and the godlike. The century's most fascinating paradox, the idea of 'The Noble Savage', attracted the attention it did because it was a challenge to the belief that only the nobly born could possibly be noble. Common people were common all through. The trivial was trivial all through. The joke of Pope's *Rape of the Lock* was its use of heroic language to depict fashionable social trivia; but it was an 'in' joke. The idea of fashionable ladies casting loud shrieks 'to pitying heaven' over the death of a lapdog seemed acceptable because ladies were delicately nurtured beings. But the idea of common people being encouraged, as they were by Wesley, to call publicly upon pitying heaven to save their souls was considered disgusting. When, in serious vein, Pope had written, 'Order is Heav'n's first law', he was speaking for his times. So he was when he wrote, 'The worst of madmen is a saint run mad'. By eighteenth century standards, Wesley was that kind of madman, inciting common people to a similar insanity. Worse still, his insistence that persons belonging to the highest ranks of society were as depraved as members of the lowest until they too had undergone conversion caused great offence. One duchess thought it 'monstrous' to be told that she had 'a heart as sinful as . . . common wretches'.

Wesley's offence was that, being an ordained clergyman of the established church, he nevertheless preached to common people that there was a wrath to come, from which their only escape was by instant conversion to an indwelling faith in the Lord Jesus as each man's personal saviour. This emphasis on conversion led to strong condemnation of Wesleyan 'enthusiasm' among the educated. The claim to have experienced 'immediate revelation' was dismissed by Dr Johnson as 'a vain confidence of divine favour or communication'.

The visible signs of conversion were an eschewal of strong drink, combined with a clean, neat appearance and a life of respectable decency. Men were to wrestle fervently against sin, adopt unwavering principles of behaviour and transform the dim, wholly exteriorised 'Our Saviour' to whom society deferred with mechanical solemnity, into a beloved 'My Saviour' on whom the converted could hang, to whose bosom they could fly, and whom they besought to 'leave, ah, leave me not alone'.

The message was the more effective because, overcoming much opposition, Wesley implanted Anglican Arminianism rather than Calvinist predestinarianism into the movement. Under Laud, the Arminian doctrine of free will had got itself entangled with royal supremacy. Wesley used the doctrine to give dignity to the humble by setting them free from the chains of their otherwise low and often wretched earthly destiny. They were free; and through that freedom they could be saved.

The Church of England was poorly equipped for the task of evangelising the lower ranks of society. Too many of its parish churches and parsonages were defensive garrisons, commanded far too often in the eighteenth century by parsons who were also squires and JPs, and for that reason scarcely distinguishable from squires and JPs who were not parsons. By contrast, Wesley fought a fifty-year war of movement against faithlessness, gin, obscenity and dirt, preaching 40,000 sermons, travelling a quarter of a million miles and still finding time for a two-hour stint of daily private devotion.

Yet the movement's novel feature was that, whereas all forms of Protestantism had, as its accidentally acquired name suggests, hitherto been a form of protest, Wesleyanism was not a protest movement, but an evangelising mission. More distinctive still, Wesley was a tireless organiser. This meant that he could not only launch a movement; he could ensure its survival after him.

Excluded from the pulpits because of his emotionalism and the type of audience he attracted, he employed to the full that gift for organisation which he himself recognised was his especial talent. Wherever he went, he left behind efficient cells of devout believers, responsible directly to himself. From 1744, the various societies met in an annual Methodist Conference. In 1784, with already over 40,000 Methodists in England and 8,000 in America, he began to supplement his lay preachers with ministers whom he himself ordained. Despite the disapproval of his own brothers, and his own disclaimers, he thus created a separated movement, adding the New Dissent of Methodism to the Old Dissent of Presbyterians, Baptists and Congregationalists. When he died in 1791, there were 136,000 'paid up' Methodists and up to a million sympathisers.

The anxieties felt by the propertied classes about Methodism were scarcely justified. Wesley's mission to save souls was the work of a high church Oxford don of ferociously conservative principles. Nevertheless, he was the first to make a bridge across the gap between the propertied and the unpropertied. He gave his converts a fuller humanity at a time when most of them were still considered outside the ranks of society, as society was normally defined. If he had done no more than get them to keep clean and not drink gin he would have done much. But, in addition, he gave them feelings, principles and a scale of values. There is thus a case for thinking that, by converting his followers to personal standards hitherto thought attainable only by the propertied classes, Wesley created the first of the modern 'classes', the lower middle class. Cut off from the gentry by their birth, they came to be cut off also from the rest of the unpropertied classes by their acquired respectability, thus developing into a separate social group. It is largely because of Wesley that to regard England since the industrial revolution as crudely divided into a middle class and a working class is to misunderstand its social structure and to make a realistic understanding of its modern history impossible.

THE GROSS AND THE ELEGANT

The Weight of the Law

THE victory of the men of property meant that the element of paternalism in Tudor and early Stuart policy towards paupers was henceforth confined within even stricter bounds. Though paupers continued to be a charge upon the properties, they were, like the crown, subject to new limitations. The settlement law of 1662 laid down that a parish was responsible only for persons who owned property within it, had been born or apprenticed there or had lived there for forty days. Persons renting land worth under £10 a year could be turned out before the forty days were up if they could not prove they had settlement rights in some other parish. To prevent an additional burden on the poor rate, pregnant women might be turned away so that their child should not be born in the parish and establish settlement rights there. If an unmarried woman became pregnant by a man from another parish, they might be forced to marry so that the child became a charge on the father's parish. Cottages might be destroyed to prevent their being occupied by potential paupers. The settlement laws were still being applied in various ways at the beginning of the twentieth century. It was discovered in 1908 that about 1200 poor persons were still compulsorily shifted every year from one poor law area to another. In the eighteenth century tens of thousands were thus moved off. The salvation of many was the lax administration of the law in London; hence, the poor of England joined those of Ireland and Scotland (which gave no relief to the able-bodied) to swell the population of the capital's overflowing alleys and cellars. The London dispensary for the sick noted that only a quarter of its patients had been born in the capital.

Nevertheless, the cost of the poor rate rose from £0.7 million to nearly £2 million a year in the century after 1688, a reminder that poverty was not a condition invented by the industrial revolution. It was estimated, even at the start of the eighteenth century, that over half the total population was liable at some time to become a potential charge on the poor rate. The result was that though most parishes showed fair concern for the infirm and aged poor, the able-bodied came off badly. Parish authorities tended to treat every wage labourer as a potential liability and, if they could, to invoke the settlement law against him or to deny him assistance unless he entered the poorhouse.

Growing pauperism perhaps contributed to the increasing severity of the penal code. Though transportation, that curious early consequence of empire, was introduced in 1719, the death penalty was society's favourite penal device. In 1688, there were 50 capital offences; a century later the total exceeded 200. By 1740, any theft of property worth over a shilling (5p) carried the death penalty. On a normal day at the Old Bailey in 1801, 13 men were sentenced to death and 34 transported for 7 years. Among those sentenced to death were a man in possession of skeleton keys who entered a house and stole articles worth £2; a Hampton blacksmith who stole a horse while it was grazing in Bushey park and tried to sell it to a Smithfield innkeeper for £10; and a boy of twelve who stole a piece of cloth worth £1.80 from premises near St Paul's. The fate of the twelve-year-old is a reminder that a high proportion of the victims of capital punishment were under 21.

Public hangings were a popular entertainment. London stopped work once every six weeks or so to watch the two-hour procession of men and women being conveyed by cart from Newgate jail in the City to Tyburn, where the roads to Oxford and to Edgware met at the north-east corner of Hyde Park. At the gallows, the nooses were fixed, the cart pulled away and the bodies left to dangle. The execution of such star personalities of the 1720s as Jack Sheppard, the highwayman, and Jonathan Wild, the London gangster, drew crowds of cup final proportions. The spectators allotted the victims the role of anti-heroes, and were liable to jeer at those who showed fear. The manly and moving dying speech was much appreciated. The upper ranks of society paid high prices for good vantage points. For them, no doubt, the occasion provided reassurance. No more solemn affirmation of the sanctity of property and the stability of the social order could be offered than the spectacle of a petty thief slowly dangling on a rope.

Public executions provided the cathartic experience sought by later generations in theatre, cinema or sports stadium. The culture of this society provided little drama except the drama of real life, little tragedy except real tragedy. The judge (whose costume dates from this time), the trial, the hangman and the gallows were, to the eighteenth century, what the figure of Death and his scythe had been to the fourteenth. They symbolised the arbitrary fate that threatened whoever was unlucky enough to be caught making private war against society. In an age when religious paintings and visual images had long been banished from old churches, and when the style of new ones evoked the atmosphere of a courtroom administering the laws of Imperial Rome, public hangings provided the one awe-inspiring occasion when all could see that the wages of sin was indeed death. All looked forward to having their feelings heightened by watching the criminal fulfil the duty that his role imposed on him, a last repentant acknowledgement of guilt before being despatched choking into the presence of his Maker.

The imaginative limitations of the culture of a time distinguished principally for its 'taste' may explain the practice of seeking amusement by going to laugh at the madmen chained up in Bedlam, the Bethlehem

Hospital. With no fictional fools to laugh at, men made fun of real ones instead. And if they laughed also at the poor fools being carted from Newgate to Tyburn that was because the need to enjoy the misfortunes of others was fulfilled here too.

Public hangings continued into Victorian times. By then they appealed principally to the criminal elements themselves, gathering to gloat, or mourn, over the death of a fellow soldier in the battle against the respectable. By then, the populace found it easier to enjoy the crude simulations of reality provided by Victorian melodrama; and, with uncanny precision, the last decade of public hangings was also the first decade of the serious 'crime story'. It was in 1868, the year public hangings were abolished, that Wilkie Collins published *The Moonstone*.

In the countryside, the acceleration of enclosure and emparking made the game laws ever more repressive. From 1671, none was allowed to kill 'game' who was not a £100 freeholder. Tenants of land were not allowed to shoot the game on it until 1831. An act of 1723, creating fifty new capital offences, included that of appearing in disguise on the king's highway. This was expressly designed to deter 'unlawful hunting' in royal forests and private deerparks, warrens and fishponds. By 1816, any poacher found guilty by a jury of being out at night with nets could be transported for seven years. Gamekeepers could enter and search houses and confiscate weapons. They were not forbidden by law to use spring guns and man traps against poachers until 1828. These penal acts, administered for the most part by JPs in the fortunate position of being judges in their own cause, restricted villagers' diet and, in addition, kept them unarmed.

Intellectual protest against the system, at least before the 1760s, was fairly easily contained. The traditional system by which nothing could legally be printed without pre-censorship by the church or the universities was allowed to lapse in 1694; but the press, though the freest in the world, was wide open to charges of sedition and blasphemy, and printing presses liable to seizure. According to Boswell, the authorities considered they had a good case in law for proceeding against Dr Johnson for defining 'Excise' in his Dictionary as 'a hateful tax levied upon commodities and adjudged by . . . wretches hired by those to whom Excise is paid', but refrained out of considerations of prudence.

The theatre was gagged. In *The Beggars' Opera* (1728) John Gay implied that Walpole's government was a gang of highwaymen; and incidentally convinced contemporaries, as well as a posterity familiar with the song, 'Mac the Knife', that 'the criminal classes' were larger and more highly organised in the eighteenth century than they probably were in reality. Gay's next work, *Polly*, was so personally offensive to Walpole that he had it banned by the Lord Chamberlain. Further, by the Licensing Act of 1737 all plays were henceforth made subject to pre-censorship by the same dignitary, a regulation not repealed until the 1960s. It was the Theatres Act of 1843 which reduced the object of stage censorship to that of protecting 'good manners, decorum or the public peace'. The original aim had been political censorship.

Complacency and Benevolence

Those who set the tone of eighteenth-century thinking were men for whom religion had been purged of enthusiasm, and whose universe, no longer magic and mysterious, was an ordered mechanism governed by unchanging laws fashioned by Newton and a Supreme Being. There was thus little conflict between religion and free thought. As Horace Walpole put it, there seemed 'as much bigotry in attempting conversions from any religion as to it'. If to this were added the perfection of the English constitution and the success of its warfare and commerce, it is not surprising that it was fashionable to believe, either with grave piety or smug complacency, that everything that was was right, that nothing ought to be changed and that, indeed, nothing could be changed.

Yet, just as Wesleyanism challenged religious tepidity, so complacency was increasingly challenged by those to whom social realities suggested that everything that happened was not invariably for the best. The eighteenth century saw the beginning of the twin movements for humanitarianism and hygiene which have shaped so much of society's actions since. Their progress was governed by their emergence within a society believing that men were free, but subject to immutable natural laws. Their aims had therefore to be fought for from below, by individuals and voluntary pressure groups. Freedom was held to imply that governments did not interfere in social problems. To do so was despotic and reminiscent of discarded Tudor laws against enclosures, or Laudian and Puritan interference with personal morals and public pleasures. It was also contrary to the natural order of things. When Johnson harangued Boswell on the matter, he defined the basis on which, both then and thereafter, community action for social betterment was usually resisted. 'Let fanciful men do as they will,' he declared, 'depend upon it, it is difficult to disturb the system of life'. And to Boswell's query, 'So, sir, you laugh at schemes of political improvement,' Johnson replied, 'Why, sir, most schemes of political improvement are very laughable things'. It is significant that Johnson has always been commended for his 'common sense'.

It is a result of this eighteenth-century attitude that 'improvement' had for so long to be advocated by individuals who, when not eccentric in fact (as they usually were), were commonly alleged to be so. They were accused of doing 'more harm than good', an accusation not without justification, given the magnitude of the problems they tried to solve by voluntary effort and the reluctance of the political nation to support them. The theme recurs in English history from the early-eighteenth century to the late-twentieth.

Anticipating Wesley's campaign for temperance, pressure built up, between 1720 and 1750, against the poisonous effects of excessive gin drinking. Doctors, magistrates, local dignitaries from industrial towns, as well as Hogarth, the painter, petitioned parliament, and constituted themselves the first in that long line of worthies whose successors write many-signatured letters of protest and admonition to *The Times*. Like all subsequent pressure-groups they were entangled with commerce. Governments had encouraged gin distilling to keep up the price of corn to the farmer. The brewers aided the campaign against it because gin drinking depressed the sale of beer. For their part, the humanitarians, being also eccentrics, further advanced the brewers' cause by denouncing tea as if it were as lethal as the swilling of gin. Typically, legislation aimed at prohibition failed in the face of riots. The solution came from increasing the excise on gin and regulating conditions of sale.

Later, the century produced the classic humanitarian campaign against slavery. This too found itself working against some economic and political forces and with others. In a politically free society not amenable to government dictate, a movement of conscience needed the alliance of commercial interests hostile to those of the plantation owners. It had to await the abolition of the rotten boroughs which gave the West Indian interest so much influence in the commons; and it depended in the end on the British naval supremacy that had made possible the slavery it was now desired to abolish. The campaign began in 1787, secured the abolition of the trade twenty years later and the emancipation of the slaves themselves in 1833, though it was not completed until 1838.

The limitations which the ratepaying mentality imposed on the poor law also stimulated private and professional benevolence. Since parishes were required to care for their sick paupers, most poorhouses were also infirmaries. It was as centres from which improved notions of medical care might be disseminated among poor law overseers that the hospital movement developed. Five great London hospitals (Guy's, the West-minster, the London, St George's and the Middlesex) were added, between 1720 and 1745, to the two medieval foundations of St Bartholomew and St Thomas. Guy's owed its origin to its founder's excessive good luck in the South Sea Bubble speculation. Many provincial infirmaries and hospitals (among them Addenbrooke's at Cambridge) date from this time. Their immediate effects were small. Institutionalisation instantly involved exposure to infection, notably typhus, which acquired the familiar name of hospital (or gaol) fever. But whereas hospitals would normally have two patients to a bed, the poorhouse at Shoreditch at one time shared three beds among thirty-nine children. Benevolence may have been more speedily effective through the dispensary movement: doctors gave physic and elementary advice to the poor about cleanliness and fresh air, though both were hard for the poor to come by in crowded towns. Scientific midwifery also may be said to date from the work of William Smellie in the mid-eighteenth century, with the consequent building, all by voluntary effort, of a number of lying-in hospitals which gradually showed the way to reduce infant mortality.

Other signs of the humanitarian spirit, as of the difficulties which faced it, were provided by the success of the former sea captain, Thomas Coram, in attracting sufficient funds from the highest in London society for the establishment of a Foundling Hospital for abandoned children. The problem was such that nearly 15,000 children were admitted between 1756 and 1760, of whom over 10,000 died. The hospital became a dumping ground for unwanted children; for a time admission had to be limited to those who could contribute £100 per child.

Jonas Hanway, a governor of the Foundling Hospital, campaigned against the use of child chimney sweeps. He tried to stop London pauper children being apprenticed to a trade which was particularly attractive to poor parents because there was no apprenticeship fee. Masters would often virtually buy a suitable child. In 1788 it was made illegal for such children to work before 5 a.m. in the summer or 7 a.m. in winter. It is indicative of the ill temper of the early nineteenth century that the evils Hanway had fought recurred during the wars with France and that all efforts at new protective legislation were rejected by the Lords. The cause had to be taken up all over again by Lord Shaftesbury from the 1830s onwards.

Hanway also secured an act forcing London poorhouses to board pauper infants with foster parents in the countryside where they might benefit from fresh air. He hotly condemned tea drinking and had such a partiality to the umbrella that he was credited with having invented it. Mocked by many for his 'goodness of heart' (the phrase was as despised as Methodist references to 'the inward light') he seems to have been the origin of the tradition by which cartoonists continued even into the twentieth century to equip with a badly rolled umbrella any person whom they wished to discredit as an interfering busybody and killjoy.

The plight of prisoners also attracted the benevolent. Early in the century there was the good General Oglethorpe, much concerned with the sufferings of imprisoned debtors, who constituted up to fifty per cent of the relatively small proportion of those imprisoned at that time. He founded, by public subscription, the colony of Georgia for selected debtors and paupers; running them into trouble, however, by denying them both rum and slaves. Later, John Howard travelled England, Wales and the continent to report movingly on the filth and horror of prison conditions. One debtors' prison he encountered was a small underground room with an open sewer running through it. A dog brought in by a prisoner to protect him from the rats was killed by them.

The century was rich in endeavour to improve literacy. The often very effective small grammar schools and the efforts of those parsons who kept school, were no compensation for the absence of the school in every village that the kirk tried to insist on in Scotland. By 1714, there were already 25,000 children attending voluntary charity schools. Robert Raikes, a newspaper proprietor of Gloucester, founded the Sunday School movement. He was emulated by Mrs Sarah Trimmer of Brentford, mother of twelve and author of many tracts; by Hannah More among the miners on Mendip; by the Pembrokeshire worthies, Sir John Philipps and the Rev. Griffith Jones, whose efforts, when extended by the Methodists and the Old Dissenters, may be said to have begun the history of modern Welsh national consciousness.

It does not do to regard these schools too dismissively merely because their motive was strictly religious and their objectives simple piety, sober behaviour and habits of subordination. Puritanism had committed the English to an intensely verbal religion and an intensely verbal culture. In the century in which Johnson produced the first authoritative dictionary of English spelling, which gave birth to the modern newspaper and the modern novel, and in which English at last finally ousted Latin as the sole official language of the courts of law, it was already evident that literacy was basic to participation in the effective life of society. The poor were thought to be outside that life. One said, approvingly, of a man who was inside it, that he was 'a Christian and a gentleman'. Only because they aimed to turn the poor into Christians, but not into gentlemen, were the charity and Sunday schools of the time even conceivable. That the principal educative influence should be the Bible was almost unavoidable, since there were few books written specifically for children. This, combined with the fearsome authoritarianism of the time, doubtless explains the earlier intellectual maturity achieved by the educated young compared with their descendants, reared by adults who turned childhood into a cult.

Coffee House and Concert Room

By the early years of the century, London already had hundreds of coffee houses, serving not merely their original purpose, but acting also as informal clubs, offices, and places of conference for newspaper editors. With a cover charge of one penny, their patrons might be craftsmen and traders come in to read the daily news or peers of the realm come to display their English spirit by talking freely to persons whom they would not dream of admitting to their houses. This open, manly intercourse was facilitated by the absence of women other than the serving girls and cashiers. Well before the end of the century, coffee houses had been formalised and specialised. Some became mathematical and scientific clubs. Garraway's coffee house had become the nucleus of the Stock Exchange and Lloyd's in Lombard Street was being transformed into its later redoubtable status from its beginnings as the coffee house favoured by sea captains and shipping agents. Others were turning into London's first exclusive, and exclusively male, clubs, with their 'coffee room' as sole reminder of their more democratic origins. But in the decades before they became institutionalised, the coffee houses enriched the quality of London social life by lessening the normal tendency of moneyed men, literary men and aristocratic men-about-town to hive off into separate coteries. The opportunities for the cross-fertilization of interests and ideas which London offered in the mid-eighteenth century was probably greater than at any other period and enabled it to hold its own with the thriving social and intellectual life of Edinburgh and Dublin at this time.

It was in the London of this period that the public concert was invented, as an institution open, like the coffee house and the assembly rooms at Bath, to whoever could pay the admission charge. The first such public concert appears to have been organised by John Bannister, in an obscure room in a public house in Whitefriars, in 1672, the admission charge being a shilling. The more celebrated Thomas Britton, a coal dealer, and known accordingly as 'The Musical Small-Coal Man', established a long-lasting series of weekly concerts in a room above his Clerkenwell shop for an annual subscription of ten shillings. Both attracted the best people and in time the best international performers appeared in London concert rooms, notably Handel, Haydn and Mozart. Dr Pepusch established another concert venue in the Strand before 1710. Hickford's Room, which opened in 1713 off Haymarket and then moved to Brewer Street in Soho, made the regular concert room a firm feature of English life by enduring until 1799. During the first half of the nineteenth century the Hanover Square Rooms dominated; in the latter half, the St James's Hall; and in the first half of the twentieth century, the Queen's Hall.

Eighteenth-century continental visitors found the public concert a strange institution. Accustomed to music as an activity provided by royal and princely patrons for the beguilement of aristocratically exclusive circles, they found it a testimony to the openness of English society that in London they would rub shoulders with persons who had been allowed in simply on the unaristocratic grounds that they could afford the admission charge or the subscription fee. They were also surprised that an entertainment so public was so exclusively musical. There were no prostitutes, no card-playing and no drinking.

The consequences were not necessarily favourable to English music or English musicians. In music, as in commerce and technology, England was so much a land of opportunity compared with caste-bound Europe that continental musicians flocked to London. The result was to establish the belief that foreigners were musically gifted, but that the English were not. Aping classical attitudes in this as in other matters, Englishmen came to regard music as something performed by hired foreigners for the gratification of the patrons of the concert room much as, in Rome, it had been performed by slaves for the entertainment of patricians. Music ceased to be a suitable accomplishment for the educated male; the 'music master' employed to teach singing to the ladies became a stock comic figure, and it was held all but impossible to find a musician who was also a gentleman. Characteristically, when Covent Garden began as an Opera House in 1847 it was officially entitled The Royal Italian Opera House. Not until the age of Elgar, Delius, Holst, Bax and Vaughan Williams, and those doughty impresarios Henry Wood and Thomas Beecham did the English shake off an idea of themselves as unmusical which would have surprised the Elizabethans.

Politer Pleasures

Urbanity and taste slimmed away some of the grossness of manners which, at the start of the eighteenth century, had succeeded to the high-pitched laxity of the post-Restoration period, lightened as it had been by its raffish sense of comedy. In the civilising of society's upper ranks, Lord Chesterfield's letters to his son did something. What Dr Johnson unfairly dismissed as an attempt to propagate the manners of a dancing master was really an effort to reassert for a different age the forgotten chivalric ideal of the harmony that should exist between nobility of birth and gracefulness of social demeanour.

More widely effective was the long reign of Beau Nash as master of ceremonies at Bath. Here, with John Wood, architect and town planner, and Ralph Allen, a resourceful business manager, Nash enabled the English to discover for the first time since the Romans the concept of the holiday resort, a place claiming not merely to restore its visitors to radiant health but to do so painlessly, and in conjunction with attractive facilities for usually expensive leisure and pleasure. In a society still formally Christian and with a conscience almost indelibly puritan, an invitation to pleasure for its own sake was unacceptable; but to advertise pleasure as concomitant with a cure for ill-health was to have it both ways. Thus, in the eighteenth century, coffee was sold as a cure for the spleen and dropsy and, in the nineteenth, cocoa commended for its 'flesh building' qualities. So, Bath was sold in the first place because its hot springs were a cure for faintings, sweatings, low spirits and the effects of intemperance. They were also good for disorders proceeding from the eating of fruit, always a suspect item of diet until the twentieth century could bring it fresh to the buyer and the discovery of vitamins give it dietary dignity. But the real attractions of Bath were its gaming room, its pump room, and its opportunities for endless dancing and social intercourse.

What distinguished it was Nash's dictatorial insistence on good manners. It was from Bath that emanated the rule of 'ladies first'. Gentlemen were not to crowd in before ladies at the ball. 'Whisperings of lies and scandals' were vetoed, as were bad manners between young and old. Men were not to wear boots or swords in the ballroom. Ladies, whatever their rank, were not to appear in their aprons, even if beautified by the most expensive lace. Equally firm discipline prevailed in the gaming room. At Bath, distinctions of wealth and birth were ignored. All who could pay the fees and were presentable were admitted to an equal footing with everybody else. It was also the rule that acquaintanceships made at Bath involved no obligation to keep them up elsewhere. This did not prevent Bath being a notable marriage market, particularly as the maximum of social mixing was so elegantly combined with the maximum of decorum. It was on the basis of Nash's success that Wood was able to plan and extend the town of Bath. Together with the London squares of the time and the contemporary development of, for example, Buxton and Tunbridge Wells, the planning of Bath suggests that England was at last on the verge of creating a dignified and ordered urban civilisation. Other towns which acquired visual dignity from their status as spas included Scarborough (older-established even than Bath), Harrogate and Cheltenham. From the diversion of resources to war and industrial growth which halted this type of urban development, save for a while in the Prince Regent's London, English town life has not recovered.

The century also gave birth to the seaside resort. In 1750, a certain Dr Russell began to proclaim the health-giving consequences of bathing in (and, mixed with cream of tartar, drinking) the sea water at the fishing village of Brighton. By the end of the century, sufferers from vertigo, melancholy, scrofula and stomach disorders joined mere lovers of novelty in the day-long journey by coach to make a stay at Brighton. By comparison with it, Bath had, at least according to the Duchess of Devonshire, become by 1800 a 'hateful' place swarming with 'old maids, old cats and bachelors'. Margate, Eastbourne, Dover, Deal and Portsmouth became watering places also. The primacy of Brighton was the result of its patronage by the Prince Regent.

An Unphysical Culture

This tentative, valetudinarian approach to the bracing pleasures of the seaside is a reminder that for all their later contribution to the world's sports and games the English were long as hesitant in their attitude to them as were continental peoples. Water was still normally viewed with deep and often justifiable suspicion. Apart from it being so dangerous to drink, it was thought typical of student folly that Cambridge undergraduates went swimming in the Cam.

Renaissance theories about the harmony of body and spirit had little positive effect. The Tudor and early Stuart mind was much given to melancholy about the body's mortality. The first Lord Salisbury mournfully wrote, 'Death is the centre to which we all do move, some diameter-wise, some circularly; but all men must fall down to the centre.' The sentiment recurs in Shakespeare and John Donne, and in the dramatist, Webster, dismissing the body as 'fantastical puff-paste'.

The ideal Renaissance male nude was androgynous. Mere physical strength was associated with crude rustics or, as in Marlowe's Tamburlaine, with brutish tyranny. Thus, the medieval fear of violent exercise survived into the eighteenth century. Even those who approved of exercise warned that unless it was moderate it would too much consume a man's substance. To perspire was bad; it dried the body. Charles II was untypical in weighing himself before and after playing tennis and in taking a loss of weight as a sign that he had had a good game.

The only pastime considered honourable was riding. It made a man conscious of his power over others. Hunting ought to involve some physical effort and courage. Bows and arrows were not honourable. Coursing for hares with greyhounds was thought appropriate for studious persons and even, provided they were not too worried about their complexions, for ladies. It was unthinkable before the fourth decade of the twentieth century for ladies to desire anything but pale complexions. To look sun-tanned would have been to resemble a peasant woman. The sixteenth century apprehensively thought bowls liable to strain the sinews, tennis ('real tennis') too strenuous, football 'all beastly fury' and skittles and quoits beneath the notice of a noble mind.

The only officially approved physical activity for common persons was archery, because of its alleged importance for national defence. In 1541, commoners were forbidden to play bowls and though lords of manors and noblemen could have private bowling greens, public ones were closed. In spite of this, bowls is the game whose technical terms occur most frequently in Shakespeare; and when official rules were devised in 1670 they were ascribed to Charles II. Bowls did not become a game for lesser folk until the eighteenth century.

Commoners had to content themselves with the traditional sports and games associated with Sundays and holydays. Shrovetide Tuesday was a great day for football. This was a general affray or riot for villagers or town apprentices. Legs and heads were broken and deaths not unheard of as the contestants pushed and kicked their way through streets with shops shuttered as if the town were under siege, or through mud and stream, wasteland and fallow. Tug of war and cock fighting were other Shrovetide delights. Easter was associated with running, jumping, throwing and wrestling. Ascension Day may have produced the evolution of the original ceremonial beating of the bounds of the parish first into a race round them and then into a race round a particular field, or on a particular course, as became common in the seventeenth century. The annual presentation of their accounts by the church-wardens was another excuse for parish games. These rustic activities were opportunities to display exuberance rather than skill, the latter being left to the usually professional morris dancers. There would be outdoor feasting, drinking, singing and dancing and perhaps a dressing up in animal skins. By Stuart times, handball, ninepins, pitching the bar, throwing the hammer and foot races were common. Archery and wrestling declined with the decline in the military spirit.

Church ales were a Tudor precedent for the church fêtes of the nineteenth and twentieth centuries. To raise funds, the churchwardens would buy, or secure the gift of, a quantity of malt, have it brewed into strong ale, and sell it to all and sundry, sometimes inside the church itself. Christmas could produce a twelve day uproar led by a Lord of Misrule chosen by the heartier village youths. They would bedeck themselves with ribbons, dress in liveries of some 'light wanton colour', put on laces, scarves, rings and bells and then, with 'hobbyhorses, dragons and other antics', dance their way to the churchyard to the sound of pipe and drums. May morning could see the ceremonial erection of a maypole 'covered all over with flowers and herbs', bound with strings and sometimes painted in variegated colours. It would be borne to the village green by oxen with nosegays on their horns. Once the pole was erected, the villagers would dance robustly round this doubtless venerable fertility symbol.

By the late-sixteenth century these activities, with their resemblance to a riot with pagan rituals thrown in, excited official disapproval. The spread of Puritanism led to reasoned doubt as to their appropriateness to the celebration of major feasts of the church and to a desire that 'holidays' should be the holy days they were supposed to be. Since merrymaking and games had long been tolerated (though not without criticism) by the old religion, they were all soon under a cloud. Thus, in 1579, the obstinately Catholic people of rural Lancashire were forbidden their pipes and minstrels and their bull and bear baiting on Sundays.

It was as calculated anti-Puritan propaganda that in 1618 James I's government issued a Declaration, or Book, of Sports. It declared that prohibition of Sunday games bred discontent, hindered the conversion of Catholics and deprived the commoner sort of their only chance of healthy exercise. Hence, though bear and bull baiting were, like bowls, still proscribed, dancing, archery, leaping, vaulting and Maytime festivities were all permitted if they did not interfere with divine service.

This made 'sports' a political issue. The first concern of the first parliament of Charles I's reign was to impose a fine of 3s 4d (16½p) or three hours in the stocks on anyone committing 'abuses' on 'the Lord's day, called Sunday'. The overt excuse was that Sunday games caused disorders and bloodshed. This was perhaps connected with the tendency of puritan-minded magistrates and their sympathisers to invade even private houses to stop music and dancing. The threat of a Puritan attempt to close alehouses on Sundays prompted Charles I to re-issue the Book of Sports in 1633 with the injunction that all clergy were to read it from their pulpits. Many refused and were deprived of their livings.

Puritans were neither ascetics nor celibates, since this would have smacked of the monastic. Because man had a duty to labour in the world, they regarded a sound body as desirable. But the only lawful form of physical activity was the work itself, the only lawful relaxation the necessary rest that would enable the work to be begun again as soon as maybe. Morally bound to do the Lord's work, for a man to play was immoral. Physical pride and profitless work were wicked. Idleness and frivolity were signs of a sick and probably lost soul.

During the Interregnum, therefore, all the old feasts of the church were abolished and a monthly one-day holiday and fast day substituted. Among the duties of Cromwell's major generals was the suppression of horse racing, cockfighting, bear baiting, drunkenness, blasphemy, stage plays, gambling dens, brothels and a superfluity of alehouses. On the whole, private activities, particularly those of the gentry, were not greatly interfered with; but horse racing was under suspicion as providing opportunity for the hatching of Royalist plots. The glum English Sunday was one of the more permanent relics of the Interregnum; but Puritan protest against the crudity of much that passed for sport was sensible enough, as was its raising of the whole question of what physical fitness was actually for. Puritan objections to bear and bull baiting may have something to do with the fact that there was a society for preventing cruelty to animals in England long before one to prevent cruelty to children.

Games of the less rollicking sort began to develop in the seventeenth century. Though its association with unpopular Scottish monarchs did it little good, golf was sufficiently played for the Buckingham family to find it worth while to acquire the monopoly of the supply of golf balls, as well that for the licensing of bowling alleys. James I's courtiers played golf at Blackheath; but that king's major contribution to sport was to establish Newmarket as a centre first for hunting and then for racing. He spent £500 on buying the first Arab horse to be seen in England.

The second half of the seventeenth century saw the start of that regular aristocratic patronage of certain games that was to characterise sport for more than two hundred years. Cricket (with a wicket) and stoolball (with a 'stool' or stump of a tree instead of a wicket) had developed, almost exclusively in the south-eastern corner of the country, and become the subject of disapproving sermons. It was established as an adult game, with a heavy curved bat and underarm bowling, after 1660; and a party of men from an English ship played a game at Aleppo in 1676. There was a cricket club at St Alban's in 1666. Cricket was usually played for money prizes; professionalism appeared early in the eighteenth century. Under Charles II, Newmarket was further developed, but racing rapidly became an activity for professional jockeys, the gentry functioning as owners and backers. For exercise, they relied on the hunt. It was the element of gambling in sport that led to the drawing up of rules in games patronised by the aristocracy. The concept of fair play derived largely from the fact that money was at stake.

Although there was some revival of country games after the Restoration, the ending of saints' days tended to limit activities of the grosser sort, though cockfights, dogfights and the tossing of hens, geese and cats continued. Cockfighting appeared to enjoy a status comparable to that of horseracing. It was an acceptable pastime at good schools, though Eton was distinguished by its annual ram hunt. This was criticised, not because it culminated in the ram being beaten to death, but on the grounds that it was so strenuous as to be a danger to the boys' health.

Town and Country

Though a self-governing commercial and maritime republic presided over by a limited monarch of foreign birth, England was also aristocratic; and society continued to take its tone from the aristocracy. Most nobles were recently ennobled, were descended from men of business, and were men of business themselves. They let others farm their lands; they derived splendid incomes from royalties on the minerals that others extracted from their land; and many of them were at pains to acquire and profit greatly from valuable building land in and around London, so that the West End and Bloomsbury still enshrine the noble names of Bedford, Cavendish, Portland and Russell, as well as those of lesser men such as Bond and Davies. But the fact that the Hanoverians provided a court life of German dullness or, under George III, of rather stuffy domesticity, the social and cultural sovereignty that in France was concentrated on a unique monarch and a dominating court was exercised in England by the great peers, principally from their handsome country houses.

They were worlds apart from the lesser gentry, the squires. These were almost wholly rural. Their boldest excursions would be to quarter sessions in the county town or, accompanied by their wives and daughters, to dances at its assembly rooms. That they were often depicted as fox hunting, beef-guzzling, port-swilling bucolics indicates not merely the superior esteem accorded to the nobility but the increased prestige of London as the centre not only of political but of fashionable and intellectual life. The writing of the time is spiced with praises of the town and scorn for the rural. Dr Johnson thought a man who was tired of London was tired of life. Horace Walpole regarded the Norfolk gentry and their wives as 'lamentable proofs' of the 'stupefying qualities of beef, ale and wine', declaring,

I here every day see men, who are mountains of roast beef . . . I shudder when I see them brandish their knives in act to carve, and look on them as savages that devour one another . . . Why, I'll swear I see no difference between a country gentleman and a sirloin . . . I have an Aunt here . . . who . . . to all intents and purposes is as beefy as her neighbours . . . you sit an hour with somebody you don't know and don't care for, talk about the wind and the weather, and ask a thousand foolish questions which all begin with, 'I think you live a good deal in the country'.

315

In similar style, Sydney Smith was to speak of the country as 'a kind of healthy grave' and Lamb to write feelingly of 'the sweet security of streets'. It would not be fair to suppose that all the country gentry were as bucolic as this suggests. To lampoon 'Tory squires' was routine among Whiggish sophisticates such as Horace Walpole and Sydney Smith. A way of life which, by the end of the century, could have nourished the novels of Jane Austen can hardly have been merely boorish.

The most enduring and admired cultural achievements of the eighteenth century were the country houses of the nobility and wealthier gentry. These had an added beauty because of their often remarkable gardens and the craftsmanship lavished, regardless of expense, on the furnishing and adornment of their interiors. Through all the many changes of taste which took place between 1660 and the early nineteenth century, most characteristic was the receptivity of the great aristocratic builders to foreign influences and the skill with which they adapted them. In the late-seventeenth century, Dutch influence was strong, as was the baroque. To this period belong the grandeurs of Castle Howard and Blenheim, both built by Vanbrugh, the former for Lord Carlisle, the latter was a national tribute to the victorious Duke of Marlborough; and Chatsworth, built for the Dukes of Devonshire. Palladian influences, domesticated first of all by Lord Burlington, were adapted first, to produce Chiswick House, and then, by Thomas Coke, Earl of Leicester, and his adviser, William Kent, for the building, between 1732 and 1765, of Holkham Hall in Norfolk. In the second half of the century the pace quickened. By 1800 there were some four hundred landed gentlemen with incomes of over £10,000 a year, from estates of 20,000 acres. Among the great houses built, improved or rebuilt during those years were Syon House, Harewood House, Woburn and Bowood. The arbiters of taste were now the Adam brothers, Syon being perhaps their most outstanding achievement.

Taste became the modish word. According to Sir Joshua Reynolds it was founded on wide reading and the Grand Tour. The latter was by now so thoroughly established that there were sufficient patrons to justify the opening of an English coffee house in Rome. The artistic appetite of the Englishman of taste led to a busy importation of countless items from abroad for the embellishment of both country houses and their gardens. Not surprisingly, the century ended with such a miscellany of 'tastes' that it could be said in the 1780s that 'the well educated British gentleman' talked and dressed in French, sang in Italian and rivalled the Spanish in indifference and the German in drinking; that his house was classical Greek, his business premises Gothic and his furniture Chinese. By the 1790s, the despised middle ages were coming back into fashion, leading to a passion for Gothic ruins and heady Romanticism, mildly displayed in Horace Walpole's Strawberry Hill and more extravagantly at Fonthill, for the millionaire,

Beckford. In this, as in so many respects, the nineteenth century was born in the eighteenth, even though the Victorians pursued their Gothic under the impression that it showed how much higher was their moral tone and how deeper their religious feelings than those of their lax and semi-pagan predecessors.

The landscape gardening of the eighteenth century resulted from the English abandonment of the geometric pattern of straight level paths, box hedges, regulated avenues of neatly shaped trees and formally shaped ornamental waters which French taste had dictated in the seventeenth century. This older-style garden was an extension of the house. Its plants were a kind of building material and its purpose to provide a setting for polite conversation. The English garden, of which the first great example was at Stourhead, planned by the banker Henry Hoare from the 1740s onwards, aimed rather at laying out an idealised landscape which strictly speaking should have nobody in it but its gazing, contemplating creator. It was an attempt to turn nature into a work of art and yet to leave it still nature, as a sculptor turns marble into a human figure but still respects its innate character as stone. The ideal was expressed by Pope and striven for in various ways by William Kent and John (Capability) Brown:

> He gains all ends who pleasingly confounds
> Surprises, varies and conceals the bounds.

Symmetry was broken up by serpentine paths through irregular plantings of trees and shrubs; by lakes of irregular, 'natural' shape; and by small temples, statues and pavilions nicely placed to surprise the eye. Kent, in particular, by adapting the French military device of the sunken fence or ha-ha, in order to dispense with walls, sought to merge the garden and the further landscape into one artistic whole. The lack of clear boundaries, sharp edges or straight lines sorted well with the hazy light induced by the moist English climate and with the undulating, changing character of the landscape as a whole; yet its original inspiration was French landscape painting and its nearest foreign parallel, Chinese. But the English garden was not bounded by its original conception. The eighteenth century was the first great age of plant collectors: the Royal Botanic Gardens were laid out by Kent in the 1730s. Scores of rose and hundreds of rhododendron species as well as many exotic trees found their way into the English garden, to ensure that the original conception of a work of natural art was not permanently overlaid by the somewhat mannered mania for statuary and stone.

The willingness thus to blend the precincts of the house with the countryside to which it belonged and the loving acclimatisation of exotic trees and shrubs suggested a genuine affection for nature in the great landowner; but it also ministered to his sense of himself, by giving him the feeling that as far as his eye could see all had been shaped to his heart's desire. The plan was also such that a vast distance had been placed between him and people in general.

The combination of country house landscape-gardening with the general movement for land improvement and ever more enclosure and for hedging and tree planting on a large scale, made a great part of the English countryside anew in the eighteenth century. The result was so visually harmonious that it was hard to believe afterwards that England's rural landscape was as man-made as its factory towns and mining villages. In England, the country was being made more beautiful just when many of its towns were about to be made more ugly; but both processes were the work of men. The 'immemorial elms' that Dutch elm disease almost banished from the English landscape in the 1970s had scarcely existed before they had been planted in such quantity (as, for example in Blenheim Park) by the great eighteenth-century landowners. The gradual elimination in the latter half of the twentieth century from many southern counties of their much loved 'natural' hedgerows was likewise a break with a 'past' that did not exist before the agricultural improvements of the latter half of the eighteenth century. Paradoxically, the 'modern' countryside acquired a less familiar, but more ancient, aspect.

The passion for gardening, so widespread in England until high land values and rival preoccupations began to erode it in the late-twentieth century, owes much to the wealthy garden makers of the eighteenth century. There is, however, a rival tradition, derived from the cottager's and mechanic's garden. With little space to hand, this emphasised flowers, which in the large garden were subordinate to the whole. This craving for colour increased when cottagers became town dwellers with even less space, surrounded by the dingy and the drab. The two separate traditions survive: one having aristocratic feeling for shape, foliage and curving 'natural' design; and the other, working class and lower middle class, athirst for 'the blaze of colour', the large-flowered bedding rose and big assertive dahlia.

4
THE ENGLISH CENTURY

Great Britain

THE Act of Union with Scotland of 1707 turned Englishmen into citizens of Great Britain and the wars between 1689 and 1763 made them beneficiaries of a Greater Britain beyond the seas. In 1739, a Scottish poet, James Thomson, wrote *Rule Britannia*; during the Jacobite rebellion of 1745 a concert audience, by spontaneously singing the recently composed *God Save the King*, turned it into the first national anthem. If at any time in their history the English may be charged with pursuing a conscious policy of acquisitive imperialism, the evidence is to be sought in the eighteenth century rather than the nineteenth.

The Union with Scotland came about chiefly because the Whigs feared the Scots might otherwise oppose the Hanoverian succession and because, if Scotland sent peers and MPs to parliament, most of them were certain to be Whigs. But it was long before the English could overcome the scorn for the Scots expressed in an early eighteenth-century remark that Scotsmen needed only eight commandments since they had nothing in their country either to covet or to steal. Initially, their poverty, clannishness and unfamiliarity with southern speech (the more ambitious of them took lessons in English pronunciation) held them back. But by the end of the century the English had been greatly enriched by the Scottish contribution to law, medicine, science, architecture and political economy. The '15 and '45 notwithstanding, the union liberated the English from their ancient fear of a Scottish alliance with a continental enemy. James II's attempt to use Ireland as a base from which to recover the crown of England in 1689 fixed Ireland in the English mind as a potential backdoor for invasion and perpetuated the tragically different view the English were to take of the Irish.

Dutch Courage

That Britain first arose 'from out the azure main' was at the command not of heaven but of William III. The events of the preceding century had shown that naval power was an adequate defence against invasion and just strong enough (though only just) to prevent the Channel coming under first Spanish and then Dutch control. For waging offensive war against, or forcing political concessions from, a major continental power it was ineffective. For more than a hundred years before 1689, the English had sought to break Spain's monopoly of trade with the

New World; but their efforts had been, for the most part, those of gallant, if legendary, losers.

The age of ineffectiveness abroad was broken by William III. He accepted the English crown in order to mobilise English naval and financial power in the service of the European coalition by which he determined to preserve Dutch independence. From 1689 to 1697 he drew England into the European war against Louis XIV known as the war of the League of Augsburg. In 1701, it was largely because he was England's king that the country entered the war precipitated when Louis XIV claimed the vacant throne of Spain on behalf of his grandson. This foreshadowed that France, already dominant in Europe, would close all the world's oceans both to the English and the Dutch.

Yet, though England gained much from the Spanish Succession war, had it not been for Dutch finance and Dutch armies, there could have been no English success and far less English glory. There were more Dutch than English among the victors at Blenheim, more Dutch than English dead at Malplaquet. It was Marlborough's particular quality to see that the war in which he figured so outstandingly was England's war precisely because it was a European war. The patriotic Tory view, however, was that English interests were being subordinated to Dutch and to Habsburg interests. The Whigs (and Marlborough) were displaced by the Tories. In 1713, at Utrecht, they made a separate peace with the French that gained the English much, but left their allies to make the best terms they could.

The war established the English for the first time as a Mediterranean power: they gained Gibraltar and Minorca. It gave them security in the Channel: there were to be no fortifications between Calais and the mouth of the Scheldt, so that in effect the French were excluded from the North Sea. It gave them at last what Drake and Hawkins had vainly battled and pillaged for: the right by treaty to trade with Spanish America, principally, though not solely, in slaves; and it gave them a foothold at the mouth of the St Lawrence.

The war's larger effects were also advantageous. France was drained of energy and resources for a whole generation, and the Dutch more permanently so. The Navigation Acts, passed in the 1650s and 1660s to prevent Dutch ships carrying British or foreign goods to British ports, were maintained throughout the war; and though the Dutch were still major carriers by sea they were never again the threat to British naval power that had justified three maritime wars against them between 1650 and 1673. Dislike of the Dutch connection, and the scant regard shown for their interests in the peace treaty, cannot disguise how much the English owed to them. There was little in the financial and agricultural techniques developed in eighteenth-century England, from the excise to the new forms of crop rotation, which had not been pioneered in Holland. Dutch investment, which starved their own industry and trade, provided an important part of British financial strength until the

1770s. The fashion for red brick domestic architecture and, less attractively, the addiction to the planting of laurel and the drinking of gin, were of Dutch origin. Dutch influence stimulated the immigration of other victims, or opponents, of Bourbon or Habsburg religious obscurantism, such as Huguenots, Germans, Sephardic Jews and Portuguese. Dutch William had brought England out into the world and had enabled it to become the open society it could never have been under rulers as glumly Catholic as James II and his son and grandson.

Deeds that Won—and Nearly Lost—an Empire

Tory dislike of continental entanglement was appeased during the long peace over which Walpole presided. But, by 1739, the patriotic Whigs felt he had lapsed into Stuartlike indifference to English commerce. London merchants and the South Sea Company were avid for markets. Sugar planters in the West Indies wanted Spanish competition eliminated. The strategically minded saw France recovering and forging close links with Spain. Their pressure forced Walpole into war with Spain. Much was made of Captain Jenkins' ear. It had, they said, been severed by the Spanish. Preserved in a bottle, it was displayed in the commons to demonstrate the insupportable brutalities to which, because of their rulers' cowardly pacifism, Englishmen sailing the high seas, their God-given element, were being subjected.

The complexities of war and foreign policy placed severe strain on the court Whigs who had ruled since 1714. Walpole and his successor, Henry Pelham, were men of peace, whom war filled with foreboding because it wrecked their hopes of keeping taxes low. Walpole was therefore an almost inevitable victim of the decision to fight Spain in 1739. But, by 1742, there was added to England's quarrel with Spain, another, created by Frederick the Great's invasion, in 1740, of the province of Silesia, which belonged to Maria Theresa of Austria. George II had little interest in England's quarrel with Spain, but much in what might happen to Hanover during a war in Germany. Accordingly, to the distress of both Pelham and Newcastle, George conducted his foreign policy not through them, but through their brilliant, European-minded colleague, Carteret, later to become Lord Granville. Plunging England into a complicated continental diplomacy, he allied with Austria, first against Spain, and then against France, thus reviving the traditions of the wars of William III and Anne. The results were disastrous. The Spanish issue was almost lost to sight. English blood and English gold were being spilled unavailingly in a dynastic continental war. George II personally led a combined Anglo-Hanoverian force to victory over the French at Dettingen in 1743; but did so wearing, not English, but Hanoverian colours. And in 1745, English troops were beaten at Fontenoy; while in expectation of French aid, Jacobite forces entered England from Scotland. By 1748 there was stalemate. At Aix-la Chapelle, the parties to the war handed back their conquests. This meant that war would certainly be renewed. Of the quarrel between England and Spain the treaty made no mention.

The Pelhams were so agitated by these developments that in 1744 and 1746 they staged what amounted to a sit-down strike against George until he consented to abandon Granville, on the grounds, not altogether just, that he was conducting foreign policy purely in the interests of Hanover. Faced with the choice between pleasing George II and losing control of the commons, the Pelhams took the risk of upsetting the king. For the commons was coming increasingly under the spell of William Pitt. The Elder Pitt combined, in his theatrical person, independence of spirit and freedom from the blandishments of corruption with a gift for patriotic oratory which at last gave a focus to country Whigs and Tories alike, since it was allied to furious denunciations, first of what he considered Walpole's pusillanimity, and then of official preoccupation with Hanover. He called Hanover 'a despicable electorate', and Carteret an 'infamous minister who seems to have renounced the name of Englishman'. This language made Pitt so objectionable to George II that, as his price for parting with Granville in 1746, he refused to let Pitt enter the ministry save as paymaster general, and not as secretary at war. Pitt supported the Pelhams loyally enough for the rest of the war and gained much personal prestige out of this minor appointment by ostentatiously refusing (unlike other holders of the post) to take more out of it than the official salary of £4000. This further strengthened his reputation as a Great Commoner whom the court could not corrupt. It was, however, the measure of the Pelhams' triumph in thus taming both George II and Pitt that, in the elections of 1747, there were only sixty-two contests and the Whigs got a majority that saw them peacefully through the remaining eight years of Pelham's life. He died just before the election of 1754 which gave the court Whigs the largest majority of the century.

Full scale war resumed in 1756. In Europe, Frederick the Great of Prussia was now England's ally against Austria and France. Outside Europe, French and British colonists wre already fighting in North America and the forces of the British and French East India Companies waging war in India.

Here was Pitt's opportunity. Already enraged that Newcastle had not made him the ministry's leader in the commons and professing to be outraged at the policy of subsidising Frederick the Great to protect Hanover, he became more and more hostile to Newcastle as the Seven Years War threatened to be as disastrous as the Austrian Succession War. The French captured Minorca, one of Britain's great naval gains in the Spanish Succession War. A neurotic government had Admiral Byng court-martialled and executed for losing the island. In a succession of desperate manoeuvres, an irascible king and a flustered Newcastle tried and failed to escape the inevitable. By 1757, faced with the threat of losing control of the commons, Newcastle had to be reconciled with Pitt and the king had to accept the consequences. From then until 1761, England's most rapacious and triumphant war was directed by Newcastle, by now an ageing hypochondriac whose principal role was to raise the money and manage the patronage, and Pitt, who conceived and saw to the execution of a strategy of almost unlimited maritime conquest. Pitt, several of whose relations were insane, alternated periods of furious energy and histrionic oratory with periods of physical and nervous prostration, euphemistically called 'gout', or, with unconvincing precision, 'gout in the bowels', or 'gout in the head'. The most melodramatic imperialist of them all, he displayed an arrogant addiction to conquest for the sake of commercial gain which a Lloyd George of his day would have ferociously denounced; and, more fortunate than Winston Churchill, he bestrode a world in which England had everything to gain and everywhere to attack, instead of everything to lose and everything to defend.

Pitt's strategy was to make the European war a large-scale diversionary operation to harass the French, so that the main business of destroying their overseas power could be pursued without fear of French attack in the Channel. To this end he subsidised Frederick the Great (a policy he had violently opposed until he adopted it himself) and perpetually attacked French ports to keep their armies at home and cut off their supply lines to their overseas possessions. His main overseas objective was Canada. To rob the French of this would deprive them and their empire of most of their colonial trade. In the event, Pitt secured much more than Canada. By 1759, Guadeloupe was taken, producing so great a plunder of coffee, ginger, cocoa, cotton and rum as to make it seem as rich a prize as all Canada. All French trading stations in Senegal were seized, offering prospects of rich trade in slaves and ivory; and at Quiberon Bay the French fleet was so signally defeated that on New Year's day, 1760, David Garrick led his entire Drury Lane company in the singing of a new, specially composed number entitled 'Hearts of Oak'. To all this was added Wolfe's capture of Quebec, and Clive's victory over the French in India at Plassey.

'We'll fight and we'll conquer again and again' was the punch line of 'Hearts of Oak' and the literal definition of Pitt's war policy. He still wanted Martinique, the richest remaining French sugar island and Mauritius, the naval base vital to their power in India. Beyond these, he wanted the rich loot of the Spanish empire: Florida, Cuba, Mexico, South America and the Philippines. Accordingly he demanded war with Spain, hitherto neutral.

War with Spain did come, in 1762; but not as the result of the pre-emptive strike against Havana, Manila and the Spanish treasure fleet that Pitt had demanded. The Spanish themselves declared war in order to help the French put pressure on the English to make peace. The situation was increasingly dangerous. Britannia's rule over the waves involved the principle that, in effect, virtually all goods shipped to an enemy power were seized as contraband of war. This high-handed English version of 'the freedom of the seas' made Sweden, Denmark, Holland and the Italian maritime states likely candidates for a European coalition against England headed by France, Austria and Spain. Pitt's colleagues and the new king, George III, therefore forced him out of office in 1761 by refusing to let him make England the aggressor against Spain. But his work survived him, if only briefly. In 1762, Martinique and all the remaining French sugar island were captured. Havana was taken and, with it, three million dollars and a fifth of the Spanish navy. Manila, the great entrepôt between China and Mexico, was overrun and pillaged.

Nevertheless, peace came in 1763, by the sacrifice of Frederick the Great and the Duke of Newcastle. To force the hand of the former, George III and his new minister, Bute, cut off his subsidy; and Newcastle, a minister for forty years and heir to the European traditions of the reign of Anne, resigned rather than support this abandonment of an ally without whom it would have been impossible to fight the war. As at Utrecht, the English made peace by deserting their strongest continental ally.

By the Treaty of Paris, England kept Minorca, additional West Indian islands, Florida, Canada, all Louisiana east of the Mississippi, and paramountcy in India. Martinique, Guadeloupe, Havana and Manila were given back to France and Spain. To Pitt, denouncing it in parliament in the awesome voice of an emaciated, flannel-encased spectre of doom, it was a peace craven and inept, and a base betrayal of Prussia. John Wilkes wrote that it was a peace that passed all understanding. That its architect was the young George III's 'dear friend' and tutor, Lord Bute, made matters worse. To the offence of an allegedly craven peace and of displacing both Pitt and Newcastle, he added that of being a Scotsman. Two months after the peace was signed he was out of office.

Yet the course of the war of American Independence, from 1775 to 1783, showed how much hostility England had aroused on the continent and how dangerous that hostility was. France, Spain and Holland all supported the rebel colonists. Sweden, Denmark and Prussia armed themselves to resist the British claim to search their ships on the high seas. The surrender of Cornwallis at Yorktown to a combined French and colonial force in 1781 was a salutary reminder of the vulnerability of British sea power when it had a hostile Europe in its rear. The British lost not only the Thirteen Colonies by the treaty of Versailles in 1783 but all the rest of their North American territory south of the Great Lakes, as well as Tobago, St Lucia, Minorca and Senegal; but for a timely victory by Admiral Rodney against the French in the West Indies, even more might have been lost.

The English never quite regained their old high-handed delight in conquering 'again and again' once the Thirteen Colonies were lost.

When, like Burke, Pitt, by then ennobled as the Earl of Chatham, condemned the government's efforts to coerce the Thirteen Colonies as futile and ignoble he began a tradition of anti-imperialism that lasted as long as the empire itself.

Age of Imperialism

The wars of the years from 1689 to 1783 have little hold on the English imagination. Blenheim is primarily a touristical 'great house', Marlborough recollected because his family name was Churchill. Wolfe still dies at Quebec in the folk memory. But Dettingen, Fontenoy, the valour of the infantry and artillery in the defeat of the French at Minden in 1749, the naval triumph at Quiberon Bay, and even Clive's success at Plassey, are interred in the least-read pages of the duller textbooks. An age disenchanted with Empire recalls the surrenders to the American colonists at Saratoga in 1777 and at Yorktown in 1781 as if they were representative occurrences. Yet the deeds that really won an empire were not performed by Elizabethan seadogs or by minor Victorian skirmishes like Rorke's Drift or Omdurman, but during the fifth and sixth decades of the eighteenth century. These were the years that settled that the English would become a Mediterranean and Atlantic power, that North America would be built on 'Anglo-Saxon' foundations, and that India would emerge into the twentieth century with English as its common language.

Eighteenth-century imperialism was ruthless and deliberately fostered by government. It was pursued, not to spread civilisation, nor to convert the heathen; such considerations intruded into Victorian imperialism, rendering it self-conscious and hesitant. It was pursued as part of an expansionist commercial policy committed to denying foreigners (and colonists) from as much of the world's trade as possible, so that England should have as large and exclusive a trading empire as could be obtained: an empire protected by trade discrimination against foreigners and colonists and by restrictions on their right to ship goods to and from England and its possessions. Policy, whether in war or peace, was directed to the crude accumulation of wealth. The balance of trade must always be in England's favour.

The policy succeeded. Dutch shipping was surpassed, the French overseas empire all but destroyed. It was an imperialism of unashamed competition and exploitation, its most coveted and valuable commodity the sugar of the Caribbean, its sinews the trade in African slaves. Unlike the predominantly dynastic policies pursued by continental powers, it was sustained by the active consent of the political nation. Only three times in the century were governments enjoying royal support and commanding the resources of the patronage system overthrown by a revolt of the commons. On each occasion the cause was popular and journalistic clamour against government incompetence in wartime. It was for this reason that Walpole was ejected in 1742, Newcastle in 1757 and Lord North in 1782. The starting point of the public career of John Wilkes was his journalistic attack on the Treaty of Paris. It was another century before the word 'jingoism' was invented; the phenomenon it described was, like the occasion that inspired it, almost an aberration in Victorian England. In Georgian England it was a consistent national mood, until the salutary calamities of the war of American Independence. After it, official British imperialism was basically defensive. The growth of empire thereafter was an uncoordinated, embarrassed and reluctant acceptance of increasing commitments by governments dragged by eager pioneers and aggressive visionaries towards a greatness that many regarded as at once costly and dangerous.

Scum of the Earth and Jolly Tars

The contrast between civilians politicking about war and the rank and file actually fighting it was extreme. The small size of the army must be related to the fact that though in the first half of the century there were not many more than a million adult males between the ages of sixteen and sixty, the number under arms in Anne's reign at times reached nearly 200,000, while from Walpole's time onwards the peacetime army usually numbered between 30,000 and 40,000. Impressment for the army declined after 1688; native forces were supplemented in wartime by foreign mercenaries. Orders were nevertheless given in 1779, in the crisis of the war of American Independence, to press all London's rogues and vagabonds into the army. The resultant enlistment of those too poor to bribe parish constables to overlook them or too stupid or lame to run away caused the regular army to encourage these new recruits to desert immediately. The device was not repeated.

The social status of army officers was largely guaranteed by the fact that from 1720 onwards commissions were obtainable by purchase, supplemented, of course, by patronage. Army officers thus tended to be less professional than naval officers, whose commissions could not be purchased. Dislike of soldiers persisted. Barracks were built from 1722 onwards, but were always opposed. The practice of concentrating and segregating soldiers was held harmful to civil liberties. The common soldier was considered the lowest of the low, his calling a sign of his unfitness for civilian employment. Wellington's later verdict that the rankers of his time were 'the scum of the earth, enlisted for drink' was, however, accompanied by a tribute to their bravery. The readiness of these despised men to fight for a country that thought so little of them testified to the low level of expectation that civilian life had to offer them.

These last considerations applied even more to naval ratings. Unlike the soldier, the sailor was popular. He was affectionately personified as a jolly jack tar more than a century before the soldier was depicted as a good-hearted Tommy Atkins. This was partly because sailors spent most of their time conveniently out of the way on the high seas, whereas soldiers were the means by which authority could oppress the people by subduing their riots. Yet most sailors were victims of the press gang, a random catch of conscripts. Subject to the immunity of certain fishermen supplying London and Westminster, all seafaring men, and watermen on rivers, were liable to repeated impressment between the ages of eighteen and fifty-five. So also were all whom the justices designated as rogues and vagabonds. Prisoners from gaols were pressed too, frequently infecting whole ships with typhus as a result. In 1795, debtors and desperate men of all sorts were pressed; their influence was alleged to have contributed to the naval mutinies of 1797. At critical periods during the war with Napoleon, the navy would impress crew-members of passing merchantmen on the high seas and, with a fine contempt for American independent sovereignty, seize men from United States merchant ships, alleging they were British citizens. Impressment died out in practice after 1815, but its legality was reaffirmed as late as 1835, in an act limiting the period of impressment to five years.

That such material was welded into a successful fighting service was due to the generally high standard of British ships and to the competence as well as the despotic authority of ships' commanders. The food was as bad as the discipline was inhuman. Crews were turned off as soon as they were no longer required, yet with no guarantee that they would not be pressed again and again in the future. The only consolation was the chance of prize money; but of that, the officers took more than the lion's share. The expedition to Havana in 1762 enriched the two principal commanders by just under £123,000 each. The ordinary seaman got £3.14.9¾d (£3.74) each. It is not unreasonable to suggest that ordinary soldiers and sailors suffered more from the hard-heartedness of the age than paupers, agricultural labourers and factory workers. When asked what was his view of 'the naval tradition', Winston Churchill said, 'Monstrous. Nothing but rum, sodomy, prayers and the lash'.

5

GEORGE III, THE POLITICIANS AND THE PEOPLE

The King and the Politicians

THE accession of George III in 1760 introduced into the high politics of the century a confusion that bewilders all but the most dedicated of students. And, although the many ambiguities of the forty years thereafter were important for the development of the English system of government, equally significant was the growth, after 1760, of a political consciousness among people in general that went on independently of the politicians at Westminster, though it sometimes irrupted upon them, usually to their great alarm. Yet in certain respects, George III, as well as greatly changing the character of Westminster politics, himself contributed, to his dismay, to the emergence of 'popular' politics.

Pitt had come to power in 1757, against the wishes of both George II and Newcastle, because of his combination of demagogy and patriotism. The spectacle of an incorruptible patriot untainted by party allegiance, contemptuous in his time both of the crown and of its ministers, rising despite their hostility to a position from which he could orchestrate a war in which victories were won all over the globe, had an appeal so wide that only the prose of a Macaulay can adequately express it. Pitt's situation 'at the close of the reign of George the Second,' Macaulay wrote,

was the most enviable ever occupied by any public man in English history. He had conciliated the King; he domineered over the House of Commons; he was adored by the people; he was admired by all Europe. He was the first Englishman of his time; and he had made England the first country in the world.

Unluckily for Pitt, he found himself outflanked after 1760 by the new king, George III. An immature young man, uncharitably virtuous, George was as convinced as the most disgruntled of Tories that the nation needed saving from the rule of a corrupt oligarchy and from costly involvement in continental war. One may suspect the only reason George III did not say, 'I am sure I can save this country and nobody else can', was that Pitt said it first. George saw himself as a truer patriot than Pitt in 1761. Pitt's grand global strategy was ruining the nation's finances, inducing war-weariness and committing England too closely to Frederick the Great. George fervently believed that Pitt was prolonging a 'bloody and expensive war' to preserve his own power and that of the Whig oligarchs who had corrupted the nation and interposed themselves between the king and his people. George was thus overjoyed when Pitt's colleagues forced his resignation in 1761 over the issue of war with Spain. Pitt's fall would have caused the king less unpopularity had George not, immediately upon his accession, appointed his tutor, Lord Bute, as a principal minister and relied on him exclusively. Bute's only qualifications for high office were that he was handsome and amiable, and had a concern for virtue as earnest as that of his admiring royal pupil. The view, therefore, that George had begun his reign by exalting Bute, a mere favourite, at the expense of Pitt, the nation's hero, was the first of the several political sins of which this most unfortunate of English kings would be accused.

The real havoc George caused, however, came when he forced Newcastle to resign in 1762. This he did by persistently conducting ministerial business behind Newcastle's back, chiefly through Bute. This meant not only that crown patronage would now be controlled by the king himself, but also that the Whig patronage system managed by Newcastle fell apart. Both George I and George II, mainly through fear of Jacobitism, had been, in effect, the chiefest of court Whigs; but George III acted as a sort of crowned 'country' Tory, trying to create, within a commons containing very few Tories, a permanent body of reliable 'court' Tories. Though most of them would be 'renegade' Whigs, whom Macaulay would duly denounce as 'a reptile species of politician', they were nicknamed 'The King's Friends'. But, by themselves, neither court patronage nor a fragmented Whig patronage could control the commons, which quickly made life so intolerable for Bute that he resigned in 1763. From then until 1770, four successive ministries came to grief, torn between the devil who wore the crown and the deep blue sea of confusion, over personalities and principles, which the commons inevitably now became.

Not until 1770 did George III find, in Lord North, a chief minister able, for as long as twelve years, to achieve the task of pleasing the king without wholly alienating the commons. Though it would be unfair to say that North took orders as faithfully as a royal coachman, there remain doubts as to whether it was North or the king who was the real head of this administration. North stayed in power partly because he was personally well-liked; partly because on the great issue of the struggle with the Thirteen Colonies, the commons felt bound to support one who, in spite of himself, was the political leader of a nation facing rebellion in North America and war on the high seas; and finally because his easygoing, irresolute character was continually kept up to the mark by the dogged, if blinkered courage of George III. When in 1782, a year after it became evident that the North American colonies had been lost, North finally resigned, it was as if a beloved household retainer were informing a deeply revered employer that he was so broken down by the burden of his duties that he had no choice but to hand in his notice.

North's fall in 1782 appeared to deliver George into the hands of a group of opposition Whigs led by Lord Rockingham. Within months, Rockingham died; and George, on personal grounds, refused to appoint the obvious successor, Charles James Fox. Fox, for scarcely less personal reasons, then formed an alliance with North to unseat George's preferred choice, Shelburne. Despite a six-weeks' resistance, George had to accept a Fox-North coalition, nominally led by the Whig Duke of Portland. George could do nothing until he had found an issue on which to dismiss this detested ministry, a reliable candidate to replace Portland, and time to use crown patronage and treasury influence to organise a successful general election. Astutely, he accused his Whiggish ministers of organising a new and outrageous form of corruption in their proposals for the future of the East India Company; and secured the Bill's rejection in the Lords by letting it be known that he would consider as his personal enemy any peer who voted for it. He then dismissed the Coalition; and invited the elder Pitt's second son, William Pitt the younger, to form an administration in December 1783.

Hardly less arrogant at twenty-four than his sovereign had been at twenty-two, the younger Pitt had already shown himself as ambitious as his father (though in a more controlled manner) no less independent and with even more administrative talent. He had been Shelburne's chancellor of the exchequer at the age of twenty-one and had ostentatiously refused to join the coalition that had removed Shelburne. As well as pointedly holding aloof from what had seemed a cynical connection between the king's most eloquent critic, Fox, and the king's most devoted 'Friend', North, he had repeatedly promoted bills, which had predictably failed to get through, to limit the patronage system. He had thus, like his father, acquired merit as an opponent of corruption; and, in the elections of 1784, the fact that the electorate rated such a man above the excessively anti-monarchical, apparently cynical and certainly dissolute Fox, counted almost as much as the success of the crown in organising Pitt and his growing band of parliamentary followers a sound majority. The size of the Pittites' electoral victory contrasted greatly with the derision with which Fox and his friends had greeted Pitt's first appearance as chief minister and the several adverse votes he suffered in the commons before the dissolution.

The King and his Ministers

After twenty-five years of devoted toil, George had learned not to pin his hopes on a political nonentity like Bute, but on the younger Pitt, an almost certain winner. But Pitt turned out a winner in a sense no one expected. The most important political development of the thirty-five years after 1784 was that from 1788 onwards George III was at first intermittently and then, from 1811 until his death in 1820, permanently, incapacitated by an obscure disease now considered to have been porphyria. Not easily distinguishable from insanity, it first attacked him at the end of 1788. First manifest in eccentricity, such as allegedly gravely saluting a tree in Windsor Park under the impression that it was the King of Prussia, it rapidly became serious enough for him to be put in a strait-jacket. Though he recovered, his capacity for business was so diminished that Pitt's personal ascendancy greatly increased. The only serious act of royal policy thereafter was George's refusal to accept, in the Act of Union with Ireland in 1800, clauses that would emancipate Roman Catholics from their civil and political disabilities. Hysterically declaring that to do so would be contrary to his coronation oath, George thereby precipitated a brief recurrence of his mental incapacity, the temporary displacement of Pitt's ministry and lasting damage to Ireland.

When Pitt came back in 1804, Catholic emancipation had to be avoided at all costs. It would drive the king mad again and, worse still, lead to a Regency under his erratic and scandalous son, the future George IV, to whom Fox was an ancient crony. Though Pitt's death in 1806 led to a Whig Ministry of the Talents, led by Grenville, including, to the king's disgust, Fox, George dismissed it in 1807 the moment they once more raised the Catholic issue; and the ministers themselves were not sorry to go, since, for all that the Whigs believed in their right to govern, they had small confidence in their capacity to do so. The Pittites came back; and stayed. By 1812, George III having by that time become a blind, white-bearded old man, forever talking of people long since dead, his son at last became Prince Regent. But, like Pitt, Fox died in 1806; and the Regent, for all his old loyalty to the Whigs, offered them no more than membership of a coalition with their rivals. This they declined; and the Regent therefore refused to dismiss the more or less Pittite government that was now being led with increasing competence by Spencer Perceval. It was, by 1812, a winning team which would shortly turn the Prince Regent in his own eyes (though in nobody else's) into the conqueror of Napoleon Bonaparte.

Despite this initial exercise of his royal authority to determine who should be his ministers, George IV, as Regent until 1820, and as king from then until 1830, often disturbed, but never really upset, the ministerial applecart. When Catholic Emancipation became inevitable in 1829 if civil war in Ireland was to be avoided, he tearfully called in aid the ghost of his 'revered and sainted father'; and, even more tearfully, gave way. The decline of monarchical power was demonstrated when William IV contrived, in 1834, the replacement of a shaky Whig government by a Tory one. The outcome was a general election that forced him to have the Whigs back again. In the 1840s, the combination of Peel's authoritarian efficiency as prime minister with Prince Albert's devotion to the ideal of 'constitutional monarchy', finally established the crown's acceptance of the principle that real sovereignty in the state lay in a cabinet headed by a prime minister accountable, not to the monarch, but to parliament.

King and Party

George III's determination to undermine their political power had raised questions the Whigs were long in solving. All the governments of the 1760s were Whiggish. This was true of a disastrous 'all party' government of 1766–68 led, though often *in absentia*, by the elder Pitt, by that time no longer the 'Great Commoner' but the unpopular pensioner-peer, Lord Chatham, hovering on the borders between sanity and madness. Similarly, North accounted himself a Whig. But the only likely future of a Whig group which refused to take orders from the crown as a matter of course was that of an opposition. But whatever else Whigs had doubts about, they firmly believed that all governments ought to be Whig governments, dominated by Whig peers and preferably Whig dukes. It was a conviction that survived the Reform Bill of 1832 and Whig assimilation into the Liberal party in the 1860s. It was thus inevitable that many Whigs should go over to the king's side in the 1760s and that more still should do so when the French Revolution and the resultant war threatened not only national security but the aristocratic principle everywhere. Indeed, almost all politicians tended to proclaim their loyalty to Whig principles. Like North, the younger Pitt regarded himself as a Whig. By the 1780s, there were so few old-style Tories left that 'Tory' became merely a word that described someone hopelessly old-fashioned. It reappeared in 1807 along with the traditional Tory slogans of 'The Church in Danger', 'Church and King' and 'No Popery' as the designation of those who opposed the desire of the Foxite Whigs to force George III to agree to Catholic emancipation. It was only slowly that it became usual to label the Pittite governments of 1807 to 1830 as 'Tory'. 'Government' and 'Opposition' or 'Pittite' and 'Foxite' were for long the more usual terms.

The opposition Whigs' second problem was that, though opposition to the king's government on particular issues or for particular reasons was acceptable, 'opposition' pursued to force the sovereign to replace his chosen ministers by persons acceptable to that 'opposition' was thought disreputable, not least by the aristocratic Whigs themselves. What the English had become used to since 1714 was one-party government mitigated by tolerated parliamentary dissent. Just as the religious dissenters were not legally entitled to hold public office, so, for half a century, Tory MPs were, though allowed to contribute to parliamentary business, more or less debarred from ministerial office. The Whigs were therefore compelled to seek a formula which would enable them to dissociate opposition from the stigma of being a 'self-interested faction' and from the prospect of permanent exclusion from office. The formula took a long time to work out.

First came an appeal to the past. The Glorious Revolution, it was said, had established a mixed constitution, with a limited monarchy. George III, the Whigs claimed, was destroying that mixed constitution by re-establishing personal monarchy, a view celebrated in the motion accepted by the commons in 1780, that 'the power of the crown has increased, is increasing and ought to be diminished'. This instantly linked the opposition Whigs of the 1780s with such noble figures in the story of English liberty as Sir John Eliot in the 1620s and Shaftesbury in the 1680s. But George III also venerated the constitution; and he could with equal justice have advanced in 1760 a proposition about the power of the Whigs identical with their resolution about him in 1780. To claim that no monarch since 1688 had made a chief minister out of a Bute, supervised a chief minister as closely as George had supervised North or created as powerful a one as the younger Pitt by a royal coup would have been fair enough. But it was never more than propaganda to describe this as a violation of the constitution, just as it was the merest slander to call George a tyrant.

Fortunately, George III's use of his powers forced the opposition Whigs to go beyond mere name-calling. Though an ever-decreasing band for the rest of the century, they did evolve the principle that the chief bulwark of political liberty was the existence within the state of two parties, both in competition for office. It was false, wrote Edmund Burke, thereby providing a Whig condemnation of the forty years of Whig rule after 1714, to believe 'that the idea of a united administration carries with it that of a proscription of any other party'. It was also, he claimed, 'Necessary often to destroy administration to support Government—remedy the disorders and confusions at the head'. Without true party, government would tend to be based upon the corruption of the venal and the proscription of the principled. True party, as Burke defined it, was 'a body of men united for promoting by their joint endeavours *the national interest* upon some particular principle in which they are all agreed', or as another Whig put it, a body of 'persons united in principle, concurring in sentiment, and bound together by affection'. Party was thus the best guarantee against faction. When party was strong, those who were out of office but in search of it would be less liable to seduction by government patronage; and, most important for the future, true party would concentrate opposition within parliament itself and thus prevent it degenerating into popular radicalism or leading to dangerous notions of democracy.

Naturally, the political practice of the opposition Whigs was on a less exalted level. It was hard to escape the impression that the Foxite Whigs opposed Pitt solely because they thought Fox and not Pitt should be in office. That Fox, the most vehement opponent of the crown, should have allied temporarily with North in 1783, and permanently with the Prince of Wales, suggested that Fox's chief political policy was that of waiting for the death of George III or Pitt, or of both. Fox's hatred of royal power and his resentment over his defeat at George's hands in 1784, put him on the side of the future in that he was forever insisting that the conditions on which a ministry should govern should be decided by the ministers and not by the crown; but it put him on the wrong side in his own lifetime. His resentment also contributed to his continuing to applaud the French Revolution long after Burke had convinced most of the political nation that it was a catastrophe; and to his opposition to the war with France on the grounds, not altogether unreasonable, that it was a war for the defence of despotic monarchy. Most of the Whig grandees, however, took their line from Burke and supported Pitt. The number of opposition Whigs soon became so small that it was said there were hardly enough of them to fill two hansom cabs.

Nor was it likely, in wartime, that a large following could be secured for a leader like Fox who, dissolute himself, identified so closely with a dissolute heir to the throne whose behaviour was popularly considered, along with that of his equally scandalous brothers, to be driving an aged royal father to insanity. Fox claimed to stand for the sovereignty of the people; but it is hard to acquit him of being principally concerned with waiting upon the day when the sovereignty of the future George IV would make Fox chief minister. When Cobbett declared in 1812 that Whiggish references to 'the principles of Charles James Fox' stood for 'almost everything and almost nothing', he was not altogether wrong. Fox's followers, however, considered only his advocacy of the removal of religious disabilities, the elimination of corruption, the abolition of the slave trade and the overthrow of despotism everywhere. Yet, during his brief tenure of office in 1806 he had time before his death only to set in motion legislation to end the slave trade, completed in 1807. Otherwise, his attitude as a minister was that of Pitt, namely that reform was not possible in wartime. Just as Fox's early habits of debauchery had, by 1806, given way to a life of quiet domesticity with a retired prostitute, his ardour for 'the people' had likewise cooled. His successors, Grenville and Grey, behaved less like Fox's heirs than his pall-bearers, acting with timorous, patrician fastidiousness and showing none of Fox's strong, if rather sulky, yearning for office. When, in 1812, after Perceval was murdered, the 'Foxites' refused to join any government they did not dominate, they were again discredited. Suspecting the Regent of bad faith, they lacked the courage to put him to the test. Lord Liverpool took over as a 'Pittite' prime minister, to hold that office for longer than any other nineteenth-century prime minister. And when circumstances at last pushed Grey into office in 1830 to preside over the crisis that produced the Reform Act of 1832, he behaved rather like a man of the highest breeding who found himself unexpectedly called upon to wash his own linen; and disgustedly resigned in 1834.

Yet, just as it was Burke's view of 'party' that would eventually be accepted, so it was with Fox's view of the role of the crown in the constitution. Equally, it was his association of Whiggishness with 'reform' and with ideas that by the 1820s would come to be called 'liberal' that enabled Whiggery to survive the profound changes of the years from 1780 to 1830 and to emerge from them as accredited champions of reform, even though their advocacy would be highly selective and often more rhetorical than real. On the other side, the prolonged resistance of Pitt and the Pittite Tories to the ideas and causes for which Fox had stood, identified the Tories as the party of law and order and of the continued subordination of the great majority of the people to the traditional ruling élite; even though their actual views were rarely more severe than those of the Whigs, themselves an even more traditional ruling élite. Various practical considerations account for the gradual emergence by the 1840s of a genuine two-party system within parliament in place of the eighteenth century's record of one-party rule followed by a confusion of factions. But, in the minds of both politicians and people, what mattered most was that the combined effects of revolution and war abroad, and industrial transformation at home, were gradually to create a real division within the political nation as a whole. What had begun as an almost private political dispute at Westminster about what George III's powers were, and reached a climax in the defeat of Fox by George and Pitt in 1784 had, by the 1830s, become a serious social and intellectual issue between proponents of tradition and advocates of change, transforming politics into a continuing national debate between those who would preserve the past and those who would change it.

King, Politicians and Popular Protest

The years when George III directed political affairs most personally were also remarkable for the two most dramatic popular disturbances of the eighteenth century: the riots associated with the slogan, 'Wilkes and Liberty' in the 1760s and the sensational Gordon Riots of 1780. The Wilkes riots were different in kind from, and the Gordon riots larger in scale than, the riots which had regularly punctuated, though they had never punctured, the century's apparently solid calm.

Riots were as much a feature of eighteenth-century life as strikes, protest marches and demonstrations became during the years after 1950. Least comparable with such modern manifestations were food riots, provoked by bad harvest and high bread prices; but these, though constituting around half the total of riots during the century, relate to economic rather than political factors. Particular to the decades before 1780 were riots directed against specific government policies. Scattered Jacobite riots at the accession of George I and during the 1715 elections induced the Whigs to pass the Riot Act of that year. This empowered magistrates to call in troops if any crowd of more than twelve refused to disperse within an hour of being ordered to do so. Defiance of such an order was added to the century's long list of offences punishable by death; and though rioters seem to have caused about a score of fatalities, over a hundred rioters were hanged and over six hundred persons killed by troops during the century after 1730.

It was, however, often hard to find a magistrate tough enough to 'read the Riot Act' to a roaring crowd; and sometimes harder still to expect local JPs, probably themselves as Tory at heart, and as suspicious of a Hanoverian-Whiggish government as the rioters they were required to suppress, to send for troops. To call out the local militia, officered by the gentry, and with an unwilling rank and file of the rioters' friends and neighbours, was not always practical either. Those who did call for troops were soon begging for them to be removed. They often caused more uproar than the rioters.

Rioters were usually neither the criminal, the hooligan nor the destitute, but respectable wage-earning labourers, independent craftsmen, shopkeepers and small manufacturers. Women often took part, exploiting the protection their sex afforded them. In general, those brought to trial after the more substantial riots of the time were of better standing than the informers put up by the authorities as witnesses against them. Rioters would gather in a noisy, marching crowd, chanting slogans and attacking the property of whoever was in some way held to be responsible for, or associated with, the grievance of the moment. They would smash windows and 'pull down' houses, by wrenching away doors and shutters. They rarely inflicted bodily harm; and some crowds would disperse with 'huzzas' all round if an officer of the militia could succeed in assuring them their grievance would shortly be attended to, or if some responsible person would offer to help them draw up a petition to parliament. Yet, whatever the grievance behind any riot, it was usually inadvisable to appear to be better off than the rioters thought proper. Most riots were something of a general protest against social injustice. Whenever agricultural or manufacturing machinery was broken by rioters in the century before 1820 the purpose was as much to impose a fine on a man for being a profiteer or for paying low wages as to attack machinery as such. When an anti-Catholic riot was in progress it might not be enough to claim not to be a papist; it was dangerous to appear more prosperous than was thought fitting in a godly Protestant. Whatever the cause of the riot, it was also dangerous to be a foreigner or, as the century progressed, a Methodist. Anti-Methodist riots occurred in various parts of the country in the 1740s.

The accession of the Hanoverians and the collapse of the South Sea Company caused riots; there were several riots against low wages on Tyneside before 1750; and among west country textile workers from 1738 onwards, three of the 1738 rioters being hanged. More typical were the so-called Gin Riots of 1736, when Walpole tried to stop the indiscriminate sale of gin. The London riots of that year seem to have begun with a riot against the employment of cheap immigrant Irish labour and then become intertwined with protests against the compulsory burial of 'Mother Gin'. This was an affront to liberty, an attack on property and an effort to reduce freeborn, gin-drinking Englishmen to the level of the common people of France, whose enslaved status was proved by their having to wear 'wooden shoes'. 'No wooden shoes!' was, for some time, the eighteenth century's parallel to the 'Fascists Out!' of the twentieth. There were riots, too, when turnpike or enclosure acts threatened local rights of way or trade, such as the turnpike riots in Yorkshire in 1753 and the enclosure riots in Wiltshire in 1758. There were riots when the calendar was reformed in 1753 to bring it into line with the Gregorian calendar used on the continent. This meant legislating eleven days out of the September of that year, and arranging for the New Year of 1754 to begin on 1 January instead of 25 March, as had been the practice when using the Julian calendar. The riots were not merely irrational. The removal of eleven days from the calendar raised problems concerning rents, leases and debts and was probably a more complex change than the assimilation of the currency to the continent's decimal system in 1971. The adjustment was evidently too much for the revenue department, which still begins and ends its calculations on 5 April, the Julian calendar's New Year's Day of 25 March. The other eighteenth-century innovation, the large workhouse serving a union of parishes, also provoked riots. In East Anglia, in 1765, two such new Houses of Industry were attacked by paupers determined that their deaths, though miserable, should at least take place in their own villages. There were riots between 1757 and 1761 against the attempt to register all men between the ages of eighteen and fifty for possible service in the county militia to supplement the regular army during the Seven Years War. An army, even locally recruited, was as detestable to free Englishmen as popery.

Though riots of this sort were less frequent than food riots, they gave colour to the Whig belief that only one-party government, involving the banishment of as many Tories from Westminster as possible and the 'lenient measures' of a studiously cautious Walpole and the 'quiet' administration of Henry Pelham, could keep the peace in a society with so much potential for strife. Unfortunately, when he broke first Pitt and then Newcastle, George III undermined the political system which had imposed that peace. For the next ten years, the strife which it had restrained spilled out into the streets not only of Westminster and London but of most of the principal towns of the kingdom, from Falmouth to Berwick on Tweed, from Shrewsbury to Great Yarmouth, from Bristol to Margate. The cry, 'Wilkes and Liberty', first raised in the London streets in 1763 would intermittently break the public peace for almost a decade.

The Wilkes and Liberty riots were an acting out by the populace at large of political rivalries previously, and for long afterwards, presented exclusively on the parliamentary stage at Westminster. Suddenly, those whom politicians regarded purely as spectators insisted, at the instigation of an accredited, if discreditable, member of the cast, on turning affairs of state into a disorderly experiment in audience participation. George III's assumption of the duties of national manager, coinciding with John Wilkes's semi-comic performance as MP-cum-journalistic propagandist for the fallen Elder Pitt, came near to turning English politics into a theatre of the absurd in which, for the first time, nearly everybody could participate.

Wilkes owed his seat in the commons to the patronage of Earl Temple, a leading pro-Pittite peer; and served his betters' cause by writing a weekly, called, with pointed reference to the king's Scottish favourite, Bute, the *North Briton*. Its first forty-four issues attacked Bute and the Treaty of Paris scurrilously enough; but No. 45 declared that for the king to call the treaty 'honourable' was a 'falsehood' and that, by attending a service of thanksgiving there for so craven a peace, the king would profane St Paul's. For once, the king, Bute (behind the scenes by now), and his nerve-racked ministers were at one. A general warrant, naming no names, was issued for the arrest on a charge of seditious libel, of everybody connected with publishing No. 45 of the *North Briton*. Wilkes challenged the legality of general warrants in the courts and won his case, with damages against the Secretary of State. Luckily for Wilkes and liberty, the case was heard by Mr Justice Pratt, an adherent of Pitt, and an opponent of George and his ministers. The other great legal figure of the day, Lord Mansfield, was a firm upholder of the prerogative.

Not wishing to go down to posterity mummified in the case books of constitutional law, Wilkes published widely his accusations against those who had imprisoned him, with full details of his arrest and of his correspondence with the government. He played it for belly laughs, too. He hoped, when taken to the Tower, he would not be lodged in the same room as a Scotchman in case he got the itch; could he be put in a room of which one earlier inmate had been a Jacobite peer; no, he would not play cards, he did not know a king from a knave. That in private company, Wilkes was a man of whom Dr Johnson could say, 'Jack has a great variety of talk, Jack is a scholar and Jack has the manners of a gentleman' is almost irrelevant. What made him a popular champion of 'liberty' was that he was also rake, gambler and pornographer, that he squinted and leered and was ugly. Many of the best loved figures of the music halls would also be leeringly ugly comics. And Wilkes, like any good comic, knew when to reach out to the public with a sudden warm embrace to show that his heart, like theirs, was in the right place. What was at issue at his trial he declared, was 'the Liberty of all peers and gentlemen and, what touches me more sensibly, of all the middling and inferior class of people, which stands most in need of protection, and whether ENGLISH LIBERTY be a reality or a shadow'.

George and his ministers eagerly assumed the role of 'straight' men feeding this political comic. They got the commons to declare No. 45 a seditious libel and, ordering it to be burned by the hangman, expelled its author from the house. Injured in a duel, Wilkes fled to France; and was then declared an outlaw for failing to answer the charge of publishing (in fact privately circulating) a pornographic poem about women. The burning ceremony at Cheapside was the occasion of a considerable riot. It caused little damage but much alarm, the crown's supporters being angered by the pointed refusal of the City magistrates to order the mob to disperse, and by the number of gentlemen who 'from windows and balconies encouraged the mob'.

More momentous riots were caused by his illegal return to England to stand for election for the county constituency of Middlesex in 1768. Though elected by its freeholders, he was at once conveyed to prison, though only after being tumultuously rescued for a while and escorted to a tavern by excited supporters. Next, the judiciary assisted his cause. Lord Mansfield decided that No. 45 had indeed been seditious libel, fined Wilkes £1000, and jailed him for twenty-two months. The commons expelled him again; and ordered fresh elections. On three successive occasions, the freeholders of Middlesex elected Wilkes. Each time the commons declared him ineligible, finally giving his seat to his defeated opponent on the grounds that the latter 'ought to have been returned'.

There were additional reasons for discontent in London at the time of the Middlesex elections. During the hard winter of 1768–9, prices were high and wages low. Sailors and hatters, glass grinders and journeyman tailors demonstrated and rioted against their conditions. The Spitalfields weavers had to be kept in check by troops; two weavers were executed for damaging silk and silk looms. The coalheavers were particularly militant, at one time besieging a Shadwell public house shouting 'Wilkes and coalheavers for ever!' Fifty coalheavers beat up two captains of colliers. But though such vigorously resentful workers doubtless swelled the Wilkite riots, they had no organised part in them. Nevertheless, there was widespread uproar at each new development in the long-running farce of the Middlesex elections themselves. Mobs swarmed the streets from Temple Bar to Hyde Park, forcing people to light up their houses in Wilkes's honour. The windows of the Mansion House were broken. St George's Fields, Southwark was filled with a great crowd, allegedly shouting, 'Damn the King, damn the Government and damn the Justice'. The Guards shot six rioters dead and thereby provoked further rioting. One woman, arrested by a constable for her persistent cries of 'Wilkes and Liberty!' threatened to break his head; and then did so. A group of merchants about to deliver a loyal address to the king had their coaches set upon by Wilkites as they proceeded to St James's Palace and were still being assaulted even inside the palace gates.

Wilkes was almost as much of a hero outside London. It was a tribute to his skilful performance as an engaging rascal being hearteningly irreverent towards the government, and a good fellow who was standing up for his rights and those of every disgruntled tradesman or independent-minded newspaper reader. Though, since his Middlesex

339

constituency covered most of north and west London, the bulk of his support was metropolitan, what he got printed in London newspapers was eagerly reproduced by the fast-growing provincial press. Floods of gifts reached him during his imprisonment. The number '45' was used nationwide in the way later generations would use the CND badge or the clenched fist. Several cities sent him salmon, each allegedly weighing 45 lbs. Norwich sent 45 lbs of tea, a private donor 45 lbs of Cheshire cheese. His fame reaching the refractory colonists of North America, Marylanders sent him 45 hogsheads of tobacco. He even received 45 bottles of wine from well-wishers in Hamburg. The number '45' was chalked on doors and houses all over London and other towns and displayed on blue cockades. In Wilkite Middlesex itself, 45 Brentford chimney sweeps sat ceremonially down to eat 45 lbs of beef, 45 lbs of ham and 45 lbs of bread, and to drink 45 pots of beer. In London, the Austrian ambassador was up-ended by a Wilkite crowd so that '45' could be chalked on the soles of his shoes. A nationwide Society of Supporters of the Bill of Rights was formed to pay Wilkes's debts. His unlovely features appeared on snuff boxes, buttons, coins, medals and coffee pots. Fifteen counties and a dozen boroughs petitioned on his behalf in 1769 and others tried to do the same. His release from prison in 1770 led to public junketings in all parts of the country. At Tewkesbury they rang the Abbey bells and fired guns. A celebration at Northampton was concluded by the dancing, by 45 couples, of a specially devised country dance called 'Wilkes's wriggle'.

That the Wilkite riots, political though they were, had no sequel was due in part to Wilkes. He was more clown than crusader, the human equivalent of an anti-government caricature, not the embodiment of a political theory. Some Wilkites advocated various kinds of parliamentary reform; Wilkes did not. After 1770 his chief ambition was to become Lord Mayor of London. Though he encouraged riots, he led none. He was a journalist, not a parliamentary, let alone a mob, orator. The politicians disliked a man who encouraged 'the middling and inferior class of people' to be irreverent about affairs of state or to think themselves entitled to take part in them. One of the reasons for the political ineffectiveness of the Whigs in opposition was their aristocratic abhorrence of 'the people' whom Wilkes had revealed as all too ready to engage in a riotous carnival of derision that mocked the senatorial airs of the ruling élite and for whom Liberty could be symbolised by a journalistic jester with a squint.

Moreover, when Londoners next went on the rampage, in 1780, the comic element was wholly absent. They were provoked by the action of a neurotic and insignificant MP, Lord George Gordon, in arranging a demonstration in St George's Fields against a Roman Catholic Relief Act, passed in 1778. This meant that Catholics could now inherit and purchase land and were no longer liable to life imprisonment for running a school. The spectacle of a large body of well-dressed, decent looking tradesmen all loudly crying 'No Popery' was, said Edward Gibbon, as if 40,000 Puritans had risen from the dead. When Gordon presented a petition to the commons against the act, the crowds besieged parliament, manhandling several peers so that they reached the chamber looking 'as pale as Hamlet'. The bishop of Lincoln took refuge in a private house from which he escaped in safety in female disguise. It was several hours before the Guards could relieve the siege. The crowd then moved on to destroy the Catholic chapels serving the Sardinian and Bavarian embassies and, on the following day, to attack the property of prosperous Catholics in Moorfields, as well as the houses of the promoter of the Relief Act and of JPs who had ordered the arrest of demonstrators. When parliament was again besieged, a justice plucked up enough courage to read the Riot Act. This led to the destruction of his town house in St Martin's Fields and his country house in Islington, and to a succession of disorders that continued for days. Newgate, Marshalsea, the Fleet and King's Bench prisons were opened and set fire to. Lord Mansfield, imprisoner of Wilkes, upholder of the prerogative and strong supporter of Catholic Relief, had his Bloomsbury Square house ransacked and his entire library destroyed. Mansfield, it was alleged, was himself a Catholic and had used his position as Lord Chief Justice to make the king a secret Catholic too, ready to break his coronation oath to relieve his new co-religionists. The riots extended to Bermondsey, Moorfields and Wapping as well as Southwark and Westminster. The Bank of England was attacked. Blackfriars Bridge, built little more than ten years earlier, was stormed, its toll houses robbed and burned. A gin distillery in Holborn, owned by a wealthy Catholic, was set alight with the consequent burning of over twenty neighbouring houses. 120,000 gallons of gin poured forth. That quantity of it which did not burn was drunk, or scooped up by the pailful, by men, women and children, a spectacle which led Horace Walpole to write that, at this stage, there were 'more people killed by drinking than by ball or bayonet'.

The government's tardiness in resorting to 'ball or bayonet' was due to a combination of legal caution and, though neither North nor the commons would consider the repeal of the detested Relief Act, sheer fright. Neither the Gin riots nor the Wilkite riots offered precedent for the sight of such flames as were now rising to the sky from the City and Southwark. The use of the Guards on an *ad hoc* basis occurred from the outset. Even so, soldiers were noticeably reluctant to fire on crowds engaged solely on destroying Catholic places of worship. Moreover, they were always outnumbered; every fatality they caused provoked yet more rioting; and their position in law was precarious. In 1736, a Lieutenant Porteous, whose troops shot six Scots who had rioted on behalf of three smugglers accused of trying to rob an excise officer, was tried for murder, found guilty and sentenced to death. A mob then broke into his prison and lynched him lest the authorities grant him a pardon. Faced with a situation which a French observer (nine years before the Fall of the Bastille) considered unthinkable in a well ordered city like Paris, the government was in not much less of a plight than that of the king of France in 1789 or the authorities in Paris and Vienna in 1848, or in St Petersburg in 1905 and 1917. It may well have been decisive that George III was totally unlike Louis XVI, Louis Philippe, the Habsburg emperor Ferdinand, or the Tsar Nicholas II. From the beginning, bristling with irate bellicosity, George III demanded action. He had no more respect for the feelings of rebellious London crowds than he had for those of rebellious American colonists. It was his resolution that finally stiffened North into allowing 10,000 troops to be used against the crowds. According to a probably conservative estimate, the troops caused up to 300 civilian deaths and wounded 200 people. Afterwards, they covered the bloodstained walls of the Bank of England with whitewash and those on Blackfriars Bridge with piles of mud. Yet, after the riots petered out, only 160 persons were brought to trial. Of the 62 who were sentenced to death, the total number hanged was 25. 85 of the 160 were acquitted. Lord George Gordon was tried for treason, perhaps because, as he was after all a duke's son, the charge would not stick. As there was no evidence that either he or his Association had provoked the uproar deliberately, he was acquitted, to end his life a convert to Judaism.

Throughout, the Gordon rioters seem to have damaged property with studied discrimination. The targets were the property of prosperous, but not poor, Roman Catholics, and that of persons favourable to Catholic Relief and to strong measures against rioters. That there should be riots for the political rights of ordinary citizens in 1768–9, but for the continued suppression of Roman Catholics in 1780, is no paradox. The eighteenth-century crowds were doubtless devoted to liberty; but they were not liberals. To bawl for Liberty in sympathy with a Society for the Preservation of the Bill of Rights in 1769 and to shout 'No Popery' after a meeting of a Protestant Association in 1780 was wholly consistent. Just as the personality of Wilkes (and, a century before him, Shaftesbury) demonstrates that Liberty may select for its champions persons of the most doubtful character, so the Gordon riots are a reminder that to adhere to apparently irrational prejudices is not a failing exclusive to persons whose views are authoritarian. By 1780, the British government had landed the country in a losing war against the American colonies and, worse still, in a war against France and Spain. Both were Catholic powers, and so dangerous to British naval supremacy that a year later, in 1781, the fight against the colonists had to be abandoned in defeat. It was a situation not wholly unlike that of the years from 1679 to 1690. The Bill of Rights was born of the anti-popish frenzy of 1679–81, and out of fear of a Catholic king at home and a Catholic France across the Channel; and it had produced the ferocious suppression of the papists of Ireland. In yelling 'No Popery' in 1780, the London crowd was asserting, at a time of national crisis, its belief in Liberty in the manner most habitual to Englishmen at critical moments ever since the 1580s. The words 'No Popery' were packed with meaning. They were the emotionally charged incantation by which people expressed their hatred of despotism at home, foreign domination and lack of patriotism. And hatred, too, for the sins of the rich. For they could not erase from their collective consciousness the old Lollard and Puritan conviction that, for them, the Catholicism of the pope symbolised the conspicuous extravagance of a privileged, hierarchical few to whom their hungry sheep would look in vain for succour.

Though, at the start, some politicians and some City magnates had supported the Wilkes campaign, no politicians countenanced the Gordon riots; and the City's attitude was expressed most notably by Wilkes's own active participation in the defence of the Royal Exchange against the rioters. The Gordon riots thus rendered less likely than ever any effective link between popular and parliamentary politics. They were held to prove that Wilkes's 'middling and inferior class' were an ungovernable rabble, to whom it would be the height of folly to allow any role in political life beyond that of spectators. It was, therefore, with their minds already made up that the rulers of England would shortly face the combined threats of the contagious ideological programme of the French Revolution and the mounting restiveness of a people about to experience the dislocations of an 'industrial revolution'.

PART SIX

CHALLENGE AND RESPONSE

Approximate Dates: from before 1760 until after 1860

1
LAND, PEOPLE AND TECHNOLOGY

Industrial Revolution—When and What?

To isolate the years from 1760 to 1830 as 'the period of the industrial revolution' is misleading. By the latter date the largest employers of labour were still agriculture, domestic service, building, and boot- and shoe-making. These occupations involved little or no power-driven machinery; none was organised on the factory system. If industrialisation is thought of as based on steam power, it cannot be regarded as fully established until the whole economy was sustained by a factory system, the steam locomotive and the steamship; and this was not the case until after the 1870s. Though, by 1851, only a fifth of all occupied persons worked on the land, agriculture still employed six times as many males as the cotton industry or the coal mines and its nearest rival as a large employer of labour was domestic service. Nevertheless by the 1870s it had long been clear that what sustained the growth of the economy as a whole and the great increase in non-industrial employment available to the much increased population was the work of that forty-three to forty-six per cent of the labour force engaged in manufacturing, mining and the other major industries.

To choose the mid-eighteenth century as a starting point also conveys the impression that before that date the English lived in an 'underdeveloped' country. In fact they were already rich enough to be able, out of their own resources, and without additional savings, to finance the whole process of industrialisation, including the canal and railway networks, the expansion of the coal, iron and cotton industries and the costs of a twenty year war with the French. The industrial revolution occurred not because the English were 'backward' but because they were already 'advanced'.

What is usually called the industrial revolution was the solution, through commercial and technological innovation, of the hitherto unsolved riddle of how to avoid the problems facing a community whose population dramatically outgrew its supply of cultivable land. One former device, that of mass migration and conquest, such as their remoter Saxon and Danish forbears had undertaken when they had left their homelands to create the English nation, was not available, even though all through the nineteenth century improved communications led to continuous emigration, particularly to the United States. The other normal outcome might be called the 'terminal' solution: society might pass through a period of inflation and scarcity, sooner or later

347

culminating in the elimination of the surplus population by famine and disease.

This latter solution had occurred in the fourteenth century, before, during and after the visitations of the Black Death. There had been a similar period of crisis from 1510 to 1660. But it is significant that, although that crisis saw continuous inflation, a lowering of the living standards of the unpropertied and many signs of social maladjustment, the final effect had been to halt population growth, but not to reduce it to its pre-crisis level. The rate of growth after 1750, however, was without precedent. The population of England and Wales grew from just over six to just over nine million in the next half century. During the nineteenth century it went up by two million every ten years. In the 1870s it rose by 3.2 million, a figure equal to fifty per cent of the whole population little more than a century before or for the whole of it in the early thirteenth century. At the end of the seventeenth century an intelligent estimate of the probable population of England and Wales by 1900 was that it would be 7.35 million. In fact it was 32.5 million.

From Plague to Epidemic

There is no agreement about what caused the population explosion of the second half of the eighteenth century. It was not unique to the British Isles and was not even an exclusively European phenomenon. Of the various reasons usually suggested some are improbable, others speculative and only two may tentatively be advanced as carrying more conviction than the others. One was the disappearance of plague, the other the more productive use of the land.

The Great Plague of 1665 acquired its name chiefly because it was the last Great Plague. There had been plagues in London of hardly less serious proportions in seven separate years between 1560 and 1637. Plague was endemic from 1566 to 1611 and from 1636 to 1648. In each of the years 1563, 1603, 1625 and 1665 the death rate rose to at least five times the normal level, killing between a sixth and a quarter of London's population on each occasion. Twice in 1665 there were over 8,000 burials in one week. There was no escape save flight; and it had been to prevent the spread of infection in this way that Elizabeth I had set up a gallows in Windsor in 1563 to warn fleeing Londoners not to endanger the safety of her court.

It seems therefore the plague had kept numbers within bounds by killing off a considerable proportion of that part of the population which migrated to large towns. London by itself tended to absorb the equivalent of the country's annual population increase, growing from 200,000 to 450,000 inhabitants between 1600 and 1660 and sustaining at least 33,000 plague deaths in 1603, 41,000 in 1625 and 69,000 in 1665. Yet, though large towns were killers everywhere in western Europe before industrialisation, they continued to be so for a long time after it.

Cholera, typhus, tuberculosis, scarlet fever, whooping cough, rheumatic fever, diphtheria and smallpox, all flourished in crowded towns, killing slowly where plague had formerly killed quickly and intermittently. Though Englishmen in general could hope to live to their fortieth birthday, those citizens of early nineteenth-century Manchester who survived to their twenty-fifth birthday were luckier than most living in that city; whereas the fortunate inhabitants of rural Surrey could look forward to surviving until they were fifty-one. There were parts of Manchester, as of Liverpool, London and Glasgow, where life expectancy was well below twenty years. In Bethnal Green in London in 1839 the average age of death of those living in the poorest households was reported to be sixteen; only the families of gentlemen and professional men would normally live beyond forty.

Rural Growth and Transformation

It seems therefore that population growth began in the countryside, independently of and ahead of the process commonly known as the industrial revolution, and that it originated in causes other than merely the disappearance of the largely urban phenomenon of bubonic plague. This seems confirmed by the fact that population grew as fast in parts of Europe unaffected by industrialism as it did in England. For every 100 Englishmen and Welshmen in 1700 there were about 163 in 1800; but (assuming the correctness of the estimates) there was an almost exactly proportionate increase in the number of Italians; and the population of Norway almost trebled in the century before 1865. Similarly, though the number of Englishmen and Welshmen went up by a half from 1700 to 1775, the numbers of the Irish and Scots doubled in the same period.

Since these increases were among a rural population, they can hardly have been due to the hospital or dispensary movements, or improvements in medicine, midwifery and hygiene. Vaccination was not generally available until after 1800, not free until 1840 and not compulsory until after 1853, even though smallpox was deadly among infants. To commit a newborn child to a foundling hospital or workhouse infirmary was, on the evidence of the mortality figures, little more than a form of infanticide. Nor did the progress in sanitation help much, even though London began to pave its streets and thus to render obsolete the sedan chairs in which dainty people had been carried to protect them from the filth of unpaved streets. Sanitary engineering before the mid-nineteenth century was limited to providing sewers for carrying away surface water. Water supplies were usually so irregular that the fact that Joseph Bramah had invented his improved water closet in 1778 mattered little, even to the wealthy, until after 1830. A cold water tap in the house was still a luxury in the 1840s.

The extent to which the increased rural population was a consequence of the increased productivity of the soil is uncertain, but cultivation had long been improving. The spectacular advances in agriculture from about 1780 were an acceleration and culmination of processes of which some had been going on since the inflationary sixteenth century. Proper drainage, better strains of wheat, selective breeding of stock, the use of the four-course system of rotation, which eliminated the fallow and provided winter feed for cattle, were all on the way to adoption before the names of Townshend, Coke and Bakewell first attracted the public acclaim which secured their immortality in the history books.

Exploitation of the land's mineral resources had likewise developed ever since the Tudors. Coal, china clay, stone, timber, copper and tin were being extracted from it, laying the rural foundations of an economy which would eventually become urban. Given that spinning and weaving, and the finishing of cloth, had long been put out by manufacturers into the homes of country dwellers, there were, already well before 1760, alternative or supplementary sources of income, apart from agriculture, for families in many parts of the country. If to this be added that enclosure was superseding open field husbandry at a quickening pace, it would seem that the old world was already being pulled out of shape well before 1760.

The slow erosion of the area of open fields which had been going on since the sixteenth century rapidly quickened in the eighteenth. By 1750, half England's arable was already enclosed. In Anne's reign, 1500 acres were enclosed by parliamentary acts; in George I's, 18,000; and in George II's reign, 319,000. Between 1760 and 1815, some seven million acres were enclosed by parliamentary action, three quarters of them during the twenty years before 1780 and between 1793 and 1815. In many, perhaps most, cases, the commissioners appointed to reallocate the land would allot some land to cottagers and squatters. In a century so devoted to the principle of property rights and in a section of rural society committed for centuries to the idea of customary rights it is unlikely that rapacity and sharp practice would suddenly become universal. Too often, however, the land allotted to cottagers and squatters would be poor land, inconveniently situated, and amount to no more than a tiny garden or potato patch. Rights of access to common and waste were not always extinguished, though, if they were, this was a serious deprivation. But enclosure usually led to more intensive exploitation of the arable and thus to increased employment. More people worked in agriculture in 1831 than in 1811; and although the number of landless men grew, the increase was far smaller than the rate of population growth. In 1831, when virtually all the open fields were enclosed, for every 100 occupiers there were 251 men with no land; but in 1700 the ratio had already been as high as 100 to 174. Nor were small farmers instantly squeezed out by the opportunities opened to the greater landlords. As late as 1851, more than half the 275,000 farmers of Britain employed no regular labour beyond that provided by their own families.

Nevertheless, poverty became greatest in areas without industry, whether such areas were enclosed or not. The cost of poor relief seems to have been heaviest in East Anglia, the non-industrial midland counties and Sussex. Thus, although more enclosures and the use of new techniques were increasing food production, it was still not possible, owing to the growth of population, to provide a bearable standard of life for those employed exclusively in agriculture. And although there were already higher wages and more jobs wherever there was rural industry, there was also even more social upheaval than that generated by enclosure; and an even faster growth of population. In industrial villages, people married earlier than in the open field economy and there was increased illegitimacy. Contemporaries were not wrong in thinking they were living through a crisis. The time seemed to be approaching when population would so increase as to produce inflation, famine, social chaos and consequent demographic decline. Yet, given sufficient energy and resourcefulness, this growing population could be used as a source of labour and of purchasing power and hence of economic expansion. The industrial revolution was a process by which a rich, ingenious and ruthless society contrived to transform the threat of social catastrophe into an opportunity to create new wealth on a scale previously unknown. For the first time, increased numbers were, in the long run, accompanied by an overall increase of prosperity. After 1780, real incomes (in average terms) did not, as in the sixteenth century, fall with increasing numbers, save perhaps in the first decade of the nineteenth century when the industrialising process was barely begun and the country was at war with Napoleon, one of whose major weapons was economic blockade. The population nevertheless almost doubled between 1800 and 1850; and this, the fifty years when the impact of industrialisation was greatest, was the only period when England's population increased at a faster rate than that of any other country in Europe.

Shortage: Midwife of Change

The industrial revolution did not so much create British industry as transform it. Since the cotton industry expanded so dramatically, from a minor activity that contributed only half of one per cent to the national income in the 1760s, into one that contributed almost twenty-five per cent of total exports by 1800, there is a long tradition of concentrating attention on it. A wider view of what happened must take in the difficulties and opportunities facing older industries. Almost all of them faced a shortage of raw materials caused by a shortage of land. Most significantly, wood had been becoming scarcer ever since Tudor times. There was a chronic lack of fuel. The cost of firewood had outsoared the rises in other commodity prices during the decades of inflation, compelling the use of coal, not only in London, but in all towns to which it could be transported by sea or navigable river. Timber was the basic industrial and domestic raw material. It was needed for house-building, furniture, casks and other receptacles in daily and commercial use, and for all forms of transport involving anything more complicated than the single rider or the pack animal. All machinery was made of it and it was vital to industrial processes. Yet already by the seventeenth century, ironsmiths, soap and salt boilers were having to use coal; it was used more and more in brewing and dyeing. The adverse chemical changes otherwise produced by using coal instead of wood compelled bakers, brickmakers, glassmakers, lead and copper smelters and finally iron smelters to adopt new techniques. The smelting of iron with coke by Abraham Darby of Coalbrookdale in 1709 at last released the blast furnace from charcoal. This change, by which the iron industry became coal- rather than wood-based, was a culmination as well as the start of a technological revolution. Significantly, the consequent expansion of the iron industry in the first half of the eighteenth century was a response to agricultural progress. Nearly fifty per cent of the total iron output in 1750 arose from the increasing demand for iron for ploughs and horseshoes.

Greater use of coal and metals, as well as the increased movement of grain resulting from greater agricultural productivity and the growth of towns, raised acute transport problems. Wood, of sorts at any rate, could be found in many places, coal in only a few. Packhorses thus gave place to waggons and carts. But these deeply rutted the unsurfaced roads and retarded the development of coach travel. Coach journeys were uncomfortable, slow and dangerous. Vehicles were overturned by the potholes and the ruts, and their wheels came off. Progress was at a rate which made them highly vulnerable to attack by highwaymen.

The most massive capital investment of the late-eighteenth century was therefore in communications. The initial task was to widen and deepen rivers to make them navigable to barges. The canal age began, between 1757 and 1764, with one canal linking a coalfield with the Mersey, and another connecting a ducal coalfield to Manchester. Involving as it did the construction of bridges, viaducts, reservoirs and countless locks, canal construction was the largest and most heroic civil engineering operation so far undertaken. It testified to immense financial confidence, if not over-confidence. The Grand Trunk Canal absorbed an investment of £200,000 and the Pennine link cost well above the original estimate of £320,000. The needs of the surveyors and engineers employed to align and construct the canals led to the establishment by the government of the Ordnance Survey. The growth of Birmingham owed most perhaps to its being the centre of a radiating network of canals. Never before had there been so important a trade centre so far from the sea. Like Manchester and Leeds, it was a representative large town of the future. Its function was neither administrative nor ecclesiastical. It was a centre neither of fashion nor of sociability, but solely of design and manufacture.

The roads were dealt with principally by allowing commercial bodies, the turnpike trusts, to surface and maintain important stretches of road in return for the right to levy tolls. Though, like the canals, the turnpikes failed to provide a rational and coherent transport system, they had, by the 1780s, begun the relatively short golden age of the horse-drawn stage coach. The time from London to Birmingham was cut by a day, that to Leeds by two days. The increase in speed was proportionate to that involved in the later change from horse power to steam power. As the eighteenth century gave way to the nineteenth, the improved roads, increasingly developed by such men as Telford and Macadam, made it possible for coaches to travel faster, to provide a safer and more comfortable ride, and to accommodate outside passengers, thus increasing carrying capacity from six passengers to eleven.

Both canal and road building were in large part a response to the insufficiency and costliness of animal feeding stuffs. Since something between four and eight acres of land under hay was needed to feed one horse, horses cost more to feed than men. Canal promoters were much given to announcing how much land would be released for agriculture because of the greatly increased load a horse could carry when harnessed to a barge. Similar considerations applied, less dramatically, to the increased effectiveness of horse power when used on smooth surfaced roads and, more spectacularly, to the development of steam locomotion after 1829. A commons committee declared in 1834 that if the country's more than a million horses were replaced by steam vehicles, 'and the means of transport drawn from the bowels of the earth instead of being raised upon its surface' land would 'be freed to feed a further eight million people'. It is a measure of the scale of the problem that, for all the capital, technology and sheer hard slog that went into, first, canals, and then into railways, there was still no reduction in the number of horses. They remained irreplaceable for personal and short distance transport throughout the century and were still used in agriculture and for the transport of industrial products in the earlier decades of the twentieth century. They thus continued to compete for food with human beings (of whom the heartiest could not really 'eat like a horse') until they were gradually ousted by the bicycle, the electric tramcar, and petrol driven buses, cars and tractors.

The spectacular rise of the cotton industry also reflected the land shortage. The new enclosure movement was mainly for arable, with beef and mutton in mind. There was thus a scarcity of raw wool, made worse, from the home consumer's point of view, by the fact that so much woollen cloth was exported that it made up fifty-seven per cent of total exports in 1700 and was still ahead of cotton exports in 1800. The high price of woollens on the home market forced an expanding population to switch to cotton. Though universally condemned as inferior to wool (except for dainty clothing, proper only to the prosperous) it was cheaper. Even when used for outer garments in the form of heavy cotton known as fustian, it offered less protection against wet and cold in an age when food, shelter and fuel were generally inadequate; and, in a time of low wages, it quickly wore out. It had its advantages as underclothing. It could be washed more effectively and, compared with woollen garments, which might even be treated as heirlooms, could perhaps be regarded as 'disposable'. This would eventually make for better personal hygiene. For the poor, however, soap was for long a costly commodity, and clean water often unobtainable.

For a people to have to import the most widely used raw material for its clothing and its export trade was manifestly inconvenient and expensive. It is a comment on the human dilemma that the teeming English multitudes of the industrial age were soon to depend, some for their livelihood, some for their basic need for bodily covering, others for their profits, and the community as a whole for its most successful export industry, on the productive soil of a continent 3000 miles away, worked by American negroes condemned to the humiliations of slavery, and on successfully competing with the spinners and weavers of the villages of India.

Since the cotton industry flourished chiefly as a provider of a cheap alternative to wool, it was in the forefront of the drive to cut costs. Devices such as Kay's fly shuttle increased the output of the domestic weaver to the point where his family could not provide him with sufficient yarn. This led to Hargreaves' spinning jenny. The jenny made the spinning wheel obsolete within a decade. But, so far from hastening the urban industrial revolution, it revivified the domestic industry, being simple enough to be used by the children of the family. The decisive innovation was Arkwright's water frame. This was so massive that it could be operated only by horse power, water power and eventually steam. It was this which foreshadowed the time when men, women and children who had been badly paid textile workers in their own homes would have to become badly paid textile workers in factories. The frame was also expensive, which meant that, in the language of later times, the 'means of production' would be within the reach only of those who possessed adequate capital. Changes of a similar nature were to take place in the woollen industry, though more slowly. This was partly because woollens were for a time on a falling market and partly because its traditional forms of domestic employment were better safeguarded, while they lasted, by the apprenticeship laws, and by gild regulations, neither of which applied to the cotton industry.

The excessive demand for natural resources necessitated the foundation of the chemical industry. Some form of alkali was essential, not only for the making of soap and glass, but in most manufacturing processes. Its normal source was potash which, for so long as wood was the normal industrial fuel, was widely available. Once there was a shift to coal burning, potash became scarce, and for most of the eighteenth century was made up for by collecting, drying and burning seaweed. The modern chemical industry dates from the establishment in the 1790s of the process of synthesising soda (sodium carbonate) invented by the Frenchman, Nicolas Leblanc. The sulphuric acid produced to make soda could also turn bones into superphosphates which helped to end the traditional shortage of natural fertilizer. Hydrochloric acid, at first only a noisome by-product of soda manufacture, was then used to make chlorine. This could bleach fabrics in hours, whereas the previous method of laying them out in the sun could take weeks. Chemical bleaching also solved the papermakers' problem of how to make paper out of coloured as well as white rag.

The timber shortage universalised the brick-built house. Coal began to replace wood in brick kilns in the seventeenth century because it was taking four times more wood to build a brick house than a timber one. A brick built house was thus at first a luxury; but once inland navigation made it cheaper to transport coal to the brick kilns, bricks became cheaper, and provided not only the shell of the house but replaced wooden lintels over windows and doors by the arched row of bricks characteristic of most smaller nineteenth century houses. Once it became cheap, brick was thought inferior to stone; hence the Regency fashion of covering facades with stucco to simulate blocks of stone. The coming of the railways later universalised not only the brick house but the slate roof.

The general use of coal facilitated one further economy in the use of the soil's resources, the adoption of gas lighting. This reduced the demand for tallow. This had become so considerable that it could be argued that, though the sheep and cattle bred by the famous stock-breeder Robert Bakewell were too fat to provide good quality mutton and beef, his improvements may well have been welcomed by the candlemakers. The spread of gaslighting was slow, except in factories, owing to the unpleasantness of the fumes.

From Waterpower to Steampower

Though it came to depend on coal, the early industrial revolution was founded on water, and predominantly powered by it, well into the nineteenth century. Water mills were used for corn milling, the manufacture of iron and paper, and the making of furniture. They provided most of the power for Sheffield's cutlery and allied manufactures in 1800 and powered the growth of Birmingham till well after that date. The design and efficiency of water wheels were so much improved that their replacement by rotative steam engines was delayed even in the textile industry. In 1839, 2,230 water wheels still survived in textile factories alongside the 3,051 steam engines. That the future lay with steam is demonstrated less by their numerical superiority than by the fact that in sum they generated over three times more power than the water wheels.

The use of steam was due in the first place to the simple fact that mining coal was harder and more complicated work than felling trees. Quite early in the eighteenth century it was already common for mining to be carried on at depths of from two hundred to four hundred feet. To drain such shafts required machinery so cumbersome that it was impracticable and uneconomic to use horse power. Savery's steam pump appeared in 1698. Newcomen and others produced more efficient variations of the Savery pump and, as well as being used to drain mines and supply waterworks, they were used, particularly in Lancashire, to blow furnaces and for a variety of jobs in textiles.

These earliest steam engines were expensive to build, extravagant users of coal, and not very powerful. Their main justification was that, unlike horses, they did not have to be fuelled with expensive food when not doing any work. Engines of this type remained in use well after James Watt had revolutionised design by his rotative steam engine fitted with a separate condenser. Though Watt's engines were up to four times more powerful, they cost twice as much to instal. Steam power was first harnessed to a cotton mill in Nottinghamshire in 1785, but only the larger textile firms in Lancashire could afford the steam engines marketed by Boulton and Watt until after 1800. Water-powered mills increased in number until 1830 and even as late as 1850 accounted for ten per cent of all cotton mills. Only after that did the water mill slowly become confused in the popular mind with the 'old mill by the stream', which had once ground corn but had ended merely as a romantic setting for the dreams of 'Nellie Dean'.

By the end of the 1880s, steampower nevertheless solved, for almost a century, the problem of coping with the enormously increased workload which society had undertaken in an effort to sustain its ever-multiplying population. Steam power finally ensured that coal and iron would replace wood as the basis of industrial power and plant. It reduced costs by concentrating industry. Ironmasters no longer sought in far country places for wood and water, nor cotton masters for fast-moving streams remote from the ports whence their raw materials came and from the markets where they sold their products. Steam power either transformed villages into towns or forced factories out of the country and into the towns. This was more than a cost-reducing juxtaposition of cotton with coal and iron. It meant building factories together in fairly large numbers in order to attract and guarantee a livelihood to the engineering firms needed to fit, maintain and repair the new and complicated iron machinery that steam power had now made essential.

The most remarkable evidence of society's success in coping with increasing numbers was that there was still sufficient wealth to support the most dramatic achievement of the industrial age, the construction of

356

nearly 10,000 miles of railway track in the thirty years from 1830. Although that figure was itself almost doubled. by 1900, the route mileage operating by the mid-1860s was roughly equivalent to that in use a century later. Railway construction absorbed, at times, half the country's investment finance, a labour force of over a quarter of a million, hundreds of millions of bricks, tons of gunpowder for blasting, and of candles for lighting the workings, and generated a demand for vast quantities of coal and iron. It is hardly to be wondered at that a people capable of such an achievement, as the climax of almost a hundred years of economic and social transformation and dislocation, should have ended by concluding there was nothing they could not do if only they were hard working and optimistic enough to try.

Progress: or Malthus Confounded

In 1798, Thomas Malthus, a Surrey parson, published his *Essay on Population*, revised and elaborated five years later. Malthus deduced, from the rural poverty around him, that population was fated always to outrun food supplies and therefore to produce permanent misery, if not pestilence and famine. Only in strict sexual continence and the postponement of the age of marriage was there much, if any, hope of salvation. The applicability of his theories to pre-industrial societies in general is a matter of debate. What seemed not to be in question was that, as far as industrialised Britain was concerned, he appeared to have been wrong.

What seemed to prove him wrong was Progress, whose mighty monuments and engines were for all to see, and whose reality was attested by indisputable statistics. Manchester's population grew from 75,000 in 1801 to 399,000 in 1861, Birmingham's from 71,000 to 351,000, Liverpool's from 82,000 to 472,000, Greater London's from 1,117,000 to 3,227,000. Prices as a whole had nevertheless fallen in the same period by 38%. Consumption per head of tea and sugar had almost doubled. In 1800, 11 million tons of coal had been mined; in 1860 the figure was 84.9 million. Cotton exports had increased about tenfold. The railways carried 30.4 million passengers in 1845 and 238.7 million in 1865. Progress was so rapid that already by 1865 the major constructional achievements of the previous half century were obsolescent. All but the most important canals fell into disuse, and there descended upon cross country roads which, not long before, had known the exciting sounds of the stage coach, a silence to be broken only by the shrill of the first bicycle bell and the honking of the first motor horn.

The Commercial Landed Aristocrats

The English pioneered this technological revolution for reasons other than their possession of large deposits of coal and iron or the appearance of an exceptional handful of 'inventors'. That the English were a rich people is also an inadequate reason; wealth is more often devoted to pleasures and palaces than blast furnaces and steam engines. The reasons lie rather in those features of English life which distinguished it from life in other European societies. One was its exceptional freedom from central control. Because the great landowners had absolute control over their land they were free to exploit it to the full. There was no obstacle to enclosure and improvement and none to their making money out of the minerals beneath their soil. They lived in—and ruled—the only country in Europe in which all minerals save gold and silver were the undisputed possession of the owners of the land from which those minerals were extracted. It was important for the social and political transformations of the nineteenth century that peers who were also mine owners had to that extent the same economic interests as mine owners who were not peers or, more significant still, might eventually become peers. All the largest coal owners were in fact in the Lords, and the biggest single owner was the bishop of Durham. The peerage dominated other forms of mining almost completely. The landed interest, in short, was an industrial as well as an agricultural interest. In some cases, as at Barrow-in-Furness, Whitehaven and Warrington, the development of an industrial town on a site owned wholly by one substantial ground landlord offered almost the only chance that it might have an overall plan. It was Lord Liverpool, prime minister from 1812–27, damned forever by Disraeli as the 'arch reactionary', who said of Watt, Boulton and Arkwright, the great innovators of the industrial revolution, that they had been 'as useful to their country in their generations as any of the legislators of old'. The great English landlords grew inordinately rich on ground rents and mining royalties; but in so doing they provided to those who leased their farms, their mines and their industrial sites, opportunities for enrichment in their turn for which foreigners were agreed the continent offered no parallel.

The Diffusion of Wealth

Because the landowners passed on to others, at a handsome profit to themselves, the opportunity for profitable enterprise, wealth in England was more widely diffused than elsewhere. The existence of a considerable body of industrious people, content by trade, industry and commerce to secure for themselves and their families a solid prosperity, was a natural consequence of this. It made for diversity of investment and a maximisation of the freedom to initiate. Decisions about innovation and economic growth were in the hands not of an authoritarian few but the commercially-minded many.

Wide diffusion of moderate wealth also made England a 'consumer society' compared with other European countries. 'All progress,' said a minor prophet of the late nineteenth century, 'is based on a universal innate desire on the part of every organism to live beyond its income'. So widespread among all classes was the wish to imitate the improving standards of their betters that it was a common source of satire and rebuke. At quite low levels of society there were signs of growing indulgence in morally debilitating 'luxuries' such as white bread, china crockery and printed cottons. Even labourers acquired a taste for tea and sugar. As early as 1796, one enraged gentleman thought the degree of luxury to which the country had sunk within a few years was 'dreadful to think of'. It reached the point where even village labourers, in the worst times of the Napoleonic wars, objected to receiving potatoes instead of wheaten bread from the poor law authorities. By 1800, many common people were already wearing clothes which imitated those of their betters, or were in fact their cast-offs. Only in the remote parts of the south and west, in the surviving long smock of the farm labourer, could there be found a costume that proclaimed its wearer to be without hope of aspiring to, or pretence of having fallen from, a better social status.

Piety and Plurality

It is often asserted that an important element in the making of an industrial society was the Puritan ethic of work, sobriety, thrift and conscientiousness. These, however, are qualities conducive principally to subordination and routine; the industrial revolution was neither made nor driven forward by men of this kidney. The Puritan virtues were principally revived not to stimulate the entrepreneurial spirit but rather to persuade the masses to keep quiet and obedient while they were being habituated to working harder, and perhaps sometimes suffering more, than previous generations. The industrial revolution was powered by the plurality rather than the piety of English society.

It is true that, in proportion to their numbers, Dissenters contributed more to innovation than Anglicans. This may well have been because Dissent gave a sense of intellectual pride and independence to all who, by temperament or conviction, dissented from society's values, but were determined to make their way in spite of the fact. Of all the original Puritan contributions to the future, its condemnation of superstition and magic was perhaps the most important. Together with the indeterminacy of Anglican theology, it helped to encourage the spirit of practical scientific enquiry. It paved the way for that rational enquiry into natural phenomena which post-Tridentine Catholicism inhibited for so long in much of continental Europe.

The Diffusion of Knowledge and Opportunity

Widespread interest in experimental science is demonstrated by more than the foundation of the Royal Society in 1660 and the work of the Dissenting Academies a century later, important though both were.

Opportunities for self-education in mathematics had existed at least since the seventeenth century. One arithmetic textbook published in 1751 ran into eighteen different editions by 1783 and remained in use for a further fifty years. Its original purchasers included craftsmen of all sorts, many of them members of the local mathematical clubs founded in various eighteenth-century towns. Several London coffee houses had been scientific clubs, where lectures were given on mathematics, experimental philosophy, electricity, 'chymistry', steam engines and methods of iron founding. In the Society for the Encouragement of Arts, Commerce and Manufacture were mingled men of all rank, from great aristocrats to mechanics, shipwrights and the humblest instrument makers. The inventions of the industrial age emerged out of a society in which there was, in proportion to the literate population, possibly more opportunity to acquire an informal but none the less informed and practical scientific education than at any time in the nineteenth century.

The idea that the industrial revolution was pioneered by brilliant amateurs with no theoretical knowledge is based partly on an artificial division between pure and applied science which is inappropriate to eighteenth-century conditions and partly on misleading propaganda by nineteenth-century proponents of the gospel of self-help. It would not do to inform the humble that they could improve themselves by a scientific education: that might cause them to demand such an education. It was better to assure them that they, too, like James Watt and George Stephenson, could achieve success if only they would knuckle down to it and keep off the bottle. The truth was that the 'self-made' men of the early industrial revolution were made by a society many of whose members were consumed not only by a desire to get on but by a genuine scientific curiosity directed, as in practice such curiosity usually is, towards making useful things that worked.

That, relatively speaking, England was a land of opportunity in this respect is attested by the large number of foreign inventors who realised that they could develop their ideas only if they came to England. English tool makers, instrument makers and clock makers, on whose skills the mechanical engineering industry was built, were much influenced by continental, particularly French, techniques. Virtually all applications of water power owed their origins to the Dutch. The alkali industry and the use of chlorine for bleaching, were based on French innovations. The railway engineering Brunels were French refugees. Almost all agricultural improvers were applying innovations made by the Dutch and the Flemish. England pioneered the industrialisation of the world because it was an exceptionally open society.

The Fortune of War

An important accelerator of the industrialising process was the war with France and Napoleon, from 1793 until 1815. Already by 1790 Britain was the world's most powerful trading nation, exporting a third of its total industrial production. Yet, for all the fluctuations and dislocations it caused, the war led to massive progress in the cotton and iron industries, the capacity of the latter being quadrupled. More important, perhaps, the effect of British naval supremacy was almost to ruin the trade of her potential competitors. Although Napoleon's blockade, from 1807 to 1812, the so-called Continental System, was designed to bankrupt Britain by cutting off her exports to the continent and choke her to death with goods she could not sell, British counter-measures to inhibit seaborne trade with, or by, Europeans, were far more damaging. At the start of the war, the British had captured the French West Indies and therefore already dominated the whole trade of the Caribbean. After 1807, British interference with United States trade was so effective that not until twenty years after the war was over did United States exports again reach their 1807 levels. That British naval policy led to the Anglo-American war of 1812 is hardly surprising. The collapse of the Spanish and Portuguese economies during the Peninsular War led, after 1808, to British domination of the trade of both those countries with Latin America.

British exporters were also exceptionally active in finding alternative markets to those barred to them by Napoleon. British trade in the Mediterranean was over eight times greater in 1812 than in 1806; and, by way of Sweden, British exports soared from just under £75,000 in 1791 to nearly £5 million in 1810 and were still over £2 million in 1812. From a strictly economic and financial point of view the overall picture was therefore more important than the intermittent setbacks, notably the commercial slump of 1811, with its 2112 bankruptcies; for these last arose from an exceptional entrepreneurial readiness to take risks at a time when the unpredictabilities of war and the severity of Napoleon's economic offensive might have been expected to discourage it. By the year of Waterloo, the total result of war and industrialisation was to give Britain a decisive advantage over the rest of Europe that was to endure for half a century.

That the French wars forced Pitt to suspend cash payments in 1797 also encouraged industrial expansion. It helped Britain to perform the unusual feat of fighting a costly war and yet to grow richer almost every year. In effect the transfer of so much gold by Britain to her continental allies in the form of subsidies had created such a shortage of bullion at home that Pitt prohibited the Bank of England from honouring its notes with cash. Had he not done so, the economy might have seized up for lack of currency. Thereafter, until cash payments were resumed in 1821, English commercial and industrial growth was financed by paper money, issued not only by the Bank of England but also by the many country banks, whose number was steadily increasing. No attempt was made to limit the number of notes issued, and in terms of face value there was about twice as much money in circulation at the end of the war as at its beginning. Thus, the industrial and commercial entrepreneur enjoyed the benefit of a cheap and flexible money supply at a time crucial for the conduct of the war and the expansion of the economy. The extent of the expansion can be judged by the fact that inflation during the war years was not more than 3.3% a year.

Inflation encouraged the entrepreneur at the expense not only of those on fixed incomes but also of the labour force, whose real wages were automatically depressed by the continuous rise in prices. Prices rose by 3% a year due to the fact that rises caused by bad harvests and trade fluctuations could never, owing to inflation, revert to their previous lower levels. Napoleon, by his interruptions of England's corn imports, has long been regarded as the patron saint of the enclosing landlord. By forcing on the government a financial policy that gave maximum advantage to the thrusting capitalist he may also be considered the godfather of the early industrial entrepreneur. And, given that the financial policy to which the war gave rise operated greatly to the detriment of the wage earning population, he also deserves a large place in the demonology of those who concern themselves with the plight of the working classes at that time.

2
SOCIAL STRESS AND POLITICAL SURVIVAL

Credits and Debits

MORE important than the statistics which show that national wealth was greater in 1860 than in 1760 and that standards of living had improved is the statistic which records an average life expectancy of forty-one years.

On the optimistic (as well as improbable) assumption that he and his successors all conformed to this statistic, a wage earner born in 1760 would probably be dead by 1800; a son born to him in, say, 1785, would be dead by 1825; and a grandson born in 1810 would die just about the time when Queen Victoria opened the Great Exhibition of 1851, an event taken as celebrating the summit of mid-Victorian prosperity. Hence, not until the fourth generation, in the person of a great grandson born in 1835, would this wage earning dynasty be reasonably certain of enjoying the benefits of such material progress as had by then become available to their class. To view the industrial revolution 'in the long run' can mislead; for it was, in the short run, a time of unhappiness for many. And a short run was the most that the many could hope for.

The industrial revolution kept more people alive; but it did not keep them alive for very long, particularly if they were wage earners. Though living standards rose, they did so neither considerably nor steadily. Real wages stagnated or declined during the French wars from 1793 to 1815, rose in the early 1820s, but then fell back by anything up to 9% until 1840. And this takes little account of the possible absence of wages altogether for many workers in the slumps of 1811, 1816, 1819, 1826–7, 1830–31 and 1836–42, nor of Henry Mayhew's opinion in 1849 that only half the country's workers were in regular employment, the rest being either half employed or without work altogether. Though more jobs were being created, the new technology was destroying the livelihood of thousands of once prosperous craftsmen. The despairing silk weavers of Spitalfields in the late 1840s echoed the thoughts of two generations of craftsmen all over England when they told Mayhew they thought the object of the government was 'the starvation of the labouring classes', that 'weavers were all a-getting poorer and masters all a-getting country houses'; or said, as one of them did, 'Every year, bad is getting worse in our trade. What's life to me? Labour—labour—labour—and for what? Why, for less and less food every month'. Remarks such as these are a reminder that it was probably not until well into the railway era that technological innovation ceased as a general rule to replace adult skilled labour by unskilled, female, or child labour.

The country's increasing wealth after 1760 went mainly to the well-to-do. The tiny minority who paid most in taxes nearly trebled their wealth; the lower ranks of taxpayers effectively doubled theirs. But though labourers' real wages are thought to have nearly doubled also between 1800 and 1850, this grossly over estimates both their real earnings and their real gains. It ignores the frequency of unemployment and the fact that 1800 was a bad year for wages anyway. Such gains were small compensation for the collapse of the employment prospects of so many skilled craftsmen made economically superfluous by new technology. Nor were they any great reward for submission to new disciplines of work combined with likely spells of illness or lack of work ameliorated neither by the possibility of personal saving nor the certainty of poor relief.

Yet those who were skilled, tough, intelligent, healthy and adaptable might do well enough. The challenge of a time of revolutionary change will defeat some but stimulate others. An early historian of the cotton industry, writing in the early 1820s, thought that 'operative workmen being thrown together in great numbers had their faculties sharpened and improved by constant communication'. Their conversation 'wandered over a variety of topics never before essayed'. They discussed 'the vast field of politics' and 'the character of their government and the men who composed it'. Formerly 'only a few degrees above their cattle in the scale of intellect they were now political citizens'. He contrasted the 'bright, shrewd, penetrating and intelligent' quality of jurors from the manufacturing districts with 'the stupidity and ignorance' of those from rural parts. 'During the last 40 years,' he averred, 'the mind of the labouring class (taking them as a body) has been progressively improving, and within the last 20 has made an advance of centuries'.

Nor was the urban scene everywhere deteriorating. Between 1785 and 1850 there were 400 acts to improve towns and markets in places outside Greater London, designed to lay pavements, to clean, straighten and widen streets and remove ruinous buildings or stop the slaughtering, or wandering, of animals in public thoroughfares. By 1800 large parts of the medieval centres of Manchester, Liverpool, Bristol, Birmingham, Sheffield, Wolverhampton and Durham were being demolished and rebuilt. In 1817 the streets of Newcastle were reported as wide, well built, and with shops remarkable for their size, elegance and air of bustle and business. There was a discernible commercial district in Manchester before 1820 and by 1850 most larger town centres were dominated by offices, warehouses and retail shops commanding high rents. When to these improvements was added the rebuilding necessitated by the railways it is evident that early industrial towns were not given over wholly to squalor.

What was objectionable was the tendency to drive the workers out of the centre and into ugly and insanitary enclaves close to their workplaces. Yet, with the increasing number of highly paid workers such as cotton spinners, engineers, boiler makers and some grades of mine and railway workers, the first shops to cater for the better-off working class began to appear. In the main, the labouring classes would avoid shops, being sure that shopkeepers were rich, but that the pedlars who followed the proletariat as they migrated from country to town were poor people like themselves. But, though working-class wives continued to buy fish, fruit and vegetables from markets and street traders, they were beginning to get bread, bacon, meat, cheese and groceries from shops. The arrival in the working class areas of shops, hitherto institutions almost wholly for the well-to-do, testifies to rising living standards.

In assessing the causes of the social and political conflicts that accompanied the industrial revolution, attention has thus to be paid not only to the phenomenon of continuing poverty and hardship, but also to the sharpening intelligence and rising expectations of the more skilled among the workers. Such men would not be patient when their political capacity was denied expression and when their rising expectations were so frequently put in jeopardy by the slumps that terminated the booms.

On the miseries, one quotation may suffice: from a speech by Lord Shaftesbury in 1873, recollecting the earlier decades of the factory system and in particular the sight of Bradford children coming out of the factory gates. 'A set of sad, dejected, cadaverous creatures they were . . . the cripples and distorted forms might be numbered by hundreds, perhaps by thousands . . . the sight was most piteous, the deformities incredible. They seemed to me, such were their crooked shapes, like a mass of crooked alphabets'.

'We, the People'

The years after 1780 were therefore stormy with conflicts similar to, and often as intense as, those between 1530 and 1660, likewise a time of rapid population growth, exceptional industrial change and continuous social dislocation. Now, as then, this complex disturbance was aggravated by a revolution in ideas and made more tumultuous by fears that an alien system of thought might be imposed upon the nation by a powerful enemy from without, aided by traitors within. Though, this time, no king of England was executed, the king of France was; and the intellectual starting point of the new ideas of the age was the deposition of the king of England by his own colonial subjects in the Thirteen Colonies in North America. True, there was, this time, no Great Rebellion at home; but in the small taverns of London, in workshops in industrial villages and towns, men everywhere talked of one. Much property and some persons were attacked; many Englishmen were hanged, transported or imprisoned because they had made evident by word or deed their hatred of the king's ministers and all who were set in authority over them. Just as English life was never the same after the crisis of 1625 to 1660, so the nature of English society and the attitudes of Englishmen towards other Englishmen are still in part conditioned by the social conflicts of the years from 1793 to 1848.

The public events that created the shift in men's thinking that had been launched in the sixteenth century by Luther's Ninety-five Theses against papal indulgences, and by Henry VIII's Act of Supremacy, were paralleled in the late-eighteenth century by the American Declaration of Independence of 1776 and the defeat of the English in the war that followed. In England, as in France, that war, which ended in 1783 with the English still masters of the seas but with the colonies freed, produced a loss of confidence in government: among Frenchmen because they had lost a war, among Englishmen because they had lost an empire. The French monarchy was discredited, the prestige of England's oligarchs was undermined. The aplomb with which the Founding Fathers had asserted that it was impossible to deny that 'all men are created equal' (because, they said, it was 'self-evident') had explosive effects among the English as well as among the colonists' French allies. The colonists' refusal to be 'taxed without representation' could hardly go unnoticed by George III's other subjects at home, most of whom were not only taxed, but governed, without representation. Moreover, the English had a parliament which, despite the emergence of a society whose wealth was increasingly produced by industry and commerce, was falling more and more under aristocratic domination. Whereas peers' sons had made up 13% of the commons' membership in 1735, a quarter of all MPs were peers' sons by 1826. By then, 115 of the 658 MPs in the commons were the direct nominees of 87 peers and a further 103 MPs also owed their seats to aristocratic influence. During the period of the early industrial revolution, therefore, England was increasingly in the grip of an aristocratic élite which, knowing itself to be living through a social and political crisis of unprecedented seriousness, acted in the united conviction that any dilution of its power would plunge the state into irremediable chaos. They were convinced by the Wilkes and Liberty riots and the Gordon riots that 'the people' was a disorderly and irrational rabble. All the popular manifestations of the decades from 1780 to 1830 were as detestable to the allegedly liberty-loving Whigs as to the government; on this point they were at one with the Pittites, so that effective parliamentary opposition was in abeyance. Hence, in the face of continuous public hostility, the English aristrocracy survived their crisis and were able to preserve their hold on society and its politics well beyond the Reform Act of 1832. Their resolve that there should be no revolution was thus more significant than the fact that their harsh rule over a nation racked by the social stresses of a rapidly changing economy and the dislocations of a long and difficult war bred such potentially revolutionary feeling in a society more and more alienated from them.

Signs of that alienation appeared among all ranks of society. There was some highly intellectual criticism of the system as such and of the economic and fiscal policies it pursued, and an attack on its antiquated law. There was a growing demand for parliamentary reform among the gentry and, more significantly, among unpropertied persons of the sort who had supported Wilkes. The war years produced intensified protest of the traditional sort, involving riots and demonstrations and, as the authorities grew less tolerant of rioting crowds, a consequent resort to secret outrages and conspiracies. To these, between 1807 and 1812, the really bad years of the war for people at home, was added a revival of the Wilkite spirit as a response to government failures and to evidence of corruption in high places.

The Lights Go Out

'We live', young Jeremy Bentham had written in 1776, 'in a busy age: in which knowledge is rapidly advancing towards perfection'. And he went on, in his *Fragment on Government*, to point the contrast that was so soon to be in the minds of many: though busy with change, England was clogged with social, legal and political anomalies. Times were changing fast; but government and legislature still relied on the faded almanac for 1689. Yet, though the clear light of reason showed plainly enough how badly parliament needed reform, the only change most parliamentarians themselves were prepared to support was the removal of some of the more glaring forms of 'corruption'. Though Burke was most eloquent on the subject, it was in fact the Younger Pitt who was more active in the 1780s in reducing the number of 'corrupting' sinecures by which government could reward its supporters. But the elimination of rotten boroughs was considered interference in the rights of property and the extension of the franchise as socially dangerous. Nevertheless, in 1776, Major John Cartwright, by publishing the pamphlet, *Take Your Choice*, advocating annual parliaments, equal electoral districts, the payment of MPs and manhood suffrage, made himself the first notable propagandist on behalf of demands which were to continue to be made for well over a century. Groups working for parliamentary reform proliferated. The Yorkshire Association, of gentlemen, clerics and freeholders was founded in 1780 by Christopher Wyvill. The Society of the Friends of the People called for 'a more equal representation of the people' and had the patronage of Charles Grey, a young Whig who, in his old age and to his great embarrassment, found himself committed by his youthful ardour to the passing of a Reform Bill for which he had by then but little enthusiasm.

These movements among the propertied classes might have had some success, given that 'economical reform', i.e. the removal of sinecures and the reduction of some official salaries, was undertaken by Burke in the 1770s and Pitt in the 1780s. What halted the movement abruptly was the outbreak of war with France in 1793.

367

The overthrow of dynastic and aristocratic power by the French revolutionaries was hailed initially as a victory for enlightenment. Wordsworth recollected that time as a 'dawn' in which it was 'bliss to be alive'. Fox impulsively called the Fall of the Bastille by far the best and greatest event in history. But the French attempt at constitutional monarchy broke down, to be followed by the French king's execution, the September massacres, the Jacobin 'Terror' under Robespierre, and a French republican war against all the rulers of Europe, into which England, too, was drawn. The Revolution rapidly became a god that failed. Only the diminishing band of Foxite Whigs retained their faith, even after Napoleon had shattered yet more illusions by making himself an Emperor. On the grounds that Napoleon had become insatiably aggressive, even Fox supported the war when in office. Though there were still, even in 1815, some who saw Napoleon's defeat as a victory for the dynasts and aristocrats from whose suffocating grip men had hoped to free themselves in the 1780s, the overwhelming majority rallied patriotically behind the war throughout its course.

The near unanimity with which the Pittite Tories were for so long sustained was based on that most merciless of conjunctions, a combination of patriotism and fear; and since these were also the basis of Robespierre's rule it is understandable that some of Pitt's victims referred to the years 1792–96 as the English Reign of Terror. Pitt's fear was based on the fact that Jacobin ideas, which had produced terror against kings and aristocrats in France and wars against them everywhere else, were also being propagated in England. Most frightening of all, they were being spread among the lower ranks of society whom it was thought that Cromwell, the Restoration and the Glorious Revolution had permanently excluded from the political nation because they lacked property and were not gentlemen. 'Jacobin' acquired, and long retained, the significance that 'Bolshevik' had in the decade after 1917 or 'Communist' in the early 1950s. Whoever could with even a tinge of truth, be labelled with the word became an enemy of society.

Battle Joined: Burke v. Paine

The conflict which raged in English society was programmed by Burke's *Reflections on the French Revolution* (1790) on one side and on the other by Tom Paine's *Rights of Man* (1791–2). Burke's reputation as a thinker was assured when his prophecy that the French Revolution would issue in bloodshed and tyranny was speedily fulfilled. What also gave him a European reputation was his view of society as an organic unity which could survive only if its roots were nourished by its past. Society was a partnership between the living, the dead, and the unborn. Its intricate, subtle nature, akin to that of a living organism, was, moreover, beyond the understanding of those whom, in a phrase that was a gift to his detractors, he called 'the swinish multitude'.

Paine, a former exciseman and Quaker, was, like many other unprivileged persons, stirred into intellectual life by the American revolution. He, more than anyone else, personified the Jacobin threat. He had a hand in drafting the Declaration of Independence and sat for a time in the French Convention. His *Rights of Man* expressed in starkest manner the optimistic downrightness of an age naive enough to suppose that all would be well with the world as soon as the last king had been strangled with the guts of the last priest. For a king to inherit a government was, he said, to inherit people as though they were flocks and herds. To appeal to tradition was to subordinate the rights of the living to 'a mouldy parchment'. The Bill of Rights of 1689 was a bill of wrongs and insults. All existing governments were based on conquest, superstition and arbitrary power. From these trumpet blasts against the present he went on to make demands for the future: a system of international arbitration to eliminate the expense of armies and navies; and a graduated income tax, with the richest paying twenty shillings in the pound, the proceeds being used to provide family allowances, state aided schools, old age pensions (granted as of right) and marriage, maternity and funeral benefits.

Thus, well before 1800, Major Cartwright had revived the political programme of the Levellers of 1640 and foreshadowed the chief political ambition of the succeeding century; and Tom Paine had drawn up a programme of social welfare which was not to be implemented till the twentieth century. In 1795–96, Paine went further still, in *The Age of Reason*, a crude attack on both old testament and new. 'My religion', he said, 'is to do good'. The morality of the old testament was condemned, the revelation of the new denied. Though the uncouth irreverence of *The Age of Reason* alienated many eager readers of *The Rights of Man*, Tom Paine's work far outsold Burke's and continued to educate and liberate the minds of thousands of artisans, mechanics and literate labourers for decades to come. Hence, to all right-thinking men of property, Paine's works were seditious and blasphemous.

Pitt's 'Reign of Terror'

In 1792, Thomas Hardy, shoemaker, founded, in a public house off the Strand, the London Corresponding Society. Within six months, its eight original members had grown to 2,000 and it soon linked together like-minded men in many parts of London and similar societies (founded earlier) in Sheffield, Derby and Manchester as well as others in Birmingham, Leeds, Nottingham, Coventry, Halifax, Newcastle and Tewkesbury. They decided, after earnest debate, that though they were only tradesmen, shopkeepers and mechanics they had the right to demand parliamentary reform. A truly representative parliament would 'bring the necessities of life more within the reach of the poor', the young would be better educated, the poor better cared for. The Sheffield group felt their purpose was 'to show the people the ground of all their sufferings' and why a man who worked 'thirteen hours a day the week through was not able to maintain his family'.

Though, on the surface, just one more movement for parliamentary reform, the Corresponding Society had three fatal distinctions. Its foundation coincided with the outbreak of war and the national panic about Jacobins; its literature applauded the teachings of Tom Paine; and its membership, though not lacking the adherence of some members of the professional classes, consisted mainly of shoemakers, tailors, watchmakers and weavers, most of them young and of an aspiring cast of mind. Since so few of them were gentlemen or clerics or freeholders, they were at once condemned as Painites and Jacobins. And since revolution, like beauty, often lies chiefly in the eye of the beholder, it is relevant that to most men of property, in the 1790s as in the 1640s, it was revolutionary for the unpropertied to ask for the vote. Other advocates of parliamentary reform had as little sympathy with the idea as other Puritans had had with the Levellers in 1647: Ireton's attack on Rainborough was repeated by Wyvill: once Painite ideas had raised up the lower classes, he wrote, 'all we now possess, whether in private property or public liberty, will be at the mercy of a lawless and furious rabble'. For almost thirty years the propertied and employing classes united in the determination to keep the unpropertied majority of Englishmen in a state of strict subordination. The alienation of the more thoughtful of those who worked with their hands during those decades had consequences which long endured.

Crudely forthright, Paine had written, 'Mankind shall not now be told that they shall not think or that they shall not read'. Dedicated and thorough, the Younger Pitt set out to give Paine the lie. Paine might, Pitt is alleged to have said, have the right of it; but it was his job to save the country from bloody revolution. Hardy, with others, was charged with high treason. Rather than see these solemn men hanged, drawn and quartered, the London jury found them not guilty. The crowd that cheered the acquittal was rather larger than the mob which had previously attacked Hardy's house in the cause of church and king and so terrified Hardy's pregnant wife that she shortly died in childbirth.

Pitt's response to the jury's decision was to suspend habeas corpus and to make it henceforth treasonable to incite hatred of king, constitution or government in speech or in writing. No meeting of over fifty persons could be held without a magistrate's permission. To defy a magistrate's orders in the matter could be punishable by death. Premises where reform was discussed could be closed down as disorderly houses. Paine had already been indicted for treason and his writings proclaimed seditious. Printers who printed or sold them were subject to continuous persecution.

Prices, Wages and People

The Pittites further aggravated matters because, unlike their Tudor predecessors, they refused to legislate to reduce economic pressure on the labouring poor. This was because the thinker of their time whom they most admired was Adam Smith. Smith's *The Wealth of Nations* had appeared in 1776, that seminal year which also saw the Declaration of Independence, Bentham's *Fragment on Government*, Cartwright's *Take Your Choice*, Tom Paine's first pamphlet (*Common Sense*) and the first volume of Gibbon's *Decline and Fall*. It was Adam Smith's work alone that commended itself to England's rulers. He advocated (along with much else that they ignored) the ending of all government regulation of internal and external trade. Already an aristocracy imbued with the commercial spirit, they at once deduced from the principles of free trade that the price of labour, like that of other 'commodities', should be left to find its own level.

Hence, when craftsmen in the woollen and other trades petitioned the government in the 1790s to compel magistrates to fix wages and limit apprenticeships as they were still required to do by the Elizabethan Statute of Labourers, they refused. Indeed, far from reviving these rarely applied regulations, they went on to abolish them altogether by acts of 1813, 1814 and 1824. The plea that there was distress among skilled craftsmen because of the competition of machines or a temporary slump, was answered by Lord Liverpool, prime minister from 1812 to 1827, with observations such as that 'evils inseparable from the state of things should not be charged against the government' or that 'human evils' were almost always 'beyond the control of human legislation'. The home secretary, Lord Sidmouth, declared, 'Man cannot create abundance where Providence has inflicted scarcity'. The government heightened the impression that it was bent on making the labouring poor suffer when it added, to its refusal to protect wages, an absolute veto on collective bargaining. In 1799 and 1800 the Combination Acts reaffirmed beyond dispute that 'combinations' or trade unions of workers against their employers were illegal.

It is significant that in wanting wage regulation restored, the workers of the time were appealing, not to principles devised for them by intellectuals looking forward to a utopian paradise to be achieved by revolution, but to the remembered past of their own community. This was even more characteristic of the food riots of the whole century before 1812. In protesting against high prices and in particular the price of bread, a commodity which might account for up to a half of their household budget, men were invoking a complex of practices sanctified by custom and common law and by statutes dating back to the sixteenth century. These required farmers to bring their corn to the local market, for some of it to be sold in small quantities to the poor, before it was offered to the dealers at the going economic price. Enactments existed requiring justices to prevent millers overcharging for flour, bakers for bread. Farmers were supposed not to hold back the sale of their crops in the expectation of a rise in prices. Such impediments to the freedom to sell so marketable a commodity as corn, flour or bread, at the best price that could be got for it was scarcely compatible with the capitalist farming of the eighteenth century. And they were wholly at variance with the ideas of free trade to which the Pittites were now dedicated. By the 1790s, theology was also being invoked to sanctify the precepts of the new economic theory. Wilberforce excused authority from all moral obligation, even in times of scarcity, to help the poor to acquire their daily bread by announcing that parliament could not alter 'the course of things as they appeared in nature' because they were 'under the dispensation of Providence only'.

This did not stop local communities feeling outraged when, faced with shortage and high prices, they saw locally-produced corn, butter or bacon being carted away to the towns while they themselves had to go without. Bad times had produced food riots in every decade since the 1740s; but they were most noticeable in 1795, in 1800–1801 and in 1811–12. Procedures, and the kind of people involved, followed the usual pattern. The poorest labourers took little part, the principals being craftsmen and their wives. They would claim to be taking the law into their own hands because the justices were failing in their duty. They would seize corn which dealers had bought, or were transporting out of the county, and organise its sale to local people at what they considered a fair price. They would collect money from those who bought this confiscated produce and pay it over to the farmer, miller or baker concerned. Perambulating crowds, as well as breaking into stores, mills and farms, or holding up waggons on the roads, might form formidable deputations demanding contributions in cash or kind from wealthy local farmers. They might enlist the services of the parish constable and entrust him with the care of the money they obtained from the sale of the seized produce. Sometimes a magistrate might be called on to preside over such sales. The mayor of Cambridge once found it politic to perform this task. Violence was used only against those who sought to resist this exercise of popular justice and usually against their produce rather than their persons. This apparently irrational destruction of commodities in a time of scarcity was considered a means of punishing the profiteer for making a profit out of the misfortunes of the poor.

Ignored though it had long been during times of stable prices, the control of prices in the old Tudor tradition seemed in the popular mind an essential part of social justice; and many landowners and magistrates thought much the same. They would sometimes order their tenant farmers to make cheap corn available in times of dearth in order to forestall a riot. But, though some old fashioned gentry might be as prejudiced against corn dealers as the common people were, the government, learning its economics from Adam Smith, was certain that corn dealers had never caused shortages. All appeals to parliament for price-fixing legislation were rejected; and food rioters were now to be dealt with by troops. In 1795, when 178 food riots were reported, the policy of the government was defined by the Whiggish Duke of Portland, then home secretary, as that of 'holding assistance in readiness as may enable Magistrates to secure the freedom of the Markets and to protect the persons and property of those who frequent them'. The Duke also informed Oxford's town clerk, who protested at the despatch of cavalry to disperse a food riot in the city in 1800, a year when there were altogether 132 such riots, 'nothing is more certain than that (riots) can be productive of no other effect than to increase the evil (of scarcity) beyond all power of calculation . . .'. A food riot was 'a violent and unjustifiable attack on property pregnant with the most fatal consequences', which it was the 'bounden duty' of the authorities 'to suppress and punish by the immediate apprehension and committal of the Offenders'.

Though, by 1800, magistrates were themselves becoming affected by prevailing economic theories and anti-Jacobin sentiment, there is not much sign that revolutionary ideas counted for much among the food rioters of the 1790s. Blood-curdling slogans had always accompanied the stormier riots. In 1743, at Henley, the cry was, 'Long Live the Pretender!' and someone in Hereford in 1767 thought it 'better to undergo a foreign Yoke than be used thus'. By the 1790s, there was a reference to 'those bloody numskulls, Pitt and George'; and, in Wiltshire in 1800, a comprehensive attack on the government, the crown, the constitution and the war ended with the splendid prayer, 'God Save the Poor and Down with George III'. Though there is evidence that some would-be Jacobin revolutionaries existed in various parts of the country, it is likely that the principal influence of Jacobinism was not so much to inflame the passions of the rioters as to harden the hearts of the authorities.

The Labouring Paupers

Rejection of wage and price regulation, the less complaisant government attitude to riots, and the serious bread crisis of 1795 put the agricultural workers of the southern counties even more at the mercy of harsh economic facts. Already an area of low wages and scarce employment, the south of England had no alternative but to extend still further the operations of the Poor Law of 1601. In January 1795, the Oxford justices in quarter sessions decided to supplement inadequate wages by cash payments out of the parish poor rate. The practice became widespread in the southern counties and became known as the Speenhamland system, after the district in Berkshire which adopted it in May 1975. Introduced as a humanitarian measure because without it the labourers might have starved, it became, by its persistence, an affront to economic and moral orthodoxy, and almost as objectionable to the labourers themselves. By the 1820s, Whigs and Tories were at one in wanting the abolition not only of the Speenhamland system but of the whole poor law. Apart from the mounting cost to ratepayers, the granting of poor relief was held responsible for adding to the pauper population by encouraging early marriage and improvident breeding. Since the Speenhamland system included allowances to a man in respect of his wife and children, it was held to flout the whole Malthusian theory that sexual abstinence by the poor was almost society's only guarantee against universal famine. The labourers objected to a system which perpetuated low wages and enabled farmers to treat them as a disposable source of purely casual work. When East Anglian labourers rioted in 1816 they demanded not only wage and price fixing but also the end of Speenhamland. They were ruthlessly suppressed.

The culmination of decades of degradingly low wages, aggravated by the stiffening of the Game Laws in 1816, and the immobility imposed on them by the Settlement Law that tied the pauper to his parish, produced the Labourers' Revolt of 1830. To their other frustration was added the use of the threshing machine. An obvious and desirable agricultural 'improvement', it further depressed the labourer. By eliminating the old labour-intensive business of threshing corn with flails, it deprived him of desperately needed winter employment. The Labourers' Revolt was the most widespread disturbance of the time. Beginning in Kent in 1830, it spread to Wiltshire and Dorset, and into East Anglia and parts of the Midlands. They burned barns and ricks, attacked poorhouses and threshing machines and drove poor law overseers out of their villages in carts. Their principal demand was for higher wages; but, inevitably, larger grievances were added, such as demands for lower rents and the end of the tithe, whose survival (two hundred years after the Levellers) did so much to alienate the rural community from the established church.

Even at this date, some of the old scale of values survived. Farmers and magistrates recognised the depths of the labourers' plight and were at first slow to act. But the newly installed Whig government sent special commissioners to the affected counties with the result that six men were executed, over four hundred transported, and a similar number imprisoned; and this in spite of the fact that the rising had led to no loss of life. Nothing so demonstrated the solidarity of the aristocracy in the face of popular discontent at this time than the fact that the Whigs so unhesitatingly put down the Labourers' Revolt just before passing the Reform Act of 1832, and drastically cut down on poor relief immediately afterwards.

The famous act of 1834 was a Poor Law Amendment Act and not a Poor Law Repeal Act because, having so recently had one Labourers' Revolt, the Whigs did not wish to provoke another. Fortunately, the way certain Nottinghamshire parishes had reduced their poor rate provided the authorities with a model which, applied nationally, might enable them to save almost as much by amending the Poor Law as by abolishing it. The Act aimed to universalise the practice adopted by the 'efficient' Nottinghamshire parishes. In future, no poor relief, other than to the aged and infirm, would be given to people in their own homes. If they were indeed destitute, they would be helped only if they entered the workhouses to be provided by newly-organised unions of parishes. Workhouses were not a nineteenth-century invention. Justices had been empowered to create them by an act of 1723, after the setting up of workhouses in Bristol and ten other cities from 1697 onwards. Their effectiveness as deterrents had been noted as early as 1725, since their introduction had much reduced the poor rate. In the workhouses planned in 1834, conditions were required to be worse than the worst conditions of life and work outside them. This would have the salutary effect of safeguarding the poor against the temptation of idleness and dependence, which was considered to have been encouraged by the Speenhamland system of 'out relief'. The sexes were to be segregated, whether married or not, and insistence on economy extended to such refinements as a refusal to toll a mourning bell at a pauper's funeral because the bellringer's fee would be an additional burden on the poor rate.

In the long run, the system could not work as planned. That the operation of the New Poor Law was to be supervised by Poor Law Commissioners appointed by the central government was much resented in the localities, not only as an intrusion by Westminster in a sphere of activity which local justices had controlled for centuries, but because, like all future assertions of bureaucratic control by central government, it was insensitive to local conditions. Many poor law guardians found the ban on 'outdoor relief' (i.e. on relief outside the doors of the workhouse) impossible to apply. This was most true in industrial areas subject to temporary periods of great unemployment. In times of acute distress the numbers of the destitute were so large that workhouses could not accommodate them all. Nevertheless, though not universally applied and slowly becoming less ferocious as the century proceeded, the 1834 Act induced a horror of the workhouse among the poor that endured well into the twentieth century.

The Critical Years

The repression of would-be reformers and agitators in the 1790s and the new severity towards rioters had secured a brief respite for England's rulers after 1800; but from 1807 to 1812 they faced renewed and mounting hostility from every quarter.

On the political front they were challenged by the virile journalistic propaganda of William Cobbett, a tough realist owing nothing to enlightened eighteenth-century ideas, and everything to his inherited prejudices as a country-bred Englishman, and to the acquired dislike of aristocratic privilege and corruption of a former NCO with a grievance against the army. Cobbett also had no time for the Whigs. Indeed the main theme of the revived reform agitation of the time was a public vote of confidence in George III's original assessment of the state of things in 1760: that crown and people were alike victims of a conspiracy on the part of an aristocratic oligarchy. Sir Francis Burdett, a wealthy patrician of such aristocratic independence of mind that as a schoolboy he had been expelled from both Westminster and Eton, became the successful populist spokesman of a new attack on bribery and the 'treating' of electors by parliamentary candidates. He was elected to the commons in 1807 after a riotous election for Westminster, which had an exceptionally wide franchise. Also elected for Westminster on the same tide of protest against corruption, was Thomas, Lord Cochrane, a spectacular and romantic naval hero of the day. His chief interest was in denouncing the rampant corruption in the navy. He himself, however, became involved in a spectacular Stock Exchange scandal in 1812. Burdett and Cochrane were political lightweights, exploiting and symbolising popular aspirations but doing nothing to satisfy them. More important was that some of the organisers of their victory were survivors of the old Corresponding Society and that among the others was the tireless Charing Cross tailor, Francis Place, who would have a part to play in every major popular movement for the next thirty years.

Two years later a scandal blew up about the Duke of York, Commander in Chief of the army and son of George III. Among various allegations spread by numerous scurrilous pamphlets was that commissions had been granted through the favours of his ex-mistress, Mrs Clarke. She was, it was asserted, a harlot whom the Duke had allowed to prostitute his patronage 'in return for the prostitution of her person'. The storm was such that the government agreed to a public enquiry. Its upshot was the Duke's resignation (though he was later reinstated), the humiliation of the Portland ministry that had tried to defend him, and general disgust at the failure of the opposition Whigs to make any political capital out of the affair. The popular clamour that broke out was of almost Wilkite proportion. The real military sensation of 1808 had been the Convention of Cintra by which British commanders (appointees of the Duke of York) had allowed the defeated French to remove themselves, their equipment and their booty from Portugal after Wellington had defeated them at the battle of Vimiero. It was not this, but the fall of the Duke of York that made a national hero of Gwylym Wardle, the independent member for Okehampton who had brought that fall about. Everywhere there were county and town meetings to applaud Wardle's triumph over the corrupt system that had for so long perverted the constitution. Typical of the opinions expressed, and by persons socially respectable enough to belong to the carriage-owning classes, was Southey's verdict that, in allowing York simply to resign, the commons had 'given a false verdict wilfully and corruptly' and had 'betrayed their trust'. A colonel of the Liverpool Yeomanry announced that 'when any question of vital corruption is agitated' the Whigs 'desert the cause of the people' and that therefore 'the people must, for the redress of grievances, rely on their own exertions'. Yet there was little to show for it all, save for an act to abolish the purchase of parliamentary boroughs for cash. Since governments always had other inducements with which to persuade owners of proprietary boroughs to part with them, even this looked better than it was.

The shaming event of 1809 was the failure, like most similar British ventures into the Low Countries, to open a 'second front' by a landing on the island of Walcheren, intended to launch a campaign against Napoleon in Belgium. In 1810, Francis Burdett's resistance in the commons to attempts to muzzle press reports on the debates on the affair led to his imprisonment in the Tower and three days of London rioting during which soldiers killed at least two of the rioters. Worse followed in 1811. Napoleon's blockade had reduced trade to a desperate condition and he seemed about to mobilise the armies of the whole continent for an assault on Wellington's forces in Spain. The year's total of bankruptcies and bank failures mounted, the government faced an uncertain future as the unpredictable, emotional Prince Regent took over his father's role, and the Whigs showed themselves incapable of providing an alternative government. Parliament itself was wholly discredited by the recent scandals and many military failures and by what seemed its total incapacity to unite the nation. And simultaneously with the attempt to create, in the Hampden Club, a new nationwide focus of demands for parliamentary reform, working men burst into a new and more alarming form of riot and secret outrage.

Industrial Secrets

Though the industrial areas had been quiet during the early years of the nineteenth century, it is unlikely that men had stopped thinking thoughts they had been ordered not to think or refrained, the magistrates notwithstanding, from reading what they had been told not to read. Nor did they stop combining in secret. It added to the alarm of government and magistrates that the more the workers were clustered together in industrial villages and towns, the more difficult it was to control them. In the larger industrial towns there had already begun that geographical separation between employers and employed, the wealthy, the not so wealthy and the poor, which was to reach its culmination in the planting of working-class families into segregated estates of council houses which began in the 1920s. As soon as urban growth started, the more prosperous moved away from the crowded and filthy areas in which factories and workshops were concentrated to more distant and salubrious parts. Gradually, it was to be only in the small country towns and in parts of London that the different ranks of society continued to live cheek by jowl. It was not simply that aristocracy and gentry had no idea what Manchester was like. Many of Manchester's own citizens did not know what life was like in the more dreadful parts of their city. Not knowing how the other half (or, more accurately the other four-fifths) lived became a national characteristic. Burke's 'swinish multitude' might, as Tennyson later wrote, be 'hovell'd and hustled together each sex like swine'; but respectable people did not frequent pig styes.

It was because the life of the labouring poor was becoming at once so teeming and inaccessible that government supplemented the vigilance of magistrates by an increasing resort to spies, informers and agents-provocateurs. Hence, the views of contemporaries and posterity alike became obscured by a cloud of witnesses who, if not always false witnesses, did not expect to be paid much for consistently reporting that all was well.

During the longish period before it generated a sufficiency of new skills, the factory system, by displacing skilled craftsmen, seemed to threaten a general lowering of both status and living standards for the male worker. The factory, of necessity, could flourish at this stage only on long hours and low pay, the latter a sufficient explanation of its heavy reliance on cheap female and child labour. Factory equipment was costly and financed wholly out of private risk capital. The violent fluctuations of wartime trade created so much intermittent unemployment that to be working long hours for low wages was to be one of the less unfortunate few. It seemed objectionable most of all because it diminished both a man's independence and his freedom. To work for wages was no new experience; but to be wholly dependent on wages was new to many. The employment of women and children was not new; but the submission of entire families to the routine of factory life was a real loss of freedom. The fines imposed on factory workers for infringing minor rules indicate how hard it was to secure submission to a regime that bore little relation to the time of day (or night) or the season of the year, a life in which there seemed only the crude choice between unceasing toil or complete destitution. The man earning money under the domestic, or putting-out, system was often underpaid; but he could pause, if he chose, to sup his ale or charge his clay pipe; the mother could turn from her domestic wage-earning to her household duties; the children could play when there was little work to be done. In the factory such intermissions were impossible. There was not, as in agriculture, a time when, because the season was not right, or the moment for the year's bigger jobs had not yet come, there was little or nothing to be done. Natural rhythms were replaced by mechanical; any slackening of pace was a sign of malfunctioning.

It would be anachronistic to say that the early factories were like prisons, since sizeable prisons were a mid-Victorian innovation caused by the abandonment of transportation in 1853. Nevertheless they could justifiably be compared to the houses of correction within which rogues and vagabonds had traditionally been confined. And in due time, the factory, where individuals were kept in custody for the purpose of earning their living, became the model for those other forms of custodial confinement which urbanisation and technology created: the school, where the young were confined in order to learn how to earn their living; the workhouse, where adults were confined for failing to earn a living; the hospital, where they were confined for being too ill to earn a living. These, along with workers' tenements, office buildings, high rise flats, luxury hotels and holiday camps, were all foretold by the industrial factory and most, two hundred years later, had become extraordinarily alike in architectural design, custodial function and insistence on uniformity, regulation and routine.

Resentment caused by the factory system is to be measured not by statistics but by its persistence. Thus, the most widely-sold piece of socialist propaganda of the 1890s, a collection of articles by Robert Blatchford called *Merrie England*, condemned the factory system outright:

I do not believe in the factory system . . . 1. Because it is ugly, disagreeable and mechanical. 2. Because it is injurious to public health. 3. Because it is unnecessary. 4. Because it is a danger to national existence.

It is the more significant that this should be found in a book which, according to its publishers, had sold over two million copies in England and abroad by 1908. What the late-twentieth century called 'poor industrial relations' would seem to have been bred into the factory system from the start.

The unrest which swept across the midlands and north from 1811 onwards was directed less against factory routine itself than against the threat of its machines to the status of the independent craftsman. It was a protest mainly against unemployment and low wages, both made more distressful by the effects on trade as a whole of the Continental System. There was considerable machine wrecking by cloth workers in the West Riding of Yorkshire, among the cotton weavers of south Lancashire, and framework knitters in the Nottinghamshire hosiery industry. Those responsible claimed as their leader a 'well beloved Brother and Captain in Chief Edward Ludd'. It does not seem that their activities were the irrational response of violent, ignorant men to the inevitability of change or, on the other hand, the partly fictitious inventions of government spies. Their methods may have been less secret and mysterious than they seemed since they often had their bases in small, inaccessible industrial villages and enjoyed there, as in the larger towns, the moral support of the people around them. Nor, as craftsmen, can they be dismissed as uncouth, illiterate survivors from a dimly rustic past. They seem, rather, to have been more than usually alert to the effects of technological change and as likely as other men bred in the comparatively open society of the eighteenth century to invoke the ancient constitution, or to have learned something from the pages of *The Rights of Man*. Luddites, like most rioters and protesters, were more likely to be from the lowest ranks of society's 'haves' than from its 'have-nots' and to have the dynamic temperament of men determined either to get on or to resist being pushed downwards. They were not desperadoes.

The Luddites caused so much alarm, however, that large numbers of troops were despatched to hunt them down and the government made machine-breaking punishable by death. In 1812 a particularly unpopular millowner in Huddersfield was assassinated. A fortnight later a mad-man with a purely private grievance against him murdered the eminently worthy prime minister, Spencer Perceval. When the news reached Nottingham, it was reported, 'a numerous rabble . . . in the most indecent manner testified their joy at the horrid catastrophe by repeated shouts, the firing of guns and every species of exultation . . . a melancholy proof of the depravity which reigns amongst many of the lower orders'. The Prince Regent received a note whose writer assured him, if Perceval's murderer were hanged, then he would be 'shot as sure as I remain an Enemy of all the damned Royal Family'. There were food riots in Bristol, Plymouth, Falmouth, Leeds, Sheffield and Barnsley. The government's information was that almost all the towns of Lancashire and the West Riding, much of the Midlands, and many towns else-where, were seething with Jacobinism. Nothing, it was thought, but the army stood in the way of the proclamation at any minute of a revolutionary republic.

Crisis Overcome

The crisis was surmounted in part because discontent, widespread though it was, had no organisation and no political leadership; and in part because, among those who ruled, there was no real loss of nerve. True, the Foxite Whigs showed their customary combination of obstinacy and pusillanimity during their negotiations with the Regent over the succession to the murdered Perceval. But this in itself sprang from their unwillingness to rock the shaking boat of aristocratic control. The result was the long-lasting premiership of the Pittite Liverpool, which kept the old system in being for almost two more decades.

The contempt the Pittite Tories aroused during the generation after 1790 would pursue them through the pages of most history books. They had grappled with insoluble social and economic problems while trying to conduct a long, arduous war which naval power enabled them not to lose but which, because of their lack of military resources, could be won only by the armies of other powers. Their conduct of the war was made more difficult by the corruption, incompetence and lack of professional-ism which characterised so much of traditional English society. Their approach to their social and economic problems doomed them to obloquy by its paranoiac insistence on law and order, combined with a grim dedication to economic and theological propositions that led them to regard the hardships of the mass of people as due to forces natural and divine whose operations would inevitably be made more severe by an attempt to render them less so. Yet their dedication was also a dedication to duty. Perceval and Liverpool were sincere, pious Evangelicals, Castlereagh, who led Liverpool's government in the commons, a serious man of great integrity. Precariously perched at the head of an aristocracy still in general as profligate as at any other time in English history, and of a nation racked with the pains of war and economic upheaval and less and less disposed to suffer in silence, they managed, but only just, to keep themselves in, and the population under, control.

It was as well, all the same, that there was a Tsar in Russia. At the end of 1810, Alexander I had denounced his alliance with Napoleon. By 1812, the main weight of Napoleon's armies moved east, first to advance upon Moscow and then to retreat from it. The Continental System broke down and Wellington's army was at last able to advance northwards through Spain and into France. Brilliant tactics by Napoleon in 1813 failed to stop the continental armies' advance upon Paris from the east. When, after the war, Tsar Alexander came to London in triumph, he was cheered by enthusiastic crowds. When the Prince Regent appeared at his side, he was hissed. This was not altogether unfair. The Tsar had not only saved Europe from Napoleon; he had probably also saved the Prince Regent's government.

Post-War Conflict

That peace in 1815 had not brought plenty was sufficiently demonstrated in 1816 by the East Anglian riots and a hunger march of unemployed miners and ironworkers in South Wales. In the same year, a large gathering at Spa Fields, Bermondsey, threatened to set up a Committee of Public Safety and to do to the Tower of London what the citizens of Paris had done to the Bastille. That government policy had not changed was demonstrated by the tougher laws against poachers; by the abolition of income tax which, unlike indirect taxes, had been paid only by the better off and therefore tolerable only as a drastic wartime expedient; and, above all, by the Corn Law of 1815. This forbade the import of foreign corn until the price of home grown wheat was high enough to indicate a scarcity little short of famine levels. The Corn Law seemed symbolic of a landed aristocracy's selfish determination to obstruct the onward march of manufacture. Industry's essential fuel was the bread that powered its workers. If bread was not cheap, wages could not be kept low, and manufacturers' prices might cease to be competitive. The Corn Law implied that Liverpool's government opposed free trade, whereas manufacturers wanted taxes on raw materials and

381

on their exports removed, to keep their prices low in the world's markets. Here was further reason for agitating to reform parliament and make it more truly representative of the nation's commercial interests.

With a government still ossified by its fear of change lest change lead inevitably to revolution, working men and others continued to demonstrate. In 1817, six hundred weavers set off from Manchester on a march to London. Since each carried a blanket, they were immortalised as 'the Blanketeers'. Only one marcher reached London. In the same year, Jeremiah Brandreth led two hundred Derbyshire labourers to Nottingham, in order, he said, to take part in a general insurrection. Three of the leaders were executed for treason.

In 1819, a demonstration at St Peter's Fields, Manchester, carrying banners bearing slogans against the corn laws and in favour of universal suffrage, was charged by troops, with the loss of eleven lives. Well publicised in advance, and intended by its leaders as a deliberately peaceful demonstration, the meeting may well have been one which the government had advised the magistrates to deal with firmly. Sidmouth subsequently insisted that the demonstration had been overtly treasonable and sent the magistrates the government's congratulations on their decision to employ troops.

There were hundreds of casualties as well as the fatalities, and the incident was christened 'Peterloo' in mockery of the government's great victory under Wellington only four years before. It scarred the memories of ordinary people deeply. Particularly sinister was the fact that the most vigorous attacks on the demonstrators were made by the Yeomanry, a civilian volunteer force recruited from the commercial and manufacturing classes of Manchester. The regulars involved, from the Hussars, were less indiscriminate, their officers doubtless aware of the regular army's vulnerable position in law when using force against civilians. The contrast between the government's outspoken support of the 'massacre' at Peterloo and the long drawn out debate about the legality of using troops to put down the Gordon Riots shows how far government standards had fallen since the 1780s.

The government lost no time in taking steps to legalise similar action for the future. The Six Acts of 1819 extended and consolidated the laws against public assembly and freedom of expression. Any house could be searched without warrant on suspicion of containing firearms. Public meetings were again virtually forbidden. Periodicals were taxed to price them beyond the reach of the poorer classes. The power of magistrates to seize literature judged seditious or blasphemous was further increased.

The measures against reading matter reflected the government's view that there was 'scarcely a village in the kingdom that had not its little shop in which nothing was sold but blasphemy and sedition'. Accordingly, there was a 4d (about 1½p) stamp tax on each newspaper or periodical; a duty of 3/6 (17½p) on each advertisement; and a duty on paper itself; while a large sum had to be deposited in advance as a surety against libel actions. These efforts to keep radical reading matter out of the masses' reach were largely unavailing. Unstamped pamphlets and periodicals continued to circulate, despite ceaseless persecution of those who printed or sold them.

It was in the conviction that Peterloo should be revenged and that the Six Acts called for a desperate response, that Arthur Thistlewood, principally at the instigation of an agent of the government (which had been shadowing him for three years) planned the Cato Street conspiracy to murder cabinet ministers while at dinner. The heads of Castlereagh, the foreign secretary, detested for his long association with the tyrannical rulers of Europe, and Sidmouth who, as home secretary, was custodian of law and order, would be publicly displayed. A provisional government would be proclaimed from the Mansion House. The plan was another re-run of the imitation of the assault on the Bastille proposed during the Spa Fields affair, and was calculated by the government's agent among the plotters to appeal to Thistlewood's rather old fashioned Jacobin republicanism.

The trial and execution of Thistlewood and four others in 1820 constituted the final major act in the long succession of confrontations between desperate government and desperate protesters. By general consent, the government had gone too far in applauding Peterloo and passing the Six Acts; and its enemies had gone too far in planning the Cato Street conspiracy. A more sober mood began to take over.

But before the rulers of England could begin to recover at least some support among an almost completely alienated nation, a whole age of popular protest was brought to its conclusion in a manner at once riotous, farcical and appropriate. The greater part of 1820 was given over to excitable demonstrations of popular support for the new queen, Caroline, a fat, raddled and vulgar woman of fifty who had lived abroad since 1814, but who now, on George III's death, returned to claim her rightful place as royal consort. Since she was so exceedingly vulgar and had so obviously been 'wronged' for more than a decade by the Prince Regent (now George IV) and his government she became, and obviously enjoyed being, the people's favourite. She was welcomed back to London as if she were Charles II being 'restored' in 1660. Excitement grew when in August 1820 a bill was brought into the Lords to divorce her on the grounds of her adultery. Given that George IV had secretly 'married' Mrs Fitzherbert, a twice-widowed Roman Catholic, in 1785, and had consorted with her and a number of other, usually elderly and well-built, ladies ever since, there was some justice in the evident popular belief that if George IV was fit to be a king, Caroline was no less fit to be a queen. The taste and magnificence of the Regent's costly purchases of paintings, silver and furniture, his patronage of such gifted architects as Holland and Nash, the transformation of Buckingham

House into Buckingham Palace, the rebuilding of a great swathe of London through from St James's to the Regent's Park, as well as his rebuilding at Windsor and the creation of the Brighton Pavilion, were the finest artistic achievements of the crown since the time of Charles I. Unfortunately, all this had taken place at a time when the standards of life of ordinary people were cruelly low and when it was believed that the government of which George was the head was denying the nation its rights. And since George and his ministers were trying to deprive Caroline of her rights too, her cause, therefore, was the people's cause. Feelings ran so high, and the proceedings against her were so squalid by their very nature that Liverpool had to drop the bill. Fewer and fewer peers could bring themselves to support it. Caroline had been cheered daily by roaring crowds on her way to Westminster Hall; acquittal led to three days of riotous rejoicing at the total humiliation of a dissolute monarch and a detested government.

Just as the first great champion of Liberty to set the capital on a roar nearly sixty years earlier had been the squinting, woman-chasing Wilkes, so the last was the fat, man-chasing Caroline. But if Wilkes signalled a beginning, Caroline marked an end. After her, Liberty, like all nineteenth-century English worthies, cultivated a high moral tone and its custodians became the most grave and solemn of persons. By the century's end the deficiencies of bad government would be publicised not by deplorable characters like Wilkes or Queen Caroline, but by the grimly respectable partnership of Sidney and Beatrice Webb. Much of the greater seriousness of popular protest during the rest of the nineteenth century derived from the circumstance that in future it would not be London but the great provincial cities that would provide the principal initiative.

3

STABILITY REGAINED

The Tories Relent

RARELY had government been so detested in England as it had been in the years after Waterloo. The drama at St Peter's Field, Manchester, had branded the king's ministers as murderers. The Six Acts appeared to legalise such butchery for the future, and to reduce England to the level of central Europe where Metternich, in that same year, was purging the universities, and the detested tyrants of Austria and Russia were inviting England to concert with them to suppress the cause of liberty everywhere. The disrepute into which the Regent and his brothers had brought the royal family was without precedent. Byron, Shelley and Hazlitt added their voices to attacks on the system. Cobbett offered, to a wider public even than Paine, a continuous journalistic assault against the politicians which they did not know how to silence.

The comparative calm that succeeded Cato Street and the affair of Queen Caroline was not due solely to an improvement in trade. It was a time of repentant Toryism, symbolised, tragically enough, by the suicide of Castlereagh who, as foreign secretary and government leader in the commons, bore more than his share of the odium heaped on the ministry. Canning succeeded him. Labelled, by some with distaste, and by others with over-optimism, with the newfangled word 'Liberal', Canning adopted and publicised a posture of opposition to the despots of Europe. By championing the independence of Latin America he uplifted the hearts of lovers of liberty and raised anew the faith of English businessmen in the limitless possibilities of trade in those parts. (There was a brief boom that burst by 1827.) Canning's followers in cabinet were Sir Robert Peel, now home secretary, and Huskisson, both of them willing to face the facts of a changing world. By 1829, Peel had mitigated the abuses in prisons, stopped the excessive use of spies, abolished the death penalty for two hundred crimes and founded the Metropolitan Police. The fact that this new force was unarmed, and initially equipped with chimney-shaped top hats of the sort that men now wore as if to confirm that the age of the factory chimney was upon them, was a measure of the government's certainty that an armed force would provoke riot. That the Metropolitan Police was the only unitary organisation Greater London was to possess until the London County Council was set up in 1888 is an indication of the priority attached to the maintenance of law and order in the capital.

Huskisson began the era of free trade by relaxing the navigation acts and mitigating the terms of the Corn Law. The government did not prevent the repeal either of the Combination Laws or of the Test and Corporation Acts. Trade unions had persisted despite the ban on them and both statute and common law had always been competent to prevent them doing much; while the Test and Corporation Acts had been a dead letter for a century.

Nevertheless, here were signs of aristocracy recovering its flexibility. Much that was indeed intelligent, and indeed Liberal, in the political life of the next sixty years derived from the Canningites. Peel may be accounted one of them, despite his refusal to see, until after Canning's death, that Canning had been right to support Catholic Emancipation; and Gladstone derived most of his political ideas from Peel, save for those that he derived from another Tory from that decade, Lord Aberdeen. Palmerston, too, was a Canningite. In a note about Metternich's pettifogging persecution of intelligent men in central Europe, he set down as accurately as any how aristocratic rule was preserved for so long in England without either revolution or counter-revolution: 'Separate by reasonable concessions the moderate from the exaggerated, content the former by fair concessions and get them to assist in resisting the insatiable demands of the latter'.

Minimal Reform, Maximum Consequences

Unfortunately, not all the Tories repented and those who did, did so too late to save their party from the obloquy that pursued it into the twentieth century. In 1829, not even the prospect of revolution in Ireland could persuade all of them to support Peel when, to avert civil war in Ireland, he secured with Whig support the emancipation of all Catholics from the old penal statutes which denied them public office and election to parliament. And it was a last ditch Tory rump, now deserted by the Canningites, and referred to by Palmerston as 'the stupid old Tory party', whose obstructiveness precipitated the political crisis of 1831–32. The elections of 1830, necessitated by George IV's death, produced a majority in the commons in favour of parliamentary reform. Wellington, leading the Tory rumpers, pronounced the existing system perfect. Lord Eldon, formerly Lord Liverpool's Lord Chancellor, gave his fellow peers a solemn warning: 'My lords, sacrifice one atom of our glorious constitution and all the rest is gone'. Reform, he said, would reduce this 'most glorious of nations' to 'that state of misery which now affects all the nations'.

Tory divisions had let the Whigs in at last, with Lord Grey as Prime Minister. Despite his youthful flirtation with parliamentary reform, Grey was fearful of its revolutionary potentialities. It was therefore with apprehension that he and the intensely aristocratic patricians with whom he filled his cabinet embarked upon the hazardous task of trying to pacify a people whose demand for reform was rendered the more vociferous by provocative Tory opposition. After fifty years of Pittite Toryism, the Lords was stuffed with peers ready to block reform. As several versions of the proposed measure were thrown out by these Tory peers, even after another election had confirmed the Whigs in power, the country burst into scattered but riotous violence. Grey pleaded with his obdurate opponents: 'There is no one more decided against annual parliaments, universal suffrage and the secret ballot than I am. My object is not to favour but put an end to such hopes'. In the end, with riots in Derby, Bristol and Nottingham, there seemed a choice only between a reform bill and a revolution. Lord John Russell, piloting the bill through the commons, insisted it was a 'final' solution, aimed to put an end to a crisis, not to launch a gadarene dash towards democracy. As Grey put it, 'only such changes would be made as would associate the middle with the higher orders of society in love and support of the institutions and government of the country'.

The 1832 Reform Act abolished a number of parliamentary boroughs with few if any electors; gave seats to some large industrial towns; and made the distribution of county seats somewhat more proportionate to population. The right to vote in the counties, confined since 1432 to forty shilling freeholders, was extended to the more prosperous leaseholders and copyholders. After it had been established that the figure of £10 would be high enough to ensure that only about one working man in ten would qualify, £10 householders were enfranchised in all parliamentary boroughs. This eventually disfranchised workers in that small number of boroughs which, under the old system, had had a wide franchise.

The Reform Bill extended voting rights to persons in town and county (for example to copyholders whose land had originally been held in villeinage) which had hitherto been denied them by the antique in-feriority of their 'rank'. And though the £10 borough franchise limited the vote to 'small manufacturers, shopkeepers, master tailors, inn-keepers, commercial travellers and dealers of all kinds,' the limitation was at least related to the living man and not to Tom Paine's detested 'mouldy parchments'. But the bill left major electoral abuses untouched. Open voting continued and with it the general exercise of influence and 'treating'. The enfranchisement of tenants-at-will in the counties gave votes to men who, by the fact of being tenants, were expected to vote for candidates approved by their landlords. Thus, county constituencies were less independent than when, as before 1832, only freeholders voted; and, while many small boroughs survived, those which once had very wide voting qualifications now had a narrower one.

Nevertheless, the effect of the Reform Bill crisis of 1830–32 was that, willy-nilly, the Whigs had at last assumed parliamentary responsibility for the leadership and control of that radical body of opinion outside parliament which the legislature had, over the previous sixty years, mostly either ignored or repressed. They had finally justified their often equivocal stance as an 'opposition' by transforming themselves, without either revolution or the destruction of the ancient constitution, into a 'natural' and legitimate party of government committed to the peaceful, piecemeal change of existing institutions. Henceforth, parliament's task would always be seen, as it had not consistently been seen before, as that of the 'improvement' of society and its institutions; and not simply, as it had been since at least 1780, that of sustained resistance to change. For even in their reforming mood of the 1820s the Tories had, on the major issues of Catholic emancipation and parliamentary reform, insisted to the end on immobility. The Reform Bill thus enormously extended parliament's field of responsibility and its effective constituency. By tradition, one of its functions had been to right the wrongs of particular individuals and communities as set forth in petitions. Now it assumed the task it was not in future to lay down: that of trying to remedy the grievances and improve the conditions of life of the whole of society, even as that society grew in complexity. Parliament came to be seen as an engine of continuous change, always in some degree responsive to pressure from without. The welfare state, the permanently high taxation and the great bureaucratic machinery of the late twentieth century were natural consequences of what happened between 1830 and 1832. The Great Reform Bill ushered in a pretty watery dawn; but it was dawn all the same.

To those who had been for so long agitating for parliamentary reform, it had always seemed, essentially, as the means to a multitude of ends. Working men saw it as a first step to the reduction of over-long working hours. To others it was the prelude to the establishment of free trade and the ending of the Corn Laws. To radicals and Dissenters it was a first step towards bringing down the established church: they wanted to abolish church rates, remove Anglican bishops from the Lords, end church endowments and the Anglican monopoly over the rites of birth, death and marriage; and they wanted a national system of education in which the church played no part. The Whigs fulfilled almost none of these aims. But merely by making token gestures towards such a programme they acknowledged the legitimacy of its objectives. And in doing so, they opened, as Peel had foretold, doors which would not be shut.

They rounded off their own favourite humanitarian campaign by emancipating the slaves in the British Empire in 1833. They began the history of government intervention in public education when, in the same year, they instituted an annual grant to the Anglican and Nonconformist bodies that provided schools for the children of the poor. In 1839 they doubled the annual grant and appointed school inspectors for the first time. In 1833 a Factory Act was passed, forbidding the employment of children under nine in most textile factories, limiting the hours of work of those between the ages of nine and eighteen and appointing four government factory inspectors. They instituted the civil registration of births, deaths and marriages; and, provided a registrar was present,

Dissenters could now be married in their own chapels. A first breach in the monopoly of university education by Oxford and Cambridge was opened up by a charter granted to University College, London, a 'godless' institution which, unlike Oxford and Cambridge, imposed no religious tests on its members. The Municipal Corporations Act of 1835 began the history of modern local government by establishing, in place of 200 more or less closed corporations, 178 municipal boroughs, each with a council elected by ratepaying householders with three years' residence. The Poor Law Amendment Act of 1834, for all its unpopularity and harshness, would prove by the end of the century to have given rise not only to the whole great public health movement, but also to have introduced a fair degree of public responsibility for the education of pauper children and for the care of the aged. Old people, terrified of ending their days as inmates of the workhouse, would eventually feel little sense of shame if terminal illness resulted in their admission to the workhouse infirmaries, many of whose premises survived as elements in NHS hospital complexes well over a century later.

All of these reforms were important in the long run. Almost all were less than the Whigs' radical followers in and out of parliament were demanding. Most sound more far-reaching in summary than when their small print is examined. Accordingly, the Whigs of the 1830s have always been more highly esteemed by historians than they were by their contemporaries. Yet, for all their hesitations and internal dissension and eventual electoral defeat, the Whigs of that decade made a sufficient mark for it to be evident to Peel, leading the Tory opposition, that his party too must change its stance. Just as opposition Whigs after 1780 had accepted Tory resistance to radical change, so opposition Tories were now compelled to accept the Whig principle of cautious concession to change. When Peel adopted the term 'Conservative' to signal this change of policy, Disraeli made a character in one of his novels say that 'Conservative government' meant 'Tory men and Whig measures'. It was a fair comment on the complete change that the 1830s had made in English politics.

Corn, Church and Aristocracy

The issue of the twenty years after 1832 was the endeavour to find out how far and how fast parliament could be persuaded to make the wheels of change revolve. The two great movements of the time, the Anti-Corn Law League and Chartism were both in their different ways the outcome of the new belief that parliament could be persuaded to respond constructively to popular pressure.

As early as 1834, Grey had found the pressure of his radical colleagues more than he could stand; and Melbourne, his successor, did little to provide an answer to the abuse their various opponents now directed at the Whigs as, from 1837 onwards, their political disunity showed up sharply against the background of a severe trade depression. O'Connell, enraged at their failure to attend seriously to the affairs of Ireland, said they were 'base, bloody and brutal'. They were accused of showing 'truckling subservience' to the Tory opposition. Disraeli said they were 'reckless aristocrats stricken with palsy', presided over by 'a saunterer and a lounger', which unfortunately was what Melbourne gave every appearance of being. Not surprisingly, therefore, the Anti-Corn Law League presented itself as a crusade against an aristocracy of idle, selfish drones and against 'that creature and tool of the aristocracy', the established church. John Bright, the League's leading orator, did not hesitate to publish the banns of marriage between Protestantism and capitalism by declaring, 'As a nation of Bible Christians we ought to realise that trade should be as free as the winds of heaven'.

The triumph of the Anti-Corn Law League in the 1840s belongs more to the history books than to history itself. The Younger Pitt had been a pioneer of free trade in the 1780s. Under Liverpool, Tories had legislated to lift some trade restrictions in the 1820s as well as to mitigate the severity of the 1815 Corn Law. Perhaps the only positive gain the League could claim was that it converted Lord John Russell; desperate in 1841 to avert a Whig defeat in the election, he suddenly declared his conviction that the corn duties ought to be lowered. As prime minister from 1841 to 1846, Peel systematically lowered or discarded import and export duties and reintroduced income tax as a way of making good any temporary loss of revenue. He did not do this because he was a dedicated reader of Anti-Corn Law League literature, but because he understood trade and finance. By 1846 there were no logical reasons, as there had long been no sound economic reasons, for keeping the Corn Laws. By that date both Peel, the Tory prime minister, and Russell, the Whig leader, were ready to get rid of them: Russell because he hoped it would win electoral support, Peel because he saw no further point in them. The sole opposition came from a majority in the Tory party, whose objections were based as much on a dislike of Peel's manner, and his rational policy towards Ireland, as on the protection of agriculture. The Whigs voted for repeal because it would split the Tories. Peel admitted that the League's arguments were unanswerable, but this related less to the principle of the thing than to the need to act in 1846 rather than, as he had intended, after another election. Even the fuss about the timing was spurious. The English were hungry and the Irish starving because of bad harvests and a potato famine. Lowering the import duty on foreign corn in the late 1840s made no difference to that. There was little or no corn to import, and the effect of Repeal on the starving and dying Irish was nil.

The League were thus men who had won a reputation for prescience by contriving to back a winning horse when it was half a length from the finishing post. And they had put their money on the wrong race. In

1849, John Bright said that the affair had proved that 'the landed aristocracy had reached its height and henceforth it would find a rival to which eventually it must become subjected. We have been living through a revolution without knowing it.' But in backing Corn Law repeal as a revolution against the landed aristocracy Bright was supporting what was not a revolution and fighting against what was largely a myth. The landed aristocracy owned much land and had great power; but had its power been based simply on agricultural rents it would have voted repeal down in the Lords. It declined to do so because the greater the landed aristocrat, the less dependent he was on the rents of agricultural land. Moreover, those aristocrats who derived a great part of their income from rents were already persuaded that British agriculture was efficient enough to have little to fear from foreign competition. The extent to which the agricultural labourer benefited from the universal belief in the virtues of cheap food which henceforth prevailed is, however, open to question.

'Fortifying Established Institutions'

Though driven from office immediately after Repeal by the Tories who had voted against it and the Whigs who had voted for it, Peel was the architect of the League's failure to transfer power to the middle class. As early as 1834 he had made a reasoned bid for command of the middle ground of English life by announcing his acceptance of the Whig view of the Reform Bill as 'a final and irrevocable settlement of a great constitutional question'. While rejecting the idea 'that public men can only support themselves in public estimation by promising the instant redress of anything that anybody may call an abuse' he gave full support to the view that the Reform Bill implied that there should be 'a careful review of institutions civil and ecclesiastical, undertaken in a friendly temper and the correction of proved abuses and the redress of real grievances'. Both in opposition in the 1830s and in office in the 1840s he had pursued this policy. In factory reform as in the rationalisation of finance, Peel, like the Tories in general, had a better record than the Whigs. His readiness to recognise a social problem when he saw one may be said not so much to have 'conserved' national unity as to have re-created it after its near-dissolution in the decades before him. He was conspicuously appropriate to the needs of the time in the further respect that, as prime minister, he distributed patronage and honours more sparingly than any of his predecessors and most of his successors. There was justice, therefore, in the reply he had given two years in advance of it, to Bright's claim that there had been 'a revolution'. The passing of Repeal had, Peel said in 1847, 'tended to fortify the established institutions of this country, to inspire confidence in the equity and benevolence of the legislature, to maintain the just authority of an

391

hereditary nobility and to discourage the desire for democratic change in the constitution of the House of Commons'.

By dragging aristocratic leadership away from its former resistance to change and its bleak dedication to a static society based on subordination, Peel did much to ensure that England would be the only European country in that age which did not have a reactionary right wing nobility. Aristocratic rule therefore continued. Peel's own cabinet contained 8 peers, 2 eldest sons of earls, 3 baronets, 1 knight and only 1 plain mister. Even in the last 25 years of the century, there were rarely less than 8 peers or heirs to peerages in the 17- or 18-strong cabinets of the time. In 1877, Disraeli thought he should be congratulated upon, and Queen Victoria thought he should be restrained from, the daring step of appointing, as First Lord of the Admiralty, a Mr W. H. Smith, who had made his money out of providing the nation's railway stations with bookstalls. Not until the 1920s was Canning's exceptional achievement in becoming Foreign Secretary as a mere commoner repeated. Middle-class values certainly permeated Victorian society; but they did so only because the aristocracy was permeated with them.

Credit for preserving the stability of English life and for preventing class rivalries from festering must also go to Lord John Russell. In a political career stretching from 1830 to 1866, during which he was twice prime minister, he was always, in the words of *Punch*, like William III, 'about to land at Torbay to save the cause of English freedom'. Forever threatening to upset the political applecart by trying to secure the instant adoption of whatever radical demand happened to be currently vocal, at various times he wanted to disestablish the Irish church, abolish church rates, introduce secret ballot, repeal the Corn Laws. Having earned the label 'Finality Jack' for insisting on the finality of the 1832 Reform Bill, he later became 'Fidgety John', the one parliamentarian of distinction to support further extensions of the franchise, introducing unsuccessful bills in 1849, 1852, 1854 and 1866. The conscious, pedantic and sometimes comic embodiment of the traditions of his aristocratic forbears, who had challenged Charles II, James II and Louis XIV in the cause of civil and religious liberty, he was a tetchy colleague, a disordered prime minister, and a rather absurd foreign secretary—though a not inappropriate grandfather for Bertrand Russell. But, while Peel and John Russell lived, it was hard to pretend that England was groaning under a 'Norman yoke' imposed by a brutal, unyielding aristocracy.

From Hierarchy to Class

The stresses of the half century after 1780 had permanently changed men's traditional view of society as a hierarchy in which each rank except the highest deferred to the rank or ranks above it. The only real demarcation line had hitherto still been the old one between the propertied, who might be held to constitute the political nation, and the unpropertied, whose lack of property was held to disqualify them from participation in public affairs. These conditions of dependency and subordination were, however, to some extent sweetened by the concepts of freedom, paternalism and community. From these notions sprang the respect paid in the countryside to custom; the existence of a common law, so named because it was common to Englishmen of whatever rank; and the belief, often honoured in the practice, that those to whom the lower orders were subordinate acknowledged responsibilities towards them: a squire might refer to 'my poor'.

Between the 1780s and the 1830s, however, the failure of aristocratic government to cushion society from the shocks of sudden and radical economic change had created a resentment powerful enough to fracture the ties of subordination by which the old society had been held together. Alienated from their traditional leaders, men looked for a new source of unity; and failed to find one. The scattered, sporadic and various character of the protests of the age, and their manifestation in sudden explosions of wrath, often provoked by peripheral issues or by the capricious exhibitionism of a Wilkes, a Gordon, a Cochrane or a Caroline, testify to the discontent of a people restlessly in search of a programme, or a leadership, that was not forthcoming. Their protests were also, for the most part, conservative. The more literate would claim to be protesting at the violation of ancient constitutional freedoms by the corrupt and the tyrannical. Those who took part in food, employment or machine-wrecking riots were possibly the most conservative of all. To them, it was their rulers who were the revolutionaries, imposing new restraints and destroying historic rights, customs and livelihoods.

By the 1820s, however, it was becoming clear that appeals to the past would be of little avail. Industrial change had fashioned a new world. The old aristocracy, though ready enough to profit by it, were seen as unfit to rule over it. Men had to discover new loyalties, new rallying cries. But though there could, as always among liberation movements, be a temporary coalition of the forces ranged against the *status quo*, there could be no enduring unity. Even before the major battles of the time, that for parliamentary reform from 1830 to 1832, and the even more symbolic campaign for the repeal of the Corn Laws in the 1840s, it was evident that England was dividing itself into 'classes'. There would be an aristocratic 'class', under constant attack but, thanks to Peel and Russell, displaying unexpected powers of survival; and opposed to them, but also to each other, a 'middle class' and a 'working class'. Both terms had first come into use in the years after 1815. Each of these new terms was a slogan rather than a label, a battle cry rather than the definition of a precise social or economic category. The 'middle class' would always consist of a wide range of 'middle classes' and the 'working class' include a large and ever multiplying assortment of 'working classes'. To use either term in the singular would always imply the collective unity of so many pluralities as to be unavoidably misleading. To regard the demarcation lines between the classes as having the rigidity of the frontiers between adjacent but hostile nation-states and as alterable only after an armed struggle would be to rely on an analogy whose falsity could be demonstrated by simple observation of reality. Classes were not entities and, when treated as such, would come to be thought of as the hereditary castes which, appearance notwithstanding, they would not prove to be in fact. The concept of class, valid as an assertion that divisions existed, became untenable if it ignored the fact that the dividing lines between classes were constantly shifting and usually so ill-defined that there was a continuous to-and-fro traffic of families and individuals across them.

The relevance of the idea of class to the generation after 1815 is, however, unquestionable. The aristocratic élite was indeed opposed by two quite different classes of people. Dynamic, upward-thrusting manufacturers and businessmen resented the stigma of social inferiority that was attached to them and the unwillingness of aristocratic government to acknowledge their paramountcy in the new industrialised society either by admitting them into full political partnership or by liberating trade from the legal shackles which still encumbered it. Doctors, surveyors, solicitors, engineers and architects, and most educated professional men, had their own particular resentment of a society in which preferment depended on patronage rather than qualification, just as the Old Dissenters and the newer generation of Methodists detested the domination of religious life by a hierarchical Anglican clergy dependent on, and subservient to, aristocratic patronage. But whereas this 'middle' class opposed aristocracy out of a sense of frustration over a lack of opportunity and a tiresome clutter of antiquated laws, the 'working' class opposed aristocracy because it positively oppressed them. To working people, indeed, the principal offence of aristocratic government was not that it impeded the unrestrained exercise of the profit motive but that it actively encouraged it to the detriment of all whose only economic asset was their labour.

But though at one with the middle classes in detesting aristocracy, working men were no less alienated from the middle classes. The middle classes were the employing classes. They were men of 'means'. Most of them had 'independent means'. Whether employers or professional men, they did not get their hands or their clothes dirty. The middle classes were neither compulsorily overworked, nor compulsorily underemployed, nor deprived of livelihood and therefore of all the means of life by the economic obsolescence of their skills. They were not potential paupers owing to the impossibility of saving out of their precarious earnings when they had any. These distinctive characteristics of the great majority of the working classes shut them off from the other classes and inevitably nourished a hatred of both. It was for this reason that the Reform Bill, essentially a successful bid by the aristocracy for the cooperation of the middle class in the task of maintaining the existing social order, was seen by the working class as a defeat. The impression was reinforced wherever there was an attempt to implement the harsh terms of the Poor Law Amendment Act. The working class shared the middle class dislike of the Corn Laws and the church; but they disliked their middle class employers even more, and still, moreover, wanted the vote. Although the Chartist movement, with its immediate demand for manhood suffrage, secret ballot, payment of MPs, annual parliaments, equal electoral districts and the abolition of property qualifications for MPs, officially emerged in 1838, its real birthday was that on which the Reform Bill received the royal assent in 1832.

To Turn the World Upside Down—or Not?

Chartism was not merely the result of the defeat of the working class in 1832. Carlyle perhaps put it best when he said, 'Chartism is a new name for a thing which has had many names, which will yet have many. The matter of Chartism is weighty, deep rooted, far extending: did not begin yesterday: will by no means end tomorrow'. It was a nationwide, if only temporary, coalition of a whole range of working-class ideas, developed or given new force by the experiences of the previous forty years. Autonomous working-class social organisations were already in existence. Trade unions, trade clubs, mutual improvement societies, various attempts at retail and wholesale cooperative movements and, at that time the most important, the benefit clubs and friendly societies, all attested the capacity of working men to create institutions of their own. Their 'class' ideas were also in the making; and in this process the trade unions, though their numbers were a fraction compared with those of the friendly societies, were naturally most active. They took over, chiefly from the fecund mind of the benevolent and paternalistic factory owner, Robert Owen, the idea that labour was the only source of all wealth and that all the value of whatever was produced was put into it by, and therefore rightfully belonged to, the workers. This proposition would take men well beyond Owen's first object of 'remoralising the lower orders' and to the rewriting of an ancient text to make it read, 'The earth is the workers' and the fulness thereof'. It was a revision that harked back to the True Levellers and forward to the 'scientific' socialism of Marx.

In the 1830s it was hoped that a national assembly elected by trade union lodges would provide the real universal suffrage, annual elections and so forth that the Reform Bill had denied, and would take over management of all trade and commerce, and eventually all political power, from the house of commons. The attempt to form such a Grand National Consolidated Trades Union in 1834 foundered. The transportation of the agricultural labourers of Tolpuddle was merely the most celebrated of the hostile actions of the employers. Moreover, the principal cause of the creation and survival of the many small unions of the time was their natural concern with their own sectional interests. To

395

try to weld them into a national organisation was, at this stage, unrealistically premature.

This failure made men turn back, during the severe slump of 1837–42, to the unfinished business of parliamentary reform. The vote should be given, not to property, but to the man himself. To deny a man the vote was to deny him 'the most valuable right that man can enjoy in society'. Bronterre O'Brien, the only considerable Chartist theorist, declared that the working class wanted 'an entire change in society amounting to a complete subversion of the existing "order of the world"'. The 1832 act was damned for transferring power to the middle class, since 'of all governments, a government of the middle classes is the most grinding and ruthless' and because the interests of the middle-class employer and those of the worker were 'as directly opposed to each other as fighting bulls'.

Unfortunately for intellectuals like O'Brien (a distinguished graduate of Trinity College, Dublin) skilled, articulate working men will behave like fighting bulls only when provoked by a rigidly hostile political system or a sudden change from fair economic weather to foul. Since 1820 the political and economic climate had improved. It was becoming clear to many that there was an alternative ambition to that of over-throwing the system: that of stringing along with it in the hope of getting something out of it. Creatures of habit save in times of exceptional stress, most men think first, not of turning the world upside down, but of providing for their women and children. These are immediate needs; and, such is their hope, these are best served by continuing to do in the future what has kept them from hunger in the past. The fewer a man's possessions, the more clamant are his family's demands upon him. The command to follow instead the cause of a utopian future by waging a bitter struggle against those in high places will ordinarily be ignored. It will be obeyed only when unusually large numbers of men are confronted with an abrupt reversal of their unambitious workaday expectations of a continuance of their usual means of livelihood, or of their customary acquiescent belief in the superior wisdom of those who run their country's affairs.

In consequence, Chartism flourished only during the bad years of 1838 to 1842 and again in the bad winter of 1847–8; and even then lost support in proportion to the degree of violence its leadership demanded. Of the various groups which advocated the charter, those most akin to the earlier middle class or artisan reform clubs shied away first. They were alienated by the explosive tactics of Feargus O'Connor who, having seen the government give way to the threat of violence in Ireland in 1829, thought the same tactic would work again. In the event, O'Connor incited to violence only to dissociate himself from it when it seemed imminent. The commons rejected the first Chartist petition in 1839; there followed riots in various places, the imprisonment of most Chartist leaders and, inevitably, outbursts of desperate oratory by those still free. O'Connor sponsored a new National Charter Association in 1840; it was repudiated by other Chartist leaders; the petition was again presented and rejected; and O'Connor lost interest. When the movement revived once more in 1848, the year when most continental capitals outside Russia were stormy with revolt, London feared the worst. The Duke of Wellington was appointed to defend the metropolis from the mass demonstration and march to Westminster from Kennington Common which O'Connor now threatened. The demonstration was thinly attended. The police had no difficulty in persuading O'Connor to abandon the march. The petition was, however, presented but, as usual, rejected. Much fun was enjoyed by men of property at what they naively supposed was the unique circumstance that the petition contained false or funny signatures and at the apparent unwillingness of would-be revolutionaries to submit to the discomforts of a dampish April day. As after the General Strike seventy-eight years later, the English were widely congratulated, not least by the English, on their phlegmatic good sense in the hour of peril.

The importance of Chartism was that it was a nationwide demonstration of working-class aspiration that owed little or nothing to middle-class leadership. It had a middle-class element to begin with; but by 1842 insistence on manhood suffrage and talk of physical violence had frightened middle-class radicals off. At the same time, though the middle classes responded eagerly to the Anti-Corn Law League, the working classes stayed aloof from it. The separateness of the two great movements of the 1840s indicated the growing detachment of working men from even the more 'enlightened' and 'benevolent' of their betters. They would no longer be 'extras', content with crowd parts in shows put on by political mavericks like Gordon, Cochrane or Caroline, or individualists like Wilkes and Wardle. And, though the Chartist peaks coincided with years of economic hardship, neither was Chartism a monster version of the old eighteenth-century food or unemployment and wages riot. Though all working-class movements would be shot through with nostalgia for some golden pre-industrial age, and though some among the Chartists dreamed of an England in which every man would live on his own farm, Chartism looked forward rather than backward. Working men were not now appealing for the protection accorded them by old laws. Now they were demanding, through a reformed parliament, the right to make new laws for, and by, themselves.

Nor were they, when it came to it, prepared to re-enact the violence that had so terrified authority during the Gordon riots. The threat of violence was in a sense an alien import, O'Connor's attempt to apply Irish tactics to a social and economic problem in England that was not, after all, a conflict between rival races divided by religious passion or the consequence of the conquest of one people by the other. The majority rejected the violence of Chartism as firmly as they had expressed their solidarity by support for its substance. And just as the Gordon riots began a long period when governments sought to repress all signs of popular protest, the peaceable outcome of the Chartist demonstration of 1848 may perhaps be said at last to have laid the ghosts of the Gordon rioters. Normally considered as marking the true beginning of 'the working-class movement', Chartism may also be looked on as the last stage in the history of that sort of popular protest which had needed a Wilkes or a Gordon before its grievances could be made nationally known.

The transformation of protesting workers from rioting 'crowd' into more or less nationally organised 'movements' whose more explosive moods could normally be contained by the police without the necessity to use armed force was also assisted by the changed attitude of government. The initial nervelessness over the Gordon riots and the precipitate violence of Peterloo were both avoided. Peel and Russell were determined to resist the Charter, but though Chartist leaders were at various times imprisoned and troops deployed, the job was discreetly done (with a judicious use of the new railways) and a concern not to provide the movement with martyrs. There was no similarity between the attitude of Sir Charles Napier, the distinguished soldier who commanded the troops used in Lancashire, and the brutality of the civilian Yeomanry of Peterloo. 'Seizing these men,' he told the magistrates, 'could do no good; it would not stop chartism if they were all hanged; and as they offered no violence, why starve their wretched families and worry them with long imprisonment?' Most working men could themselves have put their point no better than he when he angrily complained that his distasteful task had been made necessary 'by tory injustice and whig imbecility'. 'The doctrine of slowly reforming when men are starving is of all things the most silly,' he wrote, 'famishing men cannot wait'. But that was in 1839. By the later 1840s, men were for the most part rather less famished. More of them were at last beginning to share a little of the country's rising prosperity. They would want to turn the world upside down only if they could see no chance of decent prospects while it stayed as it was. By the 1850s, though the poorest of the population were still largely untouched by the rising standards of the time, the more skilled and energetic began to find they had rather less to complain about.

Calmer Waters

After the storms of the preceding decades, the stability of the years from 1850 to 1875 surprised contemporaries. Certainly, the phenomenon of a still rising population contriving to achieve an even more rapid increase of national wealth was a source of amazement abroad and of complacency at home. The orderly good humour of the hundreds of thousands who crowded to the Crystal Palace to visit the Great

Exhibition of 1851 seemed to make nonsense alike of the bloodcurdling oratory of popular protest and of the panic fear of the men in authority. Not only did quite common people come quietly to gape at the wonders of the new age of steam and manufacture: they endured with patience the regimen of buns and non-alcoholic beverages which Prince Albert had imposed on all the Exhibition's visitors; and, *en route* to and from the excursion trains that brought them to the main line termini, they troubled the police hardly at all.

Walter Bagehot thought this stability existed because the English were a 'deferential' people. This perhaps overlooked the many evidences of a lack of such deference during the preceding decades. Yet the verdict seemed true. There was only minor popular agitation when the vote was extended to all male householders in the boroughs in 1867. There was a party struggle to compete for the credit of granting the vote, but only a minor, if sharp, parliamentary argument against the principle. The 1867 Reform Act was the brainchild of Lord Derby, an astute parliamentarian and prime minister for all that he spent so much of his time studying the racing form book and the works of Homer. He left it to Gladstone and Disraeli to compete confusedly about which of them was to be acknowledged its rightful foster father. Disraeli won by being more imaginative and less pettifogging than Gladstone. As for the granting of the household suffrage in the counties in 1884, this was undertaken almost as a routine chore. By now, only Tories living in an imaginary past, and a few Liberals over-impressed by what their classical studies had taught them of the horrors of 'democracy', opposed universal male household suffrage. Realists knew it to be almost a guarantee of conservatism. From 1886 until the 1970s, if English constituencies alone are considered, only in 1906 and 1945 was the majority of seats won by other than Conservative candidates.

Patriots All

The prevailing mood of the working class in mid-century was one which united them once more with the middle class: an intense patriotism. It had long been an easy matter to raise a mob on behalf of church and crown. So, in Victoria's reign, no belief was more popular than that Englishmen were absolutely superior to all 'damned foreigners', a category which, though first and foremost inclusive of Frenchmen and Russians, also included Yankees, Irishmen, Welshmen and Jews. The Scots were an exception: they were either very romantic, or were considered honorary Englishmen for being shrewd about money (except when drinking) and good at engineering.

The great popularity of Palmerston in the two decades after 1850 attests the strength of Victorian patriotism, for the radical patriotic image he cultivated was the only Victorian thing about him. In all other respects he belonged to the eighteenth century: of casual sexual morals, he firmly believed in the game laws and the flogging of soldiers; was a quondam supporter of the Six Acts; and an opponent of further parliamentary reform from 1832 until his death in 1865. For their own outspoken opposition to the Crimean War, John Bright and Richard Cobden, the heroes of the campaign against the Corn Laws, were both rejected by an outraged electorate. Even Palmerston was hooted in the streets when in 1851 he momentarily forgot his patriotic role and had congratulated Louis Napoleon for setting up a dictatorship in France. The delight in Disraeli's diplomatic showmanship displayed by the music hall audiences which sang the word 'jingo' into the language in the mid 1870s further demonstrates the patriotism of working men who are too often credited with a class conscious bitterness they apparently did not always feel in fact.

There was more than xenophobia in the working man's participation in this tribal patriotism. Foreigners were despised for submitting to tyranny, for being poorer than the English, and for having no great navy and no great empire, but only the great armies which kept them permanently in subjection. It was thus a prejudice in favour of freedom and decent standards of living. And though more English working men emigrated to the United States than anywhere else, the sentiment of empire was nourished in working-class homes because so many members of working-class families were already 'going out to the colonies'. It is easy to forget that any Englishman, however humble, who had a roof over his head and food for himself and his family, could justifiably feel that he belonged to the greatest nation on earth. He was always being told so; and in the mid-Victorian years he had no reason to disbelieve it. True, England was a land of abysmal poverty still; but in the mid-Victorian years, the poor were largely forgotten. When Henry Mayhew first published his articles about their lives in 1849, his newspaper was so embarrassed that he was got rid of. The poor had to wait to be rediscovered in the 1880s.

4

CHURCH AND SOCIETY, 1790–1970

Dissent, Religious and Social

IN the eighteenth century, religious dissent had institutionalised political dissent. As Joseph Priestley said in 1769, 'So long as we continue Dissenters it is hardly possible that we should be other than friends to civil liberty'. Every dissenting chapel was a focus of social consciousness, providing an opportunity for the practice of some degree of self government. Dissent gave respectability to supporters of the American Revolution and (in its early stages) the French, as well as to the parliamentary reform and free trade movements. One reason why social and political change were so limited when they came, and attended by so little violence, was that Old Dissent was so conservative. It inherited the constitutional traditions of the Commonwealth men who had been outraged not only by the arbitrary acts of the Stuarts but also by the revolutionary radicalism which their own reluctant resort to arms had then produced.

This conjunction within Old Dissent of actual conservatism and potential radicalism weakened it on both fronts. The conservatism left the field open to the Methodists; the radicalism provoked a revival of the Church of England. All three great religious movements of the late eighteenth and early nineteenth centuries, Methodism, Evangelicalism and Tractarianism, were, in their differing ways, and in spite of some of their own slogans, avowedly counter-revolutionary.

Methodist Orthodoxy

As a religious body reaching out to the poor, Methodism might have been expected to identify with their social and political aspirations. Many of its adherents thought so too. But Wesley himself condemned both American and French Revolutions and his chief successor declared, 'Methodism hates democracy as it hates sin'. The inmates of Wesley's school for miners' children had to be out of their beds, winter and summer, at 4 a.m. and were taught that 'he who plays as a child will play when he is a man'. 'Whatever pains it costs,' Wesley wrote, 'break the will if you would not damn the child. Let a child from a year old be taught to fear the rod and to cry softly; from that age make him do as he is bid, if you whip him ten times running to effect it . . . Break his will now and his soul shall live and he will probably bless you to all eternity'.

This suggests a man as wedded to an authoritarian social order as a hanging judge.

Wesley was in fact all his life preoccupied with the contradictions in his message of salvation. His early upbringing had been Tory, if not Jacobite. From the ideas of passive obedience and Laudian Arminianism he was never to depart. He aimed to reform England in order to extinguish the flames of revolution, not to fan them. He considered the Wilkes and Liberty rioters who, when he refused to illuminate his house in their hero's honour, had to be held at bay by the Horse Guards, as victims of 'epidemic madness'. Yet his evangelical, Arminian message that any man could, through a New Birth to a life of purity and good works, attain to Christian perfection and assurance of salvation was anathema to those in authority. In the years before his death in 1791 the success of his mission among the unpropertied seemed to threaten a revival of the socially disruptive and 'levelling' enthusiasms which had accompanied the civil war. During the twenty years after his death it appeared scarcely distinguishable from Jacobinism. It was only by persistently proclaiming a vehement support for law and order that Methodism managed, during the anti-Jacobin years, to escape persecution and the possibility of actual suppression.

It was not therefore surprising that the Methodist annual conference was as zealous to preserve the movement from the taint of Jacobinism as its future foster child, the annual conference of the Labour Party, to preserve itself from the taint of Communism between 1920 and 1940. Politically minded lay preachers who offended in this way were expelled. The Primitive Methodists were proscribed for their political radicalism. The fact that some Luddites went to the scaffold singing Methodist hymns led to an official Wesleyan denunciation of Luddism. After Peterloo, the Methodist leadership issued a strong condemnation of the practice of 'large masses of people' being 'irregularly' collected together, 'often under banners bearing the most shocking and impious inscriptions' to listen to 'infidel principles', 'wild delusive political theories' and 'violent and inflammatory declamations'.

Yet Methodism made great headway after 1815 among both the industrial middle class and working class. Its attraction was that, while it reconciled people to the new industrialism, it also provided emotional escape from it. It taught people to be sober, hardworking, and obedient to their employers on six days of the week; and on the seventh restored their personal value by offering, to each and every one of them, the open arms of a Jesus who loved them so much that He had laid down His life for them. In this Sunday situation they could feel redeemed both by their industrious weekday respectability and by the cleansing Blood of the Lamb. Or, depending upon the quality of the preacher, they could be uplifted into a state of religious emotion or hysteria. As time went on, the fervour declined and the respectability came to dominate. The psychologically healing joyousness of early Methodism would survive longest among its black converts in North America and West Africa.

Moreover, though Wesley had been fiercely Tory, Methodism's breach with Anglicanism, and the contempt with which the movement was regarded by society's higher ranks, meant that in the long run it could scarcely do other than develop the hostility towards the established church and towards aristocratic rule which continued to characterise the Old Dissenters. Given the social classes to which they appealed, Methodists were bound sooner or later to swell the ranks of those whose political allegiance would be to the more radical among the Whigs and then to the Liberals and eventually to the Labour party. The obstinate Toryism of the earliest Methodists may well explain the movement's slower growth between 1800 and 1815; only after that time did it greatly expand again, attracting a new generation to whom Pittite Toryism and clerical privilege were alike objectionable. Thus, though, in its Tory beginnings, Methodism seemed to sanctify the principle of subordination, in its later history it would do much to give the reforming movements of the nineteenth century the moral and religious dimension which made them crusades rather than mere political campaigns.

That Methodism sought to divert some of its radical zeal into the anti-slavery movement and, from 1815 onwards, into foreign missions, reflects Methodist nervousness at the political implications of their evangelising work at home. Nevertheless, by proclaiming the principle of human equality in the religious life while ardently striving to resist whatever smacked of political egalitarianism, Methodism contributed to the process of social change by simultaneously encouraging and restraining it. To the small scale employers and shopkeepers and the more ambitious workpeople of the years after 1815, Methodism opened up the most accessible path to the respectable piety expected of all but the very poorest of nineteenth-century Englishmen. It challenged the snobbish notion that this condition was attainable only by those who adhered to the Established church. Methodism gave the new type of man a new type of status and added moral and religious force to his insistence on hard work, punctuality and obedience among his subordinates. It proclaimed that here was one whose pious prosperity had been achieved without the advantages of either privileged birth or inherited wealth and who eschewed the luxury and flummery of those who enjoyed—and usually frittered away—such advantages. Not being an Anglican enabled him to proclaim his independence of aristocracy and gentry; and in many towns even Old Dissent was sometimes too socially exclusive for him. But as the frontiersman of a new kind of society, he could make a mark for himself as luminary and benefactor in a Methodist community, because most of its members were as lacking in historical social prestige and tradition as he himself.

Evangelical Indoctrination

The Evangelical movement within the established church was more deliberately repressive than Methodism. The Society for the Suppression of Vice and the Encouragement of Religion was founded in 1795 by William Wilberforce and by that Dr John Bowdler who is better remembered for editing the ruder parts out of Shakespeare. It was a propaganda campaign to combat the spread of Jacobinism and the ideas of Tom Paine among the lower orders and to induce a greater attention to their religious duties among the upper and middle classes so that their inferiors could learn piety from their good example. Like Wilberforce himself, the Evangelicals were wealthy as well as pious and flooded the country with torrents of improving and extremely sentimental literature. Wilberforce himself, as a close political colleague of Pitt, eagerly supported the Combination Laws and virtually the whole policy of Pittite repression for as long as it lasted. He resisted Catholic emancipation and defended the Corn Laws and the Six Acts. His opposition to the slave trade and to slavery itself, as well as his share in the foundation of the Royal Society for the Prevention of Cruelty to Animals, suggest someone careful to support good causes combining the maximum emotional appeal and the minimum relevance to immediate social problems. The humanitarian work of Howard on behalf of prisoners and of Hanway for child chimney sweeps was held up or reversed; and Wilberforce, unlike that later Tory Evangelical, Lord Shaftesbury, could find sound theological reasons for being complacent about factory conditions. For Wilberforce, the principal duty of the poor was to endure their sufferings meekly. Their more lowly path, he told them, had been allotted them by God; they were 'faithfully to discharge its duties and contentedly to bear its inconveniences'. They were reminded that 'the present state of things is very short' and that 'their situation with all its evils' was better than they had 'deserved at the hands of God'. It is not surprising that Cobbett should say that the aim of the Evangelicals was to teach the poor to starve without making a noise; and that one special reason for admiring the Americans was that they had 'No Wilberforces! Just think of that, *No Wilberforces!*'

Since Wilberforce had charm, wit and personal generosity, and gained the ear of the powerful in society and politics, his influence and that of the Evangelical movement was wider than that of the socially inferior Methodists. It is from Wilberforce and the Evangelicals that the Victorians inherited their high moral tone and the nobility and gentry their new-found resolve to go to church regularly in order to encourage the lower orders to do the same. From this source came the regular habits of family prayers, particularly in households where there were many servants to influence, and of the saying of grace before meals. Old Puritan habits were thus refurbished and some of the values which the nineteenth-century aristocracy are said to have absorbed from the middle classes came originally from the aristocrats themselves. The aristocratic wickedness of the Regency period was only a topdressing; underneath there was already a deepening subsoil of earnest piety. When the Congress of Vienna met in 1815, the diplomats of Europe were astonished that, alone among them, England's representative, Lord Castlereagh, dressed quietly, went to church on Sunday, kept company with his wife and consorted with no mistresses. It was in response to Wilberforce's promptings that Lord Liverpool passed the Church Building act of 1818, setting aside £1 million for building new churches. The opprobrium which attached to George IV and his dissolute brothers in their lifetime is some indication of the extent to which their behaviour was felt to belong to a wicked past that ought to be buried. The reserved, restrained Englishman, gravely and delicately courteous towards ladies and as careful to eschew gallantry towards them as they were to avoid coquetry towards him—these stereotypes were brought to life by Evangelicalism's energetic stimulation of the fears and revulsion engendered in English minds by the twin phenomena of godless Jacobinism and working-class turbulence. These evils could be suppressed only by teaching the poor to be meek and the rich to set a good example. As Ruskin later said, it was a process of turning the Bible into a 'special constable's handbook' and making the church seem, in the words of the Frenchman, Taine, writing in the 1870s, the nation's 'moral health department'.

Since educated men of Evangelical convictions were prominent throughout the nineteenth century in commerce, the civil service, the armed forces and in politics, these convictions permeated the life of the time. Evangelicals displayed an earnest dedication to duty and a high sense of responsibility in personal and public behaviour. They contributed much to the long, slow business of establishing the ethical basis and the institutional machinery for eliminating the carelessness about public money, the more irresponsible aspects of the patronage system, and the lack of professionalism, which had been so marked in the eighteenth century. No longer was involvement in public life, or even commerce, to be considered a mere means to self-enrichment. Rather, it was now the means by which those whom God had been pleased to endow with talents should devote them, selflessly and tirelessly, to the service of their fellow men, whether they be 'unfortunates' of the more deserving sort in the cities of England or the even more unfortunate 'natives' or 'heathens' of Asia and Africa. To the conversion and civilising of these latter, Englishmen had obviously been specially called by the God who had given them so vast an empire. In any consideration of such men it perhaps needs to be remembered that the best of them were likely to impose on themselves much the same hard moral disciplines they imposed on their subordinates.

The Ideology of Industrialisation

Wesley and Wilberforce were thus to England's Industrial Revolution what Marx and Lenin were to the Soviet Union's later and speedier one after 1918. They provided the psychological and ideological motive power which turned the traditionally unruly English into a nation of dedicated toilers year by year achieving production norms that no previous society would have thought attainable. Between them, they offered a consolatory doctrine of equality: all, even the humblest, had but to open their hearts to the Lord Jesus and He would Save them. But there was no question of an unconditional passport to paradise. Grace was indeed universal. But so was sin: all men were conceived in it. The Calvinist assurance of election was replaced by a lifelong fear that grace might be forfeited for ever by a yielding to the sins of the world and, above all, of the flesh. This virtually compelled concentration on work. Enjoyment was innately sinful, since it was an indulgence of a man's own preferences (which were bound to be evil, since his nature was evil). It was a profaning of the Time which God had, out of his ineffable goodness, bestowed on man for the sole purpose of transforming his sinful soul into one fit at the last to stand in the awful presence of his Maker. Neither political commissars nor secret police were needed to exact hard work and conformity to official ideology from an Englishman on whose living room or bedroom wall he had hung the text, 'Thou, God, seest me'.

Sabbatarianism followed naturally from this creed of joy through joylessness. Since Jehovah had commanded his people not to work on the Sabbath, it was a matter of eternal life and death that they should not enjoy themselves instead. Attendance at a place of worship up to three times; an absolute ban on the reading of anything apart from the Bible or prayer book; on going for a walk; or even on visits to relatives unless they were seriously ill: these were the Sabbatarian regulations by which the godly worker and his women were protected from the temptations of drinking, card playing, singing, dancing, theatres and gaudy dress. Of course the result was a thrifty, serious minded, hardworking population. But that it worked out of an overbearing selfconfidence is uncertain: the bouncingly self-confident Victorian would more likely be found among those robust enough to resist or ignore the prevailing ideology. The first item in the questionnaire that Wesley would submit to the faithful was, 'What known sins have you committed since our last meeting?' Thus, when Hazlitt said of the Methodists that they were a collection of religious invalids, he diagnosed the condition of many of those who, in the century after 1790, took Methodism or Evangelicalism seriously.

Reason Condemned

Their ideology cultivated not only a dark night in the soul but a dark one in the mind as well. Both were anti-intellectual. Poetry and all the arts together with philosophy and political theory were tainted with temptations to faithlessness. There was reluctance in Methodist and Evangelical schools to teach writing; and, for a time, a ban on teaching it on Sundays. Reading was essential for a Bible Christian; but writing was a worldly accomplishment. Moreover, it was expensive; paper, ink and pens cost money and before penny postage began in 1840 it could cost a day's wages to send a letter across England. The poor ought not to be encouraged in such profligacy; and many a worker who could perhaps read well enough was deemed illiterate because, having little practice in writing, he could not spell. This seems to have been the fate of the canal pioneer, James Brindley, whose alleged 'illiteracy' lay in his being as bad at spelling as the shoemaker who is quoted as beginning a letter 'Sir, I Ham a very Bad Hand at Righting'.

The exercise of the intellect was inhibited because it encouraged the use of reason; and reason was held to be the antithesis of faith. 'The heart is everything and the intellect scarcely anything in the great pursuit of salvation,' wrote Lord Shaftesbury. Kingsley's advice to young women ('Be good, sweet maid, and let who will be clever') was applied to both sexes and anti-intellectualism was a marked feature of English life well into the twentieth century. Thomas Arnold had a larger mind than either Evangelicals or Tractarians, and he was not responsible for the domination of the public schools by games; but responsive nevertheless to the spirit of his times, he bequeathed to them, for something like a century after 1840, the mentally debilitating principle that the pursuit of intellectual excellence was secondary to the fashioning of morally pure Christian gentlemen. The disarming good heartedness that caused his admirer, Thomas Hughes, later to write *Tom Brown's Schooldays* and, as a Christian Socialist, to work for the legalisation of skilled workers' trade unions in the 1860s, was one of the more attractive results of Arnold's influence; but that influence did much to justify the verdict of his son, Matthew Arnold, that, above the level of 'the Populace', there were in the England of the 1870s but two sorts of men, aristocratic 'Barbarians' and middle class 'Philistines'.

'Useful Knowledge'

Fortunately, it was still permissible to pursue what was called *useful* knowledge. The abhorrence of any knowledge considered useless found vernacular expression whenever a parent ordered a child not to 'fill its head with a lot of nonsense out of books'. Botany, chemistry, mathematics and applied science, together with political economy (through which men could learn that the laws of supply and demand were eternal verities) were all acceptable, because 'useful' and 'improving'. This encouraged philistinism and a revulsion from general ideas, particularly challenging ones. It helps to explain why in England the words 'intellectual' and 'intelligentsia' became terms of abuse whereas their continental equivalents described, more or less neutrally, members of the professional middle class who made their money through their mental capacities. But if this English characteristic put a low value on learning, it put much on knowledge. The Victorians were voracious for facts; Harmsworth's *Tit Bits* would not otherwise have sold so well when it first appeared in the 1890s. It was this desire for improvement that bred mechanics' institutes, mutual improvement societies, the Society for the Diffusion of Useful Knowledge and nourished night schools, the first, late-nineteenth century polytechnics, the technical schools and the Workers' Educational Association and persisted long enough to launch the Open University in the late 1960s. Though this zeal for self improvement had become by the twentieth century an increasingly middle-class phenomenon, few workers being touched by the WEA and fewer than was hoped by the Open University, its working-class origins help to explain why those whose minds were formed by such influences bewildered their social betters. Bernard Shaw noted the fact with amusement when creating the polytechnic-trained chauffeur, Straker, in *Man and Superman*. But E. M. Forster's Leonard Bast, the humble self improver in *Howard's End*, and Aldous Huxley's Illidge, the only technically-qualified character to appear in *Point Counter Point*, were clearly created out of deep ignorance of what such men were really like.

It would be wrong to attribute the earnestness of the humbler autodidacts of the nineteenth century solely to religious influences. Anti-clerical radicalism was just as earnest at all levels. James Mill, friend of Bentham, and 'philosophic radical', advocated in 1835 a 'secularised' church with a clergy composed of 'salutary teachers of utilitarianism' and a 'secularised' Sunday designed to be scarcely less tedious than the Evangelicals' Sabbath:

There should be social amusements of a mild character such as to promote cheerfulness rather than profane merriment. Sports involving bodily strength are not well adapted to promote brotherly feeling: their encouragement in antiquity had in view the urgency of war. Music and dancing would be important. It would be desirable to invent dancing representing parental, filial and fraternal affections and to avoid such as slide into lasciviousness, which the author is always anxious to repress. Quiet and gentle motions with an exhibition of grace are what would be desired. To keep everything within the bounds of decency, the parishioners would elect a master and mistress of ceremonies and support their authority. A conjoint meal on Sunday would have the happiest effects, being a renewal of the Agapai—love feasts—of the early Christians; but with the exclusion of intoxicating liquors.

The Painites and their free-thinking successors in all classes were no less serious in mind and conduct. This was the more necessary because their detractors sought to identify agnosticism and radicalism, as they so often identified Roman Catholicism, with vice. The reflective, free-thinking weavers, shoemakers and blacksmiths, all men with time to mediate and discuss while they worked, may perhaps be claimed, not less than the religious zealots, as the earliest pace setters of the ideas of self help and self improvement.

Fortitude Fortified

No analysis of the importance of religion in the nineteenth century can overlook the extent to which it strengthened the quality of fortitude, without which life would have been unbearable in the gruelling living and working conditions of the time. Many of the social problems of the age were even less susceptible of easy solutions than those of most ages. Nineteenth-century society was caught unawares by its own biological and technological fecundity, forever grappling with problems that exceeded its capacity. When Wesley and Wilberforce urged the poor to endure without bitterness or a sense of grievance, they were in some respects telling them to do what they had always done; the fortitude of the nineteenth-century poor may well have sprung from deeper roots than could be watered by the promise of heavenly reward. Bitterness and a sense of grievance would intensify life's burdens, not reduce them; and would certainly inhibit effort. So, men might walk twenty to thirty miles a day for weeks, or even months, on end and in all weathers in search of work. Sometimes their wives walked with them; only rarely might an occasional passing carter offer a lift. Those who survived to old age often recalled their long hours and struggles with a sense of achievement rather than resentment; like the widowed Methodist laundress of seventy-five, declaring 'I've had a hard life, praise the Lord', and uttering the words with a bright, complacent smile. Overworked servant girls could recall the compensations of their days of drudgery: the excitements of the great house parties, or the pleasure of pouring tea, even for a harsh mistress, out of a fine silver teapot in a drawing room whose windows offered a view of gleaming japonica. Men would look back with no less pleasure on their two or three mile walk to school as country boys at a time when it was possible to enjoy the freedom of untrafficked roads and the beauty of the unpolluted streams by which they passed. These signs of an assumption that the world was to be endured rather than to be enjoyed, that few of its wrongs could be soon or easily righted, and that man was born to trouble as the sparks fly upward must certainly have ensured that social evils too long survived; but it also ensured that life nevertheless went on. Their descendants, who would have incredulously enquired, 'Why did you put up with it?' would discover that a contrasting way of living, based on ever-rising expectations in the here and now, with the hereafter wholly discounted, did not itself lack difficulties.

Tractarian Deviationism

Yet, as soon as the Victorian years began, serious men felt that godlessness had by no means been overcome. Some, indeed, felt that those claiming to be the most godly were themselves only minimally Christian. The young Gladstone felt there was something of anti-Christ about the Reform Bill; and the radical and nonconformist campaign against the Church of England, which the Reform Bill symbolised and intensified, produced in 1839 the birth of the Oxford, or Tractarian, movement, of which the most significant figure was John Henry Newman. He and his associates inaugurated what its opponents, had they known of the term, might well have described as a right-wing deviationist movement in English religious life. Tractarians confronted the godly English with the proposition that Protestantism as such, whether the Protestantism of Dissent or that of the evangelically orientated Church of England, was but a halfway house to atheism. Holiness that depended on inward assurance and private judgment was built on shifting sand. The Bible alone could not be the ruler of faith; it was not an authoritative text from which every man was free to extract such dogmas as took his fancy. Such authority as it had derived from the church which had adopted it. The argument that a bibliocentric Protestantism could underpin almost any set of beliefs and almost any mode of conduct that men could devise was unanswerable; its truth had been shown again and again ever since the Reformation. The solution propounded by the Tractarians, however, was unthinkable: the Reformation must be undone and the English church must revert to its Catholic origins and become once more a source of unifying authority. The logical conclusion of this view of the Established church as Catholic was to return to Rome. After infinite mind-searching, Newman took that road, as did some other distinguished Anglican clergy. Enough of them remained within the Anglican communion, however, to restore forgotten qualities to it that were to survive until swept away by the tides of latitudinarianism to which Anglicanism, like the Roman church, was subjected in the late 1960s. Though Newman was not himself a 'ritualist' in the manner of his so-called 'High' church or 'Anglo-Catholic' successors who remained within Anglicanism, there came from the Tractarians a revival of sacramental and ritualistic worship in the church as a whole which brought back some of the 'beauty of holiness' that Laud had so hamfistedly discredited.

Like the Romantic movement in the arts, Anglo-Catholicism enriched, and was enriched by, a feeling of community with the medieval past. It greatly stimulated the popularity of Victorian Gothic architecture; Anglo-Catholic influence was responsible for some of the more spectacular of the new churches of the time. The practices of some Anglo-Catholic clergy were over precious; but, apart from their influence over the church generally, Anglo-Catholic 'priests' (they gloried in the word and liked to be called, Catholic fashion, 'Father') were often rather better than other Anglican clergy at attracting large congregations in the less prosperous urban areas.

God and the Masses

Victorian religion made little progress among the working masses. Churches and chapels were built in large number; but they did not attract the poor. Much concern was expressed about these 'Dark uninstructed masses'. Mayhew asked one of them if he knew that God had made the world. The answer was earthily realistic: 'Of course Gawd Almighty made the world; and the poor bricklayers' labourers came and built the houses afterwards'. Whether the indifference of the poor and the unskilled towards the religion of their betters was a new fact or an old one, newly revealed by the Victorian zeal for social investigation, is matter for debate. But the virtual identification of religion with respectability meant that the moment one became respectable one could proclaim the fact by going to chapel and thereafter, if to respectability was added success, by going to church; but not to be respectable was to be excluded from most places of worship. One needed decent clothes before one could go to church. When one got there, one had to remember that the best pews were reserved for those who had paid a pew rent; to occupy one of them without permission could lead to an action for trespass.

Though the Moody and Sankey revival of the 1880s had a powerful, if temporary, effect on the more prosperous workers, it was the Salvation Army that came nearest to stirring the really poor. Its uniforms, its hearty bands and rousing street corner revivalism touched emotional chords otherwise plucked chiefly by the melodramas and the music halls. Greeted at first by physically violent hostility, its genuine concern, organised by very ordinary men and women, brought back to the crowded towns something of the qualities of the first Franciscans. Unfortunately, like most Anglo-Saxon forms of Christianity, it could not permanently accommodate any but the permanently repentant sinner. It was this almost universal defect which helps to explain what is called the 'hypocrisy' of the Victorians. Once one was 'saved' it was necessary to appear forever incapable of sin. This inevitably led to pretence. Even those who committed no public acts worth calling sinful were apt to persecute themselves with the fear that they were guilty of private, forgotten or unrecognised sins. Some were such spiritual and psychological valetudinarians that they raised any number of harmless peccadilloes to the status of sins. Such sickly preoccupation with the rights and wrongs of the trivia of daily conduct was a luxury which the working class in general and the poor in particular had little opportunity for.

411

Sunday School and Board School Religion

Yet, though Victorian workers did not often go to church, they sent their children in droves to Sunday schools. Between 1818 and 1888 the percentage of children attending Sunday schools rose from 4% to 75%, most of them from the working class. Sunday schools, with their voluntary lay teachers, some of them teenagers, laid down a sediment of Bible stories and of residual recollections about God and Jesus which ensured the continuing demand in adult life for the magical services of the clergy at christenings, weddings and funerals and, well into the first half of the twentieth century, the habit of sending the next generation of children to Sunday school too. Given the chronic lack of privacy in working-class homes, to send children to Sunday school also gave parents the rare opportunity of a brief period of quiet conjugality. The Sunday school 'treat'—an outing to a not too distant open space with a celebratory issue of oranges and buns—was also an attraction. Sunday school membership usually increased in the weeks before the annual 'treat'.

Board schools were also a source of Christian indoctrination after 1870. Compelled by law to be non-denominational, they necessarily relied on Bible stories, supplemented by the sedulous learning of hymns. By the beginning of the twentieth century therefore, though religion was regarded as declining, working-class children almost certainly knew their Bibles better than had their predecessors a century earlier. That this did not make them churchgoers is understandable. They had learned their religion in school rather than in church; and when they left their schools they put most of their religion away, along with the other childish things of schooldays.

Intellectual Disarray

It was during Victoria's reign that the intellectual basis of English national Christianity collapsed. Continental Biblical criticism, the findings of the geologists, and Darwin's theory of evolution induced a state of mental disarray from which religion in England was unable to recover. The new ideas had little effect on the Board school and Sunday school majority, beyond eventually confirming their adult scepticism or indifference. But the shock administered to better educated Christians was at first great. They were totally committed to the literal truth of the Bible. It was the one sure ground of their salvation, the spiritual sword with which they had defended themselves and their country against godlessness, vice and revolution. They regarded Genesis as being chapter one in the history of the world. They calculated from Biblical evidence that the creation of the world had occurred late one October afternoon in the year 4004 B.C. They tried to work out the exact dimensions of Noah's Ark and believed that Jonah had indeed been swallowed by a whale and survived the experience. They attached central importance to the miracles in the new testament and felt that to call any part of the gospels in question was to undermine the whole of their faith. The new 'higher' criticism and the scientific theories of the Victorian age therefore signalled the eventual passing away of that age of intellectual constriction which Wesley and Wilberforce had done so much to establish.

In practice, there was some readiness among bishops and clergy to accept that Biblical fundamentalism was not intellectually tenable. These mental adjustments were not communicated to the laity. A gap opened between the theology of the clergy and the theology of their congregations. It was thought dangerous to offer subtlety and doubt to flocks so long accustomed to feed only on certainties. Nor were congregations always anxious to hear social criticism from the pulpit. Most clergy therefore kept to the old routines of comfortable words and biblical exposition on traditional lines. Neither science nor politics was to interfere with religion.

Hence, in the twentieth century, the churches came to depend on three fast diminishing groups: those who were content with the most mentally undemanding of faiths; those in whom old habits of social duty and Sunday observance were still hallowed because customary; and, smallest of all, the few whose vision was too powerful to be extinguished by the intellectual vacuity of sermons, the archaism or banality of services, the social small change of jumble sale and fête, or the pale joys of happy evenings in parish halls and pleasant Sunday afternoons in chapels.

Less Often to Church

In terms of daily life, the most noticeable consequence was the decline, along with that of family prayers, of the practice of Sunday observance. The churches clung to Sunday observance in the hope of perpetuating conformity to religious tradition by trying to ensure the melancholy absence of any other social activity. Sunday trading, save for the morning and evening sale of milk, had been banned by an act of 1677; and, though exceptions from it were legislated for during Victoria's reign, the terms of the Shops acts of 1912–22, ensuring a half holiday for shop assistants, all implied that the 1677 ban on Sunday trading remained basic law. A Sunday Observance act of 1781 had banned any public entertainment to which people paid for admission. The survival of the 1677 act and the enforcement of that of 1781 gave firm legal foundation to the English Sunday. The Victorians fought a long battle to keep museums and libraries closed on Sundays and to prevent bands playing in parks. In the twentieth century it proved impossible to legislate for the universal opening of either cinemas or public houses; the matter had to be settled between the wars by local option. By that time the limitation on almost all avoidable economic activity on Sunday had become so closely woven into the pattern of English life as to survive the religious sanctions that had engendered it. One of its principal legacies was the 'double time' that trade unions insisted be paid to those of their members who worked on Sundays.

The erosion of church-going was due mainly to the multiplication in the century after 1870 of opportunities for private and social pleasures whose emergence Sabbatarians had providentially not foreseen. Cycling, tennis, golf, excursions by train and bus; Sunday games by amateurs, as local authorities were gradually compelled to open municipal playing fields; and, later, the motor car, offering greatest scope of all for 'a day out': all these conspired to lure away those whose limited lives had formerly provided the clergy with a semi-captive audience. For those denied the new Sunday activities, the Sunday newspaper, already a working-class institution by the 1850s, provided more enthralling fare than Sunday sermons. *The News of the World* loudly echoed the parson's disapproval of sin; but, less reticent and better informed about it than many parsons, it could make the delineation of vice and the record of its due punishment in the courts rather more cathartic than the efforts of the most rousing of Revivalists. In the mid-twentieth century, the English had only three popular religious festivals. In autumn, they remembered their rural past and went to Harvest Festival, unaware of participating in what was, in fact, a Victorian innovation. On Remembrance Sunday, in November, a decreasing number of them sang *O God Our Help in Ages Past* round the local war memorial. In late spring, if they could get tickets, they might sing the hymn *Abide With Me* just before the beginning of the Football Association cup final at Wembley stadium.

From the 1880s onwards, the churches sought to keep the young in the fold by blessing the growing interest in sport. This 'muscular' Christianity sought to attract 'the fellows' by encouraging them to play 'a healthy game of footer'. Later, tennis clubs, scout groups and table tennis clubs became part of church social activities, but, after the second world war, were secularised in Youth Clubs, often unconnected with a church. The muscular Christianity of the half century before 1914 suffered in the long run from its association with imperialism. This, in the first years of the 1914–18 war, turned too many pulpits into recruiting platforms.

Twentieth Century Stratagems

In the second half of the twentieth century the church tried to identify itself, not with the social order as in the past, but with national and international social change. To purge itself of the charge of exclusiveness, it espoused ecumenism. By diminishing the status of the parson it tried to appease a society no longer disposed to behave deferentially. Watched over by a parochial church council from the 1920s onwards and put in his democratic place with the establishment, by the 1970s, of church synods dominated by the laity, he was on no account now to be thought of as a priest but as a 'presbyter' or 'president'. Precluded by the spirit of the age from asserting its own authority, the church thus became even more dependent on the Bible. It therefore tried to re-habilitate the scriptures through new translations; alleging, not only the need for more scholarly versions, but, paradoxically, the surprising circumstance that, after a century of compulsory education, modern congregations were less able to understand the King James Bible than eighteenth-century cobblers and weavers. By processes marked, accord-ing to one outraged bishop, by 'persistent, prosaic and purblind pedantry,' it drastically mutilated its liturgy and ritual. It set out to make church services inward-looking family gatherings on the grounds that God was not 'out there' but 'in one's neighbour'. A handful of pop stars assisted the search for 'relevance', hoping to demonstrate that God, no longer a still, small voice, could be heard, electronically amplified, in the discotheque. The careful exclusion from organised religion of all sense of the *mysterium tremendens* caused many of the young to seek it instead in occultism, Indian gurus and drugs.

PART SEVEN

FROM PAST TO PRESENT

Approximate Dates: 1860–1975

1

NEW COMPETITORS, NEW OCCUPATIONS

Omens of the 1860s

THE gestation of the world that had come to birth by the mid-twentieth century began with a conjunction of events occurring between 1860 and 1871. None of these events took place in England; none was to England's advantage; and in so far as England tried to influence any of them, the efforts made were ineffective.

Nelson's victory at Trafalgar in 1805 had finally broken French naval power; and, though the French refused to believe it and spent well over a century pretending the contrary, the Anglo-Prussian victory under Wellington at Waterloo in 1815 had deprived the French of their military preponderance for good. The aftermath of these achievements was that the English became the world's commercial and maritime masters. For over fifty years, Europe lagged behind, economically, socially and technologically. France was, for most of the nineteenth century and beyond it, bitterly divided by its Revolutionary and Napoleonic experiences. Germany remained politically fragmented, a land without definable frontiers or perceptible national unity. The rest of central Europe was likewise overwhelmingly rural, its Habsburg rulers in Vienna characterised by long, inbred hereditary tradition by lack of imagination and frequent mental inadequacy. Russia had only its great size and huge population, assets immobilised by a ruling family which, if less tainted by insanity than the Habsburgs, was even more superstitiously committed to the ideas of the past and possessed by even greater fear of the peoples it ruled. The United States was totally involved in the travails of westward expansion and the social and economic tensions which were to explode in Civil War. It was scarcely surprising that, at a time when its potential rivals were enfeebled by immobile governments, political divisions or intense social conservatism, England should indeed be the whole world's workshop.

But notice was given that England's supremacy was not permanent when the Franco-Prussian war of 1870–71 established, on the ruins of a humiliated French army, a unitary Germany ruled from Prussian Berlin. To the making of the new Germany, as of the unitary Italy that emerged during the 1860s, the English were able to contribute little beyond equivocal words and righteous attitudes as ineffective as those of Neville Chamberlain in the 1930s, if less interferingly obtuse. For the next seventy-five years the English had to compete with the resolute drives of a Germany bent on economic and political dominance.

In the 1860s, the Civil War established the ascendancy of the North in the United States, guaranteeing the rapid industrial growth of a land far richer than England in natural and human resources and, like Germany, less hampered by leaders distrustful of businessmen. In 1869, the Union Pacific and Central Pacific railroads effected their historic junction in Utah with results, particularly in the form of American wheat exports, that contributed more to the downfall of the English landed aristocracy than the efforts of all the English radicals. A small cloud appeared in the east, too. In 1868, the shoguns abdicated in Japan and the Meiji period turned that country's face towards the twentieth century, with all that that was to involve for England's economic and political power in the world. Even in Russia, the foundations of the twentieth century were foreshadowed by the emancipation of the serfs in 1861.

Slower Growth

These were not the only warning signals to suggest that the way ahead for the English would not in future be as clear as, foreign wars notwithstanding, it had been since 1689. It had been predicted during the Great Exhibition of 1851 that on any similar occasion in the future, 'British supremacy will be manifested in every branch of Industrial Art'. But as early as the International Exhibition in Paris in 1867 it was evident that England no longer had a monopoly of industrial innovation. More disturbing to contemporaries was that the pace of expansion decelerated. The average annual industrial growth rate of from 3 to 4%, normal since the 1820s, dropped to below 1.5% in the 1880s. Exports, expanding at a rate by volume of 5% a year between 1840 and 1870, increased by only 2% a year from 1870 to 1890 and by only 1% a year in the 1890s. Though the value of foreign trade went up in the decade before 1914, growth rate did not. Growth rates above 3% were not again achieved until the years 1919 to 1939 and not surpassed until the 1950s. Productivity also fell. In 1907 it was calculated that whereas a British worker added £100 to the value of the raw materials on which he worked in manufacturing industry, the average figure for a United States worker was £500. This suggested a continuing reliance by the British on older and less efficient machinery. So did the fall in the proportion of national income devoted to capital investment at home. The mid-century proportion of 7.5% a year dropped to 4.5% and stayed at that level until 1914.

Slower growth, and falling productivity and investment, went hand in hand with falling profits and prices. The contrast with the bounding advance of the United States and Germany led to the view that the cause was the tariff system by which those countries protected their new industries against the quality and quantity of British exports. The novelty of the situation caused a despondency expressed in melodramatic and inaccurate language by Winston Churchill's father, Lord Randolph, who proclaimed in 1886 that cotton was 'sick', iron 'dead as mutton', shipbuilding 'at a standstill' and the whole of industry showing 'signs of mortal disease'. The heroic solution, appropriate to one who believed 'the age of empires is come', was offered by Joseph Chamberlain in 1903: it was to beat the United States and Germany for size by turning the Empire into an economic unit through a tariff against foreign imports, combined with preferential treatment for those from what were coming to be called the Dominions. The energy with which Chamberlain campaigned to convert the Tories and the country to his ideas, and the celerity with which the disorganised Liberal party pulled itself together to defend the gospel of free trade, meant that, as in 1846, economic fundamentals were lost sight of in a turmoil of politicking. From it, the Liberals emerged in 1906 with an electoral victory so large that the Conservatives were infuriated into obstructive bad temper for a decade.

Dangerous Prosperity

Chamberlain's threat that without tariff reform there would be industrial catastrophe and mounting unemployment seemed discredited by a trade revival after 1900. Much of this was due to the increasing wealth of a world now fast industrialising itself on the English model. Germany in particular was not only a principal industrial rival of the British but also their best customer. Accordingly, England entered upon and, more important, emerged from, the first German war with an economy still over-committed to the now ageing and in the long term contracting heavy industries which had created her wealth between 1780 and 1850. In 1913, coal, iron and steel, machinery and vehicles, ships and textiles, together constituted two thirds of all exports; their contribution to the nation's prosperity was such that Great Britain still accounted for a third of the world trade in primary products and thirty per cent of all the world's manufactures.

Hence, the coal industry, with over a million workers and plenty of recruits coming forward, saw no advantage in the mechanisation adopted elsewhere, even though output per man per shift had been falling for thirty years. The great development of steampower in the 1870s, the longstanding commitment to gaslighting, and the size of the steam-powered railway network were reason enough for the slow development of an electricity industry. The British output of five hundred motor cars in 1896 had already been achieved by the French in 1893. Having invested heavily in the Bessemer process, the steel industry relied on it long after others had abandoned it for processes that enabled steel to be made more cheaply from low grade iron ores. The excellence of British marine steam engines and the abundance of coal delayed the use of oil fired engines. Lancashire continued to use old techniques rather than the more efficient textile machinery used in the United States, Switzerland, Germany and Japan. Such machinery was being manufactured in Lancashire; but most of it was exported. There is a case for arguing that well before 1914 much of the British economy was prospering on a thriving export business designed to equip foreigners to take away its principal markets.

The strength of that economy was itself a powerful stimulus to foreign inventiveness. Most new machinery in farming, mining, electrical engineering and glass manufacture, as well as the sewing machine and the typewriter, was developed abroad. In 1914 all the khaki dyes for the army's uniforms (like all the magnetos then in use) came from Germany. Yet not all complaints of declining inventiveness or lack of drive, forward planning and scientific and technical education were as relevant as they seemed. The thirty years after 1945 were not without evidence that the eager adoption of advanced technologies did not always guarantee unbroken advance. There was a good deal of rather foolish breast-beating about the inevitable. The rest of the world was not so lacking in acquisitiveness as to remain content for ever, as it had been for about fifty years, with low standards of living while the United Kingdom dominated its trade, bought its primary products on the cheap, and made large profits by virtue of being its sole source of manufactures. The English were perhaps too ready to equate declining domination with decline as such, and spent too much thought on an introspective search for excuses and scapegoats; or detected signs, as always, that it was due to an erosion of moral standards. But, by 1914, with the anxieties of the 'Great Depression' of the 1870s and 1880s forgotten and shareholders again getting a good return, most businessmen featherbedded their minds by a sturdy faith in methods which (they said) 'had stood the test of time'.

Unfortunately, as Tennyson had reminded them, 'Time makes ancient good uncouth'. With the first German war, time took so swift a leap that by 1921 what might not have happened for another thirty years had come to pass already: the United Kingdom could no longer hope to rely unquestioningly for its prosperity on the basic industries which had sustained it during the previous hundred years. The stagnation or decline of those industries between the two wars, which condemned large numbers of their workers to long-term unemployment, was in large measure due to a failure to read signals the future had been sending out to British industry ever since the 1880s.

It would be wrong to suggest that innovation and enterprise were wholly lacking in the last quarter of the nineteenth century. But it was most evident in areas which added significantly neither to exports nor to the development of technologies that would help the growth of major new industries in the twentieth century. The period of the Great Depression saw the first appearance of what would become nationally and in some cases internationally famous household names: Lever, Boot's, Sainsbury, Cadbury, Fry, Lipton, Guinness and Bass were among them. The spread of multiple shops and the institution of the great departmental store, pioneered in London by William Whiteley, indicated an evident entrepreneurial drive in a field hitherto but thinly cultivated, that of the retail and distributive trades. It was a proper development in its way. It was time that more of the national capital was diverted from concentration on growth in order to satisfy the individual's desire for consumer goods. In the longer term, fewer Beecham's pills, fewer bars of chocolate and fewer well-stocked multiples and departmental stores and, instead, an earlier and more vigorous electrical engineering or chemical industry might have given the United Kingdom a rather firmer foundation for economic advance in the twentieth century.

As early as the 1870s, it seems, the English were showing signs of rating the enjoyment of good things in the here and now as the major benefit of life in a rich industrialised society, and one which they were unwilling or, owing to the impact of strident advertising, unable any longer to forgo. A century later it would be alleged that the desire to consume had all but stifled the impulse for economic growth that had dominated society in the decades of 'the industrial revolution'.

Rural Profit and Loss

Though more fuss was made about its difficulties at the time, agriculture as a whole adjusted to change rather better than industry. Between 1851 and 1871 it had increased its productivity faster than in the earlier period traditionally called 'the agricultural revolution'. In addition to a rapid spread of the techniques advocated in the eighteenth century, there was now a lavish use of imported fertilizers (chiefly guano) and the beginning of mechanical harvesting. This efficient period of 'high farming' led to a rapidly increased output of meat and grain, even though there were 300,000 fewer agricultural workers in 1871 than in 1851. Though the amount of imported wheat doubled, prices held steady and arable farmers did well because the growth of population kept up demand.

Starting with a period of bad harvests in the 1870s, however, wheat prices tumbled from just below 50s a quarter in 1875 to below 30s in the early 1890s. They rose little above that figure until the 1914–18 war. Farm incomes fell on average by 30%; rents by a third. There were about 3.5 million acres under wheat in 1872; by 1895 there were less than 1.5 million. Even by 1918 acreage had risen to only 2.6 million. The basic cause was that the railway and steamship, which had enabled the English to export their manufactures and investment-capital all over the world were now, under conditions of free trade, enabling wheat to be imported cheaply and in quantity from North America. Russia, desperate for foreign gold, stepped up her great wheat exports. Argentina sent meat, Australasia wool, mutton and butter; cheese came in from North America, margarine from Holland, butter from Denmark, maize from Romania. Many of these imports became possible for the first time with the development of refrigerator ships.

Since wheat accounted for half the arable output in 1870 but only a sixth by 1895, here was an unquestionable slump and indeed perhaps the one period in English life when there really was an agricultural revolution. Yet, although it is easy to make light of the misfortunes of just one group within a community, the situation was not as universally disastrous as was claimed. The fall in cereal prices cut the cost of animal feeding stuffs, so that home-bred meat, being cheaper to produce and of better quality than imported meat, held its prices. The population increased at a greater rate from 1871 to 1901. Lower agricultural prices led to higher real wages. Cheaper wheat, cheap meat and dairy imports enabled yet one more spurt in numbers to be accompanied by a rise and not a fall in living standards. This did not, however, help the wheat farmer. His wheat was no better than foreign wheat; and a rising standard of living produced a decrease in the proportion of bread consumed and an increase in milk and meat consumption. At last, in fact, the diet of all but the very poorest began to improve perhaps for the first time for four hundred years. Indicative of a better-fed population was that the greater demand for meat and butter kept the prices of both from falling much, increased imports notwithstanding. Beer consumption, standing at just over 20 gallons a head per annum in the 1820s, rose to the peak figure of nearly 40 gallons a head in the 1890s. The figures add point to Victorian temperance campaigns; to the licensing restrictions of the last quarter of the century; and to the severer licensing laws with which the English were saddled in (apparent) permanence during the first world war. But the slaking of such thirst saved the grower of malting barley from the misfortunes of the wheat growers.

The fuller development of the railways also made possible the exploitation of the urban demand for milk, hitherto drastically limited by its dependence on local dairies and cowkeepers. Liquid milk prices rose. The first large-scale milk factory was opened at Chippenham in 1891 by the concern later known as Nestlé's. This was not an umixed blessing; heavily watered condensed milk was not intended for the nourishment of young babies but often used for that purpose. Dairy farming for London could, owing to better transport, be developed as far away as Wiltshire and Somerset. In the vale of Evesham and north Kent, fruit farming expanded to serve the new consumer industries of jam making and fruit canning. The survival of that colloquial reproof to the idly self-indulgent, 'You want jam on it' is a reminder that it was the stresses placed on late Victorian farmers that allowed the humblest of house-wives the novel luxury of a jampot on the table or, if times were good, the extravagance of a pretty jam dish ('and spoon-with-it'). The switch to market gardening near the still swelling towns saved many farmers, added to the variety of the national diet and began the slow process of reducing the once dominant carbohydrates to the status of 'fillers' to be used only with caution by those who, a century later, valued their health and their appearance.

In the thirty years before 1901 the number of agricultural workers fell from just under a million to 621,000. They were a fifth of the working population in 1851 but less than a tenth of it in 1901. Yet the value of agricultural and horticultural output had increased by 10%. Overall, therefore, although much contracting, agriculture had showed a greater flexibility than industry, even if its share of the national income fell to 6.4% from the 20.3% of 1851.

Social effects were less lopsided than in previous agricultural upheavals. This time landlords suffered as well (though inevitably not as much) as tenants and labourers. The latter were forced into the towns in the last of the several major migrations from the countryside. The preponderantly urban society of the twentieth century may with some confidence at last be said to have emerged. Rural migration, however, aggravated urban poverty, itself already deepened by the higher unemployment of 1874–95 and the growth of population in the last three decades of the century. Those who remained on the land suffered from the rising prices of the decade before 1914 and from the fact that socialism, essentially an urban creed, would take little note of them. An agricultural labourer was, almost by definition, 'backward' and his condition usually described by journalists as 'feudal', as if he were some accidental survival from a distant past. Since a better deal for farm workers might raise the price of the town worker's food, the farm worker suffered the usual fate of minorities. The Tories favoured his employer, and Labour those who bought what he produced.

The fall in rents in the wheatlands meant a further decline in the importance of land as a basis of aristocratic power. Indeed, politics registered the diminution of the great landowner's authority without a stir. Estate duties began in 1889, death duties in 1894. In 1888 and 1894, almost all the ancient functions of JPs, save as non-stipendiary magistrates and licensing authorities for public houses, were transferred to county and district councils elected by ratepayers. Peers of the realm could still find themselves elected chairmen of county councils; but despite their continuing wealth and social prestige they could be sure henceforth only of the prospect of honorific appointments as lord lieutenants and high sheriffs and the expectation of presiding over, and contributing to the funds of, local football and cricket clubs. By the time they tried to use their surviving political power in the lords to resist the 'confiscatory taxation' of Lloyd George's People's Budget of 1909, peers whose predecessors had been magnates of the realm had sunk to the status of 'diehards' and 'backwoodsmen', easy targets for the radical oratory of a rural-born Lloyd George, but mainly ignored by a working class, then busily engaged in strikes against those with the real power, the owners of mines, docks and railways.

The New Proletariat

Economic development by the end of the nineteenth century was creating a society too complex to be comprehended within the simple trinity of aristocracy, middle class and working class. More than ever, peerages were rewards for large-scale business enterprise and for what were called 'services to politics'. This meant having contributed generously to party funds; having failed in the commons or as a cabinet minister; or possessing a capacity for longevity greater than that for contesting elections. More important for the future was the growth of a new lower middle-class group which might more realistically be described at this stage as an intellectual proletariat. It was called into existence by the growing scale of the retail trade, of commerce and of government administration; and by the rapid growth of state education after 1870 and by the transformation of nursing.

Hitherto, shopkeeping had been something of a craft, to which the young were apprenticed to learn the skills of blending, grading, weighing, cutting and packaging and, not only of selling, but of buying. The good shopkeeper did not advertise much, preferring a trusted and regular clientele, since long credit was the rule and price tickets unknown. When introduced, the latter were considered vulgar. The prices ladies and gentlemen paid for their purchases were a confidential matter negotiated between them and the shopkeeper. To demand immediate cash payment would cast doubt on a customer's honour and solvency. While retailing remained predominantly a service to the upper classes, its clientele and scale of operation were limited, and a shop no place for unskilled assistants.

The late-Victorian and Edwardian years saw the limited liability company and the beginning of near-monopoly. The English Sewing Cotton Company, the Imperial Tobacco Company and the Lever 'Soap trust' came into being. The development of multiple shops, department stores and branded goods revolutionised shopping and brought it into the lives of classes previously reliant upon markets, street traders and, outside the towns, on home cooking and dressmaking. It was a response to the rising wages of those in full time work between 1850 and 1900. Sainsbury's first shop opened in Drury Lane in 1869; in 1870 Oldham signalled the birth of an invaluable dietary standby for the lower classes for another century with the opening of the first fish and chip shop. Thomas Lipton, with world wide tea interests as his base, opened a chain of grocery stores throughout the country before setting up seventy new shops in London within three years in the 1880s. He was soon imitated by the International, the Home and Colonial and the Maypole. The bold words 'Boot's Cash Chemists' began everywhere to proclaim that the new retail business was directed towards the multitudes who, though uncreditworthy, usually had a bit of 'the ready' in purse or pocket. By 1909, the first Woolworth's had appeared.

The new trends, noticed first of all in the drapery business early in the nineteenth century, demanded and, owing to the growing population, secured, a large body of unskilled shop assistants, in some cases for the simple task of transferring items from shelf or drawer to counter, taking the amount of the fixed price, and giving change where necessary. These were tasks conveniently within the capacity of the earliest products of state elementary education. Though the death of the small independent shopkeeper was early foretold, he survived because the shopping habit was becoming universal. The estimated 295,000 shops of 1875 had swollen to over 450,000 by 1907.

In commerce, too, independent proprietorship and partnerships (which dissolved when one of the partners died) gave place to joint stock companies and large scale amalgamations with much capital, thus reducing the dominance of very small businesses. As industrialisation developed and the scale of operation enlarged (in part because of such practical developments as improved transport and posts, the electric telegraph and finally the telephone), administration became more complex, requiring transactions to be speedier and more accurate. Here, as in the shops, specialisation and division of labour called into existence a variety of low-grade clerical skills, such as filing and the keeping of records, and the operation of adding, stamping, sealing and duplicating machines. The invention of Pitman's shorthand, first made public in 1837, contributed to the list of office skills and, in commercial life, replaced handwriting much as, in textiles, the spinning jenny had replaced the spinning wheel. The American invention of the typewriter turned shorthand writers into shorthand typists. Remington machines came on the British market in 1874; and in the early 1880s a lady in Cincinnati invented touch-typing, so that the two-fingered 'hunt and peck' approach to typing would in future be the mark of the amateur. Between 1861 and 1911, the number of workers classified as clerks rose from just over 92,000 to almost 686,000.

The expansion of the public service also added to the number of semi-skilled clerical jobs. The 50,500 persons in government employment in 1861 had grown to 189,500 by 1913. Increased state regulation created more jobs in the Home Office, the Board of Trade and the Local Government Board, as did the state takeover of the postal and telegraph services and the introduction of old age pensions and national insurance in 1909 and 1912.

There were features common to all these new workers, and to most elementary schoolteachers and nurses. Like early factory workers, they were underpaid. The earnings of some were kept low by the semi-skilled nature of their jobs, and those of others because, like the first cotton operatives, their rates of pay were governed by the predominance of cheap female labour. Nursing was wholly female; telegraph and telephone operation wholly so save for night work; clerical work increasingly so. From the beginning, most 'typewriters' were 'lady typewriters'. An added cause of low pay was that, initially many telephonists and typists were gentlewomen of limited means in search of a supplementary rather than a subsistence income. The notion of office work as a means to enable a girl of modest gentility to earn 'a little pin money' or to help her buy little extras for the 'bottom drawer' in which she collected minor items for use after her marriage lingered on into the 1920s. The Nightingale principle that nurses be personally above reproach also helped saddle their occupation with the exiguous pay proper to girls who worked from a Victorian sense of middle class dedication and not because they had to.

Accordingly, at a time when £300 was the minimum for sustaining a modest middle class existence and when skilled craftsmen might expect £90 a year, clerks might get £80 a year, rising at best (and rarely) to as much as £200. A second division civil servant could earn £190. By 1914 the average annual salary of a certificated elementary teacher was £127 if male, £95 if female. Staff nurses were paid from £24 to £30 a year, sisters from £30 to £40 and matrons around £50, save in very large hospitals. It was hard for a nurse to get work after forty, impossible after fifty, and there was virtually no pension. A nurse incapacitated for life by an infection contracted in the wards might end her days in a workhouse infirmary. Shop assistants endured a 76 to 94 hour week in poor districts until an act of 1869 established a 69 hour week and various acts from 1911 to 1913 established a statutory half day. Before these changes, shops in working-class areas stayed open as late at night as possible, since the working hours of the poor compelled them to be evening shoppers. West End department stores, catering for the middle class, were unusual in operating a mere 56 hour week in the 1880s. Shop assistants were liable to dismissal on the spot. Male assistants were discouraged from marrying, since the expenses they thus incurred were thought certain to tempt them to rob the till. A campaign to provide assistants with seats was resisted even more stubbornly than the demand that they be given adequate (and sexually separate) lavatories. Female shop assistants were thought to be in worse physical shape at forty than domestic servants and more eager to get married than factory girls. A girl would, it was said, marry anybody to get out of the drapery business.

By contrast, civil servants enjoyed a relatively short week, sick leave with pay, annual holidays and pensions. In these respects they set standards slowly adopted for clerical workers outside government service and which, a century later, still too often served to distinguish the most junior member of a firm's 'staff' from the 'workers' who, however long-serving, rarely enjoyed these benefits. No night work, no paid overtime and a working day that started at 9 a.m. also set clerical workers apart, as did the regularity of their employment. Civil servants had the further advantage of security of tenure; but their pay was kept low because it was thought in the public interest to pay them as little as possible, to avoid increased taxation. It became a regular civil service practice to downgrade work so as to pay it less. The post office imposed a marriage bar on women in 1875 and this spread to all the civil service in the 1890s. Sacking women when they married saved money: their marriage gratuity was less costly than the prospect of their staying on to rise high in the salary scale and thus qualify for good pensions. Promotion prospects were poor for women and, owing to the permanence of government jobs, slow for men.

New Snobberies, More Working Women

All these new occupations suffered in social esteem because of one idea about society inherited from a distant past and another born of industrialism. The older idea was that those who did paid work of any kind were socially inferior to those who could afford to do no paid work at all, and that manual work was inferior to all other kinds of work. The newer, trade union and socialist contention was that manual work was the only work that mattered. Thus, most of these new occupations were despised in themselves. Though Florence Nightingale had seen to it that all nurses were angels of light and healing (but in no sense 'workers'), schoolmarms, pen-pushing clerks and jumped-up lah-di-dah office types were looked down on because, according to one trade union leader, they were 'snobs fancying themselves as gents'. They were accused of wearing top hats and carrying hymn books. They refused to associate with manual workers, even with skilled craftsmen as respectable as themselves and earning more money. Yet the threadbare keeping-themselves-to-themselves, privet-hedged gentility of these occupations was almost forced on them by employers and the public. Shop assistants had to be clean, neat and polite in an age when customers were likely to have servants to defer to them at home; only street traders dared chaff their customers in the vernacular. Clerks and lady typewriters had to keep up appearances. Their superiors would hardly tolerate cloth caps, clay pipes or, particularly from shorthand writers and telephonists, common accents. Schoolteachers could carry weight with the working class only by cultivating asperity and a certain grandness of manner. To be obviously down at heel would be poor advertisement for the benefits education was supposed to confer. Nor was it a matter merely of appearance. Without benefit of bathrooms, hot and cold water and lightweight, easily washable clothing, the working class had, as well as a distinctive look, a distinct smell. They were 'the great unwashed'. Clerks, shop assistants and elementary teachers who failed to be neat and tidy would be suspected of having a bad smell.

This intellectual proletariat was also disliked by the middle class, particularly middle class socialists. At least until 1939, 'little clerks and typists scurrying home to their poky little terraced homes in dingy suburbs' were condescendingly patronised in most circulating library novels. Before 1914 there was freqent reference to the poor showing the country would make in war owing to the decline of the English into a race of 'pasty-faced clerks'. True, they were not manual workers; but their pretence at being middle-class was considered 'pathetic'; or was laughed at, for example by an eventual Poet Laureate, for such solecisms as calling table napkins 'serviettes' and for saying 'Beg pardon, I'm soiling the doileys'.

The medieval notion that a gentleman (the old *generosus*) did not work for his living, but was what was now described as 'of independent means,' applied with double force to women. If a woman was obliged to work, though she be 'both Christian and well bred she was bound to sacrifice that peculiar position' designated by the word 'lady'. In fact, the 'woman of leisure' who spent her life first looking for a husband and then looking after him, his children, his comforts and his servants to the exclusion of any other useful activity was peculiarly distinctive of the early Victorian middle class. Women made up 34.1% of the working population in 1861, 29.7% in 1911, and 36% in 1970.

Feminine emancipation was thus achieved, less by the agitation of leisured middle-class women, whether suffragists or suffragettes, than by the increase after 1861 in the number of non-manual jobs which were within women's physical capacity. Nowhere in all the pageant of Dickens characters (Dickens died in 1870) can one find a woman clerk. By 1881 the number of so-called 'middle-class' (i.e. non-manual) jobs was 2 million, rising to nearly 4 million by 1914; but whereas the percentage of men employed in them went up by 72%, the percentage increase for women was 161. By contrast, though the total of manual workers rose from 9 to 12 million in the same period, the number of male manual workers rose by 41% compared with a rise in women manual workers of only 24%.

The new opportunities for employment; the growing expense of maintaining idle daughters in an age of increased consumer expenditure; cheap education; the growth of omnibus and tramcar services: these were the means by which women began to acquire incomes of their own which, though usually inadequate, started them off on the road towards that economic independence which by the last quarter of the twentieth century was perhaps at last within their reach.

ANCIEN REGIME

Gladstone and Disraeli

IT says much for the snail-like pace of nineteenth-century change that Gladstone's ministry of 1868–74 is said to have laid the foundations of modern England. It disestablished the church, but only in Ireland; abolished patronage in the home (but not the foreign) civil service and the purchase of commissions in the army; set up machinery for non-denominational elementary schools financed by rates levied by locally elected school boards; instituted secret ballot; and amalgamated into one supreme court of judicature the hugger-mugger of high courts inherited from the middle ages and the seventeenth century. Almost all these measures had been radical aims in the 1830s; few would have surprised, or satisfied, either Tom Paine or the 'saints' of the Barebones parliament. Disraeli, however, announced that Gladstone had 'legalised confiscation, consecrated sacrilege, condoned treason' and 'destroyed Churches'.

Gladstone presided over these reforms because, Palmerston and Russell being dead, he had gathered under his rhetorical spell that miscellany of Whigs, Peelites, radicals, nonconformists and Irish which was now called the Liberal party. It was a tribute to Gladstone's personality that he was able to hold these not very like-minded groups together long enough to pass these reforms. But the impression there-after created, that this Liberal party was the permanent and sole embodiment of all that was truest and best in the national life, though the most enduring political illusion in the average English mind, was an illusion all the same. Largely created by Gladstone, it was wholly dependent on him; and ever since he himself destroyed it, people have tried to prove that it was destroyed by the 1914–18 war, Lloyd George, the Labour party, the system of simple majority voting at elections or by the operation of some mysterious force for evil inherent in all modern history. Viewed soberly, Gladstone's long political career was devoted mainly to cutting taxes and reducing government expenditure. He led only one effective reforming ministry, from 1868 to 1874; and at the end of its term, the electorate, enjoying for the first time both secret ballot and a register that included all male urban householders, gave the Conservatives a majority in the commons for the first time for over thirty years.

Back in power in 1880, Gladstone spent from then until 1886 obstinately demanding that his followers eschew further reform in England and, instead, unite behind him first in an attack on the rights of

Ireland's English landlords and then in a crusade to establish Irish home rule. In 1886, the Whigs deserted him, as did the radical Birmingham MP, Joseph Chamberlain, otherwise likely to have eventually become Liberal leader. The defectors became Liberal Unionists and, by the 1890s, members of what was thereafter officially called the Conservative and Unionist party.

The chief result of Gladstone's career was therefore to achieve Disraeli's aim of making the Conservatives the natural governing party of the English for another century. Though Gladstone became prime minister again in 1892, he did so mainly with Irish, Welsh and Scottish votes; though home rule got through the commons, the Tory majority in the Lords vetoed it. Gladstone retired shortly afterwards, being replaced by Lord Rosebery. Rosebery owned two Derby winners and was married to an heiress; but suffered from insomnia and unmanageable colleagues. In 1895, the Conservatives were back for another decade.

Gladstone's rival, Disraeli, who was prime minister from 1874 to 1880, was subject to the delusions of others rather than of his own. Unlike Gladstone, who understood only the topsoil of his times, Disraeli divined the nature of its sub-soil. While Gladstone was the politically overgrown child of Peel, Disraeli was a ne'er-do-well parody of Palmerston. Like Palmerston, he had the route to India on his mind. He bought Suez Canal shares, and involved England, along with France, in the control of Egypt's finances. He also made a typically Palmerstonian clatter against Russia during a Balkan crisis from 1875 to 1878. The Slavs of the Balkans had rebelled against their Turkish rulers, threatening to destroy Turkey's power in Europe. This prospect was considered dangerous by both Britain and Austria-Hungary, each regarding Turkey as a buffer against Russia. For that reason, therefore, Russian influence was at work encouraging the Slav rebels. Disraeli insisted that Turkey must be defended. But when the Turks assaulted the Bulgarians, the Slav people most accessible to their capital at Constantinople, Gladstone denounced these 'Bulgarian atrocities' and called for British cooperation with Christian Russia against the cruel, infidel Turk. Disraeli was unmoved. Frustrated by lack of European support, the Russians marched against the Turks but were held up for six months by fierce Turkish resistance at Plevna in the Balkan mountains. Turkey proved after all not to need the British assistance offered by the music hall songster who proclaimed that 'we had the ships, we had the men' and had 'got the money too,' and that 'by jingo' the Russians should 'not have Constantinople'. Exhausted by Turkish opposition, the Russians made peace without actually reaching the Turkish capital. The Russo-Turkish treaty of San Stefano awarded most of the Balkans to a large, new Bulgaria, independent of Turkey, but under Russian supervision. Disraeli demanded European revision of the treaty. Russia, opposed by Austria-Hungary, denied support by Germany and in no condition to fight, gave in. By the Treaty of Berlin of 1878, Turkey was given back much of the territory that ought to have gone to Bulgaria; and, for the better security of the eastern Mediterranean, yielded Cyprus to the British for use as a naval base. Disraeli's claim that he had personally secured a sensational English victory over Russia was a fraud, but a convincing one. When he claimed he had come back from Berlin in 1878 bringing 'Peace with Honour' all true patriots cheered, in dangerous unawareness of the fact that England had triumphed over a weak and isolated opponent and in the foolish expectation that victories could be won just as cheaply in the future. Gladstone denounced the *de facto* acquisition of Cyprus as thunderously as he had the Turks' atrocities against the Bulgarians, and continued to condemn Disraeli's avowed preference for defending what he considered to be British interests as thoroughly immoral.

Tory Patriots, Liberal Idealists

Disraeli's long term political importance was thus not that he founded late Victorian imperialism but that, with the hostile collusion of Gladstone, denouncing him with frenetic passion, he reversed, for at least the next eighty years, the traditional Tory posture on foreign affairs. By imitating Palmerston (a Whig), Disraeli made the Tories for the first time the party avowedly devoted to the maintenance of British interests abroad against all comers. It is only in the sense that imperialism was a later manifestation of this policy that Disraeli can in any way be associated with it. Save for the small minority loyal to Fox during the Napoleonic wars, it was the Whigs who had wielded the 'big stick' abroad. After 1689, the Tories had been the peace party; and, from 1812 to 1846, the party of cooperation with Europe. These attitudes, thanks to Gladstone, were now made characteristic of Liberals and passed on thence to Labour. Gladstone had allowed a long standing dispute with the United States to go to arbitration. He harped on the sanctity of treaties, the rights of small nations and (like Castlereagh, Peel and Aberdeen, all Tories) on the moral rightness of concerted action with continental powers, Russia included, even though, with Bismarck at work, the concert of Europe no longer existed. Gladstone also campaigned for foreign Causes: not only the suffering Irish, but wronged Neapolitans, Bulgarians, Zulus and Afghans. Ever since Gladstone, reduction of defence expenditure has been put forward by almost all zealots as the standard solution to the problem of 'paying for' whatever social reforms they deem desirable.

This divergence between the Tories and their political opponents was constant until the Suez debacle of 1956. The indifference of Neville Chamberlain not only to the suffering victims of Nazis and Fascists but also to the blows inflicted on British prestige in the 1930s by Japan, Italy and Germany, explains why he was disliked inside as well as outside his own party and could keep himself in command of it only by excluding from his government such traditional Tories as Churchill, Eden and Amery. Those Tories who shuddered at their party's haste to dismantle the colonial empire under Macmillan and Macleod in the late 1950s and at Heath's dedication to Europe in the 1960s, were registering the shock of seeing an old tradition, dating from Disraeli, superseded by an even older one; that of the century when 'Tories' had left Europe in the lurch in 1713 and 1763 and overthrown Marlborough for being too European and the Elder Pitt for being too greedy for Empire.

Gladstone also established the tradition of selectivity which inevitably marked Liberal and Labour idealism about suffering foreigners. Having long proclaimed his fervent support for 'peoples rightly struggling to be free' he nevertheless sent an armed expedition to fight the Egyptians in 1882 when they rebelliously struggled to free themselves from Anglo-French financial domination. As a result, Egypt became the centrepiece of imperial defence and so vital that its protection dominated the British war effort in the desperate years from 1940 to 1942 and the whole empire seemed untenable when it was lost for good in 1956. Yet the seventy-year presence of British troops on Egyptian soil (which Tories were so zealous to defend) was the work, not of Disraeli, the putative founder of imperialism, who merely sent financiers there, but of Gladstone, the founding father of all who then and afterwards condemned imperialism as immoral.

Gladstone's excitable campaign in the late 1870s to pretend that it was possible for a government led by him (or anybody) instantly to reverse all earlier foreign policy and institute a new one based on purely idealistic considerations was no doubt in origin a form of self-deception. But though its consequences after he returned to office in 1880 made him embarrassingly open to charges of hypocrisy, it established an even more unfortunate precedent: electors would often be wooed in the future with the unrealistic promise that an incoming Liberal (or Labour) government would pursue a foreign (and indeed domestic) policy based wholly upon moral considerations; and with hardly less disappointing and confusing results.

To the irony that it was Gladstone who sent the British into Egypt was added another. In 1871, Gladstone at last rescued trade unions from the handicap that, as 'organisations in restraint of trade' they had no standing in the common law. But at the same time, it was reaffirmed that picketing during strikes was illegal. Hence, it was from an act of 1875, passed by Disraeli's Tories, that the trade unions derived the freedom to picket. Gladstonian Liberalism hesitated to allow the individual's right to work to be impeded by the pressures of an organised body of militant trade unionists. Disraeli showed no such reluctance. He lacked the Liberals' early-Victorian suspicion that the labouring classes were still a rather 'swinish multitude'. It was to the Tories therefore that the town worker owed both his right to vote and his right to strike.

Yet neither Gladstone nor Disraeli bequeathed their policies to their own parties. When the Liberals returned to office in 1905 they strengthened England's defences to meet the danger of war with Germany. So far from resuming the Gladstonian tradition of minimal taxation and government expenditure, the revived Liberals launched a process of increasing both that has not since been reversed. Whereas Gladstone's faith was in individual initiative, the Liberalism of Asquith and Lloyd George was sufficiently collectivist for them to be accused of creating a 'servile state'.

Salisbury's Ancien Régime

Disraeli's death in 1881 and Gladstone's disruption of the Liberals in 1886 left England for over twenty years (or, a pessimist might assert, for longer) without relevant political leadership. The obvious future Liberal leader was the Birmingham radical, Joseph Chamberlain; but it was in part to prevent his radicalism taking over the Liberal party that Gladstone had made Irish home rule the issue of the day. With Chamberlain removing himself, along with his strong midlands following, from Liberalism, and with the Whigs ceasing to bestow their wealth and prestige on progressive liberal causes, almost the only links between Liberalism and the lower classes were now habit and a declining commitment to nonconformity.

In parallel with this, Disraeli's successor, Lord Salisbury, made certain that few of Disraeli's policies were continued. Salisbury's most brilliant cabinet minister, Lord Randolph Churchill, bade fair to outmatch Chamberlain as a focus of radical opinion. He convinced himself (and many others) that Disraeli had invented 'Tory Democracy' and that this was the path the party ought to tread. Salisbury soon provoked Churchill's exit from government; and from then until 1905, Salisbury and his nephew, Arthur Balfour, both aloof patricians, provided late Victorian and early Edwardian England with an *ancien régime* under which vast territories were added to the colonial empire and government grew more and more remote from common men. With the benign pessimism of a devout Christian convinced that, though one should do one's duty, the world would always be an imperfect place, Salisbury presided over a fair amount of mildly ameliorative legislation and contrived, with Byzantine skill, to preserve the peace as England jostled with other European powers for control of Africa and East Asia. On the way he allowed to ageing queen and patriotic people the passing pageants of a Golden Jubilee in 1887 and a Diamond Jubilee ten years later; and then, too old to resist, let Rhodes and Chamberlain drag the country into the scandal of the Boer War from 1899 to 1902.

Thus, as had happened a century before, government lost touch, in the thirty years after 1886, with the aspirations of the sensitive and the articulate. Though an innocent expectation of high adventure lured some and a patriotic love of their country moved others, there are signs that it was a lack of attachment to the world they lived in that led yet others to volunteer, with a readiness now hard to understand, for the alternative experience of war in 1914. Since Rupert Brooke was a socialist intellectual, one of whose close friends became Attlee's first chancellor of the exchequer, the wide appeal of his poems has some significance. He greeted war with the words, 'Now God be thanked who has matched us with His hour' and spoke of and perhaps for his generation in finding it a 'release' from 'shame', and in turning to it 'Glad from a world grown old and cold and dreary'. The disillusionment which the war caused was derived not simply from the experience itself but from the discovery that it did not, after all, provide the escape from reality that men of many different classes had been so eager to find.

An Alternative Society?

Throughout those thirty years that combination of uncritical Bible religion with the pursuit of profit which had fashioned an industrial society came under attack from several quarters as well as falling victim to its own loss of confidence. There was a growing desire for an alternative society to that created by economic growth; a revolt of hearts and minds against the persistence of the poverty of the many amid the inordinate wealth of the few. There was a resurgence of the intellectual, aesthetic and moral revolt which had informed the writings of Cobbett, of Dickens, of some of the writings of Disraeli and most of the pages of Ruskin. We can, said the last named, perform all sorts of manufacturing processes. The one thing we cannot do is 'to brighten, to strengthen, to refine or to form a single living spirit'. Matthew Arnold held that 'the concern for making money' and for saving their souls had blinded his generation to the moral imperative of striving for a society in which all their 'fellow men, in the East End of London and elsewhere' could share 'in the progress towards perfection'. An aesthetic movement developed, often with socialist associations. William Morris and Oscar Wilde, each in his way claiming to be socialist, sought to reawaken both emotional spontaneity and artistic creativity. Gustav Holst, as well as teaching music at St Paul's Girls' School, conducted the Hammersmith Socialist Choir, inspired to do so by the teachings of Morris and Shaw. Absurdly, yet forgivably, Swinburne bade the spiritual heirs of Wesley and Wilberforce exchange 'the lilies and languors of virtue For the rapture and roses of vice'.

Such extravagances were labelled 'decadent' and, in the 1890s, 'fin de siècle'. The labels were appropriate. They were attitudes that presaged the decay and approaching end of general consent to that blinkered, compulsive sense of duty that had kept the English nose to the grindstone for so long, yet had still failed to create a society which valued justice, beauty or common humanity. There were signs, too, that many of what working men's organisations were calling 'the ruling classes' and 'the idle rich' were themselves leaving the sinking ship of early Victorian values. Society was taking its lead from the portly and raffishly Hanoverian Prince of Wales well before he became Edward VII in 1901. Susceptible to female beauty, whether English or French, he hobnobbed with persons whose passports to royal favour were that they were rich and amusing, even if they had grown rich by selling tea or owning diamond mines. Fashionable families gave up family prayers and regular church attendance. Discarding the hair shirt of duty and prudery, Edwardian 'high society' donned the over-dressed apparel of conspicuous display and began to forfeit the deference their predecessors had earned by their care for at least the externals of moral respectability.

Social criticism acquired a keener edge. While still a Liberal, Chamberlain denounced Salisbury (under whom he would eventually be a cabinet minister) as belonging to a class made rich by what other men had 'done by toil and labour to add to the general wealth and prosperity of the nation', while themselves doing nothing: they 'toil not, neither do they spin'. The 'great evil with which we have to deal is the excessive inequality in the distribution of riches' he said. Randolph Churchill, self-appointed champion of Tory Democracy, demanded increased taxation for social purposes: better housing, compulsory national insurance, museums, art galleries, baths and wash houses. Though both these voices were soon silent, the dandyish City stockbroker, Henry Hyndman, disseminating (without acknowledgment) the ideas of Marx for the first time among Englishmen, founded a Social Democratic Federation in 1884. In the following year Sidney and Beatrice Webb joined the newly-created Fabian Society and transformed it into an organisation for the propagation of their own special brand of socialism that, though inevitable, would have the 'inevitability of gradualism'. The patient, persistent accumulation of facts and figures would 'inevitably' lead to the adoption by central government of that already widespread 'municipal socialism' by which the new elected local councils provided municipal and county health and sanitary services, trams, gas, electricity, schools, libraries and hospitals.

Rediscovering the Poor

Literature, fictional and factual, poured out on the subject of the poor, a high proportion of it emanating for the first time from London. The capital's poor were being augmented by native immigrants from the stricken corn counties and by victims of East European anti-semitism. There was exceptional distress in 1879, 1886 and 1894; it is at this time that the word 'unemployment' first came into use. Its appearance indicates an improvement of understanding. Hitherto the poor were mainly thought of as an unwelcome army of occupation unaccountably quartered on the main body of the population and composed of persons so morally delinquent that if any of them pointed out that they were starving they were liable to be taken into protective custody in a workhouse. As Christianity began to disentangle itself from respectability, charity work among the poor became almost fashionable. Writers and journalists went among them in search of copy and came back with material entitled *The Bitter Cry of Outcast London* in 1883, *The White Slaves of England* in 1897 and W. T. Stead's notorious articles of 1885 on 'The Maiden Tribute of Modern Babylon' in *The Pall Mall Gazette* ('London's lust annually uses up many thousands of women who are literally killed . . . living sacrifices slain in the services of vice.'). More impressive was *Darkest England and the Way Out*, produced in 1890 by General William Booth of the Salvation Army. He denounced the Poor Law as a system by which it was only when he had nothing but the clothes he stood in that a man could secure lodging in the workhouse. He raged at the treatment of the temporarily out of work in the casual wards:

> Individuals casually poor and out of work, being destitute and without shelter, may . . . receive shelter for the night, supper and a breakfast, and in return . . . shall perform a task of work . . . as a test of their willingness to work for their living. The work give is the same as that given to felons in gaol, oakum-picking and stone-breaking . . . The stone-breaking test is monstrous. Half a ton of stone from any man in return for partially supplying the cravings of hunger is an outrage which, if we read of as having occurred in Russia or Siberia, would find . . . Hyde Park filled with strong oratory.

Longer lasting in influence was the voluminous social survey, *Life and Labour of the People in London*, published by Charles Booth between 1875 and 1903. This suggested that a third of the urban population were unable to provide themselves and their families with the barest necessities in food, clothing and shelter. Similar surveys in York in 1899 and four other towns in 1912–13 supported these conclusions. Though Booth was less shocked than is usually suggested, the fact was that, despite the sewers, the drains, the improved water supply established since the 1840s, which had virtually eliminated cholera, and the various measures against the adulteration of food and the worst of factory conditions, the total environment of the labouring poor was still a matter of dirt, disease and early death. The national figures of infant mortality and life expectancy were little better in 1900 than in 1840. In these matters the Age of Improvement was not the nineteenth but the twentieth century. Even in 1911, something like eight million people were dependent on the two million married men whose earnings even when in work were less than £1.25 a week. Most of them, men, women and children, were underfed, badly housed or insufficiently clothed, with lower standards in all three than those of families who, twenty years later, were rightly held to be in poverty because their only source of income was unemployment pay which, in 1911, did not exist. Yet the country was manifestly extremely wealthy; it seemed no longer acceptable that too many had too little of their country's riches. It was coming to be realised that the worst effect of the uneven distribution of wealth was that those with the lowest and most irregular incomes had no defence against the effects of being too ill or too old to earn a living, or of becoming, through no fault of their own, unemployed. It was seen, too, that maldistribution of wealth in itself caused unemployment. If the poorest had more money, they could buy more goods and services; and providing them with those extra goods and services would generate more employment.

Unfettering the Women

A further crack began to appear in the rigid social attitudes that industrialised society had taken over from the past. From the 1870s onwards, the middle classes began to practice birth control. Large families were a particular manifestation of middle class affluence in the mid-nineteenth century; but there now began the process by which the average of six children per middle class marriage was reduced by the 1930s to two. The practice began as a response to the increasing difficulty of getting domestic servants now that girls with a modicum of intelligence could get other work; to the cost of buying more luxury foods and paying for more expensive holidays; and to the desire for expensive new amenities such as installing running water, water closets and gas cookers. That family limitation was considered a fearful breach of moral standards, even by those who resorted to it, is shown by the longlasting conspiracy to keep the poor in ignorance of it. Working-class women, though less able to withstand the strains and consequences, continued to be burdened with the risks of excessive child-bearing for another century; yet the large size of working-class families continued to be ascribed to 'improvidence'.

This partial release of the middle-class woman from the status of a dutiful brood mare was accompanied by the first stages of her elevation above the position of a legal chattel. Until the married women's property acts of 1870 to 1893, the rule as between husband and wife was that what was his was his, but that what was hers was his as well; and that extended to her post office savings account. The husband who asked if the new acts really meant that if his wife received a legacy of a hundred pounds he would now actually have to ask her for it, was revealing much by his question. The matrimonial causes act of 1857 had at last permitted actions for divorce in the courts by those who could afford the cost; but, whereas a wife's adultery was sufficient ground for divorce, she had to prove cruelty and desertion as well as adultery before she could herself get a divorce. A wife's adultery was deemed more serious than a husband's because her misbehaviour might involve him unknowingly in legal paternity of another man's child. Though various acts between 1878 and 1902 enabled wives to obtain separation orders with maintenance from husbands guilty of serious cruelty, not until 1923 could a woman get a divorce solely on the grounds of her husband's adultery and only in 1937 could she do so on grounds of desertion, cruelty or insanity.

As well as these small beginnings, it was already noticeable by the century's end that the wholly dependent and submissive woman was being replaced by a 'New Woman'. As early as 1879, it was observed that the phrase 'May I have the pleasure of dancing with you?' was giving way to the less chivalric 'Shall we take a turn?' and that young ladies no longer responded with 'I shall be very happy' but could be heard making the straightforward (if not 'forward') reply, 'Thank you, yes'. By the 1890s, the society magazine *The Queen* was describing the fashionable young women of the time as 'sharp, wide awake, aggressive, self-assertive' and as standing no nonsense and needing no help. And a fair way down the social scale, the bicycle was taking women out and about without their chaperones; and so many of them travelled alone by train that, in the 1880s, the Great Western Railway put on 'Ladies Only' compartments.

It was logical that women no longer be denied the vote. They could already vote in local elections, and in 1907 they became eligible to sit on town and county councils. Their continued exclusion from parliamentary voting rights provoked the Women's Social and Political Union to launch from 1905 onwards the campaign of violence that gave to Englishwomen the dubious distinction, by several decades, of being the first aggrieved twentieth-century minority to conduct an urban guerrilla movement.

The cause of the delays which gave rise to the fury of the militant suffragettes was that both Tory and Liberal parties were divided on the issue so that neither government nor opposition leaders could sponsor the enfranchisement of women. Campbell-Bannerman, Liberal prime minister from 1905 until his death in 1908, favoured it but Asquith, who then succeeded him, did not. Just as Gladstone had thought that for women to vote would 'trespass on their delicacy, their purity, their refinement, the elevation of their whole nature,' Asquith believed that woman's 'natural sphere' was 'not the turmoil and dust of politics but the circle of social and domestic life.' Lloyd George and Sir Edward Grey, the Liberal foreign secretary, were in favour; so was the Tory leader, Balfour, as Disraeli had been. But both parties felt that votes for women was not a cause likely to commend itself to the existing all-male electorate. Although no women at all could vote, neither could the forty per cent of men who were not householders. A young artisan who had been earning his living since his early teens might have no vote whereas other males could vote who, because they enjoyed independent means, did not work at all. Yet a step-by-step approach was also not acceptable to the Liberals. They rejected a proposal to enfranchise the wives of £10 householders as likely to increase the anti-Liberal vote. An attempt to give votes to all women householders might well have the same effect and could be said to be unjust to working males who were not householders. Lloyd George saw the dilemma: the Liberal party would, he wrote, have to give the vote to working men's wives as well as to spinsters and widows, since any more restrictive female enfranchisement would spell 'disaster for Liberalism'.

There were other anomalies in the electoral system. Occupation of business premises, as well as residential, conferred entitlement to vote, so that business men had more votes than one. In addition, graduates could vote for university MPs as well as for their local candidate. But there were great obstacles in the way of a comprehensive reform of the electoral system since, if a partial enfranchisement of women would harm the Liberals, abolition of plural voting would harm the Tories. From 1910 onwards, the Liberals depended for their parliamentary majority on the votes of Irish Nationalists, who would resent the diversion of parliamentary time from the home rule bill they were insisting on. Apart from his own personal dislike of the idea of votes for women, Asquith was continuously harassed by the problem of Ulster. Of his two most dynamic ministers, Lloyd George was exhaustingly involved in creating a national insurance scheme and Churchill revelling in the thrills of being in charge at the admiralty. The government's failure to do anything for women's suffrage because it could not find the time simultaneously to reform the unsatisfactory male suffrage is as understandable as is the rage of the suffragettes.

The treatment of female law breakers by Asquith's government further illustrated the difficulties that Liberals faced when deciding which of the world's good causes they ought to support. Coming into office in 1905 as champions of unjustly treated Afrikaners and indentured Chinese labourers in South Africa, they stayed to authorise the forcible feeding of imprisoned suffragettes.

3

WAR, APPEASEMENT AND WAR

Supremacy Challenged

OMINOUSLY but appropriately, the twentieth century opened with the British fighting a war and finding it unexpectedly difficult to win. The Boer War of 1899–1902 was the product of exceptional circumstances. Simultaneously, there were, at the southern tip of Africa, a determined people of European stock resolved to resist British imperial expansion, and a small but hardly less determined British group bent on removing that obstacle and, most unusually of all, enjoying at the very least strong moral support at Westminster. This had been provided by Salisbury's Colonial Secretary, the Liberal Unionist, Joseph Chamberlain. Like Cecil Rhodes, the South African millionaire who had founded Rhodesia, Chamberlain believed in the special mission of the Anglo-Saxon race to develop the whole of Africa 'from the Cape to Cairo'. The two resentful Afrikaner republics of the Transvaal and the Orange Free State were an impediment to that mission. Also of concern was German encouragement of these Boers. This might lead to German interference at the Cape and endanger the security of the long sea route to India.

The difficulty the British experienced in overcoming Afrikaner resistance during the war revealed weaknesses in army organisation which first the Conservatives and then, after 1905, the Liberals took steps to improve. The reforms had to be undertaken, however, within the limitation that alone among the European peoples the English were resolutely opposed to conscription. That the British won the Boer War in the end and, though widely condemned as aggressors by continental countries, were subject to no outside interference, was a tribute to their continuing naval preponderance.

This naval supremacy was confirmed when, during the Russo-Japanese war of 1904–5, the Japanese eliminated Russia as a naval power by destroying the Russian Far Eastern and Baltic fleets. Despite the recent initiation by the Germans of an ambitious programme of naval building, and a growing unease about Germany's industrial competitiveness, England was in a strong position internationally when the Liberals took office in 1905. Its strength was increased rather than diminished by the fact that alone among the great powers England had no commitment to defend any major ally in Europe and was in process of reducing outstanding causes of friction. By the 'entente cordiale' of 1904, a twenty-year quarrel with France about Egypt had been amicably resolved. Russia's defeat by Japan, at that time Britain's only ally of importance, was to lead in 1907 to an Anglo-Russian 'entente' which did much to reduce England's longstanding dread of a Russian threat to India by way of Persia and Afghanistan. The traditional nineteenth-century fear that Russia might take Constantinople was also over. Secure in possession of Egypt, neither the admiralty nor the foreign office were any longer interested in the matter. That England, so diplomatically and navally secure between 1905 and 1907, should by 1914 have felt in such great danger that it appeared vital to enter a war against Germany is a somewhat less obvious matter than is usually supposed.

The two most obvious novel factors from 1905 onwards were a changed naval policy by the admiralty and a change of personnel at the foreign office. In 1906, the admiralty launched the Dreadnought, a big-gun ship which could fire at a range beyond that of the torpedo and which, as well as outgunning other capital ships, was, owing to its turbine engines, also faster. The original idea was to produce between ten and fourteen such battleships before the Germans could produce similar vessels themselves. Moreover, the Dreadnought programme created the further problem for the Germans that before they could sail ships of a similar type into the North Sea they would have to reconstruct the Kiel Canal, a task they did not complete until 1914. Despite heavy building by the Germans, and a temporary cutback in Dreadnought building when Campbell-Bannerman's Liberal government first came to power, England maintained its lead in capital ships of the Dreadnought type; but at increasing cost and with increasing irritation because the Germans repeatedly refused any limitation of this naval arms race. The function of the rapidly growing German navy was unclear. Reasonably enough, the English saw its only purpose as that of threatening them. The Germans' insistence that they needed a navy 'for the general purposes of power' was not reassuring.

The Dreadnought policy like that of allying with Japan in 1902 and of settling colonial differences with France in 1904 (and with Russia in 1907) arose out of the prime Tory concern to protect the empire and the naval supremacy on which it was wholly dependent. None of these policies was undertaken with continental Europe in mind. But, by the end of 1905, the foreign office, headed previously by officials suspicious of France and sympathetic to Germany, passed to the control of men who were pro-French and deeply concerned with the threat to the continental balance of power posed by the unpredictable diplomacy and growing strength of Germany. This new attitude was either shared or absorbed by the incoming Liberal foreign secretary, Sir Edward Grey. Though one of the group known as Liberal Imperialists, which had been led by Rosebery and to which Asquith also belonged, Grey conducted an almost entirely European foreign policy, devoting himself ceaselessly to attempts to maintain the continental balance so that the need would not arise for England to defend it by military means.

From the start, however, Grey interpreted this policy as requiring him always to give diplomatic support to France against Germany, in part because, though France had an alliance with Russia, he doubted Russia's capacity to act as a reliable ally either in peace or war. In 1905, and again in 1911, the Germans precipitated two unnecessary international crises by attempting to obstruct French efforts to make themselves the predominant power in Morocco. By the entente, Grey had undertaken to support French ambitions in Morocco; but in both crises he put so much diplomatic support on the side of the French that the Germans were forced to abandon their pressure. Again, though he always insisted that there could be no peacetime alliance with France, Grey undertook in 1912 that, in a war against Germany, France could rely on the British navy to defend the French Channel coast.

Yet, when war came in 1914, it arose out of matters irrelevant to British interests either imperial or foreign. A teenage Austro-Hungarian citizen, trained in Serbia as a freedom fighter in the cause of liberating the Serbs of Bosnia from Austrian rule, assassinated the heir to the Austro-Hungarian throne. The military chiefs in Vienna insisted that this proved beyond doubt that Serbia was a dangerous threat to the survival of the Austro-Hungarian empire and must be militarily crushed. In this resolve they were supported by the military leaders of their German ally. This support was given either in spite of the certain knowledge that Russia, for a variety of reasons not all of them sensible, would fight if Serbia were attacked; or perhaps because of this certainty. Nineteen-fourteen was about the last year in which the Germans could rely on numerical superiority to the Russians, owing to the fact that the Russian army was being considerably increased. With precipitate haste, the Germans therefore hustled themselves into declaring war on the Russians and then with even less ceremony forced a war on the French as well. This was because the so-called Schlieffen Plan, originally drawn up by the German High Command twenty years before, laid down that a war against Russia could succeed only if Russia's French ally was defeated within six weeks.

The contrast between the quick military reflexes of the continental powers and the slow, sober cogitations in London was extreme. Grey alternated solemn warnings to the French that British intervention on land could not be considered automatic, with hardly less earnest intimations to his colleagues that his own position and the honour of the country made such intervention inescapable. Few members of the Liberal government, though perhaps not as few as some of them later alleged, knew much about Grey's conduct of foreign affairs; and the first instinct of many Liberals (though not of the Conservatives) was for neutrality. But the Schlieffen Plan required the Germans to attack France by marching through Belgium; and Grey was able to secure parliament's support for war against Germany by emphasising, not his policy of supporting France for the sake of the balance of power but by representing, not very accurately, that England was bound by treaty to go to war to defend the neutrality of Belgium, which had been guaranteed by the European Great Powers since 1839.

The Plans that Failed

Virtually none of the participants supposed themselves to be embarking on a four-year war that would produce millions of casualties. Had they realised as much, it is unlikely they would have started the war. Accordingly, the real cause of the war of 1914–18, which would lead to the disappearance of four of Europe's oldest royal dynasties, may be said to be the irrational expectation that it would be a short war. The only precedents in favour of this self-deception were the short Austro-Prussian war of 1866 and the Franco-Prussian war of 1870–71. Neither of those wars had been fought in circumstances remotely like those of the Europe of 1914.

Nevertheless, as the continental regulars and reservists were mobilised, Englishmen volunteered by the thousand, and with such eager haste that the authorities were overwhelmed. Everywhere, Europeans swept into war in 1914 with the unthinking self-confidence of societies altogether over-persuaded by the technological achievements of the preceding hundred years that no task was beyond the capacity of courageous, determined men to undertake, no personal or national challenge that could not be overcome.

Almost all the plans came unstuck. The planned French advance on Berlin got no further than the French frontier. The Schlieffen plan was carried out only in part, and thoroughly mismanaged. The Germans could not hold back the Russians. The Austrians could not even beat the Serbians. The British mopped up most of the German merchant fleet, but their Dreadnoughts could not destroy the German High Seas fleet because the Germans kept it in port. The less than 100,000 regular soldiers of the British Expeditionary Force, so far from helping any successful actions by the French, were entangled in a French retreat and confused the Germans by proving themselves among the most effective fighting troops in Europe. But the most they could do was to fall back in line with the French. By the winter of 1914, though Paris was saved, almost all Belgium and one-tenth of French soil were in German hands; those fighting on the Western Front were condemned, despite great loss of life on both sides already, to the long-lasting miseries of trench warfare on a line from Switzerland to the Channel.

There was no possibility of a compromise. The Germans would not give up what they had gained but were unable to advance much beyond their original line. Their Anglo-French opponents could not drive the Germans back but were nevertheless determined to recover the occupied territory. The repeated failure of the many Allied offensives to break through the enemy line and the tremendous casualty lists that resulted from them, scarred the memories of a whole generation, dictating the character of British foreign policy when the war was over and of Britain's strategic policy when war was resumed in 1939.

Both then and afterwards, army commanders and the General Staff were held almost personally responsible for sending men to their deaths in tens of thousands in attempts to gain a few paltry miles or salients. The high command were said, wrongly, to be for the most part cavalry officers, mindlessly sacrificing the infantry with callous indifference, in the vain hope that they could open a breach wide enough for the élite to charge through in a gallant, romantic dash to glorious victory. The truth was that a long war of this sort not having been planned for, no attention had been given to the problem of how advancing troops could survive against the deadly combination of machine guns and barbed wire. Aircraft were still primitively fragile; and the reluctance to use tanks until late in the war derived as much from the normal inefficiency of newly-invented machinery and from inexperience in their tactical employment as from any stupidity on the part of the General Staff. The British Commander-in-Chief, Sir Douglas Haig, had little to offer except his highly professional dedication to duty; but it is hard to see how the army's morale could have survived at all amid its troglodyte miseries without intermittent injections of hope, however unjustified. The morale of British forces proved in practice more stable than that of the French and more enduring than that of the Germans. The most conspicuous of those who unrealistically pinned their hopes on the large-scale break-through were Nivelle, the French commander whose offensive of 1917 reduced his army to a state of mutiny; and Ludendorff, the German commander whose failure to achieve success with his 'Big Push' of 1918 led him to insist that the German civilian government sue at once for peace on whatever terms were going, in order to prevent the disintegration of his army.

The war at sea also failed to work to plan. The British fleet barely managed to avoid losing the war's one big-ship battle, at Jutland in 1916; but the German fleet was sufficiently discouraged not to attempt a second encounter. More important was that German use of the sub-marine all but negated a strategy based on big ships. The German decision to wage 'unrestricted' submarine warfare against virtually all forms of shipping, enemy and neutral alike, threatened the very survival of an England that depended on foreign food and on supplies from the United States. Fortunately for the British, Lloyd George, as prime minister, was able to reduce merchant shipping losses by getting the admiralty to adopt the convoy system. Submarine attacks on neutral shipping were also an important factor in drawing the United Sates into the later stages of the war on the Allied side.

When the armistice Ludendorff had sought came into force on 11 November 1918, the Germans were still in occupation of large areas of territory both in the west and the east. Their surrender was unexpected;

and since there had been no fighting on German soil (except in the east in the early stages) there was some basis for the German feeling that they had not 'really' been defeated. This would enable Hitler subsequently to ascribe a surrender forced on the German government by Ludendorff, to an evil 'stab in the back' by Jewish-socialist conspirators. Furthermore, on the eastern front, the Germans had won a great victory. Incompetent management of the war led first of all to the overthrow of the Russian Czar and then to the Bolshevik coup d'état of October 1917 which installed Lenin and Trotsky. Convinced that his main task was to create a Marxist Russia and that socialist revolutions were imminent all over Europe, thus making matters of territorial sovereignty irrelevant, Lenin had agreed to the treaty of Brest-Litovsk with Germany in March 1918. This ceded vast areas to the Germans; and though the Germans withdrew from them after the November armistice, the Soviet Union did not get them all back until 1940. In short, the Russians had in effect lost the war, thus postponing until 1945 the embarrassment they would have been bound to cause the rest of Europe had they been one of the victorious powers in 1918.

Appeasing the Germans

In 1919–20, France aimed for a peace settlement that would complete by other means the total German defeat that had not in fact taken place. Germany would be permanently subjected. To make up for the elimination of Russia by defeat and Bolshevik revolution, France would ring Germany round with a number of small but well-armed newly-made states, all of them clients of the French. Early in 1918, however, Woodrow Wilson, the United States president, had issued his Fourteen Points, following them with various high-sounding promises which led him to be greeted by the war-weary Europeans as a saviour. The peace he delineated would be absolutely fair and just to both vanquished and victors. It would set up a League of Nations which would prevent war and achieve disarmament. It would bring about a 'world safe for democracy', based on 'the self-determination of peoples'. Much public opinion, not least in Germany, assumed that Europe was about to be redeemed for all time by a combination of 'forget and forgive' with the liberation of all Europe's oppressed national minorities.

It was in an attempt to inject some rational elements into the treaties in spite of the understandable bitterness of the French and the confused impracticalities of Wilson's cloudy moralisings, that the British policy of appeasement of Germany was first conceived: in 1919–20, and by Lloyd George. It was a policy from which the British did not depart until 1939, and one not inherently objectionable until Neville Chamberlain made it seem so. It was certainly not his invention.

Lloyd George, though not in principle opposed to war, had never been reconciled to the kind of war that had been waged in the west since

1914. Like Churchill, he was sickened by the slaughter on the western front and though, despite ugly quarrels with the generals, he had been unable to prevent it during the war, he wanted to make sure the British should not undergo the experience again. He believed that an attempt by France to dominate Germany would lead to another war in the west. With Wilson's support he successively scaled down French demands. They could not create a separate Rhineland state, detached from the rest of Germany. They could not even administer the Rhineland. The best he would allow them was that it should be under Allied military occupation for fifteen years and that it should be demilitarised, so that Germany should never station troops there. When France demanded a permanent guarantee of British military assistance against Germany, Lloyd George declined; officially because the United States would not give a similar guarantee. Against Wilson, Lloyd George insisted that the new state of Poland should have as few Germans in its borders as possible; and refused to allow Danzig, Poland's natural outlet to the Baltic but a wholly German city, to pass under Polish sovereignty. Instead, he had it made a Free City under League of Nations control. Lloyd George and his colleagues hesitated long before agreeing that the Sudetenland, an area heavily populated with Germans, should be included within the new state of Czechoslovakia which had emerged from the collapse of Austria-Hungary. He tried, in various ingenious ways, to reduce to reasonable proportions the total reparations to be demanded from Germany, in spite of political pressure at home and from the United States. He was reduced to trying to dodge the issue by setting up a Reparation Commission to fix the final sum; although giving the public impression that it would name a large one, his intention was that it should decide on a smaller one.

Lloyd George could not dominate the settlement. Adroit at fixing things, he brought no air of moral authority to the proceedings and was over-burdened with problems at home. Accordingly, Germany was deprived of all her colonies; was so thoroughly disarmed that her army was scarcely large enough to maintain public order; was forbidden to unite with the new, small all-German Austrian republic; and not allowed to negotiate with the Allies, but merely to accept the treaty of Versailles. This enabled Hitler to claim that it was a 'Diktat' and not a 'real' treaty.

The resolve of the British not to press too hard on the Germans grew stronger as the French continued into the post-war period their insistence on exacting reparations. Before 1914, Germany had been England's best export market; an economically depressed Germany was bad for trade. Lloyd George tried vainly, at conferences at Cannes and Genoa in 1922, to change the French attitude. In 1923, alleging Germany's failure to pay reparations on the due date, the French invaded and occupied the Ruhr. This French attempt to convince the Germans they had actually lost the war failed owing to the passive resistance of the German population and the runaway inflation the German government then encouraged. The British, so far from supporting their wartime ally, said the French action was illegal.

The British policy of appeasement had its greatest success when, following a change of government in France, an agreed plan to reduce and rationalise reparations was drawn up; and when, in 1925, the treaty of Locarno was signed. Britain, France and Germany all affirmed their permanent acceptance of the frontiers established in western Europe by the peace settlement. A year later, Germany's international rehabilitation was formalised by her admission to the League of Nations as a member of its Council. A further lightening of reparations in 1930 was accompanied by the ending, five years ahead of the date fixed by the treaty of Versailles, of the Allied occupation of the Rhineland.

Despite many French reservations, the financial chaos caused in Europe and in Germany in particular, by the Great Depression and the collapse of the New York stock market in 1929, led to reparations in effect being abandoned altogether at a conference at Lausanne in 1932. In 1930, an international conference on Disarmament had opened. From the start, again despite French alarm, it took seriously the German complaint that, since total disarmament was not being planned, Germany should be allowed at least some measure of rearmament to give her 'equality of status' with other powers. When, after Hitler had come to power, he withdrew Germany from the Disarmament Conference (and from the League of Nations) it was not, as he claimed, because German rearmament was being obstinately obstructed, but because progress was being made towards its achievement by international agreement. A plan, sponsored by the British prime minister, Ramsay MacDonald, would have offered Germany almost as big an army as its military men thought they could train and equip, at any rate before about 1935. What Hitler was afraid of was that the French might sabotage the whole thing by publicly revealing how much they knew of the extent of Germany's secret rearmament, then being carried on with the cooperation of the USSR.

The Unappeasable Not Appeased

During 1935 and 1936 attention was diverted from Germany to Italy. In those years, Benito Mussolini, Italy's 'Duce', was transformed from a highly esteemed potential ally of France and Britain against Hitler into a potential enemy likely to cooperate with him. Mussolini invaded Abyssinia. This was a breach of the Covenant of the League of Nations, which the peace conference had set up to provide 'collective security' for states which became victims of aggression. The French saw no reason for denying Abyssinia to the Italians if it would keep Mussolini from allying with Hitler. The British, however, took the lead in opposing

Mussolini and were responsible for a League of Nations decision to impose sanctions on Italy. This was chiefly because the National government of the time, then presided over somewhat nervelessly by Stanley Baldwin, was faced with a General Election in 1935; and an enormous passion for the principles of the League of Nations was being displayed not only by virtually the whole of the Labour party but by many influential persons outside it. Baldwin therefore needed to go to the country claiming that he, too, fully supported the League.

Once the election had been won, however, the British faced the obstinate fact that the French would not agree to oil sanctions against Italy. Accordingly, one last attempt was made to appease Mussolini by the so-called Hoare-Laval plan to give Mussolini rather more of Abyssinia than he had then managed to conquer. The plan was abandoned in the face of a general outcry that it was 'rewarding the aggressor' and a betrayal of the League. With partial sanctions ineffective and oil sanctions vetoed by the French, nothing more could be done. Mussolini not only conquered Abyssinia but showed every sign that he would treat the 'effete democracies', which had so bungled their feeble efforts to stop him, with undisguised contempt in the future.

Hitler made the most of the confusion among his enemies. In 1935 he denounced the treaty of Versailles and announced the introduction of conscription in Germany. The British promptly demonstrated their own low opinion of how Germany had been treated in 1919. Within weeks, they signed a naval agreement with Germany, in effect condoning German naval rearmament, provided the German navy's strength did not go beyond thirty-five per cent of British naval strength. Thus further encouraged, Hitler marched German troops into the Rhineland in 1936, at the same time denouncing Locarno, cleverly confusing the issue by offering non-aggression pacts with all and sundry.

At this point, according to conventional wisdom thereafter, Hitler could and should have been 'stopped'. But in denouncing Versailles and re-militarising the Rhineland, Hitler was performing actions to which the British had long had no objections in principle; and the French, with Italy hostile and Britain indifferent, were unwilling to act alone. However militarily weak Hitler's Germany was in 1936, armed resistance by the French over the Rhineland would have received little support from public opinion and, by proving that Hitler was right in his otherwise mendacious claim that the democracies wanted to keep Germany 'in shackles', would enormously have increased his prestige among his own people.

In 1937, when Baldwin retired, Neville Chamberlain became prime minister. His mind was made up. Not only did he believe war to be wrong in itself because cruel and wasteful. He believed the first German war had been a catastrophe into which England had blundered by sheer inattention to diplomatic detail. He was determined to end the drift and muddle into which international relations had sunk since 1934 and to make absolutely sure that England did not blunder into a European war for a second time.

Towards Europe itself he was indifferent. The practicalities which concerned him were imperial and strategic; and by 1937 the strategic problems that faced the government were serious. In November 1936, Hitler and Mussolini joined together in an association which Mussolini melodramatically described as 'the Rome-Berlin Axis'. In the same month, Hitler formed with Japan the so-called Anti-Comintern Pact. The Japanese had been much affronted by the ineffective but much publicised League of Nations opposition to their annexation of Manchuria between 1931 and 1933, and were about to embark on the full scale war with China that was not to end until 1945. And though both these pacts of Hitler's were said to be aimed against international Bolshevism (i.e. the Soviet Union) they foreshadowed a potential anti-British coalition which, in time of war, it would be impossible to defeat. To defend the Far East against Japan, the Mediterranean against Italy, and western Europe against Hitler was, as the British chiefs of staff told Chamberlain in 1937, an impossibility. Chamberlain therefore set to work to eliminate every possible cause of friction with at any rate the two potential European enemies as briskly as he could, with a frigid, stubborn conviction that he was doing the right thing and a chilly contempt for all opposition even if it came from members of his own cabinet.

When the Spanish Civil War broke out in 1936, the British and French governments resolved that it should not spread beyond the borders of Spain itself and organised an international non-intervention agreement. This meant in practice that Britain and France gave no help to the Spanish Republican government but that Mussolini went on giving military and other aid to the rebels led by General Franco despite signing various agreements that he would do no such thing. This made so little difference to Chamberlain that when Anthony Eden, his foreign secretary, resigned in protest at attempts to make agreements with a man who kept breaking them as a matter of practice, Chamberlain was relieved to see Eden go. Though gaining nothing much beyond a reduction of the amount of anti-British propaganda broadcast to the Arabs by Italian radio, Chamberlain was convinced that he was success-fully wooing Mussolini away from his support of Hitler.

Simultaneously, Chamberlain continued to let Hitler be informed that British support would be willingly forthcoming for a number of changes in European boundaries that might be pleasing to Hitler, provided they were undertaken peacefully and by agreement. The idea was mooted in several quarters that since it was so unfair that Germany should have no colonies, something ought to be done about that too.

But, in 1938, mainly as an impulsive gesture of rage at discovering that its head of state was not amenable to his dictation, Hitler invaded and annexed Austria. Since this was a consummation Chamberlain had regarded as desirable and had no power to stop, he could do no more than regret the method by which this *Anschluss* had been brought about. But when, soon afterwards, it became clear that Hitler was threatening by force to 'liberate' the 'persecuted' Sudeten Germans living (as they had done for centuries) in Bohemia and Moravia, which had been part of Czechoslovakia since 1919, Chamberlain spent the summer of 1938 trying to achieve a pro-German solution to the issue that would not involve the use of force. For months, diplomatic pressure was put on the Czechs to make concession after concession to the strident Nazis of the Sudetenland. This was even after an official British mission had established that the Sudeten Germans had little to complain about.

Nothing had any effect on Hitler. Three million unfortunate Germans were, he said, being 'persecuted' in the Sudetenland and he would not tolerate it. This merely stiffened Chamberlain's resolve. He took the then unusual step of making a personal visit to Hitler, and by air. Learning that Hitler demanded 'self-determination' for the Sudetens (which would mean their transfer to Germany), Chamberlain flew back to London, got the agreement of the cabinet and returned to Germany only to discover that Hitler wanted even more. Since France was pledged to support Czechoslovakia if attacked by Germany, and Britain could hardly stand aloof in any Franco-German war, Chamberlain turned, as a last resort, to his new friend, Mussolini. Only too willing to get in on the act, Mussolini persuaded Hitler to agree to a four-power conference at Munich. Here, with the least possible delay, it was arranged that the Sudeten German borderlands of Czechoslovakia should be given to Germany forthwith. The Czechs were told of the agreement after it had been made and that if they resisted they would do so alone. To register publicly that the crisis had been settled without war, Chamberlain also got Hitler to sign 'a piece of paper' promising that all future Anglo-German differences would be settled peacefully. 'I think,' Chamberlain said, 'it is peace for our time'.

'Munich' made appeasement, hitherto a respectably neutral term, a word of ill-repute perhaps for all time. It was not simply that it had settled the crisis at the expense, and over the heads, of the people of Czechoslovakia, among whom were thousands of Germans who were social democratic opponents of Nazism. Munich was in no real sense the outcome of peaceful negotiation. One side had conceded all that the other demanded, and under threat. Chamberlain and his French opposite number, Daladier, had been given what was in effect an ultimatum, and had freely accepted it. Hitler's aim ever since 1933 had been to ensure that everything that was thereafter gained by Germany would be gained not with, but without, international cooperation, so that it could be seen as proceeding from the unfettered will of an all-powerful Führer who, single-handed and in defiance of the whole world, had once more made Germany a great and mighty state that owed nothing to anybody. It was pointless to expect Hitler to act by international agreement. He was determined to do the opposite. Since he had no intention of being appeased, concessions did not appease him. Having got the Sudetenland, he would now make fresh demands elsewhere. That he had said he would do no such thing was irrelevant.

It was not that this point had not been made. As early as April 1933, Chamberlain's own half-brother, Austen, joint architect of Locarno when foreign secretary in 1925, had made it plainly:

Germany is afflicted by this narrow, exclusive, aggressive spirit, by which it is a crime to be in favour of peace and a crime to be a Jew. This is not a Germany to which we can afford to make concessions.

Neville Chamberlain, however, seemed scarcely able to realise this, even when his policy had manifestly failed.

The main issue of 1939 was to be Danzig. But Hitler was temporarily diverted by the collapse of the much weakened Czecho-Slovak state in March 1939. In particular, both Hungary and Poland had designs on Slovakia, the eastern part of the country. To ensure German control of the situation, Hitler marched into the Czech capital, Prague, and turned the Czech provinces of Bohemia and Moravia into German protectorates; Slovakia became a nominally independent state. As had been forecast, Munich had destroyed Czechoslovakia.

Since this was of no great concern to him, Chamberlain was at first disposed merely to grumble that he ought to have been consulted. Then, suddenly realising that Anglo-German consultation was what Munich was supposed to be all about, he sharpened his tone. 'Is this the last attack on a small state or is it . . . a step in the direction of an attempt to dominate the world by force?' The obvious response, that this was a silly question to which the answer was 'neither', was not made. Instead, repentant of their jubilation over the 'deliverance' of Munich, the politically-minded switched instantly to the view that appeasement had failed and must be abandoned. With an incoherent combination of rashness and hesitation, Chamberlain moved forward in the wake of this new tide of opinion.

He began precipitately. Acting upon false rumours of Hitler's intentions, he announced in March 1939 that Britain would guarantee the independence of Poland, Greece and Romania. Hitler continued with his new propaganda campaign: Danzig and at least part of the former German lands in Poland must become German. To show his opinion of Chamberlain's guarantees and grumblings, Hitler annexed the German city of Memel, which had been ceded after 1918 to Lithuania; and denounced the Anglo-German naval treaty of 1935.

It soon became apparent, however, that Poland could only be defended in any real sense with the help of the Soviet Union. Reluctantly, negotiations were opened with the Soviets. Hitler countered by offering the USSR a non-aggression pact and a share of Poland, as well as the return to the Soviet Union of the three Baltic States it had lost at Brest-Litovsk. Having thus made it strategically impossible for the Poles to be defended, Hitler pressed on. The Poles, unlike the Czechs, regarded their country as a Great Power. They would concede nothing to Hitler. That there was no second 'Munich' was a Polish decision.

Germany invaded Poland on 1 September 1939. Unwilling to accept that he had fallen into a trap of his own making, Chamberlain delayed declaring war until two days later. Hitler was alleged to have been taken aback by the news. It was certainly odd: the whole basis of British foreign policy since 1919 had been that it had no interest in the affairs of eastern Europe. Chamberlain mournfully told the nation by radio, 'Everything I have worked for . . . has crashed in ruins'. So had British foreign policy; and so, if war were persisted in, might the British Empire.

The war that was declared on Germany in September 1939 was, as the Americans correctly if somewhat impertinently christened it, a 'phoney war'. Since the previous German war was held to have 'proved' that an offensive strategy led to defeat, the British and French waited for the Germans to take the initiative against them. In the meantime, economic blockade might quite possibly 'starve' the Germans. They might even be obliging enough to rebel against Hitler, a prospect hitherto considered by the British as certain to lead to a Communist Germany. When real war came, it was begun by Hitler. On 9 April 1940, German troops entered Copenhagen, and, on the following day, Oslo. They took The Hague and Brussels on 14 May and 17 May respectively, and were in Paris by 14 June. Already, by that date, the only British troops left alive on continental soil were prisoners of war. Hitler's *Blitzkrieg* had succeeded where the Schlieffen plan had failed. France had been defeated in a matter of weeks.

Victory Won, Supremacy Lost

One long term consequence of the Second World war was that the six years of deprivation while it was going on and the six years of austerity to which it led created a chasm between those who lived through those twelve years of rationing, shortages and voluntary and involuntary self-sacrifice and those who were too young to have experienced them. The generation gap between the mature survivors of that time and their children, experiencing the continuously rising standards and expectations of the twenty-five years that followed was wider than such gaps usually are. It contributed much to the social difficulties of the 1950s and 1960s; and to the general rebelliousness of the emancipated young against elders long conditioned to 'going without' and to 'putting up with things'.

Nevertheless, the second world war, even during the phoney war, was also chock full of movement, drama, spectacular catastrophes and gigantic to-and-fro encounters on land and sea and in the air. This war of tanks, and heroic deeds by Spitfire pilots, of aircraft carriers and saturation bombing, of blazing cities, wrecked homes, flying bombs and rockets, of underground agents, partisan fighters and resistance movements, of combined operations and mammoth surrenders, as well as of colourful and resourceful commanders in all arms of the services, bequeathed to those who survived it or merely heard about it an excited fascination with violence. There was little of that emotional revulsion against war that had followed the ending of the long agonies of the trenches in 1918. Opponents of nuclear weapons notwithstanding, there was little of that sense of high ideals betrayed or of lives gone to waste that lay so heavily on the minds of those who survived the earlier war. Not eager, innocent volunteers, but systematically classified conscripts made up the bulk of the armed forces from 1939 to 1945. Until Churchill became prime minister in 1940, and France had fallen and the BEF come home weaponless from Dunkirk, the atmosphere under Chamberlain was as unimaginative in war as it had been in peace. Whatever Chamberlain's private virtues, they remained private: his public image was prissy when not vinegary. Churchill made an immediate difference because of his exceptional mixture of the impudent, the pugnacious and the grandiloquent. But he, though broader in vision and more generous in his sympathies than Chamberlain, relied mainly on historic appeals to national greatness. Concern either for 'resisting Fascism' or for rescuing European Jewry from the scourge of Nazi anti-semitism played almost no part in the shaping of British foreign policy, in the declaration of war, or in its conduct until well towards its end. By a strange paradox, the war did not become a crusade until it was almost over. The freeing of the inmates of the Nazi concentration camps by British soldiers was one of the results of the war; it had not been one of its aims. A major factor in the dislike that Chamberlain and his fellow appeasers aroused at the time was their studied public indifference towards any of the victims of the Nazi persecutions of the 1930s, culminating in their treatment of the Czechs as importunate nuisances. It was an attitude they dearly wanted to display towards the Poles. The British ambassador to Berlin much regretted the fact that the diplomatic situation in the late summer of 1939 made it impossible for him to say 'boo to Beck', the Polish foreign minister.

But the Fall of France gave the English, for almost the first time since 1588, the bracing experience of feeling that the only asset they had was a will to survive. As elsewhere, the bombing of cities did as much to raise morale as to depress it, ending more effectively than the conscription of the labour force the traditional semi-hostility between those in uniform and those who kept to their 'civvies'. The mood changed again when Hitler invaded the USSR in 1941. In the popular mind it was this, rather than the more important entry of the United States at the end of that year that guaranteed 'we' were bound to win in the end. For the rest of the war there was a continuing suspicion that the Russians were 'doing all the fighting' while the British upper classes were 'Colonel Blimps' dragging their feet. The fall of Hong Kong and the surrender at Singapore seemed to confirm this unwarranted suspicion. Montgomery's value as a morale booster lay precisely in his success in persuading the general populace, as well as the rank and file in the Desert Army's fight against Rommel in North Africa, that he did not care a damn about anybody as long as he was free to keep his 'chaps' fully 'in the picture'.

The pro-Soviet fervour of the time was expressed in the insistent demand that the British should 'Open a Second Front Now'. Fortunately, Churchill had been as resentful as had Lloyd George over the endless slaughter in Flanders in the earlier war and had damaged his reputation almost until after he became prime minister by his advocacy of the bungled Gallipoli expedition of 1915 that had failed to open up an alternative and more mobile front in south-eastern Europe. Churchill properly insisted, in spite of Stalin's gibes and Roosevelt's importunings, that no assault on western Europe by land should be undertaken until there had been time to accumulate an overwhelming supply of men and material. It is thanks to Churchill that, because the British experienced nothing like them in the Second World War, it is the battles of the Somme and of Passchendaele of 1916 and 1917 which retain their hold on the national memory as the most gruesome and deadly of the British army's ordeals.

In 1945, when, with the Soviet army in Berlin, Hitler committed suicide and the Nazi forces surrendered, and a few months later the Japanese surrendered after the dropping of two atomic bombs by the United States, it was even clearer than it ought to have been in 1918 how illusory it was to suppose that it was 'we' who had won. What had been true of 'our' defeat of Philip II of Spain, of Louis XIV of France, and of Napoleon, was true also of 'our' defeat, first of the Kaiser's Germany and then of Hitler's: for all the effort, sacrifice, maiming and death that were involved, there was no moment in either war when 'we', unsustained by others, could have achieved victory. As for imperial greatness, there was truth as well as ill-will in H. L. Mencken's sour verdict in the 1920s that 'The British won most of their Empire without having to stand up in a single battle against a civilised and formidable foe, without grave or dreadful risk, and without the slightest risk of the conqueror being made the conquered'. In their only two overseas encounters with 'natives' of European stock, the War of American Independence and the Boer War, the English, with no allies to aid them, lost the first war and suffered humiliating defeats before officially winning the second.

The United Kingdom's capacity to act as a world power had always depended on the fact that, in a divided Europe, French and Dutchmen were as eager as Englishmen to fight Spain; Dutchmen, Germans and then Russians no less willing to fight France; and first Frenchmen and then Russians and Americans to fight Germany in the twentieth century. England's political power in the world had also depended, since the beginning of the nineteenth century, on Russia's value as an ally in a crisis (notably in 1812 and 1914); and on its weakness as an opponent (most notably in the Crimean War of 1854–6 and as a revolutionary Bolshevik power immediately after 1917). It had depended, too, on the readiness of the United States to abstain from the exercise of its political potential outside the American continent save in moments of extremity as in 1917 and 1941; and then to assert that power on both occasions in ways disastrous to England's enemies, even though the interests the United States thereby protected were their own rather than England's. But by 1945, the Soviet Union and the United States had been transformed by war into developed, independent powers capable of overshadowing all others. And in the continents of Asia and Africa, the emergence of Japan, and the dissemination far and wide of those major European exports, Anglo-Saxon ideas of liberty, and Marxist critiques of capitalism and Imperialism, were no less pregnant with change. England and western Europe had invented modern power-politics, modern industrial economics and modern concepts of liberty and social justice; but now, from all parts of the world their inventions were about to be turned against them. The brief period during which the talented, thrusting peoples of the small western peninsula of the Eurasian land-mass and its British offshore island had dominated the rest of the world was coming to an end. In 1938, the decision that there should not then be a great war likely to engulf the whole world was made by the political leaders of the United Kingdom, France, Germany and Italy, meeting at Munich. In September 1939, the ultimate decision that such a war should in fact be precipitated was effectively made by the house of commons at Westminster. This conformed to a pattern of history that had existed for two hundred and fifty years. By 1945 it was evident that future history would follow a different pattern.

4

THE PEOPLE'S FLAG

Socialists and Collectivists

THE ineffectiveness of late Victorian ideas and aspirations is shown by the melancholy record of the middle-class socialism and trade union militancy to which the period gave birth. The two were forced by the inadequacies of Liberals and Tories into the creation of what, by 1905, was being called the Labour party. Under its makeshift roof they were to cohabit uncomfortably through the twentieth century, often quarrelling, sometimes barely on speaking terms, each in turn claiming the right to wear the trousers, and never consummating a perfect union because their declarations of mutual affection were less frequent and more formal than their demand to be allowed to pursue their own separate aims.

Like 'democracy', 'socialism' was a word whose meaning depended on whichever Humpty Dumpty happened to use it. Virtually any government expenditure on purposes other than defence, public administration, justice and law and order was called socialist by somebody. So also were regulations to limit the rights of landlords or the freedom of employers to hire and fire their workers. When, in 1888, Lord Salisbury suggested that the state ought to concern itself about the condition of housing among the poor, even he was accused of being socialist. In the 1890s, the Liberal MP, Sir William Harcourt said, famously, and to modern minds fatuously, 'We are all socialists now'. All he meant was that the state had been interfering in a piecemeal way in public health, factory conditions and mass education for some sixty years.

England had entered the nineteenth century with a government that regulated its people less and did less for them than any continental government. Even by the end of the century the average able bodied adult male worker who did not pay income tax, become drunk and disorderly, serve in the armed forces or write many letters, hardly came into contact with government. If he failed to have his child vaccinated or did not send him to school he might attract attention; but even so, both vaccination officer and school attendance officer were locally appointed. Accordingly, the Poor Law Amendment Act of 1834 had been condemned because it was thought it might impose central control from London; the use of government inspectors rather than local justices to enforce factory acts was resisted; and so, even more persistently, were all public health acts. Because state action was 'socialistic', most so-called 'municipal socialism' was an attempt to keep central control at arm's length. Much health and housing legislation merely permitted local authorities to act if they chose. It was only when the local government acts of 1888 and 1894 created county and district councils, and when the education act of 1902 abolished the school boards, that this 'municipal socialism' ceased to be administered by a jumble of *ad hoc* bodies reluctantly set up by a parliament convinced of the moral value of local and individual liberty.

Both parties contributed to the increase of state power and regulation. Harcourt himself, as Liberal chancellor under Rosebery, pioneered the process of 'soaking the rich' by introducing, in 1894, a steeply graduated property tax, payable on the death of its owner. State power increased in other ways, too. The Conservatives had passed acts to protect merchant seamen, for the inspection of weighing machines, for the punishment of the owners of insanitary premises and to forbid housemaids to sit on window sills when cleaning their employers' sash windows. By 1905 there was sufficient state interference and municipal socialism to provide a reasonable basis for the Fabian case for a better organised and more comprehensive socialism run by the state.

Since socialism was an alarming word, the word collectivism was thought more respectable. After their return to power in 1905 the Liberals made some play with it. By that time, socialism, which hardly meant anything different, had become associated with a Labour party. As labels, socialism survived because the Labour party survived and collectivism passed away with the collapse of the Liberals after 1916. This is a pity, for collectivism would have said more to the English about how their society was being changed than did the word socialism. That all their governments since 1905 have been collectivist is certain. Whether any has been socialist is arguable.

Filling the Radical Gap

The disappearance of relevant radicalism from the Liberal party leadership in the 1880s and 1890s created a gap which Keir Hardie tried to fill by founding an Independent Labour Party in 1893. More vital results flowed from the obtuseness of the Tories in refusing to support the trade unions' right to strike which they had themselves bestowed on the unions in 1875. Fearful of foreign competition and alarmed by falling profits, employers in the 1890s took a strong line against unions. A National Free Labour Association appeared in 1893 to provide blackleg labour for employers faced with strikes. In 1897 the Court of Appeal upheld an injunction granted to an employer to prevent his premises being picketed. Engineering employers cooperated to counter a strike in July 1897 by a lock-out which lasted until January 1898, when the union capitulated. In response to these pressures the TUC congress of 1899 voted by a narrow majority to discuss with sympathetic bodies the idea of getting better representation for 'labour' in parliament. It was Keir Hardie who persuaded the consequent conference in Farringdon Street,

459

London, to work for 'a distinct Labour group in Parliament'. Even so, the Labour Representation Committee then created spent most of its time deliberating on which Liberal candidates to support in that year's election.

What powered the emergence of a more independent move was the notorious legal decision granting damages to the Taff Vale Railway Company against a railwaymen's union for losses caused to the Company by a strike; and, more important, the refusal of Balfour's conservative government to repair this culminating breach in that Tory act of 1875 which had appeared to give strikes full legal protection. This combination of employers' pressure and Tory indifference led to the new Labour movement being swamped with trade unionists who saw themselves merely as an industrial workers' pressure group. In the same way, many leaders of the ILP thought of themselves not as socialists but as liberals particularly pledged to press the demands of industrial workers against Tories and employers. They were 'Labour' because a Tory-dominated parliament had deprived them of their chief weapon against employers; and because, since a separate parliamentary group was being formed, association with it would enable them to exercise greater influence over the Liberals, under whose umbrella a few trade union MPs had usually sat in the commons since 1874. Half the Labour MPs of 1911 had first entered the commons as Liberals. As Bernard Shaw remarked, an empty stomach did not automatically induce an intellectual conviction of the existence of a class war. Labour's objective was fairness rather than revolutionary social reconstruction, its basis lying in morality rather than economics. When, forty years later, Aneurin Bevan said the movement was either a 'moral crusade' or it was nothing, he well defined both its weakness and its strength. Thus, the tactics by which the movement's secretary, Ramsay MacDonald, ensured that Labour candidates would in some constituencies not be opposed by Liberals and that in others Labour would not oppose Liberals, accorded with the real character of the Labour party. It was a major contribution to the defeat of the Tories in 1906, and the establishment of a collectivist Liberal government, first under Campbell-Bannerman, and then under Asquith.

Socialism Discerned

Yet, from the outset, the Labour party was not merely a small group of third-class passengers in a Liberal railway train. The support of the unions emphasised the difference of class and aim. This was put with some directness by Blatchford in *Merrie England*:

To be a Trade Unionist and fight for your class during a strike and to be a Tory or a Liberal and fight against your class at an election is folly . . . During a strike there are no Tories and no Liberals among employers. They are all Capitalists and enemies of the workers . . . You never ask an employer to lead you during a strike. But at election times, when you ought to stand by your class, the whole body of Trade Union workers turn into blacklegs and fight for the Capitalists and against the workers.

The support of the ILP signified a deeper moral feeling and a broader sympathy whose origins were defined, with unaccustomed clarity, by Ramsay MacDonald when he wrote in 1920 that the growth of the Labour party was due

to the rise within Labour organisations of an intellectual class of workmen who were influenced a good generation later than the intellectual classes by the literary and spiritual movements . . . embodied in the works of Carlyle and Ruskin.

With more characteristic gush he had claimed in 1911 that 'Some of the best literary and artistic work of the last century has been but as drum taps to which the step of Socialism kept time,' going on more realistically to write:

Socialism is not found in the slummy and most miserable quarters in towns, but in those quarters upon which the sun of prosperity manages to shine. It is the skilled artisan, the trade unionist, the member of the friendly society, the young workman who reads and thinks, who are the recruits to the army of Socialism.

In her schoolmarmish way, however, Beatrice Webb would allow no credit even to the most thoughtful of unslummy young workmen. Socialism, to her, owed nothing to 'the sweated worker or the so-called aristocracy of labour'. Indeed 'no section of the manual workers' created socialism. It was born of 'a new consciousness of sin among men of intellect and property' producing 'a growing uneasiness amounting to a conviction' that

the industrial organisation, which had yielded rent, interest and profits on a stupendous scale, had failed to provide a decent livelihood and tolerable conditions for a majority of the inhabitants of Great Britain.

With middle-class ideas and ideals, trade union sectionalism, collectivist Liberalism, the aspirations of intellectual workmen, together with a strong infusion of Victorian sentimentality, all closely involved in its birth and nurture, it is not surprising that Labour did not often speak with one voice. The movement as such was forever at odds with the parliamentary party. Preoccupied with their guerrilla campaigns against employers, trade unionists often regarded Labour MPs who were not themselves trade unionists as 'intellectuals', ignorant of working-class realities. The Independent Labour Party, until its virtual demise in the 1940s, and the extra-parliamentary rank and file who kept the movement alive in the constituencies, were always liable to surges of emotionalism deeply embarrassing to parliamentary leaders, compelled to conform to political realities. The nonconformist strain in the movement could lead to indulgence in moving, but largely meaningless, sentimentalities about Labour politics being 'the Gospel expressed in social terms'. When that calculatedly aspirate-dropping Labour Cabinet minister, J. H. Thomas, founder of the NUR, said of his party colleague, George Lansbury, famous for his Christian pacifism, "'is bleedin' 'eart goes to 'is bleedin' 'ead," he was being cynically uncouth, but also diagnosing a characteristic of many others in the party as well.

The emergence of Labour as the alternative governing party to the Conservatives can be attributed to the Franchise Act of 1918, which at last gave universal male suffrage and increased the electorate from the 7.7 million of 1910 to 21.4 million. But Labour's political advance owed even more to the policies pursued by the Tories between the retirement of Salisbury in 1902 and the coming to power of Baldwin in 1923. The Labour party in parliament all along owed its position less to any success it had in representing the diverse aspirations and interests of those who voted for it than to the collapse of the Liberal party as a result of the political manoeuvres of the Conservatives.

Tory Tactics and Liberal Dilemmas

Having failed to appease the unions after the Taff Vale case, Balfour went on, by various political miscalculations, to lose the 1906 election so handsomely that no parliament has since had so few Tory MPs. But during the campaign he had said it was everyone's duty to see that 'the great Unionist party should still control, whether in power or whether in opposition, the destinies of this great Empire'. It was soon clear that by 'everyone' he meant the Tory majority in the Lords. The party used that majority to wreck or mutilate so many Liberal bills as to appear opposed to all social reform. They deepened the impression by refusing to pass the so-called People's Budget proposed by Lloyd George in 1909 because, partly to finance new social insurance schemes, it steepened direct taxes on the rich and threatened to tax profits on the sale of land. This enabled Lloyd George to attack landlords and peerage in language so vividly denunciatory that his speech on the subject at Limehouse was stigmatised as having contributed to the permanent 'debasement of politics'. The outcome was that two elections were held in 1910, one on the issue of the budget and the second on the issue of reducing the power of the Lords. Significantly, the electorate showed little gratitude for the Liberals' reforms, little enthusiasm for collectivism (now damned by the Tories as 'socialism') and no great conviction that peers were very wicked. By the end of 1910 Tories had as many MPs as the Liberals. The Asquith ministry depended for its majority on 42 Labour and 82 Irish Nationalist MPs.

Although usually treated as a major 'constitutional' issue, the 'Lords v. Commons' controversy of 1909–11 was essentially a political conflict between the Liberals and their Irish and Labour allies on one side and the Tories on the other. Though both Liberals and Tories contemplated doing so, neither side used the ultimate weapon at its disposal: the Liberals did not create several hundred new peers and thus swamp the Tory majority in the Lords; and the Tory peers decided in the end not to reject the Parliament Act. What therefore emerged was a weak compromise that left the constitution of the Second Chamber unreformed. The Lords could no longer vote on financial measures but, unrepresentative though they remained, they retained a two-year suspensive veto over other legislation. To meet the charge that during the seven-year interval between general elections the commons itself might become unrepresentative, elections would in future be held every five years; with the result that, with their two-year veto, the Lords now had the power to render any government of which it disapproved ineffective after only three years in power.

In the complicated political manoeuvring that went on it was, in the end, not the People's Budget so much as the issue of Ireland that mattered most. The Irish disliked the budget (it taxed whiskey) but they did like the Parliament Act because it meant that the Liberals could now no longer avoid the issue by sheltering behind the Lords' veto. It was this prospect that got the Parliament Act through the commons.

Amid these and all the other preoccupations of the government, the more important issue of the suffrage was wholly lost sight of. Those anomalies in the electoral system which disfranchised all women and three-fifths of the men were untouched. It was left to the Lloyd George Coalition to give the vote to all males with six months' residential qualification in 1918, and at the same time to enfranchise women over thirty provided they were householders or married to a householder. The act of 1918 added more people to the electorate than any of its predecessors. Women were given the vote on the same terms as males aged twenty-one or over in 1928. Only with the election of a Labour government commanding a majority of parliamentary seats for the first time was plural voting by businessmen and graduates abolished in 1948, along with the six months' residential qualification. The parliamentary voting register, compiled twice a year, would in future also serve as the register of local government electors. Henceforward, therefore, the right to vote in local government elections was no longer confined to ratepayers.

The immediate result of the Parliament Act, however, was that the Tories could no longer use their majority in the Lords to hold up Irish Home Rule. After two years' delay by the peers it would become law regardless of them. Denied their constitutional weapon, the Tories employed instead the threat of civil war by exploiting the passions of armed Ulster Protestants determined not to be governed from Catholic Dublin. They were able to use this threat because of strong Ulster Unionist sentiment among senior army officers, causing doubts about the government's capacity to put down a rebellion. Asquith, magisterially convinced that the whole operation was bluff, kept cool; but it was in those two years rather than in Mosley's heyday in the 1930s that the United Kingdom came nearest to facing a quasi-fascist threat. An unpleasing alliance of determined imperialists, anti-liberals, anti-socialists, many of them markedly anti-semitic and anti-working class, was in the making. And although the affair went into cold storage with the outbreak of European war, Tory behaviour in those two years provided political ammunition for their opponents for another quarter of a century.

Though such a Tory party could not expect, and did not seek, to appease the Labour movement, its policy from 1914 to 1922 brought Labour fully into the political arena because it was in those years that the Tories destroyed the Liberal party. On the grounds that Asquith had failed to prosecute the war against Germany with sufficient vigour, the Tories drove Asquith into admitting them into a Coalition government in 1915. In 1916, by dubious manoeuvres, they engineered his replacement as prime minister by Lloyd George. Then, with the war over and its aftermath proving economically and socially disappointing and disturbed, Tory back-benchers, in 1922, compelled their leaders to ditch Lloyd George. Thus, Asquith was blamed for failing to prevent war and then for not waging it efficiently; and Lloyd George, though 'the man who won the war', was held to have lost the peace by failing either to satisfy post-war workers' discontents or their employers' desire for high profits and a docile labour force. In consequence, the Liberal party virtually collapsed, its downfall hastened by the hostility between the many Liberals who remained loyal to Asquith and the fewer Liberals whom the Asquithians regarded as mere personal hangers-on of Lloyd George, the deceitful Welsh wizard who had betrayed his party chieftain. Already, in the 1918 election, those among the electorate who had not voted for the Coalition of Tories and Lloyd George Liberals had given Labour 22.2% of the votes cast. From 1922 onwards, therefore, Labour became the second party in the state by default.

Liberal Epitaph

Many typewriter ribbons have been worn out in attempts to find explanation for the apparently astonishing fact that the Liberal party, so triumphant in 1906, nevertheless shrank to such relatively insignificant proportions after 1918. Yet perhaps personal and ideological divisions were rather more normal to the Liberal party than unity and electoral victory. Perhaps it was always the Liberals' weakness that they trafficked so freely in ideas and values and claimed to be above 'interests'. The rank and file of Liberals were on the whole the less coherently organised sections of the community. Liberalism was strong in rural areas, particularly the Celtic lands and the West Country, where dislike of Tory landlords was coloured by varying degrees of suspicion of the

English ruling class as a whole. It included non-socialist trade unionists and small, provincial businessmen resentful of Tory big business and finance. Such Liberals would value free trade because, to them, it meant above all low taxes and cheap food. Liberalism also still relied greatly on nonconformists; these, though still as offended as ever by the privileges and pretensions of the Church of England, were a less powerful force nationally than they had been. Many of them, in fact, were very soon drawn into the Labour movement.

Liberalism also continued to attract a varied assortment of idealists from all ranks of society who felt passionate about peace and social justice. Although, therefore, the party of change, its leaders tended to be educated, thoughtful persons with a tradition, often inherited from a longish line of upper-middle-class or aristocratic forbears, of conscientious commitment to the principles of tolerance and the liberty of the individual, but always within the context of the improvement, but not the re-shaping, of the society into which they had been born. They believed, too, that politics should be conducted by moral men for moral ends for the good of all and never for the particular benefit of any one interest within it. Their devotion to values made them cautious, their openness to ideas made them disputatious. The gap between the Liberal Imperialists, who looked to Lord Rosebery, and the rest, some of whom were dubbed 'Little Englanders', and that between Gladstonians who still sought to give Ireland home rule and those who wanted the issue indefinitely postponed made the parliamentary Liberals an ineffective body for most of the 1890s. The ill-success of the Boer War, Chamberlain's attack on free trade principles, and the straightforward, robust good sense of Campbell-Bannerman, were the principal reasons why the Liberals were able to ride to power in 1906 on a wave of general dissatisfaction that, in fact, they had no particular programme for dealing with.

The incapacity of the Liberal leadership to throw itself energetically into the prosecution of the German war was a harking back to its inability to make up its collective mind about the Boer War when in opposition, and was reminiscent of the attitude of their Foxite predecessors between 1790 and 1814. After Asquith's fall from power in 1916, his followers displayed the same solemnly nostalgic loyalty to him that the Grenvillites had showed to the memory of Fox after his death in 1808, a similar political ineffectiveness and a like propensity for blaming that ineffectiveness on the wickedness of others. The correspondence of the dejected Liberals of the 1920s reveals the same combination of a conviction that government had fallen into the wrong hands (Lloyd George's, or Bonar Law's or the socialists') with a patrician unwillingness to sully themselves by too much contact with a world where, they believed, 'values' had been debased. Just as they had little to contribute to the conduct of war, those few who felt they had something to say to the working classes after it, men such as Addison, Wedgwood Benn and

C. P. Trevelyan, transferred to Labour. From beginning to end, they, no less than Labour and far more wholeheartedly than the Conservatives, the more intelligent and aristocratic of whom always liked him, could never forgive Lloyd George for his determination to 'get things done'. Their distaste for him ran fairly deep, well before he became prime minister. Lloyd George later claimed that it was the Liberal cabinet itself that put up the strongest resistance to his People's Budget of 1909. Like Gladstone, Liberals were attracted by broad issues, not bread and butter problems of public administration and detailed social reform, let alone the crude imperatives of war. Correct as they were in believing that liberal values of moderation, impartial government and individual freedom were everywhere being threatened, they had little to offer but melancholy regret. Sir Edward Grey, steadily going blind, largely as a consequence of his own decision to ignore the risk to his sight of a long stint as foreign secretary; and Asquith, conveying in his unhappy old age after 1918 'a faint aroma of banquets and brandy' and talking 'with an air of distant wisdom as though a bank of clouds separated him from the common run of humanity'; these are sadly symbolic of the fading of a long and dignified political tradition. Its post-mortem survival depended, in the years between the wars, on the innately liberal attitudes of Baldwin and of MacDonald, both of them much disliked by their own followers for the lack of cutting edge in their tactics that such liberalism carried with it.

The Unions and the Party

The growth of trade unions increased the vote for the Labour party for the reason suggested by Blatchford. Once a party with a monopoly of trade union support existed, other parties would at once begin to seem anti-trade union parties and as middle-class and non-manual workers' parties. Once initiated, the new alignment was perpetuated by the intenser trade union militancy that followed the late-Victorian emergence of general or industrial unions among unskilled or semi-skilled workers, such as gasworkers, dockers and railwaymen. Semi-skilled workers were now more numerous in industry and a number of strikes, of which the classic example was the London dock strike of 1889, successful because of good discipline and wide public support, enabled them to narrow the gap between their own pay and that of skilled craftsmen. Earning only half as much as unskilled workers in the 1890s, they were earning two-thirds as much by 1914. Craft unions thus sought to protect their differentials; and all unions were provoked by the fact that the decade before 1914 was the only considerable period since 1815 when real wages failed to rise. Real national income per head grew at an annual rate of only 0.1% in those years, compared with a rate of 2% in the forty years before 1894, 1.1% from 1924–39 and 2.2% in the ten years after 1953. There resulted bitter strikes by, among others, miners, railwaymen, cotton spinners, boilermakers, seamen and dockers. The total of working days lost in strikes from 1910–14 was over twice that for the whole of the previous ten years; and only in 1921 and 1926 were more days lost through strikes than in 1912. The most significant outcome was the formation in 1913 of a Triple Industrial Alliance of miners, railwaymen and transport workers, pledged to support one another in an industrial dispute by launching a 'sympathetic' or general strike. The chasm thus opened between employers and employed in the major industries could benefit only the political party almost all of whose funds came from the trade unions. Active trade unionists would now vote either Labour or not at all; for though Asquith's Liberal government wrung repeated concessions from reluctant employers, it had also from time to time invoked the police and moved troops about. The fact that Labour MPs were impotent spectators of the struggle was thus paradoxically without relevance.

The 1914–18 war had strengthened this paradox. The Labour party split. Of those who supported the war, two or three, notably Arthur Henderson, joined the coalition government. Others, because they were pacifists or, like MacDonald, in favour of a negotiated peace, went into limbo. By 1915, the trade union leaders agreed to dilution of skilled by unskilled and female labour, to compulsory arbitration and to the outlawing of strikes. Manual workers nevertheless showed no disposition to turn against their chosen political and industrial leadership. Trade unionists certainly became more militant than their leaders, with their shop stewards playing a more energetic role than in the past; and union membership rose from just under four million to just over eight million. Labour's share of votes cast, which had been between 7% and 8% in 1910, was up to 22.2% by 1918, rising continuously until 1929. In that year, it secured 37.1%, a percentage only slightly below that obtained in the elections of 1974.

Two Disasters: 1926 and 1931

The story of the Labour movement from 1906 to 1931 was, therefore, one of an ever increasing rank and file devotedly loyal to a chronically timid leadership. With the end of the war and the short boom that followed it, the staple industries, facing, with outdated techniques, the strains of the more competitive but contracted international trade of a dislocated world economy, sought to reduce costs by bringing down wages. Selected by their unyielding employers to be immediate victims of this process, the miners determined to resist. In 1926 they insisted on dragging the TUC into a general strike on their behalf. In doing so, they ignored the several clear signs they had been given that the leaders of the other unions had no stomach for such a fight. The contrast between the unanimity and zest with which the rank and file answered the call, and the unpreparedness of the TUC confirmed, as does the whole history of the Labour movement in those years, that if it was exaggeration to say that ordinary Englishmen had been lions led by donkeys in wartime, it was not so far from the truth if applied to their leaders in peacetime. The General Strike, which began with enthusiastic support, was called off after nine days; but the miners chose to stay out for the rest of 1926. Technically having been locked out by their employers for refusing lower wages, they gave in district by district, by which time many other workers who had responded to the call for a General Strike had likewise been taken back, if at all, at lower wages than before.

Similar disillusionments were provided by the Labour party. The ineffectiveness of its first short period in office in 1924 was doubtless pardonable, since it was not even the largest party in the commons. Its incapacity to make even token efforts to deal with unemployment when again in office from 1929 to 1931 and its intellectual bankruptcy in the face of the financial crisis, were not. The easy way out was to blame it all on MacDonald's 'betrayal' in exchanging his premiership of a Labour government for that of a 'National' government almost wholly reliant on Tory votes. It would be nearer the truth to say that the Labour leadership suffered, along with all intellectual persons of the years after 1880, from the delusion that to transform ideas into words was to transform society. Even the miners' leaders of 1926 seemed to think that slogans were enough. And just as he was the great exemplar of the belief in the 1920s that peace and disarmament could be talked into actually happening, MacDonald was as authentic a representative of late Victorian socialism as were the Webbs who so disliked him. The Webbs thought they could drown capitalism with wave upon wave of books and pamphlets and investigators' reports, lecture upon lecture at the London School of Economics and article upon article in the *New Statesman* (they founded both). MacDonald hoped, by romantic oratory, to talk it to death. They were alike in believing that everything would stand still until their opinions became everybody's opinions. They were unprepared for the problems that, because it was subject to change and therefore to tension and conflict, society would throw up in the interim. It is no accident that the spectacle of the General Strike and the collapse of Labour in 1931 affected the Webbs in the way disappointment with the Stuarts had affected the Puritans. They set sail for a distant shore, seeking, and finding, subject only to a perfunctory question mark, a 'New Civilisation' in the USSR. Commitment to Utopia (they forgot the word meant 'nowhere') had been so inbred into the more earnest men and women of the time that, when 1931 and the Depression signalled the end of the ever-progressing world they had taken for granted, the Webbs were merely the most elderly of the flood of intellectual emigrants of the 1930s who, in search of a world that would conform to their dreams, went mentally east as their forbears had gone physically westward. To be anti-Conservative and anti-fascist in the 1930s, but neither a Communist nor a fellow traveller, required more control over their emotions than some could manage.

5
TWO NATIONS

Electric Progress

THE vulnerability of general statements about conditions of life in any period of history is well illustrated by the contrasts of the years between the two German wars. For more people than ever before, these were the best of times; and it is in part because this was so that they seemed, for many others, to be the worst of times. Though regarded then and afterwards as an era of nerveless government and economic stagnation, it was in reality a time of economic advance. Seen in retrospect as a time of hideous foreign menace which evoked only the alternative responses of cowardly concession or neurotic hysteria, it was a time when English life was less violent, less inhumane and, for large numbers, pleasanter and more cheerful than it had ever been before.

The economy did not decline between 1919 and 1939. Total production exceeded the levels of 1913 every year from 1924 to 1939. In 1913, output per head had been double that of 1850; it was over three times as much by 1937. Income per head, though barely back at 1913 levels by 1924, was 26.5% above them by 1938. Though the average working day was an hour less than in 1913, real wages increased by between 20% and 33%. There was an almost continuous rise in standards of living, of which a larger proportion than before was enjoyed by those regularly in work.

Much was done to make good the failure to develop new industries during the half century before 1914. Much of the new expansion was based on electricity, an industry which, though backward in 1918, was on terms with foreign rivals by 1939. The Central Electricity Board, set up in 1926, provided the country with a number of strategic power stations linked by a grid of high transmission cables. Owing to the greater glamour of aeroplanes and cars, electricity pylons impinged little on the consciousness of the time, except by way of complaints that they sometimes 'desecrated the countryside'; but they changed life and work more intimately than either, more so even than steam engines. The fewer than 0.75 million electricity users of 1920 had become nearly 9 million by 1938. Electricity revolutionised the home by bringing power to it. It eliminated the dirt and hard work inseparable from the use of its common predecessor, coal; and, by powering vacuum cleaners, electric irons and in due course washing machines and refrigerators, contributed to the decline of domestic service. This was still the largest form of female employment in the 1930s and there were more domestic servants

470

in 1931 than in 1851. But whereas before 1914, 14 or 15 of every 100 workers was a servant, the 1.5 million domestics of 1931 were only 7.5% of the work force. The 350,000 servants of 1951 were only 2% of all workers. Ten years after that they were becoming as rare as the men once employed by gas companies to turn on the street gas lamps, also made redundant by electricity.

The contribution of electricity to cleanliness in those homes and districts where it was available (sometimes at as low a charge as a farthing or about one tenth of 1p a unit) heightened the contrasts between the booming and the depressed parts of the country, between the newly housed and the badly housed, and between the suburban and the slum housewife; and it was the technological foundation of the characteristically antiseptic domestic interiors of the 1930s. The overhead wires used by trams and trolleybuses, like the pylons that stalked the countryside, were the only environmental drawbacks of electricity. This distinguished it from other sources of power. Its only aesthetic concession to the past was the radiant heater disguised to look like logs burning in a grate. This was despised by the discriminating.

Internal Combustion

Before 1914 the car industry had been composed of small firms, often deriving their initial skill and impetus from the making and repairing of bicycles and motor bicycles. There were nearly 200 different models of cars. Many were custom built for the rich and eccentric. With the protection of a tax on foreign cars, Austin and Morris turned to mass production; Ford's set up their production unit at Dagenham in Essex. Under 100,000 cars were produced in 1921, over 500,000 in 1937; the number of models fell to 20. Almost the whole output was for the home market, engines produced to cope with the United Kingdom horse power tax being unsuitable abroad. Accordingly, the truly symbolic cars of 1919 to 1939 were not the fast, stylish ones with noble headlamps but the Austin 7 and the bullnosed Morris with its hazardous dickey seat. Also almost wholly of the period was the motor cycle with sidecar.

Like the bicycle, motor cycles and cars brought new skills and interests to sections of a population allegedly deprived by industrialism of the deep satisfactions of working with their hands. Along with the novel pastime of making a wireless set from circuits published in popular magazines, the 1920s did much to gratify the instinct that Max Beerbohm, disguising an ancient prejudice in *fin de siècle* disdain, had described as 'common to all stupid people, the instinct to potter with machinery'. By 1939 private motoring was popular enough to require those ancillary phenomena which entitle the internal combustion engine to be regarded as exceptionally disfiguring in its effects on the environment. It produced petrol stations and wayside cafes, both usually hideous; and in the plusher counties the sometimes sleazy roadhouse.

To say that it led to traffic jams is to overlook that these had always existed in English cities. But unpleasant results flowed from the choking of the streets with cars. Potentially fast, they had to be restrained. Traffic police, speed traps, traffic signals, pedestrian crossings and parking regulations made their appearance. With their apparatus of legal penalties they did more than any other development in history to bring ordinary citizens into the cognisance of police and magistrates. That cars were potentially the fastest means of personal locomotion provoked demands for the environment to be changed to release that potential. The bypass and the arterial road made the crooked straight and the rough places plain; but it was not until after 1945 that the car insatiably demanded the disruption of urban areas and the degradation of adjacent property that had been characteristic of much Victorian railway building.

Though, because of its dependence on the home market, ministering eagerly to the private motorist, the petrol engine also served the great majority as yet unable to afford personal transport. Motor bus and delivery van broke the rural immobility and isolation that had followed the nineteenth-century flight of so much work, labour and amenity from country to town. They both marked, however, an intermediate stage. The growth of private motoring after 1950 reduced the motor omnibus to the status of an unreliable last resort for those too poor, too infirm or too young to own a car at all, or not rich enough to have more than one car per family. The years between the wars were golden years for most forms of public transport. The ubiquity of the delivery van was hardly less brief. After 1950, the bulky lorry would convey commodities to shops, thus adding to the malformation of towns by rendering most urban streets impassable without elaborate parking restrictions and disruptive through-routes and freeways, while customers, even when not personally motorised, were treated as such. By the 1970s, local authorities would confirm the status of pedestrians (mostly female) as second-class citizens by allowing them access to the 'traffic free shopping precincts' of which they boasted only after first driving them underground by steps and ramps to subways which would stop them 'interrupting the traffic flow'. And the petrol engine remained lethal. Of all male deaths in the 15–19 age group in 1961, 43% were due to road accidents, two-thirds of them among motor bike users.

Other Novelties

Other fields showing technical progress included aluminium, whose use increased sixfold, its versatility and strength making it valuable alike for aircraft, machines, cooking utensils and as a conductor of electricity. The chemical industry emerged from the war to make belated but rapid advances, producing explosives, dyestuffs, fertilisers, industrial gases, medicines and, by the 1930s, plastics. These last were manifested only at this stage by the marketing of bakelite, originally invented in 1908. Bakelite ashtrays and wireless sets were praised for being 'so light' but condemned as cheapjack until, in the 1970s, they became collectors' items as specimens of what had come to be called 'art deco'. The production of glass expanded to meet the need for windows and plate glass created by the building industry, for toughened motor car windscreens, for the new habit of delivering milk in bottles and the demand for electric lamps. Boot and shoe making flourished, a sure sign of rising standards, as did the hosiery industry, particularly with the introduction of rayon. The shortened skirts, which revealed ankles by 1919, knees by 1925 and calves all through the 1930s, made the 'silk clad leg' the erotic symbol of the age. Accordingly, rayon was marketed as 'artificial silk'. It caused unease; it was said to enable shopgirls to look as elegant as debutantes. The misapprehension could, however, soon be corrected by a transfer of attention from the look of the leg to the sound of the voice. Further proof of rising prosperity was that canned vegetable consumption rose from 24,000 tons a year to 193,000, while that of canned and bottled fruit increased sixfold. Tinned peach slices, married to that other innovation of the time, the mass-produced ice cream, gave birth to a new delicacy, perpetuating the name of the decade's most widely known operatic Dame just as one of its favourite biscuits, despite the rival appellation of 'squashed fly', still immortalised Garibaldi among millions who had not heard of the Risorgimento.

Apart from a year or two at the end of the 1920s, building boomed, contributing greatly to England's rapid recovery from the Great Depression of 1931–33. Building accounted for between 20% and 30% of the four year drop in unemployment figures from the three million peak of 1931. By 1919, there had been an estimated national shortage of up to a million houses, mostly for the less well off. The war had stopped building. Much working-class housing was at last now being considered unfit for occupation. Wartime rent restriction had made private investment in building houses to let unprofitable. By 1939 some 4.5 million new dwellings had been built, three-quarters by private builders for owner occupiers, the rest by local authorities to be rented by 'council' tenants. The housing boom stimulated the demand for new roads, for drains, for water supply, new furniture and furnishings and, since all had gardens, for lawnmowers, turf, seeds, privet and roses. Virtually all wired for electricity, they instantly attracted the many vacuum cleaner salesmen of the time, eagerly demonstrating the virtues of the machine which 'beats as it sweeps as it cleans'. The proud mortgagees could themselves be as clean as their carpets, for bathrooms at last became standard in new houses, with hot water from gas, electric heater or a 'back boiler'. This ensured that they would·derive maximum benefit from the invigorating lather of Lifebuoy, or the gentle kind produced by the Palmolive that would enable every wife to 'Preserve Her Schoolgirl Complexion'.

New Spenders and Savers

The wider diffusion of basically lower middle class standards was due partly to some redistribution of wealth by higher rates of income tax and partly to the ability of trade unions to maintain the higher wage levels achieved towards the end of the 1914–18 war. Although wage earners continued to take 40% of the national income, the fact that they were only 71.4% of the population in 1938 compared with 78% in 1900 meant that they were doing a bit better. There was also less diversion of national wealth into overseas investment and a continuing absence of substantial investment in home industry. Older industries attracted hardly any investment; many of the newer ones were launched by firms that were initially small. The relative decline in the incomes of the rich, and the small return on investments, all produced a tendency to spend rather than save; and this naturally encouraged industries and services ministering to pleasure and the creature comforts.

Though diffusion of wealth had been going on for centuries, the production of consumer goods had been principally sustained by the very rich and therefore predominantly concerned with costly luxuries, sometimes of elaborate craftsmanship and artistry. The initial (pessimists said permanent) effect of a downward extension of purchasing power is a decline into vulgarity. It is still a received truth that the aristocratic eighteenth century was an era of exquisite taste and craftsmanship; that the increased spending power of the Victorian middle classes led to an accumulation of pointless knick-knackery and a mania for overfed males and over-dressed, under-exercised females; and that once it became possible for classes below them to buy mass produced objects the country was submerged under a flood of the cheap and tawdry. This explains the lopsided view long current about the 1930s. People who wrote books at that time felt much relieved in their minds by their capacity to display righteous anger and, at times, a creditable, if ineffective, sympathy for the unemployed. But for the new society emerging from the decay of the old they had only contempt. All new houses were 'jerry built'. The mass produced furniture (often in limed oak) that filled them was 'shoddy'. Time has largely disproved these propositions. The houses built between the wars looked worse than they were mainly because of bad environmental planning. In essentials —such as the possession of bathrooms, the larger amount of light they let in, and in their labour saving convenience, they represented, even when they were council houses, the highest standard of domestic housing hitherto seen in the world outside the United States. And the tastelessness of their decor is no longer taken for granted. It may be inevitable that any new group which finds itself for the first time with money to spare will be an easy touch for whoever can most loudly advertise the most gaudily tawdry rubbish. But the 'Tudorbethan' gables and mock beams of 1930 semi's, the crinoline lady 'cosy' covering the telephone, the plush, lush cinema interior with its ascending and descending mighty organ player, emitting tunes of awful banality amid slowly changing beams of coloured light, were all symbols of the liberation of large sections of society from the burdens of endless work and graceless living which had been the experience of most since the 1790s.

Anticipating the consumer society ahead, came the early development of hire purchase. This, by taking 'the waiting out of wanting' over forty years before the phrase launched a new credit card, heralded the slow passing of Victorian thrift. But, between the wars, aware that in buying things 'on the never-never' people were breaching a whole social and moral code, 'Mr Drage', who specialised in hire purchase furniture, promised to deliver it 'In a Plain Van' so as not to scandalise the neighbours.

Moreover, even to say there was not much saving is to say that in fact more of it was being done by classes previously unable to save. Saving, like consumption, spread downwards, so that half the country's total investment was now 'small savings' by the lower middle class, chiefly in building societies and insurance companies. The assets of these institutions rose from £607 million in 1919 to £1760 million in 1937. Investment in building societies largely financed the building boom.

Fewer Babies, Cheaper Imports

The new spenders and savers had two advantages, one which had declined by the 1970s and another which by then was threatening to disappear. First was a precipitous decline in the birth rate which, for that period only, greatly outweighed the effects of the falling death rate. About a million babies were born every year before 1914. After 1919, despite an increased total population, only up to 700,000 a year were born. The rate dropped from 23.6 per thousand in 1914 to 15.1 in 1938. This argued that birth control spread at the same time as other hitherto mainly upper-class privileges. It was still rather an undercover matter of discreet mail order or 'rubber goods' shops. But the practice was encouraged by the fact that, among all but the poorest, the infant mortality rate fell rapidly. The overall rate in the 1880s had still been as high as 145 per thousand. By 1911 it was down to 110. By 1937 it had fallen to 67 and, if the much higher rates among semi-skilled and unskilled workers are discounted, the effective rates for all other classes was below this figure. Life expectation was also greater. In 1871 it had been between 43 and 47 years and in 1911 between 57 and 60. By 1938 it was between 61 and 65. Yet, although there were more of the elderly than there had been, the decline in the proportion of the population that consisted of children under 14 was greater than the rise in the proportion of the elderly. This meant that proportionately there were more people than usual aged between 15 and 64 and therefore able to work—

but with fewer dependants among whom to distribute their earnings, a factor which in itself was reckoned to have raised standards of living by 12½%.

An even greater advantage was the low price paid for imported raw materials and food. Primary producers abroad suffered badly in the early 1920s because of the ending of the boom they had enjoyed during Europe's war. They continued to suffer during the late 1920s because Europe's population rose less rapidly than in the past and because continental countries imposed tariffs to protect prices for their own over-large peasantry; and they suffered even more during the Great Depression, when the prosperity of industrial countries collapsed. For the United Kingdom consumer this made the 1920s and even more the 1930s seem a golden age when everything was wondrously cheap. It is therefore necessary to recall, as well as the low prices of the time, that the average wage was just under £4 a week and that the old could remember even lower prices, but also lower wages, before 1914.

Going to the Office

Those who enjoyed the new consumer society did not consist merely of the producers in new industries. The deflation of the times worked also to the advantage of the intellectual proletariat, whom it was now possible, despite their continuing conformity to the maxim that he who owned nothing but his labour was 'a worker', to label 'lower middle class' with less inaccuracy than in the past. The salaried class emerging after 1870 grew enormously after 1918, both in public service and in industry, particularly with the greater number of large firms emerging from the new industries and the tendency to near-monopoly. This meant that many who before 1914 might have been entrepreneurs now became salaried managerial employees. It further increased the demand for semi-skilled office workers. The new industries generated what were, by comparison with the generally small concerns of the nineteenth century, economic giants such as Courtauld's, Celanese, ICI, EMI, Pilkington's and Bowater's. Railways, breweries and banks underwent amalgamation; and in pursuit of economies of scale the new monsters outdid the alleged reliance of the civil service on 'red tape' by an insatiable appetite for paper, and for people to type memoranda, reports and directives. The age when the man of business 'did his books' in the evenings and communicated with an employee by shouting through the door for 'Joe' or 'Mr Bicket' gave way to one in which, in larger firms, only a highly qualified accountant could understand the company's finances. Procedures now had to be settled by interdepartmental conferences with shorthand writer in attendance. Now no words exchanged between individuals were deemed valid until confirmed by a memo dictated to another shorthand writer, typed by her with several extra copies (because the branch in Doncaster and the sales manager in

Hereford would create hell if they were not told about it) solemnly signed, transmitted, and then as solemnly read and initialled, with every copy thereafter dutifully filed by separate filing clerks. All this, multiplied hundreds of times a day in every largish concern, was supplemented by an interminability of telephonic communication, channelled through private switchboards manipulated by determined young women connecting, rejecting, holding and switching calls, like army commanders moving artillery and tanks from centre to left flank, from right flank to centre, in the course of a major battle.

The estimated increase of administrative staff in industry was from just over one million to 2.21 million between 1911 and 1931. The number of salaried persons rose by 35% between 1920 and 1938 compared with a 14% rise in the number of wage earners. By 1938 salaried workers were over a quarter of all those employed. This indicated a shift of manual workers' children into the salaried class and a continuous rise in the employment of unmarried women.

The Other Nation

Unhappily, Disraeli's celebrated dictum that the kingdom was divided into two nations, 'the rich and the poor' was in some ways more obvious than ever. All the tendencies which created distinct geographical demarcation lines between industrial and residential areas, between areas of heavy industry and light, between areas of good housing and of bad, between regions rich in social amenity and those lacking in them, between the prosperous and the deprived, were reinforced during the 1920s and 1930s. The war of 1914–18 produced a disruption of world economic development wholly disadvantageous to those parts of the kingdom on which the industrial revolution had been based and which, while containing the largest resources of traditional skills, often provided the least healthy physical environment. Cotton, shipbuilding and coal never recovered their pre-war prosperity and iron and steel endured a long, painful period of adjustment. Falling export markets, foreign tariffs and increased overseas competition struck industries which had seen no need to modernise before 1914 and were therefore now less efficient than their foreign rivals. The Depression of 1931–33 was, for these industries, an aggravation of an already depressed condition, leading to the virtual abandonment of all hope of remedy. By 1927 there were already over a million unemployed; in 1932 and 1933 around three million; and as late as 1938 little less than two million.

More significant than the totals, was the concentration of unemployment in particular industries and therefore particular places. In 1936 the average percentage of unemployment in all trades was 12.5. But whereas in the south-east it was only 5.6%, in the north-east and the north-west it was over 16. In Scotland, Northern Ireland and Wales the percentages were 18, 23 and 28.5% respectively. Specific towns could provide starker contrasts. In 1934, when the national average was 16.6% unemployed, Jarrow, dependent wholly on shipbuilding, had 67.8%, Gateshead had 44%, Motherwell in Scotland 37.4% and Merthyr Tydfil in Wales 61.9%. The corresponding percentage for High Wycombe in Buckinghamshire was 3.3, for Birmingham 6.4, Luton 7.7, and for Greater London 8.6. Whereas before 1914 poverty as such had seemed society's gravest problem, after 1919 it was the inequitable phenomenon of apparently irremediable long term unemployment in particular parts of the country.

The significance both then and for the succeeding half century of the intense localisation of 'mass' unemployment is hard to exaggerate. Its mere existence accelerated the decay and aggravated the environmental backwardness of the places it affected. New industries shunned the 'Depressed Areas'. Their community services and above all their housing were in a parlous condition, because the local authorities derived little revenue from the rates on their cheap, rundown property but were required to spend heavily on the relief of much local poverty. The most energetic inhabitants removed themselves to the prosperous midlands and south—if they could. Reversing the trends of the previous 150 years, population rose by 18% in London and the home counties, but only by 11% in the midlands. Lancashire's rose by less than 1% and in Northumberland and Durham it declined. The new industries did not need the coal, the raw materials or the skill and muscle of the male labour of the depressed areas. Devoted to the home market rather than to exports, they established themselves in areas of prosperity, not only to be nearer their well-heeled consumers but because neither they nor their employees cared to live and work in parts of the country afflicted with dole queues, slums, low grade shops, obsolescent mines, mills or factories, or amid unremedied environmental deficiencies left over from the previous century.

In consequence, to them that had, it was given. The suburban outer ring of London was the fastest growing area of the country, its 20% of the kingdom's population enjoying in the 1930s five sixths of the increase in new factories, a third of all factory extensions and 40% of all new factory jobs. Birmingham also did well; and other principal cities which were large centres of administration, civic and commercial, suffered less than the depressed areas in which they were situated. This applied to the 'better' parts and suburbs of Liverpool, Cardiff, Glasgow and Newcastle. The worst sufferers were often the inhabitants of smaller towns which had been the industrial villages of the early nineteenth century (and in many cases, particularly in some mining areas, still retaining that character) and dependent on one particular industry. New industry naturally shunned such places. The people in them were not working and could not consume. The unemployed were thus, in the economic sense, non-persons twice over.

The concentration of the problem in specific areas was one reason why nothing much was done about it. In that it was out of sight, it was usually out of mind and a kind of social and economic apartheid prevailed. The concern for the poor manifest in polite circles between 1880 and 1900 had arisen largely because these were particularly difficult years in the metropolis itself. Now, as in the early phase of industrialisation, social and economic malaise was scarcely noticeable in the booming capital and not obtrusively obvious in other great cities. The average unthinking beneficiary of the rising prosperity of the south-east shrugged the problem off by asserting that many of the unemployed were 'unemployable' (which in a sense was true, since they had skills or muscles for which the economy could find no use) and that 'some of them' were 'as well off on the dole as they would be working' (which in a period of low wages was also often true). There was no pressure on government to take remedial action because whatever was done would cost money and, by increasing taxation, reduce the purchasing power of prosperous consumers, as well as the profits and jobs of the industries which relied on them and which alone kept the economy expanding. The National government of the 1930s and its Labour opponents were alike in thinking that not much could be done. The National government's concern was to keep unemployment pay as low as possible, to avoid encouraging idleness and the need for higher taxes. Labour and the trade unions rarely got beyond demanding that unemployment pay be increased, or hoping that the falling birth rate and the possibility of raising the school age or lowering that of retirement might eventually cause the problem to disappear. Some found consolation in viewing the situation as marking the 'death throes' of capitalism, from which in some undefined way would emerge a 'socialist solution'.

The unemployed had no effective voice. There was a National Union of the Unemployed; but since its leadership was Communist it was resolutely opposed by the trade unions and Labour party. Even when, in 1936, the men of Jarrow dramatically marched to London, the citizenry of the capital barely noticed their arrival; and their red headed woman MP, Ellen Wilkinson, was regarded unfavourably by the Labour party in the commons for having marched part of the way with them. In general, with their self-respect and their psychological stamina undermined by their loss of status as breadwinners or by the absence of any chance of achieving that status, they became despairing and lethargic. Their sense of alienation from the prospering majority would express itself only later, when the shake up of the war and the urgent demand for their skills to which it gave rise put heart into them again. They and their families may be said to have looked back in anger ever since; perhaps not least because at the time they were reduced to the flaccid passivity expressed in Louis MacNeice's dejected lines, 'All we want is a packet of fags When our hands are idle'.

Favourite Politician

The emasculation of the unemployed by the process of denying them work but at the same time doling out just enough to stop them starving, as well as the cosiness of the salariat and the workers in the newer industries, gave the period after 1922 a character that, beneath all the mania for novelty, remained politically conservative until 1945 and socially stable almost until the 1960s. Neither those employed in the new service and consumer industries nor those who consumed what they provided (they were often the same people) were in powerful trade unions; nor did they have serious political affiliation. They had little in common with traditional Tories, whom they stereotyped as 'the rich', or with Labour, which they regarded as 'all for the working classes' (from which they preferred to exclude themselves) or as 'Reds'. They found their natural political leader in Baldwin. Baldwin was the most effective spokesman of the Tory revolt at the Carlton Club in 1922 that broke the Coalition and rescued the people from the disturbingly energetic dynamism of Lloyd George. They turned to him to restore normality after the unnerving experience of ten months of Labour government in 1924. As prime minister from then until 1929, he piloted the nation through the perils of the General Strike. He 'put country before party' and joined a National Government under MacDonald in 1931 to prevent financial disaster. As prime minister from 1935 to 1937 he averted the danger that an American divorcée might become queen-consort. An underrated prime minister, Baldwin said, in 1935, 'I sometimes think, if I were not leader of the Conservative party, I should like to be the leader of the people who do not belong to any party'. Here was an ideal prime minister for the growing numbers of new people and their wives who no more wanted the ferocious sort of Tory who had howled down Asquith before 1914 than they did the 'common chaps' put up by Labour. Baldwin realised this. He had sat on the Tory back benches before 1914, disapproving of the divisive, wrecking tactics of his party at that time, later describing them as 'Diamond Jubilee diehards'. Resolved not to antagonise Labour, it was Baldwin and not, as legend persists in asserting, Chamberlain, who used in public the prayer book's words, 'Give peace in our time O Lord'—in 1925 and about industrial unrest. Sneered at or groused about by party zealots such as Churchill, who wanted him to do battle against Labour, the unions, Indian nationalists and European dictators, Baldwin thought only of the people who belonged to no party. Their non-political absorption in domestic joys and woes was the basis of a national stability that would be shattered by men and measures which intensified social conflict. The reward for his genuine, instinctive preference for doing nothing to upset them was the support they gave the patriotic cause during the General Strike and the overwhelming vote they gave the National government in the crisis year of 1931.

When that government at once reduced unemployment benefit and cut the pay of civil servants, teachers, the police and the armed services, the resulting protests hardly rose above a murmuring grumble. The only effective action, which in fact caused the government to limit its cuts to a maximum of ten per cent, was a technical mutiny (it was a sort of stay-in strike) by naval ratings at Invergordon. As was true of the unemployed, most of those penalised in this way fell back on the inherited virtues of the past—deference to those in authority and fortitude born of the experience that life was to be enjoyed when one could, but endured when one must. They were hardly yet touched by the concept of 'rising expectations'; only by surprise that they had done as well as they had, and by the fear that they might lose what had been so recently acquired.

Favourite Newspaperman

If Baldwin was their favourite politician, Max Aitken, Lord Beaverbrook, was their favourite journalist. His *Daily Express* was so much the newspaper of the a-political newly-prosperous that it became the first of the dailies to reach a circulation of three million. It outpaced the *Daily Mail*, a more emphatically political newspaper, which had been the first to sell a million copies through its vehement espousal of jingoistic imperialism before 1914. The *Express* also beat off the challenge of the *Daily Herald*, which, though the first daily paper to sell two million, did so perhaps as much by inaugurating a fierce sales-promotion contest with its rivals as by its support of Labour and the unions. The *Express* won readers by assuring them that everything was going their way, dismissing 'jeremiahs' and 'prophets of gloom' as unworthy of notice, and insisting that any unpleasant news its able correspondents reported was nothing to worry about. Beaverbrook could tell his readers in 1938 'there will be no war this year—or next' and increase his circulation nevertheless. It was the sort of 'news' his readers preferred. A Canadian-Presbyterian Dr Pangloss, his confidence in the immaculacy of his readers' political virginity was so great that he cheerfully employed radical journalists and the biting political cartoonist, Low, whose work was diametrically opposed to normal Beaverbrook policies. Such devices, like Beaverbrook's running attack on Baldwin for not adopting a policy of 'Empire Free Trade' assured readers that here was one after their own heart: against socialist cranks, comfortingly hostile to ideas of any sort, suitably philistine about the arts, but not a bit pompous, stuffy, conformist or 'posh', like the stuck-up people who read and wrote for *The Times* and the *Daily Telegraph*. *Express* articles were bright, brief and 'human'; above all they contained nothing 'improper'. This marked it off from the *Daily Mirror* which, by the end of the 1930s was setting forth on that 'forward with the people' policy that would carry its circulation beyond even that of the *Express*.

The 1930s have been depicted as a mean, sordid and bloodstained decade. To readers of the *Express*, their country was presented as one vast, happy inane. Only if the unemployed went into the reading room of a public library (if there was one), in search of warmth that did not have to be paid for out of their dole money, were they much more likely to see the *Express* than its readers were to visit a depressed area. It could not untruthfully be said of such areas that, for most people, they were what Neville Chamberlain called Czechoslovakia, 'a faraway country of which we know nothing'.

6

TIDYING UP THE PAST

Liberal First-Aiders

THE twentieth century saw the gradual abandonment of the nineteenth century's use of deterrence as society's main weapon against poverty. It was increasingly seen to be ineffective because it ignored many of the fundamental causes of poverty; and once the poor had votes (adult manhood suffrage came in 1918) their needs could no longer be disregarded.

The introduction of state old age pensions in 1909, and state health and unemployment insurance in 1912, are usually considered to have initiated the change. They were possible because it was being grasped that old age, unemployment and sickness were the principal causes of poverty and that the principle of deterrence that still lingered in the practice of the Poor Law not only lacked humanity but was ineffective. Like most nineteenth and early twentieth-century social reforms, the initiative in locating the real causes of a problem and the devising of ways to overcome it came from the conscientious and patient observations and enquiries of members of the middle classes, particularly in the professions. Improvements in public health and education were all taken up by publicly acclaimed politicians only after decades of pressure by local medical officers of health, Poor Law relieving officers, factory and school inspectors. The investigations of socially conscious people like Booth and Rowntree and the Webbs, and the endeavours of hardworking civil servants like William Beveridge, who collaborated with Churchill in 1909, and W. J. Braithwaite, the idealist who worked with Lloyd George in 1911–12: these provided the foundations of administrative reforms for which their political betters received most of the credit.

A Royal Commission had been set up to consider the Poor Law in 1905, and by 1909 produced a majority and a minority report. Both revealed a fairly censorious attitude towards the poor. One group wanted casual wards closed because they encouraged shiftless people to go on being shiftless. Elderly alcoholics with dirty habits and habitually immoral persons should receive no cash assistance but be permanently institutionalised. The 'kindly instincts of impulsive humanity' were deplored because they helped keep the poor free from the disciplinary supervision of the workhouse. The other group, led by Beatrice Webb, wanted the Poor Law abandoned, on the grounds that to try to deter paupers by making their conditions worse than the worst conditions outside was impossible without doing them physical harm. They wanted specialised local government services to end a system by which money from the poor rate was, they said, being used to subsidise insanitary and vicious habits and to encourage children to be brought up in drunken, dissolute homes at the public's expense. Nevertheless, there was agreement that reforms were needed. The evidence exposed the existence of appalling housing conditions, widespread casual labour and inadequately low wages. The Poor Law swept the sick, the infirm, the children, the tramps and the mental defectives all within the one category of 'pauper'.

No systematic overall reform followed the report of the Poor Law Commission. Even though its publication stimulated the growing unease of the social conscience, that anything was done at all was due almost entirely to the independent energies of the two youthful Liberal cabinet ministers, Lloyd George and Winston Churchill. While at the Board of Trade from 1908 to 1910, Churchill and Beveridge introduced state-run labour exchanges which made casual work easier to obtain by reducing the time and money spent on the traditional nineteenth-century working-class practice of travelling from place to place in search of work. Trade Boards were set up in 1909 to fix minimum wages in four non-unionised occupations, the so-called 'sweated' trades. It was the first fresh government intervention in wage rates for centuries.

The two measures that followed, old age pensions, introduced by Asquith and implemented by Lloyd George, and national insurance, wholly Lloyd George's responsibility, ensured Lloyd George immortality and in the matter of insurance justifiably so; his hard work and sustained skill in placating various sectional interests with objections to the scheme, such as doctors, trade unions, insurance companies and friendly societies, were regarded as exceptional even by his opponents.

In part, however, both measures were devices to shift the burden of poor relief from local rates to either the central government or the workers themselves. The old age pension was fixed at five shillings (25p) a week and granted to all over seventy, subject to their having no record of regularly avoiding work and only a very small income from other sources. The fact that the pension was non-contributory, and that by 1913 three-fifths of all those over seventy were receiving it, caused much disapproval; but though the cost to the exchequer was double the estimates, the number of the aged depending on the poor law guardians fell considerably. The pension was several times raised from 1920 onwards and there were still some old people in the 1970s whose only unconditional state benefit it was.

Health insurance, covering sick pay and free medical attention, was made compulsory for about thirteen million manual workers earning less than £160 a year, as was unemployment insurance for about 2.5 million workers in various trades, notably building, in which employment was normally intermittent. Contributions to the scheme were by weekly insurance stamps stuck on a card, part paid for by the worker and part by the employer, with a supplement added by the exchequer. It was thus a means of keeping people off the poor rates and, by the use of the contributory system, a somewhat paradoxical attempt to make self-help a statutory obligation. Since the workers were inclined to believe that employers could recoup their contribution to the scheme either out of their labour costs or by putting up prices, national insurance was not the instantaneously popular innovation that the old age pension was from the moment of its introduction.

The End of the Poor Law

The sudden arrival of mass unemployment from 1920 onwards put an end, by making it impracticable, to the traditional policy of deterrence. In that year, unemployment insurance was extended by Lloyd George's Coalition to virtually all those earning under £5 a week, though domestic servants, the self-employed, civil servants, the police, railway-men, the armed forces and (until 1936) agricultural workers, were all excluded. But the insurance fund could finance unemployment benefit for only about 4% of workers and for a limited number of weeks; and by the spring of 1921 the two million unemployed made up 15% of insured workers and some of them were to be jobless almost permanently. To apply Poor Law principles to so many often skilled men and their families was out of the question: the local rates could not stand it. Nor would the unemployed. Trade unions and the Labour party were now forces to be reckoned with. The strikes of 1919–21 were on a greater scale than those of 1911–12. The aftermath of war had produced social disorder all over Europe and a chilling fear of Communist revolution everywhere. Governments had no alternative but to go on handing out public money to the unemployed long after the fifteen weeks during which their insurance entitled them to benefit had come to an end.

Called variously 'uncovenanted', 'extended' or 'transitional' benefits and then 'unemployment assistance', this 'dole' was at all times subject to a means test and liable to be reduced because of earnings by others in a man's household, such as a teenage daughter working in a shop. Bitterly resented though the means test was, the fact that almost half the registered unemployed were regularly provided with cash from government funds for the relief of poverty was a revolutionary break with the principles used against the poor since 1834. Appropriately, a century after the Poor Law Amendment Act, an Unemployment Assistance Board, staffed by civil servants, was set up to administer the dole on a national basis. Loathed because it administered the means test with bureaucratic thoroughness, it was nevertheless the foundation of the post war government departments of National Insurance and of Social Security.

Meanwhile, the Poor Law itself collapsed. Many locally elected guardians of the 1920s were overwhelmed by the need to relieve the poverty that unemployment inflicted on those not covered by unemployment insurance. Relying wholly on local rates, they found themselves maintaining 1.5 million people in 1922 and again in 1926, as well as the aged and infirm poor. In the latter year three Poor Law authorities went bankrupt.

After 1929, the aged and infirm no longer depended on the many Poor Law unions of 1834 and their traditional guardians, but on public assistance committees of county councils. By 1934, responsibility for the relief of all the able-bodied poor, whether insured or uninsured, had been taken over by the Unemployment Assistance Board. The duty placed on the UAB was significantly defined as that of maintaining 'the employability of those able and willing to work' so that they might 'when opportunity offers' resume 'their places in industry'. Thus the pseudo-moralistic principle of deterrence gave way to an economic though not avowedly humanitarian principle: the unemployed were to be stored in a condition of low-temperature finance until the economy was ready to take them out and use them again.

Beveridge and the Better World

The Second World War revived in ordinary minds the capacity for social criticism which had atrophied in the 1930s. The pre-1939 system was considered to be wholly discredited. It was held to have failed to prevent an unnecessary war and to have done nothing about unemployment. The story of the war was experienced as being, almost to the end, one mainly of defeats and retreats. The adulation of the Soviet Union found among some public school intellectuals in the 1930s was replaced by a more widespread and equally unquestioning admiration of the heroism of the Red Army. This induced a vague feeling that a system of government which was 'all for the workers' had a lot to recommend it. The sense of class difference was sharpened among many conscripts by a suspicion that those who had attained commissioned rank had sometimes been raised up for reasons not always self-evident. A sense of democratic togetherness among civilians was strengthened by their common endurance of danger from the air, their universal submission to the rigours of rationing, the black out and long hours of work, and their enforced part-time enrolment in home guard, air raid precautions or fire watching duties. Encouraged by much middle-class propaganda designed to demonstrate the beneficent effects of planning better cities, better schools and more clinics and welfare centres for mothers and young children when the war was over, there emerged a general feeling that 'we' were 'fighting for a better world', using the word 'world' in its most insular, if not domestic, sense.

Only this amalgam of not wholly rational ideas can explain the enthusiasm that greeted the publication in November 1942 of a somewhat rhetorically written report by Sir William Beveridge on the future of state insurance. Despite its initial coldness, Churchill's government created the administrative structure needed to implement the Beveridge proposals, creating a Ministry of National Insurance just before, on the tide of an optimistic belief that to drive the Tories out would usher the better world in, the 1945 election swept Labour for the first time into power as well as office.

The combined effect of the Beveridge Report and Labour's legislation of 1946–48 was to coordinate, extend and universalise, in one central government department, the bits and pieces of administrative apparatus for dealing with poverty that had emerged since 1900. This included not only the old UAB and public assistance committees but workmen's compensation, started in 1906, and the widows', orphans' and old age contributory pensions system, first devised in 1926 by Neville Chamberlain and Winston Churchill and several times extended after that; this already compelled those insured for national health to contribute for a retirement pension. From 1948, everybody over school age was to be compulsorily insured by one weekly insurance stamp for benefits during unemployment, sickness, or incapacity due to industrial injury, for retirement and widows' pensions, and for death and maternity grants.

Beveridge had specified that to defeat the 'Giant Want' there should also be government-financed family allowances, a national health service and, through management of the economy on Keynesian lines, a policy of full employment. Family allowances were provided for by an act of Churchill's government in 1945. Payable to all mothers for each child after the first, they reflected the fact that, owing to ignorance of, and male prejudice against, birth control among the working classes, the poverty of the 1930s had afflicted a disproportionately large number of children. To complete the tidying up, a national assistance board was set up in 1948 to give money 'as of right' to whoever could prove need. After 1966, this and the ministries dealing with pensions and insurance were combined into one Department of Health and Social Security.

National insurance benefits were soon devalued by inflation. Increasing them, as in the 1920s, made nonsense of the insurance principle. The stamp became a regressive and ever-increasing poll tax for benefits that bore little relation to need and were frequently not in fact enjoyed. Sickness benefit was simply deducted from many salaried workers' pay by their employers. The pension, on the grounds that it was for retirement, was withheld from men over sixty-five and women over sixty if they went on working; those who were retired had their pensions curtailed if they chose to do more than a little paid work. A large number of the elderly came to depend on 'assistance' or 'supplementary benefits' because they were too old to have qualified for a pension, or had no other means. Many of this group did not apply, unpersuaded that it was theirs 'of right' and resentful of official enquiries as to their 'need' which, though less wide-ranging than the means test of the 1930s, appeared harassing and humiliating and beset with form-filling rituals that frightened them.

By the late 1960s a flat rate contribution allied to a low flat rate benefit was no longer acceptable; and inflation debased retirement pensions faster than governments were willing to increase them, given the cost of dealing with a population of whom by that time so large a proportion was elderly. How to perpetuate a system based largely on the proposition that most employed persons would never earn enough, or never be sensible enough, to insure themselves and their dependents against misfortune and old age—as the better off had long been doing and still continued to do—proved a complex task. Its outcome, a mainly graduated scheme, first implemented in 1975, appeared to ordinary people not greatly less anomalous than its predecessor and even less comprehensible.

Nationalised Health

By 1945, a century of spectacular advance in medical science had produced, to accompany the belief that poverty was curable, the conviction that disease was conquerable too. Improvements began with the use in surgery of anaesthetics (first ether, then chloroform) after the mid 1840s. Before that, the surgeon's most desirable skill was speed (fifty-four seconds for removal of a stone from the bladder and about twelve for a leg amputation were good figures) plus a capacity to regard a patient's cries of agony as 'good, healthy screams'. By encouraging surgery, anaesthetics also increased the risk of post-operative death until antiseptics and sterilisation of instruments developed from the 1860s, with the discovery of microbes and the work of Pasteur and Lister. Inoculation and immunisation followed the isolation of specific disease bacilli in the 1880s by Koch. Henceforth not only could smallpox be prevented but also other killer diseases such as cholera, typhoid, rabies, diphtheria and, eventually, polio. The history of modern analgesic and preventive drugs began with the supersession of opium and belladonna by commercially produced aspirin after 1899, the discovery of insulin and penicillin in the 1920s and the mass production of the sulphonamide antibiotics in the 1940s. Since the latter were peculiarly specific against respiratory diseases they contributed, along with better housing conditions (where these existed) to the decline in deaths from pneumonia and what was then always called 'consumption'. The proportion of deaths due to tuberculosis dropped from 10% of the total in 1900 to under 5% by 1940 and to less than half of 1% by the 1960s. Infant mortality per thousand fell from 105 per thousand in 1910 to 64 in 1930 and to 18 in 1968. The death rate fell from 18.4 per thousand in 1911 to 11.8 by 1950.

It was in the context of growing evidence that previously fatal or crippling disease could be prevented or cured that the national health service was devised by Aneurin Bevan in 1948. Medical and hospital care should be free for all. Hence the health service provided free hospital, specialist, general practitioner, dental, ophthalmic, midwifery, maternity and child welfare services to all. Initially, drugs, medicine, spectacles and dentures were also free; later, charges were made for these except for the young, the poor and, in certain cases, the old.

It would be wrong to suggest that before 1948 such services were available only to the well off. A school medical service had existed for forty years. Maternity and child welfare services had been provided by local authorities since at least 1918, and the care taken by the state for the welfare of mothers and young children under difficult wartime conditions from 1939 to 1945 was of a standard that could not be abandoned in peacetime. Medical, specialist and hospital treatment had previously been charged for but, in a rough and ready fashion, according to the patient's ability to pay. The poor were expected to show much gratitude and extreme deference to those who so charitably attended them for a mere tithe of the sums that could have been extracted from them had they been well off; and the middle class could also fare badly, since doctors expected them to pay a substantial fee, particularly as, in accordance with genteel tradition, the bill was presented only after a decent interval, and often paid after an interval that was less than decent. The poor patient put his half crown on the surgery table at the end of the visit. The expulsion from the system of the rather bullying charity that was often meted out to the poor, and of the heavy doctor's bills that could wreck a middle-class family's finances, were gains that were too soon lost sight of. Though doctors' surgeries became appallingly overcrowded in the generation after 1948, perhaps only those who experienced the wards and outpatients' departments of hospitals of the days before the national health service could comprehend the extent of the change it initiated. The continuing and ever-growing inadequacy of the system thirty years after its creation could be ascribed to rising expectations, a communal unwillingness, which the financial policies of governments encouraged, to pay for anything better and to the social tensions which, by the 1970s, afflicted the internal management and the external relations of all large scale organisations and services, whether public or private.

Remembering Clause Four

Taken aback to find itself really in power in 1945, the Labour government of Clement Attlee realised with something of a start that it was the residuary legatee, after thirty years, both of Liberal collectivism and the early Fabian socialism that so closely resembled it. Sidney Webb and Arthur Henderson had written state ownership into clause four of the party's 1918 constitution, and the Attlee administration hastily decided to fulfil the by then venerable hope that coal mines and railways should 'one day' be nationalised. Gas, electricity and civil aviation were also taken over. Inadvisedly, Labour failed to take over iron and steel until their political repute was in decline. The recovering Tories were able to postpone nationalisation until 1950 and unscramble the industry in 1953. Labour nationalised it again in 1967.

From the start, nationalisation proved so disillusioning that Attlee's successor as party leader, Hugh Gaitskell, tried to get the concept removed from the party programme. One reason for popular dislike was that, like national insurance and the health service, the nationalised industries created, not more democracy, but less. Before 1948, trade unions and friendly societies had assisted in the administration of health insurance. Local authorities had financed, and local communities had supported, county and cottage hospitals. Municipalities had operated their own gas and electricity undertakings. Now, insurance was run wholly by civil servants. The health service and hospitals were run by nominated regional councils whose principal raison d'être was to act as employers to doctors and consultants because, like medieval bishops refusing to acknowledge the temporal power of the state, medical men refused to become direct employees of the government. The nationalised industries were run by public corporations of exalted persons nominated by the government but answerable to it, and to parliament, only as regards overall policy and not in respect of day to day operation. The public at large were supposedly represented by users' councils; but these were mostly window dressing.

The device of the ministerially appointed public corporation had two purposes. One was to enable its top managers to be paid more than top civil servants without causing top civil servants to ask for similarly high salaries. The other was to stifle any notion that either those who worked for, let alone those who relied on, a nationalised body should have a share in running it. As a result, ordinary people developed feelings of resentment towards gas, electricity and railway boards out of proportion to the incompetence they sometimes displayed. It was believed that they were less efficient than their pre-1939 predecessors (which was by no means true) and people even showed signs of imagining that, before nationalisation, railways had made good profits. The employees of nationalised concerns seemed to like them no more than dockers liked dock employers or car workers liked car manufacturers. The transfer from private to public ownership did little for industrial relations or to persuade railwaymen's, miners' or power workers' unions to forgo the right to strike whenever they chose to.

7

CLASSROOMS FOR CLASSES

Teaching the Poor to stay Poor

THE war greatly stimulated the nation's normally sluggish attitude to education. The 1944 Education Act, piloted by R. A. Butler, Churchill's minister of education, was put into operation by Labour in 1947, to prove the basis for much expansion and even more controversy for the rest of the century.

The controversy was at least as old as the setting up of the state aided, rate maintained board schools in 1870; and even at that date it was a controversy about class barriers and not, as is usually claimed, the relatively peripheral matter of the survival of the traditional influence of the church over the education of the poor. From 1833 onwards, the state paid annual grants to the large Church of England Society and the much smaller nonconformist one that maintained schools for poor children and by so doing acquired powers of inspection and control. There was already an 80% literacy rate by 1870 and the Newcastle Commission of 1861 reckoned that the 2.5 million children then receiving 'elementary instruction' was as reasonable a number as could be expected. Yet, though 75% of these children left school at ten, a third of them put in less than 100 days' attendance a year and though only a quarter were thought to be getting a 'good education', compulsory schooling was not recommended. 'Independence' was 'of more importance than education' and a child's wages could keep a family off the poor rates. By 1870, however, it was evident that 60% of all working-class children were not being formally educated at all and that the religious societies lacked the funds to cope with them. The locally elected, rate financed, government aided school boards were created by Forster's Education Act of 1870 to fill this gap.

The basic objective of the new system was that board school and voluntary, or church, school education should be neither free nor compulsory and that it should be strictly limited to the minimum instruction in reading, writing and arithmetic sufficient to fit pupils for the menial employments appropriate to their lowly social status. From the start, however, payment of 'school pence' was remitted for the poorest; and after 1891 the government made it possible for fees to be abolished in all but the least well-endowed church schools. Fees ended altogether in 1918. Compulsion was enforced by a Tory act of 1876 and a Liberal one of 1880, but only up to the age of ten, the employment of children under that age being made illegal. Children between ten and thirteen could leave school or work part time if they passed 'the labour examination'. They could leave at thirteen if they had a good attendance record. And however poor their record, whether of attendance or attainment, they could leave at fourteen. The minimum leaving age was raised to twelve by 1899 save in agricultural areas; and despite some initial trade union objection that the end of part-time working by children would reduce working-class living standards, full time schooling until fourteen was the rule from 1918 until 1947.

The issues of fees and restricted education were tied to considerations of class. It was pointed out in 1870 that to build lots of free schools for the poor was unfair to the lower middle class, who paid for their children's education. The Clarendon Commission on the nine major public schools, and the Taunton Commission on the miscellany of schools between the public schools and those catering for the poor both recommended in the 1850s that the practice of charitably allotting certain places in these schools to poor children should be stopped. This, it was thought, would save poor children from being embarrassed and rich ones from being corrupted. The Taunton Commission delineated the structure of English schools as they were to be for another century. First grade schools were those which, like the public schools, would educate, to the age of nineteen, sons of men with considerale income. Second grade schools would educate, until they were sixteen, boys destined for the army and all but the top positions in medicine, law and other professions. Third grade secondary schools should enable the sons of small tenant farmers, smaller tradesmen and superior artisans to leave school at fourteen and become clerks. With private schools thus carefully graded to cover such a wide range of social classes, the maximum that the publicly financed board schools would be allowed to provide was a minimum. Their allotted task was to produce a docile, Bible-reading population with rudimentary attainments and no more.

Some school boards had other ideas. In 1880, Sheffield's school board opened a higher grade school for children over ten. By 1894 the country had sixty-three such schools. The best of them could offer Latin, French, mathematics, geography, shorthand, book keeping, chemistry and electricity. Such schools were deplored. They gave too much godless science, and too little religious, teaching. They took pupils away from the Taunton second and third grade schools. They also competed with those of the county councils, anxious to get the control of technical education that had been permitted to them in 1889. The upshot was the so-called Cockerton judgment by which the courts declared it illegal for school boards to finance the teaching, out of public funds, of anything beyond the basic three Rs.

Few Are Chosen

The resistance to broadening elementary education was stiffened by the 1902 Education Act. Named after Balfour, it was chiefly the work of a strong-minded civil servant named Morant, whose influence on policy in the decade after 1899 affected the state education system for most of the twentieth century. He abolished school boards altogether, transferring responsibility for elementary education as originally conceived, to county, borough and urban district councils; and empowered county councils to aid or maintain not only technical but also secondary schools.

Upon all publicly financed or aided secondary schools Morant imposed the curriculum laid down by Taunton as appropriate to the genuinely middle-class school. No school would be recognised as 'secondary' (i.e. get public funds) if it devoted more than a third of its time to mathematics and science. Higher grade board schools thus had to jettison their vocational, technological emphasis. The private grammar schools, which habitually neglected such subjects, easily qualified for finance. To impose middle-class traditions more firmly, it was ruled that, if two languages other than English were taught, one had to be Latin; and the minimum fee was to be £3 a year, to make it clear, in Morant's words, that the education provided was of 'a superior quality' —i.e. inappropriate to the children of manual workers, for whom £3 might represent two or three weeks' wages. An official report in 1906 condemned attempts by some counties to provide 'higher elementary' courses in former board schools because they tended 'to make a boy a little above his job'. Morant then suggested strengthening society's defences against the peril of an over-educated labouring population by making secondary fees higher still.

Thanks largely to the indefatigable Fabian, Sidney Webb, however, scholarships into technical schools already existed; and in 1907 the Liberals made all secondary schools reserve 25% of places for scholarship children from elementary schools. With the development after 1918 of sixth-form work, leading to generous state scholarships and county council grants, an exceptional pupil could get from elementary school to university by the late 1920s. To do so, however, he had to 'pass the scholarship' at 10+, the general schools examination creditably in a range of specified subjects at sixteen and, at eighteen, at the very least pass a higher schools examination with distinction. No more than one state school pupil per thousand ascended to the Everests of Oxbridge in this way between the wars. Only four elementary school pupils per 1,000 reached university at all; and only six per cent of all secondary school pupils, who themselves included only one out of every twelve of the children in state schools, did so.

Nevertheless, the scholarship system and their then relatively modest fees enabled the secondary schools between the wars to raise the sons of some postmen, train drivers, small shopkeepers and low-paid clerks into the sweet middle-class security of banking, accountancy, the clerical and executive grades of the civil service and the teaching profession. Girls who did well were usually directed into teaching or nursing. These schools were the first organised device since the decline of the monastic schools in the later middle ages for recruiting into the higher ranks of society young people bred below the level of the gentry or the affluent middle class. They did something to blur the sharp edges of the rigid class distinctions set up in the nineteenth century. They recovered educational opportunities from which public and provincial grammar schools had been progressively excluding poorer children since Tudor times; and, being based on examinations, were less fortuitous than the patronage system of the eighteenth century. Hence, Sidney Webb thought them 'the greatest capacity catching machine the world has known', making a major contribution to 'national efficiency' and giving children from the lower middle and working classes the chance to prove they could hold their own with the children of the wealthy.

Selection or Differentiation?

From the start there were objectors. Keir Hardie thought this highly selective system would put particular children 'through a class machine in order to make them effective guardians of the vested interests of the possessing classes'. At a less political level, secondary grammar schools were thought 'snobbish'. The obsessive concern of headmasters (and headmistresses) with the minutiae of speech, dress and deportment and their often frenetic zeal to make their pupils 'keep up the tone of the school' by never behaving in any way like 'common' people did not mollify this hostility. More important, selective secondary education downgraded elementary schools without in practice really creaming off their ablest pupils. Clever children from poorer homes were not always encouraged to 'take the scholarship'. Many working-class parents whose children were offered secondary places declined them because they might be deprived of the child's earning power for anything from two to seven years and would certainly, grant or no grant, incur extra expense. This particular factor continued to operate against the chances of working class children being educated beyond the school leaving age long after the reforms of the 1940s and 1950s.

In view of this, the 1924 Labour government set up the Hadow Committee. This recommended in 1926 that elementary education as such should end at eleven, and that some form of secondary education should be devised for all children. Instead of a system which, by selecting only a handful, rejected the majority, there should be one that enabled all to go forward, but by different paths. Accordingly, by 1939, there were, as well as junior technical schools, a number of senior or central schools for abler children over eleven who had not got to grammar schools. The Norwood Committee, on whose report the 1944 act was based, elevated this circumstance that some children over eleven were already here and there being sorted into three types of school, grammar, technical and senior (or 'central' or 'modern') to the status of a psychological absolute.

The committee pronounced it self-evident that only some children 'loved learning' and 'understood the relatedness of related things'. These should have a traditional grammar school education. Others, described in words expressive of the faint distaste of a classically educated committee headed by a Provost of Eton, as having 'an uncanny insight into the intricacies of mechanism', should have a technical education. The rest should have a 'modern school' education; but to define what should be done for children too intellectually limited to understand 'the relatedness of related things' or the 'intricacies of mechanism' proved beyond the committee's own understanding. Nevertheless, on All Fools' Day 1947, the school leaving age was raised to fifteen; all grammar school fees were abolished; and all children over eleven in the state schools were immediately declared to be receiving free secondary education. Education below that age was to be labelled 'primary'.

Comprehensive Confusions

Although the rickety new structure was called 'tripartite' (once rendered in a perceptive schoolboy howler as 'tripartheid') it soon ceased to be so because so many junior technical schools were closed: either they had unsuitable premises or were said to offend the ghost of Morant by being 'too vocational'. In practice, between 15 and 20% of pupils went to grammar schools, the rest to modern schools after being sorted by an examination at 11+, usually based in varying degrees on what were optimistically called 'intelligence' tests. Though much was heard of 'equality of status' and 'parity of esteem' between the two sorts of school, to go to a secondary modern was, for both parents and pupils, to have 'failed the 11+'. To go to a grammar school was to have 'passed it'. The developments of the next twenty-five years reinforced this view. As success in public examinations became more and more the basic professional qualification, and the number of universities and university places grew, to fail to go to the grammar school, with its well established tradition of getting pupils through examinations and into universities, was to make a child a non-starter in the business of getting on in the world; or at least to impose severe handicaps on him. Nor was it possible to persuade rational minds of the justice or feasibility of trying to base the whole of a child's future on a test taken at the age of eleven.

Inevitably, therefore, the Labour party turned back to those ideas of a common system for all children which had largely been lost sight of after the establishment of the scholarship system forty years before. The small proportion of working class children in sixth forms and universities added force to this trend. The idea of sending all children to a comprehensive school large enough to provide wide-ranging courses for those wishing to stay on till they were eighteen early gained ground in London and elsewhere; and by the 1970s was on the verge of universal adoption. Some areas preferred devices such as common schools up to sixteen and an 'open' sixth form college for sixteen to eighteen-year-olds.

The long and genuinely difficult argument for and against comprehension prejudiced grammar, modern and the emerging comprehensive schools alike. A truly comprehensive school needed to 'comprehend' the local grammar school. But this undermined grammar school morale where it was likely to happen and deprived comprehensives of able pupils where it did not. As decision was deferred by controversy, the secondary moderns suffered further loss of esteem and some neglect by authorities bent on building and equipping comprehensives. Secondary moderns were not, save in a few favoured areas, given time or opportunity to develop a coherent and generally acceptable form of education suitable to the majority of the nation's children.

More Old School Ties

Once grammar school fees were abolished in 1947, middle class parents lost their right to buy their children places in such schools. But not many parents who could afford otherwise were prepared to let their children stay in state primary schools long enough to run the risk of being condemned at eleven to what seemed the second-class citizenship of attendance at a secondary modern. The Butler act thus revived the previously rather sagging reputation of independent schools and, as affluence grew, the demand for places in them increased. Between 1900 and 1939, the minor public and preparatory boarding schools and the small private day schools of the prosperous areas often had poorer academic standards than state primary and grammar schools, specialising instead in what was called 'turning out boys (and girls) of the right type'. Even the top public schools suffered scathing attacks from their own more intellectual and literary former alumni. But good independent education rose in prestige after 1947 through its more conscious pursuit of traditional academic standards. These, save in the grammar schools, showed signs of being submerged beneath the powerful waves of anti-intellectualism which emanated from the educational theorists who dominated both teacher training and curriculum development in the state system. Thus, not only did the 1944 act fail to add greatly to the number of working-class children in grammar, higher and university education; it widened the gap between state education and private, restored the reputation of the latter, and left undiminished the monopoly of the high places in English life enjoyed by those educated in the best public schools. It thus perpetuated the marked division of the English into two wholly different societies.

The social objectives of most independent schools were based on those of the nine public schools studied by the Clarendon Commission of the 1860s which (in order of their foundation between 1382 and 1611) were Winchester, Eton, St Paul's, Shrewsbury, Westminster, Merchant Taylors', Rugby, Harrow and Charterhouse. Most were boarding schools and so were most public schools founded afterwards. By tradition, therefore, well-to-do Victorian children were cared for by a nanny and governess until at the age of eight or nine they were sent off to a preparatory boarding school which would prepare them for admission to a public boarding school at twelve. This, almost until the 1950s, made admission to Oxford or Cambridge, if applied for, virtually certain. The ability to pay the fees and a character vouched for by previous attendance at a good school needed to be supplemented by only minimal academic attainments. This did not mean that intellectual excellence was neglected either at public schools or at Oxbridge, merely that both were, within a limited income group, comprehensive institutions with the low pupil-teacher ratio that made it possible to detect and nourish the gifted and yet give adequate attention to average or less than average pupils. Many of the latter took 'ordinary' and not honours degrees at Oxbridge. The suggestion that undergraduate standards declined after 1950 because numbers were swollen by state school pupils thus had little substance. Virtually all such students took honours degrees.

After 1947, independent public schools faced an increased demand for places from parents fleeing the state system and stiffer competition for university places from state school sixth formers, since the latter got those places by qualifying for local authority grants as a result of above-average examination successes. This in turn made university entrance standards more rigid and examination-based. Both developments forced academic standards up in public schools and the preparatory schools which fed them.

Two Ways of Life

Independent schools could cope with this not only because they could pay better salaries than state schools but because they inherited a tradition older than those created by Arnold at Rugby and by Thring at Uppingham in the nineteenth century. This was that the sooner a child ceased to behave like a child and learned to stand on his own feet the better. Before the nineteenth century, children were expected to think and behave as mature people at an age when, by the 1970s, they would have hardly begun primary school. Lord Chesterfield had informed his son in 1741, on his ninth birthday, that he was now no longer a child but a youth and must therefore turn from 'toys and playthings' and direct his mind to 'serious objects'. There was no special children's clothing until the end of the eighteenth century and even then not to dress a child as a miniature adult was thought eccentric. Nor was there children's literature; when it began, it was evangelically obsessed with sin and death.

Over two centuries later, the English well-to-do seemed likely to retain this attitude for as long as they could pay the ever-increasing fees. They continued to send their eight- or nine-year-old children to spend most of the year at preparatory boarding schools to lead an institutional life that other parents and children by then considered unsuitably restricted and regimented. In such schools they might still be taught Latin, French and mathematics at a pace and in a manner which, in the state system, would be thought psychologically harmful.

State education moved in the opposite direction, originally because it was believed that the old elementary schools had 'crammed' bright pupils for 'the scholarship' and neglected the rest; and because most teachers damned their usually better paid grammar school colleagues as concerned only with instructing their pupils in how to pass examinations. These beliefs were strengthened by the colleges where state school teachers were 'trained' in theories of child and educational psychology (public school teachers rarely underwent 'teacher training'). Formal teaching ('sitting children in rows') was condemned. Primary education should be largely a matter of 'joyous activity based on play'. Children should not be 'forced' to learn to read before they were 'ready'; they should at all levels be enabled to 'discover' knowledge for themselves and not learn things at the behest of a teacher, since this was 'authoritarian'. Education should be 'child centred'. Mere learning must be subordinate to developing the emotions, the imagination and good social relations. Books must be supplemented, if not superseded, by poster paints, visual aids, drama and school visits, not excluding the chartering of ships to take pubescents *en masse* to the Mediterranean.

The origin of most of the 'new' ideas is traceable to the early nineteenth-century Romantic concept of the child as 'trailing clouds of glory' and of childhood as an experience to be valued, and valued highly, for itself and not as a mere tiresome prelude to adulthood, to be terminated as soon as possible. The result was the gradual replacement of the child cruelty of John Wesley and the buttock-beating public school headmasters of his time by an attitude to children which, to traditionalists, seemed intellectually undemanding and sentimentally indulgent.

Communications Gap

A more abiding difference was that a minority were driven at an early age to cope with the problems of life in a closed community of their peers and that their home life was thereafter a matter of relatively short interludes. The majority by contrast remained enclosed within the family, usually until their mid-teens and often until marriage. The public schools encouraged the self-reliance, assertiveness and articulacy of the rich particularly as the system was, thanks to Arnold, self-governing, putting a high value on those who developed 'qualities of leadership'. The homes of the less affluent provided a more cosy nurture; and a concentration on 'doing one's best for one's kids' that could lead too easily to an unthinking response to advertisements asserting of any commodity that 'kiddies love it'. The young tended to depend overmuch on the services of their 'mums'. Though the ideas and feelings of the state-educated majority would be real enough, their lack of verbal fluency (of which, indeed, the more consciously working-class were wont to boast) meant that they would fail to understand, or be understood by, their fluent 'betters', whose voices seemed too smooth, too patronising, too lacking in sincerity, too glibly pompous. The gap contributed to the lack of communication between the independently educated, who managed society, and the state educated majority, who were managed or employed. Even in 1970, the 2½% of the child population educated in public schools still got 35% of Oxbridge places, provided 71% of leading company directors, 90% of a typical Tory government and half of an average Labour cabinet; and their share of entry into the highest grade of the civil service was as large as ever. The creation of the new universities in the 1960s was of little immediate help. Public school pupils tended to avoid them, while state school pupils felt uneasy about those older universities which, despite real efforts to reassure them, they still regarded as public school preserves.

Backbench mutterings notwithstanding, the Labour party could find no means of eliminating the social division which its own educational philosophy after 1947 had done so much to widen. In 1975, however, it tackled the anomalous but vulnerable 'direct grant' grammar schools. These were old established schools which, after 1947, received finance direct from government funds and were thus independent of local authorities. They continued to charge fees, but allotted a proportion of their places free to children of high ability from state primary schools. They continued ostentatiously faithful to traditions of academic excellence. But now, they were told, their grants would be withdrawn. They faced the alternatives of absorption within the state system as comprehensive schools, or of becoming fully independent and thus able to admit only pupils of parents who could pay the inevitably much-increased fees.

Education for What?

Yet both state and independent systems shared a common hostility to the world of work, and to manufacturing industry in particular. Since education now exercised some of that sovereignty over men's developing minds once exercised by the church, this in a sense affected economic life rather as did the medieval theologians' condemnation of charging interest on loans. Public school distaste derived from the old belief that trade and manufacture were ungentlemanly. This had been rationalised as a belief in 'a liberal education'; but this meant, basically, that public and grammar schools gave particular people a vocational training for a particular group of learned occupations. The early nineteenth century cleric who said of a classical education, 'It enables us to look down with contempt on those who have not shared its advantages and also fits us for places of emolument not only in this world but in that which is to come' was also defining 'a liberal education'. Owing to their conception by Morant, state grammar schools were in much the same mould. Even when science developed in schools it was pure science rather than applied. Medicine (and certainly dentistry) ranked even lower. Only after 1960 did engineering and applied science come to be thought of as authentic intellectual disciplines. Engineering was otherwise thought fit only for mentally under-endowed persons who happened to be 'good with their hands'. The writer, Maurice Baring, was fond, in the 1920s, of mimicking Dr Warre, headmaster of Eton, preaching in Lower Chapel: 'And you boys—whatever you may be in after life—*whether* you may be great statesmen—or *whether* you may be lawyers—or whether you may be writers—or even if you're only enginEERS . . .'. The manner of the utterance was no doubt amusing enough; the content was both typical and significant.

In elementary schools, an anti-manufacturing bias was built-in from the start. Every attempt to educate poor children was fought for against employers wishing to retain a supply of cheap labour. Every poor child kept at school after the minimum leaving age was a brand saved from the burning. Schools everywhere proclaimed they were educating 'for life' or 'for leisure'; never for a job or even a career. There was virtually no careers advice in English schools until the 1960s; and, though universities boasted appointments boards, they had only by then ceased to be the objects of derision they had been in earlier decades of the century.

While it was right that education at all levels should instil values other than those of material gain and should develop pupils' mental and creative talents as much as possible, the gulf between the way the English were schooled and the kind of life most of them lived after full-time education had ended added to the tensions of the late-twentieth century. Anti-authoritarian and child-centred theories may have aggravated the problem. An educational philosophy that treated working life as an unfortunate adult postscript to the joys and opportunities of childhood or as a mere tiresome interruption of leisure and pleasure was perhaps something of a luxury for an industrial and trading nation wrestling with the competition of powerful economic rivals.

8

THE PURSUIT OF PLEASURE

Games Nationwide

IN the century after 1870 education was not the only challenge to the primacy of work. One reason why its effects were less dramatic than was hoped was that though in some ways education promoted, in others it was overshadowed by, the democratisation and commercialisation of leisure. No longer did radicals sturdily assert that work was 'noble'. Less and less was it seen as man's means to salvation or defence against the devil. The upper classes began the process in the late-nineteenth century by making an institution out of 'the week end'. A century later, work had, for many, become that part of their life they were forced to endure in order to finance not only life's necessities, but also its significant leisure.

The transformation of games from a university and public school privilege at one end, and an occasional local pastime at the other, into organised national activities depended on progress in communications. Without the penny post (from 1840) and the halfpenny postcard (from 1871) national organisers could hardly keep in touch with local clubs or they with their members and supporters. The growth of a national press also contributed, as did the railways, along with buses and, owing to their large carrying capacity, which made them ideal for handling football crowds, tramcars. Hence, as early as the 1860s, the two major football codes replaced the confusion of local ones. The Football Association was formed in 1863. The F.A. cup competition began in 1871, with 15 clubs competing; in 1880 there were 54. By 1890, professional teams were admitted. The 1899 cup final had a gate of 74,000. The separate rugby code was also devised in the 1860s: the rugby union started with 20 clubs in 1871. In 1893 came the professional rugby union, later known as rugby league. Cricket was popularised nationally by William Clarke's itinerant All England XI in the late 1840s. Commercial sponsors sent a professional cricket side to Australia in 1861–2. The county championship began in 1871; the first test tour to Australia was in 1877. By 1884 every English county had its county side and by 1900 cricket was a business, its players and its ethos a part of the national consciousness.

It was the affluent middle class who civilised public school football and turned cricket into a study as exacting as the classics. In the 1860s, Eton boys devoted 4½ to 6 hours a day to study and 5 to cricket. Harrow had up to 24 hours cricket a week and Rugby up to 15. Public schoolboys took their games with them into the church, commerce, the army, the civil service and overseas, as well as to evangelical mission work in the slums. The committee that devised football's rules and divided its codes in 1863 were all public school men; several were clergymen. The industrial middle class also contributed. Preston North End football club was founded and financed by a local mill. County cricket clubs depended on the landed nobility. Lord Lyttleton gave Essex a ground out of his estates. Lord Darnley financed Kent in the 1860s, Lord Belper and the Duke of Portland patronised Nottinghamshire. Lord Sheffield subsidised Sussex and test tours to Australia. Lancashire, Surrey and Yorkshire were unusual in having large lower-class support from the start. Apart from the now abandoned Bramall Lane cricket ground in Sheffield, Surrey's Oval ground at Kennington was almost the only county cricket ground laid out in a working-class area. In the main, games were a consequence of suburban rather than early urban growth, owing to the high cost of land in central areas, a circumstance which would deny their inhabitants open spaces and playing fields for decades.

Gentlemen and Players

Games were encouraged for moral reasons. Cricket, it was thought, would keep boys out of mischief (especially sexual mischief), lay up a store of strength and health against old age and produce a race of robust men with active habits, brisk circulation, manly sympathies and exuberant spirits. 'Be the peer never so rich and the labourer never so poor,' one enthusiast wrote, 'the field is a neutral ground where both meet in fellowship without the one compromising his dignity or the other being reduced to subservience or adulation'. According to Lord Harris, another patron of Kent cricket, games taught men 'first to obey, and eventually to command, thereby helping to form those capabilities which go to make a good soldier'.

It was not quite like that in practice. The middle classes soon turned against association football when they discovered it was rapidly being taken over by the working classes and therefore becoming professionalised. That gentlemen should work for money was bad enough but that they should associate with those who played for money was unthinkable. The result was a decline in the standards of amateur football, a withdrawal of amateur clubs from major competitions and a firm educational tradition that good schools played rugger rather than soccer. Recognition that hardly any adults could afford to play serious football regularly without payment was not finally achieved until the abolition of the amateur football cup competition as late as 1974.

Obviously, men capable of running trade unions could also form football clubs. Sheffield United was founded by working cutlers, Manchester United by local railwaymen. Coventry City began as a Singer's works team. Tottenham Hotspur, Chelsea, Leeds United, Millwall, Bury and Stockport County were formed by meetings organised by working men in pubs or public halls. Such practical improvements as shinguards, the goalnet and the referee's whistle were initiated by working men.

Soccer was condemned as encouraging absenteeism and making the English a nation of spectators. The coming of football pools in the 1930s further aroused moral censure. It was not until the 1960s that the game began to attract the kind of lyrical enthusiasm previously peculiar to cricket. Erudite professors declared the game both art and science. This arose in part from the discovery from the 1950s onwards that soccer was the most universal of English exports, reaching parts of the world closed even to those other contemporary English contributions to global culture at that time, English actors, pop culture and young fashions.

Other factors, however, worked against it. It became too tensely involved in too many international competitions. A razor's edge win in the world cup in 1966 hardly compensated for defeats inflicted at various times by the United States (once), Hungary and Poland, disasters unthinkable even in the 1930s, when it was still believed that only persons of British stock were robust enough to play manly games. The cult of sport had buttressed not only religion and virtue (defined, in this context, as 'good, clean living') but also the racism that was always inherent in even the loftiest sort of imperialism. Prowess in sport was considered irrefutable demonstration of the superiority of 'the Anglo-Saxon race'. A writer on cricket in the 1890s did not doubt that foreigners were cowards. 'Who could imagine,' he wrote, 'the phlegmatic Dutchman with his . . . round stern, chasing or sending the ball whizzing through the air like a cannon shot . . . As for . . . the effeminate inhabitants of cloudless Italy, Spain and Portugal . . . instead of the bat their backs would be turned for stopping an approaching ball from the sinewy arm of a first class bowler'. It was through games that ordinary Englishmen most easily expressed their arrogance in the fifty years before 1939 and in the thirty years after 1945 began to unlearn that arrogance; and, as far as football was concerned, to lose a little of their enthusiasm. Attendances at League football games declined from over 39 million a year in the late 1950s to just over 25 million a year in the 1970s. Contributory to the decline was the revival among younger supporters of the violence which had characterised football in the middle ages and from which the Victorians had managed to rescue it.

Unlike amateur rugby union and professional football, cricket did not become a 'one class' game. It had always needed a work force of professionals, to prepare the pitch, do most of the bowling and be available to bat some way down the batting order if the amateurs lost their wickets too quickly. The classes thus worked together in cricket and only sharply separated off in the annual game between amateurs ('The Gentlemen') and the professionals, designated, with increasing accuracy, as 'Players'. Significant of the game's development was that whereas the Players XI rarely defeated the Gentlemen before 1885, the

Gentlemen rarely won after that date. As the county championship extended, more professionals were employed. Cricket was earlier than football in offering one of the few chances working men had of rising from the harsh world of factory or mine. Thus, of those two legendary Lancashire cricketers, Hornby and Barlow, Hornby, an ex-Harrovian, was so much the gentleman that he refused to play against the Australians in 1880 on the grounds that they were not true amateurs. Barlow, a professional, had started life as a factory worker, beginning his shift at 4.30 a.m. so as to give himself time to develop his cricket.

'Shamateurism' was, however, as old as the game itself. The great Dr W. G. Grace of Gloucestershire, perhaps the first national sporting personality other than a prizefighter, is thought to have made more money out of cricket while playing as an amateur than any other cricketer including, according to Australian sources, Bradman. In respect of loss of earnings and of expenses for himself, his wife and two children he received £3000 for touring Australia in 1873–4 and regularly took fees of £20 when playing for his county. Less colourful figures might later be employed on administrative tasks in the county club to ensure that, though they were paid, it was not for actually playing. Not until the 1960s was the gap between Gentlemen and Players finally closed. Until then, amateurs and professionals had separate dressing rooms, stayed in different accommodation when travelling, and were carefully distinguished on score cards and in county reports. Amateurs had their initials printed on the former and were called 'Mr' in the latter; professionals were referred to solely by their surnames, to show they were the club's employed servants.

Decades before the 1960s, the game's prestige was in professional hands. By 1914, the typical professional, once a convivial, truculent fellow with often dirty flannels, was suggested rather by a man such as Wilfred Rhodes, whose 'well cut grey flannel suit', 'polished brown shoes' and 'deeply tanned face' were declared to make him look like a 'young captain in the 60th Rifles'. Men of similar mould, like Jack Hobbs and Frank Woolley, and later on Walter Hammond and Len Hutton, established as a fact that players could indeed be gentlemen.

More complex than football in that its skills and tactics are intricately related to time (spreading over three or five days in major games), the weather and the state of the wicket, cricket was absorbed overseas only in the Antipodes, the Indian sub-continent, South Africa and the Caribbean. At home it was saved in the 1960s by a return to commercial sponsorship and by limited over and knock-out competitions, providing an impatient populace with 'results', unlike the frequent drawn games of traditional encounters, though with the loss of some of the game's refinements. Yet one day 'League cricket' had long flourished in Yorkshire, south Lancashire and Staffordshire. League cricketers played Saturday games as part time amateurs, each club relying heavily on a star professional. In the more democratic spirit of the industrial areas, supporters revered, and clubs cosseted, their professionals. Among the most famous of them was the great West Indian all-rounder, Sir Learie Constantine.

Alternative Pursuits

No other team games challenged football and cricket. Rowing was too costly and, despite the popularity of the annual Oxford and Cambridge Boat Race, so class-ridden that virtually all its regattas were barred to persons engaged in manual work until well into the 1960s. Tennis became popular after the first Wimbledon championships (for men in 1877 and women in 1884) but was long excluded from boys' schools, partly because it was also a girls' game and partly because it was not a team game. Since it did not cultivate 'team spirit' it was morally suspect. It played a notable part in country house life in the thirty years before 1914, and between the wars spread to the new semi-detached suburbs where, with the occasional flannel dance thrown in, it provided pleasing opportunities for courtship and flirtation. After 1939 it declined as a pastime. Working wives had too little time, and the young associated its traditional spotlessly white uniform with snobbish conformity. It also suffered because British superiority over foreigners was lost sooner at tennis than at other games. By contrast, soccer and, to a lesser extent, cricket and rugger, kept a stronger hold on the young. Football and cricket matches continued to be played by innumerable small clubs in and around every town and in most villages. Neither was properly defined as a mere 'spectator sport'.

Spreading affluence after the mid-1950s popularised alternative pastimes once reserved to the wealthy. Few were team games. Squash rackets, once exclusive to executives, to whom it gave maximum exercise in the brief pauses their arduous duties permitted them, was the 1970s' fastest growing sport. The growth of skiing, rock climbing and sailing also testified to the diffusion of once exclusive opportunities. So did the popularity of the foreign package tour after the 1950s. This had hardly been envisaged when a week's holiday with pay became statutory in 1938. At that time, the annual holiday still meant a week (or perhaps a fortnight) at the seaside, in lodgings or boarding house.

'High' Culture

Technological change not only fused local sports into national ones, but had similar effects on culture, though in unexpected ways. The accepted view of 'culture' was (and often still is) that it was exclusively that 'high' culture, expressive of noble themes, which burgeoned during the Renaissance and which was, like noble feelings, the peculiar property of aristocratic minds. Art originally thought deficient in such qualities (as the eighteenth century thought Shakespeare) was admitted into the canon only if hallowed by time. By the late nineteenth century this had also, since it was a bourgeois age, sanctified that middle-class invention, the novel; but it was sometime before, succumbing to his sentimentality, educated opinion ceased to find Dickens 'vulgar'. Though working men could be good craftsmen, the masses were regarded as without culture. The answer to Wordsworth's rhetorical question about the solitary Highland lass at work in the fields ('Will no one tell me what she sings?') was that nobody knew or wanted to know. This applied even more to workers in industry. Hints reached the upper classes that sailors sang shanties and that rude rustics chorused incomprehensibly in dialect over their cans of ale. But that early industrial workers, like American negro slaves, had work songs, was so little realised that their rediscovery has only just begun. The awakened interest, at the end of the nineteenth century, in the folk songs of pre-industrial rural society reinforced the belief that the industrial masses had no culture. Earnest middle-class socialists, and others seeking to 'improve' the workers always thought in terms of getting them to love Chaucer, Shakespeare and symphony concerts. Forms of creative expression native to the working class itself were regarded with an energetic hostility in state schools for a full century. This antagonised thousands of working-class children into stubborn resistance to education, and to a 'culture' that seemed, and indeed was, 'alien'.

After 1870, nevertheless, improved communications, increased leisure and purchasing power promoted a two-way cultural traffic. High culture was more widely diffused. State grammar schools and expanding higher education, particularly after 1950, did much. So did the provision of well-stocked free local authority lending libraries and the low prices of books in England, of which the most remarkable example was the pioneering by Penguin of sixpenny paperbacks of quality fiction and non-fiction in the 1930s. The early gramophone, radio, television, longplaying records, and the hi-fi boom from the mid-1960s, all helped to liberate the English from their strange belief that only foreigners made good musicians. The establishment after 1945 of a government subsidised Arts Council aided music, the theatre and ballet; some of its finance helped save provincial repertory theatres from extinction.

More revolutionary was that, for the first time, society in general was made conscious of, and slowly responded to, cultural forms emanating from the working class. Manifest first in the music halls, it was more widely extended by the cinema, which, for the first twenty years of its history, was almost wholly of and for the working class.

'Low' Music Hall

Music halls developed in the second half of the nineteenth century out of male glee clubs or in certain working-class taverns which, as well as providing space for dancing, offered vocal or instrumental 'turns' or perhaps 'tableaux vivants' in which girls posed in a state of vaguely classical undress. Gradually, drinking was transferred from tables in the auditorium to adjacent bar or promenade. Fire regulations and the building of a proscenium reduced the number but increased the size of what were now 'halls' and by 1914 were 'palaces of variety', 'hippodromes', 'pavilions' or 'empires'. Women were early admitted into the audience and some halls' previous function as places of resort for prostitutes was gradually suppressed, though not in London's Stoll and Alhambra music halls until 1916. By that time, the larger halls with their 'fauteuils' and their lavish decor foreshadowed the later super cinemas. Even the small ones had dispensed with the jolly chairman who announced the 'turns' and kept the audience in good humour.

The halls were national institutions because transport facilities enabled professional performers to travel easily from town to town to do their acts and, in London, to appear in several halls in the same evening. Hence music halls were the first means by which Lancashire audiences could hear cockney sentiment and humour at first hand, a west country audience hear Scottish jokes in Scottish accents and metropolitan society take pleasure in the skills of working-class entertainers from parts of the British Isles they had never seen. For the first time, indeed, the working class could show the rest of society that it had a talent both to amuse and to touch the emotions. Music hall stars became national figures, applauded by the open-minded among all classes, royalty not excluded.

In its heyday before 1914 and in much that survived long after the halls themselves closed down, music hall was the first, and perhaps also the last, purely working class cultural manifestation wholly native to the British Isles. It suggested men and women who did not greatly conform to middle-class and socialist stereotypes. They expressed, with strong, uninhibited sentimentality, their love for their mothers, wives, sweethearts and comrades, and a touching devotion to 'home', often interpreted not as where they actually lived, but as where they thought they had come from, or would one day like to go back to—little grey homes in the west, with roses round the door and situated where fields were always fresh and green. Robustly salacious, they rejoiced in the humour they extracted from bashful young men, blushing brides, dragon-like mothers-in-law, large women who dominated small husbands, and vixenish wives having rows with tippling, barmaid-loving menfolk; as well as chamber pots, women's drawers and men whose trousers fell down. Jests of this variety provoked shrill shrieks from the women, a phenomenon audible still among studio television audiences. They also sang patriotic songs about soldiers, sailors and the queen, which sorted ill with the idea of a nation bitterly divided by class. They took a high spirited delight in the absurd, laughed at themselves and at 'the toffs' and all with a rumbustiousness which ought to have dispelled the belief that the entire working class was composed of men bent and twisted with industrial disease and women slowly dying of successive pregnancies. The music hall, on the stage and in the auditorium, revealed that many working-class women were physically formidable, loudly aggressive and boisterously good-hearted.

The Cinema: from 'Low' Culture to 'High'

The strong appeal of the cinema to the working class in the first twenty-five years of the century derived partly from its early boycott by the cultured. It transferred to celluloid the ethos of Victorian music hall and 'low' melodrama. Film makers were themselves uneducated men. It was no accident that Chaplin, like Stan Laurel, was nurtured in, and never evolved far away from, the well-timed clowning and heavy sentimentality which was characteristic of English music hall; or that Mary Pickford was called, in the authentic language of music hall, 'the world's sweetheart'.

The cinema could provide what could not be offered elsewhere: the prolonged, helter skelter chase and the excitingly contrived fight. Almost inevitably, even without the virtual monopoly the United States acquired when European film making stopped from 1914 to 1919, this was done best by American film men. Their minds were inhibited by fewer traditions of 'high' culture than the least educated of Europeans. Their own myths were enough. In addition to music hall slapstick, raised to delirious heights, they offered the 'western', in its early guise as 'the cowboy film'.

For fifty years the film industry sold its products by a frenzied build-up of 'stars'. Once, men and women had been retainers, hangers-on and dependents of great noblemen. During the nineteenth century they idolised political figures: young English ladies tried to snip Garibaldi's flowing locks and young men would tramp across a whole county to hear Lord Palmerston or Mr Gladstone. The populace goggled at peers' mistresses. Traffic was blocked in Kensington when Lord Hartington's delicious mistress, Skittles, rode along Rotten Row in her skin-tight riding habit. By the end of it they divided their attention between royally favoured lovelies like Edward VII's Lily Langtry and the curvy but decorous girls of the chorus at the Gaiety, some of whom married into the nobility. But the cinema made gods and goddesses out of the small-town backstreet people themselves. Young men no longer got themselves up like 'toffs'. The shop girl who dressed above her station no longer looked 'like a duchess' but a film star. Film stars became for ordinary people (and not only the young) 'the glass of fashion and the mould of form, the observed of all observers'. Democracy needed, and was given, a democratic pantheon. In England, the only real-life star to match the celluloid ones for popular appeal between the wars was the Prince of Wales. Perhaps it was his resemblance to the unreal glamorous ones that led him finally to assume the essentially cinematic role of The King Who Gave Up All For Love.

By the 1930s, the coming of sound had brought escapism and sophistication, both valuably therapeutic to a world economically and psychologically deflated. Refined out of its exclusively working-class nurture, the cinema attracted even wider audiences. Thousands went two, three or four times a week. Cinemas had great advantages over music halls and theatres. There were more of them, providing greater choice. Performances were conveniently continuous. Prices were so low that three hours' entertainment could be got for as little as 2½p in warm, comfortable and sometimes garishly luxurious surroundings. The back rows could be put to good use by courting couples and occupants of the best seats were not, as in the theatre, expected to wear evening dress.

In the second half of the century the cinema declined in mass appeal. This was due to television, to which the film industry could only reply by heavy concentration on either costly and not always successful Mighty Spectacles and by promotion of excessive violence and 'frank' sex. This did not reverse the process by which cinemas were closing down, during the 1950s, at the rate of four a week. A more respectable reason for the loss of the old automatic mass audience was that after 1945 the cinema was invaded by intellectuals. Much influenced by continental film makers, the cinema started to become part of 'high' culture. Going to the cinema became more like going to the theatre. Prices went up; continuous performances were less usual; audiences were more discriminating. The cinema had become the first universally accepted cultural form to have arisen from purely working-class origins. The television authorities continued to show old films in quantity nevertheless, conjecturing correctly that there was a large audience for them among those too young or too old to think of the cinema as 'art'.

Radio: 'Middle' Culture

Radio developed differently in England. The monopoly granted to the BBC in the mid 1920s enabled its director general John Reith to operate it as a public service concerned to protect traditional standards of morality and culture. Committed all the same to attracting a wide audience since the emergent radio industry would otherwise attack its monopoly for failing to boost the sale of sets, the BBC could neither ignore popular taste altogether nor fully satisfy the small but growing minority for whom 'high' culture was the only culture. That its programmes satisfied nobody in particular was its greatest virtue. It broadcast material from a broad range of the cultural spectrum, excluding only the avant garde and the blatantly vulgar. Intellectuals complained that it devoted too little time to the music of Schoenberg (which was to do some injustice to Sir Adrian Boult) and almost none to readings from James Joyce or lectures on humanism. It was alleged to be so dully middle-class that by the 1930s more and more of the lower orders preferred to listen to the commercially-sponsored mass-appeal programmes of Radio Luxembourg. This, with continental sinfulness, regularly broadcast variety programmes on Sundays, which the sabbatarian Reith forbade. Worse still, the BBC's view of what was vulgar extended to sanctions against a comic who let slip a 'damn' and to insisting that another, claiming to have been discovered naked in his bathroom by his aunt, could properly say that he had thereby nearly lost his 'prestige' but not on any account his 'honour'. Nevertheless it made standard symphonic and chamber music available to a large audience for whom concert-going was impossible. It raised standards of appreciation by the high quality of its drama and its varied talks made it for some a miscellaneous source of adult education.

It also preserved the music hall tradition. The first radio comics were essential, if tepid, music hall: a henpecked Yorkshireman called 'John 'Enry', a comic BBC 'charlady' and a pair of cross talk comedians. Tommy Handley, who had begun in music hall, successfully transferred to radio the music hall's gift for verbal nonsense. With radio to keep them before the widest of audiences, such essentially music hall performers as Gracie Fields, George Formby junior, Will Hay, and many others, ensured that the native tradition did not die out with the closing of the music halls, but survived by adapting itself to a changing society. Thoughtful people, however, did not approve. The *New Statesman* condemned the BBC's 'bawdy vaudeville' along with its 'bowdlerised talks'.

Jazz and Quasi-Jazz

Another new element in popular culture also had working class origins, among the negroes of the North American South. Though, like a strict religious sect, jazzmen refused to number more than a handful of the elect among the faithful, ragtime and jazz, however adulterated, revolutionised the musical taste of all but the minority wholly committed to western musical traditions as they had evolved since the Renaissance. The unregenerate had hitherto relied on watered-down, over-sweetened versions of the music of 'high' culture. Throughout the twentieth century many continued to do so. Music hall and drawing room ballads were clearly poor relations of the arias and lieder of 'highbrow' music. The works of Gilbert and Sullivan, dating from the 1870s, the operettas of Lehar, musical shows such as *The Belle of New York*, *The Maid of the Mountains*, *The Desert Song*, the heart-melting creations of Ivor Novello and later still the ineffable *Sound of Music* all proved how abiding was the appeal of 'straight' romantic music allied to equally romantic story lines.

Jazz, however, imported new elements: voices that mimicked instruments and music that imitated voices, pyrotechnic improvisations, outrageous high spirits, the brooding melancholy of the alienated and the deprived. Its rhythms were a compelling incitement to excitable dancing. But since the result was usually to produce a great deal of noise (the 'shrieking of devils and goblins,' Sir Thomas Beecham thought) most people born much before about 1910 found it hard to endure. Though 'real' jazz was, by the 1970s, a minority cult, its early commercial derivatives created, after 1919, a gap between the cultures of old and young well in advance of that created by the advent of post-1950 'pop'.

The 'jazz' of the post-1919 'jazz age' was an English dilution of what had already been diluted on Broadway. Its principal media were the gramophone and radio. From the start, the BBC regularly broadcast 'dance music' by what hostile critics called 'jazz bands'. By the 1930s they had become 'orchestras' and fallen victim to the 'glamour' which, in retrospect, made that decade's style seem so insipid. If the symbolic 'jazz' figure of the 1920s was a black man with a saxophone, that of the 1930s was the (usually white) crooner. Jazz had got into a boiled shirt and smarmed its hair with brilliantine.

With jazz influences as its motive force, the dancing craze of the 1920s released the inhibitions of the more prosperous young and encouraged others to try their hand at forming small dance bands of their own to play at clubs and works' socials. But as the sound became sweeter and the lyrics less banal (as in Cole Porter and Rogers and Hart) jazz-based music acquired, like the cinema, an adult status that made it no longer the private possession of the young but rather a reservoir of nostalgia for those no longer young.

'Pop': a 'Youth' Culture

In the 1950s, new technology, the slow disappearance of war-engendered austerities and the great increase in teenage incomes combined to wrench popular music away from its moorings in the harbour of yesterday's memories. Jiving, twisting and rock 'n' rolling, the young were swept away from their elders in a deafening roar of over-amplified sound. Compass and sextant for this age of discovery were the long playing record, played on what was no longer a gramophone but a record player, and the transistor radio. Both ensured that when not communally involved with their new music the young could be so privately. Before 1939, families had gathered round both gramophone and wireless as once they had gathered round the piano. Now, while parents were set down before the television, the young listened alone to their record players and transistors.

In its earlier phases, pop had an affinity with the boisterousness of the charleston and black bottom of 30 years earlier, girls being twisted and hurled about by boys known as 'Teds' from their unaccountable indulgence in clothes parodying those of Edward VII's reign. But, as it

511

developed, pop rarely dispensed gaiety. Limited in verbal and musical range, it concentrated on volume and iteration, savagely assaulting the nerve-endings of its immature audiences, inducing hysteria, and stimulating or perhaps crudely sublimating, half-felt drives towards sex and violence. George Gershwin had said that he wanted his songs to be for young girls sitting on New York fire escapes on hot summer nights dreaming of love. 'Pop' asserted a heavily breathing desire devoid of subtlety and concerned not with dreaming of love but with grabbing at it. The dancing it provoked was often a matter of vague solo undulations. Girls did not, like their jazz-mad predecessors, 'kick their heels about'. They were 'sent' instead. When not screaming, they moved their arms and bodies in ways suggesting unskilful belly dancers engaged in a public display of total self-absorption. Bawling and contorting himself aggressively, Mick Jagger, chief Rolling Stone and former student of the London School of Economics, perhaps spoke for his generation: '*Hey, you,*' he shouted, '*Get Off of My Cloud*'.

Being small, pop groups were numerous. Astute agents, elaborate electronic aids, gimmicky 'gear', painted faces, bizarre hair styles, an aggressive up-raising of large, phallic guitars and a studied uncouthness, often secured a place 'in the charts' for limited talents. But the quantity of pop was so vast that it was unlikely it would all be rubbish. In matters cultural, quantity is often the necessary concomitant of quality. A minority of pop stars graduated into traditional 'showbiz' and the legitimate stage. Others, starting as purveyors of loud noises to brash kids like themselves, enriched pop with unexpected intelligence and musicianship. The Liverpool-bred Beatles, though characteristic of their time in boasting a few O level passes, belonged wholly to the tradition that had created music hall and, while provoking world-wide hysteria, progressed from the mere registering of high decibels to much inventiveness. To Gershwin's girls dreaming of love, they added Eleanor Rigby, past dreaming of it. For the jokey jazz stereotype, 'Sitting on Top of the World' or 'Keeping his Sunny Side Up', they substituted the brooding Fool on the Hill.

Ragtime, jazz and pop each contributed to the emergence of an open, plural culture, divorcing it from class and freeing it from exclusive traditions. Youthful addiction to these successive fashions did not inevitably foreshadow a lifetime obsession with 'second best'. It did not preclude the acquisition of discriminating taste in 'real' music later on. Culturally, both jazz and pop added rather than subtracted.

The effect of technology upon culture was widely condemned for destroying regional, and indeed national, culture and for substituting a banal, commercialised uniformity. Yet it could also be said that the effect of technology and commercialisation upon leisure and the arts was to make available, for the first time, an exceptional variety of occupations, interests and enjoyments, cutting across social barriers and offering new opportunities for freedom of choice, of self-expression and self-development. It would be shortsighted to see in all this nothing but evidence of a process of mindless vulgarisation.

Mass Newspapers: Rise and Decline

The most venerable and self-congratulatory medium for the dissemination of popular culture was the daily press. Its acquisition of its national character depended on the abolition of newspaper and advertisement taxes by Gladstone, the introduction of steam printing in the 1850s, the use of wood pulp from the 1880s and the new facility for nationwide distribution provided by the railways.

The pioneer modern newspaper was the middle-class *Daily Telegraph*, with a circulation in the 1860s of 140,000. Condemned for its 'sensationalism', it was the first paper to launch an energetic circulation campaign. The *Daily Mail*, appearing in 1896, brought newspaper reading, at ½d a copy, to the lower middle class and launched the process of turning the English into avid newspaper buyers. The hostility of the educated classes to the *Mail* arose from their inherited belief that public affairs and politics were exclusively their business and that the less the common people knew about them the better. The *Mail* sought to maximise circulation by sensationalising national events and whipping up patriotic hostility to foreigners (especially Germans). By starting an annual Ideal Homes Exhibition it struck a deep chord in its readers' hearts; and by offering its £1,000 prize to the first intrepid aviator to fly the Channel promoted itself as immensely forward looking.

But a sensational popular press long predated the *Mail*. Founded in 1843, the *News of the World*, a Sunday paper, sold 100,000 copies by 1850, 3 million by 1900 and, by 1950, over 8 million, a figure never reached by a daily. Well into the twentieth century, it was the principal paper of the working classes. They did not buy dailies regularly until the heyday of the *Daily Mirror* between 1940 and 1964. In its devoted attention to crime and scandal, the *News of the World* continued into the new century the long established working class passion for life's seamier goings on, previously catered for by occasional bloodcurdling broadsheets about the latest stranglings and the last hours of condemned criminals on the scaffold. The mass dailies modified this tradition. To secure the respectable lower middle class market they deferred to Puritan susceptibilities by publicising the scabrous through the medium of 'campaigns' against it. This, however, differentiated them from the 'reputable' press and helped preserve the division between 'popular' and 'quality' newspapers. This was expressed most class-consciously in the *Daily Mirror*'s choice of the slogan, 'Forward with the People' and in the claim of *The Times* to be the paper for the 'Top People'.

The popular press owed its success to the skill with which it combined avoidance of 'the posh' with a steady opposition to 'socialism'. Labour had solid support only from the *Daily Herald* which, with 50% of its finance coming from the TUC, was a mass circulation daily from 1929 to 1964. From the 1940s, the tabloid *Mirror* promoted a brash working-class style; but the *Herald* died, to be transformed at once into the *Sun*, outselling the *Mirror* with the aid of its daily presentation of pictures of scarcely-clad 'girlies'. Thus, after 1964, the entire daily press was, when not positively against Labour, certainly not committed to it.

Yet the political influence of the popular press was possibly less than either its owners or critics supposed. No newspaper was financially dependent upon a political party. That they were mostly owned by millionaires enabled newspapers, as Baldwin once memorably reminded them, to display political independence, irresponsibility or indifference. They thus helped to preserve in the twentieth century the old eighteenth-century objections to 'bought' journalists no less than to 'bought' politicians. Realistically considered, newspapers were advertising media which also subsidised a news and leisure reading service for well-defined readerships. The test of a newspaper's survival power was its capacity to attract enough revenue from advertising to compensate for the high printing costs forced on it by powerful printers' unions, an over-large labour force and for the fact that copies were sold to readers below cost. The popular national dailies which ceased publication in the 1960s did so because their circulations were falling towards, though still in excess of, a million copies a day. Nor, since there was a loss on every copy sold, were expensive campaigns to increase circulation always economically justifiable.

Popular dailies enjoyed mammoth circulations only in the absence of effective competition. They understood this and, as soon as the BBC was set up, they prevented it from broadcasting news bulletins before 6 p.m., by which time the day's papers were all safely sold. This ban continued until the war established BBC bulletins as national, if not international, institutions. The continuous broadcasting of news bulletins throughout the day on radio and television, and the advent of commercial television in the 1950s, and commercial radio in the 1970s, drew off much profitable advertising from the national press. Though local weeklies continued to flourish, journalism was otherwise a contracting profession. That the daily press was controlled by only eight major newspaper concerns, still dominated by millionaires, certainly preserved it from being in the pocket of any one political power group. But, in a declining market, national dailies began to lose so much money that survival was seen to be in the hands of an unaccountable oligarchy. Yet the danger to press freedom now seemed to come, less from the maligned press tycoons, than from their employees. To safeguard their vulnerable livelihoods, journalists began demanding a closed shop to deny access to the daily press to all who were not members of the one particular union (or who were not willing to provide unpaid copy by contributing to the correspondence columns). Printing and allied unions resolutely defended their highly paid jobs against management attempts to cut labour costs when introducing new processes. In consequence, newspapers were increasingly liable to intermittent suppression by official or unofficial strikes by aggrieved journalists or printers. In 1926, Baldwin had made the *Daily Mail*'s printers' refusal to print an anti-trade union editorial a sufficient excuse for breaking off the negotiations with the TUC that were intended to avert the General Strike. Fifty years later, censorship or suppression of the press in this way was commonplace. Freedom of the press, therefore, seemed to require rather more than an absence of official censorship or of millionaire proprietorship. It seemed to demand that all the powerful institutions within a society, whether or not they were part of the machinery of government, should be on bad terms with the press and that they should have almost no power to control it.

The declining sales of mass dailies and the still greater fall in the circulation of serious periodicals and magazines should induce no careless decision that the printed word was necessarily in general decline. Paperbacks proliferated. The crowded interiors of bookshops indicated there were too few of them. Public libraries flourished. Cinema, radio and television damaged the 'quality' press less than the popular, and increased the sales of almost every book they turned into play or serial.

The Mind Benders

The establishment of a popular culture was dependent even more on national advertising than on national newspapers. Politically, universal suffrage created an electorate too large for politicians to bribe or influence in the old person-to-person manner, and a newspaper industry too rich for them to buy. Economically, the technological changes which made it possible to can, bottle or package consumer products of every kind from tea, sugar and milk to hair oil, jam, vegetables and patent medicines, opened up possibilities of high profits to manufacturers and low costs to consumers which only national advertising could maximise. The growth of great cities involved large shops and chain stores, so that they too needed more advertising to shift their greatly increased stocks; and more and more these were composed of nationally advertised goods with brand names believed to guarantee reliability.

Criticism of the bland uniformity of branded, packaged goods needs weighing against the widespread fraud and adulteration from which poorer consumers suffered in the days when 'chalk and alum and plaster' were 'sold to the poor for bread'. It was not for nothing that late Victorian advertisers so persistently warned against 'worthless imitations' by 'unscrupulous dealers'. Claims such as that these villains would sink to the depths of palming off ordinary braces on unwary men who had asked for a special brand of patent ones were doubtless 'good copy' rather than genuine warnings; but the antique caution 'See that the bottle bears the facsimile signature of the Proprietors and avoid worthless substitutes put in the market to impose upon the public' was a comment on consumer vulnerability as well as on manufacturers' hopes of imprinting a brand name firmly on the public mind.

Once begun on a national scale, advertising had no choice but to grow. Without it there could have been no national press. Its role in this regard reached its most spectacular in the give-away colour supplements of the quality Sundays. Without advertising there could hardly have been a fast growing car industry, let alone the doubling between 1950 and 1959 of the proportion of families with vacuum cleaners, the trebling of those with refrigerators, the tenfold increase in washing machines and the increase of television ownership from 1% to over 80% in barely twenty-five years. More than any other influence, advertising determined how twentieth-century people lived. Compared with it, schools and colleges, universities and churches, politicians and leaders of opinion laboured largely in vain. More than these it directed in detail how people spent or saved their money, the clothes they wore, what they did with their leisure, how they measured their social status, and the extent of their participation in the common life of their time. Over the century it pressurised the purchase of more, and usually more elaborate, commodities: from gas stoves to electric heaters, from linoleum to fitted carpets, from Zonophone gramophone records to hi-fi stereo systems, from penny-a-week insurance to investment in unit trusts, from beer to vodka, from cage-like corsets to bras and briefs, from meat extract to vitamin pills, from dumb bells to saunas, from steel nibbed pens to ballpoints, from Monkey Brand which cleaned floors to products which deodorised the genitals. Whoever would not, or could not, conform to the styles of life it propagated was at once under suspicion as wilfully eccentric, neglectful of wife and children, psychologically incapable of coming to terms with the world around him or, worst of all, classifiable within an income group so low that, like society in general, advertisers felt it more decent to pretend that it did not exist.

By the late 1960s, 2½% of the national income, almost the same as that then devoted to old age pensions, was spent on advertising, two thirds of it on publicising virtually identical products by pretending they were different from one another. Arguably defensible as necessary, first to establish, and then to secure, the large markets that made low costs possible, advertising seemed increasingly to be using verbal and visual talents for frivolous and wasteful ends: wildly elaborate and often unhelpful (if not deceptive) packaging; pretentious 'prestige' advertising (English cathedrals or bosomy calendar girls); and desperate efforts to present particular cars, perfumes, drinks, cigarettes, chocolates or beef cubes as industrial society's equivalents of a primitive society's love potions and aphrodisiacs.

9

TOILS OF SISYPHUS

Recovery from War

THE paradox of 1931–39 was that one part of the nation grew steadily more prosperous while the other remained in poverty. The paradox of the thirty years after 1945 was that the population as a whole came to enjoy a higher standard of living than ever before, but within a national economy that was continuously in crisis. Moreover, though highly successful in terms of its own past record, the United Kingdom economy seemed less successful when its performance was compared with that of other industrial countries after 1945.

Ending the war bankrupt in 1945, the United Kingdom was tided over, on stiff terms, by an American loan and then by the injection of cash into western Europe as a whole by the Marshall Plan of 1947. Under Attlee's Labour governments of 1945–51, consumer demand was held back by continued rationing, by import restrictions, and by government control of vital raw materials, most of them compulsorily diverted to the export trade and to such social purposes as council housing and school building. Wages were kept within bounds by large food subsidies. Even this was barely enough to cope with the inflated costs caused by the Korean War. Worse than that, disproportionate armament increases were then undertaken, since the United States administration needed this gesture for fear that Congress would force it to leave Europe defenceless against the presumed Soviet intention of overrunning it. Worst of all, the government had already secretly committed the country to the huge cost of developing a so-called 'independent nuclear deterrent'.

Nevertheless, overall industrial production was, by 1950, almost twice that of 1924. And though world scarcities induced inflation, earnings rose only slightly higher than prices and usually lagged behind them. In a nation whose wartime sense of community was still not dissipated, the TUC was able to secure a measure of wage restraint because the government, which exuded late Victorian social earnestness, communicated to ordinary people a humdrum impression of being dedicated to their welfare. No government that so repeatedly restricted people's comforts and luxuries proved so difficult to dislodge. In 1950 its majority was down to 5 overall and in 1951 the Conservatives gained an overall majority of 17. Yet, in the latter election, Labour gained a higher percentage of votes cast (49.2) than it had had before or was to achieve again; and the highest number of votes (about 14 million) any party has obtained in any general election in history. .

Compulsions of Growth

The underlying economic problem persisted despite the remarkable economic advances between 1951 and 1964, during what Labour was to call 'thirteen years of Conservative misrule,' presided over by Churchill (1951–55), Eden (1955–57), Macmillan (1957–63) and Douglas-Home (1963–64). The dilemmas became more obvious during Wilson's Labour governments of 1964–70 and Heath's Conservative one of 1970–74 and appeared to presage disaster as Wilson formed and maintained a minority Labour government as a result of the two elections of 1974. All governments were committed to growth. Growth certainly occurred; and, in the 1950s, at a faster rate than ever before. Industrial output from 1948 to 1960 rose annually by 3.7%, which bettered the high rates of the nineteenth century and of the years between the wars. It was over double that between 1877 and 1914. From 1950 to 1966 the value of the nation's 'gross domestic product' increased by almost 50%, chiefly through an acceleration of that shift from old industries to new which had marked the 1920s and 1930s. Even the 'declining' older industries improved output with better technology.

There was, however, a new urgency about growth after 1945. The need to switch from war to peace production, the swallowing up of most of the country's overseas investments by the costs of the war and its new and humiliating status as a debtor nation were no more, in sum, than a starting pistol. The need to produce and export became even more compelling with the rapid revival of competition as other industrialised or semi-industrialised peoples recovered from defeat and foreign occupation. Most of these necessarily invested in the newest technology. None was encumbered with a multiplicity of entrenched trade unions or had banking and financial systems traditionally interested in investment other than in manufacturing industry. None, save France, was burdened with a disproportionate attachment to 'defence commitments' inherited from an imperial past. None had a currency which, as a principal medium of international exchange, foreigners were liable to imperil by turning into dollars whenever the economy with which it was linked appeared particularly unstable.

To keep abreast of these problems, it seemed imperative for the economy to 'earn more' by ever more exports. But to export more meant, first, importing more raw materials, and then, as British technology lagged behind that of newly expanding countries, expenditure on new capital equipment as well. This inflated both costs and export prices. British export prices therefore rose proportionately higher than those of continental countries and became less competitive. Industry suffered cash shortages which precluded adequate investment in the new equipment by which alone it could increase productivity. Throughout the period, Britain produced some of the world's best scientists and economists; too little of their ability was put to practical use. Good on research, the economy was weak on development, principally because long term investment was repeatedly held up when governments put curbs on spending and on credit in order to halt inflation or to save the balance of payments and the stability of sterling.

'Stop-Go'

A major constraint on growth was a government commitment to full employment and higher living standards, a commitment to which trade unionism gave an institutional strength that was difficult to resist. Manual workers were organised above all to prevent a return to the inter-war situation where the cost of economic progress was borne by mass unemployment. Social and economic policy during the thirty years after 1945 was conducted under the shadow of the 1930s. Yet, though living standards rose sufficiently to enable the facile to talk of a candy-floss, affluent, assertive, acquisitive, throw-away society, the facts were that, though wages rose (thus aggravating the uncompetitiveness of exports) they did so less than in continental countries, which could more readily absorb them because of the higher productivity achieved through long-term investment in advanced technology. Standards rose in the United Kingdom; but, relatively, they declined.

The old orthodoxy of allowing a boom to go on till it bust, bringing deflation and the low wages and unemployment that went hand in hand with low prices, was socially unacceptable. For one thing, almost half the working population was employed in providing goods and services for the other half. A collapse in productive workers' purchasing power would spread unemployment like a forest fire. But governments could, it was now affirmed by the Keynesian economists, 'manage' the economy. Hence there came government-controlled 'stop-go' policies. The 'stop' was designed to damp down home demand in order to reduce inflation ('take the heat out of the economy') until the balance of payments looked healthier. Once that had happened, there would be a 'go'. Credit became more easily available and a new opportunity was said to be open for rapid and continuous 'export-led' growth. The 'white heat of the technological revolution' would blast the land into a permanent orbit of high prosperity. But 'stop-go' proved less and less effective. Each period of 'go' was shorter than the last. Inflation continued, despite the 'stops'.

The confusion was worsened by governments' handling of the nationalised services and industries. Government expenditure provoked inflation. Therefore during every 'stop' that expenditure was cut. This deprived nationalised industries of finance and created an enduring legacy of low wages and low productivity due to the impossibility of a planned investment programme. Industry needed gas, coal, electricity, steel and efficient transport and communications. It could be sure of none of them. Governments could not decide whether public utilities should be 'commercially profitable' or be subsidised services. They

519

injected cash into aviation for some purposes and withdrew it from others without inspiring confidence that either policy was correct. They could not decide whether railways should be greatly contracted and motorways greatly multiplied; or the former preserved and the latter limited. They displayed an enthusiasm for atomic power stations which was scarcely justified by the amount of energy they actually produced. After expanding the coal industry, they scaled it down in favour of oil, only to find that an escalation of Middle East oil prices had suddenly made coal the king again. They sought to disguise real costs by preventing economic charges being made for telecommunications, gas, electricity and certain foods. They prejudiced the political effectiveness of the social services by inadequate finance and by inflicting poor management on the national health service and local government welfare services.

'Stop-go' did ensure growth and did prevent periodic collapses into slump. But it made certain that growth would be slow because of the perpetual uncertainty that led to too little of the national wealth being diverted into capital investment, industrial and social. By the early 1970s, the British were accused of technical backwardness and of tolerating the survival of too much that was archaeologically primitive in an environment shaped by the early industrial revolution.

The situation was dramatically worsened by the sharp rise in oil prices imposed by the oil exporting countries in 1973. By piling inflation upon inflation and bringing with it the prospect of a worldwide halt to economic growth, it imperilled not only the British economy but also the stability of its society.

The Collective Bargainers

In the relations between government and governed, the problem was manifested chiefly by successive attempts to control, limit, squeeze or freeze incomes, partly to preserve full employment, and partly to halt the upward price spiral that made exports uncompetitive and engendered yet more wage demands that then pushed prices up still further. In that, until the mid-1970s, they avoided mass unemployment, these devices prevented bad from being worse; but apart from the success of official and unofficial strikes in breaching incomes policies, there was virtually no way by which such policies could be made to appear just. Wages and salaries at any given moment are no more than the product of a chaos of historical accidents. Income restraints and freezes perpetuated capricious injustices at all social levels, aggravating the discontents of an age of ever-rising prices; and they generated fiercer struggles for better pay whenever the policy was relaxed.

The growing sense that, in an increasingly interdependent society faced with intractable economic problems, wages and salaries should no longer be privately arranged by what was euphemistically called 'free collective bargaining', was soundly based. As Attlee's good Sir Stafford Cripps had often solemnly explained, no one should ask for a larger share of the national cake without realising that this would make somebody else's smaller. But by the 1970s society had been made to realise how dependent it was on the labour of particular groups of workers and how determined their union leaders were to maintain and improve their members' standard of living and to assert that, if this policy created problems, they were problems for others to cope with. Embattled dockers blew Wilson's 1966–70 government economically 'off course', causing Wilson himself to accuse the dockers of being 'politically motivated', as if government policies had not inescapably made wages a 'political issue'. Electricity power workers and coal miners plunged the land into the cold and the dark in 1972 and gained all they had wanted. In 1973, with railwaymen augmenting the general dislocation, the miners struck again, against the prices and incomes policy of Heath's Conservative government, forcing him into an election which he lost. The Labour government that followed at once ended the three-day working week to which coal and fuel shortage had reduced the country's industry, but by adopting the 'common sense' procedure of once more letting the miners have what they wanted. Their defeat in 1926 had thus been amply revenged. The effect was to make trade union leaders seem like 'overmighty subjects' who, with the support of economically armed retainers, could over-awe law and government because they commanded the loyal acquiescence of a dependent membership whose whole livelihood derived from the 'good lordship' the unions insisted on imposing on them.

The tension grew as, first Wilson's governments from 1964 to 1970, and then Heath's from 1970 to 1974, tried to pass laws to incorporate into trade union practice, and into 'free collective bargaining', some formal regard for the economic situation of society as a whole. Labour tried a Declaration of Intent by which, in 1964, government, employers and TUC all promised to be moderate. Within two years the government had nevertheless to freeze incomes. The same government tried to frame a legal code of industrial relations. It was blocked by trade union opposition. Heath's government got an Industrial Relations Act on to the statute book in 1972. Bitterly detested and as far as possible flouted or ignored, it contributed much to the Conservative defeats of 1974 and was repealed by the incoming Labour government at once. Labour pinned its hopes on what was called a 'social contract' with the unions. The TUC would use its influence to moderate wage claims, in some not very clearly defined fashion, provided the government pursued policies which met with TUC approval.

This refusal of trade unions to accept legal limitations upon their privileged position in law deepened the general unease. Trade unionists appeared to be free to strike, officially or unofficially, sometimes without notice, and with no risk of being found guilty of any breach of contract.

They interpreted the right to picket as including the right to picket premises and supplies access to which might enable the community to defend itself against the worst consequences of strike-induced shortages or danger to life and health. All proposals to limit these rights were labelled 'strike-breaking' and denounced as infringements of what was solemnly, if not very accurately, called 'a man's right to withdraw his labour'.

To the other members of the community, strikers began to appear not, as in 1889 or 1926, as victims, but rather as aggressors, demanding and almost always seeming to get, an increased share of a total national income which inflation was steadily devaluing. These reactions explain the fall in both Conservative and Labour votes in 1974. Tories lost votes for provoking, and then failing to control, this apparent reign of misrule; Labour lost votes for supporting it. The percentage of the electorate voting Conservative in February 1974 was equal to the previous lowest of the century; that in October 1974 was the lowest. Labour's percentage vote of 37.2 in February 1974 was its lowest since the disaster year of 1931. Its percentage in October 1974 (39.3) was the lowest since 1935.

The malaise was infectious. If powerful manual workers' unions could coerce government and society, others felt forced to imitate them. Nurses, hospital technicians, firemen, dustmen, sewage workers and teachers, all traditionally underpaid, marched the streets behind angry banners all the more significant for being hastily put together only the day before, unlike the elaborate banners with which trade unions sought to pretend they were being treated in the 1970s as if the year were 1819, 1889, 1911, 1921 or 1926. Hospital cleaners went on strike to try to force the Labour government to forbid the treatment of private patients in national health service hospitals. Hospital doctors came close to withdrawing their labour to stop the government doing what the cleaners demanded. Had Sir William Harcourt been alive in 1974, he would have said, not 'We are all socialists now', but 'We are all syndicalists now'—seeking to use workers' power to determine who should govern and how they should govern.

Certainly, the unions' insistence on treating government and law as enemies, and the rest of the community as hostages, had disturbing implications. Their legal immunity and their apparently scant respect for the sovereignty of government recalled the medieval church. By 1974, Harold Wilson seemed something of a latterday King John, agreeing with the barons of the TUC that the first article of a new Great Charter should be, that not 'holy church' but 'sacrosanct trade unions' should be 'free'. The demands for the most extensive picketing rights and the most comprehensive closed shop regulations, like the alacrity with which some workers from time to time 'walked out' should any of their number be accused of a minor offence while at work, appeared something of a modern parallel to benefit of clergy.

With a greatly increased foreign indebtedness; with threats that standards of life might fall below those of Mediterranean peoples the English had once imagined to be so much sapped by the sun that they could neither work nor play football; with mounting Welsh and Scottish pressure for home rule; with the ordinary defence mechanisms of the state proving unable to prevent murder in Ulster or Irish-made bombs exploding in English towns; with Arabs pouring inflated oil prices on the flames of home-fuelled inflation; with industry running out of cash and shares falling in price as if it were 1931 again, it was perhaps not surprising that a contributor to the *Spectator* could write, in January 1974, that the country faced 'a transcendentally awful crisis,' or that *The Times*, surveying so much social disruption, should sadly declare five months later, 'These are mournful times for democrats'.

An Ungovernable People?

The signs were that the powerful unions had set an example so widely followed that the English (and the United Kingdom as a whole) were beginning almost to appear ungovernable. Ever since Magna Carta, the system had, save for the years from 1640 to 1660, been based on a consent that derived from a balance between freedom and subordination. The balance had often been precarious; but it had never quite broken down. It had been constantly and consciously adjusted, to ensure that the governed could treat those who governed them with the kind of deference which, though frequently punctuated with the expletives of riot, demonstration or strike, manifestly still survived into the England of the early 1950s. By the 1970s, that deference seemed to be fast disappearing, and consent seeming to be withheld. Whether this was a permanent or only a temporary condition, no one could be sure.

Yet there were understandable reasons for the decline of deference and the erosion of consent. It is possible to detect two broad ideological camps in late-twentieth century England and to suggest that, in conditions of continuing inflation and contracting world trade, a clash between the two was more than probable. Both ideologies, though reflected in them, were more subtle than differences of class or political allegiance and both were grounded in history. One tradition was that of individual initiative, allied to a tradition of public service. The minority bred in this tradition, or educated into it, inherited from the propertied classes of the remoter past the belief that they and, ideally, they alone, should govern, manage, administer and, either as professionals or as well-wishing voluntary workers, minister to, the rest of society. The latter in its turn should serve and defer to them and accept as normal the privileges and comforts to which their superior position and (as they would argue) their greater responsibilities entitled them.

The rival ideology, though the men of Kent of 1381 and those of East Anglia of 1549, like Lollards, Levellers, Luddites and Chartists, would have found it familiar enough, was largely the product of the 150 years

523

of intense urbanisation after 1820 and the technological changes which, after 1880, had created a common, popular culture and, through advertising, a common consciousness of the luxurious living which, though on offer to all, was easily accessible only to some. Its essential characteristic was a sense of solidarity, encouraged by trade unionism and the shared closeness of traditional working-class environments. It involved a deep commitment to social justice, or at any rate, to a conception of 'fairness'; and it was strengthened by a sense of alienation which rising standards of living did little to diminish and which the increasing size, power and remoteness of large scale organisation did much to increase.

The two ideologies could co-exist so long as managers appeared to be successful; but in the thirty years after 1945, government, whether central or local, and enterprise, whether private or nationalised, seemed, rightly or wrongly, not to have been at all well-managed. Conflict could be avoided, too, if the relative privileges of the managers and decision-makers were balanced by an assurance among the managed that their livelihood was not in danger, their savings not likely to become of little worth, and their wages or salaries never less than sufficient to guarantee a secure and steadily improving standard of living. The affluent parts of England between the wars were full of families in this happy position. The fact helps to explain the quietude of that time. But all these certainties, and the harmony they ensured, were imperilled by inflation. The less secure majority of the population —manual workers, intellectual proletariat, lower middle class—increasingly turned to the ideology once peculiar to the skilled worker in his trade union. They began to develop a similar solidarity and a similarly intense sectionalism.

In consequence, governments were confronted by a discordant clamour of rival sectional interests. Each occupational group, industrial or salaried, looked to itself, wary (or simply envious) lest others might 'leapfrog', erode 'differentials' or undermine the historic dogma that manual work must always be paid less than intellectual. These solidarities bred an intensely defensive conservatism. Technical change and innovation, as a product of the rival ideology of the managers, was resented because of its potential threat to traditional work patterns, acquired skills or particular employments. As, during 1975, unemployment rose, the demand that jobs be protected by government finance, sometimes regardless of whether a real demand still existed for the goods or services those jobs would provide, grew louder. Economic pressure might demand that, to survive, technologies were needed that might reduce the labour force. Such developments were often resisted.

Simultaneously, the morale of the traditional higher ranks in administrative and economic life was being undermined by fiscal inroads upon their wealth and income, by a mounting propaganda that represented their mere existence as manifestation of an apparently objectionable phenomenon known as 'élitism' and by their feeling that their inability to combat union pressure in any of its various forms deprived them not only of status but of their capacity to innovate and initiate. Government and industry found their policies attacked, obstructed or ignored much as James I and Charles I had found their policies paralysed by parliamentarians and justices in the 1620s. As the tasks of political and economic decision-making became ever more complex, those who had to make the decisions found themselves less and less able to carry them out. At almost all levels of society the ideology of service was in retreat. Those who managed society were coming to feel that they could not serve; those who were the managed seemed to be saying that they would not serve.

Which Way to Consent?

The reconciliation of these discordant elements was the allotted task of the TUC and the Labour party. Neither was very efficient at the task. The TUC had little power over individual unions, and there was no constitutional machinery by which it could exercise more than informal control of government policy. The Labour party could consult and defer to them; but it had no power over the trade unions. Nevertheless, the Labour government was probably correct in judging that the creation of a cooperative consent among its miscellany of supporters (and that 60% of the electorate which had declined to vote for it in either of the 1974 elections) provided the only reasonable chance of a way forward. Without that consent, there would be small hope of defeating inflation, avoiding mass unemployment or of dealing with those social shortcomings from which so many of the poorer members of the community continued to suffer. But, as the social contract of 1974 failed to halt inflation, 1975 saw a return to more customary devices. Limits would be set on wage rises. The nationalised industries could raise their prices to an economic level so that their real costs should be made apparent; local authority and other public expenditure would be firmly held in check. But this, though it might contain inflation, might also fail to win the approval of any one of several powerful trade unions. It would increase unemployment; it would perpetuate the already well-established contrast between private affluence and inadequate or mismanaged social expenditure; and, of itself, seemed unlikely to divert funds away from consumption and into capital investment, or from labour-intensive to new capital-intensive technologies. For the moment, the English remained divided most by what they were most agreed upon. The division that separated those who believed in private enterprise from those who wished to restrict or abolish it was as nothing to the divisions the English had created for themselves by their unanimous demand, irrespective of class or political affiliation, for ever-improving personal and domestic standards of living.

10

HOMES WITHOUT HEROES

The Past Lives On

ONE contribution to the unsettled state of the English mind was that the huge colonial empire, much of it created with such deceptive ease after the 1870s, collapsed as the ironical consequence of a successful war. The rapid accumulation of so much territory with relatively little effort between 1875 and 1914, and the unchallenged domination of the Middle East achieved after the war of 1914–18, had bequeathed illusions which, though held in check for a time by Baldwin and Chamberlain, had led the English to imagine that merely to declare war on Germany in 1939 was of itself a sufficient gesture and that, once 'we' had won, continued greatness was assured. Churchill did more in wartime than stir up intense and energetic patriotism at home. He laboured ceaselessly to secure the United States' cooperation without which victory was unthinkable, and then struggled unremittingly to prevent British interests being largely disregarded by a Roosevelt unsympathetic to those interests. Nevertheless, the facts (as he had too much political sense to admit and too much historical sense not to see) were against him. His less than enthusiastic attitude to the Beveridge Report reflected his fear that there was in the nation at large too little understanding of how war had accelerated the diminution of Britain's economic power and how much weaker was the United Kingdom's capacity to behave as a political great power.

Soothing talk about power having merely been 'transferred' to India and Pakistan in 1947, and bland hopes of the emergence of a new, multiracial Commonwealth to replace the old British Commonwealth also kept old ideas of world leadership alive. The success of Nasser's daring obduracy in the Suez crisis of 1956, and the sensational fact that the British action against Egypt was condemned, not only by the United States, but by both India and Canada, were profoundly shocking to the popular mind. The rapid dismantling of the empire in Africa that followed the Suez debacle had hardly been envisaged at the start of the 1950s, and perhaps excited relatively little opposition because the Suez affair had so starkly uncovered the realities of the British position. Yet a referendum in 1956 would have shown a substantial majority in favour of Eden's action against Nasser. To express opposition to it at the time was to invite social ostracisim.

Imperial Realities

Yet, long before submarines and aircraft began to imperil the naval supremacy which held the empire together, official policy at Westminster had almost always been based on the premise that, in a hostile world, that empire could not be defended by force. Despite the flow of imperialist rhetoric, the notion that the empire had at any time been thought capable of surviving in 'splendid isolation' has no foundation. Gladstone was wiser than his detractors not simply because he hated braggart jingoism and the cost of great armaments but because he saw that empire could neither be indefinitely extended nor long preserved, by the use of force. Joseph Chamberlain's quite different idea of a closer imperial federation showed that he too understood that a loose, shambling structure like the British Empire could not hope to be permanently dependent for its safety upon the armaments or the economy of the home country.

And, amorphous, world-wide and almost indescribably varied as the British Empire was, an underlying principle was nearly everywhere detectable. The idea of imperial permanence was based on the belief that, everywhere, the British were doing good and that, in the end, since the varied inhabitants of the empire were bound to realise the merits of the institutions and values the British were commending to them, they would absorb the values, adopt the institutions and, while still acknowledging the ultimate sovereignty of the crown, do so as wholly self-governing peoples. Already, well before 1939, the ties linking the mother country and the old colonies of settlement, or as they had come to be called, 'the Dominions', were ties mainly of sentiment. Not that the sentiment was sentimentality. Forces from Dominion countries came swiftly and voluntarily to the home country's assistance in all its twentieth-century wars. The necessity of avoiding war until he was sure the Dominions would voluntarily support it was always an important element in Chamberlain's dealings with Hitler.

Though the economic links with the home country were sometimes more and sometimes less close than sentiment might have dictated, the political relationship had been given brilliantly subtle definition in the Statute of Westminster of 1931, based on a formula produced by the elegant mind of Balfour. Its terms made no attempt to disguise the fact that Canada, Australia, New Zealand and South Africa were equal in status with Great Britain or that, though associated with the home country and with one another within a Commonwealth of Nations, each was free to go its own way if it wished. It made it plain that none of the Dominions was amenable to any form of political oversight by Westminster. Even so, it was hard for outsiders to believe that its bland language meant what it said. It also failed to secure the approval of the Irish. They underlined their refusal to have anything to do with it by remaining firmly neutral from 1939 to 1945. From first to last, the Irish would regard themselves, with some reason, not as partners in empire but as victims of it.

The dependent empire consisted in the main of areas of non-white population and was mainly concentrated in Africa and the Caribbean; but it also included a wide scatter of strategic possessions in all the world's seas and oceans, ranging in size and importance from St Helena to Malta, Cyprus, Aden, Singapore and Hong Kong. The whole miscellany was governed in the last resort by the colonial office in Westminster. Even in the dependent empire, however, varying degrees of local self-government or local self-administration existed; and it was the theory, at least after 1917, that eventually they should, where practicable, be handed over to local rule by the inhabitants when a majority of them so desired. It was assumed that the British would be judges of when it was practicable, and of whether the inhabitants of a particular colony were sufficiently acquainted with British standards to be thought fit for freedom. As late as the early 1950s the time when the non-white colonial populations of Africa would be capable of governing themselves was thought to be far in the future. The men on the spot usually, and the man in the street almost always, inclined to the view that they would never be capable of it.

Yet in 1923 Westminster refused to grant self-government to the white settlers in Kenya, on the stated grounds that Kenya was 'an African territory' and that 'the interests of the African natives must be paramount'. The opposite policy was adopted in Southern Rhodesia at the same time for almost accidental reasons. Still then administered by the financially unprofitable Chartered Company launched by Rhodes in 1889, the territory was thought of as a potential extra province to add to South Africa. But in 1922, the white inhabitants voted, out of fear of Afrikaner domination, for responsible self-government instead. The policy adopted by the white minority after self-government, that of excluding Africans from political rights and, more important, from ownership of most of the land, was based on South African precedent. Worse still, Westminster, having granted responsible self-government, had, as events after 1965 showed, no means of taking it away.

India was in a category of its own. Much of it was 'British India', administered until 1858 by the East India Company, but thereafter by a Secretary of State for India in Westminster, and a Viceroy in India itself who represented the Crown. The rest of the sub-continent was ruled by a number of Indian princes, each watched over by a British 'Resident' and, like British India, subject to the Viceroy. Attitudes to India varied. Cool, eighteenth-century Englishmen found India exotically interesting and had a certain respect for its culture. The early nineteenth-century English were convinced that Indians could, if honestly governed and systematically trained and educated in English ways, gradually learn to govern themselves in the best English fashion. The Indian Mutiny of 1857, however, cast doubt on this complacent, if benevolent, view of the

Indians. The later growth of an Indian nationalist movement deepened British suspicions. These increased as, during the early twentieth century, there emerged a potentially explosive division between those Indians who were Hindus and those who were Muslims.

Nevertheless, governments in England, from 1919 onwards, embarked on a frustrating attempt to conduct India step by cautious step towards self-government. Every proposal was opposed at home as premature and in India as inadequate and accompanied by disorders which the imperial authorities suppressed. The abandonment of India was, when it actually came, precipitate. Politically conscious Indians made the most of Britain's difficulties during the Japanese assault by way of Burma. Alliance with the United States rendered the British vulnerable to the American view that European powers ought never to have had empires in the first place, and ought not to cling on to them after a war fought to liberate the oppressed. Financially exhausted by 1945, the British could not afford to hold India against its will, least of all given that by now the army in India was already largely Indianised. All that delayed Indian independence was the inability of Indian politicians to decide among themselves to whom exactly their country's government should be transferred. In the end, the solution of partition into two states, India and Pakistan, was arrived at only when the British announced their imminent withdrawal whether Indian politicians had made up their minds or not. Nevertheless, the granting of independence was not solely a product of post-war policies. Though the 1945 Labour government was firmly committed to Indian independence, it was implementing a course of action which had been earlier foreshadowed, in words at once passionate and compassionate, by both the Younger Pitt and Stanley Baldwin. The granting of independence to India was followed rapidly by the independence of Burma and Ceylon. Burma, unlike the others, withdrew from the Commonwealth at once.

As well as the Dominions, India and the dependent empire, England had acquired a strategically important 'unofficial' empire in the Middle East as a result of the decline of the Turkish Empire in the late nineteenth century and its disappearance in 1918. This included Egypt and, after 1919, Palestine, Transjordan and Iraq. Egypt was granted nominal independence in 1922 and a more substantial form of it in 1936. The other three areas were held as mandates under the League of Nations and were intended to become fully independent when considered 'fit' for self-government. Iraq became independent in 1932. Transjordan, though not completely free until 1946, seems not to have found the British presence particularly objectionable. Palestine proved intractable. In the course of various uncoordinated diplomatic manoeuvres between 1915 and 1917 the British had involved themselves in three commitments: to hand over virtually all the Middle East to its Arab inhabitants; to partition it with the French; and to provide a national home in Palestine for the Jews. The French were pacified (though the inhabitants were not) by getting control of Syria and Lebanon. The Arabs, however, were reconciled to the presence neither of British nor Jews. The Jews inevitably sought to transform the 'national home' into a Jewish state, above all after the advent of Hitler. Alone among the races subjected to Nazi brutality they, who had suffered the most, had lacked the essential means for the defence of a people's identity provided by the diplomatic and military machinery of a sovereign state of their own. In such a situation it was not within the capacity of any third party to provide satisfactory government. Various solutions proposed by the British in the 1930s aborted; hounded after 1945 by Zionist terrorism, Arab fury and universal moral indignation at their failure to solve the insoluble, the British withdrew in 1947. The subsequent history of Israel and its neighbours demonstrated that two equally desirable objectives, the rights of Arabs in their homeland, and of Jews to a sovereign state, were not made reconcilable by the mere absence from the scene of the 'British Imperialists'.

Nasser's triumph, in seizing and keeping the Suez Canal for Egypt in 1956 in defiance of the British will that he should fail was like the sound of a shrill alarm clock summoning a sleeper to abandon the world of dreamland for that of reality. Macmillan, who succeeded the luckless Eden as prime minister in 1957, soon began, all the time giving an impression of insouciant statesmanship, a rapid process of 'decolonisation'. The dismantling of the old dependent empire continued, with only the mildest expressions of dissent, throughout the 1960s. It is unlikely that the process would have provoked so little opposition had not Britain's isolation in the Suez affair in 1956 brought home to the English that their imperial past could not survive in a greatly changed world. The greatest hostility to the proceedings came from South Africa and Rhodesia. Told by Macmillan in 1960 that the 'wind of change' compelled attention to be paid to African nationalism, the South African government determined to pin its faith, not on multi-racialism, but apartheid; left the Commonwealth in 1961; and declared itself a Republic. Rhodesia set to work to preserve white dominance for as long as it could. But, between 1956 and 1971, the government at Westminster gave independence to Ghana, Malaya, Nigeria, Cyprus, Tanganyika, Trinidad and Tobago, Uganda, Kenya, Malawi, Malta, Zambia, The Gambia, Singapore, Guyana, Botswana, Lesotho, Barbados, Aden, Mauritius, Swaziland, Tonga and Fiji. By no means all, but certainly most, departed without preliminary violence and few with a notable aftermath of anti-British feeling. Significantly, the majority of these yielded territories had had less than a century of subordination to Westminster. They had been acquired during the heady, feckless age of late-Victorian imperialism, when Englishmen, for some thirty years or so, forced their normally unenthusiastic rulers to plant the Union Jack wherever traders, adventurers, missionaries and self appointed visionaries told them they ought to, if only to keep out the Germans and the French.

The British imperial record need not be excessively apologised for. Cruelty and arrogance were certainly included in the record. But this is true of almost every nation that, by having any territory at all, proclaims by that very fact that it has taken land that was once somebody else's. There is hardly a people in the world who have not at some time or other set out, under their own particular Moses or Joshua, to snatch some Promised Land without regard to the opinion of the local Philistines that it actually belonged to them. By a strange quirk, the rightminded were slow to apply the word 'imperialist' to those who acquired great territories by continuously expanding their frontiers overland, reserving it instead as a term of abuse applicable only to Europeans, and above all the English, for doing the same thing after first sailing ships across seas. Nothing in British imperial history had consequences for indigenous peoples on the scale of those resulting from the westward expansion of the United States or the eastward march of Czarist Russia. Whatever may have been done to Maoris and Australian aborigines by those who settled on their lands, Malay, Hindu, Muslim and African customs and culture survived submission to British rule. Inca and Aztec culture are subjects only for archaeologists, North American Indians for last ditch acts of repentant protection. It does not seem likely that the descendants of the Mashona and Matabeles who submitted themselves to Cecil Rhodes will suffer a similar fate. Against the disservice the British did the human race by prosecuting the slave trade must be set their energy in organising its suppression. Against the confusion they caused by encouraging the migration of Chinese to Malaya, and of Indians to East and South Africa and the Caribbean, must be set their advocacy of multi-racialism, however awkward the ideal proved when transformed from one designed for export into one for home consumption. And against its many and frequent illiberal actions must be set its widespread dissemination of liberal values into every continent.

From Empire to Europe

The rapid succession of ceremonies at which, during the 1960s, the Union Jack was hauled down in all parts of the world, as Governors-General in plumed hats retreated punctiliously into the past, gave rise at home to a certain feeling of national purposelessness; and, with black and coloured immigration into the country proving one of the more abiding legacies of the imperial past, a certain disturbed perplexity. The popular mind seems to have drowned its unease in the sound of its own noisy laughter as members of radio's Goon Show transformed the upholders of the imperial tradition into the gullible, patriotic fool, Harry Seagoon; the pathetically eager boy scout, Bluebottle, forever being blown up and 'deaded' for his pains; and Colonel Bloodknock, the permanently sozzled and forever outwitted representative of imperial military ineptitude. Yet a great deal had been lost besides the overblown pretensions of the past. Both in India and elsewhere, imperial and colonial administration had offered meaningful employment to many who were excluded from such work at home. The Indian Civil Service and the Colonial Civil Service, like commissions in the Indian army, though never ranked with the Home Civil Service or commissions in the best English regiments, had given many men of middle-class origins opportunities they could not expect to aspire to at home. For others in the social scale, service in the rank and file of the army in India and elsewhere offered an experience and a sense of national and social superiority greater than were available to those enlisting in the much reduced post-imperial forces. Moreover, possession of empire induced a general feeling of responsibility, a feeling that to be 'British' was to be permanently under public scrutiny as a member of a great and valiant race dedicated to maintaining law and justice over less fortunate peoples all over the world for their own good.

Inevitably, loss of status and opportunity had a certain enervating effect. There was perhaps a feeling of belonging to a society aware that history was no longer working in its favour, and disinclined to respond with much energy to the challenge of a world grown so different and so demanding. Only yesterday, 'we' were an imperial race superior to, and admired by, all others. Now, it seemed, there was barely an advanced country to which the English were not, for some reason or other, held to be 'lagging behind'. Some of this was exaggeration. Often, the real 'English disease' was not a failure to 'work hard enough' but a nagging itch to indulge in self-deprecation and to bemoan, or to make repetitive jokes about, lost glories. Some at least of the allegations the English made about themselves were symptoms of the disease rather than the disease itself.

Europe became a new source of discomfiture. There was pique at being kept out of the EEC; then, bewilderment as to why the United Kingdom was in it and uncertainty as to whether membership was to continue. It would be rash indeed to guess what the positive reasons were for the majority in favour of remaining in the Community which emerged from the referendum on the subject in 1975. It might perhaps be construed as a grudging admission that the past was, after all, beyond recall. If so, it was an admission accompanied by few signs of cordiality towards the future that was said to lie ahead. And, through all the manifest changes, and amid all the uncertainties, one inherited conviction seemed hardest of all to dislodge: the paradoxical belief that England was still a rich country whose social evils could be put to rights if only some magic formula could be found by which its wealth could be redistributed.

Home's History

It could well be claimed that the once powerful slogan 'For King and Country' was now effectively replaced by another: 'For Wife and

Kiddies'. Though the censorious spoke of a heedless pursuit of material luxury, most people, in the twenty years after Suez, devoted themselves to a single-minded concentration on the home. It was endowed, at breakneck speed, with power-driven machinery, expensive consumer durables, warmth of a kind previously unattainable in so uncertain a climate and every available device for the reception and reproduction of musical and other forms of entertainment. This withdrawal into the encapsulating warmth and comfort of home was not reduced, but merely made mobile, by the motor car, the housing of which became a major function of any 'desirable residence'.

This intense home-centredness was, historically, still relatively new. The concept of the home had begun to emerge only from the seventeenth century onwards, to become a cult in the life of the Victorians, for whom the song 'Home, Sweet Home' ranked next in public esteem only to the National Anthem and the Hallelujah chorus. In priding themselves that the French had no equivalent for this beautiful English word, they unconsciously asserted that a 'home' was a luxury that less fortunate peoples could not yet afford.

The home, as it evolved after about 1700, slowly became transformed into a phenomenon with minimal social and eventually no economic function. Once, 'home' was the shelter where the poor man lay at night side by side, not only with his wife and children, but also with his chickens and his pig. Even the rich were slow to acquire withdrawing rooms and sleeping quarters of their own to set themselves apart from the political, military or administrative household of which they were the head. Normally, the larger the establishment, the greater the mingling of different social ranks within it, and the less privacy there was for everyone. There might be magnificence or grandeur, but not comfort. The place where an ordinary family lived was, for most of history, an adjunct to, or simply just was, a manufactory, a workshop, a productive unit within the textile industry, a counting house, a wholesale or retail shop; and in each of these capacities it was likely also to be an apprentice training school.

Even as it slowly detached itself from whole time economic activity, the home continued to fulfil functions now excluded from it. It was where daughters and servants learned domestic crafts and management. As often as not it was, for younger children at least, a school. From the Puritan age until the end of the nineteenth century it might be something of a gathered church. It was a dairy, a bakery, a lying-in hospital, a funeral parlour, an old people's home. It provided the only residential or hotel accommodation normally available to poor relations, unmarried relations, itinerant friends and acquaintances, and distressed gentlefolk. Until well after the advent of the gramophone it was also a concert room and a dancing salon. If its owner was a Justice of the Peace it could also be a magistrate's court.

With the progressive transfer of these activities to specialised premises elsewhere, home became for ordinary families what Le Petit Trianon had been for Marie Antoinette and Malmaison for the Empress Josephine, a retreat devoted to private leisure and pleasure. When, in 1921, Lord Lee of Fareham presented his country house at Chequers for the use of England's prime ministers, he was directing attention to the fact that a prime minister had by then become one of the few important people left in the country who still lived at his place of work. 'Number Ten' provided historical evidence that 'to go out to work' was a recent innovation and 'having a home to go back to' a once too expensive luxury. When reflecting on the squalid houses put up for the earliest factory workers, account might be taken of the fact that, insupportable though many of them were, they were the first 'homes' in the modern sense that poor people had had.

The Domestic Male

Slowly, as the home ceased to be an economic unit, marriage also began to lose its economic character. Traditionally, a woman was married off to a man because her father, being mortal, could not guarantee to provide for her throughout her life. The man married the woman because he needed someone to manage or serve his household, to add her land or dowry to his wealth, to perpetuate his name, and provide for his old age by carrying, and caring for, an adequate number of children. Most marriages were, to a greater or lesser extent, 'arranged'. Virtually all were based on some balancing of economic niceties, to determine how he could add to her social or economic status and how she could add to his. The virtual disappearance of a system by which only the very poor or the very feckless would marry merely for love is almost wholly a twentieth-century development.

These changes worked against male authoritarianism in the long run, though reinforcing it in the short. At first, the paterfamilias continued to enjoy the authority that had once been his by virtue of being the head of a household that was also to some extent an economic enterprise. Though he sent his sons out into the world, and got his daughters married off, as soon as possible, he could not fire them until then and he could not fire his wife at all; but they were all his dependents, and society approved and indeed required their total subordination to him. Nevertheless, the sharp separation of home from work inevitably feminised the home, causing it to be seen as peculiarly the woman's domain, even when its chief purpose was to minister to the comfort of the male. If of the servant-employing class, the male was only secondarily concerned with domestic management. In the best establishments servants were kept out of the way. One reason why the more menial of them had to rise so early was to ensure that his start to the day should not be disturbed by their sounds, or even their sight. In working-class homes the tradition, not yet quite dead, was that the man gave no help at all with 'women's work'. He expected his wife (with his elder daughters' help if they were around) to be, not only a domestic servant and a child-minder, but a child disciplinarian as well. Hence Shaw's view of the home as 'the girl's prison and the mother's workhouse'; and the opinion that the working-class woman's life was one of 'drudgery and sensuality'.

The increasing significance attached to home suggests that the competitive struggle to keep up with the demands made on them by a thrusting industrial society imposed strains which men could bear only if they had a private retreat from which all signs of that outside world were excluded. If the English early came to be thought peculiarly concerned to preserve the private life, it may be less because they were snobbish than because they were earlier forced to realise that if they had no home in which to hide from an industrialised society for part of every day, their personalities might collapse under its burdens or its tediums. Further, by a psychological division of labour, the man at work was allotted the qualities of assertive aggression, while the woman at home was made sole custodian of those gentle, tender and compassionate virtues that 'economic man' was precluded from displaying. But the more home-centred society became, the more susceptible men became to 'home influence'. The social history of the twentieth century is in part the history of the domestication of the male. During the same period, as women themselves became 'emancipated' from full-time domesticity by going out to work, masculine and feminine roles tended to become fused. The effects of no longer specifically charging either sex with fostering the 'feminine' qualities have not yet been worked out.

Romance and Sex

Since the other factors which stabilised the home had begun to disappear, the late twentieth-century home could be held together only by affection. Devotion of man and wife, and of both to their children, became even stronger cultural imperatives. Once, marriage had been kept in being by a common economic or financial interest and by fear of social ostracism. Once, the whole family might constitute a common economic enterprise: sons learned their fathers' trades, daughters their mothers' skills at home management; and all the young would learn their letters, their Bible and their duty of obedience to God and society from a childhood of obedience to parental authority. Now, sons do not see their fathers at work; some do not even know what work their fathers do. With mothers as often as not going out to work and girls doing the same, they do not watch their mothers do much cooking. As for teaching the children, schools take care of that; and the complexities of modern work can hardly be taught in flat, maisonette or council house.

The twentieth-century family transmits few skills, and much of the knowledge and culture it hands on comes in by way of 'the media'. Unlike the family of the past, it scarcely ventures even to lay down rules, for deference decayed in the family in parallel with its decay in the world outside. Compared with its original functions, the home does hardly anything at all except compulsorily require mutual love from those who, however divergent in their interests or contrary by temperament, happen to find themselves in it. It is not surprising that the youthful psyche is often a confused conflict between extreme dependence and defiant aggression and liable to react unpredictably when released into the world of work or propelled into what Anthony Powell called 'the crushing melancholy of the undergraduate condition'. What is surprising is that the system works as well as it does, and that the minority who can afford to send their children to boarding schools are considered by the rest of the country's mums and dads as lacking in feeling.

The love out of which the modern marriage and home are made was first of all 'pure' and romantic love, end-product of late-medieval chivalry; but by the 1970s it had become a compound of romance and sexuality, blended in varying proportions. The arranged or economic marriage could often create love. If it did not, marriage as an institution was buttressed about by adultery or prostitution, hypocritically, guiltily or sensitively concealed. In the twentieth century, the supportive roles of these two institutions became increasingly taken over by that of divorce. Just as people now went to church largely because they wanted to and not because society expected it, so, though social pressures to preserve rather than end a marriage were still strong, people remained married because they wanted to rather than because society insisted that they did so. Those whose hopes of lasting love were unfulfilled now sought, by divorce, to go back to another and more promising square one to start again. Since, however, divorce was still disapproved of, the positive programme for combating it was to sexualise romantic love and to disseminate advice on how to achieve so refined a sexual technique that the bedroom should be a place of constantly renewed physical, if not gymnastic delight, and for both partners. Until the twentieth century, married love was often mainly a matter of men using women for breeding purposes or for the satisfaction of male desire. The wife's role was that of submission to duty. Though common women might enjoy the proceedings, ladies ought not to. With the spread of birth control and the growth of female independence, it became fashionable to insist that both male and female must be assured of total sexual gratification within their marriage. This new imperative was made somewhat awesome by the earlier age at which couples married and the greater life expectancy to which they could now look forward. The words 'till death us do part' took on an altogether greater significance. A marriage could be expected to last much longer than in the historical past; and throughout the long lifetime together that couples now had in prospect they were apparently committed to the energetic pursuit of orgasm well into old age.

Emphasis on sexual performance could create, as well as diminish, personal problems and induce a disregard for the value of a long-shared partnership in humdrum ups-and-downs; and it added to the burdens of the young. Marriages not being arranged, they now, far more than in the past, had to find their mates very largely through their own unaided initiative. Modern marriage was thus even more dependent upon chance than before. Perhaps this was, eugenically, as it should be; but the contemporary emphasis on sexuality put pressure on the young to assure themselves as soon as possible of their sexual competence. While many teenage sexual unions were intended to be, and often became, permanent, experimentation tended to become almost mandatory in a cultural climate where sex was so extensively valued. Generalisations about 'premature sexual experience' among the young were, however, unreliable. Statistics of illegitimacy, for example, now have an accuracy that makes it impossible to draw comparisons with times when a daughter's bastard might be registered as born to the girl's parents, or simply be left to be 'found', only to die in an infection-ridden foundling hospital or in a ditch. The casual youthful and adult copulations, the slum incests, the compulsive drunkenness, brawls and brutalities, and the prostitution of girls and children in the urban life of the eighteenth and nineteenth century are, as they mostly were at the time, immune from exposure under the social microscope of statistical survey; but enough is known of them to induce much suspicion of appeals for a 'return to the higher standards of the past'.

Life Without Rules

Life in the 1970s tended to be one in which the only rules and formalities were those imposed by the bureaucracy. Private life had lost most of them. This partly followed the decline of domestic service. The keeping of servants compelled formality, because it meant that, even at home, every family was, according to its status, conducting some of its private life in the presence of outsiders who were inferiors. Formality was required of children in order to maintain paternal authority. They stood in the presence of their parents. A boy at boarding school would write to ask his father's permission to return home for the holidays. Even when he was married, a man might sign letters to his father, 'I am, honoured Sir, your obedient and dutiful and obliged humble servant'. The regular morning greeting exchanged by an unusually devoted brother and sister of ducal family was, 'How is your ladyship this morning?'—'I am quite well, I am obliged to your Grace'. Sir Edward Marsh, patron of Georgian poets in the early twentieth century, was rebuked by an aunt for signing a letter to her with merely his Christian name because, to sign oneself thus was, she averred, a privilege exclusive to princes and princesses of the blood royal. At Eton in the nineteenth century, boys did not recognise the existence of one another's Christian names and sent letters to one another beginning, 'Dear Sir'. The use of Christian names by schoolboys in general came only after 1945. Even humble women referred to, and addressed, their husbands by their surnames. Respectable nineteenth-century people surrounded social intercourse with the most elaborate safeguards against unauthorised intrusions upon their status and privacy. They allowed others into their residences only on days when they were 'at home'. Nice rules were laid down about how long they should stay, where they should put their hats and walking sticks if male, and what should be talked about. Exquisite rituals attended the leaving of visiting cards. The right number to be left varied according to the sex and status of caller and recipients and there was the further complexity that in certain circumstances the corner of one or more of the cards had to be turned down.

The telephone in itself was enough to end all that. It did not ring politely at front doors, but insistently, within private interiors, demanding immediate attention to whoever chose to dial a number. The old titles and forms by which people deferred to one another's age and status fell out of use. The word 'lady' ceased to designate a woman who did not work and became attached to certain women who did. Institutionalised catering was done by 'canteen ladies'; homes and offices were no longer attended to by charwomen but by 'cleaning ladies'. Because it was thought such distinctions were no longer relevant, the introduction, 'Meet John and Mary' would be made to serve whether John and Mary were engaged, married or merely cohabiting, were a duke and his duchess, mere office colleagues or an eminent lawyer whose wife was a celebrated female don. For similar reasons, hats and caps, once clearly indicative of male status (downwards from top hat by way of trilby and bowler to cloth cap) almost disappeared, so that men could no longer raise them either to females or to the Cenotaph; and the female hat itself was seen chiefly at weddings and at Royal Ascot.

Tomorrow's People

The demolition of old formalities was hastened by the new status of the young. More higher education for some, and more money for most, rendered them more susceptible to the commercial and political exploitation of their normal desire to appear different. The freedom to express youthful disapproval of authority and the old which, in the 1920s, had been the prerogative of Oxbridge undergraduates and their sisters, was democratised. Yet it was by no means only the working-class young who became rebellious. The middle class young turned against trim, well-cared-for homes as forcefully as others against less privileged environments. Their larger numbers of middle-class students made universities more like the explosive universities of the continent than the staunch upholders of the *status quo* that Oxford and Cambridge had been when, in the mid-nineteenth century, the central European universities were launching so many revolutions. The merely ritual disorderliness of Oxbridge undergraduates knocking off policemen's helmets in Piccadilly on Boat Race night gave place to student 'protest' and demonstrations. In so frequently demonstrating outside the United States embassy, they revealed how true had been the opinion of Oscar Wilde's Lady Bracknell that if education were ever taken seriously in England it would 'probably lead to acts of violence in Grosvenor Square'. In the 1950s, students marched for nuclear disarmament and in the 1960s for Ho Chi Minh. Soviet Communism having become one more 'establishment' the rebellious young now declared themselves to be Trotskyists or Maoists. The pictures of Lenin and Stalin their dissident public school predecessors might have put up in the 1930s were replaced by posters depicting Che Guevara. They demanded a control over their teachers such as university students had not had since the fourteenth century and, when impeded by the law, complained of 'police brutality' by 'fascist pigs'.

This headline-seeking minority were only the flames and fury that diverted attention from more important changes among the young, many of whom were more serious, less class-ridden and more inter-nationally-minded than their predecessors. Many of them nevertheless seemed anxious to constitute on a national scale a new version of the rebellious sub-culture of the London apprentices of Tudor and early Stuart London. They transformed their personal appearance into a carefully cultivated display of social criticism. Clothes became defiantly proletarian when not deliberately grubby. Yet, while some, in T-shirts and jeans, appeared to have been cast for bit parts in a grim, realistic play about the oppressed and under-privileged, others became brightly colourful. Younger men at last broke free from the subfusc costume appropriate to an economy based on coal and on smoking chimney stacks and no longer so regularly formalised their social gatherings by putting on the penguin uniform of black contrasting with spotless white, by which the rich had been used to proclaim how much cleaner their linen was than that of the grimy poor. And though both sexes favoured sheepskin-type coats, giving them the look of Mongolian nomads, the girls too had an alternative mode. Ministered to by Mary Quant and a burgeoning of boutiques they took over control of fashion from traditional *haute couture*, enjoying with uninhibited individuality the variety of styles which mass production and their newly acquired cash permitted them. Though eschewing 'glamour' they nevertheless felt free in the 1960s, thanks to the invention of tights, to expose even more of their thighs than the girls of the 1920s, wearing a miniskirt merely as a brief pelmet to overhang the region where their bodies bifurcated. Yet, with that clairvoyance that pertains to female fashion, skirts began to descend to calf level and beyond, almost simultaneously with the deepening of the economic crisis in 1975; perhaps indicating that same sense of a party being over that had accompanied the lowering of hemlines in 1930.

Spirit of the Times

Much of the disapproval of the supposed demoralisation of the English by the twin evils of affluence and 'permissiveness' in the third quarter of the twentieth century derived from too myopic a view of recent history. England had pioneered the industrial revolution by becoming a land dedicated to intensive capital investment and to debased standards of living for the majority. Its transformation into a consumer society concerned with the wider diffusion of domestic comforts and 'luxuries' had become apparent by the 1870s. The acceleration of this transformation from the mid-1950s was remarkable only because it had been halted, for many by the Depression of the 1930s and, for most, between 1939 and 1953, by the exigences of the war and of recovery from it. The only novel feature of the 'affluent society' after 1950 was that, for the first time, it extended to most of the population. This naturally provoked unfavourable comment from those so accustomed to thinking of 'the lower classes' as 'the poor' as to regard it as in the nature of things.

It is pertinent therefore to note that in the historical record the desire for freedom and the desire for opportunities for increased personal consumption go together. Personal liberty is not to be identified solely with the right to print, read and say what one likes. It also involves the right to butter and jam on one's bread, more than one pair of shoes, several changes of underwear, armchairs instead of stools or benches, refrigerators instead of larders, and washing machines instead of mangles and coppers. It is noticeable that modern dictatorships are as anxious to protect their populations from the temptation to want consumer goods as from the infection of dissident opinions. In a free society men may aim to possess more than they have. In the authoritarian state they must be content with what they have got until authority decides otherwise. For the English to congratulate themselves on belonging to a free society while condemning most of its members for wanting to increase their personal expenditure is illogical and authoritarian.

Moreover the affluence of the period produced both personal and social advantage. By the early 1970s, personal incomes commanded over 75% more goods and services than in the early 1950s. The number of dwellings without lavatories fell from 7% to 1%; the number without bathrooms from 30% to nine. Only one home in eight had the telephone in 1950; by 1970 it had been installed in 50% of the country's homes. The expectation of life rose from 66 to 69 for men and from 71 to 75 for women. The infant mortality rate per 10,000, which stood at 276 in 1950, was down to 139. The proportion of the population having three or more weeks' holiday a year rose from one-third to two-thirds. If these figures are compared as, strictly speaking, they should be, with those for the 1930s or for 1913, they represent a social revolution which might well be considered a matter more important than the persistence of considerable inequality. In addition, a much larger proportion of national resources was devoted to improving the environment. Rivers ceased to be wholly poisonous to fish; in spite of the visual brutality of much, though not all, of its new building and the stink of the petrol engine notwithstanding, urban England became altogether cleaner and brighter, its blemishes consisting chiefly in a mindless indifference to litter and much often drink-induced vandalism. More of the national income was devoted to the arts, through subsidy by the state, by commerce and by industry, as well, though too often on a miserly scale, as by local authorities. English music, and the best of English theatre, were more admired abroad than for centuries.

As for 'permissiveness', the whole century since the 1880s had seen the slow liberation of the private life from the authoritarian restraints of a hierarchical society committed to the repressive moral code which seems inevitably associated with a system in which human beings are required to serve the imperatives of intensive capital investment without which, apparently, the industrialisation of a largely rural economy cannot be achieved. This liberating process, like the spread of affluence, was checked, though more decisively, between 1930 and 1953. The Depression, and the frightening spectacle of the totalitarian systems that then came to dominate continental Europe, inhibited 'liberal' thought by seeming to make nonsense of all assumptions that the world would inevitably 'progress' under the influence of enlightened 'thinkers', and men of intellect and good will. Though to a lesser degree than European peoples beyond the Rhine, the English succumbed in the 1930s to mind-dampening appeals to unity and patriotism. Throughout the decade, there was no effective political opposition to a government allegedly 'National'. The coming of war concentrated the English mind on immediate perils and though plans for radical reconstruction proliferated, they withered in the smothering atmosphere of unimaginative solemnity created by Attlee's Labour government after 1945, under its oppressive commandment 'export or die' and amid fears of imminent annihilation engendered by the atomic bomb, the Korean war and the menace of Soviet Communism.

Between 1930 and the end of the Churchill-Attlee era by 1955, the world was full of iron facts that made a mockery of idealistic plans for a benignly progressive future. The happy, harmonious Utopia that William Morris had projected in *News from Nowhere* in 1884 was replaced by the nightmare futures of Aldous Huxley's *Brave New World*, published in 1932, and George Orwell's *Animal Farm* and *1984*, both appearing in the late 1940s. Too fearful, and too preoccupied with immediate difficulties to indulge in schemes for making the world a better place, the

English passed through a period of stability which, though taken for granted by those who saw their successors rebelling against it, was quite untypical. It was a period when they were more docile and well-behaved than ever before in their history. Not even in the celebratedly stable 1850s had society known so little violence or contained so few drunks.

This social stability was much assisted by the absence of corruption and adventurism in public and political life after the fall of the Lloyd George Coalition in 1922. Before Baldwin had established himself, twentieth-century politics had often been unsavoury. The years of the First World War, like those just before and just after it, were disfigured by such unpleasant characters as the megalomaniac Alfred Harmsworth (Lord Northcliffe) and rogues like Pemberton Billing, Horatio Bottomley and Maundy Gregory. Lloyd George himself, lacking a political base as prime minister, relied more and more on his temperamental preference for the dubious short cuts natural to a rural Welsh *arriviste* of quick intelligence. English traditions of respect for monarchy, parliament, peerage and correct administrative procedures were wholly foreign to him; his lack of respect for them created an ugly rivalry between those who resented his methods and those who flourished by imitating or condoning them. But Baldwin, MacDonald, Neville Chamberlain, Churchill and Attlee, with all their shortcomings, were conspicuous for their old-fashioned sense of propriety. Unlike Asquith in 1916, Chamberlain did not, when replaced by Churchill in 1940, lead his followers into a wilderness of sulky disaffection to deprive his successor of adequate political support. Churchill's maverick personality was nevertheless anchored to a strong and almost romantic regard for the sanctities of marriage, monarchy and parliament. The outcome was that standards of propriety among top politicians became so exacting that, even in the era of 'permissiveness' three ministerial careers were terminated because of breaches of the traditional sexual code which, compared with those indulged in by nineteenth-century politicians unscathed, were trifling.

By the mid-1950s, however, as they found their pay packets becoming fatter, the English decided it was time to start enjoying themselves. The years of sacrifice, shortages, courage, resolution and austerity had culminated by 1956 in their being condemned by the United Nations and outfaced by an Egyptian. Encouraged by the advertising industry, then rejoicing in the advent of commercial television, they seized on Harold Macmillan's words, 'you've never had it so good', and determined to prove him right—failing to notice that he had used the words in the traditional context of an appeal for restraint.

The twenty years after Suez, though quite unlike the twenty years before it, were a louder and more orchestrated recapitulation of the period before 1931. Just as virtually all the crazes and daring ideas of the 1920s were excitable variations on social and intellectual themes already audible by 1913 but then muted by wartime, so, in this later carnival, the voices were mostly newer than their mesage. Of the theatrical successes of the later 1950s, one was Sandy Wilson's musical, *The Boy Friend*, an infectious, affectionate pastiche of the self-conscious merriment of the upper class young of the 1920s. The other was John Osborne's *Look Back in Anger*, a play remarkable for making, though in more rebarbative language, attacks upon English society that would have been deemed almost routine had they been made in 1927. Equally appropriate was that the 1960s, like the 1920s, should witness public trials of the works of D. H. Lawrence, a writer whose entire output pre-dated 1931, and that there should be a judicial *cause célèbre* about the publishability of *Lady Chatterley's Lover*, a book completed in 1928. The publicity given to drug-taking echoed the metropolitan uproar caused by Noel Coward's play on that same subject, *The Vortex*, produced in 1924. Even the language of denunciation had the familiarity of an only half-forgotten popular song. Aldous Huxley's stern censoriousness in 1927 (in *Proper Studies*) would have excited no surprise had it come from the lips of a Malcolm Muggeridge in 1967: 'Our modern savages have no taboos of any sort. They copulate with the casual promiscuousness of dogs; they make use of every violent emotion-producing sensation for its own sake, because it gives a momentary thrill'.

What was new about the 1960s was that these alleged 'savages' were no longer, as in the 1920s, a privileged minority. The roses-and-cream-complexioned debutantes and Oxford-bagged public school youths who went to jazz-mad night clubs, organised wild parties and uttered emancipated ideas in the 1920s were rich, sometimes stylish, often talented and usually members, or hangers-on of, the best families. But whereas the night club was priced to keep almost everybody out, the discotheque was priced to let almost everybody in. Aldous Huxley's copulating 'savages' had been a very small tribe, their numbers limited in more senses than one by their then exceptional familiarity with birth control. But now the tribe had members in all parts of society. Divorce ceased to be the privilege of the moneyed classes or the occupational hazard of cinema stardom. Persons of humble birth and ordinary talent could have as many love affairs, and as many wives, as Bertrand Russell. In matters of sex, moralists whose cry had once been, 'Woe unto you, ye rich,' now found it necessary to denounce all the income groups.

To multiply freedoms is to multiply risk. There was always a seamy side to the so-called 'swinging' years. They stimulated a mood of financial acquisitiveness that expressed itself in, among many other things, a reckless speculation by the rich in property development. Universal contraception, legalised abortion, easier divorce, relaxed censorship of stage, screen and print, and some mitigation of society's legalised hostility towards homosexuals, inevitably put the feckless at risk. The presence in the community of many vocal defenders of 'traditional' values ensured the continuance of much commercially profitable furtiveness in matters sexual. Strip clubs, pornographers, dubious abortionists and purveyors of blue films or of drugs, soft and hard, did well out of the atmosphere of excitement generated by the conflict between the allure of a new 'permissive' society and the inevitable campaigns for the return of a more authoritarian one. Violence, a product of factors more deep-seated than a mere erosion of deference or a dislike of conventional timidities, was far greater than in the previous thirty years and more likely to be imitated because so much more widely and rapidly publicised. Yet the English reputation for being law-abiding was comparatively modern. In 1826, and without much exaggeration, one of the country's leading magistrates described 'the people of Britain' as 'the most criminally-disposed race in the whole of the civilised world'.

The victims of the new age of relaxed rules were more numerous, more vulnerable and less stylish than the casualties of the years before 1939. The comparatively rare figure, such as Brian Howard, clever young Etonian of the 1920s, proceeding through homosexuality to drugs and suicide as a brilliantly gifted failure, gave place to a dismal regiment of lower middle-class drop-outs and drug takers, lured to disaster not from the likelihood of fame but from the prospects of comfortable normality. Yet the majority emerged from these years unscathed. Already, by 1970, the deplored rock 'n' rollers of the late 1950s were on the threshold of a middle age not noticeably less nostalgic or less lacking in *gravitas* than that of their parents had been.

Nevertheless, by the mid-1970s a change of mood seemed called for. There was a sharp break among the industrial countries of the west in the otherwise continuous post-war history of ever-rising incomes and growth rates. All faced an intractable combination of inflation and unemployment; and, as in 1931, economic theorists offered no agreed solution. In England, inflation seemed the major problem. Between 1971 and 1974, incomes had risen by 15.4%, but industrial production by only 8%. This, combined with the oil crisis, signalling perhaps the beginning of a new Revolt of Islam against the western nations' dominance, led to attempts to deal with a situation in some ways like that of 1931 by somewhat similar methods and slogans. With the renewed talk of belt-tightening and of the nation's 'need to pay its way' came the first reduction of living standards (by about 5.7%) since 1945.

The country's passage through this new phase was both facilitated and impeded by the fact that the Labour party did not behave as it had done in 1931. Its leaders, once again heading a minority government, did not surrender to a coalition dominated by their opponents. They stayed, endeavouring to control the situation. But to try to hold back inflation could increase unemployment; attempts to reduce unemployment could increase inflation; and neither consequence was acceptable to the trade unions to whom the Labour government was subservient. The unions were determined that the manual worker should not, as in the 1930s, bear the burden of a slow, fitful recovery by meek capitulation to large-scale unemployment and the low-wage economy that went with it. Nor, and this seemed a permanent characteristic of the work force, would they respond in deferential humility to a perpetuation of the tradition that those employed in mines, on assembly lines, or in the drearier and dirtier of jobs should, on the grounds that there was a national crisis, automatically cease to demand higher living standards.

In consequence, the workers' revolt continued, more often than not as a form of guerrilla strike activity, with the union hierarchy marching rather reluctantly wherever a fury of shop stewards led them. Those whom the trade unions could not control, the government could not control either. It had long been the conventional wisdom that throughout the twentieth century, the power of government over its citizens was continuously increasing. By the mid-1970s it seemed, in some ways at least, that this might not be altogether true.

One paradox bequeathed by the past remained. England's oldest institution, its monarchy, survived. True, it had done so, despite expostulatory outbursts by Queen Victoria, by yielding up its power: separation of 'the crown' from the person of its wearer became almost total. Disraeli and Lord Salisbury wooed Victoria in her later years into assuming the role of a non-political symbol of nationhood. Edward VII became king too late and for too short a time to reverse the trend. George V and Queen Mary, forced by war to detach the monarchy at last from its German connections, were temperamentally suited to preserve an appearance of stability in the midst of much social change. Edward VIII's hopes of making monarchy 'smart' were soon dashed, but George VI and his Queen made it, though still relatively 'old-fashioned', altogether kindlier and less stuffy. Elizabeth II, though perhaps, like Victoria, at her happiest in her more private hours, continued the new tradition. The survival of monarchy kept the politicians in their place. It prevented them from organising for themselves that loyalty of the masses for men of power which is so often the sign of a society whose truest freedoms have been lost.

Postscript

The last pages of this book were drafted well before the leadership of the Conservative party was transferred from Edward Heath to Margaret Thatcher and before Harold Wilson had exchanged prime ministerial office for membership of the Order of the Garter. Having begun with the arrival on these shores of the legendary Hengest and Horsa, the book therefore ends with the departure from the political high places of the not yet legendary Harold and Heath. Starting with the Roman retreat from Britain, it reaches an appropriate conclusion in the year the English voted to 'stay in Europe'. Any attempt to assess events later than that would have been premature. To judge the book's last pages in the light of developments after 1975 is a task for the reader.

A NUMBER OF BOOKS

THE books named in the following pages are included either because I consulted them while writing this History or because those interested in particular themes or periods may find them useful. Some are large general works, some are large specialist works, some, like those on economic history, demography or the church, may be fairly technical. Others, by contrast, are slight and amiable. Few, given the exercise of a little patience, will fail to inform or stimulate; most will do both.

Parts I–III (410–1509)

General
Sir Frank Stenton, *Anglo-Saxon England*, O.U.P., 3rd edn, 1971.
P. H. Sawyer, *From Roman Britain to Norman England*, Methuen, 1978.
H. R. Loyn, *Anglo-Saxon England and the Norman Conquest*, Longmans, 1962.
D. P. Kirby, *The Making of Early England*, Batsford, 1967.
P. Hunter Blair, *An Introduction to Anglo-Saxon England*, C.U.P., 1956.
Christopher Brooke, *From Alfred to Henry III, 871–1272*, Nelson, 1961.
George Holmes, *The Later Middle Ages, 1272–1485*, Nelson, 1962.
Du Boulay, *An Age of Ambition: English Society in the Later Middle Ages*, Nelson, 1970.
M. H. Keen, *England in the Later Middle Ages*, Methuen, 1973.
J. R. Lander, *Conflict and Stability in Fifteenth Century England*, Hutchinson, 1969.
Charles Ross, *The Wars of the Roses*, Thames & Hudson, 1976.
C. M. Loades, *Politics and the Nation, 1450–1660*, Fontana, 1974.

Constitutional and Legal
F. W. Maitland, *History of English Law before the time of Edward I*, 1898, reissued C.U.P., 1968.
A. Harding, *Law Courts of Medieval England*, Allen & Unwin, 1973.
Lapsley, *Crown, Community and Parliament in the Later Middle Ages*, Blackwell, 1951.
K. B. McFarlane, *The Nobility of Later Medieval England*, O.U.P., 1973.

Economic and Social
Sir John Clapham, *Concise Economic History of Britain*, C.U.P., 1957.
M. Postan, *The Medieval Economy and Society*, Weidenfeld & Nicolson, 1972.
W. Bonser, *The Medical Background of Anglo-Saxon England*, Wellcome Historical Medical Library, 1963.
G. C. Homans, *English Villagers of the Thirteenth Century*, Harvard University Press, 1942.
Philip Ziegler, *The Black Death*, Collins, 1969.

F. J. D. Shrewsbury, *A History of the Bubonic Plague in the British Isles*, C.U.P., 1970.
W. E. Meade, *The English Medieval Feast*, Allen & Unwin, 1971.
T. Baker, *Medieval London*, Cassell, 1970.
M. Holmes, *Elizabethan London*, Cassell, 1969.
J. C. Drummond and A. Wilbraham, *The Englishman's Food*, Cape, 1939.

The Church
Bede, *Ecclesiastical History*, Penguin, 1965.
J. Godfrey, *The Church in Anglo-Saxon England*, C.U.P., 1962.
Z. N. Brooke, *The English Church and the Papacy from the Conquest to the Reign of King John*, C.U.P., 1931.
D. Knowles, *The Monastic Orders, 943–1216*, C.U.P., 1940, and *The Religious Orders in England* (three vols.), C.U.P., 1949–59.
W. A. Pantin, *The English Church in the Fourteenth Century*, C.U.P., 1955.
K. B. McFarlane, *John Wycliffe and English Nonconformity*, English Universities Press, 1952, and *Lancastrian Kings and Lollard Knights*, O.U.P., 1972.

Parts IV and V (1509–1815)

General
S. T. Bindoff, *Tudor England*, Penguin, 1950.
Roger Lockyer, *Tudor and Stuart Britain, 1471–1714*, Longmans, 1965.
G. R. Elton, *England under the Tudors*, Methuen, 1955.
G. M. Trevelyan, *England under the Stuarts*, Methuen, 1904.
Christopher Hill, *The Century of Revolution, 1603–1714*, Nelson, 1961.
J. Carswell, *From Revolution to Revolution, 1688–1776*, Routledge & Kegan Paul, 1965.
Christopher Hill, *From Reformation to Industrial Revolution*, Weidenfeld & Nicolson, 1967.
J. R. Western, *Monarchy and Revolution: The English State in the 1680s*, Blandford, 1972.
J. H. Plumb, *The First Four Georges*, Fontana, 1966.
W. A. Speck, *Stability and Strife: England, 1714–1760*, Arnold, 1977.
Richard Pares, *King George III and the Politicians*, O.U.P., 1953.
J H. Brewer, *Party Ideology and Popular Politics at the Accession of George III*, C.U.P., 1976.
G. Rudé, *Paris and London in the Eighteenth Century*, Fontana, 1970, and *Wilkes and Liberty: A Social Study of 1763 to 1774*, O.U.P., 1962.
A. D. Harvey, *Britain in the Early Nineteenth Century*, Batsford, 1978.

The Reformation
A. G. Dickens, *The English Reformation*, Batsford, 1964.
P. Heath, *The English Parish Clergy on the Eve of the Reformation*, Routledge & Kegan Paul, 1969.
S. E. Lehmberg, *The Reformation Parliament*, C.U.P., 1970.
G. W. O. Woodward, *The Dissolution of the Monasteries*, Blandford, 1966.
P. McGrath, *Papists and Puritans under Elizabeth I*, Blandford, 1967.
H. G. Alexander, *Religion in England, 1558–1662*, University of London Press, 1968.

Civil War and Interregnum

Lawrence Stone, *The Causes of the English Revolution*, Routledge & Kegan Paul, 1972.

J. R. Hexter, *Reappraisals in History*, Longmans, 1961.

Lawrence Stone, *The Crisis of the Aristocracy*, O.U.P., 1965.

Conrad Russell, *The Crisis of Parliaments, 1509–1660*, O.U.P., 1971.

Ivan Roots, *The Great Rebellion, 1642–1660*, Batsford, 1966.

Christopher Hill, *God's Englishman: Oliver Cromwell and the English Revolution*, Weidenfeld & Nicolson, 1970, and *The World Turned Upside Down*, Temple Smith, 1972.

Robert Ashton, *The English Civil War, 1603–1649*, Weidenfeld & Nicolson, 1978.

Economic

D. C. Coleman, *Industry in Tudor and Stuart England*, Macmillan, 1975, and *The Economy of England*, O.U.P., 1977.

L. A. Clarkson, *The Pre-Industrial Economy in England, 1500–1750*, Batsford, 1971.

C. Wilson, *England's Apprenticeship, 1603–1763*, Longmans, 1965.

Social

K. Charlton, *Education in Renaissance England*, Routledge & Kegan Paul, 1965.

L. L. Shucking (trans. B. Battershaw), *The Puritan Family*, Routledge & Kegan Paul, 1969.

D. Brailsford, *Sport and Society from Elizabeth to Anne*, Routledge & Kegan Paul, 1969.

Stella Margetson, *Leisure and Pleasure in the Eighteenth Century*, Cassell, 1970.

Dorothy George, *England in Transition*, Penguin, 1953.

P. Laslett, *The World We have Lost*, 2nd edn, Methuen, 1971.

Lawrence Stone, *The Family, Sex and Marriage in England, 1500–1800*, Weidenfeld & Nicolson, 1977.

Parts VI and VII (1780–1975)

General

A. D. Harvey, *Britain in the Early Nineteenth Century*, Batsford, 1978.

Asa Briggs, *The Age of Improvement, 1783–1867*, Longmans, 1959.

J. R. Hobsbawm, *The Age of Revolution, 1789–1848*, Weidenfeld & Nicolson, 1962.

G. Kitson Clark, *The Making of Victorian England*, Methuen, 1962.

G. M. Young, *Victorian England*, 2nd edn., Methuen, 1953.

E. L. Woodward, *The Age of Reform, 1815–1870*, 2nd edn., O.U.P., 1962.

L. C. B. Seaman, *Victorian England: Aspects of English and Imperial History, 1837–1901*, Methuen, 1973.

L. C. B. Seaman, *Post-Victorian Britain, 1902–1951*, Methuen, 1966.

A. J. P. Taylor, *England, 1914–1945*, O.U.P., 1966.

C. L. Mowat, *Britain Between the Wars, 1914–1940*, Methuen, 1955.

Political

N. Gash, *Reaction and Reconstruction in English Politics, 1832–52*, O.U.P., 1965.

D. Southgate, *The Passing of the Whigs, 1832–1866*, Macmillan, 1962.

Jasper Ridley, *Lord Palmerston*, Constable, 1970.
James Prest, *Lord John Russell*, Macmillan, 1972.
N. Gash, *Sir Robert Peel*, Longmans, 1972.
Philip Magnus, *Gladstone*, Murray, 1954.
Robert Blake, *Disraeli*, Eyre & Spottiswoode, 1966.
Robert Blake, *The Conservative Party from Peel to Churchill*, Eyre & Spottiswoode, 1970.
R. R. James, *The British Revolution, Vol I, 1880–1914*, Methuen, 1977.
J. Grigg, *Lloyd George: The People's Champion, 1902–11*, Eyre Methuen, 1978.
H. Pelling, *Short History of the Labour Party*, 2nd edn, Macmillan, 1965.
Beatrice Webb, *Diaries, 1912–24* and *1924–32*, 2 vols, Longmans, 1952, 1956.
Roy Jenkins, *Asquith*, Collins, 1964.
Lord Beaverbrook, *The Downfall of Lloyd George*, Collins, 1963.
M. Bentley, *The Liberal Mind, 1924–29*, C.U.P., 1977.
H. Montgomery Hyde, *Baldwin, The Unexpected Prime Minister*, Hart Davis, 1973.

Economic

R. Wilkinson, *Poverty and Progress*, Methuen, 1973.
J. D. Chambers & G. E. Mingay, *The Agricultural Revolution, 1750–1880*, Batsford, 1966.
A. E. Musson and E. Robinson, *Science and Technology in the Industrial Revolution*, Manchester University Press, 1969.
E. P. Thompson, 'The Moral Economy of the English Crowd in the Eighteenth Century', *Past and Present* no. 50, 1971.
P. Mathias, *The First Industrial Nation, 1700–1914*, Methuen, 1969.
S. G. Checkland, *The Rise of Industrial Society in England, 1815–1885*, Longmans, 1964.
S. B. Saul, *The Myth of the Great Depression, 1873–1896*, Macmillan, 1969.
R. H. Breach and R. M. Hartwell, *British Economy and Society, 1870–1970*, O.U.P., 1972.
S. Pollard, *The Development of the British Economy, 1914–67*, Arnold, 1969.

Social

Harold Perkin, *Origins of Modern English Society, 1780–1880*, Routledge & Kegan Paul, 1969.
E. P. Thompson, *The Making of the English Working Class*, Penguin, 1968.
R. J. White, *From Waterloo to Peterloo*, Heinemann, 1957.
D. Alexander, *Retailing in England during the Industrial Revolution*, University of London Athlone Press, 1970.
Dorothy Davis, *History of Shopping*, Routledge & Kegan Paul, 1966.
Muriel Jaeger, *Before Victoria*, Penguin, 1967.
J. F. C. Harrison, *The Early Victorians, 1832–51*, Weidenfeld & Nicolson, 1971.
Geoffrey Best, *Mid-Victorian Britain, 1851–75*, Weidenfeld & Nicolson, 1971.
P. Quennell (Ed.) *Mayhew's London*, 2 vols, Spring Books, 1949, 1950.
Gertrude Himmelfarb, *Victorian Minds*, Weidenfeld & Nicolson, 1968.
Basil Willey, *Nineteenth Century Studies*, Chatto, 1949.
Owen Chadwick, *The Victorian Church*, 2 vols, A. & C. Black, 1966, 1969.
B. Semmel, *The Methodist Revolution*, Heinemann, 1973.
D. Fraser, *The Evolution of the British Welfare State*, Macmillan, 1973.

D. Fraser (Ed.), *The New Poor Law in the Nineteenth Century*, Macmillan, 1976.
Steven Marcus, *The Other Victorians*, Weidenfeld & Nicolson, 1966.
Henry Blyth, *Skittles: The Last Victorian Courtesan*, Hart Davis, 1970.
Fried and Elma (Eds.), *Charles Booth's London*, Penguin, 1971.
W. F. Mandle, 'Games People Played: Cricket and Football in England and Victoria', *University of Melbourne Journal of Historical Studies*, vol. xv, no. 60.
L. Holcombe, *Victorian Ladies at Work*, David & Charles, 1973.
Flora Thompson, *Lark Rise to Candleford*, O.U.P., 1954.
E. Royston Pike, *Human Documents of the Age of the Forsytes*, Allen & Unwin, 1969.
J. Burnett, *Useful Toil*, Allen Lane, 1974.
D. Holbrook Jackson, *The Eighteen Nineties*, Harvester Press, 1976.
J. Ryder and H. Silver, *Modern English Society: History and Structure, 1870–1970*, Methuen, 1970.
Janet Roebuck, *The Making of Modern English Society from 1850*, Routledge & Kegan Paul, 1973.
Raymond Williams, *Culture and Society*, Penguin, 1963.
Raymond Williams, *The Long Revolution*, Penguin, 1965.
Richard Hoggart, *The Uses of Literacy*, Penguin, 1958.
Henry Pelling, *History of British Trade Unionism*, revised edn., Penguin, 1969.
G. A. Hutt, *Post-War History of the British Working Class*, Gollancz, 1937.
J. Stevenson and C. Cook, *The Slump: Society and Politics during the Depression*, Cape, 1978.
J. B. Priestley, *English Journey*, Heinemann, 1933.
L. C. B. Seaman, *Life in Britain Between the Wars*, Batsford, 1970.
M. Muggeridge, *The Thirties*, Hamish Hamilton, 1940.
A. A. Jackson, *Semi-Detached London*, Allen & Unwin, 1973.
R. Barker, *Education and Politics, 1900–1951*, O.U.P., 1972.
R. Mander and J. Mitcheson, *British Music Hall*, Gentry Books, 1974.
E. S. Turner, *The Shocking History of Advertising*, revised edn., Penguin, 1965.
I. Pinchbeck and M. Hall, *Children in English Society*, Vol II, Routledge & Kegan Paul, 1973.
M. Sissons and P. French (Eds.), *The Age of Austerity*, Hodder & Stoughton.
H. Hopkins, *The New Look*, Secker & Warburg, 1963.
A. Sampson, *The New Anatomy of Britain*, Hodder & Stoughton, 1971.

Imperial Problems

A. G. L. Shaw (Ed.), *Great Britain and the Colonies, 1815–65*, Methuen, 1970.
C. J. Lowe, *The Reluctant Imperialists*, Vol. 1, Routledge & Kegan Paul, 1967.
C. J. Bartlett (Ed.), *Britain Pre-Eminent*, Macmillan, 1969.
J. Morris, *Pax Britannica*, Faber, 1968, and *Farewell the Trumpets*, Faber, 1976.
C. Howard, *Splendid Isolation*, Macmillan, 1967.
G. W. Monger, *The End of Isolation*, Nelson, 1963.
G. S. Graham, *The Politics of Naval Power*, C.U.P., 1965.
H. G. Nelson, *Land and Power: A Study of British Foreign Policy, 1916–1919*, Routledge & Kegan Paul, 1963.
Martin Gilbert, *The Roots of Appeasement*, Weidenfeld & Nicolson, 1966.
Elizabeth Monroe, *Britain's Moment in the Middle East*, Chatto, 1963.
Colin Cross, *The Fall of the British Empire*, Hodder & Stoughton, 1968.
J. B. Watson, *Empire to Commonwealth, 1919–1970*, Dent, 1971.
M. Edwardes, *The Last Years of British India*, Cassell, 1963.
Hugh Thomas, *The Suez Affair*, Weidenfeld & Nicolson, 1967.

INDEX

Note: Acts of Parliament, whether referred to in the text as Acts, Laws or Statutes, are listed under *Acts of Parliament*. Regnal dates are given for English monarchs from 1035. Dates preceded by 'p.m.' indicate the years during which a political leader held office as Prime Minister.